D1564814

Wilhelm Liebknecht

Wilhelm Liebknecht, 1826–1900
(photo supplied by the IISH.)

Wilhelm Liebknecht

and the Founding of the German

Social Democratic Party

Raymond H. Dominick III

The University of North Carolina Press

Chapel Hill

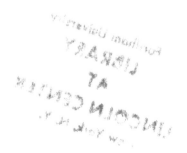

© 1982 The University of North Carolina Press
All rights reserved
Manufactured in the United States of America
ISBN 0-8078-1510-1

For reasons of economy, this book has been printed
from camera-ready copy prepared by the publisher,
who accepts full responsibility for this format.

Library of Congress Cataloging in Publication Data

Dominick, Raymond H., 1945-
   Wilhelm Liebknecht and the founding of the German
Social Democratic Party.

   Bibliography: p.
   Includes index.
   1. Liebknecht, Wilhelm Philipp Christian Martin
Ludwig, 1826-1900. 2. Socialists--Germany--Biography.
3. Sozialdemokratische Partei Deutschlands--History.
I. Title.
HX273.L6D65   335'.0092'4 [B]   81-16329
ISBN 0-8078-1510-1   AACR2

To Anne, Ray, David, and Lynn,
each of whom, in various ways,
supported me and this project

Contents

Acknowledgments

While researching and writing this biography of Wilhelm
Liebknecht, I have been helped by many people and institutions. First, I owe thanks to my teachers, especially to
the late Professor John Snell and to Professor Lamar Cecil.
Professor Cecil also read the typescript for this book and
made valuable suggestions for improvement, as did Professor
Andreas Dorpalen. Their criticism strengthened this work
considerably.

Second, I am indebted to the staffs of the various
archives that I visited. Each of the following institutions
contributed to this study in important ways: the Internationale Instituut voor sociale Geschiedenis at Amsterdam;
the Archiv der Sozialen Demokratie at Bonn-Bad Godesberg;
the Generallandesarchiv at Karlsruhe; the Stadtarchiv at
Frankfurt; the Hessisches Hauptstaatsarchiv at Wiesbaden;
the Stadtarchiv at Giessen; the Institut für Zeitungsforschung and the Stadt- and Landesbibliothek, both at Dortmund;
the Bundesarchiv, Aussenstelle Frankfurt; and the Hessisches
Staatsarchiv at Marburg. Indispensable photocopied material
was provided by the Schiller-Nationalmuseum at Marbach a.N
and by the Bundesarchiv in Bern.

Third, I am grateful to those agencies that supported
me financially during the decade that I worked on this project.

A Woodrow Wilson Dissertation Fellowship funded my first research trip to Europe. Since that time, the Ohio State University has contributed several times to facilitate my continuing labors. In 1976, the Research Committee of the Mansfield Campus provided a travel grant that helped to finance a second research trip to Europe, and more recently the same agency helped to underwrite the cost of this publication. The College of the Humanities of the Ohio State University in Columbus awarded a generous subsidy for the same purpose.

Fourth, I owe thanks to Babette Mullet, Linda Linn, Sally Hunt, Yolanda Allen, and Ruth Thornton, each of whom worked conscientiously and patiently in preparing the typescript for this book.

Preface

Perhaps Wilhelm Liebknecht's achievement in helping to build
the world's first mass-based and avowedly Marxist party would
convince every historian that his career deserves thorough
scholarly treatment. From a vantage point in the latter
part of the twentieth century, few matters loom larger than
the evolution of Marxist theory and practice. There is,
however, another question of perhaps even more consequence
to which Liebknecht's career addresses itself. That issue,
first raised in modern times by revolutionaries over two
hundred years ago and not yet resolved, is whether democracy can be established and survive, or whether it will be
trampled by dictators. If the answer to that question is
related to the triumph of Marx's disciples in this century,
it is equally entwined with the nearly simultaneous fascist
flight from freedom in Liebknecht's homeland of Germany.
Liebknecht, a nineteenth-century German social democrat,
stands at the fountainhead of two currents, Marxism and German
nationalism, whose swollen waters eventually swept through
and demolished the institutions of self-government. Yet
Liebknecht represented tributaries to both streams that were
tolerant, humanitarian, and democratic. An account of his
successes, an analysis of the limitations of the policies
he pursued, and an evaluation of his legacy should contribute

to an understanding of both the awesome catastrophe and the
ultimate potential of self-government in Germany and elsewhere.

Liebknecht excelled neither as a statesman nor as a
maker of revolutions but rather as the builder of a political
party. As a young man he fought in the revolutionary crusade
in 1848, but he spent his mature years working with nonviolent
tools. Employing organizational effort, oratory, and journalism, he helped the German workers' movement mushroom from
an inconsequential sect in the 1860s to become the most popular party in Imperial Germany. Yet his advocacy of revolutionary change, combined with the authoritarian constitution
of the Second Empire and the failure of his party to attract
a majority of the voters, barred him from a peaceful acquisition of the reins of government. Even so, Liebknecht advised
against renewed revolutionary violence. He thought that
public support, measured by the gauge of elections, would
indicate when his party had gained sufficient strength to
force a socialist reorganization of society. In his opinion,
that time did not arrive before his death. Consequently he
spent his efforts in the uncharted territory between the
roles of moderate reformer and revolutionary firebrand.

Consider for a moment the problems that confronted this
pioneering project. How, why, and to what extent should
a revolutionary socialist participate in elections and par-
liaments? To what degree should party members be allowed
to dissent from official ideology? If the party leaders
disagree among themselves, who should define orthodoxy and
how should discipline be enforced? More generally, how should
the goals of socialism be translated into daily, legal, political activity?

Liebknecht always tried to answer questions such as these

in a nonauthoritarian manner. He encouraged open discussion inside his party, and he defended the right to hold dissenting viewpoints. In reaching decisions, he preferred persuasion and open voting at annual party congresses to intimidation, expulsions, or ukases from the elite to the membership. His democratic inclination in resolving intraparty controversies contributed as much to the character of German social democracy as did the specific outcomes of those controversies.

What follows in this work will be a description of why Liebknecht gravitated toward radical politics and how he contributed to the organization, appeal, and consequent growth of the social democratic party in Germany. Until now, his labors have been misrepresented in the historical record. That misconstruction commenced even before he died, as his political comrades and rivals composed memoirs that created an image of the past to serve their own ideological viewpoint or personal reputation. Liebknecht protested ineffectively against a few gross misstatements,[1] but after his death others could fabricate tales and color the interpretation of his work without fear of contradiction. Thus grew up a mass of "primary" sources, often misleading in their depiction of Liebknecht, by which subsequent investigators sometimes have been deceived, and the intentional warping of interpretations of Liebknecht's life and work has increased with the passage of time.

Today Liebknecht and his party are much studied throughout Germany, but not in the service of antiquarian curiosity, much less in the search for impartial accuracy. Rival historians presently are resurrecting two completely different Wilhelm Liebknechts. Marxist-Leninists mainly in the German Democratic Republic exhume a Liebknecht who admonishes his

descendants to hold fast to the class struggle and to settle
for nothing less than the violent overthrow of the capitalist
system. Partisans of moderate social change domiciled in
West Germany reclaim a reformist Liebknecht, one who preaches
the possibility of gradual and peaceful evolution into
socialism.

Liebknecht's statements are especially unsuited for
this sort of extrapolation across generations. Every word
he uttered or wrote aimed at the exposure of some abominable
feature of his own setting, the semi-feudal Second German
Empire. As conditions changed, his tactics accommodated
them. Consequently, Liebknecht left no internally consistent
corpus of tactical advice. His quotations, taken out of
context, can be misunderstood.

In the following narrative, Liebknecht's statements
will be treated as responses to the unfolding problems of
the nineteenth century. Stressing the changing agitational
needs that he faced should dissipate most appearances of
self-contradiction in Liebknecht's thought. His oft-maligned
flexibility, his willingness to compromise, allowed the German
social democratic movement quickly to outgrow the rivalries
that fragmented contemporary socialist parties in other countries. Far beyond the authorship of any particular theory,
Liebknecht proudly cited this unity for the German working
class as his most important achievement.[2]

Wilhelm Liebknecht

Chapter 1

Becoming a Student Radical

REVOLUTION AND REACTION IN METTERNICH'S EUROPE

On his twenty-third birthday, Wilhelm Liebknecht sat in the prison at Freiburg in Breisgau, where Grand Duke Leopold of Baden had established a special commission to investigate and to try charges of high treason. Liebknecht was one of thousands whose case dragged slowly through the administrative channels. Because more important revolutionaries had not yet gone to trial, his prosecution was not likely to begin for at least another month. Leaving his fate--and that of the German Revolution of 1848-49--momentarily unexplored, we may examine first how and why young Wilhelm had stepped outside the law and become a revolutionary.

In prodding Liebknecht toward radical politics, the condition of a continent played at least as large a role as did unique personal experiences. For when Liebknecht plunged into overt rebellion in 1848, he did not act alone, as a conspirator or assassin, to impose his will upon reluctant circumstances. On the contrary, when he committed himself to insurrection, he joined a raging tide of revolution so strong that his failure to have become involved would be remarkable. In that tempestuous time, artisans, lawyers, and professional people, peasants, soldiers, and students all flocked together to challenge the established order of

inherited privilege. The street battlers, the younger radicals who risked their lives in confrontations with loyal government troops, had like Liebknecht been born while Prince Klemens
von Metternich orchestrated the affairs of monarchical Europe.

Urbane and reasonable, a master of subtle argumentation
and diplomatic arrangement, Metternich became the agent of
a decaying Austria's fortunes, doing his best to undo the
changes wrought by twenty-five years of revolution and warfare. For the dangerous triad, Liberty-Equality-Fraternity,
this refugee from the Rhineland enforced the substitution
of legitimacy, the inherited right of certain dynasties to
rule by the grace of God. For the much rearranged political
boundaries within Europe, he proposed, insofar as feasible,
to relocate territorial frontiers in conformity with the status
quo ante 1789. Recognizing that subversives were hardly
extinct and that they would not respect dynastic frontiers,
he conducted an international concert of sovereigns whose
purpose was collectively to quash insurrection wherever it
threatened a "dear brother" in the family of rulers.

During Metternich's long tenure as Europe's most important minister, the political, social, and cultural cleavages
unleashed by the Great Revolution in France were often driven
from view by governmental suppression, but they were never
really narrowed. For Metternich was fighting not merely a
transient dislocation in the European order but rather a con-
geries of challenges that soon would inundate everything he
defended. In the burgeoning cities, the nonaristocratic
classes clamored for a say in government. In the countryside,
the continued bondage of the peasantry in central and eastern
Europe alienated the largest segment of the population. From
Athens to Brussels, a swelling chorus of articulate leaders
demanded that Metternich's international system be dismantled

and that the map of Europe be redrawn according to the
principle of national self-determination. Compounding these
other discontents was an earthshaking alteration in the economic character of Europe. Inexorably the primacy of the
agrarian aristocracy and the security of the artisan guilds
crumbled before the unprecedented dynamism and wealth of merchants and industrialists. In every regard, Metternich, the
monarchs, and the aristocrats fought like Luddites against
powerful engines of change. It is a tribute to the prince's
ingenuity, if not to his breadth of vision, that he survived
in power as long as he did.

Metternich's success crested in the first decade after
the Congress of Vienna. In his native Germany, he sabotaged
the constitutional movement in Prussia, and in 1819 he persuaded the other thirty-eight states in the Germanic Confederation to endorse his notorious Carlsbad Decrees. To enforce
these repressive decrees, a central invesigative committee
was established at Mainz. With virtually limitless authority,
its sole purpose was to probe allegations of illegal thought
and action. Armed with a network of spies and informers,
holding suspects in indefinite "investigative detention,"
Metternich's minions vigorously parried sedition with repression.

With time, this cloak of reaction began to fray around
the edges. First the Greeks, then the Belgians defied the
Vienna settlement and successfully revolted for national independence. In Paris, the mob rioted once more, facilitating
the substitution of a reputedly more liberal Orleanist ruler
for the reactionary Bourbons who had been restored at the
Congress of Vienna. Unsuccessful upheavals simultaneously
shook Poland and Italy. Even several German states, in
Metternich's own backyard, caught the revolutionary infection.
In Brunswick, the ruler was driven to abdicate. In other

principalities constitutions were promulgated or liberalized to forestall popular violence. By the 1830s the principle of legitimacy had taken a beating.

Conditions were not yet ripe, however, for a general overthrow of Metternich's system. Because the economy remained relatively prosperous, the mass of the population slumbered through these events. The most daring of the revolutionary projects, the assault on the Diet at Frankfurt in 1833 by a handful of conspirators, objectively had no chance to unseat the interlocking directorate of sovereigns. A successful revolution required the help of the peasants and the urban poor. Hard times, not speeches and pamphlets, comprised the only sure instigator for those people.

In *Vormärz* Germany (before the watershed of the 1848 Revolution), republican--not to mention socialist--agitators remained a minority within a minority. Even among the politically aware elite, only a small segment advocated revolutionary change. These faint voices sounded most frequently in the western German states. There French influence, constitutional government, and more advanced economic development combined to foster a more liberal atmosphere. In Baden, for example, influential professors such as Karl von Rotteck and Karl Theodor Welcker used scholarly works, university lecture halls, and seats in the legislature to spread the "light of reason," the doctrine of natural rights and the advocacy of more power for the elected representatives of the people.

Perhaps inadvertently, they lent respectability to the rantings of more radical agitators. The vanguard of the democratic movement, at that time an extremist viewpoint, also operated in Baden. There, fiery orators like Friedrich Hecker

and icy intellectuals like Gustav Struve exorted the people
to rule themselves. The government of Baden, abiding by the
most liberal constitution in the Germanic Confederation,
usually tolerated a remarkably intense political agitation.
When the ministers indulged in occasional fits of repression,
it was an easy job for the agitators to slip across the border
into France or Switzerland. Small wonder that the revolutionary currents of 1848 swept hundreds of outsiders, including
Liebknecht, into the struggle for freedom in Baden.

Baden was not Liebknecht's birthplace. He was born about
fifty miles to the north at Giessen in the state of Hesse-
Darmstadt. Metternich's Congress of Vienna had created this
Grand Duchy of Hesse. Before 1789, the tiny forerunner of
that state had consisted of only a scattering of pinpoint
territories north and south of the Main River, near its junc-
tion with the Rhine. The title of this petty principality
had been merely Landgrave. During the Napoleonic reorganization of western Germany, the Landgrave had maneuvered skillfully and acquired substantial additional property. After
1815, many of his lesser neighbors were not restored. Instead
Hesse-Darmstadt was consolidated into two noncontiguous blocs
of territory around--but not including--the Imperial Free
City of Frankfurt. The central government resided at Darmstadt. Two provincial centers for administration were located
at Mainz and at Giessen.

The Grand Duchy stood squarely in the liberal part of
the Germanic Confederation. Like its southeastern neighbors,
Bavaria and Baden, Hesse-Darmstadt received a constitution
during the early years of the Restoration. The disturbances
of the 1830s spread constitutional government to the states
to Hesse's north, thereby creating an unbroken chain of relatively progressive states from Baden to Hanover. It would

be easy, however, to exaggerate the liberalism of these governments. In Hesse, for example, the constitution was so hedged with property requirements that, out of a population exceeding 600,000, only a thousand men were sufficiently rich to hold office, and even these few were nominated indirectly in a multi-stage election. Furthermore, the power of the elected delegates to the state legislature was carefully counterbalanced by the prerogatives of hereditary and appointive officeholders. On balance, political arrangements in Hesse remained too backward to satisfy any but the most conservative. Nevertheless, the very existence of a legislature provided a focus for political aspiration and discussion.[1] Inside the Diet at Darmstadt, Heinrich von Gagern, who later chaired the Frankfurt Assembly, led a swelling liberal opposition to the grand duke's government.

In much of Germany, the universities provided an epicenter of more radical unrest. At Giessen, Hesse boasted a distinguished school whose faculty included, among other luminaries, Justus Liebig, the pioneer of organic chemistry. In the early 1800s enrollment stood under 400, and the faculty numbered only 25; by 1848, the student body had grown to 570. Although small by modern standards, this institution comprised almost 10 percent of the population of Giessen, and its students were well connected. In *Vormärz* Germany, higher education remained a prerogative of the well-born, and well-paying, influential careers remained a monopoly of the educated.

The University of Giessen, however, was a dysfunctional cog in this machinery of privilege. In the decade before 1848, its faculty disseminated seditious ideas along with a classical *Bildung*. The students, in 1815, had formed one of the first *Burschenschaften*, those radical fraternal

organizations devoted to the political unification and moral
regeneration of the fatherland. The inspirational local leader,
a lecturer in civil law named Karl Follen, penned poetry exorting
Germans to "call yourself up from slavery's wasteland to the
heaven of freedom." His disciples, sporting shoulder length
hair and black berets, were infamous: one of them murdered
the reactionary poet, Kotzebue, in 1819.[2] As a result the
local society was forced officially to dissolve, but it actually
persisted underground. In the following decades, student
strikes and riots periodically reminded the authorities of
the subterranean existence of a radical student band called
Die Schwarzen.

The subversive ideas emanating from the university encouraged extramural activities of a similar sort in and around
Giessen. In 1834, some radical students and a few artisans
joined together in the conspiratorial Society for the Rights
of Man. As part of the society's revolutionary agitation,
its members authored an incendiary appeal to the peasants
and distributed it throughout the countryside. The prospects
for this call to class warfare seemed bright in Upper Hesse,
for its agricultural population was among the poorest in
Germany.[3] Fearing a jacquerie, the authorities swept into
action, arresting several members of the society and causing
its leader to flee to Strasbourg.[4] But other radical democrats who were connected with the propaganda efforts in nearby
Baden remained active in Hesse throughout *Vormärz* Germany.

LIEBKNECHT'S ROAD TO RADICAL POLITICS

Such was the atmosphere of political fermentation that bubbled
around Giessen in the years following Liebknecht's birth.
He was born on 29 March 1826, and except for short excursions
to nearby towns like Marburg, he did not leave Giessen for
the first nineteen years of his life. As an adult he reflected
on how he had learned to know every stone and stream in the
streets and surroundings of his birthplace.

His native city was a walled town, comprised of half-
timbered houses that huddled along tangled alleys. Its sky-
line was dominated by the Renaissance style facades of a
cluster of public buildings and a handful of church spires,
the tallest among which stood across the street from the Liebknechts' house. Census records from the early 1800s state
that the town walls enclosed 740 dwelling houses, and that
6,500 people resided there. By mid-century, that number had
increased to 8,700.[5] The Lahn River, whose headwaters originate
less than forty miles to the northwest of Giessen in the Wester-
wald, flowed placidly through this setting, providing cheap
transportation to the Rhine River fifty miles downstream.
As the Lahn nears the Rhine, the terrain becomes mountainous
and the river slices a steep valley, but at Giessen the countryside opens into a broad expanse of gently rolling and heavily
cultivated farmland. Three hills within eyesight of the town
protrude sharply from the surrounding landscape. Each is
crowned by a ruined citadel, reminders of Hesse's feudal past.

The Liebknecht family tree sank deep roots into this
Hessian soil. Wilhelm's great-grandfather, Johann Georg,
had immigrated to Giessen from the nearby region of Thuringia
in 1707 in order to take a chair in mathematics at the

university. Johann Georg Liebknecht was an outstanding scholar,
a friend of Leibniz, and a member of both the Prussian and
the English academies of science. He was a prodigious *paterfamilias* as well. Outliving his first wife, the professor
married again (both marriages were to ladies of local descent),
and he sired twenty-one children. Wilhelm's grandfather was
the ninth child of the second marriage. He became a government
attorney and married into the Kempff family, who ran the local
postal service. His son, Friedrich Ludwig, born in 1790,
grew up while French troops occupied Hesse-Darmstadt. After
their departure, he secured a job as a government registrar,
a career that required him to work both at Giessen and at
Darmstadt. Presumably on his travels in the neighborhood
of Frankfurt, he met Catharina Hirsch, a lady from Hanau,
thirteen years his junior, whom he married at Darmstadt in
1822. Between 1823 and 1830, they produced five children,
only three of whom lived beyond infancy. In the intermingling
of birth and death that prevailed in the early nineteenth
century, the third child was born five months after the death
of the second. Preceded now only by an elder sister, this
son was given the name, extensive even by the standards of
the day, Wilhelm Philipp Martin Christian Ludwig Liebknecht.

These facts, taken from the records of the Evangelical
Church in which Wilhelm was christened,[6] indicate nothing
in the family background that should have predisposed the
youth for a career in revolution. On the contrary, his lineage
linked him firmly to the privileged establishment of his day.
There are, nevertheless, grounds to speculate that liberal
sympathies were harbored in his home. His father was a bureau-
crat, and the bureaucracy, especially in western Germany,
often dabbled in enlightened thought in the post-Napoleonic

era. There is even some evidence that the Liebknecht family
gave sanctuary to Polish refugees fleeing the failed revolution in that country in 1831.[7]

In any case, parental influence did not long survive
in Wilhelm's childhood. Beginning when he was five, a series
of personal tragedies befell him, severing whatever ties he
may have had to a distinguished past and a secure future.
In October 1831, his mother, who was only twenty-eight, died.
Fourteen months later his father followed her to the grave.
The paternal grandmother, aged seventy-two, undertook the
care of the three surviving children, but she died in May
1834. The wardship for the children then was given to Karl
Osswald, a *Kandidat* in theology who had been a close friend
of Wilhelm's father. Presumably a government pension helped
to provide for the children. Still, the family home, which
Johann Georg had acquired a century earlier, had to be sold
to pay accumulating debts and to provide a trust fund for
the future.[8] Thus, even the physical symbol of Wilhelm's
roots in the past was auctioned off before he was ten.

These repeated deathly onslaughts must have made an enormous impression upon young Wilhelm, though it is difficult
to say with certainty precisely what the short- or long-term
consequences of the traumas were. As an adult, Liebknecht
seldom wrote anything about his childhood. That reticence
may have resulted from repression of painful memories, or
it may have stemmed from a socialist's disdain for the personal element in history. In either case, we are left with
very few indications from Liebknecht himself about how he
felt or how he coped when his family fell apart. He did once
remark that his childhood had been "somewhat too strict and
too far removed from the pleasures of youth."[9] On another
occasion he recalled that the lack of close emotional ties

as a child had accustomed him to solitude and made him somewhat restrained in expressing his emotions.[10] Beyond Liebknecht's
own limited observations, one can assume that Wilhelm must
have emerged from childhood with considerable emotional insecurity. But how he dealt with this difficulty can best be told
as we follow the story of his life.

When Liebknecht later commented on his experiences during
the 1830s, he did sometimes mention the death of a relative,
but he did not refer to a member of his immediate family.
Significantly, he singled out the fate of his uncle, the
Reverend Friedrich Ludwig Weidig, as having made a "deep,
perhaps a decisive impression" upon him.[11]

Weidig typified the revolutionary democratic underground
that operated in Upper Hesse during Liebknecht's childhood.
He studied theology at the University of Giessen, and like
so many others he left that school infected with the virus
of rebellion. Already in 1820, in connection with the Kotzebue
assassination and its association with the Giessen *Schwarzen*,
the Mainz investigative committee had probed his politics.
Although he was exonerated at that time, a decade later evidence began to accumulate that he was a key figure in a variety
of subversive activities. He helped to organize the mammoth
nationalist demonstration at Hambach in 1832. A year later
he was among the planners of the ill-conceived coup at Frankfurt. After that incident, the authorities arrested Weidig
and held him for fifty-five days, reluctantly releasing him
for lack of evidence. Shortly thereafter, he joined the
Society for the Rights of Man at Giessen, participating in
the composition and dissemination of revolutionary tracts.

In 1835, a member of this society betrayed Weidig and
other members for money; a wave of arrests came in April.
A fortunate few escaped, but Weidig was seized at night and

taken to prison at Darmstadt, where he remained in investigative detention until 23 February 1837. At 7:30 A.M. on
that day, the jailer found Weidig with his throat repeatedly
cut. A piece of glass lay nearby, and a despondent suicide
note was scrawled on the wall, written with the reverend's
own blood. Weidig's supporters immediately assumed that he
had been harassed and driven to suicide; some even alleged
that he had been murdered. The embarrassed grand duke's
government hastily published an official explanation, but
it did nothing to quiet the bitter protests muttered throughout Germany.[12] Although the Weidig case became a cause célèbre,
it would be hyperbole to imagine an eleven-year-old Wilhelm
(who had never met Weidig) vowing to avenge the injustice
dealt to his uncle by becoming a revolutionary. Yet there
are two ways in which Liebknecht's own emphasis upon the
personal impact of this event may contain at least symbolic
truth.

     First, in the realm of Liebknecht's psychology, the
domain of his irrational processes, the judicial murder of
Weidig (for such Wilhelm thought it was) may have triggered
a lasting hostility to the state in the following way. Wilhelm
already had lost three parental figures. According to Freudian
theory, as a child he would have felt responsibility for
and consequent guilt from these deaths. In general, one
way to escape such a painful burden of guilt is to transfer
responsibility to some external agent, as a scapegoat, thus
externalizing the self-destructive passions that result from
the traumas. Weidig's death may have enabled Wilhelm sub-
consciously to identify the state as the guilty party in
his earlier losses, thereby providing an emotional foundation
for his commitment to revolution.

If this psychological hypothesis seems too farfetched,[13] it is probable that, in stressing the abominable treatment of Weidig, Liebknecht meant to summarize his impression of the political conditions he experienced as a youth. Surely Weidig's was not the only case of injustice known to him, and only a few years later he found himself threatened by those same sinister forces that had disposed of his uncle.

Liebknecht's rebellion sprang from intellectual reflection and from emotional commitment, not from the direct experience of economic hardship. It needs to be stressed that neither a socioeconomic class analysis nor a simple theory of deprivation can clarify Liebknecht's eventual hatred of the prevailing order. By birth he belonged to the elite. Although his material circumstances must have worsened somewhat when his relatives died, he did not fall into poverty. On the contrary, his resources sufficed to allow him to complete his studies at the gymnasium and to attend classes sporadically at various universities for four year years thereafter. Even the death of his guardian in 1845 apparently left him solvent, because two years later he had enough cash to book passage to America. When he subsequently cancelled his reservations and forfeited three-fourths of his payment, he accepted that loss with equanimity. In the months following, he still was able to work without pay as a volunteer teacher and to make loans to his friends.[14] He did not confront poverty until after 1848, when he was already a revolutionary.

Aside from the impact of childhood bereavement and the observation of political repression, it was education rather than poverty that comprised the vital third cause for Liebknecht's gravitation toward radical politics. His studies began conventionally enough, at the gymnasium in Giessen.

From 1835 until 1842 he pursued the typical classical cur-
riculum, excelling in Latin, Greek, German, history, and religion
Overall, he was graduated first in his class. His teacher
commented, "Through exemplary conduct, a good disposition
and uninterrupted, active diligence, Liebknecht has won the
love and respect of his previous teacher in the fullest measure;
in political regards he is not suspicious."[15]

No immediate break in Liebknecht's lifestyle came after
graduation. For the next two years, he continued to live
in Giessen, taking courses in theology and philosophy at
the university.[16] The first apparent rupture in his life
since the death of his grandmother came when he was nineteen.
At that time, Liebknecht's guardian died. A few months later,
in the autumn of 1845, Liebknecht left for Berlin with its
famous university and urban attractions.[17]

The Prussian capital, 250 miles from Liebknecht's home
town, was even further removed in terms of its size, economy,
and composition. Berlin already had become an industrial
center with a population approaching 400,000. Clearly segregated from the old aristocracy and the vibrant bourgeoisie,
there huddled a mass of impoverished workers. As immigrants
from the overcrowded countryside continued to pack into Berlin,
the city's population swelled by 30 percent in the 1840s
alone. Slums, crime, and prostitution all prospered.

At the time of Liebknecht's arrival in Berlin, the ominous
news was spreading that a major part of the potato crop throughout Europe had been utterly destroyed by a fungus. Uncontrol-
lably, the cost of living skyrocketed by 61.4 percent between
1844 and 1847. In the short span of eighteen months, nearly
200,000 Germans abandoned their homes, many to seek a more
tolerable life in the New World. Those who stayed behind

were hungry and seethed with discontent. Less than a year
after Liebknecht's visit to Berlin, the popular anger erupted,
as the citizens of the Prussian capital defied the cavalry
and ransacked the markets, appropriating the city's food
supplies for themselves. Only after four days of riots--the
so-called potato rebellion--were the troops able to restore
order.[18]

For Liebknecht, Berlin meant more than pubs and coffee-
houses, soldiers, and students; it also introduced him to
the unhappiness of the urban working class. As it happened,
his course of studies meshed perfectly with his social observations. He enrolled at the university in October 1845,
studying *philosophische Wissenschaft* during the winter semes-
ter.[19] Among the distinguished lecturers he heard were Schelling
and Grimm. More influential, however, were his readings.
Eagerly he digested Ludwig Feuerbach's relentless materialism
and David Strauss's demystifying *Life of Jesus*. Those teachers
convinced him to abandon religion altogether.[20] Having clam-
bered over that formidable hurdle on the path to revolutionary
commitment, he turned to the French socialist Saint-Simon,
whose influence in Germany was enormous in the 1840s. There
he imbibed his first theories of class struggle, in Saint-
Simon's terms, the war between the "producers and the parasites."
With relish, he explored Saint-Simon's arguments for a cooper-
atively organized and technocratically managed utopia.[21]
His attitude was consequently quite receptive when he encountered Friedrich Engels' recently published *The Condition
of the Working Class in England*. "This book," Liebknecht
later remarked, "with its burden of facts and of logic opened
a new world to me, or more accurately: it gave me firm ground
to stand on."[22] So long as one does not attach too much

philosophical precision to the word, it seems reasonable
to accept Liebknecht's recollection that, while in Berlin,
he became a "conscious socialist."[23]

Studies did not monopolize his time in Berlin. The
dizzying surroundings of that bustling city led him "into
the maddest madness of student life."[24] Aside from the carous-
ing and heavy drinking common among students, he also dabbled
in romantic poetry.[25] Inevitably, he met comrades who encouraged his revolutionary aspirations. Of special importance
were the Polish students, whose nationalist cause required
rebellion against three autocrats: Prussian, Russian, and
Austrian. In 1845, Wilhelm became sufficiently attached
to a Polish woman to remember her name fifty years later.
He later traced his lifelong sympathy for the Polish cause
to associations he made while in Berlin.[26]

Liebknecht left that city on 28 March 1846, on the day
before his twentieth birthday. His departure coincided with
an uprising of the Polish population in the Republic of Cracow
and throughout the Austrian province of Galicia. On his
trip back to Giessen, he made a little excursion through
Saxony toward Bohemia. When he arrived at the Austrian border,
the authorities held him for questioning, even though his
pass was in order. Because internal rebellion raged at that
very moment, the guard asked Liebknecht about his opinion
on the Polish uprising. His answer apparently was unsatis-
factory, for the authorities would not admit him to the country.
Liebknecht never clarified whether he actually had intended
to rush to the aid of the insurgent Poles, but it is a possible
explanation for his hasty departure from Berlin. Later he
described the incident with the Austrian border guard as
his first "serious conflict" with the state authorities.[27]

Although Wilhelm had stayed in Berlin for only half a year, he returned to his home town with a far greater awareness of the thunderheads that were accumulating in the political atmosphere of Europe. When he reenrolled in the university at Giessen, he plunged immediately into student radicalism, joining the recently founded corps, "Allemania."[28] In the tradition of *Die Schwarzen*, this club preached devotion to a united and democratic fatherland. That creed made the members long for a chance to challenge the established authorities.

The opportunity for a confrontation came in August, though in retrospect the provocation hardly seems inspiring. It seems that local police clashed with a few rowdy students at a dance.[29] While the authorities debated whether a city or university authority should review the incident, the highly politicized student body staged mass demonstrations in support of their comrades. Members of "Allemania," including Liebknecht, played the major role in organizing those protests.

When the university senate singled out several students for disciplinary action, the entire student body went on strike. Following the tactics used in previous clashes with the authorities, the young men paraded out of town en masse and camped amidst the ruins atop the nearby Staufenberg.[30] The alarmed university senate could think of nothing more creative than to summon a detachment of cavalry from the garrison at Butzbach. With battle lines now drawn, both sides glowered unflinchingly, waiting for the other to capitulate.

Liebknecht recaptured the flavor of this event in a brief article he wrote in 1898. As in most student strikes, a spirit of idealistic dedication combined with an almost

festive atmosphere. "The weather was marvelous. . . . The
beer flowed in rivers . . . ," he recalled. How glorious it
was, with "nature in full magnificence, the wide prospect,
the romantic ruins . . . and the youthful pride in fighting
for the right. . . ."[31] In serious conversation about the
proper strategy to follow, Wilhelm persuasively advocated
a daring challenge to the senate: accept nothing less than
a complete amnesty and unconditional withdrawal of the troops.
At his insistence, a deputation was chosen to carry these
demands in a petition to the rector.[32]

That administrator only reluctantly received the students.
He began the meeting with a lecture in which he set forth
stringent conditions for the students' return to school.
Exasperated, Wilhelm boldly interrupted, telling the rector
he must either accept or reject the students' demands. The
startled senate momentarily fell silent. Then the rector
turned with his haughtiest expression toward Liebknecht.
In an icy tone and using the German diminutive, "Wilhelmchen,"
he told the students that they were dismissed.[33]

The strike at Giessen continued for a few more days.
As the attention of all Germany turned to this uproar, the
faculty senate squirmed uncomfortably. Meanwhile, the townspeople, who sympathized with the students for political reasons
and for economic considerations, pressured the rector to
yield to the student demands. After a four-day contest of
wills, the senate's resolve wilted. In its capitulation,
it agreed to all of the students' demands, securing in return
only a promise that "Allemania," whose membership had provided
six of twelve persons on the student steering committee,
would be dissolved.[34]

Liebknecht was unable to savor his victory over the
university senate. Because of his prominent role in the
strike, he feared reprisals from the faculty. Consequently,
he considered an option that 16,500 Hessians chose in the
1840s: immigration to America. A decade earlier, disgruntled
radicals in Giessen had established an "immigration society,"
its purpose being the establishment of an ideal German state
in the New World.[35] Liebknecht was among the followers of
this group. He and his comrades bought flintlocks and learned
to shoot them; they vigorously followed a course of physical
conditioning; and each studied a practical skill (Liebknecht
apprenticed himself as a window fitter).[36] Yet for unknown
reasons the elaborate plans for a foreign colony collapsed
in the autumn of 1846. At that time Liebknecht set out not
for faraway Wisconsin, as had been planned, but rather for
nearby Marburg, a university town only twenty miles up the
Lahn River, in neighboring Hesse-Cassel.

He enrolled at the University of Marburg on 21 December
1846, ostensibly to study philosophy.[37] In that town, dominated by the brooding castle in which Luther and Zwingli
had failed to reconcile their differences, Leibknecht paid
little heed to formal studies. Instead he concentrated upon
acquiring knowledge that would buttress his radical opinions.
Seeking like-minded companions, he first joined the student
corps "Rhenania." When school officials proscribed it, he
gained membership in the fraternity, "Hasso-Nassovia."

In blending into these groups of his peers, Liebknecht
exhibited a personality trait that remained with him for
life. Needing the emotional support of good friends, he
could never become a reclusive theoretician or a detached
mastermind of revolution. His memoirs recall with affection

the fellowship and singing, the hard drinking and the late
night philosophical discussions that he enjoyed with his
fellow students in these corps.[38] His comrades in socialist
organizations later provided the same warmth, becoming almost
a surrogate family.

Within a short time after his arrival at Marburg, Liebknecht ran afoul of the authorities. The first incident
involved some petty vandalism, the smashing of some street
lights, but it was followed by a more serious political demonstration. The site of this protest was the citadel that
supervised the town from the mountaintop above. In recent
years, its dungeon had housed a famous political prisoner,
Sylvester Jordan.

In the aftermath of the riots in Hesse-Cassel in 1831,
the frightened government had called upon Jordan to author
a constitution. Eight years later, demonstrating how the
political climate had changed, the police arrested Jordan
for "demagogic agitation." When he was at last freed after
a six-year internment, Jordan was a shattered man. According
to Liebknecht, "the fate of Jordan, whose fate I had to connect
with the fate of my uncle [Weidig], made an extraordinary
impression upon me."

To demonstrate their solidarity with the victimized
Jordan, late one spring night in 1847, Liebknecht and a few
companions sneaked up the steeply inclined cobblestone roads
to the gate of the fortress. As the bells in the twin spires
of the Elizabethskirche below chimed midnight, the lads yelled
repeated cheers and vivats. Then they scurried away.[39]

A more tolerant era, a more lenient government, could
have dismissed the incident as a prank. But Metternich's
Germany aimed at crushing all dissent, however trivial,

and the network of spies and informants set to work investigating this outrage. Liebknecht soon heard that a retired
officer who had testified against Jordan some years earlier
now had named him as the instigator of a revolutionary conspiracy that ran underground throughout central Germany.
When friends warned Liebknecht of his impending arrest, having
seen the fate of those unfortunates who were thrown into
the prisons, he fled the city. Casting about hastily for
a sanctuary, he decided to sail to America.[40]

Young Liebknecht now could romantically imagine himself
sharing the fate of Weidig, or Jordan or any of the hundreds
of political prisoners persecuted by the petty sovereigns
of Germany. For two years, he had waded deeper and deeper
into the currents of student radicalism, rejecting religion
and monarchy and challenging authority in general. His provocative actions quickly reduced the options open to him
until, by the summer of of 1847, he was left only with arrest
or flight. With enormous sorrow, he shared a parting drink
and song with his friends in Marburg. Then he set out for
the New World.

Chapter 2

Joining the Armed Revolution

FROM A SCHOOL IN SWITZERLAND TO A BATTLEFIELD IN BADEN

If nearly two hundred thousand distressed Germans in 1846
and 1847 had not emigrated, a revolution might have started
sooner, lasted longer, or been more vigorous. Hard times
battered Germany between 1845 and 1848. Food prices increased
50 percent in those years. Unemployment in some places exceeded
half of the work force. In these bleak conditions the persistent critics of political repression at last found popular
resonance. The peasants and artisans became convinced that
the prevailing economic structure offered them no hope, so
many of them either left the country or marched toward revolution.

Economic circumstances, however, had nothing to do with
Liebknecht's decision to leave Germany. He was a political
refugee. After fleeing from impending arrest at Marburg
in July 1847, he passed through Giessen and went to Frankfurt,
where he booked passage to America. Accompanied by a single
friend, he boarded a train to Mainz, where he planned to
depart for Rotterdam. On the train, facing him in the coach,
sat a well-dressed gentleman, who gave Wilhelm his card.
Dr. Ludolf, headmaster of the Fröbel Institute at Zurich,
it said. Ludolf politely inquired about Liebknecht's

destination. The would-be immigrant proudly announced his
ambition to immigrate to Wisconsin. As the conversation
continued, Liebknecht and Ludolf learned that they shared
radical political convictions. The founder of Ludolf's school
in Zurich was the brother of Julius Fröbel, who was prominent
in the democratic faction in Baden and who soon would champion
the leftist cause as a delegate to the Frankfurt Assembly.
Ludolf depicted his school as a beehive of exile activity.
Liebknecht was awestruck by the names Ludolf mentioned;
Fröbel, Herwegh, and Ruge, who visited Zurich frequently,
were demigods to the young rebel. Ludolf must have been
impressed too, for he offered Liebknecht a position as a
volunteer at the institute. He eagerly abandoned his ambiguous
plans for a farm in America and accepted the offer in Zurich,
and the decision engendered relief.[1]

On 13 July, Wilhelm reported his arrival to the Zurich
police.[2] Against the backdrop of the jagged Swiss Alps,
domiciled in a small room overlooking Lake Zurich, Liebknecht
began his exile. He enthusiastically plunged into his first
job.

His employer, the Fröbel Institute, had been established
in 1833, when the town authorities invited a group of progressive educators from Germany to set up a model school.
The teachers agreed to apply the principles of Pestalozzi
and Rousseau, which prescribed a nonauthoritarian setting
in which a child's innate curiosity and talents could blossom.[3]
As Liebknecht worked with his twenty-one students, Wilhelm
discovered that he possessed the sine qua non for this type
of instruction--"patience." He loved to teach. In the 1890s,
he commented that teaching would have been an alternative
career.[4]

Liebknecht's acquaintances at the school soon introduced him to their radical friends. Julius Fröbel arranged a job for him as a correspondent for the left-leaning *Mannheimer Abendzeitung*. Previously Liebknecht had written a couple of unsolicited articles for the leftist press in Baden, but this official connection formally inaugurated his journalistic career. The arrangement surely was facilitated by Liebknecht's refusal to accept payment. For the young idealist, writing for the cause of a united and democratic Fatherland was its own reward.[5]

These articles from the *Mannheimer Abendzeitung* are the earliest surviving documents by Liebknecht. Approximately sixty-five of his essays appeared between September 1847 and March 1848.[6] They vividly depict his baptism into revolution, first in reflection, then in action.

Liebknecht's career as a correspondent flourished at least in part because of the exciting events he reported. At the moment he arrived in Zurich, the Swiss were hurtling toward civil war. The constitution of Switzerland, instituted and internationally guaranteed as part of Metternich's grand design, established a loosely woven confederation of twenty-two cantons. On one side within this trilingual buffer state stood the progressive elements. They favored a centralized, liberalized constitution and even some social reform. Opposite the progressives were mustered the patriarchs, most prominent among whom were the wealthy oligarchs of the trading centers and the hierarchy of the Catholic Church. The showdown, when it came, faintly echoed the religious wars that had shaken Europe two centuries earlier. Seven Catholic cantons banded together in a *Sonderbund* to defy an edict from the majority of the states that expelled the Jesuits. In the autumn of 1847, both sides eagerly resorted to arms.

Events in Switzerland attracted international interest, because wary Europeans wondered if the Great Powers would intervene. As the conflict escalated, the *Mannheimer Abendzeitung* encouraged longer and more frequent reports from Liebknecht. His initial commentaries brusquely dismissed religion as a smoke screen behind which the true political and social issues were hiding. To him, the war was "a fight of the free against the men of reaction," and he predicted, "The bulwark of reaction will become its sarcophagus, and the black cloaks of the Jesuits will be their funeral shrouds."[7] To his audience in Baden, he depicted the Swiss struggle as inseparable from German interests. "Mankind has now well comprehended how its interests, how its enemies, are everywhere the same. . . . From all lands, free men must offer their hands to heartfelt fraternity, to the common struggle."[8]

The military campaign in Switzerland commenced on 10 November. In three weeks, the outnumbered and outmaneuvered *Sonderbund* army collapsed. Liebknecht witnessed some of the fighting and detailed the clash of troops. When the military outcome was assured, he advised the Swiss Diet concerning the reorganization of the Confederation.

Most urgent, according to Liebknecht, was the modernization and centralization of the army. Intervention, orchestrated by Metternich on behalf of the defeated reactionaries, seemed imminent and probably would have occurred had not revolution soon incapacitated governments everywhere. The Swiss therefore had better prepare themselves to resist, Liebknecht admonished.[9]

On the domestic front, he advocated a typical radical program, including progressive taxation, absolute freedom for the press,[10] and free public education. He argued,

"Popular education is the only basis upon which more extensive reforms can be securely grounded. As soon as a people has begun to be intelligent, it ceases to be a plaything for the priests *and other reactionaries, and then can we first speak of a sovereign people, of a true democracy.*"[11] Although Liebknecht later decided that a socialist revolution would have to precede a satisfactory reorganization of the educational system, he always retained his faith in the influence of teaching to dispel the superstition and prejudice upon which the inegalitarian order of Europe was constructed.

There was more than idealism and radical democracy in Liebknecht's outlook, even at this youthful stage of his intellectual development. Although socialist ideas were tangential to his main concerns in the articles he wrote in 1847–48, they were nonetheless apparent. (They might have been more prominent still if he had written for a socialist instead of a democratic newspaper.)[12] From his reading of Saint-Simon and Engels, he had absorbed an awareness of economic influence in politics. In his admonitions to the Swiss radicals, he left incontestable evidence of his socialist convictions. Railing against the wealthy financiers at Basel, he asserted, "*Science* already has destroyed [private] property; *practice* now must follow the theory."[13] Of course, he recognized that few people yet subscribed to a socialist creed; but even as he made that concession, he trumpeted his belief that he marched in a socialist vanguard that in the future would include the vast majority of Europeans.[14]

Five days before revolution erupted in Paris, the *Mannheimer Abendzeitung* published Liebknecht's prediction that the whole continent was on the verge of an apocalyptic confrontation between radicalism and reaction. Characteristically tendentious and sanguine, he declaimed, "The spirit of

of freedom, in league with the proletariat, will demolish
the old forms, and on bloody foundations, the structure of
a new and better social order will be erected."[15]

By February 1848, evidence for this prediction was everywhere to be seen: civil war shook Switzerland, rebellion
rocked Sicily, rioters rampaged in Bavaria. When news came
that the mob in Paris had deposed Louis Philippe, eager exiles
throughout the continent celebrated in anticipation of a
new and greater 1789.

On 23 February, Liebknecht sat enjoying a game of cards
when a friend burst breathlessly into the room and announced
that the barricades were springing up in Paris. Afraid that
momentous events might pass him by, Wilhelm scampered to
his room, packed a few provisions for a trip, grabbed the
flintlock that he had bought for hunting in Wisconsin, and
dashed off to ask for directions from Julius Fröbel. Fröbel
advised that he hurry to the current center of action, to Paris.
He wrote a letter of introduction for Wilhelm, commending
him to the revolutionary poet, Georg Herwegh, who in recent
years had resided in Paris as an exile.[16] Thus armed with
a flintlock and revolutionary credentials, Wilhelm sped off
toward France.

Faithful to his readers in Baden, he continued to send
dispatches to the *Mannheimer Abendzeitung*, thereby cataloguing
his immersion in the insurrectionary tide. On 1 March, he
published his intention to go to Paris.[17] His first report
from that city was dated 9 March. He told his audience how
Herwegh and the horde of German exiles exploded with republican
enthusiasm. After helping the French to dispatch the last
defenders of Louis Philippe, they began organizing themselves
into an expedition to fight for freedom in the fatherland.
Liebknecht wrote a description of their 6 March demonstration.

According to his account, between 4,000 and 6,000 participants marched to the Hôtel de Ville, where patriotic songs were sung and speeches were made toasting the French, the German, and the world republics. That evening, in the Café de l'Europe, discussions were held that led to the creation of a German Democratic Society. Its members pledged themselves to devote all their energy to the regeneration of the fatherland.[18]

In a move that symbolized both the poetic aspirations and the military incompetence of the budding German Legion, the members elected Herwegh as their president. For several weeks, subordinates jockeyed for position, recruits paraded to and fro, and Herwegh lobbied to win assistance from the French Provisional Government. At last, early in April, the minister of the interior contributed 5,000 francs simply to be rid of the foreign troublemakers. Thinking himself to be well-equipped, Herwegh ordered his troops to the Rhine.[19]

Exciting newspaper accounts of these events, such as those written by Liebknecht, may have helped to inspire the Germans to begin their own uprising without waiting for assistance from abroad. In mid-March, demonstrations in Vienna toppled Metternich with surprising ease. That once mighty Prince skulked across Europe in a disguise, seeking asylum in London alongside the Citizen King. Only four days later, in Berlin, the vacillating Friedrich Wilhelm IV lost control of his capital city. Finding himself a virtual prisoner of the angry crowds, he had no choice but to promise a constitution. With the two most powerful German states thus incapacitated, revolution proceeded pratically unopposed elsewhere in the Confederation.

From the outset, the revolutionary ambition in Germany was complex. In some cases, its components became self-contradictory. There were the economic complaints of the underclass--the protests against unemployment and hunger from the urban poor; the outrage among the artisans who were being destroyed by competition from industry; and the bitterness of the peasants about rents and personal servitude. There were political demands of the educated and articulate-- ranging from the moderately liberal prescription for a constitutional monarchy to the red-hued cry for a democratic republic. Also there was the troublesome national issue: the hope that the nebulous community of German-speaking people could be forged into a single political entity. To complicate matters still further, there were thirty-nine local revolutions, each with its own purposes and framework, and each competing with the national arena for attention and effort.

In this welter of confusing aspirations and activities, the course of events in Berlin, Vienna, and Frankfurt was decisive. But the revolutionary democratic movement began and ended in Baden, where Liebknecht was an active participant.

Even before the mobs had their way in Vienna and Berlin, a group of fifty-three self-appointed government-makers met at Heidelberg to discuss how best to exploit the revolutionary situation. Hoping to spread the upheaval that was just reaching Baden, they called upon representatives from all the German states to meet at Frankfurt at the end of the month. In this way, they intended to render the Diet of the Confederation vestigial. The selection process for the resulting meeting, historically known as the *Vorparlament*, was haphazard. Prussia sent the largest delegation; Austria, the smallest. Reflecting both geographical proximity and political enthusiasm, Hesse-

Darmstadt and Baden sent the second and third largest missions, respectively.[20]

At Frankfurt, despite the pleas of Baden's radicals, the delegates declined to take any action other than to call for elections to a national assembly on 1 May. Fearing that counterrevolutionaries might use this delay to reconsolidate their forces, a handful of republicans decided to proclaim a republic in Baden.

The insurrection was led--if that term may be used for such a poorly arranged venture--by Friedrich Hecker and Gustav Struve, both of whom had attended the meeting at Frankfurt, and both of whom had departed simmering with frustration. An odd couple of revolutionaries, the former was a charismatic leader, the oratorical hero of mass demonstrations that had been held periodically in Baden for the preceding several months. Struve, by contrast, was a cold intellectual. In retrospect, both men were a bit out of touch with reality. On separate missions to Switzerland in mid-April, they raised expeditionary forces. Hastily and without any common planning, they both invaded Baden.

Simultaneously, Herwegh's legion was bearing down on Baden from the West. From various locations in Switzerland, still other would-be heros of the revolution, including Franz Sigel and Johann Philipp Becker, recruited and led their own independent guerilla armies. Altogether, approximately 8,000 rebels menaced the grand duke's regime. Like bees, though perhaps with less coordination, these ill-equipped and inexperienced detachments swarmed over the mountainous countryside.

Meanwhile, the Grand Duke received invaluable assistance from the supposedly defunct Diet at Frankfurt. The assembled representatives of Germany's princes voted to send troops to

shore up Baden's defenses. Friedrich von Gagern, brother
of the newly installed liberal minister of Hesse-Darmstadt,
commanded the relief force. He and his men caught up with
Hecker's band on 20 April. Although Gagern was killed as
the fighting began, his trained soldiers easily routed the
rebels. A few days later, Struve wasted his 4,000 men in
an assault on a battery at Freiburg. On the twenty-seventh,
Herwegh's corps of about 650 exhausted guerillas stumbled
upon 300 soldiers sent from neighboring Württemberg. Despite
their numerical disadvantage, the professionals again mauled
the amateurs, killing 30 and capturing 370.[21] The poet-
commander gracelessly slipped away unharmed before the fighting
ended. Summarizing the lessons of this abortive republican
uprising, one of Herwegh's lieutenants observed, "One does
not command troops in verses, nor will they be fed or clothed
with them."[22]

Liebknecht was not among any of the detachments of rebels
that were routed in Baden. He had participated in the organization of Herwegh's legion, but illness had forced him to
remain behind. After he had recuperated, he hurried to Strasbourg, but arrived only in time to meet the defeated remnants
of his legion.[23]

After this debacle, the flotsam and jetsam of the failed
crusade washed back across the Rhine into France and Switzerland. In this frustrated crowd, Liebknecht anxiously surveyed
the European scene. Throughout the summer, from Paris, Prague,
and Custozza, he heard the news of counterrevolutionary victories. He heard the embittered rebels exchange recriminations
and self-exculpatory explanations of the catastrophe. He saw
some, like Hecker, tire of the bickering and leave for America.
Undaunted, Liebknecht remained with those who were trying
to organize another insurrection.

His connections in Zurich provided the framework for this effort. In that city he enrolled in the recently founded "German National Union," a band of exiles who demanded a democratic fatherland. By mid-summer, Liebknecht had become the secretary of the group.

The Zurich organization was active and ambitious. In mid-June it dispatched a delegation to a congress of similar democratic clubs at Frankfurt. As a result of that meeting a liaison to the Central Union of Democratic Unions in Berlin was established. Inspired by the example of that agency, Liebknecht and his friends drew nine clubs from other Swiss cities into a German Democratic Union in Switzerland. A manifesto of principles issued by this society on 13 September 1848 announced its intention to implant a republic in Germany.[24] A few days later Liebknecht learned of a planned *Putsch* that meant to implement this vision. In Basel, Gustav Struve was readying a second assault on Baden. In mid-September, Liebknecht joined him.

The connection with Struve became important for Liebknecht. The son of a Russian councillor of state, Struve had renounced his heritage and now stood defiantly on the left wing of the revolutionary movement. Although he was no communist, he did think that people had a right to economic justice, and he propagandized for it with amorphous slogans like "adjustment of the relations between capital and labor."[25] Unlike his good friend Hecker, who won audiences by the force of his personality and appearance, Struve had no charisma. An ascetic vegetarian whom Liebknecht found to be somewhat oriental in appearance, he won disciples by his intellectual power. Liebknecht learned much from him and always retained a high regard for his efforts.[26]

Struve's organizing efforts had no chance for success, and the plot was doomed before Liebknecht lent a hand. The defeat in April had gutted the left wing, leaving 3,500 in prison in Freiburg and thousands more in exile. Furthermore, with 30,000 soldiers quartered on the population of Baden, the princes had proven that they were still in control. Moreover, the economic crisis had ended and gradual prosperity deflated the revolutionary enthusiasm of the masses. There would be no reenactment of the Great Fear, or the attack on the Bastille, much less of 10 August 1792. But no revolutionary was ready to admit these facts during the summer of 1848, least of all Liebknecht, who had yet to taste battle. Alongside Struve, he passionately sought an opportunity to fight for German unity and freedom, and the chance came in September.

At that time, popular disgust with the docility of the Frankfurt Assembly erupted into riots in several German cities. The assembly, after a brief show of backbone, had capitulated to Prussia's meek foreign policy and ratified an armistice with the king of Denmark. That accord terminated a war begun four months earlier with the purpose of bringing two duchies owned by Denmark, Schleswig and Holstein, into a united German state. The armistice at Malmö disappointingly foreshadowed a Danish victory.

As in 1833, radical conspirators stormed about in Frankfurt, attacking the Paulskirche where the assembly met, and Prussian troops were called in to save the "legitimate" government. When news of these events echoed down the Rhine Valley to Basel, the attentive Struve decided the time had come to gamble.

    After consulting with his friends, including Liebknecht,
on 21 September, Struve marched across the Rhine bridge near
Lörrach in the extreme south of Baden. Up went the posters
proclaiming the German republic. Out went the order for
conscription, calling all men between the ages of eighteen
and fifty-four to arms. Into the neighboring countryside,
Liebknecht and others were dispatched to carry the news and
to organize the recruits. Within two days, Struve had concentrated perhaps 4,000 adherents at Lörrach. Counting the
detachments being raised by his lieutenants, he may have
had a potential army as large as 10,000.

    Unfortunately, Struve had learned few tactical lessons
from the embarrassment of the preceding April. Again, he
did not wait to consolidate his forces. Instead, on 24 September, he marched toward Freiburg, hoping to free the several
thousand veterans of the April uprising who were jailed there.
Twelve miles north of Lörrach, near the village of Staufen,
he encountered 800 government troops blocking his path.
Although his men exhorted the regular soldiers not to fire,
a battle occurred. Without cannon, discipline, or leadership, Struve's force was routed. He and his wife escaped
the field and fled again toward Switzerland. At Schopfheim,
only a few miles short of his goal, he was betrayed to the
authorities and arrested.[27]

    Liebknecht was nearby with a band of several thousand
volunteers when news of the defeat at Staufen reached his
force. This demoralizing report caused his legion to desert.

    Discretion dictated that Liebknecht head for a sanctuary
across the Rhine, but he had already been deprived once of
the honor of fighting for the revolution, and he was determined "to risk goods and blood and life, to die for the

Republic."[28] Proudly he later recounted how, "weapons in
hand," he had rushed to Struve's rescue. Within hours, he
was "surprised and overpowered" by government troops.[29]

Some have found Struve's expedition foolhardy; others
described it as comic.[30] One analysis linked it to the Frankfurt uprising, describing both as events that terrified the
middle class and provoked the counterrevolution.[31] Actually,
that counterrevolution had been underway for several months,
and its successes are what make Struve's coup so hopeless.
If the timing for a *Putsch* was poor, circumstances nevertheless became even less favorable later. By December, the
royal armies had regained control in Vienna and Berlin. Thereafter, the revolution limped along on borrowed time.

Except for a breakdown in communication, Liebknecht
would have been executed on 25 September. Two days earlier,
the grand duke had decreed martial law for the southern part
of his duchy. Drumhead courts were ordered summarily to
try and to execute sentence upon all armed rebels within
twenty-four hours after their capture. Unaccountably, the
troops in the south had not received the order when Struve,
Liebknecht, and the others were caught. Consequently, the
prisoners escaped a military trial and instead were dragged
off to Freiburg to join the incarcerated army of defunct
revolutionaries.[32]

IN THE REICHSVERFASSUNGSKAMPAGNE

For eight months, while the revolutions in Vienna, Berlin
and in Frankfurt were suppressed, Liebknecht awaited his
trial at Freiburg. The administration of justice was slow

because the overburdened investigators had to interview and
prosecute over 3,500 cases.[33] Not much is known about conditions in the prison. However, the local population sympathized with the prisoners and conspired to help them in various
ways. Escapes occurred occasionally. After one such episode,
the authorities interviewed young Ernestine Landoldt, the
daughter of the prison pastor.[34] Whether she was a suspect
or merely a source of information is unclear. In any case,
she befriended Liebknecht and their friendship blossomed
into romance. The tumult yet to come soon separated the
infatuated couple for several years, but in 1854 Liebknecht
married her.[35]

While legal procedures and personal drama played themselves out at Freiburg, the democratic elements still at
large in Germany regrouped for a last stand. In November
1848, Julius Fröbel had founded the *Zentralmärzverein*, a
revolutionary league whose core was comprised of leftist
delegates to the Frankfurt Assembly. By the following March,
it counted over 400 local branches, with a membership exceeding
20,000. As a result of energetic agitators like the Mannheim
lawyer, Lorenz Brentano, this strength was concentrated in
Baden.[36] On 21 April 1849, when the Prussian monarch dis-
dainfully rejected the imperial crown proffered by the stag-
gering Frankfurt Assembly, the *Zentralmärzverein* again raised
the standard of rebellion. Within days, street fighters manned
the barricades in Saxony, in the Bavarian Palatinate and
in the Prussian Rhineland. When the experienced and well-
organized republican movement in Baden joined the campaign,
it seemed momentarily to have some chance for success.

With the return of spring, the Badenese limbered up
for their third revolt. As it happened, the collapse of

the Frankfurt Assembly coincided with the trials of Struve
and his comrades, events which stirred much excitement locally.
Struve's wife, Amalie, had unaccountably been released by the
authorities (perhaps they had no procedures for dealing with
female revolutionaries), and she had been whipping up the
rebellious spirit among the soldiers garrisoned at Rastatt.
Gustav, who was imprisoned there, went to court late in April.
At the trial, his defense attorney, who was Lorenz Brentano,
skillfully turned the proceedings into an indictment of the
government. The five-year sentence meted out to Struve thus
only gave Amalie more effective propaganda for her agitation.[37]

Hoping to exploit the climate of discontent to extort
concessions from the grand duke, Brentano and his friends
in the *Zentralmärzverein* arranged a public demonstration
at nearby Offenburg on 12 May. The crowd, numbering about
30,000, endorsed calls for the immediate recognition of the
constitution written by the Frankfurt Assembly, the appointment
of Brentano as Prime Minister of Baden, and the prompt election
of a constituent assembly to write a new constitution for that
state.[38] Amid the self-congratulatory jubilation at Offenburg,
news arrived that the troops at Rastatt had mutinied.

Throughout Baden military rebellion spread quickly and
soon struck the fortress at Freiburg, where Liebknecht's
prosecution was scheduled to begin on 12 May. As he was
escorted from his cell through the city, Liebknecht felt
the excitement of the throng that lined the streets. Everywhere, soldiers and citizens cheered his passage. When he
arrived at the courtroom, a chief witness of the government,
worried about the shifting political winds, whispered nervously
to Liebknecht that he would not testify. Somewhat dazed,
Liebknecht then was seated on a bench alongside several

comrades from the September *Putsch*. The men eagerly exchanged greetings and news. Noticing that the crowd had fallen silent, they looked up as the state's attorney rose to speak. In a subdued voice, he declared that the charges, which ranged from thievery through murder to treason, had been dismissed. The delirious spectators then carried Liebknecht and his friends out of the courtroom.[39]

In the palace Grand Duke Leopold anxiously studied the collapse of his authority. When riots broke out in his capital on 13 May, he abandoned the city, at night, riding in an ammunition wagon. The next day, the distressed ministers he had left behind called upon Brentano to come to Karlsruhe and form a ministry. Thus did the apparatus of an entire state fall to the rebels.[40]

With revolution alive in much of southern Germany, with Austria still at war in Hungary, and with rebellion about to reignite Paris, the campaign for the Frankfurt constitution did not seem doomed from the outset. But if it were to succeed, its leaders would have to assume an energetic offensive, spreading the revolution before its enemies could react. Leftists like Struve hoped that the current crusade would galvanize the republicans in the same way that a foreign threat had invigorated the French cause in 1793.

Unfortunately, the head of Baden's provisional government feared precisely this outcome. Recalling the Terror, Brentano was determined to steer a moderate course. At every opportunity, he left an opening for accommodation with the departed grand duke (even keeping his palace securely locked in his absence). Accordingly, he hesitated to launch a military campaign beyond Baden's borders. When his attitude prevailed, the death warrant for the revolution was written.[41]

Liebknecht's experience at Freiburg in the first days
after his liberation exhibits in miniature the reasons for
the failure of the third Badenese revolt. Near that city
were encamped several hundred soldiers from neighboring Württemberg. The local revolutionary committee, which Liebknecht
quickly had sought out and joined, decided to send a delegation
to these soldiers to invite them to enlist in their revolution.
For this dangerous task, a deputy named Fehrenbach and young
Liebknecht were chosen. Outfitted with a red, black, and
gold sash to symbolize German unity, and accompanied by a
large crowd, the two men approached the Württembergers. They
called upon the soldiers to do their duty to the fatherland,
abandon their officers, and join the Badenese troops in defense
of the Frankfurt constitution. Predictably, the Württemberg
officers ordered their troops to arrest Liebknecht and Fehrenbach, but the soldiers refused. Liebknecht left the meeting
convinced that a detachment of soldiers from Freiburg could
drive off those officers and win the troops for the revolution.
Back in Freiburg, he told the makeshift authorities as much.
"All in vain," he later recalled. "Nothing happened." The
Württemberg commander "took his batallion to safety--a magnifi-
cent opportunity slipped by, and truly, we had few opportunities
remaining. . . ."[42]

Disgusted by this indecisiveness, Liebknecht left Freiburg
for Karlsruhe, where the important decisions were being made.
There he sought out Struve, and became his adjutant.[43] From
that office Liebknecht participated in the struggle between
the radicals and the moderates as well as the ensuing collapse
of the revolution.

Brentano's ministry fostered an initial harmony after
its assumption of power. Trying to consolidate support for

his provisional government, Brentano enlarged the important
state committee to thirty members, including Struve. He
ordered elections for a constituent assembly to be held on
3 June. He even ordered a small-scale invasion of Hesse-
Darmstadt, though he called a retreat at the first sign of
resistance.

This early cooperation did not last long. As Brentano
hedged and hesitated, Struve and his supporters became
increasingly impatient. Anticipating a break, on 1 June,
Brentano and his faction in the state committee voted to
delegate all power to a smaller, five-member directorate.
Brentano chaired that new body; Struve was excluded. When
the elections for the constituent assembly two days later
returned no mandates for Struve's group, he and his friends
were sure that Brentano had falsified the results.[44]

On 5 June, the radicals at Karlsruhe founded their own
club. Jacobin in inspiration, it was christened with the
cumbersome name, the "League of Decisive Progress." The
members selected a ten-man delegation, among whom was Liebknecht, to confront Brentano and demand an immediate revolutionary offensive. According to Liebknecht's recollection,
he and Brentano already had "collided once, in prison at
Freiburg," where Brentano tried to serve as Liebknecht's
attorney. At this June meeting, tempers flared again. "'I
remind you that martial law has been declared,'" Liebknecht
recalled Brentano saying. That statement implied the threat
of a drumhead trial and summary execution for enemies of
the government. "This infuriated me," Liebknecht continued.
"I attacked Brentano, shouting at him, 'Martial law exists
for you too!' He seemed to believe that I wanted to assault
him personally; he stepped back and blanched."[45] With that,
the league delegation stormed out to take its own council.

Fearing for his government--and perhaps for his life--
Brentano decided to launch a preemptive strike against
Struve's band. He had to move with caution, however. The
Karlsruhe militia was commanded by Johann Philipp Becker,
a red republican and an ally of the League of Decisive Progress.
Furthermore, *Freischärler* swarmed through the town, and their
sympathies lay unanimously with Struve. Under these perilous
circumstances, Brentano apparently struck a bargain with
conservative elements in the regular army. Just hours after
his exchange with Liebknecht, he arranged for the occupation
of Karlsruhe and the arrest of his antagonists.

Prowling the streets, Liebknecht recognized the signs
of a coup d'etat in the making and hurried to inform Struve
and Becker. They refused to believe the youth, assuming
that Brentano lacked the nerve and the resources for such
a daring move. Later that evening, these three and dozens
of their comrades were arrested and transported to the dungeon
at Rastatt.[46]

For the next three days, Liebknecht sat again in prison.
He was charged with plotting to assassinate Brentano, though
the only evidence offered was that he had worn a knife to
their meeting. When the investigative interview occurred,
Liebknecht laughed at the charge, and denied that he was
an assassin. However, he asserted that if it were within
his power, he would arrest Brentano as a counterrevolutionary
and try him under martial law.[47]

Meanwhile, within Brentano's circle of advisors, serious
disagreement emerged about the wisdom of the coup. Amand
Goegg, who had connections both to Brentano and to Struve,
pointed out how Baden's military strength had been crippled
by the recent arrests. Probing for an acceptable compromise,
he suggested an arrangement that was quite beneficial to

Brentano. According to Goegg's proposal, Becker, Struve, and their partisans would form a company of soldiers and march north to engage the advancing Prussians. By this time, that enemy already had crossed the Rhine and threatened Heidelberg. Consequently, Brentano's reservations about spreading the revolution had become meaningless. Furthermore, if the zealots went north, Brentano would regain a free hand in Karlsruhe, so he agreed to the bargain on 10 June; as a precondition for their release, so did Struve, Becker, Liebknecht, and the other league members.

Liebknecht now enlisted in Becker's artillery brigade and fought at Heidelberg. Fresh from victories in Dresden, Elberfeld and Kaiserslautern, 100,000 Prussian soldiers surrounded the republicans in Baden. Far outnumbered, with limited supplies and experience, the rebels nonetheless fought stubbornly. Aided by fugitives from the collapse of the revolution elsewhere, the insurgents waged a spirited campaign that lasted for almost a month.

Heidelberg fell first about 20 June and with it the line of defense along the Neckar River. As the defeated rebels streamed southward, Brentano urged the newly elected constituent assembly to sue for peace. Fresh from the battlefield, Struve persuaded the delegates to reject that course. Bitter at this defeat, Brentano stalked across the border into Switzerland.[48] Later he immigrated to the United States and was even elected to Congress.

The desperate men he left behind tried to establish a new line of defense anchored by the fortress at Rastatt and stretching along the Murg River to the mountainous frontier of Württemberg. This whole effort hinged upon the assumption that the Prussian army would respect the neutrality of

Württemberg. It did not. Instead, it passed the rebel flank
and attacked from the right and rear of Baden's defenders
on 29 June. Outflanked and outnumbered four to one, Liebknecht
and his comrades scattered.[49]

Some rebel units fled into the fortress at Rastatt,
where they held out against a Prussian siege until 22 July.
The remaining rabble retreated toward the Swiss border. At
Freiburg, on 3 July, Liebknecht found Struve. The latter
had just reversed his stand on continuing the war and convinced
the remaining delegates to the constituent assembly to call
a halt to what remained of the resistance.[50] Through the
evening, he and Liebknecht sat together at a local hotel
with eight other veterans and Amalie. They hesitated to
leave, even though enemy troops darted through the streets,
because they hoped that a few more friends might locate and
join them for the final flight. At last, about 3:00 A.M.,
this handful of survivors scurried toward the Rhine. At the
shore, they buried their weapons together, in case they got
another opportunity to use them. Then the dispirited group--
about the same size as the one that had tramped across the
bridge at Lörrach the previous September with such high hopes--
paddled across the Rhine toward France.[51]

Behind him, Liebknecht left Baden occupied by 100,000
foreign troops, mostly Prussian. After resistance collapsed,
the victors started executing the rebel ringleaders. Two
of Liebknecht's friends, Max Dortu and Friedrich Neff, were
among the victims. Before October at least twenty-five and
maybe dozens more prisoners had been liquidated by the vic-
torious counterrevolution.[52] Many survivors, including both
Brentano and Struve, soon would follow Hecker to the new
world. By mid-summer of 1849, the German democratic movement
lay shattered.

LIEBKNECHT'S REFLECTIONS ON THE REVOLUTION

There are no contemporary sources to indicate what Liebknecht
thought about this colossal defeat. Twenty-five years later
he wrote his first essays about the failed revolution. By
the 1870s, however, reflections on that insurrection had
become a staple in his agitational repertoire. Of the twenty-
nine substantial pieces he wrote, major portions of ten treated
the events of 1848–49. He was the author of a biography
of the revolutionary martyr, Robert Blum, and published several
shorter essays commemorating the insurrection; every 18 March,
the various newspapers he edited carried banner headlines
and provocative editorials celebrating the humiliation of
the Prussian monarch in 1848. In addition, several of the
brief autobiographical articles that he wrote shortly before
his death described his experiences during the revolution.[53]

This collection of sources, including even those few
of an autobiographical nature, must be used carefully in
trying to build an accurate reconstruction of what Liebknecht
learned from the 1848 Revolution. First none of these works
was written until long after the events it describes. Second,
with the exception of the short memoir essays, none discusses
the author's own role in the spectacular doings he describes.
Furthermore and most important, everything that Liebknecht
wrote was directed at a present agitational need.[54] To consider these writings as objective pieces of the historical
record would be a serious mistake. Liebknecht's remarks
on 1848 were either inspirational, designed to instill revolutionary virtues in the masses, or they were polemical,
trying to refute some conservative aspersions about the
revolution.[55]

Right-wing historians in nineteenth-century Germany blamed the failure to establish a nation-state in 1848 on an inherent flaw in the practice of popular sovereignty, at least as it applied to Germany. Insurrectionary madness, they argued, was un-German and futile besides. According to these apologists for elitism, only an authoritarian master craftsman, an iron-willed statesman, a Bismarck, could forge genuine national grandeur.

Liebknecht, detesting such premises and conclusions and intending to rekindle hope for a democratic and socialist Germany, aimed his articles on 1848 at rehabilitating the image of "the people" as an active historical force. Noble peasants and earnest artisans, who devoted themselves selflessly to the cause of a united, republican Germany, fill the pages of his recollections. To counter the conservative position that these innocent and law-abiding people were duped by conspirators and manipulators in 1848, he stressed the unrehearsed character of that uprising. According to Liebknecht, 1848 witnessed "perhaps the most spontaneous [ursprünglichste], the most indigenous [urwüchsigste]," of all revolutions, "in which the people most exclusively directed itself."[56] Unlike some other tacticians of insurrection, Liebknecht did not connect this observation about spontaneity with the failure of the revolution; he did not conclude that the masses were weak and had to be directed from above. On the contrary, he simply thought that the people needed to be better enlightened and organized.

After his own socialist perspective had matured, Liebknecht argued that, because of Germany's economic backwardness, the class consciousness of the workers had not yet developed sufficiently in 1848 for the successful conclusion of the revolution. The revolutionaries were not factory workers, but artisans. They aimed not at socializing the means of production, but at saving handicraft from the onslaught of industrial capitalism. As Liebknecht observed, "The ideal lay not in the future, but rather in the past."[57] Although Marx and Engels had published their *Communist Manifesto* in February 1848, Liebknecht asserted that it had little effect on the course of the revolution.[58]

As an early Marxist historian, Liebknecht helped to map out the communist interpretation of the 1848 revolution. In the overall structure of his analysis, especially regarding the description of class struggles, Liebknecht differed little from Marx and Engels, but there are two subtle shades of disagreement.

First, Liebknecht attributed more influence to the actions of individuals than did Marx or Engels. Liebknecht's *magnum opus* on the revolution, the biography *Robert Blum*, with its focus on one individual contrasts with Marx's *Class Struggles in France*, where impersonal class struggle dominates all else. This observation offers early evidence for a point that will be developed more thoroughly as this narrative progresses: Liebknecht remained uncomfortable with a deterministic application of Marx's ideas about class struggle.

Second, Liebknecht evaluated the revolution differently from Marx and Engels. Engels disparaged the events he witnessed, particularly the final upheaval in Baden. Liebknecht, however, thought that Engels "undervalued the whole movement, in which marched many talented people and much altruistic spirit."[59] The attitude of these two men diverged most markedly regarding Struve, whom Engels despised and whom Liebknecht admired. Engels and Marx were notoriously scornful toward anyone, even potential allies on the left, who did not share their precise ideological formulations. Indeed, they were seldom charitable in their handling of any public figure. By contrast, Liebknecht simply was more tolerant, both personally and ideologically.

Judging from his subsequent words and deeds, Liebknecht extracted three new perspectives from the 1848 rebellion. First, having buried his flintlock in the bank of the Rhine, he never again participated in a violent revolutionary act. Nor did he directly encourage anyone else to do so. In his future pronouncements, he usually implied that bloodshed in the next revolution would begin only when the government, desperate to defend its prerogatives against its own citizens, resorted to some sort of counterrevolutionary coup d'etat.[60] Under such circumstances, he advised the people to defend themselves, but the bulk of his later comments on the use of force warned against a premature resort to arms. Drawing conclusions specifically from the events of 1848, Liebknecht lectured that "the emancipation of labor cannot be the work of a minority which the majority of the people opposes."[61] A "*party of agitation*" was what Liebknecht strived to build after 1848: a "propagandistic party" is how he described it, "which tries to achieve victory through the *spread of its ideas*, not through childish *Revolutionsmacherei*."[62] This orientation protected Liebknecht against the slippery descent into conspiracy or terrorism that attracted some disillusioned and defeated veterans of 1848.

Second, Liebknecht henceforth designated Prussia as the archenemy of democratic socialism. When Prussian soldiers trampled the rebels throughout Germany, Liebknecht concluded that Austria had been displaced as the number one villain

of contemporary German history. However, Liebknecht's anti-
Prussianism cannot be equated with south German particularism.
He simply thought that Prussia was politically the most backward and militarily the strongest state in Germany. Consequently, its elimination or weakening, by revolution or by
international conflict, would greatly enhance the chances
for a successful nationwide revolution. This outlook inocu-
lated Liebknecht against Bismarck's brand of Junker-dominated
German nationalism.

Third, Liebknecht concluded that the proletariat could
only rely upon itself for liberation. Although Prussia was
the most intimidating military enemy of the revolution, Liebknecht believed that state would have been defeated in 1848
except for a shift in class relationships. He observed that
the middle class, heretofore the enemy of monarchy and aristocracy and accordingly a champion of change, had turned
conservative in the midst of the recent struggle. "The 'third
estate' of 1789 split into the bourgeoisie and the proletariat
and the bourgeoisie suddenly discovered that its place was
. . . on the side of the first two estates. . . ."[63] Liebknecht
thought that the middle class had accepted, if not encouraged,
the massacre of lower-class insurgents in Paris in June of
1848. Similar catastrophes in Vienna, Berlin, Frankfurt,
and Baden only proved that the conservative reorientation
of the men of property was international.

Chapter 3
Exile

LEADING THE WORKERS' CLUB IN GENEVA

For the battered German revolutionaries, one insight was
inescapable: aside from the Prussian soldiers, nothing had
done more to kill their insurrection than the chasm that
had cracked open between the comfortable classes and the
working people. Pondering this phenomenon, commentators
both inside Germany and in exile tirelessly debated the so-
called social question. Although proposed answers ranged
from monarchical paternalism to revolutionary socialism,
everyone knew that the poor had to be placated.[1] In this
decade of definition for Europe's reawakening social consciousness, Liebknecht studied with Marx. Twelve years of
study with him in London completed Liebknecht's role as a
revolutionary understudy.

Although Marx and Liebknecht escaped from the collapsing
revolution simultaneously, they did not meet immediately.
Marx fled to Paris, but the increasingly conservative authorities there did not tolerate his presence. In August they
directed him either to settle in isolated Brittany or to
leave the country. Given these choices, Marx opted for immigration to London. Liebknecht, on the other hand, first
found refuge in Switzerland and did not meet Marx in the
British capital until mid-summer of 1850.

By July 1849, Liebknecht knew the Swiss scene too well.
With the swarm of posturing rebels engaged in endless recriminations, the situation differed little from the previous
summer, except that in 1849 the European revolution was dead.
Because he desired a change of surroundings and because the
authorities in the north of Switzerland resented his recent
revolutionary escapades, Liebknecht decided to settle somewhere
in the south, choosing Geneva, where a radical government
directed the affairs of the canton.[2]

Upon his arrival, a local democrat helped Liebknecht
and his comrades rent a villa. His means of support for
affording such luxuries has little documentation. He occasionally worked as a translator and tried to learn type-
setting, but after a painful three-day apprenticeship he
decided that the "sacrifice was too great" and gave it up.
That experience was as close as he ever came to joining the
working class. In a memoir article written fifty years later,
Liebknecht referred vaguely to money he received from Giessen
while in Geneva. He did not specify the source.[3] Actually
he may have shared in some money that Struve thoughtfully
had salvaged from Baden's treasury. Unemployed, but comfortable, he could pursue politics full-time.

In 1849, Geneva remained a small, preindustrial city.
The permanent residents were practically inundated by the
incoming tide of vanquished revolutionaries: Engels, Mazzini,
Herzen, and Liebknecht's former captains, Struve and Becker.[4]
In the egalitarian environment of exile, Liebknecht drank,
talked, and argued with these men. His education in the ways
of subversion accelerated in Geneva.

Aside from a drinking club humorously labelled the
Schwefelbande, his primary arena of action was the German

Workers' Educational Union in Geneva. Societies like this
one had sprung up in the exile communities throughout Europe
during the 1840s. In 1848, Liebknecht had been affiliated
with the society at Zurich,[5] and he renewed that association
in the Geneva organization.

The nature and purpose of these educational societies
varied from place to place. In London and in Germany, at
least a few were loosely connected to the secretive Communist
League, which had been formed in 1847 by a merger between
Marx, Engels, and other professional revolutionaries. By
contrast, the Swiss organizations and many of the ones in
Germany were established by philanthropic businessmen, scheming
politicians or idealistic educators. These middle-class
patrons hoped that education would soothe the workers while
teaching them the virtues of laissez-faire economics and
government of, by, and for the propertied.

In the Geneva educational society, Liebknecht promoted
a preexisting tendency toward politicization and class consciousness; gave speeches to the members about republican
institutions, about proportional representation, and about
the *Communist Manifesto*; analyzed current events in Germany
from a socialist perspective; and quickly won a following.
The positions he advocated, however, rapidly sparked conflict
with the more moderate members of the society, who, led by
Moritz Hartmann, were classical liberals.

From a political and from a social viewpoint, the development of most enduring significance in Europe between 1848
and 1870 was the amputation of the more moderate middle-class
spokesmen from the workers and their radical leaders. This
surgery was part of the redefinition of political ideology
that followed the debacle of the revolution. The argument

between Liebknecht and his rivals in the Geneva Workers'
Educational Union is an early illustration of this major
intellectual and political pattern.

To elucidate the issues, the Union arranged to have
the main protagonists, Hartmann and Liebknecht, confront
each other in a debate. After the speeches, a vote would
decide the winner. Speaking first, Hartmann discussed the
recent revolutionary failure. In his interpretation, the
Frankfurt Assembly in 1848 had constituted the legitimate
government of Germany. Moreover, it had been effective
until "anarchists" like Struve, Liebknecht, and others had
incited lower-class violence. That specter had terrified
most reasonable people and had forced them to abandon the
cause of democracy, making it easy for the Prussian armies
to defeat the divided rebels. The lessons were obvious:
selfish class interests should be subordinated to the universal
struggle for democratization; that struggle, wherever possible,
should be pursued through parliamentary channels. The assembled
crowd cheered Hartmann's conclusion enthusiastically.

Liebknecht, filled with trepidation, mounted the rostrum,
but as he spoke, his confidence returned. He believed that
blame for the revolutionary failure lay not with the extra-
parliamentary actions that he and other revolutionaries had
taken, but rather with the treachery of the middle class.
He vividly described how Brentano's cabal in Baden had sabotaged the struggle there. From that observation, he denounced
the bourgeoisie. The men of property were a selfish minority.
They would use the working class as canon fodder and then
abandon it at the critical moment. Never would they offer
the workers anything but perpetual economic slavery. To
illustrate his point, he charged that the pious but propertied

defenders of democracy at Frankfurt had completely ignored
the social issue. If the workers were not forever to be
duped by middle-class manipulators, they must pursue both
democracy and socialism, and they must battle for those aims
as an independent social class.

When the applause ebbed at last, the vote was taken.
Over three-fourths of the audience endorsed Liebknecht's
arguments. In an organization that was originally led by
middle-class members, he had won an endorsement for social
democracy and for a class orientation for the society's politics.[6] Shortly thereafter the members elected Liebknecht
as their president. Hartmann and his handful of disciples
sullenly withdrew from the organization.

LIEBKNECHT'S STYLE OF LEADERSHIP

Groups and leaders differ in their actions, deeds, and characteristics.[7] One type of leader aims first and foremost at
integrating members into the group. By contrast, there are
other leaders who will readily sacrifice internal harmony
and cohesiveness in the pursuit of the group's external aim.
Still another type of leader may be concerned first with
self-gratification and self-promotion and lead a group only
as an incidental by-product of his personal aims. For such
a leader, group integrity or group ambitions are secondary
to personal satisfaction.[8] Although these three types may
overlap (Liebknecht pursued all three at one time or another),
he most often operated as the first. That type is called
an "affective" leader, one who specializes in emotions, in
keeping the membership happy and together.

To be an "affective leader," one must have the proper personality. Liebknecht's nature corresponded neatly to the needs of such a leader. By all accounts, he exhibited a modesty that was most attractive in a person with his extraordinary talents. This humility enabled him to avoid the petty personal squabbles that often rend embryonic political movements. Furthermore, Liebknecht genuinely valued his friends and would not sacrifice them lightly. He relished long conversations with them over a few beers. At such encounters, he won respect and affection more by his willingness to listen than by his own forcefulness.[9] Engels, who knew Liebknecht well, believed that beneath his conviviality lay a well-concealed core of insecurity that made him seek approval and acceptance more than the average person.[10] Yet Liebknecht was a warm, outgoing man whose personality acted as a cement in every group he joined. Moreover, he possessed an unfailing optimism that he passed out like a life preserver to depressed comrades.[11] His sense of humor, reflected in the way he chuckled at himself in his memoirs, made him a welcome guest at any social occasion.[12] Collectively, these characteristics served him well in performing an integrative function in every organization to which he belonged.

With such traits, Liebknecht was better able than most to head a collection of bickering émigrés. Indeed, his were perfect attributes for the leader of any newborn party. Before ideology is well-defined and organization clearly structured, before the tangible rewards of membership in the association accrue, someone must convince potential recruits that joining and staying in the group is worth the effort and aggravation. That usually was Liebknecht's job.

The talents required for success within the leadership circle are not identical with those needed to recruit supporters on a large scale. The former, more private area calls for a set of almost intimate personal skills; the latter task demands a public presence that is compelling for audiences comprised of strangers. Liebknecht was fortunate in being at home both behind the scenes and on stage.

To influence crowds, leaders may rely either upon a charismatic appeal aimed at the audiences' emotions or they may employ reasoned and persuasive arguments directed at the audiences' intellect. Again these typifications overlap, because the style of delivery colors content. Still, Liebknecht emphasized the rational approach. He never asked his audiences to suspend their critical judgment. On the contrary, his speeches and writings depended upon a logical reception for their effectiveness. Emotional encitement through drama or pathos sometimes intruded, but it never dominated his presentation.[13]

His delivery resembled that of the teacher he had briefly been in Zurich before the revolution and which he would become again for fifty years in various workers' educational societies. He crowded every talk or essay with illuminating examples drawn from an impressive cultural range. Lessons from Plato, More or Michelet were blended with those from Marx. Somewhat pedantically, he sprinkled foreign phrases into his public remarks. Always he seemed to try to raise the cultural level of his audience while he scored a political point. With examples, with patient repetition, and with the simplest of logical structures, the dichotomy, he tried to convince his listeners that one must choose either the evils of capitalism or the benefits of democratic socialism.

Liebknecht was not one to whom oratory came naturally. He admitted that he had "never been fond of speaking," even among friends. Yet there was something "wonderfully intoxicating" about the "enthusiastic acclamations of a meeting numbering thousands" who were spellbound by a "hypnotic power and filled with his thoughts and feelings. . . ." But Liebknecht was careful not to let himself be carried away by this emotional gratification. He knew that the masses could be deceived, that audiences were fickle, and concluded that reason and honesty, not acclamations from the crowds, were the only reliable guides in composing his own public pronouncements.[14]

Liebknecht's physical endowments for addressing large groups were adequate but not overpowering. He was short of stature until, in his twenties, a late spurt of growth catapulted him up to an average height for his day, five feet, six inches. Conscious of his inferior size, Liebknecht had exercised hard as a boy. He remained trim and in good health throughout his life.

His face improved with age. In youth, its neat oval shape was dominated by the pale, full cheeks. In the only surviving portrait from those early years, all the features, but especially the small mouth, seemed a bit too closely crowded toward the center. The resulting visage, though handsome enough to attract a few sweethearts, lacked dramatic power. While in Swiss exile, he added a full, coarse beard, which squared his chin line and created an expression of determination. Partly hidden under the moustache, his pursed lips now seemed to say he was thinking about something. The light brown eyes, which peered intently from under baggy lids, conveyed an air of trustworthiness and sincerity.

As wrinkles gradually appeared, they only reinforced these
impressions, and when his hair turned gray he could claim
an aura of experience as well.

Without moving pictures or any sound recording of his
voice, we cannot say very much about Liebknecht's oratorical
techniques. Though he eventually attracted enormous crowds
and held their attention, he was not renowned as a passionate
speaker. Still, he projected his voice well enough to reach
several thousand listeners. Furthermore, he had stamina.
That quality was indispensable in an age where short speeches
lasted an hour and marathon performances could spill over
from one day to the next.

In the public arena, then, Liebknecht's ideas, his confidence in them, and his persuasive presentation of them won
recruits. Inside the leadership circle of the various parties
he joined, his mellow, accommodating, and optimistic personality supplemented his intellectual power in winning loyalty,
trust, and admiration.

EXPULSION FROM SWITZERLAND

With a base of support in Geneva, Liebknecht began to build
a national organization for the German Workers' Educational
Union in Switzerland. In August 1849, while still secretary
of the Geneva league, Liebknecht co-signed a circular to
similar clubs in other Swiss cities. This dispatch was an
attempt to revive the short-lived nationwide structure of
the previous summer. The circular called upon exiled German
democrats to organize for political education, and it suggested
Geneva as the seat for a central directorate. On 16 October,

Liebknecht, who by now was president of the Geneva society,
sent a second letter to the nineteen other local bodies.
It proclaimed the twofold aim that he foresaw for a national
association: "First to bring the fundamentals of social
democracy to clear consciousness among the members of the
union, and second, to exert every effort to disseminate and
to realize the fundamentals outside [in society as a whole]."[15]

Some of the responding clubs feared police harassment
if they joined in such boldly radical agitation. Liebknecht
scorned their timidity. "Every democrat is bound to give
his life for the holy cause of liberty, equality, and fraternity, and our case is a long way from life and death. . . ."
To another reticent society he declaimed, "propaganda is
the most important means for founding the social republic."
To abstain from this work would be tantamount to treason
for Liebknecht.[16]

Characteristically, Liebknecht was not very precise
about what the content of this propaganda should be. In
a statement foreshadowing his whole career, he urged that
divisive discussions of dogma be postponed. Instead he urged
his comrades to concentrate upon constructing a viable organization. In a twenty-five point program that he proposed
for that organization, twenty-three of the items dealt with
structure rather than creed.[17] Organization first and intellectual clarification thereafter describe Liebknecht's priorities and work in the 1870s and later as well as they do his
labors in 1850.

Equally typically, Liebknecht insisted upon a democratic
form for his Swiss association. As the "highest legislative
authority," he recommended an annual party congress. Each
local club would send a single delegate to this meeting. A

simple majority vote would settle all contested points. This
structure, applying popular sovereignty to intraparty affairs,
became the cornerstone for all of Liebknecht's future political edifices.

Liebknecht's prompting and his proposal were persuasive.
Of the nineteen clubs he contacted, seventeen agreed to enlist
in his German Workers' Educational Union. Total membership
soon climbed from 365 in December 1849 to 560 early in 1850.[18]
To President Liebknecht, it was appropriate to call the first
congress.

On 1 February 1850, Liebknecht issued a call for a convention at Murten. An acceleration of the union's timetable
was necessary because of unspecified events in Berlin, which
pressed "toward a decision with force. . . . It is now our
duty to think about the revolution, for it is perhaps closer
than some believe." Yet, after these incendiary remarks,
he proposed only one specific order of business for the union's
first meeting: the creation of a "workers' newspaper."[19]

Liebknecht traveled by train to Murten on 20 February,
planning to preside over his first workers' party congress.
Surprisingly, he found no delegates to greet him at the platform. Alone, he sought out Der Schwarzer Adler, the inn where
the meeting was to take place. Again no comrades. Instead
he was approached by an unfamiliar man who identified himself
as a government official, and said that on the orders of
the Swiss Bundesrat, all delegates had been arrested. Liebknecht would have to come along to the prison at the cantonal
capital, Fribourg.[20]

The Swiss government thought it had good reason to arrest
Liebknecht's band. Twice in 1848, German exiles had mounted
attacks on Germany from Swiss soil. The various German states,

led by Baden, now insisted that the troublemakers be extra-
dicted or at least expelled from the continent. The Swiss
ministers, only recently promoted to office by civil war,
were worried that the great powers might use the émigrés'
plots as an excuse to invade their country. In addition,
some German exiles, who resented the penetration of socialists
into the educational societies, alleged to the Bundesrat that
Liebknecht and his comrades were proceeding to Murten to
plan another uprising in Germany. Karl Vogt, former leftist
leader at the Frankfurt Assembly, a friend of Moritz Hartmann,
was among the informants,[21] and considering recent happenings,
the Bundesrat could not ignore the charges.

The government in gathering evidence confiscated copies
of Liebknecht's correspondence with the various local societies. Although these communiqués revealed a fervent hope
for a future revolution, nothing in them indicated any plans
beyond organization and agitation. When his jailers told
Liebknecht of the charge against him, he composed a vigorous denial and sent it to the Bundesrat. "We are convinced
that revolution cannot be fostered through conspiracies and
intrigues." He swore that his band would never participate
in any upheaval that did not already have the "great majority
of the people" behind it. The arrest therefore must be a
"misunderstanding," and he concluded with a request for his
prompt release and for permission to hold the congress at
Murten.[22]

After a six-week investigation, the judges concluded
that, in the event of renewed revolution, Liebknecht's association intended to overthrow "not only the thrones but also
the social institutions of Germany." Because these subversives

were not Swiss citizens, the Bundesrat ordered the expulsion
of Liebknecht and over 200 other members of his union.[23]

Having rejected immigration to America as "desertion,"
and having been forbidden to travel to Geneva to collect
his possessions, he crossed France unescorted (with a pass
requiring him to check in with the police in every town along
his route), and in mid-May boarded a channel boat for England.
"The romanticism of exile was now over, . . . and on the
hard London pavement [he] abandoned the rest of [his] political romanticism."[24]

WITH MARX IN LONDON

When Liebknecht arrived in London, the British Empire stood
magnificently at the peak of its power. From recently acquired
Hong Kong to older strongholds like Gibraltar and Toronto,
the Union Jack announced British sovereignty. From all of
these domains, fabulous wealth cascaded back to the mother
country. In celebration of her economic grandeur, England
erected the famed Crystal Palace exposition in 1851. To
display the wonders of her industry and her commerce, the
nation built in Hyde Park a splendid birdcage-like construction of iron framing 400 tons of glass. The contents told
the awestruck viewers that the British Empire was the mightiest,
the most dynamic, and the richest state the world had ever
known.

Meanwhile, to the immediate south and east of Hyde Park,
2.6 million people, packed cheek to jowl, jostled for space
in Europe's most populous urban center. Rural overpopulation
and employment opportunities in industry attracted ever more

newcomers. Another half-million jammed into London between
1850 and 1860. At mid-century, in the nation as a whole,
a majority of the English population for the first time resided
in towns and cities. By 1860, only 19 percent of the work
force earned a living in farming, fishing, or forestry. By
contrast, 39 percent of those working were employed in manufacturing, a proportion unsurpassed before or since.[25]

Living conditions for the urban work force in London
were near their worst ever in the 1850s, when Liebknecht
experienced them. The massive influx of people crushed against
the limitation of available housing. Model dwellings for
workers, which gradually relieved some of the overcrowding,
were begun only a decade later. As yet, escape to outlying
districts was impossible for most, because public transportation was not introduced until the 1860s. The only interim
solution was to subdivide existing structures, giving a
floor--or a room--of existing one-family houses to each incoming family. The psychological anguish generated by such
a crammed environment can hardly be overestimated. Health
hazards also abounded. Until 1849, cesspools handled all
sewage disposal in London. As the number of inhabitants
mushroomed, that circumstance became intolerable. Alas,
the public sewer system constructed in the following years
dumped its contents directly into the Thames. As a result,
each summer's heat and drought brought an unbearable stench
to the city. Even worse, since the river supplied London's
drinking water, the newly installed sewer system merely
recycled disease. Small wonder that cholera epidemics killed
over 10,000 Londoners in 1849 and again in 1854.[26]

In London, Liebknecht suffered penury and lived among
the poor. Only with difficulty did he stitch together a

living from journalistic piecework and private language lessons.
Frequently he had to beg his editors for advances or beseech
his friends for a loan.[27] Sharing the impoverished immigrants'
life in the squalid Soho district, where a single water pump
operating only one-half hour a day served several thousand
people and where seven people typically shared a single room,
Liebknecht understandably interpreted English politics from
the underside.

This abominable situation must be borne in mind when
studying Liebknecht's attitude toward England and toward
industrialization. His primary impression of England was
not of her praiseworthy devotion to civil liberties or of
her practice of constitutional government but rather of
the poverty and exploitation of her poor.[28] Indeed his disgust with socioeconomic conditions colored his political
observations too. In the 1850s he told English audiences
that the political conditions in England were "not a bit
better than in Germany, . . . the only difference being that
[the] Germans knew [their] public affairs were miserable,
while Englishmen did not know it. . . ."[29] In political
correspondence written for German newspapers in the 1850s,
he consistently denounced the English "aristocratic regime"
and Lord Palmerston's practice of parliamentary minuets.
Repeatedly he forecasted that the enraged populace soon would
tear the privileged from their seats of power.[30]

Liebknecht's confidence in such predictions was reinforced
by what he learned from Karl Marx. Liebknecht met Marx in
mid-summer of 1850 at a picnic sponsored by the local chapter
of the far-flung German Workers' Educational Union. The London
variety of that agency ran a dormitory for impecunious refugees,
and Liebknecht stayed there during his first months in London.[31]

Marx's membership in the Communist League connected him to the educational society, which recruited members for the smaller and clandestine league. At that moment, Marx sought supporters because he anticipated an imminent showdown with his rivals in the Communist League. So at the picnic, after a brief phrenological survey of Liebknecht's skull, he agreed to meet with him for a longer interview the next day. During that discussion, which Liebknecht recalled as a long "examination," he had to prove his hostility to "petty bourgeois democracy" and "south-German sentimental haziness." Apparently he succeeded, for he and Marx, along with Friedrich Engels, drank and talked together through the night and into the next morning.[32]

The relationship between the thirty-four-year-old Marx and Liebknecht, who was ten years his junior, began and remained one of teacher and student. Gradually, however, an emotional attachment suffused their relationship. By the end of the decade, the men were more than companions in the pursuit of truth: they were friends.

In 1896, Liebknecht published *Karl Marx: Biographical Memoirs*, where he recounted that for twelve years he had been an almost daily visitor in Marx's household. That period, according to Liebknecht, transpired "at an age when we are most susceptible to deep and lasting impressions, . . ." Nonetheless, he asserted, he never treated Marx as an "idol." He had known too many "great men so early and so intimately that my belief in idols and human gods was destroyed . . . very early." These observations notwithstanding, he said that Marx made the most "imposing impression" upon him of anyone he ever met, and proudly he remarked: "I was his pupil in the narrower and wider sense of the word; I was his friend and confidant. . . ."[33]

In the first half of the decade, the Marx family lived
at 28 Dean Street. Liebknecht found an apartment a few steps
away at 14 Church Street, a short alley halfway between Soho
and Leicester Squares. The only redeeming feature of this
deteriorating neighborhood was its proximity to the British
Museum. So often did Liebknecht run errands to that institution for Marx that his daughters for whom Liebknecht often
sat nicknamed him "Library."[34] Marx's wife, Jenny, became a
surrogate mother and sister who helped him endure the pain of
poverty and exile.[35] Together with other exiles, the Marxes
and Liebknecht enjoyed weekly family picnics on the outskirts
of London. When Marx moved his family to the more pleasant
northside suburbs later in the decade, Liebknecht followed.[36]
Liebknecht learned continuously, and Marx later recalled
that he had "crammed" Liebknecht during the period of the
latter's exile.

Although Marx and Liebknecht doubtlessly were closely
associated, there are reasons to suspect that Liebknecht
exaggerated their intimacy somewhat in his memoir. Because
Marx was quite famous by the 1890s, it would have enhanced
Liebknecht's reputation to do so. Furthermore, Engels, the
only man who could corroborate or contradict his recollections, had died the previous year. In a slightly arrogant
and perhaps jealous tone, Liebknecht wrote that Engels "was
the only one who visited nearly so often and so intimately
with the man and family Marx as [he] did . . . --and Engels
only nearly. . . ."[37] In a separate and demonstrable distortion in his memoir, Liebknecht claimed that, over a span
of three decades, he and Marx had experienced only two quarrels
worth mentioning. Actually there were at least five serious
disagreements.[38]

The published correspondence between Marx and Engels
indicates a slow growth in Liebknecht's importance and a
persistence for his second-rank status. His name was first
mentioned in passing by Marx in January 1851, but the initial
reference in a political context did not occur until March
1853, when Marx was trying to reconstruct a faction for himself. In a list of potential supporters, he mentioned Liebknecht
sixth and last, describing him as "tough" and "useful." As
time passed, references became more frequent; but as late
as 1858, a year still could pass with no mention of his name.[39]
One of Liebknecht's friends in the 1850s scorned his position
vis-à-vis Marx as a "playball--an ass serving as a packmule
and afterwards ridiculed."[40] That evaluation surely underestimated Liebknecht's status. Nevertheless, Marx did not view
Liebknecht as his own equal nor did he consider him to be
as close an associate as Engels. Frequently Marx disparaged
Liebknecht in his letters to Engels, but never did he criticize Engels to Liebknecht.

Regarding the relationship between Marx's ideas and
those of Liebknecht, the latter boasted that he was "never
orthodox or doctrinaire,"[41] but in this regard he claimed
to be following Marx, who himself declined the label of a
Marxist.[42] Ideas shared by Marx and Liebknecht greatly outnumbered areas of disagreement. As noted in the preceding
chapter, Liebknecht's articles in the *Mannheimer Abendzeitung*
in 1847 and 1848 indicate that, in addition to purely political
democracy, he already advocated socialism. In comments made
to the "New Workers' Society" in London in 1852, he articulated three more specific thoughts that are Marxist fundamentals: (1) all social and political institutions originate
from an economic substratum; (2) the victory of the proletariat

and the introduction of socialism are inevitable; and (3)
that goal will be achieved by concerted class action, not
by conspiracies.[43]

Yet, Marx and Liebknecht differed. Marx thought of
himself as a scholar. Having earned a doctorate, he aimed
at intellectually demolishing bourgeois economics, exposing
class exploitation, and proving the inevitability of a successful communist revolution. His theories would thus offer
a potent weapon for the proletarian arsenal. Exhibiting
faith in the efficacy of ideas, he devoted most of his energy
to writing, and his efforts as an organizer were minor.

Although Liebknecht respected the power of ideas, he in-
verted Marx's emphasis. Liebknecht was an organizer first and
a theoretician second. He had left the university without
a degree, and the weaknesses of his philosophical understanding
sometimes led to conflicts with Marx or Engels. In 1870,
for example, Liebknecht protested to Marx about an insulting
letter he had received from Engels. "I have not finished the
course of education like Engels. . . . Before I was through
with the theory I was plunged into the practice. . . . Under
such circumstances it is obvious that I have not studied
Hegel so thoroughly as Engels, but that is no shame for
me. . . . And if I even disdain these studies a bit, so Engels
will have to leave me my private opinion."[44]

Parts of Marx's *Weltanschauung*, especially the more
philosophically abstruse parts, remained completely foreign
to Liebknecht. He probably never saw the *Philosophical Manuscripts* or the *German Ideology*, because they were not published
during his lifetime. The seminal "Theses on Feuerbach" were
not printed until 1888, far too late to mold Liebknecht's
ideas. Although he had the unique opportunity of talking with

Marx, he did not have the chance to read and reflect upon much of Marx's earlier writings. Liebknecht never grappled seriously with the philosophical or psychological dimensions of alienation, nor did he relish discussions of Hegelian dialectics or natural science. He knew Marx as the author of the *Communist Manifesto* and *Capital*. Besides, being an activist, he understandably focused on topics of immediate and obvious political importance: economic exploitation and revolutionary tactics.

Liebknecht was more flexible than Marx in both theory and tactics. On more than one occasion, he volunteered to leave all theoretical guidance of his party in Marx's hands, and he hoped to devote his own efforts to the daily business of organization, which was "overwhelming."[45] Instead Liebknecht repeatedly found himself writing socialist programs. Recognizing that some of his work had provoked criticism from Marx, Engels, and others, near the end of his career he conceded privately that he had made some mistakes in his lifetime, ". . . but I was never a man of cliques and never 'orthodox.'" To underscore the point, he added, "And no dogmatist. Some will criticize me for that," he recognized, "only I know that it has put me in a position to render great service to the party. . . ."[46] He meant specifically fusing together disparate viewpoints and feuding people, in other words, the work of an "affective" leader.

Marx and Engels believed that the "services" Liebknecht performed were transient triumphs bought at the expense of longer lasting success.[47] Occasionally their exasperation at his practices provoked harsh remarks. Referring to an article in one of Liebknecht's newspapers, Marx exclaimed, "How a man I crammed orally for fifteen years (he was always

too lazy to read) can print such rubbish . . . would be
incomprehensible, if Liebknecht were not a South German and,
as it seems, had always mistaken me for his old superior,
the 'noble' Gustav Struve."[48]

Liebknecht created his own variant of Marx's ideas,
adapted to suit the needs of his own political style and
environment. Theoretical principles remained important.
Without knowledge of Marx's "laws of development," Liebknecht
asserted that "social democracy would sink to the level of
impotent-sentimental philanthropy."[49] To justify bending
Marx's ideas to accommodate unruly conditions, he might have
quoted Marx in self-justification: "The philosophers have
only interpreted the world in various ways; the point, however,
is to *change* it."[50]

Neither Marx nor Liebknecht were successful at changing
the world in the 1850s. Both worked in the more modest arena
of the Communist League. Even there, their efforts were
unfruitful. Factionalism split the organization and contributed to its early collapse in 1852.[51] Marx's partisans
in London, including Liebknecht, briefly tried to establish
their own "New Workers' Society," but it folded in less than
a year. For the following eleven years, Marx concentrated
on his research to the almost total exclusion of practical
politics.[52]

Liebknecht could not follow his teacher into seclusion.
In 1853, despite Marx's disapproval, he drifted back into
an educational society led by Marx's rivals. Soon he rose
to a position of leadership, becoming chairman of the West
End branch.[53] For the next several years he gave weekly
lectures to this group on economic themes and current politics,[54]

but despite his best efforts, membership declined. No membership roll exists, but one can infer from public reports of
meetings that at most only a few dozen men participated by
the end of the decade.[55]

In his efforts to combat dwindling attendance, Liebknecht
sometimes accepted recruits whom Marx detested either personally
or ideologically. Furthermore, he took liberties in distorting
Marx's message in order to make it palatable to some potential
members. Informed of these irregularities, Marx reproved
Liebknecht. In the ensuing argument, Liebknecht recalled
that he had "maintained [his] right to serve the party in
a way that seemed most appropriate" and declared it "crazy
tactics for a workingmen's party to seclude itself away up
above the workers in a theoretical air-castle. . . ."[56]

This blow-up ruptured the tie between Liebknecht and
Marx for several months, but the two eventually buried their
disagreement and worked together on a newspaper that Liebknecht founded in May, 1859. The paper, christened *Das Volk*,
was financed by the scanty recources of the West End Educational Society. Marx overcame his reservations about the
personnel surrounding this venture because he needed some
public forum desperately.[57] He had just published his *Critique
of Political Economy* and hoped to use *Das Volk* to break what
he saw as a conspiracy of silence regarding his book. Furthermore, he and Engels wanted some way publicly to comment upon
the exciting international scene, particularly the war in
Italy. Consequently, Engels began contributing financially
to *Das Volk* by the end of May. By mid-June, he and Marx
became regular contributors. With Liebknecht's support,
soon they were practically running the enterprise.[58]

Under the guidance of Liebknecht, Marx, and Engels,
the most pronounced tendency of the newspaper was anti-

Napoleonic propaganda. Marx had already publicized his low
opinion of the French emperor in *The Eighteenth Brumaire
of Louis Bonaparte*. Now that "little" Napoleon was posing
as the champion of national self-determination in Italy,
Das Volk was determined to expose the hypocrisy of his posture
as a friend of the people. In their conception of international
affairs, the editors mirrored the opinions of the British diplomat and commentator, David Urquhart, whom both Marx and Liebknecht greatly respected.[59] In this interpretation, Russia was
the arch-villain (a view popularized in England by the Crimean
War), and Napoleon was her agent, either consciously or unconsciously.

Primat der Aussenpolitik was the primary and somewhat
surprising orientation of this fledgling newspaper. Nevertheless, the editors found space in one issue for excerpts
from Marx's *Critique of Political Economy*. Two months later,
two installments of a review article by Engels appeared.[60]
The financial collapse of the newspaper aborted a planned
third installment of Engels' review.

The circulation of *Das Volk* was small. Published in
German, potential readership was limited in London. Members
of the educational societies comprised almost the whole list
of possible subscribers. Despite Liebknecht's prominent
role in the West End organization, he could not attract many
subscribers.[61] Indeed the newspaper openly provoked some
members of the society. *Das Volk*, by clearly stating its
position on the issues, alienated many individuals. First
rival workers' groups and then members of Liebknecht's own
faction took issue with the paper's content.[62] On 18 June,
the beleaguered journal had to assert that it was a private
venture, not a party organ, and accordingly was responsible

for its opinions to no one but itself. After that announcement, news of the educational societies slowly disappeared
from the inside pages. Separated from its core constituency,
the paper could not meet its obligations and was forced to
cease publication on 20 August.

As *Das Volk* limped toward its demise, Marx and Engels
vented their frustration in criticism of Liebknecht. With
characteristic venom, Marx denounced his protégé's journalistic
incompetence, gratuitously remarking that he was "unreliable
and weak of character." Engels added charges of financial
mismanagement.[63] Although no record of Liebknecht's opinion
of his co-workers has survived, the short-lived journalistic
experiment clearly did not promote harmony; but neither did
it cause permanent damage. In fact, before *Das Volk* closed,
it opened a controversy that drove Marx and Liebknecht once
again into a close alliance.

The controversy in question was Marx's notorious polemic
with Karl Vogt. This tangled affair, often confusing in
its details and petty in its rhetoric, was concerned with
a crucial issue: could or should a leftist endorse an authoritarian patron of national self-determination?

Napoleon III's artful policies first raised this question.
Unlike earlier conservatives, the second Emperor of the French
recognized the need to cultivate mass support for his government. Among the measures he took to generate that support
was the exportation of domestic unrest through a glorious
foreign policy.[64] This purpose, reinforced by traditional
anti-Austrian sentiment in France and a hunger for Savoy
and Nice, led Napoleon into the Austro-Italian War in 1859.
In an effort to win a favorable international opinion for

his military campaign, Napoleon contacted and bribed influential figures, hoping that they would enlist a broad spectrum
of support for his expedition.

Among the men he recruited was Karl Vogt, a university
professor born in Giessen who now resided at Bern. Vogt
had championed German national unity and democracy at the
Frankfurt Assembly. When the decaying assembly regrouped
at Stuttgart, its members elected him one of the five *Reichs-
regenten*. After the military victory of Prussia, he had
scrambled to safety in Switzerland.

In exile, Vogt's attitudes careened toward the right.
Already in 1850 he was influential in effecting the expulsion
of Liebknecht and the other radicals from Switzerland. By
the end of the decade he had forgotten his commitment to
democracy and enlisted in the Napoleonic crusade for nationalism. On 1 April 1859, he sent a circular letter to various
veterans of the 1848 German Revolution, including those in
London, urging them to endorse neutrality for the German
states in the imminent conflict in Italy.

That circular was discussed at a lecture in London given
by David Urquhart on 9 May. Among those participating were
Marx, Liebknecht, and Karl Blind, who had participated in
the various Baden revolutions. Everyone present denounced
Vogt's stance, but Blind went a step further. He alleged
that Vogt had offered him money to write favorable propaganda
for the emperor of the French and that Vogt himself had accepted
such bribes directly from Napoleon.[65]

Armed with this intelligence, Marx and Liebknecht denounced
Vogt on the front page of *Das Volk*. The two-column accusation
charged that he had received "4000 gulden" to betray the
cause of international democracy.[66] Vogt replied in a Swiss

émigré paper, where he alleged that Marx was a police spy
and that *Das Volk* worked as an agent provocateur for the
authorities.[67]

This bitter feud might have spent itself in the obscure
pages of exile journals if Liebknecht had not raised the
stakes in mid-June. At his printer's office, he discovered
the handwritten draft of a pamphlet, *Zur Warnung*, which cor-
roborated the charges against Vogt. From the handwriting
and from the comments of the printer's staff, Liebknecht
concluded that the honorable Karl Blind had composed the
anonymous warning. Relying upon that impeccable authority,
he dispatched a copy to the world-renowned Augsburg *Allgemeine
Zeitung*, for which he had been a London correspondent since
1855. That distinguished journal, which harbored pro-Austrian
sympathies, printed *Zur Warnung* on 22 June.

In a letter he sent to the *Allgemeine Zeitung*, Vogt
indignantly denied the charges made against him. Even though
that newspaper printed his denial, he filed a slander suit
against it.[68] The anxious editors then turned to Liebknecht
for proof of his accusations. Liebknecht turned to Blind,
who denied that he had written *Zur Warnung*.

In a panic, Liebknecht beseeched Marx for advice and
assistance. To Liebknecht's surprise, Marx agreed to help
and set about mustering evidence for the impending trial.[69]
As he told Liebknecht, the case concerned Napoleon's subor-
nation of renowned democrats and consequently was important
to "*every* German revolutionary."[70]

Despite the best efforts of Marx and Liebknecht, no
evidence could be found at that time to prove that Vogt had
received money from Napoleon. Blind and Julius Fröbel publicly stated that Vogt had offered them money to write favorable

essays about the French cause,[71] but that allegation was immaterial at the trial. The judicial proceedings in October oddly produced no resolution, with Vogt's charges being dismissed on a technicality. But no proof was given of the allegation that he was Napoleon's hireling.[72]

At this point, Liebknecht's role in the controversy ended. The polemic, however, had hardly begun. Shortly after the court case closed, Vogt published a widely read and republished pamphlet, *My Action Against the "Allgemeine Zeitung."* Because the worst imaginable calumnies against Marx were printed here, conservative newspapers throughout Germany eagerly quoted excerpts for their readers. Stung by Vogt's scurrilous lies, Marx devoted an entire year to researching and writing a counterattack. To his great disappointment, when *Herr Vogt* appeared late in 1860, it hardly received any attention in Europe. Marx had to admit that it had been "a real shame to waste my time on such a wretched affair."[73] A decade later, when evidence from the deposed Napoloen's personal papers proved that he had indeed bribed Vogt, aside from Liebknecht and Marx few people cared.[74]

The Vogt affair is edifying mainly as an example of the pettiness and futility of exile politics. And yet, the feud with Vogt was the most significant matter in which Liebknecht was involved, despite a decade of political effort in London.

His personal life provided scant solace for his political frustrations, and his financial situation became worse around 1860. First his careless reporting cost him his job with the *Allgemeine Zeitung.*[75] Shortly thereafter, the Civil War in the United States forced several newspapers for which he had been writing to close.[76]

Practically penniless, without prospects, he now also had his family to consider. Since 1854 he had been wed to Ernestine Landoldt, his sweetheart from the Freiburg prison. During their years apart, Liebknecht had sporadically courted an English woman while corresponding with Ernestine.[77] Abruptly decisive, in 1853, he asked Ernestine to share his life in exile. "To live lonesome among men, to be alone amidst the throngs of London without a soul to whom we can entrust our feelings, our wishes, our hopes, that is dreadful, that is unbearable." Ernestine hesitated. Accustomed to middle-class comfort, restrained by her mother, and remembering her father's religion, she knew that Liebknecht demanded an enormous sacrifice. At last, in August 1854, she made up her mind and came to London. The couple married with Roman Catholic rites on 17 September 1854.[78]

Marriage did not bring bliss. Poverty appalled the twenty-two-year-old bride. The birth of a son in 1856 only increased her worries; the baby died after little more than a year.[79] When their daughter Alice was born in November 1857, Ernestine insisted upon taking her to Freiburg as soon as she could travel. Once there, she did not want to return to her husband and his miserable existence.[80] She eventually rejoined him. Nevertheless, domestic problems probably compounded Liebknecht's dissatisfaction in the early 1860s.

Such personal and financial difficulties, as well as the sterility of exile politics, made Liebknecht seek a drastic change in his life. Fortuitously, an opportunity surfaced in 1861, when Wilhelm I ascended the Prussian throne. Eager to inaugurate his reign with a generous gesture, the new king granted amnesty to political opponents of the regime, including most veterans of the 1848 revolution.[81] Informed of this news,

Liebknecht slowly and cautiously made his preparations to end the years of exile and return to his native land.

Chapter 4

Establishing a Political Identity in Germany

THE FIRST CLASH WITH BISMARCK

Within a month after he arrived in Berlin, Liebknecht learned
that Wilhelm I had summoned Otto von Bismarck from the embassy
at Paris to become minister-president of the beleaguered
Prussian cabinet. Considering Bismarck's record of hostility
to popular sovereignty, no one doubted that he would try to
quell the rebelliousness in the lower house of parliament,
where at that moment a majority of the deputies were defying
their king over a proposal to reform the Prussian army. Working
without material resources, relying upon newfound and fragile
political connections, Liebknecht intended to incite such rebelliousness and to prod its careful leaders into outright revolution. Consequently, he collided with Bismarck and was severely
bruised. Liebknecht needed twenty-eight years to build an
organization that could fight the Iron Chancellor on an equal
footing.

The first confrontation between Liebknecht and Bismarck
came unexpectedly, only a few weeks after both men settled
into Berlin. The battleground was the *Norddeutsche Allgemeine
Zeitung*, a newspaper owned and edited by August Brass. Brass,
who was known as a red republican from the 1848 upheaval, had
founded his publication in the Prussian capital in 1861, and
had hired Liebknecht as his English correspondent.[1]

By May 1862, Brass urged him to come to Berlin to join the full-time staff.[2] To insure a fruitful collaboration, Brass elucidated his editorial guidelines and asked Liebknecht if he could accept them. Brass was primarily concerned about the Napoleonic menace to Germany's peace and independence, and he promised to combat "any movement in Germany . . . which presently could lead to a revolution, i.e., to a split between the crown and the people, because this [split] would mean not only the weakening of Germany but also the *strengthening* of Bonapartism." Consequently, Brass pledged to support "*any* government which opposed Bonaparte, . . ." even if [he] "should meet the *Kreuzzeitungspartei.* . . ."[3]

Surprisingly, Liebknecht swallowed this startingly anti-revolutionary platform and agreed to work with Brass. Perhaps he comforted himself with Brass's anti-Napoleonic zeal and relied upon Brass's subsequent promise to combat the exclusion of Austria from Germany and to resist the *Nationalitätenschwindel* in general.[4] He may also have believed that he could influence the stance of the newspaper from within. And he may have been desperate to leave London for any new undertaking. In any case, on 14 July, he asked Brass to check with the police to insure that the recent royal amnesty excused his offenses. When Brass wrote back with the desired assurance two weeks later, Liebknecht set out for Berlin, traveling at the expense of the *Norddeutsche Allgemeine.*[5]

Hardly had Liebknecht settled into his new job when he began to suspect Bismarck's influence on the newspaper. Bismarck took an active interest in the Prussian press from his first days as minister-president. Like Napoleon III, he understood the value of a positive public image. Accordingly, during his long tenure as the head of state, he entrusted press

affairs to the political department of the Foreign Ministry,
an agency he directly supervised. Although he often resorted
to legal suppression of unfavorable opinion, he also consistently encouraged friendly journalists. Sometimes the encouragement took the form of money, as when Bismarck bribed Liebknecht's old friend, Julius Fröbel. At other times, news leaks
or other preferential treatment were used. One of the newspapers Bismarck successfully recruited (whether for money is
uncertain) was the *Norddeutsche Allgemeine*.[6]

By November 1862, at the latest, Liebknecht was convinced
that his boss served Bismarck.[7] He later described how he
obtained conclusive proof. One evening as he and his close
friend, Robert Schweichel, worked late at the editorial office,
a messenger from the Ministry of War arrived and demanded to
see Brass. Because Brass was absent and the matter seemed
urgent, Schweichel offered to accept the written note that
the emissary carried. Imprudently, the messenger handed his
note over to Schweichel. Once alone, Schweichel and Liebknecht
broke the seal to discover a personal communication to Brass
from Albrecht von Roon, the minister of war. Confident of
his connections, Roon requested publication of the note's contents in the next issue of the *Norddeutsche Allgemeine*.

That was the "corpus delicti," Liebknecht later reflected.
The next day he and Schweichel cornered Brass and confronted
him with the evidence of his perfidy. Unabashed, Brass admitted
and even defended his ties to Bismarck.[8] Like Julius Fröbel,
Johannes von Miquel and dozens of other prominent ex-revolu-
tionaries, Brass joined ranks behind Bismarck's banner, trading
his democratic ideals for the hope of success in national unification.

On 20 November, after a mutual exchange of recriminations,
Brass accepted resignations from Liebknecht and Schweichel.[9]

Thus, within three months after his repatriation, Liebknecht found himself unemployed, penniless, and entirely without prospects. Like other forty-eighters, he could have joined Bismarck and prospered. Even after he left the *Norddeutsche Allgemeine*, Brass offered to pay for his essays, especially if they were socialistic enough to conjure a red spectre. Liebknecht saw through that ploy. He knew that Bismarck only meant to intimidate the rebellious bourgeoisie, "to grind [it] between the Junkers and the proletariat as between two millstones."[10] He would have no part in that treachery.

THE POLITICAL SCENE IN PRUSSIA

When the skirmish between Liebknecht and Brass occurred, Prussian politics was complicated. Even before 1848, Prussia had inherited a typical threefold division of political opinion: conservative, liberal, and democratic. To be sure the boundaries between these viewpoints were murky, but the confusion generated by that ill-definition was nothing compared to the controversy created by what was called the social issue. When Liebknecht returned to Germany, no one publicly advocated abandoning the poor and the unfortunate to starvation. Conservatives, laissez-faire liberals, and democratic socialists agreed that something had to be done for the lower classes, especially for the artisans. Battered by increasing competition with modern industry, the handworkers' shops were turning belly up with unseemly frequency.[11] Amid the ruins of guild production, would-be leaders of the masses sought an economic alternative that would help the skilled craftsmen keep their dignity and livelihood.

In all three political camps, a similar solution surfaced; producers' cooperatives, owned and managed by the workers, would be erected for mechanized manufacture.[12] For the liberals, these ventures had to be self-help enterprises. Hermann Schulze-Delitzsch, the foremost advocate of this viewpoint and for a time the most popular man among the artisans of Germany, advised the workers to husband their meager resources, to organize their own businesses, and to compete with the middle-class entrepreneurs.[13] By contrast, some paternalistic conservatives like Hermann Wagener called for state assistance to the infant, collectively owned industries.[14] Countless worker petitions that flowed into Bismarck's ministry showed the readiness of the laborers to take economic assistance from a monarchical government.[15] Recognizing an opportunity to steal a march on his liberal enemies in the Chamber of Deputies, the minister-president advised his king that royal help for the working class could dispel the pernicious influence of Schulze-Delitzsch and his middle-class patrons among the masses.[16]

For some years, the working class pondered the alternatives of state-help and self-help. To appreciate Liebknecht's work in the 1860s, it is necessary to remember that three possible political orientations resulted from these two economic choices. From self-help arose two options: integration of the working class as a left wing of the liberal movement or the development of an independent proletarian party. Acceptance of state-help, on the other hand, could have integrated the workers into institutions of the authoritarian state,[17] and it was against this third, undemocratic possibility that Liebknecht battled most vigorously.

In the 1860s, the confusion about political and economic issues was compounded by controversy concerning the unresolved national question. At least four distinct camps confronted each other on the matter of German unity. The most tradition-laden of these four were the particularists. They favored the status quo, with practical sovereignty vested individually in each of the thirty-nine members of the Germanic Confederation. Standing slightly closer to centralization were the federalists, who wanted an invigorated Diet of the confederation but who feared the domination of Germany by either Austria or Prussia. Then there were the partisans of a centralized state led by each of those two powers: the Prussophiles, *kleindeutsch*; the Austrophiles, *grossdeutsch*.

In this time of molten ideologies, Liebknecht worked to forge a coalition of elements that could establish a *grossdeutsch*, socialist republic. In that effort, he could choose among a wide range of potential allies, depending upon which issue he chose to stress. If he focused on the national issue and operated in simple opposition to Bismarck and his plan for Prussian hegemony, Liebknecht might cooperate even with conservative particularists. Although antagonism toward Prussia was the sole cement in such an alliance, Liebknecht actually did collaborate with reactionary Hanoverian monarchists later in the 1860s.[18]

Likewise, Bismarck could seduce some unlikely allies if he concentrated on German unification, and he used nationalism to his advantage, encouraging Prussian particularists, liberals, and even some socialists to abandon their traditional alliances. On three separate occasions between 1862 and 1865, Liebknecht learned to his dismay that several trusted members of the socialist party also supported Bismarck.

Bismarck's allies made several attempts to recruit Liebknecht too, but he rejected all overtures. Firmly *grossdeutsch*,
Liebknecht opposed the amputation of the Austrian Germans uncom-
promisingly. Firmly democratic, he could never support the
enemy of liberal freedoms. In Marxist terms, he believed that
Germany tottered on the brink of a somewhat belated middle-
class revolution. Like his mentors, Marx and Engels, he believed
proper strategy currently dictated encouragement of the liberal
opposition to the crown. As Engels wrote in 1865, the workers
needed the bourgeois freedoms--freedom of the press, of assembly
and so forth--"like the air they breathe." If the bourgeoisie
proved too cowardly to carry forward the fight for these freedoms, then the lower class would have to pursue the struggle
against Bismarck by itself.[19]

LIEBKNECHT'S VIEWS ON NATIONAL UNIFICATION

After leaving the *Norddeutsche Allgemeine*, Liebknecht penned
anti-Prussian, anti-Bismarckian paeans for various newspapers
outside Bismarck's realm. Several nonsocialist sheets, including the *Oberrheinische Courier*, the *Schweizerischen Volksfreund* and the *Osnabrücker Zeitung*, shared his hostility to
Prussian hegemony, and they published his articles.[20] The
paltry wages they paid staved off starvation, and their modest
circulations gave him at least a small audience in the furious
argument about national unity.

Concerning the content of these hundreds of articles,
Liebknecht confided to Marx, "Naturally I do not write directly
for our principles [but rather] mainly negatively, against
Bismarckian and Progressive Prussianism. . . ."[21] Understanding

this statement as a caveat that these essays are an incomplete reflection of Liebknecht's ideas, one can still learn something of his agitation from them, especially concerning national unification. For although he could not smuggle socialist comment into his journalism, his writing was neither colorless nor impartial. On the contrary, almost every sentence smoldered with anti-Prussian passion.

In his remarks, Liebknecht gave sophisticated political instruction to his readers: Bismarck could not be understood as a "feudal" type of leader; the minister-president despised the small-minded, particularistic Junkers; he aimed at a centralization of power that would allow him "free play for caesaristic leaps and bounds in every conceivable direction," and to achieve this end would use modern, nineteenth-century manipulative means, even if they "reaked a bit of 'democratic oil' or even of revolutionary sulfur."[22]

Liebknecht's commentary tracked Bismarck's escalation of tensions through the war against Denmark in 1864, into the controversy over the administration of Schleswig and Holstein in 1865, and to the brink of war with Austria in 1866. When a joint Austro-Prussian army seized Schleswig and Holstein from Denmark, he moaned that it was a "national misfortune" that this "separation has come about through the enemies of German freedom and unity."[23] As arrangements for administration of the occupied duchies tangled into a Gordian knot, Liebknecht complained that the matter of national unification had become a "plaything for dynastic interests."[24] Repeatedly he insisted that only the German people could achieve genuine unity.[25]

Bismarck knew that Prussian aggrandizement inspired substantial opposition on the left. So before his showdown with Austria he took steps to secure his left flank on the domestic front. In the spring of 1866, he publicly endorsed a national assembly elected by universal male suffrage. Liebknecht was not moved. How, he asked his readers, could the mortal enemy of the Prussian parliament sincerely champion a democratically elected legislature?[26] In March 1866, Liebknecht announced his analysis of Bismarck's plan: "*internally*, regarding the Chamber of Deputies, a purely negative policy, maintenance of the constitutional appearances, disregard for the Chamber decisions, avoidance of every use of force; *externally*, great actions, so that the people by and by would forget the constitutional conflict, annexation of Schleswig and Holstein, with the 'last means' of a war against Austria."[27]

From the outset, Liebknecht had tried to immunize his readers against the contagion of Bismarck's spectacular diplomacy. Consistently he lambasted the abuse of nationalism by "despots who lust after conquest," and always he advised his audience that "freedom [stood] above the nationality principle."[28]

Liebknecht's bitter opposition to Prussia did not originate in particularistic sentiments, nor did it spring purely from *grossdeutsch* sympathies. He saw Prussia as *the* archenemy of revolution in Germany; "1849 had already shown that Austria was crippled, and Prussia had to assume the court martial work." He regarded a further consolidation of resources under Prussian control as a catastrophe. If the Prussian army were strengthened, if the middle class and particularistic opposition to Bismarck were allowed to languish, no successful revolution could occur "until the German proletariat would become capable of governing. *But until then we would have*

to wait *a few generations*!" he exclaimed. "I proceed from
the viewpoint that the fall of Prussia is the victory of
the German revolution." "And against this Prussia," he confided on another occasion, he was willing to lead "even
Hanoverian particularism into the field."[29]

SCHISM IN THE WORKING-CLASS MOVEMENT

Liebknecht's anti-Prussian campaign comprised only a tiny
part of his work between 1862 and 1865. While in Berlin,
he continuously conducted a two-fold campaign. First, he
tried to exploit the national issue to incite Bismarck's
enemies: proletarian, bourgeois, or even aristocratic.
Second, he struggled to construct the nucleus of a working-
class, democratic, socialist party.

In 1864, Liebknecht emerged as a man of considerable
influence in working-class circles. Records of public speeches
and references in various correspondence solidly attest to his
importance. Because he was not the charismatic type of leader
who enlists a following overnight, he must have been diligently nurturing his political connections for months. The
few letters from Liebknecht to Marx that have survived from
1863 corroborate this backward extrapolation.[30] Nevertheless,
it remains sadly true that much, much more is known about
the workers' movement in these early years than about Liebknecht's part in it.

In the early 1860s, throughout the industrializing society
of western Europe, proletarian associations consolidated
like crystals from a supersaturated solution. In England,
France, Germany, and elsewhere, labor leaders organized

the declining artisans and the growing number of factory
workers. By the end of 1864, an International Workingman's
Association (IWA) had been built to bind these various leagues
together. Karl Marx stood at its head.

Three streams flowed together to create this reemerging
workers' movement. First was the legacy of 1848. In almost
every local workers' club that sprang up, the most important
figures were men who had fought for the red republic in 1848.
The returning corps of exiles, including Liebknecht, was
the most important cause of the resurrection of a German
workers' movement.[31] The experienced revolutionaries usually
tried to goad the labor movement from passive introspection
or economic rumination into political activity. Berlin and
Leipzig were the most important centers of their efforts.
By November 1862, leaders from both cities, armed with mandates
from massive public meetings, had agreed upon the need to
convoke a pan-German workers' congress.

That development terrified the second category of contributors to the revival of the workers' movement. These
were the liberals, the middle-class friends of the laboring
class. In many locales, well-to-do sponsors had initiated
workers' educational societies to propagate technical skills
and to extol the virtues of the apolitical, self-help cooperatives that Schulze-Delitzsch advocated. By this effort,
the liberals hoped to enlist a mute legion of followers who
would intimidate the government into granting the constitutional concessions that they demanded. By late 1862, hundreds
of these local workers' societies had leaped into existence.
Yet, the propertied patrons of these associations worried
about their own success. For in many of the clubs, the workers
groped toward radical and independent political action.[32]

Hoping to exploit that development to weaken his parliamentary enemies, Bismarck arranged a third tributary to
the workers' movement. Although small and doubtless dis-
pensable, the minister-president's ministrations to the embryonic labor organization are symbolically significant. They
underscore the observation that the working class faced three
political alternatives at the moment of its political crys-
tallization: either independence or ties to the liberals
or an alliance with the conservatives. To coax developments
toward this last-named direction, Bismarck hired an agent
provocateur named Eichler to burrow his way into the budding
workers' movement. Soon he surfaced in the front ranks of
those labor leaders who advocated the pan-German workers'
congress. In November 1862, when the workers in Berlin became
convinced of Eichler's connections to the government, they
publicly repudiated him, thus ending his brief career,[33]
but this episode was only the first of many direct interven-
tions in the workers' movement by Bismarck.

As in his handling of the press, Bismarck treated the
workers movement with a combination of courtship and judi-
ciously applied repression. When bludgeoning proved necessary,
he had available a sledgehammer resolution of the Germanic
Confederation from 1854. That decree banned any and all
organizations that professed "political, socialist or communist purposes." The same document proscribed connections
between organizations in various localities, regardless of
their purpose.[34]

To avoid dissolution, most of the workers' clubs that
appeared in the 1860s advertised themselves either as "educational societies" or as organizations of a particular craft.
To remain within the law, they had to forego overt political

activity and regional superstructures. Because the police
attended every public meeting, discussion of radical subjects
had to remain muffled.[35] Given these facts, one must assume
that, when an avowedly political and independent workers'
party appeared and survived, it did so with the explicit
forbearance of the Prussian ministry.

In the spring of 1863, Ferdinand Lassalle slid into
the leadership of the politicized part of the German workers'
movement, his way having been carefully prepared by the work
of a committee in Leipzig. As a result of his inspirational
efforts, a fledgling workers' party, the General German Workers'
Union (ADAV, the *Allgemeine Deutsche Arbeiterverein*), was
founded at a meeting attended by twelve delegates in Leipzig
on 23 May. Even as he accepted the presidency of this movement, Lassalle entered into fateful secret conversations
with Bismarck.

On the surface, Lassalle seemed to have many experiences
and beliefs in common with Liebknecht. Accordingly, on the
surface, his talks with Bismarck seem incomprehensible.
Lassalle, one year older than Liebknecht, grew up in much the
same political environment. Like Liebknecht, he had joined
the *Burschenschaften*. Both men studied at the University
of Berlin about the same time, although apparently they did
not meet. Both knew and respected Karl Marx. In the 1860s,
both claimed to work for the emancipation of the working
class and the creation of a democratic, socialist society.

These similarities notwithstanding, telling differences
between Liebknecht and Lassalle became apparent in 1859,
before they even met. In that year, they crossed literary
swords over Napoleon's war in Italy. While Liebknecht took
an anti-Napoleonic, pro-Austrian stance, Lassalle urged Prussia

to exploit the fleeting opportunity offered by Austria's distraction and expel the Habsburgs from Germany. Already Lassalle stood in the *kleindeutsch* camp.

When Lassalle learned that Liebknecht endorsed a common German front against France, he warned Marx that Liebknecht must be an agent of the Austrian Emperor, Franz Joseph.[36] Lassalle's Prussophilia and Liebknecht's *grossdeutsch* convictions remained a barrier during their subsequent political contacts, and may partially explain why Liebknecht did not contact Lassalle for over a year after his return to Germany, even though both men lived in Berlin. Only Lassalle's political success finally induced Liebknecht to shake off past grievances and approach him.

Lassalle's rise in German workers' politics was meteoric. Prior to his involvement in the ADAV he had never spoken in a workers' club. Aristocratic in demeanor, he detested contact with the laborers in their usual haunts, the shops, pubs, and slums of the cities. He had "absolutely nothing of a *Volksmann*" about him.[37] A single pamphlet he had written on the worker question in 1862 called him to the attention of the leaders of the organizing committee in Leipzig. In December 1862, they invited him to lead the movement they were promoting. After hesitating for three months, Lassalle agreed to cast his lot with the lower class.[38]

Self-indulgent and autocratic, Lassalle accepted this challenge mainly to gratify his own ego. Because he used politics primarily for personal satisfaction, the resulting personal style built another barrier between him and Liebknecht. As president of the ADAV, Lassalle successfully insisted upon dictatorial control over the organization. For reasons both personal and political, Liebknecht would have preferred a collective leadership and the institution of frequent and sovereign party congresses. Moreover, the impoverished Liebknecht despised Lassalle's ostentatious lifestyle, with his lavishly furnished apartment, his annual vacation in Switzerland, and his liaisons with the aristocracy.[39]

These irritations aside, on matters of political substance Liebknecht could find much in Lassalle's early agitation that he endorsed. Lassalle's first programmatic statement in connection with the ADAV, composed as an "Open Reply" to a political inquiry from the Leipzig committee, unequivocally said the workers could "expect the fulfillment of their legitimate interests only with *political* freedom." Regarding the ongoing liberal struggle against the crown, Lassalle advised the lower class to support the Progressives when they shared a common interest and to drive them forward at all times under the threat of losing popular support. To put a political club in the fist of the working class, he called for universal suffrage for all adult men. To insure that weapon would be wielded effectively, he advocated the organization of all laborers into a General German Workers' Union. That agency would then proselytize for government sponsorship of worker-managed cooperatives as a "preparatory measure" for the solution of the social issue.[40]

Lassalle's political intent in this manifesto has long been the subject of controversy. Because it explicitly adhered to legality and because it proposed a sane way to reduce class conflict, Lassalle himself described it as "thoroughly conservative." Yet, he hoped that the document would generate revolutionary results. He reconciled those apparently contradictory thoughts by believing that the ruling class would

never act sanely, that it would never make calculated concessions to avoid losing everything.[41] He should have realized his mistake on May 11, when he received a brief note
from Bismarck.

The minister-president told the ambitious labor leader
that he was soliciting the opinions of "independent" men
concerning the "situation of the working classes."[42] In
his first recorded reply, Lassalle sent Bismarck a copy of
the statute and program of his ADAV. In an ebullient mood
he suggested that Bismarck might well "envy" the authoritarian edifice that he, Lassalle, had constructed for his
"Reich." But Lassalle continued, and he was serious: "This
miniature picture" should demonstrate "how true it is, that
the *Arbeiterstand* feels itself instinctively inclined to
dictatorship. . . ." More, he suggested that if the crown
adopted a "genuinely revolutionary and national direction,"
it might transform itself from "a monarchy of the privileged
elements into a social and revolutionary peoples' monarchy!"[43]

Bismarck saw the opportunity for manipulation that
Lassalle offered, and during the following months he invited
the ADAV president to frequent clandestine conversations.
Under Bismarck's influence, a gradual but noticeable shift in
Lassalle's orientation occurred. Slowly the anti-Manchester
kernel that lay behind his social thought, a perception that
might have led to useful dialogue, receded. In its place
came shrill attacks upon the liberals' politics. As time
passed, Lassalle's public protestations of loyalty to the
Prussian state became more fervent. After a brush with the
authorities as a result of a mass rally in Solingen, he ostentatiously telegraphed Bismarck and asked for his assistance.
As the Solingen incident forewarned, in this game Bismarck

held all the cards. After all, he controlled the legal system, and Lassalle was arrested for high treason in the autumn of 1863. In vain Lassalle pled for help from the minister-president. Calculatingly, Bismarck left the ADAV president to wriggle his own way out of the charge. At his trial the following March, being desperate to prove his loyalty to the throne, Lassalle publicly endorsed the idea of a "people's monarchy."[44]

By that time, Lassalle had rendered himself superfluous to Bismarck. After repeated requests for an interview were ignored, the crestfallen ADAV president gave up trying to contact the minister-president. To his enamorata, the Countess Hatzfeldt, he conceded that he had been outmaneuvered. Bismarck had segregated the social element of the workers' demands from the dangerous liberal political ideals being voiced in the Prussian Chamber of Deputies. Now he could approach the workers directly. If he succeeded, Lassalle concluded, "Bismarck alone would have the power and would have to reckon with no one, not with the people, the Chamber, nor the [workers'] movement."[45] Nor with Lassalle, he might have added. The despondency that arose from this insight probably contributed to Lassalle's decision to fight that bizarre duel in August 1864 in which he died.

By quantitative measurement, Lassalle had not achieved very much when he died. His ADAV counted less than 5,000 members. Moreover, Lassalle's liberal opponents had rallied their forces into a competing league, the Union of German Workers' Unions (VDAV, the *Verein deutscher Arbeitervereine*). Its founding congress held at Frankfurt am Main on 6 June 1863 attracted almost ten times as many delegates as the Lasallean gathering two weeks earlier. The VDAV membership

probably was four times as large as the ADAV roll at the
time of Lassalle's death.[46] And at the center of political
gravity, in the Prussian capital, the liberals' disciples
definitely held the upper hand.[47]

To overcome this embarrassing weakness, Lassalle had scheduled an agitational assault on Berlin for late October 1863.
His efforts briefly increased membership, swelling the local
chapter to perhaps 200 members.[48] Among the new recruits was
Wilhelm Liebknecht.[49] Unlike most of the other enlistees, Liebknecht remained in the organization after Lassalle left town.

There is little evidence to indicate what Liebknecht
had been doing in Berlin since his break with the *Norddeutsche
Allgemeine* the preceding November. Joined by his wife and
daughter, he had settled into an apartment at 13 Neuenbergerstrasse, and was employed as a free-lance journalist. Engels
occasionally sent a few pounds. Liebknecht's scarce resources
had to stretch still further after 28 October 1863 when his
wife bore a second daughter, who was named Gertrude.

While struggling to make ends meet financially, Liebknecht
had hesitated to become involved in local workers' politics.
His reluctance stemmed from disgust at the political backwardness of the existing clubs. In each of the several unions
in Berlin, the influence of Schulze-Delitzsch predominated.
Frequently at public assemblies and in the pages of liberal-
dominated press, Schulze-Delitzsch warned the workers to
avoid politics entirely. Otherwise, he cautioned, a red
spectre might again materialize, as it had in 1848, terrify
the middle class, and lead to the triumph of absolutism. In
Geneva a decade earlier, Liebknecht had argued against that
same viewpoint, which then was championed by Moritz Hartmann.
He was reluctant to fight tired old battles again. In May
1863, he told Marx he had not yet bothered to visit the local

workers' societies, adding, "You will have heard from
Lassalle how wretched they are."[50]

Partly as a result of Lassalle's agitation, partly as
a result of trends that antedated his efforts for the ADAV,
the workers' movement in Berlin became more aggressive and
dynamic in the course of 1863. Artisans and skilled workers,
who were threatened by the accelerating pace of industrialization, became more militant and began to organize. Unable
to abstain from politics for long, Liebknecht contacted the
executive committee of one of Berlin's largest craft organizations, the printers' union. In October, that union invited
him to speak to one of its gatherings.

Reporting on his remarks to the printers' union in a
letter to Marx, Liebknecht explained that his position was
"very delicate." Because Schulze-Delitzsch's ideas were so
widely accepted, it was necessary to focus criticism upon him.
Liebknecht felt that to successfully attack Schulze-Delitzsch,
he had to "beat the drum just as strongly against the Junkers."
Otherwise, he would be "suspected by the workers of being
a tool of the feudalists. . . ." Like the movement he sought
to foster, Liebknecht fidgeted uncomfortably between two
fires, the liberals and the conservatives. Making the situation still more tedious, he told Marx, "a word against Bismarck
will be the signal for my deportation."[51] Because Liebknecht
was not a Prussian citizen, the authorities could expel him
at any moment by a simple administrative order.

About the same time that Liebknecht first addressed
the Berlin printers, he also joined the ADAV. However, he
did so intending to work for his own *grossdeutsch* republican
socialist vision and not for Lassalle's authoritarian rump
of a Germany. From his first days in the ADAV he strove
to construct an internal, anti-Lassallean opposition.[52]

Older accounts of the antagonism between Lassalle and
Liebknecht misleadingly argued that only the national issue,
kleindeutsch vs. *grossdeutsch*, separated the two labor leaders.[53]
Clearly, the issue of revolutionary tactics played a decisive
role too. Liebknecht illustrated this point in a published
memoir recalling a confrontation he had with Lassalle.

In April 1864, the ADAV President invited Liebknecht
and about twenty other party members to a dinner. After
eating, Lassalle arose and proposed a political toast concerning the chronic constitutional crisis. According to
Liebknecht, Lassalle declared that "the bourgeoisie is the
only enemy, and we should swear to fight the enemy to death,
and not even to recoil from an alliance with the monarchy."[54]
Outraged, Liebknecht leaped to ·his feet, exclaiming that
he would never fight on the side of Bismarck. This explosion,
which doubtless ruined everyone's digestion and spoiled
Lassalle's send-off from Berlin, dealt with revolutionary
tactics, not with national unification.

Tactically, Liebknecht chose to work within the ADAV
rather than to fight its president from outside, because
the workers' movement already was fragmented and he had no
wish to attack and possibly to cripple the part which, at
least in terms of politicization, comprised its most advanced
elements. Liebknecht did not even necessarily aim at unseating
the ADAV president. His hope was to change the goals of
the party. If that could be achieved through persuasion,
so much the better.

During 1864, Liebknecht pursued two simultaneous tacks
inside the ADAV. On the one hand, at every public and private
opportunity, he expounded his own political philosophy (but-
tressed by Marx's authority) and tried to rally the opposition

to Lassalle. With special emphasis, he trumpeted Marx's contribution to the workers' movement and made it clear that Lassalle was a derivative thinker. Always, as he told Marx, he kept his "distance" from Lassalle. "When the Bismarck regime is ended," he confided to his mentor in London, "and we can afford to be messy, the break will probably be unavoidable, for I do *not* believe that he [Lassalle] will support the revolution."[55]

At the same time, Liebknecht privately pressured Lassalle to become more democratic and to abandon his affiliation with the *kleindeutsch* cause. Until the alternative of persuasion could be explored fully, he restrained his less patient friends from an open rupture with Lassalle. He intended to bring the ADAV president together with Marx in September 1864, counting upon Marx's overpowering presence to sway Lassalle.[56] If Marx could not do so, only then did Liebknecht plan to unleash an intraparty rebellion. A general congress of the ADAV, which Liebknecht called the "life-nerve" of the organization, was scheduled for autumn. By then, if persuasion and intimidation had failed, with careful preparation Liebknecht hoped to be able to oust Lassalle and abolish his dictatorship.[57]

Lassalle's unexpected death on 31 August demolished Liebknecht's plans. Instead of a weary and confused opponent, Liebknecht now had to contend with a martyred hero. With surprising speed and ease (considering the circumstances of his death), a personality cult grew up around the fallen leader. His assorted slogans--the iron law of wages that proved the futility of labor unions, the description of all nonworkers as a reactionary mass that barred temporary cross-class alliances, the panacea prescription for state-sponsored

productive associations that, combined with his references
to the social monarchy, invited the workers into docile acceptance of an authoritarian state--all these became inviolable
scripture to the ADAV faithful. Furthermore, in his testament Lassalle admonished his followers to "hold fast to the
organization! It will lead the *Arbeiterstand* to victory!"
Thus a fetish for the present ADAV dictatorship joined his
legacy too.[58]

Trimming his sails to the new winds, Liebknecht tried
to exploit Lassalle's death for his own advantage by attempting
to have Marx elected as the new president of the ADAV. The
scheme was not as preposterous as it might appear. Liebknecht's
praise of Marx's merits had won much attention and respect
in the ADAV for this theoretician. Now several prominent
party members backed his election. Thus, Marx probably could
have won the presidency, even had he chosen to remain in
London.[59]

As it happened, in September 1864, Marx was preoccupied
with efforts to build an international working-class organization. However much he would have appreciated some type
of mandate from the ADAV,[60] he would not spare the time that
leading the Lassallean legion would require. Besides, he
disagreed with much of the Lassallean ideology. Consequently,
he vetoed his nomination and left Liebknecht to fend for
himself.

Probably, Liebknecht did not consider running for the
presidency of the ADAV, because he was unknown outside Berlin
and his candidacy would have had slight chance of success.
When the local chapters of the ADAV voted on 1 November,
they followed the directions in Lassalle's will and elected
Bernhard Becker as their president. Only absolute loyalty

to Lassalle had recommended this bumbling figure. Under his
incompetent administration, the ADAV fell apart within four
months.

Liebknecht's upcoming battles with Becker and with other
aspirants to the Lassallean mantle contributed mightily to
the swelling anarchy inside the ADAV. In addition to Becker
and Liebknecht, at least two other ambitious Lassalleans lusted
after the leadership of the league: the Countess Sophie
Hatzfeldt, Lassalle's bereaved lover, and Johann Baptiste
von Schweitzer.

The Countess Hatzfeldt fancied herself to be the executor
of Lassalle's legacy. Although she is usually mentioned only
briefly in histories of the labor movement, she retained considerable influence in the ADAV until 1869. Hatzfeldt's immediate object in 1864 was to immortalize Lassalle and to see
that his work continued. To that end, she commissioned Liebknecht to write a pamphlet clarifying Lassalle's last days
and legacy. While helping Liebknecht with his research, she
disclosed the conversations Lassalle had had with Bismarck.
Before Liebknecht could recover from that shock, she urged
him to pick up the fallen standard and champion Bismarck's
expansionist plans.

Appalled, Liebknecht broke off relations with the countess.
On 16 February 1865, he complained to Marx that the countess
had "so lied and intrigued on all sides that, if her gender
did not protect her, she would deserve to be thrashed."[61] The
countess proved to be a streetfighter herself. First, she
arranged to have Liebknecht harassed financially.[62] Then,
at least Liebknecht believed, she urged the Prussian government to deport him.[63] For the remainder of the decade,
Hatzfeldt and her partisans continued to snipe at him.

Liebknecht briefly cooperated with the second rival to
Becker: Johann Baptiste von Schweitzer. Unfortunately, he
was even more compromised by Bismarck than Lassalle had been.
Schweitzer had a checkered past, personally and politically.
For most of his life he eked out a living as a playwright.
His political career lasted less than a decade, coinciding
exactly with the era of Bismarck's aggressive diplomacy and
wars. A déclassé aristocrat, he was always strapped for funds.
Machiavellian in his politics, Schweitzer was a perfect actor
for Bismarck's political stage. Insofar as he had a guiding
vision, it consisted of a united Germany. Before 1859, he
had been a conservative Austrophile. The Franco-Italian victory in that year, by exposing the Habsburgs' weakness, turned
him into a *kleindeutsch* republican. He started his republican
agitation at Frankfurt am Main, being among the earliest members
of the workers' club there. His efforts ended abruptly in
1862, however, when unsubstantiated charges of embezzlement
against him were followed quickly by a conviction for attempted
child molestation.[64] As a result of these embarrassments,
Schweitzer temporarily withdrew from politics.

A year later, when Schweitzer sought admission to the
Frankfurt chapter of the ADAV, the local members blackballed
him. Fortunately for Schweitzer, Ferdinard Lassalle intervened on his behalf and secured his enrollment. Apparently
the president had been impressed by Schweitzer's most recent
novel, which had been dedicated to Lassalle. Under Lassalle's
patronage, Schweitzer won a position of influence in the ADAV.
He was included in Lassalle's plan for the summer of 1864
to found a party newspaper. Of course, Lassalle's unexpected
demise put Schweitzer in jeopardy. To secure his own base
of influence, Schweitzer adopted the plan for a newspaper
as his own.

Money for the project did not come from the party.
Schweitzer's personal associate, Baron Johann von Hofstetten,
contributed the necessary cash, allowing the paper to be
established as Schweitzer's personal property.[65] And Hofstetten received money from the Prussian minister-president.
On 3 April 1866, Bismarck gave to Hofstetten an unsecured
personal loan, without interest, repayable *sine dei*, in the
amount of 2500 thalers. It was to be used as caution money
so that Schweitzer's newspaper, which recently had been confiscated, could resume publication. Without a doubt,
Schweitzer knew where this money came from. In the spring
of 1866, he repeatedly requested an interview with Bismarck.
It is not known whether the interview ever was granted. At
least the government did accommodate Schweitzer by releasing
him from prison in May 1866, after he had served only half
of a one-year prison term.[66] With the Austro-Prussian war
only weeks away, Bismarck needed to have Schweitzer and his
newspaper active in the field.

Contemporary allegations frequently surfaced claiming
that, in private, Schweitzer boasted of his ties to the
police.[67] After investigating charges that Schweitzer served
the Prussian government, the 1872 ADAV Congress concluded
that no "definite facts" proved his treachery; nevertheless,
the report continued, "great, impressive grounds incontestably
exist to distrust Dr. von Schweitzer." The same congress
then passed a motion censuring and expelling him.[68] The
public record of Schweitzer's service to Bismarck also is
impressive. On the eves of war with Austria and of war with
France, Schweitzer's newspaper loudly championed the Prussian
cause. Bismarck could have devised no more effective means
of gutting lower-class opposition to his wars of conquest.

Furthermore, in 1867, in a runoff election for a Reichstag seat, Schweitzer urged his supporters to back Bismarck instead of his Progressive rival, thus helping the minister-president to win election.[69]

In 1871, diagnosing the difference between the socialist faction that Liebknecht had built and Schweitzer's ADAV, Bismarck remarked that the former was inspired by international socialism but the latter was not. With the ADAV, he said, "not only is a material understanding still possible, but a timely intervention by the state will also succeed in reconciling the majority of the workers with the existing order. . . ."[70]

Even though Schweitzer's perfidy could not be foretold in 1864, when he first approached Liebknecht with a proposal that they collaborate on a new publication, Liebknecht held back. Instinctively he distrusted Schweitzer and his wealthy benefactor, Hofstetten. After some dickering, he made his participation contingent upon Marx's inclusion. To Marx he wrote, "The question is now: do we use the newspaper and the Union for a while, with the intention that both means of agitation ultimately come into our hands? Or: should we engage the battle now? I am prepared for both."[71]

As the prospect for a newspaper became more tangible, and as Marx, preoccupied by his work for the IWA, hesitated, Liebknecht took a more positive attitude toward working on Schweitzer's newspaper. "It would be folly," he wrote to Marx, "*not* to use the opportunity which [the newspaper] offers us. . . . I am firmly convinced," he added, "that the newspaper ultimately will come entirely into our hands."[72]

Cautiously, Marx agreed to lend his name to the newspaper only after a satisfactory statement of editorial policy had been prepared. The resulting tripartite declaration

of principle, carried on page one of the first issue, demanded:
(1) the abolition of the political debris of the middle ages
and the promotion of "solidarity of popular interests throughout the whold world"; (2) the creation of a "whole, mighty
Germany" as a "free people's state"; and (3) the "overthrow
of the domination of society by capital--we hope to achieve
the control of the state for labor."[73] Marx took Liebknecht's
presence on the newspaper's staff as insurance that this
editorial policy would be followed.[74]

Christened *Der Sozialdemokrat*, Schweitzer's slim sheet
first appeared in mid-December. To Marx's disgust, the very
first page printed a panegyric to Lassalle. Even more bother-
some, the same article included a flattering comment about
Lassalle from a private letter that Marx had written to console
the Countess Hatzfeldt. Lassalle "died young--in triumph--like
Achilles," *Der Sozialdemokrat* quoted Marx as saying.[75]

Liebknecht composed a lengthy epistle in which he tried
to smooth his friend's ruffled feathers. At the moment, he
explained, because of her financial resources and because
of the popular influence of her deceased lover, the countess
and her *Lassallerei* had the upper hand. "Either the newspaper
could not be founded or it had to lean on the Lassallean union
for the present," he observed. Then he promised that Lassalleanism gradually would disappear from the sheet, "but it cannot
be done all at once."[76]

Hardly had this tempest subsided when *Der Sozialdemokrat*
again provoked Marx's anger. This time the newspaper's Paris
correspondent reported charges being made locally that the
agent of the IWA in France was a tool of Napoleon. Of course
Marx reproached Liebknecht for failing to censor that slander.
"I can do nothing about opponents of the [international]

'Association' writing for the paper," Liebknecht replied,
shrugging his shoulders. "You knew that as well as I did
from the beginning."[77]

Differences of opinion inside the socialist camp never
upset Liebknecht greatly. Time and patient educational effort,
he was convinced, could cure misconceptions. However, he
would not tolerate flirtation with the reactionaries. Slowly
it became apparent to Liebknecht that Schweitzer was playing
precisely that game.

The first public proof of Schweitzer's sympathy for
Prussia came in articles that he published in *Der Sozialdemokrat*.
Already in the second issue, adopting the fashionable *Realpolitik* stance of the day, he dismissed all arguments of
legality and morality concerning the tangled controversy over
Schleswig and Holstein. "The deed alone decides in politics,"
he declared. The joint occupation of the duchies which existed
at that moment was untenable, and a Prussian annexation at
least would bring the German question closer to solution.[78]
Escalating his rhetoric slightly, on 8 January he praised
the Prussian ministry on two counts: for pursuing the "domi-
neering politics of a genuine great power" and for making
a solution of the national issue more "urgent."

Schweitzer then spelled out his solution to that issue
in a five-part editorial series called "The Bismarck Ministry."
His first installment staked out his position on the constitutional struggle. "Parliamentarism means the rule of
mediocrity. Caesarism at least means daring initiatives,
at least masterful deeds."[79] Challenging the liberal claim
to represent the people, Schweitzer's second installment proclaimed that "the population in Prussia is predominantly
royalist. . . . The dynasty and its current ruler can justly

be considered as the culmination point of the ascending scale
of the traditional elements, as the center of gravity, . . .
as the heart and brain of the organism. . . ."[80]   Surveying
the international scene, Schweitzer's series depicted the
historical inevitability of Prussia's absorption of Germany.
According to *Der Sozialdemokrat*, a Prussian minister who failed
to exploit the present opportunity deserved the anger of
Frederick the Great and the ridicule of his contemporaries.[81]

Even if one concedes accuracy to Schweitzer's evaluation
of Prussian potential, it must be stressed that he increased
that potential by disheartening the domestic opponents of
Bismarck. One hardly incites revolutionary resistance by
touting the strenth of the counterrevolutionaries, and
Schweitzer gained nothing for the workers' movement by his
publication of this pro-Prussian propaganda.[82]

By mid-February, Liebknecht had heard more than enough.
He first tried to persuade Schweitzer to repudiate Bismarck.
Arguments in private achieved nothing. Like August Brass,
Schweitzer actually defended his support for Bismarck.
Indeed Liebknecht found himself alone in the ADAV leadership
in his opposition to the minister-president. That isolation,
combined with Liebknecht's strong and persistent need for
personal acceptance, made his position an agonizing one.[83]
But principle finally triumphed. On 16 February he broke
with the countess. That evening he read Schweitzer's third
installment of "The Bismarck Ministry." Finding it reactionary beyond belief, he resigned from *Der Sozialdemokrat*
the next day.[84]

Liebknecht's decision sparked an intraparty rebellion
that nearly unseated the pro-Prussian leadership of the ADAV.
The first shock waves shook *Der Sozialdemokrat* to its founda-

tion. On 23 February, Marx and Engels published their own
resignation from Schweitzer's sheet. Widely reprinted in
Germany, their declaration denounced Schweitzer's "royal
Prussian ministerial socialism." In particular it complained
that *Der Sozialdemokrat* should have attacked the "ministry
and the feudal-absolutist party at least as bravely as [it
attacked] the Progressives."[85] Every other prominent contributor to *Der Sozialdemokrat*, save one, quickly followed
with resignations.[86] Circulation of the newspaper plummeted
to about 400.[87] The ADAV fared little better than Schweitzer's
newspaper. By the end of February, four distinct factions
had coalesced around Becker, Hatzfeldt, Schweitzer, and
Liebknecht. A free-for-all followed.

Tactically, at this time Liebknecht would have preferred
to abandon the ADAV altogether and organize his followers
into a new party. Unfortunately, police approval was needed
for every new association. Liebknecht knew that approval
would never be forthcoming. Besides, he feared that a public
rupture with the Lassallean organization would increase the
chances of his deportation. Consequently, he tried to take
control of the ADAV.[88] In Berlin at least, he succeeded for
a time.

Liebknecht rallied his supporters in the ADAV and in
the printers' union around the tactics he had advocated since
1862. On 28 February 1865, braving Bismarck's wrath, he outlined his position again to a public assembly in Berlin.
Challenging Schweitzer's recently published position, he argued
that Bismarck's "caesarism" was "nothing but absolutism, . . .
absolutism which strives to win the hungering masses through
'bread and games,' through socialistic sham concessions. . . ."
According to Liebknecht, the working class, "which wants freedom

and justice," had to reject this caesarism. Currently in
Prussia, the Progressives struggled for political liberty,
for the rule of law, and for popular control of finances and
the army. Those positions, Liebknecht exhorted, served the
interests of the working class. Although the Progressives
had proven cowardly in the current struggle, and although
the workers' political and economic demands went far beyond
what the liberals advocated, these facts, Liebknecht said,
were no reason for the working class to throw itself into
the arms of those who were even more reactionary than the
Progressives. Liebknecht warned the workers away from the
"people's monarchy." If such a state offered assistance to
the workers, very well, he said: take what was offered, but
do so without thanks. "Material improvement without freedom
would be the exchange of free wage slavery for black slavery."
Only a "free people's state" could genuinely help the masses.
"Therefore neither with the Progressives nor with the government. *Neither, nor*--the workers must build an independent
party." Then the workers will "march straight ahead in the
proud awareness that the working class is the defender of
the holy flame of freedom; that it is the true Progressive
party. . . ."[89]

The showdown between Liebknecht and Schweitzer shredded
the Berlin chapter of the ADAV. Its membership dwindled to
about fifty. By mid-March, Liebknecht controlled what was
left.[90] In a desperate attempt to regain the initiative from
Liebknecht, Schweitzer and Becker buried their differences
and attempted a coup in the local organization. On 29 March,
President Becker dismissed the incumbent plenipotentiary in
Berlin, who had been won over to Liebknecht's side, and
appointed one of his followers.[91]

Becker's ploy backfired. The outraged Berlin members, incited by Liebknecht, met and passed a group of resolutions denouncing both Becker and Schweitzer. Only one unidentified member cast a dissenting vote. The first resolution declared that *Der Sozialdemokrat* was not edited in the spirit and according to the principles of the workers' party. It applauded the resignations by Liebknecht and the other contributors. A second resolution branded President Becker a "vile slanderer and incurable idiot." It also demanded his expulsion from the ADAV. A third repudiated the Countess Hatzfeldt. A fourth statement renounced alliances with either the liberals or the reactionaries. Over Liebknecht's objections, it also reaffirmed the members' allegiance to Lassalle. But in the context of the other resolutions, that concession scarcely diminished the lustre of Liebknecht's victory.[92]

The anti-Becker, anti-Schweitzer insurrection spread beyond Berlin. According to the *Allgemeine deutsche Arbeiter-Zeitung*, a newspaper loosely connected to the VDAV, the large Lassallean organization in Altona endorsed the rebellious resolutions of the Berlin ADAV. To that VDAV newspaper, *Der Sozialdemokrat* seemed to have "played out its role," and the ADAV appeared to be disintegrating.[93] In mid-April, the wave of Liebknecht's success crested. He found himself swamped by speaking invitations from workers' craft unions and local political clubs.[94] Yet, for several reasons, he was unable to extract a lasting victory from his momentary triumphs.

First, Liebknecht lacked organizational talent. Never in his long career did he build his own party from the precinct level. Instead he preferred to attach himself to someone else's structure and redirect it toward his own goals. He excelled at public speaking, at journalism, and at recruitment in general, but he did not have the self-reliance or decisiveness to erect his own political edifice.

It seems especially odd that Liebknecht did not found a section of the IWA in Berlin. That body might have provided a viable kernel for organizational growth. Responding to Marx's urging, he promised on several occasions to labor on behalf of the International.[95] His tangible efforts, however, were few. He did propagate the International's ideas, and in that sense the IWA may have provided the "cyrstallization point" for his anti-Lassallean agitation that he later recalled in his memoirs,[96] but Marx surely remained dissatisfied. In June, he chided Liebknecht, "The International Association proceeds very well *despite* the 'enormous support' that it receives from Germany."[97] Not until November 1865 did friends of Liebknecht form a section of the IWA in Berlin.[98] By then Liebknecht no longer lived in the Prussian capital. He had been deported.

In fairness, it should be recalled how much Liebknecht feared deportation. To organize on behalf of the IWA or any party of his own would have invited his own expulsion. Furthermore, since the IWA was still young, small and disjointed, it could scarcely have provided the sound nationwide network that Liebknecht so desperately needed.

Liebknecht's organizational reticence aside, his rivals retained important assets that he lacked. Schweitzer had a newspaper and national organization at his disposal, allowing easy communication to a large audience in Berlin and elsewhere. For Liebknecht, communication with the Berlin members proved difficult; communication with other areas proved impossible. The dictatorial Lassallean organization had channelled all party communication through the president.

No lateral connections between various localities had been allowed to develop. So aside from a very few personal acquaintances whom he reached through private correspondence, Liebknecht had no entrée into the other chapters of the ADAV.[99]

These facts restricted Liebknecht's efforts to a limited life in Berlin. Still, his insurrection inside the Lassallean league did not abate of its own accord. On the contrary, it was crushed by the Prussian authorities. Already in March the police in Berlin had harrassed Liebknecht's public appearances and interrupted his speeches.[100] Their intimidation escalated dramatically early in June, as Liebknecht was arrested and ordered to leave Prussia within eight days. He appealed the decision; the authorities waited. "It looks to me," he observed, "that they want to let the sword hang over my head. . . ."[101]

Even this heavy-handed threat did not deter Liebknecht from his denunciations of Bismarck. In a speech to a public assembly of workers on 19 June, he criticized the potential for caesaristic manipulation of universal suffrage. Lassalle's universal palliative, according to Liebknecht, had proved to be only a disguise for despotism in the Second French Empire.

Shortly after this address, the authorities ordered Liebknecht to leave Prussia.[102] Leaving his wife and daughters behind (the police gave Ernestine a special dispensation because of her poor health), the battered revolutionary set out for Hamburg, where his friend Robert Schweichel lived. Friends in the Berlin printers' union voted a resolution of thanks for his hours of teaching in their ranks and donated a 100 thaler gift to cushion the economic shock of deportation.[103] Such testimonials, heartwarming though they were, were small consolation for the loss of practically every political connection Liebknecht had.

In the marathon bout between Bismarck and Liebknecht, the minister-president had won Round One. Not only had Bismarck repelled the dim threat of working-class rebellion, he had actually enlisted several influential labor leaders in his service. Bismarck's subversion of the radical movement repeatedly pulled the props out from under Liebknecht's projects. Among his immediate associates, Brass, Lassalle, Hatzfeldt, Becker and Schweitzer all ducked out of the revolutionary column to endorse a Prussian conquest of Germany.

With hardly any close supporters, Liebknecht doggedly championed democracy, socialism and *grossdeutsch* national unity as inseparable goals. His faint but unflagging voice urged the German people to repudiate Bismarck's authoritarian showmanship and to mold a free, people's state with their own hands.

Tangible triumphs from his three years of sparring in Berlin were few. Yet he had cultivated the ground for great achievements. In the long run his determined anti-Bismarck campaign contributed to the revolutionary orientation of the workers' movement. His expulsion from Prussia made him a popular martyr in that cause and eventually drove him to Leipzig, where he made the crucial political acquaintanceship that enabled him to become a leader of national importance.

Chapter 5

Helping to Build the
Social Democratic Workers' Party

MODERN PARTIES AND PROFESSIONAL POLITICIANS

At age forty, Liebknecht at last found enduring and fruitful
political connections. Just to the south of Prussia, in the
Kingdom of Saxony, he assembled the components of the socialist
party. His organizing work there was part of a momentous
pan-European phenomenon, the emergence of nationwide, mass
political parties.

Before the 1860s, political factions generally had been
transient alliances among personally prominent individuals.
These gossamer networks had had no permanent organizational
structure, and only sporadically had they approached the public
with propaganda. The extension of the franchise changed all
that. To survive, political clubs now had to lure votes from
a broad segment of society. To that end, spokesmen for conservative, liberal, and socialist viewpoints each spelled
out specific proposals and a coherent *Weltanschauung* that
were designed to win popular support. Ceaseless propaganda
and recruitment efforts coalesced around the party platforms.
In turn, these efforts spawned big bureaucracies and official
party presses. The resulting organizations sustained a new
profession, the full-time politician.

Even revolutionaries could pursue this career, if they were willing to agitate within legal limits. Earlier insurrectionary bands had usually been little more than conspiracies, comprised of a few wild-eyed outcasts who had counted upon fortuitous circumstances to provide an opportunity to seize power. The new type of revolutionary party, which originated in Germany in the 1860s, renounced this futile plotting and scheming. It worked instead to lay the foundation for a successful revolution in the future by agitating, by organizing and by expanding. From the 1860s until his death in 1900, Liebknecht dedicated himself to these tasks. His was a pioneering effort to accommodate Marxist theory to daily, legal political labor.

Liebknecht's assumption of this new role, a revolutionary representing a mass-based party that operated inside the law, created two new categories of problems for him. First came those that concerned his relationship with his comrades. Liebknecht now found himself constrained by the filaments of his own organizational web. No longer a lone operator, he now regularly had to consider the opinions of others and to take into account the probable organizational consequences of his intended actions. These limitations were the price of acquiring organized backing. The second set of problems incumbent upon Liebknecht's new role were those associated with defining a proper relationship to the existing state. To avail himself of the opportunities for legal agitation, Liebknecht had to muffle his rhetoric somewhat, but there were questions about how far he ought to go in muting his revolutionary appeal and to what extent he ought to accept and to participate in the institutions of the prevailing order. These were important issues in Liebknecht's career in the latter 1860s, and they molded the rest of his political life.

JOINING BEBEL AND THE VDAV

To organize his potential constituency into an effective
political force, Liebknecht pursued a flexible, two-part
strategy between 1865 and 1869. On the one hand, he continued his work in reeducating and realigning the various
proletarian factions. In Saxony he planned to rally advanced
elements from both the ADAV and the VDAV around the principles
of Marx's International.[1] To do so he would have to steal
some of Schweitzer's following from the Lassallean band, and
he would have to extirpate the apolitical and self-help ideals
in the VDAV. That project took four years to complete. On
the other hand, he still had to address the festering issue
of national unification. In this area, his tactics remained
the same as those he had used in Berlin, although he found
firmer allies in Leipzig. In addition to the workers, he
cooperated with local democrats, particularists, and Austrophiles. The democrats were especially vital in Saxony. Unlike
Prussia's liberals, some of Saxony's bourgeois leftists championed radical reform, including a republican constitution
and universal suffrage. For four years Liebknecht personally
belonged to the party of south and central Germany's left-
liberals. From these democrats he received far-reaching
exposure, political introductions, electoral support, and
money. He hoped too that he could recruit some of these
men for the socialist cause. By contrast, the particularists
and Austrophiles were merely circumstantial comrades-in-arms.
Liebknecht and these allies tilted at a common enemy, Prussia,
so they occasionally shared resources and shouted encouragement to each other. But no organizational ties bound them
together.

Despite the number and variety of his anti-Prussian
allies, Liebknecht was unable to stop Bismarck's advance.
By contrast, the other half of his strategy, the establishment of a proletarian party, did succeed. Industrialization
helps to explain both outcomes: while it prodded the particularists toward the dustbin of history, it also fostered the
growth of an urban working class.

In the 1860s, the socioeconomic landscape of Germany
changed enormously. At an increasing rate, the overcrowded
peasantry disgorged its discontented to countries abroad
or to cities at home. For example, the internal migration
bloated Berlin to over half a million residents by 1860.
Another quarter million people were packed into the Prussian
capital by 1870. With ever greater numbers congregating
in the cities, urban politics became the crucible of Germany's
future.

Industry was the magnet that drew people to the cities.
In a remarkable surge of growth, Germany's index of industrial production soared 46 percent in the 1860s alone.[2] Spokesmen for the burgeoning manufacturing enterprises lobbied effectively for the consolidation of a national market. The industrialists also demanded the abolition of the tattered remnants
of guild regulation, saying that these archaic restrictions
retarded the nation's material progress. When their demand
was implemented during the 1860s, mechanized manufacturing
steamrollered Germany's unprotected artisans.

As their economic opportunities vanished, handworkers
desperately grasped for economic alternatives. The socialist
movement, preaching a gospel of radical transformation,
attracted most of its initial converts from among these artisans. Thus industrialization drove the "normal," integrated,

and respectable members of a substantial social class toward
radical doctrines. That development allowed the revolutionary
movement to transform itself from a collection of outcasts
into a modern mass party.[3]

The early workers' movement had its most vigorous centers
in Berlin, in Hamburg, and in Leipzig. Liebknecht, after his
expulsion from the first of these cities on 24 July 1865,
sampled the opportunities at Hamburg. He had friends there,
and he found the anti-Prussian political climate congenial
enough, but he was unable to find employment. Consideration
of Ernestine and his two daughters, whom he temporarily had
left behind in Berlin, forced him to try elsewhere. His
Hamburg acquaintances gave him the names of a few left-liberal
editors in South Germany. Armed with these prospects, he
set out for the Saxon city of Leipzig in mid-August.[4]

When Liebknecht came to Leipzig, it had approximately
100,000 inhabitants and was already well advanced in the
process of industrialization.[5] The resulting socioeconomic
fermentation had made Leipzig the center, along with Berlin,
of the agitation for a workers' congress in 1862. A year
later Lassalle had founded his ADAV with a congress in Leipzig.
Liebknecht mentioned the *Regsamkeit* of the Leipzig workers
as a prime inducement to settle there. Furthermore the local
authorities, anxious to defend Saxony's independence, welcomed
all enemies of Bismarck.[6]

Shortly after his arrival Liebknecht reported to Engels
about local conditions. The ADAV languished, he said, relating
that the schism that had begun in Berlin had done its work in
Saxony also. According to Liebknecht, Schweitzer's disciples
in Leipzig numbered thirty; the "opposition union," fifty.
Neither approached the size of the local VDAV chapter. That

club "originally rested on 'Schulze-Delitzsch's principles,'"
Liebknecht wrote, but now it had "almost completely emancipated itself" from bourgeois ideals. According to Liebknecht,
its membership stood at 350. Because of its increasing ideologi
cal sophistication and because of its impressive size, Liebknech
decided to concentrate his working-class agitation in the VDAV
chapter rather than in either faction of the Lassallean band.[7]

The VDAV, born three weeks after the ADAV, now was two
years old. From its inception it had been schizophrenic. On
the one hand, it was a protégé of the liberals. Men like
Leopold Sonnemann, who was simultaneously the prosperous
editor of the *Frankfurter Zeitung* and chairman of the VDAV,
hoped to use the VDAV to block the creation of an independent
working-class party.[8] Yet, alongside the docile and generally
apolitical acceptance of liberal tutelage among many of Sonnemann's protégés, there coursed a current of class consciousness and muffled militancy. Displaying a newfound political
decisiveness, in September 1865 the VDAV congress reversed
prior union policy and urged the members to campaign for the
right to vote and for democratic freedoms in general.[9]

Along with the politicizing of the VDAV came a change
in leadership that was most important for Liebknecht's political future. In July 1865, August Bebel became chairman of the
Saxon district. Subsequently, he would become Liebknecht's
most trusted, most competent, and most durable political ally.

Bebel's political development encapsulates the resurrection of the German workers' movement. Born in 1840, he was
too young to have much personal recollection of 1848, of the
Reichsverfassungskampagne, of Marx's or of Engels' role in
that revolution, or of much that had been so decisive in
shaping Liebknecht's attitudes. He came to the workers'

movement as an artisan, a woodturner. After his obligatory
years of travel as a journeyman, he had settled in Leipzig
in 1860. When the workers' educational society opened there
in 1861, he was among its earliest enlistees. The members
elected him to their executive committee in 1862. A year
later he attended the founding congress of the VDAV at
Frankfurt. In February 1865, he was chosen to be chairman
of the Leipzig chapter, and six months later he became chief
of the entire Saxon organization.[10] In his memoirs, Bebel
insisted that he was inching toward a social democratic ideology
before he met Liebknecht. Nevertheless, when Liebknecht shared
his wealth of revolutionary experience and his education--both
formal and informal--Bebel's conversion to radical politics
was accelerated considerably.[11]

Liebknecht recalled that he met Bebel on the second day
after his arrival in Leipzig. The two men were mature and to
some extent set in their ways; they disagreed about some important political issues, and did not immediately become close
friends.[12] Still Bebel asked Liebknecht to work as a paid
lecturer for the VDAV. In that club Liebknecht delivered lectures on English trade unions, on the English and French revolutions, on Marx and on Lassalle, and on current political
issues. According to Bebel, his talks quickly became the most
popular that the union offered.[13] Through these talks and
through sharing agitational trips into the surrounding territory, Bebel and Liebknecht gradually forged their friendship.

The relationship between Liebknecht and Bebel was symbiotic.
Liebknecht gave Bebel the ideas that hastened his intellectual
development. Bebel gave Liebknecht an organizational forum.
The capabilities and personalities of the two men were likewise
complementary. Bebel had a flair for organization where

Liebknecht had little.[14] Bebel's usual attitude was calcu-
lating, realistic, and detached; he staked out his aims and
marched resolutely toward them. He was a goal-oriented figure.
Concomitantly, he was apt to provoke hostility, and he became
frustrated and depressed when fruits from his labors were not
quickly forthcoming. He praised Liebknecht for his "unshakeable optimism." Whenever his optimism became unrealistic, as
it sometimes did, Bebel could be counted on to bring it back
to reality. After Bebel developed his intellectual self-
confidence, he set high standards of doctrinal purity for the
party. When schism threatened as a result, Liebknecht frequently preached conciliation. When Liebknecht's concessions
seemed too substantial, Bebel would impose a harder line.

Bifurcation of leadership, such as that represented by
Bebel and Liebknecht, is a predictable occurrence. It results
from the potentially contradictory nature of two important
tasks of any group: setting external goals (instrumental)
and maintaining internal cohesion (affective). Because the
two tasks can compete, often a different individual leader
assumes each role.[15] In a schematic abstract of the German
workers' movement, Bebel could be described as the primarily
instrumental leader; Liebknecht most often functioned as the
affective. Any group functions best when the instrumental
and affective leaders cooperate closely. Fortunately for
the cohesiveness and growth of German social democracy, the
friendship between Bebel and Liebknecht survived all spats to
endure for thirty-five years. That friendship deserves part
of the credit for the extraordinary unity of the German workers'
movement.

THE CHEMNITZ CONGRESS: TRYSTING WITH THE LEFT-LIBERALS

Liebknecht and Bebel built their faction amidst a tangle of
organizational and ideological alternatives. Battles between
their VDAV and Schweitzer's ADAV plagued their project, and
two other parties competed with the VDAV for their attention
and loyalty. Between 1865 and 1869, aside from belonging to
the VDAV, both men were members of the left-liberal German
People's Party and the International Workingman's Association.
Four years were needed to extract a German Social Democratic
Party from this complicated mix of friends and rivals.

The German People's Party (the *Deutsche Volkspartei* or
DVP) sprang up in southern and central Germany almost simultaneously with Liebknecht's arrival in that area. Its founding
congress was held at Darmstadt in September 1865, when about
forty leftists of various political persuasions met there to
coordinate their efforts. Liebknecht attended this meeting,
although he remained in the background. Soon he became
acquainted with the party's most distinguished figures:
Sonnemann in Frankfurt, Ludwig Büchner in Hesse, Johann Jacoby
in Berlin. When a parallel political organization in Württemberg merged with the DVP in 1866, Liebknecht's political
network spread still further.[16]

Because the People's Party and the VDAV shared a pro-
democratic and anti-Prussian stance, they often sponsored
demonstrations jointly. Within a few months, Liebknecht
surfaced as the principal speaker for both parties at these
rallies. For the first time he addressed large public assemblies, with audiences of 5,000 being common, and he discovered
his talent to inspire the masses.

In his speeches, Liebknecht could not avoid concen-
trating on the national issue. By 1866, all politically
aware Germans sensed the imminence of a frightening upheaval.
In Schleswig and Holstein, the relationship between Germany's
two great powers was strained by the burden of joint occupation.
Because most Germans resented the potential collision between
Prussia and Austria as a needless civil war, popular hostility
to both the Habsburgs and the Hohenzollerns sparked and flared.
Liebknecht fanned the coals of that hostility. At a mass
assembly in Leipzig on 5 May 1866, he exclaimed, "The solution to the national issue is not 'either Prussia or Austria'
but rather 'neither Prussia nor Austria.'" For Liebknecht,
the people of Germany had to erect a democratic, *grossdeutsch*
state for themselves.[17]

The People's Party and the VDAV sidled toward an amalgamation around that idea. In these tense times, Liebknecht
and other leaders in both parties believed that guaranteeing
the unity of the democratic forces had to be the first priority.
Accordingly, with Liebknecht's approval, Bebel led the VDAV
Executive Committee in urging its members to join the People's
Party. He also promoted the formation of "popular unions"
that would include all social classes throughout the fatherland. Those recommendations were made on 10 June, just four
days before the outbreak of the Austro-Prussian war.[18]

Liebknecht's strategy in 1866 was predicated upon the
widespread expectation of revolution in that year. Bebel,
Marx, and Engels shared Liebknecht's belief that insurrection
was imminent.[19] In April, even Wilhelm I complained to Bismarck
that "the popular agitation against the war" was "assuming very
unpleasant dimensions."[20] A month later a republican zealot
wounded Bismarck in a disturbingly daring assassination attempt.

When war finally broke out on 14 June, most informed Europeans doubted that Bismarck could survive the battle. Liebknecht made his intimate alliance with the left-liberals in anticipation of a complete political explosion.

Bismarck recognized that his provocative diplomacy had led his enemies to organize and had raised the spectre of revolution. To confound his leftist enemies, he proposed the establishment of a national assembly elected by universal manhood suffrage to replace the old Germanic Confederation. With the same purpose and at the same time, he funded the reestablishment of Schweitzer's *Der Sozialdemokrat*.

Employing its usual guise of *Realpolitik*, the ADAV sheet discouraged revolution. In a remarkable piece of defeatism, it announced that the Lassallean league was "in such sad shape . . . that to speak of a forceful socio-political advance under such circumstances would be laughable." Having dismissed the possibility of a democratic resolution of the national issue, Schweitzer asserted that one could only choose between Austria and Prussia. The ADAV editor advocated a Prussian victory because of Bismarck's constitutional reform proposal.[22] Schweitzer's agitation helps explain why no revolution occurred in 1866.

However, it was the stunning success of the reorganized Prussian army that preempted all plans for insurrection. In only three weeks of fighting, the Austrians, and with them the hopes for Bismarck's overthrow, were driven from the field. On 23 August, in the Peace of Prague, the defeated Habsburgs agreed to dissolve the Germanic Confederation and to leave Prussia free to unify Germany north of the Main River. For the moment, Liebknecht's home at Leipzig lay under Prussian occupation.

Ever active, Liebknecht wielded his pen against the
Prussian invaders. In coordination with both the VDAV and
the DVP, he had planned to found his own newspaper since
June. The awaited opportunity came late in war-torn July,
when the *Mitteldeutsche Volkszeitung* became bankrupt. With
little but enthusiasm to fund his venture, Liebknecht took
over the paper. The first edition was printed in August.

Liebknecht composed his journal delicately, trying to
avoid proscription by the occupying Prussians. To Marx he
explained that "the smallest show of opposition will cause
our suppression; but as to the *social* question we have full
elbowroom. . . ." Accordingly, he printed no criticism of
the conquerors. Instead he published purely socialist commentary, including Marx's Inaugural Address to the International.
But despite his circumspection on the national issue, after
only about two weeks of publication, the authorities closed
his shop.[23]

This setback only steeled Liebknecht's determination
to resist the undemocratic unification of his fatherland.
Far from modifying his tactics to meet the new situation
that the Peace of Prague created, he redoubled his efforts
in their prewar channels. Pursuing the campaign to create
a broad democratic front, he participated in a congress of
all anti-Prussian leftists that convened at Chemnitz on 19
August 1866.

The Chemnitz meeting illustrates the grand strategy
that Liebknecht pursued. It brought together members of
the DVP, the VDAV, and even a few ADAVers until Schweitzer
persuaded them to withdraw.[24] Organizationally, those were
the elements that Liebknecht hoped to weld into a belligerent
coalition. He envisioned the DVP as an umbrella for all anti-

Prussian, democratic factions. Its structure would be loose-
knit, a federation of distinct member parties. (For example,
the VDAV continued to operate separately after the Chemnitz
meeting.)

The DVP never developed an effective national organization, although it held annual national congresses. Nor did
the party effectively organize at the local level. It remained
more of an old-style political faction, a combination of
regionally prominent individuals rather than a bureaucratic,
mass-based party. In Saxony, Wilhelm Liebknecht, August Bebel,
and Otto Freytag comprised the executive committee of the
People's Party.

Doctrinally, the DVP adopted a specific and wide-ranging
program. In this regard at least, it conformed to the more
modern style of political agitation. In its purely political
points, the platform approved at Chemnitz could hardly have
been more radical. Its opening statement demanded the "unrestricted right of self-determination for the people," and
endorsed universal, equal, direct, and secret suffrage for
adult men. The platform called for a parliament "with the
greatest fullness of power," and it advocated the "unification
of Germany in a democratic form of government. No hereditary
central authority." Regarding the social issue, Point 5 of
the Chemnitz Program demanded: "Promotion of the common
welfare and emancipation of labor and the laborer from every
oppression and every constraint." To "improve the situation
of the working class," it called for "freedom of emigration,
freedom to exercise a trade, and a common German citizenship."
Reflecting the vogue of the cooperative movement, the program
advocated "promotion and support" of the "producer's cooperatives, so that the antagonism between capital and labor
can be smoothed over."[25]

Although Liebknecht's precise role in composing the
Chemnitz program cannot be documented, he was satisfied with
its provisions.[26] From his viewpoint, this program pulled a
politically shy VDAV toward a democratic commitment, and it
produced a recognition of the social issue from the DVP.
Although far from a perfect reflection of his own thought,
the Chemnitz Program stood closer to Liebknecht's own ideals
than anything that either the DVP or the VDAV had acknowledged
previously.

Still, Liebknecht suffered attacks on two fronts for
the alliance he built with the left-liberals. The ADAV newspaper, *Der Sozialdemokrat*, frequently blasted the "half-
socialist *Volkspartei*" for failing to recognize that all
nonworkers comprised a "single reactionary mass."[27] For
the remainder of the 1860s, Schweitzer gleefully exploited
Liebknecht's ties to the People's Party to argue that he was
not a socialist at all.

Meanwhile, in England, Marx and Engels also scowled
at the Chemnitz Program. Prior to 1866, like Liebknecht,
they had conceded the necessity of cooperating with the left-
liberals, but Prussia's smashing victory caused them to change
their minds. Henceforth they regarded Prussia's ultimate
triumph in all of Germany as a foregone conclusion. Although
they regretted the inevitable increase in Prussia's power,
they admitted that the revolutionary moment had passed. Thus
the raison d'être for the liberal alliance had evaporated.
Besides, Engels believed that Bismarck's victory had "simpli-
fied the situation" by eliminating the "uproar of the tiny
capitals."[28] At last the opportunity existed to create truly
national parties. Socialists should seize this chance, Marx
and Engels thought, to consolidate an independent proletarian

party. For the next four years they complained to each other
and to Liebknecht about the way his agitation blurred class
distinctions.[29]

The clash of viewpoints between Marx and Liebknecht
resulted in part from the divergent attitudes of the theoretician in his study and the agitator in the field. Liebknecht
defended his tactics: "I am not dealing here with pure,
schooled communists but rather with communist *recruits* who
still have certain prejudices that must be treated with consideration."[30] In addition to this need to match his rhetoric
to what his audiences might accept, Liebknecht had to promise
success for concerted action. It might be proper for Marx
as an expositor of the laws of economic development to forecast a lengthy recess in revolutionary activity, but to concede
defeat on the national issue even while the struggle continued
would have been lethal for Liebknecht's agitation.

Furthermore, Liebknecht believed that caesarism remained
the chief danger to Germany's healthy political evolution.
In the latter 1860s, Bismarck's government courted the lower
class with allusions to economic concessions. Schweitzer
and the ADAV made such state socialism the cornerstone of
their social program. Consequently, Liebknecht worried that
the workers would be persuaded to sacrifice political democracy for material well-being. Then, in the Marxist scheme,
bourgeois freedom would not develop and the government would
have a free hand to repress all its critics, regardless of
class. Liebknecht designed his own agitation in a dialectical
relationship to that of Bismarck and of Schweitzer. Both
could best be combatted by stressing the struggle for political
democracy. If this agitation were to have any chance of success, the small and immature proletariat would need allies

outside the working class. Thus, Liebknecht thought that
the democratic coalition had to be maintained, even if that
tactic meant that rigorous discussion of the social issue
would have to be postponed.[31]

Liebknecht's resistance to Prussian expansion led him
into some questionable political positions. For instance,
even as late as 1869, he insisted that the exclusion of Austria
from Germany was "provisional, temporary."[32] More dubious
still, he hailed the changes that defeat had produced in
the Habsburg regime as the onset of a bourgeois revolution
from above. He even cautioned Austria's workers to be still
lest they upset the course of reform.[33] Bebel later recalled
how Liebknecht, "always a man of extremes," had gone overboard
both in his denunciation of Bismarck and in his praise of
Austria. "It was only natural that Schweitzer exploited these
weaknesses of Liebknecht . . . ," he sighed.[34] Marx and
Engels agreed that Liebknecht's remarks sometimes constituted
a political embarrassment. Referring to a newspaper Liebknecht
founded in 1868, Marx remarked that it was "too narrow-minded
[and] southern. (Liebknecht does not have enough dialectic
to strike at two sides simultaneously.)"[35]

A specific example of the contortions that Liebknecht's
opposition to Prussia sometimes produced came during the
elections to the Constituent Assembly for the North German
Confederation. The People's Party and the VDAV nominated
Liebknecht as one of their candidates, but he did not even
survive the first round. In the runoff in his district, a
pro-Prussian moderate liberal and an anti-Prussian particularist aristocrat confronted each other. In private, Liebknecht advocated covert support for the particularist, arguing
that social democrats ought to help their weaker enemies,

the particularists, against their stronger enemies, the
Prussophiles.[36] Subsequently, Liebknecht's newspaper sympathized with public demonstrations on the birthday of the
deposed king of Hanover, and it celebrated electoral victories
of Guelph candidates.[37]

These particularist and Austrophile sentiments were
only aberrations on the surface of Liebknecht's democratic
socialism, and they were induced solely by the unresolved
nature of the German question. Once that issue was settled,
they immediately evaporated. The same could be said of
Liebknecht's four-year association with the DVP. It was
preceded and followed by decades of a purely proletarian
orientation. If Liebknecht clung tightly to these bourgeois
allies in the latter 1860s, it was only with the hope of
fostering a successful revolution. All the while, he continued to cultivate class consciousness among his lower-
class supporters.

THE NUREMBERG CONGRESS: BIDDING FOR WORKING-CLASS SOLIDARITY

In September 1864 a motley assortment of French anarchists,
English trade unionists, and German exiles had met at St.
Martin's Hall in London to construct the first International
Workingman's Association (IWA). Karl Marx finagled the mandate
to write an Inaugural Address and a Provisional Statute for
this polyglot organization. The resulting meld of opinion
included some phrases that Marx himself found distasteful.
To Engels he confided, "It was difficult to state the matter
in such a way that our opinions appear in a form acceptable
to the present standpoint of the worker's movement. . . ."[38]

As Liebknecht later did in the Chemnitz Program, Marx accepted
a statement of principle that, in some respects, polluted his
own theories. Like Liebknecht, he hoped later to alter the
organization and its ideology from within. But unlike Liebknecht's political affiliations in Saxony, Marx's International
advocated a rigid class orientation. "The emancipation of the
working class must be achieved by the working class itself";
so said the initial paragraph of Marx's Provisional Statute.

Liebknecht's deviation from Marx's class-bound example
has led some commentators to minimize his efforts on behalf
of the International altogether.[39] Liebknecht decided,
probably some time in 1865, to spread the IWA's ideals but
to do little for its organization. His choice contributed
to the limitation of enrollments by Germans in Marx's organization to a modest number probably never exceeding 385.[40]
Marx and Engels believed that Liebknecht paid insufficient
attention to the IWA, and they complained about it chronically.
Looking back in 1872, Engels observed that the relationship
between the International and the German workers' movement had
always been a "purely platonic one."[41] The IWA penetrated
the minds of many German laborers, but it did not preempt
their organizations.

Tension over the success or failure of the International
strained the relationship between the London exiles and Liebknecht,[42] but their friendship endured this trial. The three
comrades continued to correspond often throughout this period,
and every time a conflict arose between Liebknecht and other
German agitators in the International, Marx and Engels backed
Liebknecht.

Shortly after settling in Leipzig, Liebknecht collided
with his most important rival in the IWA, Johann Philipp

Becker, who had been Liebknecht's commandant during the
Reichsverfassungskampagne. Becker, who still lived in exile
in Geneva, was trying to organize a federation of all German-
speaking sections of the International. As part of his project, he proposed Geneva as the headquarters for this national
group. Undercutting his plan, in January 1866, Marx and
Engels authorized Liebknecht to bypass Becker and to deal
directly with the General Council in London in all matters
concerning Germany. On 22 September 1868, Marx officially
appointed Liebknecht as "correspondent and plenipotentiary"
of his organization, making it plain that Becker enjoyed no
superior authority.[43] A year later, when Becker made a last
attempt to bring the German workers' movement under a Geneva-
based central office, Marx helped Liebknecht quash that plan.

Liebknecht earned Marx's support. Although he did not
enlist droves of members in the IWA, his recruitment probably
accounted for several dozen of the small membership total.
His role in preparing the Berlin section has been discussed
previously. In Leipzig, he enlisted at least a dozen additional members, including the whole executive committee of
the VDAV.[44] More importantly, Liebknecht agitated consistently
and effectively on behalf of Marx's principles. He arranged
a reprinting and distribution of the *Communist Manifesto* in
1865.[45] His *Mitteldeutsche Volkszeitung* printed Marx's
Inaugural Address in 1866. When he secured another newspaper
in 1868, its first two issues printed excerpts from Marx's
recently published *Capital*, and the journal made frequent and
extensive subsequent references to that work.[46] In his
lectures in the workers' educational society and at larger
mass meetings, Liebknecht always called his audience's attention to Marx's theoretical achievements.[47]

There were good reasons why Liebknecht did not do still more for the International. First, he feared that the existing law of associations, which prohibited branch sections of any federation, could be used to disband any publicly organized sections of the IWA.[48] He also worried that affiliation with the International would alarm the DVP and upset its alliance with the VDAV.[49] Finally, available resources, talents, and time could only stretch so far. Liebknecht and Bebel chose to concentrate their efforts on reeducating their portion of the existing German workers' party, the VDAV.[50]

On 8 February 1866, when Liebknecht and J. P. Becker first agreed to cooperate in their work for the International, Liebknecht explained his strategy to his old comrade-in-arms: "My plan is to bring the old Lassalleans together with the ex-Schulzeans under the roof of the International Workingman's Association, which will without a doubt succeed."[51] Liebknecht contributed to the eventual success of this scheme as an agitator and as a journalist.

Late in 1867, Liebknecht began spending most of his time setting up the *Demokratische Wochenblatt*, the first issue of which appeared on 4 January 1868. Sources in the People's Party seem to have provided the caution money and the initial bankroll, for the first issue of this paper published the Chemnitz Program as its own platform. That programmatic proclamation was signed, "The Executive Committee of the People's Party in Saxony, W. Liebknecht, A. Bebel, O. Freytag." The weekly newspaper soon became self-supporting, as its circulation increased from its initial 700 subscribers to 1,100 within only a few months.[52]

From this time forth, journalism joined public speaking as Liebknecht's primary vocation in the various party

organizations to which he belonged; he seldom sought or held
other administrative posts. The small sum, forty thalers per
month, that the newspaper originally paid Liebknecht helped
to meet some of the expenses for himself and his family;
eventually he would earn a comfortable living from his journalism on behalf of the party. In addition to improving his
financial condition, the *Demokratische Wochenblatt* also gave
an institutional base to Liebknecht's growing power inside
his party.

Liebknecht's success as a journalist originated in his
sparkling style. It was witty, erudite, vigorous, incisive,
and inspirational. His craftsmanship with words was perfectly suited to recruit new members to the infant movement.
His journals were not newspapers in the present sense of
the word. Liebknecht made no effort to present "the news"
objectively and comprehensively. His articles always were
editorial interpretations of events; the front page carried
a "Political Review" column, which Liebknecht almost always
wrote himself. Here appeared a potpourri of comments, primarily relating to international affairs. In the *Demokratische
Wochenblatt*, the anti-Prussian crusade was conducted in this
column. The inside pages of that publication presented an
unrelieved congregation of assorted news blurbs. Headlines
and varied spacing were practically unknown until late in
Liebknecht's journalistic career.

News of workers' meetings was rare in the early issues
of the *Demokratische Wochenblatt*, and when it was printed
it was buried in the inside pages. In the first few months
there were almost no theoretical essays about socialism. The
newspaper was, after all, the mouthpiece of the DVP, not the
VDAV. It was a "democratic," not a "socialist" weekly.

Predictably Marx and Engels grumbled about the nonsocialist orientation of the *Demokratische Wochenblatt*. After seeing only three issues, Engels threw up his hands in disgust at what he called the *suddeutscher Urinhalt-Föderativrepublikanismus* of Liebknecht's newspaper. Although Marx was, as usual, somewhat milder in his criticism, he shared Engels' frustration.[53] Yet Liebknecht did not write for convinced socialists; he wrote to win converts. Consequently, he only gradually increased the distinctly socialist content of his newspaper.

However, even at the outset in his first issue, he heralded Marx's *Capital* as an "epoch-making work which, for the first time, gives the social aspirations of the working class an unshakeable scientific formulation. . . ."[54] A few weeks later, he published a two-part review of the book by Engels.[55] In August, he published a four-part commentary on Marx's prize project by Joseph Dietzgen.[56]

The first reference by name to the IWA did not appear until 29 February 1868, and it was only a brief business notice from the General Council. The International was mentioned in eleven of the additional fifty-one issues of the *Demokratische Wochenblatt* in that year. In 1869, that organization appeared in about every third issue of Liebknecht's paper. There was thus a trend toward more references; and they became more substantial.

The same gravitation toward a more socialist stance manifested itself in the newspaper's relationship to the German workers' movement. After one year of publication, on 5 December 1868, the *Demokratische Wochenblatt* announced that henceforth it would serve as joint organ for both the DVP and the VDAV. With this change, it began printing a

regular column on "Labor Matters." When the VDAV merged
into the Social Democratic Workers' Party in August 1869,
the *Demokratische Wochenblatt* announced that it henceforth
would be the exclusive property of that party.[57] Those members
of the People's Party who did not adhere to the new organization were simply abandoned by the newspaper. Liebknecht
took a left-liberal newspaper, steadily escalated its socialist
content and within twenty months brought it into the possession
of an avowedly social democratic party.

During 1868 and 1869, Liebknecht increasingly concentrated
his efforts on the workers' movement. As a result of Bebel's
political talents, the VDAV flourished. In October 1867, Bebel
had narrowly defeated a middle-class liberal candidate for
the presidency of the entire union.[58] Nourished by the new
president's administrative skill, membership in the VDAV
approached 13,000 by the summer of 1868. Encouraged by this
growth, Liebknecht and Bebel decided to implement Liebknecht's
long-standing plan: to herd the advanced elements of both
the VDAV and the ADAV together under the roof of the International.

Enormous obstacles blocked the path of any rapprochement between the ADAV and the Bebel–Liebknecht faction. In
organizational structure, the Lassalleans and the VDAV represented opposite principles. The ADAV was centralized and
dictatorial; the VDAV, federalist and democratic. Concerning
the unfinished business of national unification, the Lassalleans
remained pro-Prussian; the VDAV, intractably *grossdeutsch*.
Regarding participation in the legislature of the North German
Confederation, Schweitzer showed far more willingness to work
for quiet, piecemeal change in an undemocratic state than did
Liebknecht. Moreover, personal antagonism among the leaders

of the rival factions became an increasingly important barrier
to cooperation. These observations notwithstanding, Liebknecht was determined to heal the crippling schism in the
workers' movement. Developments inside the ADAV dictated
that he would have to negotiate with the slippery Schweitzer
to achieve that aim, for Schweitzer had won the presidency
of the Lassallean league in May 1867.

Under Schweitzer's guidance, membership in his faction
had increased from 2,508 in May 1867 to 7,274 in August 1868.
Part of the renewed success of Schweitzer's union may have
stemmed from programmatic alterations. At the ADAV Congress
in May 1867, the delegates adopted a new platform which prominently featured demands for internationalism and for political
democracy alongside the traditional Lassallean social commentary.[59] Liebknecht's greatest reservations about the ADAV
had been the weakness of its commitment to political democracy.
With the new pronouncements from the Lassallean faction, the
ideological reasons for his fight with Schweitzer melted away.
Further encouraging a rapprochement, in the spring of 1868,
Der Sozialdemokrat published a series of twelve articles
that analyzed and praised Marx's *Capital*. Even Marx was
favorably impressed by the content of these essays.[60] Thus,
the prospects for bringing the ADAV and the VDAV together into
the IWA were propitious.

Bypassing the obstacles to a merger, Liebknecht arranged
to meet personally with Schweitzer. The two erstwhile comrades
and more recent rivals hammered out an agreement in Berlin in
the summer of 1868. On 17 July, Liebknecht reported to Marx,
"I have concluded a kind of alliance with Schweitzer under
the following conditions: 1. You are the head; 2. The
Allgemeine Deutsche Arbeiterverein either will join the

International Workingman's Association or (if that is impossible) acknowledge it." Point two was to occur at the upcoming
ADAV Congress at Hamburg in August. Two weeks later the VDAV
assembly would meet at Nuremberg. There, Liebknecht told Marx,
"the proposal will be made and adopted to enter the International Workingman's Association."[61] A more reasonable solution to the rift in the German workers' movement could hardly
have been devised.

With this important preparatory labor concluded, Bebel
secured an endorsement of the IWA's program from the VDAV
executive committee. Even at this late date, confusion still
prevailed in that body. Incredibly, the committee first
invited Leopold Sonnemann to prepare the program draft proclaiming adherence to the International. Fortunately for
the penetration of Marxism into the workers' movement, he
declined. Then the party directors chose Liebknecht's old
comrade Robert Schweichel to write a program proposal along
the lines of the IWA Statute. He was also selected to speak
on behalf of adoption at the Nuremberg Congress. Because
opposition was expected, Bebel wanted a referee who had a
"conciliatory" disposition. He would chair the conference
and consequently could not carry the discussion in the program
debate. Among his close associates, he found Schweichel's
demeanor better suited to persuading the wary than was Liebknecht's "daredevil nature."[62]

Temporarily free from pressing business, Liebknecht now
allowed himself to become preoccupied with personal matters
for several weeks. His first wife, Ernestine, had been sickly
for years. Early in 1867, her consumption had worsened, and
she had died in May. For the next year, Liebknecht had tried
to raise his two daughters with the assistance of a housekeeper.

Then, on 30 July 1868, he married for the second time. He
had met his bride, Natalie Reh, while campaigning for the
Tariff Parliament elections in Darmstadt. Nine years his
junior, Natalie was the daughter of an attorney, a distinguished
man who had been a temporary vice-president of the Frankfurt
Assembly. Natalie's mother was born a Weidig, a relative of
Liebknecht's persecuted uncle.[63]

Liebknecht described his fiancée as "very clever, healthy
and good natured, 29 years old and an outstanding housewife."
In typical socialist fashion, he explained his decision to
marry in terms of utility; he either had to take a wife or be
separated from his two daughters.[64] The marriage became an
indispensable support for him. His wife stoically accepted
his political dedication and helped in his work, especially
when he was jailed. At those times, she handled his correspondence, smuggling essential materials in and out of the
prison. She also earned money for the family by writing and
translating articles for the socialist press.[65]

The newlyweds took their honeymoon trip during the first
three weeks of August. In Liebknecht's absence, the *Demokratische Wochenblatt* did little to agitate for the upcoming
meeting at Nuremberg. Consequently, the work of doctrinal
clarification remained to be done at the congress.

In 1868, the VDAV still contained many middle-class
disciples of Schulze-Delitzsch. When the party representatives convened at Nuremberg on Saturday, 5 September, one
delegate even confessed that he was "perhaps the worst thing
a worker could imagine--a banker!"[66] Such men--and there
were several at the meeting--uncompromisingly opposed the
platform of the International.

Against this backdrop of divided opinion, the vote for chairman of the congress was a test of strength. When sixty-nine of the ninety-four ballots endorsed Bebel, he promptly railroaded through the approval of a prearranged order of business, which carried the program issue as its first point.[67]

At the Sunday morning session, Schweichel presented and explained his program proposal. Its first two paragraphs quoted exactly from the IWA Statute. Rebuking the middle-class liberals, point one said that "the emancipation of the working class must be achieved by the working class itself. . . ." Attacking private ownership of the means of production, point two traced every form of subjugation suffered by the working man to his "economic dependence on the monopolists. . . ." Casting aside the attempts by the property owners to create an apolitical proletarian party, the third point stated, "Political freedom is the most indispensible precondition for the economic emancipation of the working class."[68] Finally, Schweichel proposed the "union" of the VDAV with the International Workingman's Association.

The debate that followed Schweichel's speech reflected the irreconcilability of opinion inside the VDAV. Seven delegates detailed their opposition to the proposal; six spoke for it. Then, as the last speaker, Chairman Bebel recognized Liebknecht.

In lengthy remarks, Liebknecht defended his support for the International's program. To him, the "only bone of contention" was the "*inseparability of the political and the social movement*." As they had for years, he said, middle-class politicians still tried to steer the workers into the harmless channels of consumer and producer cooperatives. Liebknecht claimed that *Capital* had demonstrated the selfishness

of the bourgeoisie. Marx had proved that bourgeois wealth
originated in "unpaid labor" and consequently was nothing
but "theft committed against the workers. . . ." While the
capitalists grew fat on this illicit system, the workers
starved, Liebknecht said. As evidence for his point he cited
a recent study by a Saxon doctor, who concluded that life
expectancy for the average weaver was only twelve to thirteen
years, and malnutrition was to blame. Liebknecht taunted
the bourgeois delegates: "And you want to help a class that
finds itself in such a condition with palliatives, with consumer unions and the like. . . ."

Liebknecht explained: "Only the concentrated power of
the collectivity, that is to say the state, can solve the
social question." The current state belonged to the rich.
It was merely *politically organized class domination.*"
Before any genuine social reform could occur, this state
would have to be revamped in the direction of "equality and
justice." Having grasped this fact at last, the German workers
had "unfurled the banner of democracy."

Liebknecht knew these comments were provocative. His
unusually hard line probably stemmed from the following considerations. He knew that most members of the VDAV were
workers and would accept the new program. The withdrawal of
a few middle-class members thus was a loss he could accept,
especially since he anticipated an imminent merger with the
Lassalleans. The severing of ties to a middle-class ideology
had to be taken if the alliance with the ADAV was to be effected
Although Liebknecht acknowledged the DVP as important and he
remained proud to be a member, he argued that the time had
come for the "democratic People's Party simply to unite with
the democratic workers' party. . . . Unity has previously been

urged. Good--unity with friends, but separation from enemies."[69]

After Liebknecht's call for a clear-cut decision, schism was unavoidable. Sixty-nine delegates (the same number that had voted for Bebel as chairman) approved the new program. Forty-six dissented. More importantly, these dissenters claimed to represent 7,000 of the VDAV's 13,000 members. These Schulzean diehards composed a formal protest against the programmatic action of the Nuremberg Congress in which they reasserted the value of self-help principles, repudiated the adoption of any definite political program as an unacceptable fetter on freedom of opinion, and rejected class politics in general, arguing that workers' societies should promote "love of the Fatherland and a civic sense of community."[70] In various south-German towns these secessionist clubs lingered on for several years as reminders of the time when middle-class liberals controlled much of the workers' movement.[71]

Thus, Nuremberg did not carry a complete VDAV into the International. Somewhat surprisingly, it also did not end the association between the VDAV and the DVP. When the latter organization held its annual congress at nearby Stuttgart on September 19 and 20, Sonnemann led the delegates in declaring their adherence to the Nuremberg program by a vote of thirty-five to two.[72] In the *Demokratische Wochenblatt*, Liebknecht used the Stuttgart Congress to prove that there were "at least as many social democrats within the People's Party as outside of it."[73]

In September 1868, Liebknecht's grand scheme for building a pan-German social democratic party appeared to be making substantial progress. Much of the VDAV had leapt leftward and had dragged the DVP along with it. All that remained for Liebknecht was to cement the alliance with the Lassalleans.

At first, matters seemed to progress satisfactorily
on that front too. At its congress at Hamburg, the ADAV
adhered to the IWA Program as promised. On 12 September,
the *Demokratische Wochenblatt* announced: "Since the Allgemeine Deutsche Arbeiterverein has declared its agreement
with the aspirations of the International Workingman's Association, now a way has finally been found in which the collective workers of Germany can march forward, fraternally united,
in closed ranks." Yet, despite this auspicious start, Schweitze
had no intention of merging the ADAV with Liebknecht's faction.
Either fearing for his own position in the movement or acting
on behalf of Bismarck, he deliberately sabotaged the approach
toward working-class unity.

THE EISENACH CONGRESS: ASSEMBLING A SOCIAL DEMOCRATIC FACTION

In the autumn of 1868, Schweitzer maneuvered craftily on two
fronts. First, inside his own faction, he coopted the growing
trade union organization. Second, he launched a surprise
attack against Liebknecht and his party.

In Germany, trade unions followed the proletarian political movement. Not until 1868 was there substantial strike
and unionizing activity, and an abrupt decline in real wages
was probably more responsible for this development than was
agitation by either the Lassalleans or the VDAV.[74] Nevertheless, once the unions became active, they offered an enormous
auxiliary and recruiting ground for the political parties.
The VDAV moved before the Lassalleans to penetrate the trade
union movement. In April 1868, it publicly advocated the
establishment of union strike funds according to the English

model.[75] The ADAV lagged behind at least in part because
its ideology, trumpeting the then-respectable "iron law of
wages," preached the futility of strikes. Official doctrine
notwithstanding, Friedrich Fritzsche, a prominent Lassallean,
had organized 10,000 tobacco workers by the summer of 1868.
From this base of strength, he demanded that the ADAV sponsor
a national trade union congress in the autumn. When the
Hamburg party congress balked, he threatened to act on his
own, outside the ADAV.

This show of independence alarmed Schweitzer. To preserve his grip on as much of the workers' movement as possible,
he announced that he would sponsor the trade union congress
in his capacity as Reichstag deputy. On 30 August, *Der Sozialdemokrat* published a call for delegates to convene at Berlin
on 27 September. Thereafter almost every issue of Schweitzer's
sheet printed a front-page editorial extolling the virtues
of trade unions.[76]

With this first component of his plan arranged, Schweitzer
fit a second arrow into his bow and took aim upon the unsus-
pecting Bebel and Liebknecht. In the first days of September,
those two were submerged in the work surrounding the Nuremberg
Congress. Either they failed to notice Schweitzer's machinations with the trade unions or they expected to be included
in the Berlin Congress. On 12 September, the *Demokratische
Wochenblatt* still celebrated the impending agreement between
the ADAV and the VDAV.

A day earlier, Schweitzer's newspaper had started its
foray against the VDAV. Commenting that the Nuremberg Congress had been badly fractured, *Der Sozialdemokrat* reported
that delegates representing a majority of the VDAV membership
had repudiated the program of the International. In his
next two issues, Schweitzer made plain his design. First,

he printed the protest that the apolitical, self-help dissenters had issued at Nuremberg. Because he did not publish
the program actually adopted by the majority of the delegates,
the protest of the secessionists appeared to Schweitzer's
readers to be the outcome of the Nuremberg Congress. Then,
on September 15, he denounced the "hazy twaddle" of the Nuremberg Statute. Having thus handed his followers a rationale
for rebuking the VDAV, he fired off a letter to Karl Marx,
flattering his theories and soliciting his advice on a variety
of subjects. In this way Schweitzer hoped to protect himself
against an untimely IWA endorsement of his VDAV rivals.[77]

Schweitzer's strategy flabbergasted his rivals and succeeded spectacularly. He was able to carry through the creation
of Lassallean labor unions, centralized and dictatorial in
structure, with himself as president and Fritzsche as first
vice-president.[78] His ploy brought an estimated 142,000
workers under ADAV influence. Not until November could the
VDAV arrange a competing congress of unions. Starting later
and appearing schismatic, its recruiting efforts limped far
behind those of the ADAV.[79]

Betrayed and outflanked, Liebknecht was infuriated. In
the *Demokratische Wochenblatt*, he tried to regain the initiative
begun at Nuremberg. Replying to Schweitzer's ridicule that the
Nuremberg Program was "hazy twaddle," he wrote that the program
was "nothing more and nothing less than the Marxist teachings
that you, Schweitzer, with byzantine ardour, exalted in your
newspaper and at the Hamburg General Assembly. . . ." Wielding
the Nuremberg Program like a sabre against Schweitzer, the
Demokratische Wochenblatt summarized the newly proclaimed
principles of the VDAV: "that the social and political movements are identical, that socialism only can be realized in a

democratic state, that every so-called 'social democrat'
who prostitutes himself for the goodwill of caesarism and
who tries to bar the workers from the path of political
duty . . . is a traitor to the cause of socialism and of
democracy.

    "Understand, Herr von Schweitzer?"[80]

    With new urgency Liebknecht now repeated previous pleas
to Marx for a public repudiation of Lassalle's teachings.
"Now the time has come to bring everything together under
one roof. . . . In your pronunciations to the German workers'
movement, *demand unity* of the social democratic elements
(with the sharpest program), and declare anyone to be a traitor
who, . . . from sectarianism, cult of personality, ambition,
or even worse motives attempts to thwart unification. . . ."[81]
Two weeks later, he reported his side of the recent events to
Marx. Calling Schweitzer a "scoundrel," he explained, "I
kept faithfully to my promise not to attack him [Schweitzer].
Our resolution at Nuremberg removed every obstacle to the
union and reunion of all honest 'Soc. Demos.' If Schweitzer
had been honest he would have grasped the opportunity; but
instead of that he began to attack us in the paper, and to
exclude us from his [Trade Union] 'Congress.' So I had no
choice but to accept the war. . . ."[82]

    Despite the evidence of Schweitzer's perfidy, and despite
Liebknecht's request for some public sign of favor in his
contest with the ADAV president, Marx refused to help. He
believed that the authority of the General Council depended
upon its impartiality in internecine feuds like the one raging
in Germany.[83] In accordance with this stance, he wrote to
Schweitzer on 13 October and offered to arbitrate between
him and the "Nuremberg majority."[84] Even though Schweitzer

ignored this offer, Marx never issued a public pronouncement
on the battle between the ADAV and the VDAV. For the moment,
he and Engels chortled privately over the rivalry for their
benediction that now engaged both Schweitzer and Liebknecht.
Only in private did they make their preference for their
friend over the ADAV president known.[85]

Left only with domestic resources, Liebknecht resolved
to "be *very* friendly with the [Lassallean] union, but with
Schweitzer," he said, "there will be no armistice any more."[86]
In the *Demokratische Wochenblatt* he pelted Schweitzer with
abuse. But significantly he adopted a flattering tone toward
the ADAV membership.[87] With this approach Liebknecht exploited
the autocratic structure of the Lassallean league to his own
advantage. Since the death of Lassalle, many ambitious members
of the ADAV had chafed against the presidential dictatorship.
Liebknecht intended to incite these men to an intraparty
rebellion. There, in the realm of organization rather than
that of sociopolitical theory, lies the key to understanding
Liebknecht's eventual success at Eisenach.

Liebknecht first applied his strategy during a by-election
to the Reichstag in February 1869. In that contest, the
Leipzig executive committee of the Bebel-Liebknecht faction
publicly backed the Lassallean candidate, Wilhelm Hasenclever.
Hasenclever repaid the favor by publicly urging unification
of the ADAV and the VDAV. When Hasenclever triumphed in the
election, the *Demokratische Wochenblatt* hailed his victory
as that of a man who "strives for the union of the factions
of the worker party, which have been separated simply through
intrigues and misunderstandings."[88]

Having cultivated a few contacts inside the ADAV, Liebknecht next decided upon a daring move. On 18 February, he
publicly challenged Schweitzer to a debate in any public

assembly. He promised to prove two charges: (1) that since
1864, Schweitzer, "be it for money or out of inclination,"
systematically had sought to stifle the organization of the
workers' party and had served the designs of "Bismarck's
caesarism"; and (2) that Liebknecht and his friends cease-
lessly had tried to promote unity while Schweitzer always
had undermined it. Liebknecht also proposed that the General
Council of the International judge the case between Schweitzer
and himself.[89]

Schweitzer did not respond to this challenge. As preparations were made for the next congress of the ADAV, its president sat behind bars. An assistant who edited *Der Sozialdemokrat* in his absence assured his readers that the ADAV
President would not let Liebknecht's challenge pass unanswered.[90]
With only that vague encouragement, Bebel and Liebknecht took
the train to Barmen-Elberfeld, where the ADAV gathering was to
be held.

The meeting opened on Easter Sunday. Schweitzer, who
had been released from prison a few days earlier for the
publicly stated reason of poor health, chaired the assembly.
As the first order of business, he called for a vote on a
resolution allowing Liebknecht and Bebel to address the delegates. In a tense roll call, it passed 30 to 27.

Liebknecht's oratory then filled the morning session,
and it overflowed into the afternoon. As promised, he lodged
his two charges against Schweitzer. In detail he recited
the litany of Schweitzer's sins: his violation of the accepted
program on *Der Sozialdemokrat*, his endorsement of Bismarck,
his infamous public insults to the VDAV, and his treacherous
abortion of the merger that had been scheduled for the preceding autumn. Bebel followed with a much shorter speech.

Mainly, he attacked Schweitzer for excluding the VDAV from
the Berlin Congress of Trade Unions.[91]

Stubbornly Schweitzer refused to respond to the charges
against him. With no refutation at all of what Liebknecht
and Bebel had said, he called for a vote of confidence from
the assembly. Although forty-three delegates endorsed his
leadership, fourteen disgruntled representatives abstained.
Those abstaining represented over one-third of the ADAV membership. More importantly, some of the most prominent Lassalleans
joined in the abstention.[92]

Dissatisfaction with Schweitzer's silence fed the festering intraparty resentment against his dictatorship. Immediately after the vote of confidence, the delegates discussed
a reorganization of their union. Many Lassalleans envied the
more democratic structure of Liebknecht's faction, and they
insisted upon a restructuring of their own party, giving much
more power to the fifteen-member executive committee than to
the president.[93]

For the moment Liebknecht was satisfied with the outcome of the unrest he had encouraged. Rather than risk a
new assault, which might provoke the Lassalleans to rally
behind their beleaguered leader, Liebknecht proposed a cease-
fire. In the *Demokratische Wochenblatt*, he wrote, "Since
we have well-grounded prospects for unification . . . of the
various factions of social democracy, in order not to impede
the work of unification, from now on we will publish no further
attacks on Herr von Schweitzer . . . ; whereby we of course
anticipate that no attacks will be launched from the other
side."[94] A few days later, Bebel and Schweitzer met in Berlin
and formalized the armistice.

About the same time, with chracteristic ebullience,
Liebknecht informed Marx that his sortie at Barmen-Elberfeld

had destroyed Schweitzer's dictatorship.[95] Four days after
that, he told J. P. Becker: "Schweitzer is undone--he will
still intrigue a bit, but the dictatorship is over and unification can no longer be prevented."[96] He and Bebel now maintained continuous contact with several dissatisfied Lassalleans.
Despite the public truce, they conspired to pull these men
from the ADAV and to join them in establishing a new social
democratic party.[97]

Even as their design developed, a worried Schweitzer
took a desperate step that drove the dissenters from his
party. On 18 June, his newspaper carried a banner headline
proclaiming "Restoration of the Unity of the Lassallean Party."
These grandiose words referred to a reconciliation between
Schweitzer and the Countess Hatzfeldt. In recent years the
countess's faction had become negligible. Consequently, she
was ready to rejoin the ADAV on almost any terms. For his
part, Schweitzer used this occasion to reinstitute the "Lassallean organization." That phrase meant abolition of the
new powers for the executive committee created at Barmen-
Elberfeld and resurrection of the presidential dictatorship.
In a plebiscitary charade, he gave the membership five days
to register a yes-or-no vote on these terms for the "Restoration of Unity."[98]

Schweitzer's intraparty critics replied with rebellion.
Wilhelm Bracke, who had founded the ADAV in Brunswick and
had been a longtime critic of Schweitzer, contacted Bebel
and Liebknecht immediately. These three men hurriedly arranged
to meet at Magdeburg on 22 June. Other prominent ADAV defectors, including August Geib, Samuel Spier, Leonard von Bonhorst, and Theodor York, joined them there. All except Bonhorst had previously registered their displeasure with

Schweitzer by abstaining from the vote of confidence at
Barmen-Elberfeld. All had favored the reorganization of
the ADAV. With their work in the Lassallean league undone
by Schweitzer's coup, the group at Magdeburg proposed a congress to circumvent Schweitzer and to unite all factions
of German social democracy.[99]

Bracke authored the necessary manifesto, which appeared
in the *Demokratische Wochenblatt* of 26 June. Therein, he
charged Schweitzer with conspiratorial intrigues to restore
his own power. Specifically, he assailed Schweitzer for
failing to consult the executive committee concerning the
arrangements with Hatzfeldt, and ridiculed the absurdly short
time allowed for the referendum. At the core of the matter,
the signatories of the manifesto simply refused to accept
a reinstitution of the presidential dictatorship. They called
instead for a congress to meet at Eisenach on 7 August to
create a united and democratic workers' party. Significantly,
all the issues cited as motivating this action were organizational in nature. Matters of program were not even mentioned.

Liebknecht's task now was to win as many Lassallean converts as possible. To achieve that end, he and Bebel paid
a considerable price in concessions to the mavericks in the
ADAV. In the call for the Eisenach Congress, ADAV signatories
received top billing. August Geib, the Lassallean leader in
Hamburg, chaired the proceedings at Eisenach. Bebel and
Liebknecht even supported Bracke's hometown, Brunswick, as the
site for the executive committee, the highest authority in the
new party. Regarding ideology, the Lassalleans also received
at least as much as they gave. Bracke was named to co-author
the program proposal along with Bebel. The delegates at the
congress added the Lassallean demand for state-sponsored

producers' cooperatives to the adopted program. Moreover, Liebknecht confided to Marx that he had agreed to abstain from all attacks upon Lassalle for "about ¼ year."[100]

Marx issued no protest, public or private, against this compromise with Lassalleanism upon which the Eisenach Congress was founded. In this phase of his career, he too was practicing doctrinal flexibility. Only later, after his heterodox International had exploded in his face, did Marx question the wisdom of compromise.

The willingness to compromise always characterized Liebknecht's career. In 1869, it served his cause well. Over sixty Lassalleans publicly endorsed the Eisenach Congress. Among their number were Friedrich Fritzsche and Theodor York, presidents of two of the largest Lassallean labor unions.[101] Thus did Liebknecht recoup the loss of the preceding September. Liebknecht probably exaggerated when he told Marx he had captured three-fourths of the ADAV membership;[102] nevertheless, by August the ADAV lay crippled and the future apparently belonged to the Eisenachers.

The ADAV constituted only one of the working-class organizations that had to be considered in preparing the Eisenach Congress. There remained the ticklish relationship with the IWA, and especially with J. P. Becker in Geneva. Becker had championed the doctrines of the International tirelessly, and, like all politicians, he expected some deference for his efforts.[103] When Schweitzer's coup precipitated the crisis in June, Liebknecht wrote to Marx, "*Becker* wants us absolutely to subordinate ourselves to him; I have told him categorically that we deal directly with the General Council [of the IWA]."[104]

Becker must have realized that his last chance for retaining any influence in Germany had arrived. To preserve his position, he published an organization proposal for Liebknecht's party in his newspaper, *Der Vorbote*. It prescribed an extremely loose structure in which all local associations had to deal with the Geneva central authority, which in turn would correspond with the General Council in London.[105]

Liebknecht and Bebel were indignant at this idea. Both wrote to Marx asking for his intervention on behalf of an independent German party.[106] As usual, Marx sided with his comrades in Leipzig. In the General Council of the IWA, he specifically denounced Becker's organization proposal.[107] Engels later explained that the German party was too "powerful and independently significant" to be subordinate to the Geneva section.[108] Armed with the support of the IWA, Liebknecht met privately with Becker and persuaded him to renounce his claim to leadership of the German movement.[109] An open disagreement was avoided, Becker's organization proposal was disregarded, and he continued gallantly to champion the Eisenach Congress in his newspaper.[110] That convocation ended his political significance in Germany.

Marx also worked with Liebknecht and Bebel to find a mutually acceptable form of merging the new German party with the IWA. At Eisenach, Liebknecht advised the delegates to adhere to the International only "in so far as the Law of Associations allows." This ambiguous phraseology was to be accompanied by encouragement of individual membership in the IWA. The delegates then gave Liebknecht a mandate to represent the new party at the next congress of the International.[111] With that, the matter of affiliation with the IWA was considered closed. Marx and Engels apparently accepted this vague arrangement.

Having conciliated the Lassalleans as much as possible
and having sidestepped Becker's organizational proposal,
there remained the preparations for the congress itself.
The selection of a site was simple. Eisenach stood near the
geographical center of Germany. Moreover, it was not notoriously associated with either the ADAV or the VDAV. Consequently, that town could be counted upon to draw the maximum
number of delegates, and a congress bearing its name would
symbolize a new beginning rather than a victory for either of
the preexisting parties.

The planners of the Eisenach Assembly knew that ADAV
loyalists would try forcibly to break up the congress. That
tactic, although often associated with the subsequent Weimar
period of German history, was well established in the rivalry
between the two working-class parties during the 1860s. On
21 July, August Geib urged Bebel to send as many local friends
as possible from Saxony and Thuringia to the Eisenach Congress: protection in numbers would be needed, he feared.[112]

Liebknecht used the *Demokratische Wochenblatt* to enlist
those numbers. Contrasted to the skimpy treatment that the
Demokratische Wochenblatt gave to the Nuremberg Congress,
the affair at Eisenach received saturation coverage. The
Demokratische Wochenblatt published the initial call for
the congress. It carefully listed the support of each additional ADAV defector. It ran a regular column entitled
"Contra Schweitzer-Hatzfeldt (Mende)," wherein the distortions
printed in *Der Sozialdemokrat* were refuted.[113] With each
piece of reporting implicitly or explicitly disavowing responsibility for splitting the workers' movement, the *Demokratische
Wochenblatt* depicted Eisenach as a congress unifying the proletarian party in Germany.

In addition to his journalism and his behind-the-scenes
negotiating, Liebknecht made one other vital contribution
to the preparation for the Eisenach Congress. He personally
arranged for the inclusion of the Austrian social democrats.
Since November 1868, he had corresponded with Heinrich Oberwinder, the leader of the embryonic Austrian socialist movement. In the summer of 1869, Oberwinder immediately endorsed
the Eisenach proceedings, agitating on behalf of that congress
in his newspaper, the *Volkstimme*.[114] He also arranged for
Liebknecht to address a public rally in Vienna.

At least 6,000 men attended Liebknecht's speech at
Zöbel's beerhall on 25 July. His initial remarks were similar
to those he had delivered at Barmen-Elberfeld in both purpose
and content: the discrediting of Schweitzer. He added an
indictment of Schweitzer's most recent treachery in his merger
with Hatzfeldt, concluded by touting his own *grossdeutsch*
sympathies: "Austria must return to Germany, not however to
Bismarck's Germany but rather to a free [Germany], united on
democratic foundations."[115]

After the rally, Liebknecht jubilantly told Bebel, "From
Austria we will receive at least 30,000 votes, so that if
Schweitzer comes with falsified votes, he will be chopped
down with massive legitimate ones."[116] As it turned out,
Liebknecht underestimated the Austrian count. Of the highly
inflated 155,486 members claimed in the Eisenach protocol,
80,000 were identified as Austrians.[117]

These numbers insured that ADAV disrupters could not
outvote the sponsors of the Eisenach meeting. More violent
tactics remained a possibility. On Saturday, 7 August, 263
delegates came to Eisenach to create a new party. Approximately 100 Lassallean loyalists arrived simultaneously, determined to thwart that development.

Bebel, Liebknecht, and their friends convened a special
preliminary session to discuss how to handle the ADAV threat.
The protocol of this meeting claimed: that two deputies were
sent to the beerhall where the Lassalleans were gathered;
that there they extended a hand of friendship to their rivals;
and that the Lassalleans were drunk and obnoxious, and they
rebuffed the emissaries of peace. So the preliminary session
had to assume that the Lassalleans would be disruptive. Thus,
new yellow passes were issued to each delegate, and August
Geib was designated in advance to chair the opening evening
session.

At the first official meeting later that day, the Eisenachers and the Lassalleans crowded into the same beerhall.
Confrontation came immediately. Several ADAV delegates loudly
demanded validation of mandates before the election of officers.
Despite the apparent reasonableness of this request, Geib
pushed through a cloture motion and called for a vote on the
chairmanship. The indignant ADAV delegates stomped, whistled,
and sang the Marseillaise. Amid the confusion, Geib declared
his own election as chairman and adjourned the congress until
the next morning.[118]

On Sunday, policemen guarded the door to the meeting
hall. To be admitted, delegates had to produce the yellow
passes that had been issued at the preliminary session.
Fuming, the ADAV delegates skulked away and convened their
own meaningless conference. In Der Sozialdemokrat, Schweitzer
dismissed the congress of the "followers of Herr Liebknecht"
as a rump session of Austrians held under police patronage.[119]

After the hectic weeks of preparation and the tension
of the first sessions on Saturday, the remainder of the Eisenach
Congress was rather bland. Most important decisions had been
made in advance by Liebknecht, Bebel, Bracke and Geib.

Grievances about the dictatorial Lassallean organization were the primary reasons for the maverick Lassalleans' merger with the VDAV. Between the ADAV rebels and the VDAV there were no organizational disputes. Both groups wanted an association that would negate Schweitzer's one-man rule.

The organization proposed and adopted at Eisenach dispersed power among three agencies, the highest of which was the annual party congress. That body had the decisive voice in all matters, except when it altered the party statute or modified the fundamental political principles of the association. Decisions like those had to be made by a plebiscite of the membership.

Membership was defined in the broadest possible terms. To be enrolled, one had only to pay a monthly contribution of one groschen or subscribe to the party newspaper. No further commitment was required. These members, who needed no credentials in revolutionary theory or practice, elected the delegates to the party congress.

Each party congress was to designate a site for an executive committee and a separate site for the control committee. These two bodies were to run the organization between congresses. Their actual membership was chosen by comrades in the respective towns that the congress designated. (This provision was a reaction against the dispersion of the ADAV's executive committee members throughout Germany. That arrangement had rendered the Lassallean executive committee impotent.) The five-member Eisenacher Executive Committee managed all party business between congresses. The eleven-member control commission, on the other hand, was a watchdog over the executive. It was empowered to hear all complaints against the executive committee and could suspend all or part of that committee, if it found that drastic step necessary.

All of these provisions were designed to prevent the
concentration of power in a few hands. A measure with similar
intent was instituted regarding Liebknecht's own domain, the
party press. The Eisenacher organization statute barred the
editor and staff of the party newspaper from membership in
the executive committee or control committee. Again,
Schweitzer's example, combining the ADAV presidency with
the editorship of *Der Sozialdemokrat*, offered a negative
model for the Eisenachers.

The press itself was instructed to mirror opinion inside
the party. All members' contributions were to be printed,
so long as space permitted and the party program was not
violated. Complaints about rejection of contributions or
"tendentious coloration of submissions" could be submitted
to the control commission. In the last instance, the party
congress could dictate to the party organ.

At the Eisenach congress, the delegates decided to adopt
the *Demokratische Wochenblatt as the* official organ of their
party. After 7 October, it would bear a new name, *Der Volksstaat.* During the discussion of this matter, one delegate
suggested founding a completely fresh journal. He worried
about the old ties between the left-liberals and the *Demokratische Wochenblatt*, saying that Schweitzer surely would
exploit this weakness. In his longest speech at the congress,
Liebknecht rose to explain and defend his political past. He
assured the delegates he was far more radical than Schweitzer.
Specifically, he boasted of his membership in the "communist
party," adding somewhat petulantly that he had been a socialist
before most of the delegates even knew the word. The congress
apparently accepted Liebknecht's defense, for it chose Leipzig
as the site for the party newspaper. No vote for editor

occurred, the selection being left to the executive committee. Yet it must have been clear that Liebknecht would continue in that job.[120]

The Eisenacher organization statute was welded to the party program as part of a single document. The official proposal had appeared in the *Demokratische Wochenblatt* on 31 July. It was Bebel's composition, although his writing must have incorporated the thoughts of Liebknecht and Bracke.[121] Bebel dominated the discussion on both the organization and the program at Eisenach, and he managed to steer his proposal through the treacherous ADAV-VDAV antagonisms with remarkably few changes.

The core of the Eisenach program remained that of the International, but there were some significant changes. At the head of that platform, alone as Part I, stood the bold statement, "The social democratic party of Germany strives for the institution of the free people's state." In his remarks at the congress, Liebknecht said that the term "people's state" could only mean a republic. "I myself am a republican," he affirmed, "and I am convinced that there is not one in this assembly who is not a republican."[122] But in this and in other parts of the Eisenacher Program, in the face of legal realities, prudence dictated some circumlocution.

Part II of the Eisenach Statute relied heavily on the program of the IWA. However, the assertion that the workers had to free themselves was deleted. In its place stood a moralistic indictment: "The present political and social conditions are unjust in the highest degree and therefore ought to be combatted with the greatest energy." The following three points were almost identical in the Nuremberg and Eisenach Programs, except that the latter added a specific

call to abolish the wage system and to give the worker the
full fruits of his labor. Point five of Part II in the
Eisenach Program was original. It stressed the importance
of a "unitary organization" as a precondition for successful
political struggle. That statement may have been a concession
to the Lassallean addiction to organization. The last point
of this theoretical section declared that the social democratic
party of Germany adhered to the IWA "insofar as the Law of
Associations allows."

Part III announced nine short-term demands. The first
point called for universal, equal, direct and secret suffrage
only for all adult "men." The remaining points in this section
could have been found in any left-liberal platform of the
day: referenda, abolition of inherited privilege, substitution of a citizen militia for the standing army, full freedom
of the press, and so on. The only mildly socialistic proposals
called for a limited working day (although even an approximate
maximum was not specified) and the substitution of a progressive
income tax for all indirect levies. Conspicuously, the program
draft did not include Lassalle's panacea of state help for productive associations, but delegates to the congress discovered
this omission. In one of only two significant changes made by
the delegates, the Lassallean associations were added as a
tenth item in Part III.[123]

The Eisenach Program indicates how Liebknecht's party had
come to terms with the needs of daily political agitation. It
had divided its aspirations and placed them in two separate
baskets. The first contained a theoretical statement of things
ultimately desirable. It included a republican system of
government and socialist redistribution of the nation's wealth.
The Eisenachers implicitly conceded that realization of these

demands lay far in the misty future. The party made no prog-
nostication about *how* they would be implemented. Instead it
offered its second basket, which contained specific radical
changes that conceivably could be achieved within the capitalist
framework, even within a monarchy. This schizophrenic platform did not explain the connection between theoretical and
practical parts. Thus, it was possible to focus exclusively
on immediate reforms. That aspect of the Eisenacher program--
and of subsequent programs adopted by German social democrats--
allowed the party eventually to preempt the left-liberal movement in Germany. Gradually the social democrats became the
main vehicle for legal political protest.

From a Marxist viewpoint, the haziness of the line between
bourgeois democrats and socialists was not necessarily unfortunate at that stage of development. The socialists could
gain an enormous base of sympathizers through ambiguity in
their program. The next task lay in educating these sympathizers, in making them over into committed socialists. That job
belonged to the leaders, to men like Bebel, Bracke and Liebknecht. But these men were themselves unsure of their theories.
Evidence of that fact emerged at the Eisenach Congress, when
the party discussed its future name.

The planners of the congress had chosen to call their
creation the Social Democratic Party of Germany. At Eisenach,
the maverick Lassalleans noticed the exclusion of the term
"worker" from the title, and they protested against it. Bebel
tried to overcome their objections by noting that many socialists were not manual laborers. Probably he hoped to avoid
direct provocation of his friends in the People's Party. On
the initial vote on the party's name, Bebel's viewpoint won
a majority. Then, in rapid succession, several ex-Lassalleans

threatened to resign their mandates. A new vote hastily was
taken, and the congress unanimously adopted the title, "Social
Democratic Workers' Party" (*Socialdemokratische Arbeiterpartei*
or SDAP).[124] Leaders who were this reluctant to advertise
the class orientation of the SDAP would be unlikely to educate
the members toward a revolutionary Marxist viewpoint.

Because of the lack of theoretical clarity of the Eisenachers, their congress did not mark the birth of a social
democratic working class party in Germany. Left-liberals
like Sonnemann continued to hover around the party.[125] Another
crisis was needed to delineate the explicitly socialist commitment of the SDAP.

THE BASEL CONGRESS: JETTISONING THE MIDDLE-CLASS ALLIES

At the Nuremberg and Eisenach Congresses, Liebknecht had
marched confidently at the head of the column of his comrades.
Thanks to his education and experience, he had a better sense
of direction than most of his fellow travellers on the road to
a social democratic creed. By the autumn of 1869, however,
his own agitation had helped to draw a cluster of comrades
around the viewpoint he represented. Soon some of these men
surged ahead of Liebknecht, dragging him toward a position he
would have preferred to defer.

After the success accomplished at Eisenach, Liebknecht
wanted a pause, a breathing-space, before any further ideological clarification. Specifically, he wanted to maintain his ties
to the bourgeois left-liberals a while longer. The goal of
that cooperation, a republican Germany, had yet to be attained.
Consequently, for tactical reasons, he planned to soft-pedal

the SDAP's socialist sentiments and to stress the party's democratic political platform. In this latter realm he could count
upon continued cooperation with the People's Party.

Liebknecht's more adventurous comrades, particularly the
ex-Lassalleans, raced ahead of him on this issue. They had
always been more hostile to the left-liberals than had the
Bebel-Liebknecht faction. Within a few months after the
Eisenach Congress, they forced Liebknecht to choose between
his proletarian comrades and his left-liberal allies.

The precipitating cause for this excruciating choice
originated at Basel. On 6-11 September 1869, the International
Workingman's Association held its congress in that Swiss city.
The Eisenachers sent Liebknecht and one ex-Lassallean, Samuel
Spier, to represent them at this meeting. The Basel Congress
passed two resolutions that articulated the communist challenge
to property owners everywhere. First, the delegates affirmed
the "right and duty" of society to transform private agricultural holdings into collectively owned farms. Second, the
congress called for an international organization of labor
unions.[126] Thus were property and profit both threatened.

Although Liebknecht joined the majority in endorsing
both resolutions, he stated that scientific validity for
socialist propositions could not be proven by majority votes
and that only careful study and theoretical argumentation
could establish socialist truth. In any case, to him a "penny
of practice" was "worth more than 100 pounds of theory."[127]
Typically, Liebknecht shunted theory into a corner when its
consequences became uncomfortable.

Inevitably, the left-liberals in Germany were alarmed by
the Basel resolutions, and a few of their newspapers urged the
SDAP to disavow them.[128] Liebknecht responded with intentional
equivocation. On 29 September 1869, in the last issue of the

Demokratische Wochenblatt, he tried to quiet his fidgety
allies by drawing a distinction between principles and practice. He conceded that the Basel resolutions stated *as a*
theory the right of society to convert private property into
common ownership, but the resolutions designated no means
of implementation and remained, at least temporarily inconsequential.

Samuel Spier delivered this same argument to skeptical
delegates at the People's Party Congress in mid-October. He
urged the congress not to permit a "theory" to prevent cooperation against the common enemy, Bismarck. The People's Party
then voted to ignore the Basel resolutions as a "purely theoretical expression of opinion . . . , so long as the Congress of
the Social Democratic Workers' Party does not assert the contrary."[129]

Meanwhile, Liebknecht avoided a public commitment on the
Basel resolution through sophistry. To the question, what
position did the SDAP take on agricultural property, Liebknecht
answered, "none." He encouraged individual members to take a
position, but as yet, he said, the party as a whole had made no
decision. He concluded that the Basel decision, "like all
decisions of a theoretical nature, has binding power only for
those who have voted for it."[130] What was truly remarkable in
his attitude was this: he asserted that individual members or
chapters of the SDAP were free to retain their own opinions
even when and if a party congress endorsed the Basel resolutions. After all, Liebknecht wrote, the SDAP "consists of free
men, not irresolute tools."[131]

On the SDAP executive committee, the majority repudiated
Liebknecht's laxness and vacillation.[132] Liebknecht tried to
mollify them by pleading for patience. "I myself am a communist

and am therefore in agreement with the resolutions in principle. . . ." Still, he argued that the rural masses were
not yet ready for such a frank statement of the ultimate aims
of the party and reminded Bracke, "We do not need the peasants
to make a revolution, but no revolution can succeed if the
peasants oppose it."[133]

The first test of strength between Liebknecht and the
party directorate had arrived. On the executive committee,
Leonard von Bonhorst and Samuel Spier shared Liebknecht's
viewpoint.[134] They might have won time for Liebknecht's
hedging on the Basel resolutions, but the police intervened to
undercut his position. Bonhorst was imprisoned early in November
On 16 November, Liebknecht was incarcerated for three weeks as
a result of a conviction for delivering a fiery speech of the
preceding May which the authorities concluded circulated "lessons dangerous to the state."[135] With only Spier left at large,
SDAP resistance to ratification of the Basel decrees withered.

In addition to the change of constellation of forces
inside the party, two other considerations drove the SDAP
toward an explicit endorsement of the Basel resolutions. First,
as the maverick Lassalleans in the executive committee had
feared, Schweitzer exploited Liebknecht's tergiversation. *Der
Sozialdemokrat* sneered, "The emissaries and tools of bourgeois
democracy in Germany, with Herr Liebknecht at their head, vainly
attempted to prevent the Basel Congress from formulating decisively socialist resolutions." Crowing that collectivization
of agricultural property belonged to the "ABC's" of socialism,
Schweitzer asserted that Liebknecht's faction was not a social
democratic workers' party, "but rather a bourgeois or reactionary party."[136] The second pressure driving the SDAP toward
acknowledgment of the Basel resolutions originated in Bavaria.

In December 1869, disaffected elements of the ADAV in Augsburg and Munich declared their independence from Schweitzer.[137]
The Eisenachers hoped to lure these latest Lassallean deserters
into its camp, but the Bavarians obstinately declared, "There
can be no talk of joining the so-called 'Social Democratic
Workers' Party' . . . until it has completely emancipated
itself from every tie to the People's Party."[138]

It was no coincidence that *Der Volksstaat* began pelting
the People's Party with criticism precisely at this time. In
February, Bebel wrote a series of articles in which he lambasted the liberal editor of the formerly friendly *Demokratische
Korrespondenz*. Here he succinctly summarized the difference
between bourgeois and social democracy. The former, he wrote,
sees political democracy as all that a citizen can demand.
But what good is democracy, Bebel asked, if one is starving?
"Social democracy therefore considers political freedom not
as an end but rather as a means to an end," he wrote; "social
democrats consider the end as the institution of economic
equality. . . ."[139]

Swimming with the tide inside his party, after his release
from prison, Liebknecht swung around to an endorsement of the
Basel decisions and a repudiation of the People's Party. Unfortunately the sources are insufficient to reconstruct his conversion in detail. Pressure from the ADAV and the Bavarian situation certainly must have been important factors. The demands
of his colleagues within the SDAP must have played a major role,
too. Nevertheless, nothing would have convinced Liebknecht if
he had not accepted the validity of the Basel decisions. He
had, after all, voted for collectivization at the IWA Congress
in September. Only his tactical scheme to maintain the alliance
with the DVP had caused him to hold back on encouraging endorsement of the decrees by the SDAP.

The first public proof of Liebknecht's newly decisive
attitude came in a speech at Leipzig on January 13, 1870.
There he assailed his former left-liberal allies with a devas-
tating critique. In what must have been a personally painful
admission, he conceded that the People's Party could never
"shatter the North German Confederation." Turning to a lecture
on Marxist fundamentals, he continued, "Purely political
parties today are no longer capable of existence." Germany's
present government, which Liebknecht labelled "caesarism,"
"rests on the exploitation of class antagonisms," he explained;
"it therefore has an economic basis. A party that does not
comprehend this is incapable of fighting it [caesarism]. . . ."
He predicted that the People's Party, which he claimed had
come together only to resist Bismarck, would "be shredded
between the millstones of social democracy and the National
Liberals."[140]

In a speech on 12 March at Meerane, Liebknecht tied
these observations together with an endorsement of the Basel
resolutions. These remarks, augmented by additional evidence
and statistical material, were published as a pamphlet under
the title, "Zur Grund- und Bodenfrage." The contents constitute a detailed communist confession.

In this pamphlet, Liebknecht introduced his observations
on property with an historical overview of that institution.
With such an approach he intended to show his audience that
the Basel resolutions dealt with a "problem thousands of years
old."[141] He also wanted to prove that the ownership of property
was an historically malleable arrangement. Demonstrating his
erudition, he cited Plato, Christ, Duns Scotus, and Immanuel
Kant among the critics of private property. For his audience,
he hoped that the prestige of these commentators would remove
the "frightening" visage from the Basel resolutions.

Liebknecht said he knew that the very word "communist" terrified many of his listeners. To these people, he exhorted, "Instead of cringing like an old woman holding her hands over her eyes, show some manly circumspection. . . ."[142] The subject of land ownership should be investigated as a question of utility: whether the present system of land ownership was conducive to the general welfare or whether collective ownership promised to be more beneficial to the majority.

The bulk of Liebknecht's essay consisted of a statistically supported indictment of private ownership. According to Liebknecht, in areas where holdings were small and widely dispersed, as in France and southwest Germany, the peasants suffered from chronic debt, a miserable lifestyle and even a declining birthrate. Moreover, the inefficiency inherent in small plots robbed the whole nation of potential wealth. On the other hand, in areas of consolidated farms like England and northeastern Germany, a few prospered while the masses sank to the level of a rural proletariat. So poor were the peasants in Prussia that almost one-half of the military draftees were rejected each year for physical inadequacy.[143] Some blamed the plight of Europe's peasants on overpopulation, Liebknecht noted. But he argued that "overpopulation, insofar as the word has any meaning, is a relative notion. . . . In our advanced lands, to speak of overpopulation only means using an incorrect expression for unjust division of the wealth." With "rational social institutions," he continued, "the world could support a population perhaps six times as large as its present number of inhabitants."[144]

Liebknecht agreed with the advocates of modern farming techniques who hoped that proper use of the soil would greatly increase productivity, but he saw those costly methods as only another advantage for the large landowner. The debt-ridden

peasant could never afford expensive implements or fertilizers.
Consequently, he would become relatively even more inefficient.
Eventually he would succumb to competition from the handful
of land barons. Only collective ownership could combine the
benefits in efficiency of modern large-scale farming with prosperity for the many instead of the few. Thus economic interest
dictated that sooner or later private property would be taken
over by the toiling masses themselves.

If the state voluntarily renounced its class character
and became a People's State, Liebknecht said that collectivization might occur "gradually" and "without forcible damage to
private interests." However, if the state stubbornly retained
its defense of bourgeois property rights, the impoverished
masses eventually would have to choose between starvation and
"smashing the state. . . . That is revolution. . . . Reform
or revolution--the final goal will be reached in either case."[145]

When discussing expropriation, Liebknecht explained that
he was referring only to the fate of the major landowners. The
small farmers were a different sort of producer and had to be
treated differently. Education would be used to persuade these
petty landowners to renounce their property. Communes would
be established on state lands to demonstrate the superiority
of collective ownership. In every possible way, the peasants
would be led to accept socialism voluntarily.

Liebknecht knew that some in his audience would fear regulation by the state. The present oppressive state had bestowed
a bad reputation on that word, he admitted, but different social
orders produce different states. In a social democratic society,
each citizen could say, "I am the state, we all are the state."
He assured his listeners that a social democratic state would
"apply no coercion" against its own citizens.[146]

Liebknecht summarized his lengthy remarks by calling for
the oppressed in city and countryside to join together against
the capitalist exploiter: "Instead of raising their hands
fratricidally, suicidally against us, may the working people
of the countryside comprehend what the working people of the
cities proffer, and united with them build a new world in the
old."[147]

Liebknecht's "Zur Grund- und Bodenfrage" quickly became
a classic in the agitational repertoire of social democrats,
thus helping to solidify the SDAP, but it also demolished
Liebknecht's liaison with Germany's left-liberals. The denoue-
ment of his four-year affair with the DVP came at the SDAP
Congress on 4-7 June 1870. At that gathering, Bebel introduced a lengthy resolution that declared the "communal necessity" of collectivization of farmland and called for the
collectivization of state and church lands as a transitional
stage toward communal ownership of all farmland. The resolution carried with minimal debate.[148]

THE DEMISE OF THE INTERNATIONAL

Shortly after the Basel resolutions helped to precipitate
the permanent rupture between Germany's left-liberals and the
socialists, doctrinal disagreements and personal rivalries
within the International erupted into a bitter feud that killed
that organization outright. The disintegration originated in
an irreconcilable rivalry between Marx and Michael Bakunin. In
1868, that seemingly ubiquitous Russian anarchist had surfaced
in Switzerland. Within a year, he and a band of followers had
successfully petitioned Marx for membership in the IWA.[149] No

chance existed for prolonged, genuine cooperation between Marx
and Bakunin. Perhaps the two shared a goal in the liberation
of mankind from all oppression, but the paths that each advocated to that end seldom crossed.[150]

Already at the Basel Congress in September 1869, Bakunin
and the Marxists skirmished publicly over the economic demands
of the party. From Basel, Liebknecht wrote to Marx in London
equating Bakunin's intrigues with those of his own archrival
Schweitzer. Liebknecht promised that he would eliminate
Bakunin.[151]

During the course of discussions about the right of
inheritance at the Basel Congress, Bakunin urged the congress
to address only economic issues, explaining that social, not
political revolution was the proper proletarian task. To
Liebknecht, that viewpoint sounded distressingly like
Schweitzer's argumentation. Somewhat heatedly he admonished
the anarchists, "To preach social revolution without political
[revolution] is to do the work of reaction. . . ."[152]

The confrontation between Bakunin and Liebknecht had
a personal dimension too. In the least honorable episode of
his carer, during the summer of 1869, Liebknecht had privately
spread the charge that Bakunin was an agent of the Russian
government. Bakunin successfully insisted that the Basel
Congress hold a court of honor to clear his name. This tribunal censured Liebknecht for his irresponsible rumormongering.
According to Bakunin, Liebknecht then apologized, and the two
shook hands.[153]

Still the feud festered. A few months later a Bakuninist
newspaper blasted the General Council, Marx's own domain, for
failing to arbitrate the long-standing quarrel between the
ADAV and the Eisenachers. Taking sides itself, that newspaper lambasted the liberal connections of Marx's friend,

Liebknecht, and backed the Lassalleans.[154] Thus began a neglected but important connection between Bakunin and the ADAV that lasted for the next five years.

Gradually, in Marx's mind, the various actors in the ADAV, the SDAP and the IWA became polarized: Marx and his supporters, including Liebknecht and the Eisenachers, and Bakunin's faction, including the Lassalleans. Despite the diversity of opinions inside the latter group, Marx discerned enough similarities to lump anarchists and authoritarians together as "sectarians."[155] Early in 1870, in a "Confidential Report" to all sections of the IWA, Marx repudiated Bakunin's "sectarian" activities inside the International. The same circular branded Schweitzer's ADAV with the same label, and it especially lambasted the Lassalleans' inflexible organization and their cult of hero worship surrounding Lassalle.[156] This "Confidential Report" was Marx's first denunciation of the ADAV, and it was circulated only to a limited audience. Liebknecht thanked Marx for his belated support, but he could not resist adding, "If you had acted one year earlier [before the Eisenach Congress], Schweitzer would be buried in the Prussian Press Bureau and the International would not have exploded."[157]

In the spring of 1870, Liebknecht and Marx collaborated to hound the Bakuninists from the IWA. To that end, they planned to hold the 1870 congress of the International at Mainz, where a sizeable SDAP delegation could be used in a vote to expel the anarchists. In return for his help in this matter, Liebknecht expected Marx publicly to repudiate the Lassalleans.[158]

Bismarck's diplomacy unexpectedly interrupted these machinations. Preempted by the Franco-Prussian War, the congress at Mainz never occurred. Instead, the various

protagonists in the IWA redirected their energies in support
of the revolution in France. Hurrying to Lyon, Bakunin tried
unsuccessfully to smash the state by revolutionary decree.
In London, Marx championed the Paris Commune with his biting
masterpiece, *The Civil War in France*. When the war ended
and the Commune lay in ashes, the Marxist and the Bakuninists
still stood glowering at each other inside the International.

Using the excuse of intense government repression throughout Europe, Marx arranged a clandestine conference of the IWA
to meet in London in September 1871. Liebknecht later complained that Marx's deliberate secrecy precluded attendance
by any SDAP delegates. "I had to believe that you wanted to
hold the conference *privatim*," Liebknecht said.[159] With loyal
supporters dominating the small London Conference, Marx ram-
rodded a series of resolutions through the assembly that were
intended to crush his enemies.[160] His actions provoked a
chorus of disapproval from all non-Marxist elements of European
socialism. Bakunin's disciples convened at Sonvillier in
Switzerland in November 1871, where they issued a widely circulated condemnation of Marx's dictatorial methods.[161] In
Italy, Spain, and even in London, Marx won the hostility of
vocal radicals.[162] Only Germany remained to him, and there,
too, his critics attacked. Joining the anarchist clamor, the
ADAV newspaper printed the various denunciations of Marx then
reverberating through Europe.[163]

The Lassalleans had two reasons to attack the beleaguered
London exile. First, they hoped to embarrass their German
rivals, the Eisenachers, by discrediting Marx. Liebknecht and
his comrades had boasted of their ties to the founder of scientific socialism, and now, through Marx, they were vulnerable.
The second Lassallean motive for chastising Marx revolved
around the claim to paternity of the German workers' movement.

Because Marx was Lassalle's most important rival for that
distinction, the ADAV newspaper derided Marx as an idle philos-
opher without practical capabilities. The same article praised
Lassalle's uniquely effective blend of theory and practice.[164]

Battered by the abusive barrage, Marx moved to regroup
his forces. Complaining about the "purely platonic relationship" between the SDAP and the IWA, he revoked Liebknecht's
plenipotentiary status for Germany and undertook direct correspondence with the few sections of the International in that
country.[165] Liebknecht responded laconically to Engels,
"Numerous individual memberships [in the IWA] in Germany are
not to be expected and *entre nous*, I also think them to be
unnecessary."[166]

Ten days later, Liebknecht answered Engels' charge that
the Germans did less for the IWA than did the French. Liebknecht explained that the French workers had no organization
except the IWA and that their organizational weakness had
caused the failure of the Paris Commune. If the German workers
had begun that revolution, "by God we would have gotten farther
than the French and specifically thanks to our organization;
with as good an organization [as the SDAP], the Commune would
not have died."[167]

Thus, Marx and Engels got little help from Liebknecht in
their struggle to keep control of the IWA away from the anarchists. Seeing no chance to save the International for themselves, the Londoners decided to raze their organization
rather than let it fall into enemy hands. They implemented
that decision in September 1872, when sixty-five delegates
convened for a carefully orchestrated congress of the International at the Hague. Because of legal problems in Germany,
Liebknecht was not among the three SDAP representatives.

Under Marx's careful direction, the delegates first expelled
Bakunin. Then they voted to transfer the headquarters of the
IWA to New York, safely beyond the reach of Marx's enemies.
That latter decision effectively killed the First International,
leaving Liebknecht and the SDAP as the only sizeable, organized
band of Marx's friends anywhere.

PATTERNS OF CHANGE IN LIEBKNECHT'S POLITICS

An overview of Liebknecht's intraparty labors between 1865
and 1872 may be presented as a tale of six cities. At Chemnitz
in 1866, Liebknecht helped to build an anti-Bismarck alliance
comprised of democratic elements throughout Germany. To that
end, he endorsed an organization, the People's Party, which
touted democracy but soft-pedalled class conflict. Meanwhile,
regarding the working class, he planned to promote a revolutionary class consciousness inside the growing VDAV and to
arrange an eventual merger with the ADAV. The first of those
schemes culminated at Nuremberg in 1868, when the assembled
delegates adopted the principles of the International as
their own. However, Schweitzer sabotaged the second step, the
anticipated union of the working class parties. His treachery
led to a public confrontation with Liebknecht and Bebel at
Barmen-Elberfeld. At the 1869 ADAV congress in that city,
Liebknecht thoroughly indicted Schweitzer, and he incited
the aspirations for intraparty democracy that were harbored
by many ambitious Lassalleans. His tactics encouraged their
revolt and facilitated the enrollment of many ADAV mavericks
into the SDAP at Eisenach. Only a few weeks later the Basel
Congress of the IWA spotlighted an insurmountable contradiction

in Liebknecht's recent strategy. That congress's resolution
endorsed collectivization of private property and starkly contrasted the divergent economic interests of Liebknecht's
middle- and lower-class allies. Soon he had to choose between
involvement with the predominantly bourgeois People's Party
or with the more proletarian SDAP. His decision in this
matter, embodying consideration of the welfare of the Eisenacher party and reflecting substantial pressure from his
peers in the Eisenacher leadership, offers the first clear
illustration in his career of how organizational calcula-
tions could induce him to modify his tactics. Early in
1870, he opted for the SDAP and broke with the DVP, thereby
helping to bury the cross-class coalition whose creation
he had fostered only four years earlier. Now his only political affiliation outside the SDAP was the International. When
Marx maneuvered to abort that association at the Hague in
1872, the Eisenachers, organizationally speaking, were left
standing alone.

For Liebknecht, the net result of this six-city odyssey
was a shift in his political emphasis and style, away from
the national and toward the social issue, away from a coalition
that transcended economic classes and toward an exclusively
working-class orientation, and away from multiple organizational allegiances and toward integration into the leadership
of a national social democratic party.

Throughout these years Liebknecht adeptly channeled his
labor where it was most likely to be successful, shifting his
concentration as new opportunities arose. From 1865 to 1866,
the national issue overshadowed every other political question. Measured against that colossal standard, the small

and doctrinally confused VDAV appeared puny indeed. To enhance his own influence and to fight for the democratic preconditions for socialism, Liebknecht therefore orchestrated cooperation between his left-liberal friends and his working-class comrades. Meanwhile, the VDAV matured, and an opportunity for an alliance with a large bloc of Lassalleans arose. By the end of the decade it seemed both necessary and worthwhile to trade the left-liberal alliance for a solid and growing proletarian party. A less flexible politician might have missed both the earlier opportunity with the DVP and the later opportunity involving the VDAV and a part of the ADAV.

Although flexible, Liebknecht was no mere opportunist. Consistently he battled Prussia's advances and Bismarck's flirtation with the working class. Equally consistently, he championed *grossdeutsch* social democracy. As a result of his efforts, the SDAP emerged as a vehicle for those latter ideals. Unfortunately, its establishment necessitated the termination of Liebknecht's four-year tryst with the left-liberals at an especially inopportune moment. For the disintegration of that alliance, which had been fashioned explicitly to resist Prussian hegemony, came just months before the Franco-Prussian War. Its demise must have delighted Bismarck almost as much as it pained Liebknecht.

The Party Leadership, ca. 1872
Frontispiece of Wilhelm Bracke, Jr., *Der Braunschweiger Ausschuss im Lötzen und vor dem Gericht* (Brunswick, 1872)

Chapter 6

Battling Bismarck's Conquests

While Liebknecht helped to build the SDAP, he also struggled
to insure that his own thorough rejection of Bismarck's plans
and policies would prevail in his new party. Consistently,
in all his agitation, he dismissed Bismarck's constitution
for the North German Confederation as a fraud, a sham cleverly
designed to deprive the people of real self-government. Indignantly, he censured Bismarck's foreign policy as a bloody
violation of genuine national self-determination. Always he
crusaded for the institution of a socialist republic in his
fatherland.

In these campaigns against the growing caravan of Bismarck's successes, Liebknecht inevitably transgressed beyond
the boundaries of dissent that the authorities would tolerate.
With increasing severity, the courts of various German states
dealt stiff prison sentences to the unruly agitator. Still
Liebknecht persisted, employing every legal opportunity to
expound his message of resistance and revolutionary change.
His obstinate opposition to Bismarck eventually produced
a conviction for conspiracy to commit high treason, a fitting
symbol of the state of war that had arisen between Liebknecht
and the rulers of his native land.

LIEBKNECHT'S VARIED VIEWS OF THE REICHSTAG

Liebknecht's introduction to the legal realities of the North
German Confederation was a harsh one. After the Peace of
Prague, the Prussian government had issued an amnesty, and
Liebknecht--perhaps a bit naively--believed that the new
decree superseded the order that had expelled him in 1865.
In January 1866, he had travelled to Berlin secretly and
illegally, but in the autumn of that year, when he came again
to the Prussian capital, he saw no need to hide his presence.
Instead, on 2 October, he gave a public speech. The police
arrested him that evening. For the next seventeen days he
sat in jail, awaiting a hearing. When Liebknecht finally
came to court, the judge sentenced him to three months in
prison for violating the 1865 deportation order.[1]

    The prison conditions that Liebknecht endured were humane.
Liebknecht wrote to Ernestine that he was well fed, warmly
clothed and had plenty of fresh air. He said he even was
putting on a little weight in jail, and "genuine muscle tissue"
at that.[2] Inmates were allowed fairly free postal communication with the outside world. They also could borrow almost
any reading material they chose. With this "intellectual
nourishment," Liebknecht became accustomed to using his prison
terms for study and for writing.

    Yet Liebknecht agonized over the welfare of Ernestine
and his daughters. Fortunately, friends in Leipzig offered
some financial help.[3] Ernestine also turned to relatives
for support. They responded with clothes, money, and advice.
Her brother asked when Liebknecht would "come to reason,"
and Liebknecht's sister hoped that he would return to Giessen
"and give up his newspaper writing entirely." Ernestine's

mother, apparently hoping to exploit her son-in-law's absence
for a spiritual purpose, begged her daughter to baptize the
second grandchild.[4] Meanwhile, under the strain of separation
from her husband, Ernestine's feeble health collapsed. When
Liebknecht came home, he found his wife severely ill with
tuberculosis. By March, she was bedridden. Ernestine died
at the end of May.[5]

Her death gave a new, personal dimension to Liebknecht's
hatred for Prussia. On 8 June, he wrote to a friend in Berlin,
"Without my expulsion from Prussia and then later my arrest,
she would still be fresh and healthy. May the day of reprisal
not wait too long!"[6] To blame Bismarck must have eased Liebknecht's own burden of guilt in this matter.

For the next few years, Liebknecht's anti-Prussian zeal
knew no bounds. In 1868, in a speech in the Prussian capital
itself, he denounced Bismarck's wars of conquest: Prussia's
victories had buried freedom in northern Germany, and they
had fractured the German nation. "Prussia is not the founder
of German unity," he exclaimed, "it is the obstacle to the
same." To his Berlin audience he admonished, "You have the
task to remove this obstacle to German unity, this State
of Prussia. Here in Berlin stands the chief enemy. . . .
Do your duty!"[7]

Liebknecht's family tragedy, overlaid upon his abiding
red republican convictions, made his accommodation to daily,
legal agitation in Bismarck's budding Reich extremely difficult. The constitution that Bismarck handed down in 1867
made matters no easier.[8] The new political arrangements
vested the sovereignty of the North German Confederation in
a Bundesrat composed of delegates who were appointed by the
governments of the member states. In no way was this Bundesrat

responsible to the people. A hereditary ruler and his appointees
comprised the executive department of government. No provision
was made for popular influence upon these men. The sop for progressive opinion was the Reichstag. Although elected by universal suffrage, it had little power. The constitution carefully prohibited its intervention in military or foreign affairs.
Moreover, its laws could be vetoed by the Bundesrat. At most
it could refuse to pass the budget, but the recent constitutional crisis in Prussia warned of the futility of that tack.

From its inception, Liebknecht ridiculed Bismarck's
government as a parody of democracy. In a despotic state
like the North German Confederation, "without freedom of the
press, without freedom of association, subjected to the sabre
of the policeman and soldier, *universal suffrage can be nothing
but the plaything and tool of absolutism*!" Calling Bismarck's
creation a "coup d'etat" comparable to that of Napoleon III
in 1851, he lampooned the Reichstag as the "fig-leaf of absolutism."[9]

Liebknecht's denunciations of Bismarck's handiwork reached
a crescendo in a speech he made in Berlin on May 31, 1869.
Under the title "No Peace with the Present State," his newspaper summarized his strident remarks. "Under no circumstances and in no sphere may social democracy negotiate with
the enemy. . . . To negotiate with enemies in principle means
to sacrifice one's principles. . . ." After assailing all
aspects of Prussian leadership, particularly its militarism,
Liebknecht issued a warning reminiscent of Bismarck's "iron
and blood" speech. "Socialism is no longer a question of
theory," he exclaimed, "but rather simply a question of power,
which is to be solved not in parliament but only in the streets,
on the battlefield, like every other question of power." Lest

anyone miss his meaning, he explained that "revolutions are not made with the gracious permission of the authorities; the socialist ideal cannot be accomplished within the present state; it can be brought into existence only by overthrowing the existing state."[10] These intemperate remarks provoked another indictment and conviction, this time for "circulating lessons dangerous to the state." Liebknecht served his three-week sentence in November 1869.

Despite his disparagement of the parliament of the North German Confederation, Liebknecht had stood for election to the Reichstag in February and again in August 1867. On his second attempt, he succeeded in winning a mandate to represent the Stollberg-Schneeburg district in Saxony. With only two brief interruptions, henceforth Liebknecht continuously held a seat in the Reichstag.

Although Liebknecht did not believe in the possibility of legislating socialism, he participated in the Reichstag for several reasons. First, as a deputy he had freedom of speech. When impolite antagonists in the Reichstag heckled and interrupted his remarks, he exclaimed, ". . . I speak from this place, the only one in Prussia in which freedom of speech exists, not to you: I say it to you openly, I speak to the people outside."[11] Newspapers could print his remarks which, if made by private citizens, would have resulted in a jail term. Second, parliamentary immunity allowed him to travel to Berlin legally. Third, electoral campaigns provided educational opportunities as well as numerical demonstrations of strength.[12] When some members of the DVP advocated abstention from the elections to the Tariff Parliament of the *Zollverein* in 1868, Liebknecht disagreed. The elections

provided an opportunity to show opposition to Prussia, he
reasoned, and nothing could be gained by leaving the political
field entirely to one's enemies.[13]

The purely negative practice of parliamentary activity
that Liebknecht preached in the late 1860s can be clarified
by contrasting his attitude and actions with those of the
ADAV President Schweitzer. Both men were elected to the
legislature in 1867, and it did not take long for them to
clash over proper parliamentary tactics. When the Reichstag
convened early in October, the Lassallean leader introduced
a bill to prohibit child labor, to institute a ten-hour working
day, to provide for safety inspection of factories, and to
eliminate the truck system. Liebknecht refused to support
Schweitzer's bill. He explained his attitude to Marx by
saying, "Bismarck should not be given an opportunity to play
the protector of labor and to expand and to sharpen his police
system."[14]

In Reichstag debate, Schweitzer ridiculed his rival's
negativism. "According to [Liebknecht's] viewpoint," Schweitzer
said, "no laws at all should be made because the North German
Confederation should not exist at all." Schweitzer proclaimed
that his ADAV had nothing in common with "Herr Liebknecht and
his friends, the dispossessed princes and the envious foreigners. . . ." In a personal reply, Liebknecht said at least
he was not a "twin of Herr Wagener," the conservative apostle
of producers' cooperatives.[15]

In fairness to Liebknecht's position, it should be noted
that, for a man with his creed, the chances for constructive
legislative activity at that time were nil. For example,
when he advocated abolishing the standing army and installing a

militia on the Swiss model, the right side of the house laughed
so loudly that he could not continue his speech. A few days
later, he rose to endorse a common citizenship for the North
German Confederation, a proposal that would prevent deporta-
tions of the sort he suffered in 1865. Again, outrageous dis-
courtesy greeted his remarks. At last, in frustration he
shouted, "You take such things very lightly. I came back to
my house [after my prison term in 1867], I found my wife
dying, she died, and those who expelled me [from Prussia] . . .
have the death of my wife on their conscience!"[16] After these
initial futile attempts at rhetorical persuasion, Liebknecht
quit addressing the house. By 1870, he was skipping entire
sessions of the legislature.

For a time, Liebknecht's deprecation of parliamentarism
won wide acceptance in his political party. At his urging,
a congress of his comrades in 1870 explicitly instructed its
delegates to the Reichstag to conduct themselves "in general
negatively and to use every opportunity to expose the debates
. . . in their complete nullity and to unmask [them] as a
farce."[17] Despite the stridency of Liebknecht's stand in the
late 1860s, his subsequent statements on this issue exhibit
a considerable capacity for tactical tergiversation. Already,
in 1872, he openly admitted that he had revised his earlier
position somewhat. He called his speech of 31 May 1869, in
which he denounced parliament and predicted street battles,
a *Gelegenheitsrede*. Its uncompromising tone, he now said,
sprang from the need to foil Bismarck's seduction of the
working class. But after the initial inoculation of antiparliamentary sentiment, Liebknecht was prepared to be less
hostile toward the Reichstag. In 1894, he even called that
body an "independent power with which every government must

reckon." Perhaps anticipating criticism for his inconsistency, he added almost flippantly, "Other times--other tactics."[18]

Liebknecht's evolving attitude about parliamentarism speaks directly to the accommodation between revolutionary theory and legal political practice. Soon after 1869, several changes in the political environment induced him to rethink his ideas about the Reichstag. First, in 1871, Schweitzer resigned as head of the ADAV. That party gradually had been articulating a more positive opinion on political democracy. Consequently, Liebknecht felt less need to argue against the statist threat inside the workers' movement. About the same time Prussia defeated France and secured an irrevocable hold on Germany. With the revolution once again postponed for the foreseeable future, Liebknecht accepted at last the disagreeable facts that Marx and Engels had swallowed in 1866. As the futility of continued resistance to Bismarck's conquest became undeniable, the intensity of the pain from Ernestine's death also subsided. Both those conditions enabled Liebknecht to speak more favorably about the imperial parliament.

Still, Liebknecht never really renounced his reservations about compromising with his enemies. On some occasions when discussing parliamentarism, he neglected to emphasize his negative thoughts; on others, he virtually shouted them. There is not a clear pattern of change over time in this area of Liebknecht's thought. The speeches (or secondary accounts) reveal the most contradictory impressions.[19] Always, changing circumstances and present agitational considerations colored his opinions.

Liebknecht summarized his viewpoint in 1886 in the Reichstag: "Gentlemen, when I am asked whether I believe in

parliamentarism, I can say yes and I can say no. If by parliamentarism is meant that . . . , on the basis of an honestly
managed universal, direct franchise, a popular representation
meets, which brings the popular will completely and fully to
expression and to implementation, then I am a disciple of
parliamentarism. But if I think of falsified parliamentarism,
a parliamentarism that either does not rest on the direct,
universal franchise, or where the expression of the popular
will is manipulated from above by influences of a social,
political or economic nature and the will of the majority
does not decide--yes, gentlemen, from such parliamentarism
I cannot promise a peaceful solution to the social question."[20]

Liebknecht's anti-parliamentarism has been ridiculed as
quixotic or worse. In his lifelong disdain for the Reichstag
he did not change the constitution of Germany one iota. Nevertheless, his critical efforts left an important legacy. Even
though he did not immediately alter the German political
framework, he did steer part of the infant workers' movement
away from the authoritarian temptation. Consequently, the
stewardship of democracy in Germany was able to pass from
a faltering liberal faction to the growing workers' party,
where it survived all Bismarck's attempts at extinction.

LIEBKNECHT'S LONELY OPPOSITION TO THE FRANCO-PRUSSIAN WAR

When war exploded between Prussia and France in July 1870,
the SDAP faced a wrenching test of its anti-Bismarck orientation. To be sure, because both combatant states in this
conflict were not only capitalist but monarchist as well,
neither should have expected help from social democrats.

Nevertheless four formidable considerations weighed in favor
of SDAP support for the Prussian war effort. First, Bismarck's
adroit diplomatic and public relations maneuvers permitted
Prussia to pretend to fight a war of national self-defense
on behalf of all Germans. Second, national unification for
Germany shimmered as a tempting prize for the successful
conclusion of these hostilities. Third, Bismarck's antagonist,
Napoleon III, was a perfect villain, especially from a socialist viewpoint. The assassin of the French Republic, the
betrayer of the Italian national cause, the protector of
the Pope, the Mexican adventurer, the intriguer whose designs
upon the left bank of the Rhine were a matter of public record--
better credentials for an enemy of Liebknecht's party could
hardly be imagined. Fourth, as a result of the preceding
considerations, public opinion in Germany overwhelmingly
endorsed Prussia's crusade. Under such circumstances, could
Liebknecht's party ostracize itself by refusing to back
Bismarck?[21]

Liebknecht's answer was unequivocal: social democrats
should resist any and every war arranged by monarchs. That
French leftists should oppose their emperor's machinations
was self-evident. More than a decade earlier, in his writings
for the *Augsburger Allgemeine Zeitung* and for *Das Volk*, he had
insistently warned of the Napoleonic menace to Europe's peace
and freedom.[22] More recently, in his *Demokratische Wochenblatt*,
he had prophesied aggression by Bonaparte as a ploy to defuse
the growing domestic discontent in France. If Napoleon attacked
Prussia, Liebknecht hoped that the French people would renounce
their reactionary ruler and install a republic in his place.[23]

These anti-Napoleonic observations did not mean that
Liebknecht had inched toward Bismarck's camp. On the contrary,

he saw absolutely no difference between "Bismarckian and Napoleonic caesarism." Both systems of government were enemies to their respective peoples. Should these undemocratic rulers and their coterie of advisors precipitate a war, Liebknecht urged his proletarian comrades in both countries to seize the opportunity to eliminate the circumstances that "make it possible for any Bonaparte or Bismarck to disturb the world peace and to plunge hundreds of thousands of men into death. . . ."[24] In other words, he hoped war would breed revolution.

Liebknecht's opposition to any dynastic war was reinforced by his consistent antimilitarist sentiment. Illustrating that conviction, at the Nuremberg Congress he had proposed a ringing resolution that repudiated the standing army as a matter of principle. A professional military, he said, "gives to the princes the power to fight wars against the will and against the interests of the peoples. . . . The standing army [was] the source of dynastic wars of conquest abroad . . . [and] of the suppression of law and liberty at home." The aroused delegates at Nuremberg unanimously endorsed Liebknecht's call for a citizen militia to replace the professional military establishment.[25]

When the Franco-Prussian war erupted, few Germans adhered to Liebknecht's revolutionary, antiwar commitment. For Bismarck had arranged events to portray Germany as the innocent victim of an outrageous attack by a wild-eyed Emperor of the French. In this way, he planned to allay domestic opposition to the war and to insure that the south German states would lend their armies to the Prussian cause. After provoking Napoleon with a Hohenzollern candidacy for the throne of Spain and adding an insulting, public diplomatic dispatch from Ems, Bismarck relied upon the momentum of the French response to propel Napoleon into war. Stupidly, the Emperor of the French rushed into battle ill-equipped, without allies, and wearing the mask of the aggressor.

The events on the eve of battle were reported in Liebknecht's newspaper, *Der Volksstaat*. Reflecting the ebb and flow of diplomatic tension, his journal saw no immediate threat of war as late as the issue dated 9 July 1870, but on 13 July, *Der Volksstaat* adopted a more nervous tone. Liebknecht suspected that Bonaparte had constructed a trap for Prussia with the intention of provoking war. The next issue of *Der Volksstaat*, dated 16 July, mirrored a short-lived relaxation of tension between France and Prussia before the avalanche of events leading to war. On 12 July, the Hohenzollern candidate had renounced the throne of Spain. In his newspaper, Liebknecht celebrated this humiliation for Prussia: "The North German confederation is bankrupt," he exulted, "and if Germany is not to remain a contemptible plaything for foreigners, the work of 1866 must be undone and a democratic basis created upon which the unity of the entire German race may be achieved." Whether war or peace threatened, Liebknecht missed no chance to blast Bismarck's policies.

As it turned out, his diagnosis of the international situation published on 16 July was embarrassingly incorrect. On 13 July, Bismarck had released his edited and inflammatory version of the Ems telegram. On 15 July, the indignant French Chamber of Deputies had voted 285 to 6 to fight.

Contrary to appearances, Liebknecht was not days behind the news. Instead, the date on the masthead of each issue of *Der Volksstaat* was always at least three days later than when the issue actually had gone to press. The first opportunity for *Der Volksstaat* to comment on the French declaration of war came on 20 July. Its editor now believed that French

aggressiveness, manifested in the conduct of her ambassador
at Ems and in her prompt declaration of war, validated his
earlier suspicion that "Bonaparte wanted the war." At this
time, like most Germans, Liebknecht exported the immediate
responsibility for the conflict to France.

Even so, he began to agitate against the war. Along
with Bebel and other local comrades, he hurriedly arranged
a regional congress of the SDAP in Saxony. On 17 July, that
assembly, attended by over one hundred delegates, unanimously
denounced this dynastic war. "Never will we forget," their
resolution proclaimed, "that the workers of all lands are
our *friends*; but the *despots of all lands* [are] *our enemies*."[26]

Shortly thereafter, in *Der Volksstaat*, Liebknecht expounded
his analysis of the causes of the war and announced his prescription for proper proletarian tactics: "Through the humiliation of Prussia, Bonaparte wants to secure his shaky throne
[and] prepare an 'internal Sadowa' for the social-republican
movement in France. The December-throne [Bonaparte's rule]
is the cornerstone of reactionary Europe. If Bonaparte falls,
so falls the chief representative of modern class and sabel
domination. If Bonaparte triumphs, European democracy is
conquered along with French [democracy]. Our interests thus
demand the destruction of Bonaparte. Our interests stand
in harmony with the interests of the French people."

Some social democrats stopped their analysis of issues
and tactics at this point, but Liebknecht continued. In an
excellent dialectical argument, he asserted that "the War
of 1870 [was] the inevitable fruit of the War of 1866." To
ignore Prussian responsibility was to overlook a major tributary to the present slaughter. Besides, such an oversight
would invite the workers to identify with Bismarckian caesarism

in a putative war of national self-defense. Rather than ally
with either Bismarck or Bonaparte, Liebknecht cried, "First
the reckoning with the French coup d'etat, then with the German."[27] Liebknecht's 1870 stance foreshadowed Lenin's strategy
during World War I: convert the war between capitalist powers
into a civil war on behalf of social democracy, but in 1870
in Germany, this seed had no chance to germinate because of
Prussia's prompt military victory.

On 20 July, Wilhelm I convened the Reichstag of the North
German Confederation to have it approve credits for his war.
Liebknecht came to that session believing that Bonaparte had
outwitted Bismarck and pulled Prussia into the war. Nevertheless, he intended to vote against the credits. As it turned
out, Bebel convinced him to abstain rather than cast a negative
ballot. Persuasively, Bebel argued that a negative vote might
be construed as support for Napoleon.[28] In the Reichstag on
21 July, Bebel briefly announced that he and Liebknecht would
abstain from the ballot on the war credits. Perhaps fearing
harassment, he did not state his reasons orally. Instead
he submitted a written declaration to be included in the stenographic report of the session.

Bebel later claimed that he drafted this statement, with
Liebknecht making only minor changes.[29] Be that as it may,
the declaration corresponded quite closely to what Liebknecht
already had printed in Der Volksstaat. It alleged that the
present war was being waged in the interest of the Bonaparte
dynasty, just as the "War of 1866 was fought in the interest
of the Hohenzollern dynasty." It declined to support the
war credits because that action would seem to be a "vote of
confidence" in the Prussian government. Because Prussia's
"wicked and criminal" acts in 1866 had "prepared" the present

conflict, that government deserved no support. Bebel and
Liebknecht bravely declared that, "as social-republicans and
members of the International Workingman's Association," they
opposed "every dynastic war." While Bismarck's clever diplomacy swept most Germans into chauvinistic paroxysms, Bebel
and Liebknecht publicly affirmed their aim to "unite all
oppressed people, regardless of nationality, into a great
brotherhood. . . ." In conclusion, they announced their hope
that the "peoples of Europe, instructed by the current unholy
events, [would] make every effort to win the right of self-
determination and to eliminate the present sabel and class
domination. . . ."[30]

Some German socialists diametrically opposed the viewpoint expressed in this declaration. For example, the ADAV
president once again championed Bismarck's designs. Schweitzer's
newspaper described Louis Napoleon's "attack" as an assault on
the "German people," and more bizarrely, as a "war against
socialism. . . . And every German who throws himself against
the breaker of the peace fights not only for the Fatherland,
he fights too against the chief enemy of the ideas of the future,
[therefore] for freedom, equality and fraternity."[31] Other
Lassallean spokesmen carried a similarly pro-Prussian message
into public assemblies throughout Germany.[32]

More worrisome for Liebknecht, the ex-Lassalleans in
his own party's executive committee also rallied to Prussia's
side in the war. A public assembly met in the executive's
home town, Brunswick, on 16 July, and it passed a resolution
that vigorously distinguished between the French and German
roles in provoking the present conflict. Napoleon, the Brunswick resolution said, was a "frivolous breaker of the peace";
the German nation, on the other hand, had been "insulted and

attacked." The citizens of Brunswick therefore regretfully
accepted the "war of defense as an unavoidable evil."[33]

Four days later, all five members of the executive committee fired off a policy directive to *Der Volksstaat* in which
they ordered Liebknecht to edit his newspaper in conformity
with the 16 July Brunswick resolution.[34] To elucidate the
public position of the SDAP, the Brunswick directorate then
composed a manifesto that appeared on 24 July. In this document, the Eisenacher Executive promised to defend the fatherland so long as the French soldiers "menaced" Germany and
added that "the striving of the German people for national
unity also [was] justified." In conclusion, the directors
vaguely "hoped" that the new German state would "not be dynastic but rather a social democratic People's State."[35]

Bracke and the other members of the party directorate
worried that Liebknecht's opposition to the war would isolate
and cripple their infant party. "If Liebknecht continues
in this way," Bracke predicted to Geib, "at the end of the
war we will have [only] a dozen inveterate social republicans
and a few Saxon particularists. . . ."[36] Already on 22 July,
when it became apparent that Liebknecht was not following
the editorial guidelines of the executive, Bracke intimated
to Spier that Liebknecht might have to be removed from *Der
Volksstaat*.[37] A few weeks later he explained his viewpoint
to Geib: "Either we [the Executive] have the responsibility
and stand above the editorial staff . . . or Liebknecht does
not have to bend. . . . Then we have the Liebknecht monarchy
and the Executive consists of men of straw."[38]

So the Franco-Prussian War occasioned a major intraparty
battle between Liebknecht and his newspaper on the one hand
and the elected party officials on the other. Conflicts like
this one were to become a regular feature of Liebknecht's

career. At stake was his independent influence, his ability
to make policy. Although he was willing to compromise,
Liebknecht would not let his newspaper become an uncritical
channel of communication from the executive committee to the
members.

Exasperated by Liebknecht's insubordination, late in
August, Bracke appealed to Karl Marx to decide the debate
between the SDAP Executive and its newspaper. Concerning
the Franco-Prussian War, Marx hovered near the position of
the Brunswick committee. To Engels he confided his opinion
that "the French need thrashing." A Prussian victory, he
argued, would allow the consolidation and centralization of
the German workers' movement. It would also transfer the
"center of gravity of the western European workers' movement
from France to Germany," a transfer Marx wanted because he
thought the German workers were "theoretically and organizationally" superior to the French.[39]

Already on 23 July, the IWA had published a declaration
by Marx concerning the war. Although Marx had condemned Napoleon as the immediate aggressor, he carefully pointed out
Prussian responsibility in the background to the conflict.
This part of Marx's remarks encouraged Liebknecht to interpret
the declaration as reinforcement for his own position.[40] But
Marx's prescription for proper proletarian tactics actually
approximated that of the Brunswick Executive, even to the
point of advocating support for what he called the national
war of self-defense. Indeed Marx incorporated parts of the
16 July Brunswick manifesto into his own statement.[41] Although
Marx and Engels initially hailed Liebknecht's dramatic opposition to the war credits, they soon tired of their friend's
negative attitude. To them, the outcome of the war was far

more important than the matter of who or what caused it. By
mid-August they were counting the blessings of a Prussian
victory.[42] There could thus be little doubt which side they
would support in the fight between Liebknecht and the SDAP
directorate in Brunswick.

Seen against this curtain of intraparty criticism,
Liebknecht's opposition to the war appears even more courageous.
Liebknecht must have foreseen that he would have to endure
assaults from enemies outside his own faction. It came as no
surprise, for example, when Lassallean leaders in Leipzig
incited a mob that stoned his house.[43] Far more painful and
doubt-provoking for Liebknecht was the opposition from his
own comrades. To the executive committee, he privately stressed
the common ground, emphasizing that the entire SDAP opposed
dynastic wars. He conceded that sentiment in Prussia differed
from opinion in southern Germany, and he recognized that it
must be difficult to separate one's self from "local opinion."
Typically, he preached unity. Without discussing how the
present disagreement might be resolved, he pleaded that the
quarrel be ended, "or at least a public outbreak avoided."[44]

At the same time, he continued to use *Der Volksstaat* to
denounce the war. Being too prudent to challenge the executive
committee directly, Liebknecht instead printed declarations
from antiwar rallies throughout Germany.[45] More provocatively,
he published a charge by a Brunswick social democrat alleging
that the 16 July prowar meeting in that town had been comprised
primarily of nonsocialists.[46] To add international support
to his position, Liebknecht announced that the "Liebknecht-
Bebel declaration in the Reichstag [was] thoroughly approved
by the General Council of the International Workingman's Association."[47] Because the organization statute of the SDAP
directed *Der Volksstaat* to print all member contributions

that conformed to the party platform, and because that platform articulated the party's internationalist commitment,
Liebknecht could print these antiwar resolutions and challenge
the executive committee without committing a formal breach of
discipline.

The numerous manifestos published in *Der Volksstaat* reveal
a lack of enthusiasm for the war, especially in the lower
class. In addition to the evidence of antiwar sentiment in the
SDAP journal, a batch of similar resolutions appeared in Becker's
Der Vorbote. Several of these resolutions explicitly repudiated
the nationalistic declarations of the SDAP Executive Committee.[48]
Although no reliable indexes of public opinion are available,
Liebknecht and Bebel may not have been as isolated as Bracke
believed.[49]

However public opinion may have been divided, it must
be remembered that none of the German socialists could have
supported aggression to achieve national unity. At least
in their public utterances, Schweitzer, Marx, and the Brunswick directors of the SDAP cited Prussia's defensive posture
as the justification for fighting on her side. Consequently,
for Liebknecht the issue of responsibility for the Franco-
Prussian War remained a matter of burning concern, even though
he personally opposed the war regardless of who started it.

That concern later led Liebknecht to investigate the
notorious Ems Dispatch, which had inflamed passions on both
sides of the Rhine and precipitated the hostilities. In August
1873, *Der Volksstaat* published his first detective's report on
this matter. It pointed out that, within only a few days after
the appearance of the infamous telegram, the French ambassador
had denied the accuracy of the account of his meeting with
King Wilhelm that this document contained. That encounter had

been in no way so hostile as the telegram alleged, the French
ambassador asserted. He especially denied that he had been
insulted by the Prussian ruler. Because the dispatch about
this meeting at Ems had been released to the public, Liebknecht concluded that it had been intentionally colored to
provoke French anger. Proof of this suspicion came in 1876.
In that year, General von Roon published his memoirs. Therein
he admitted that the Ems telegram had indeed been altered at
the Wilhelmsstrasse. *Der Volksstaat* used this admission to
conclude that Bismarck bore the blame of the Franco-Prussian
war.[50] The socialist party press soon published Liebknecht's
accusatory articles as a pamphlet entitled "The Ems Dispatch,
Or How Wars Are Made." Summarizing his indictment against
Bismarck, Liebknecht wrote, "the genuine Ems Dispatch was
peace. The falsified Ems Dispatch was war."[51]

After retirement from office, Bismarck admitted his provocative editing of the Ems Dispatch. Liebknecht was elated.[52]
He believed that Bismarck's admission would forever silence
the 1870 arguments of his intraparty critics. He could hope
too that the German public had learned a lesson that might
inoculate it against a future chauvinistic fever.

Unfortunately, few Germans cared about Bismarck's manipulations. His eventual confession of dishonesty made barely
a ripple, and some newspapers actually praised him for performing a patriotic duty. The lesson Liebknecht expounded
was soon erased like an untrodden path. Germany, including
her socialists, forgot how governments can manufacture circumstances to make themselves look like the victim of international aggression. Despite Liebknecht's preaching, the
gate to the *Burgfriede* of August 1914 remained open.

THE SOCIALISTS CLOSE RANKS IN OPPOSING CONQUEST

Well before the Franco-Prussian War ended, Prussian plans
for aggrandizement at the expense both of her southern German
neighbors and of France became apparent to all. The realization that Bismarck pursued an expansionist design eventually
convinced every German socialist to oppose the war. In this
development, the battle at Sedan constitutes the watershed.

On 2 September 1870, after some bitter fighting near
Sedan in the Meuse River Valley, an enormous French army surrendered. Napoleon III was among the 104,000 prisoners taken
that day. Hearing that their monarch had surrendered his
sword to his "dear brother," Wilhelm of Prussia, the ever-
volatile Parisians promptly proclaimed France to be a republic.

"The stroke in Paris has completely changed the situation,"
Liebknecht wrote to Bracke on 5 September. Now a reactionary
Prussian monarch was assailing the citadel of liberty in France.
Liebknecht suggested a conference with the executive committee
to discuss suitable new tactics. "There is much to consider
and between the Scylla of duty and the Charybdis of treason
is a damned narrow gap."[53]

On the same day that Liebknecht wrote this letter, the
executive published a second manifesto on the war.[54] The
tone of the proclamation remained chauvinistic: "so long
as the Napoleonic armies had threatened Germany, it was our
duty as Germans to support the 'war of defense, the war for
the independence of Germany.'" In an alarming aside, the
manifesto even asserted, "such a war of defense does not
exclude that one attacks the enemy. . . ." It then celebrated
the "unprecedented courage" and the "splendid contempt for
death" of "our brave army whose sword has once again freed

France." But after this patriotic preamble, the executive
committee sidled toward Liebknecht's position. It now advocated an immediate cessation of hostilities and an "honorable"
peace with France. "In the name of the German Social Democratic
Workers' Party, we hereby raise a protest against the annexation of Alsace and Lorraine." The executive committee explained
that the amputation of that territory would perpetuate French
plans for revenge, drive her into the arms of Russia, and
ultimately confront Germany with a war on two fronts. Concluding with a paraphrase of Marx's remarks, the SDAP directors
commented, "This war has transferred the center of gravity of
the continental workers' movement from France to Germany."
The German workers therefore bore a tremendous responsibility
in refashioning the peace of Europe, and the executive exhorted
them to work "quickly and energetically" for a prompt and
harmonious settlement.[55]

After Liebknecht had studied this manifesto, he sent
a brief note to Bracke and his colleagues. He still believed
that the tone of the declaration displayed an excess of nationalism. Nevertheless, he agreed that in the substantive matters,
the manifesto "hit the nail on the head. Hurrah!"[56]

On 11 September, *Der Volksstaat* published the manifesto
of the executive committee on page one. Liebknecht commented
editorially that "The German war of defense is at an end; if
the war continues, it is a war of conquest, a war of monarchy
against the republic, of counter-revolution against revolution,
which is aimed as much at German democracy as at the French
Republic."

The bold and united agitation of the SDAP soon provoked
government repression. On 9 September, the military commander
of the district surrounding Brunswick used his emergency powers
to arrest the entire executive committee. His troops

incarcerated the five SDAP chiefs at the fortress of Lötzen, where they were held until the following spring. At the same time, the Prussian police-president began to prod the Saxon government to arrest Bebel, Liebknecht, and Adolf Hepner, their assistant on *Der Volksstaat*.[57] In all likelihood, only their Reichstag mandates temporarily protected the former two.

Undaunted by the lengthening lists of political prisoners throughout Germany, Liebknecht redoubled his agitation against Prussian conquest. Beginning on 21 September, every issue of *Der Volksstaat* carried a headline demanding

> **A Just Peace with the French Republic!**
> **No Annexations!**
> **Punishment of Bonaparte and His Accomplices!**

Liebknecht used the theme of punishment for Napoleon III to smuggle antiroyalism into his newspaper. He called for the return of Napoleon to the French people, who would then try him as a common criminal.[58]

Liebknecht carried his anti-Prussian agitation into the Reichstag too. On 26 November, he observed with irony that the Prussian army now stormed the French Republic while Napoleon III lived in style, enjoying the king's hospitality at the castle of Wilhelmshöhe, near Cassel. When challenged as a Francophile, Liebknecht exclaimed, "It is truly more honorable to be the brother of the French people and the French worker than [to be] the 'dear brother' of the scoundrel at Wilhelmshöhe."[59]

Even though Liebknecht did nothing overtly illegal to resist the war, the Prussian government did not long tolerate such telling verbal assaults. On 7 December, *Der Volksstaat* quoted an "authoritative source" in Berlin who predicted a new wave of searches and arrests in Saxony. On 17 December, Bebel, Liebknecht, and Hepner were taken prisoner on charges

of conspiring to overthrow the monarchy and establish a
republic in Germany.

For the next three months, these three rebels sat in
solitary confinement while the authorities investigated their
case. Because the party directors and numerous other comrades
also had been jailed, the SDAP practically collapsed. When
the annual congress met in August 1871, the executive committee's report to the membership documented how administrative
chaos within the SDAP had combined with the war fever and
police persecution to wreck party finances. In 1870-71, party
income plummeted to about one-quarter of its 1869-70 level.
Not until 1872 did it approach the prewar level.[60] Party
membership suffered tremendously too, falling from 11,000
in 1870 to 6,100 in 1871. It did not regain the 1871 level
until after 1875.[61] Still another temporary casualty of the
Franco-Prussian war was Liebknecht's *Der Volksstaat*. In October
1870, the newspaper announced on its front page "a significant
decline" in circulation. The format of the paper shrank to a
single page.[62] Subscriptions tumbled from a peak of 3,000
to only 1,200 early in 1871. Fortunately for Liebknecht's
journalistic career, the nationalistic fever soon receded and
circulation recovered to 4,200 by that summer.[63]

When the SDAP was at its nadir early in 1871, Bismarck
scheduled elections for the Reichstag of his new German empire.
With its entire leadership in prison, Liebknecht's party had
few campaigners skilled enough to combat the impact of Prussia's
military success. Trying to bolster his spirits, Liebknecht's
friends wrote to him that his chances for reelection were
good.[64] But when the ballots were counted, Liebknecht had
polled only 3,891 votes;[65] his opponent, a Progressive and an
old rival of Liebknecht named Dr. Heinrich Minkwitz, had garnered 5,204. The elections were a debacle for the whole

workers' movement. Bebel and a lawyer named Schraps, both
of whom represented the SDAP in Saxony, were the only socialist
candidates elected. The vote for both the Eisenachers and the
Lassalleans combined comprised a feeble 3.2 percent of the
total.

PEACEFUL REFORM OR VIOLENT REVOLUTION?

Having apparently put the socialists to flight, the authorities released Liebknecht, Bebel, and Hepner on 28 March 1871.
No specific date for a trial was set. The government already
had crippled the SDAP, and it is possible that no further
legal action was intended if the socialists behaved themselves.

Already, however, momentous events were unfolding in
Paris that demanded Liebknecht's public reaction. Early in
March, the National Guard in the French capital had repudiated
the defeatist leadership of Adolphe Thiers and the National
Assembly at Versailles. This rebellion escalated into the
notorious Paris Commune. For two months, Europe gaped at
the spectacle of raw class struggle in France.

Der Volksstaat was surprisingly slow to recognize the
significance of the events in Paris. For most of March, it
gave extensive but unenthusiastic coverage to the Commune.
Only in April, when Liebknecht was released from jail and
resumed his position as editor, did the SDAP journal become
a vigorous partisan of the Parisian workers.

The preceding September, *Der Volksstaat* had quoted an
admonition to the Paris proletariat from its "London Correspondent." This statement had warned the workers against trust-
ing the bourgeoisie. The parties and individuals who led the

present French Republic, it had cautioned, were the same as those who had assassinated the Second Republic in 1848.[66] Against this backdrop, in April 1871, Liebknecht hailed the emerging commune in Paris as a manifestation of proletarian self-reliance. Every issue of *Der Volksstaat* in April 1871 carried front-page stories defending the deeds of the representatives of Paris's lower classes. Eager to purify the public image of this ostensible workers' government, Liebknecht insisted that it was neither bloody nor *rauberisch*. On the contrary, he said, it was comprised of dedicated workers who received only workers' wages for their services.[67]

While the communards struggled vainly to free themselves from the tightening noose of German and French armies, Bismarck convinced the newly-elected Reichstag in Berlin to ratify his proposed constitution for the Second German Empire. This constitution extended the structure of the North German Confederation to all of Germany (excluding Austria, of course). On 14 April, against only seven negative votes, the dutiful deputies approved the document. Bismarck had succeeded. Prussia had absorbed Germany.

In *Der Volksstaat*, Liebknecht tried to belittle the importance of Bismarck's victory. "Next to the mighty events that transpire in Paris the Berlin Reichstag shrivels into the most ridiculous insignificance." The Parisians performed a "tragedy of world-historic proportions," while the Deputies in Berlin acted out a "comedy of puppets. Yes, Paris has the floor, for Paris is the chief city of the world, despite Kaiser Bomba [Wilhelm I] and his city-wasting friends."[68]

But rhetoric alone could not protect Paris against her enemies. On 21 May, troops loyal to Thiers and the National Assembly gained entrance to the French capital. During the

following week, the Commune was defeated. While the regular
army lost about 1,000 of its number dead, it killed between
20,000 and 30,000 communards. After the guns fell silent,
the courts swung into action. Additional hundreds of Parisians
were condemned to death. Approximately 8,000 were sentenced
to transportation to the colonies.

Even as the French rebels were being routed from their
barricades, Bebel picked up their standard in the Reichstag.
In a speech to that body on 25 May, he boldly adopted the
slogan of the Paris proletariat for himself and for the SDAP:
"War to the palaces, peace to the huts," he cried, "death
to poverty and to the idlers."[69]

The Paris Commune had an enormous impact on German politics. Henceforth, conservative politicians, panicked by this
lower-class insurrection, were haunted by visions of an international revolutionary conspiracy. The socialists, on the
other hand, saw proof of the internationality of capitalist
repression in the defeat of their French comrades. The nature
of the new German Reich confirmed this insight for the SDAP.
Writing in *Der Volksstaat*, Liebknecht observed that the par-
liaments handed down previously by Bonaparte and currently
by Bismarck were fundamentally the same in their "impotence
and servility." The only reason for the existence of either
body, Liebknecht asserted, was to clothe "military absolutism,
which is [too] repulsive in its naked form."[70] Although Bismarck corralled most Germans into his empire, he never persuaded Liebknecht that his rule was legitimate. The continuous
campaign of legal harassment with which Bismarck badgered
the socialists stiffened their will to resist.

But the brutal realities of the costs of class conflict
that were revealed by the events of 1870-71 produced a second,
less often noticed and somewhat contradictory effect upon

Liebknecht and the SDAP. The bloody repression of the leftists
in Paris and the prospect of years in prison at home made the
German socialists cautious. As Liebknecht commented, "If it
is naive and even foolish to demand that, in order to implement our principles, we first have a well prepared and sealed
majority in our pockets, so it is still more naive to believe
that we can realize our principles against the will of the
overwhelming majority of the population."[71]

For Liebknecht and his party, elections became the baro-
meter of public opinion. Despite the dismal showing in the
initial elections to the Reichstag, the social democrats strived
indefatigably for the magic 51 percent of the popular vote. At
no time before 1900 did any leader of the German workers' movement even suggest a minority revolution. The socialists'
patience originated at least in part from the revelation of the
awful price for failure.

Subsequent repression inside the German Empire had an
equally dampening effect upon the revolutionary ardor of some
of Liebknecht's comrades. The trial of the Eisenacher Executive Committee in the autumn of 1871 is a case in point. In
this proceeding, the government charged eight Brunswick social
democrats with conspiring to introduce the republican form
of government into Germany. Alleged connections to the IWA
figured prominently in the government's case.[72] At the trial,
the defense introduced a notarized letter from Karl Marx deny-
ing that the SDAP had ever enrolled as a body in the International.[73] Speaking on behalf of all the defendants, Wilhelm
Bracke insisted, "There may have been republicans among the
founders of the International, but the introduction of the
Republic is not its purpose."[74] The various defendants swore
too that they never had advocated or done anything illegal.

Explicitly and repeatedly, they renounced the use of force
to obtain their political objectives. As their gospel in
matters revolutionary, they cited the statist and peaceful
proclamations of Lassalle; they ignored Marx completely.[75]
After this virtual retraction of revolutionary intent, despite
a guilty verdict from the jury, the judge dispensed lenient
sentences ranging from five to sixteen months. After appeal,
even these sentences were reduced, and all defendants were
set free in consideration of time already served.[76] The government did not need to make martyrs of men as pliable as these.

    The intimidating influence of this trial radiated beyond
the walls of the courtroom, and it is discernible in a widely
circulated speech, "Zu Trutz and Schutz," that Liebknecht
made to a Crimmitschau assembly on 22 October 1871. He stressed
the organic, evolutionary nature of change in society. "History is revolution in permanence--it is becoming, growth,
change, progress--continual alteration. . . ." Putting the
most innocuous interpretation imaginable upon his beliefs,
he continued, "Revolution, movement is life. The nonrevolution,
cessation, is death."[77]

    In "Zu Trutz und Schutz," as in most of his major
addresses, Liebknecht touted Marx's historical insights. However, he significantly diverged from Marx by proposing a specific and peaceful means of transition from capitalism to
socialism. In 1871, Liebknecht suggested the state-sponsored
consumer and producer associations offered a possibility of
evolution into socialism. Competition from these associations
could drive the capitalists out of business: "The capitalists
must either enter the associations or their capital will lie
there dead and be lost for them and for society. . . ."[78]

    At this moment of impending judicial confrontation, prudence dictated that Liebknecht and his comrades advocate peaceful means of implementing their program. At other times, Liebknecht disparaged the possibility for nonviolent reform. As in his attitude toward parliamentarism discussed above, volatile circumstances determined Liebknecht's view on the inevitability of violent revolution.

Liebknecht's more moderate pronouncements usually surfaced when government repression was most severe. During the era of the antisocialist law, for example, he wrote that "universal suffrage had led to the substitution of propaganda for barricades and putsches."[79] About the same time, he asserted that a well-intentioned statesman who preached toleration and compromise could make "the peaceful solution of the social question child's play."[80] However, when government repression relaxed, Liebknecht suggested that genuine social reform could only be achieved "against the more or less violent resistance of the holders of privileged positions."[81]

Behind Liebknecht's vacillation concerning the use of violence lay one important consistency. He always believed that the option for or against force lay with the ruling class. In October 1871, he argued that all popular violence from the Peasants' War to 1848 had been provoked by government brutality.[82] More manipulative revolutionaries might object that Liebknecht's viewpoint could steer the workers' movement into a tactical doldrum, and it is true that Liebknecht never developed a theory of when and how the workers should seize the initiative in the conquest of power. Nevertheless, considering the almost ceaseless counterrevolutionary plots brewing at the Wilhelmsstrasse, Liebknecht's advocacy of defensive tactics for the working class was well adapted to conditions in the German Empire.[83]

Moreover, Liebknecht's refusal to be ironclad in his prognostications about violence left open the opportunity to encourage peaceful reform, to sound both reasonable and flexible. If the state voluntarily abdicated its class character and somehow moved to serve all its citizens equally, Liebknecht said he would be delighted. If it did not, he predicted that economic need eventually would drive the masses to revolution. "Reform or revolution," he wrote, "the final goal will be reached in either case."[84]

Between "Zu Trutz and Schutz" in October 1871 and Liebknecht's next major address, "Wissen ist Macht--Macht ist Wissen" delivered at Dresden in February 1872, a noticeable change of tenor occurred. In the interim, the surprisingly lenient treatment that the courts gave to the SDAP Executive Committee probably encouraged Liebknecht once again to toughen his public pronouncements.

The ostensible subject for "Wissen ist Macht" was education, always a subject dear to Liebknecht. "The school can be the most powerful means of emancipation," he cried in this speech, "and the school can be the most powerful means of subjugation."[85] Germany's schools, he charged, were designed only to produce "raw material for the barracks." From that springboard, he launched an attack on Prussian militarism. Contrasting the fat military budget of the Reich to the paltry outlays for education, he assailed Prussia's recent wars as a blight on German pretensions to *Kultur*. Only one month before his own trial for high treason, he boldly exclaimed, "We must do away with (*hinwegschreiten*) state and society." Returning to his original theme, he recalled how during the 1860s some "false friends" had counselled education as the panacea for working-class discontents. "We answer: through freedom to education," he said. "Only in the free people's state can the people obtain education. Only when the people gain political power by fighting [will] the doors of knowledge open to them."[86]

ON TRIAL FOR HIGH TREASON

The momentum of these strident sentiments swept Liebknecht toward his confrontation with the law of Saxony. A year had elapsed since his release from investigative detention. His trial for conspiracy to commit high treason stood on the docket for 13 March 1872.

Amid much excitement, the trial of Liebknecht, Bebel and Hepner opened at Dresden, the capital of Saxony. Sensing the public tension, *Der Volksstaat* had urged party comrades to avoid any disruption of the proceedings. So it was a large but well-mannered crowd that fought for space in the gallery when the doors to the courtroom opened at 8:30 a.m. Dozens of privileged guests and newspaper correspondents already packed the narrow balcony around the high-ceilinged chamber. Shortly after nine o'clock the president of the judicial panel and his three colleagues on the bench marched into the hall. The three defendants followed, taking their place in a stand to the left of the judges. Directly across the room, on the judges' right, sat the twelve men of the jury.

In the opening session, the prosecuting attorney submitted his lengthy brief, which set forth the allegedly illegal deeds of the defendants. This document summarized the republican aspirations of the workers' movement since the early 1860s. The program and agitation of the IWA, the congresses at

Nuremberg and at Eisenach, and dozens of excerpts from the
Demokratische Wochenblatt and *Der Volksstaat* comprised the
bulk of this indictment. Even published comments about the
Paris Commune, which had been made after the closure of the
initial investigation, were included in this summary of the
evidence. In conclusion, the prosecutor asserted that he
would prove that the defendants had prepared a treasonable
undertaking, a "forcible attack against the Kingdom of Saxony
and the other member states of the German Reich."[87]

This initial morning session set the tone for all that
followed. When the president read a short identification
of Liebknecht prepared by the Giessen police, Liebknecht seized
the opportunity to complain about the distortions in that
document. As his remarks expanded, he built toward a confession of political principle. "You see, Herren judges and
jurors, I do not deny my past, my principles and convictions.
. . . I say it here freely and openly: since I have been
able to think, I have been a republican, and I will die as a
republican."[88] The bemused judges had no wish to interrupt
such self-incriminating comments, so Liebknecht continued:
"A two-fold ideal has guided me since youth: a free and united
Germany and the emancipation of the working people, . . ."
Only he did not want to be misunderstood as an intriguer or
an assassin. "I am not a plotter by profession," he insisted,
"nor a traveling mercenary of conspiracies. Call me a soldier
of revolution--I have nothing against that."[89]

With such bold affirmation of his ideals, Liebknecht
turned the trial into a seminar on his beliefs. He carried
the burden of the defense, speaking approximately three times
as much as Bebel; Hepner had very little to say. For fourteen
days, Liebknecht lectured the courtroom--and through the journalists, the nation--on the principles of social democracy.

Embedded in these lectures, the defense tactics were
straightforward but shrewd. Liebknecht pointed out that since
the entire party archive had been confiscated when the SDAP
Executive Committee had been arrested, no secrets could be
hidden from the state. And he defied the court to prove a
single treasonable act. The judges did try to tie Liebknecht
to specific violations of the law. Had not the party statute
been designed intentionally to circumvent the law of associations? the judges asked. Yes, Liebknecht conceded, but
"circumvention of the law is no violation of the law." "On
the contrary," he explained, "it is proof of the intention
. . . to observe the law."[90] Scornfully Liebknecht exclaimed,
the prosecuting attorney "tries to prove criminal *aspirations*,
seditious *tendencies*, from which, with time, sooner or later,
criminal *dealings* would have to proceed. . . ."[91]

Meanwhile, in his lengthy testimony, Liebknecht articulated the fundamentals of scientific socialism. He lectured
that economic change breeds social and political change. In
schoolmasterly fashion, he traced the displacement of the
feudal state by the bourgeoisie, and he predicted the institution of the "free people's state by the proletariat."[92]
Proudly he noted that Dr. Karl Marx had established the certainty of that transformation. When asked about the inevitability of violence, Liebknecht gave his usual voluntaristic
reply: "Whether the [transformation into socialism] will
occur in the way of reform or revolution is dependent not on
us but rather on our opponents. . . . If they agree to our
just demands, then there will be no revolution; in the other
case, I offer no opinion on what will happen."[93]

When the judges directly asked Liebknecht if he would
fight for the establishment of the republic, Liebknecht appealed

to the 1848 example. He recalled that, at that time, the
princes had forcefully undone the majority decisions of the
Frankfurt Assembly. In a case where violence was used against
the elected delegates of the nation, Liebknecht proclaimed
that he would always fight on the side of the parliament.[94]
Adding a note of irony, he observed that the Prussian government recently had overthrown more German thrones than any
revolution, and yet it was he who was on trial for treason.
Wryly he observed, "There is still humor in world history."[95]

Through the press, Liebknecht's discourses reached the
nation. (Not until 1874 did the press code of the Second
Reich prohibit coverage of trials in progress.) *Der Volksstaat*
hastened to capitalize on this propaganda opportunity. Every
issue printed transcripts from the trial, and after the proceedings had ended, the SDAP journal continued to report the
reactions of other newspapers for another month. Nonsocialist
sheets also gave thorough coverage to the case. Although some
lampooned the defendants as hopeless visionaries, they, perhaps inadvertently, conveyed the socialists' convictions of
democracy and justice to a broad public.[96] By printing transcripts of the proceedings, all newspapers helped to circulate
Liebknecht's creed. (Recognizing this fact, one newspaper
abruptly ceased all reports in mid-trial.[97]) None but the
most conservative journals believed that the prosecution had
established grounds for conviction.[98]

On 26 March, after summations by the defense and prosecuting attorneys, the judges asked the jury to retire and
reach a verdict. The social status of the twelve members
foretold their decision. Seven merchants sat on the panel.
The remainder included a noble landowner, three smaller farmers
and a gameskeeper.[99] These men deliberated only two and a

half hours. Discounting only a charge of subverting the military, they found Liebknecht and Bebel guilty as charged. The
court president then sentenced these two defendants to two
years' imprisonment. The less prominent Hepner was acquitted.

Throughout Germany, this verdict aroused sympathy for
the socialists. Even before the trial ended, the lively journal, *Kladderadatsch*, published a stirring poem called "The
Inquisitors." In spite of judicial repression, in spite of
scorn and hostility, in spite of threats, it promised the
triumph of Truth, "in spite of everything."[100] Indeed, the
guilty verdict helped the socialist cause far more than an
acquittal could have done. From Germany and abroad, con-
dolences and congratulations inundated Liebknecht.[101] His
performance in the courtroom certainly contributed to the
fifty-percent increase in SDAP membership that occurred between
1872 and 1873. Among the more prominent converts won by his
testimony were the liberal hero from Berlin, Johann Jacoby,
and the future leader of the party in Bavaria, Georg von
Vollmar.[102] Surveying the agitational triumph that resulted
from the trial, Hepner felt compelled to apologize publicly
for his acquittal. "The difference between [Bebel and Lieb-
knecht] and myself," he explained, "was simply that . . .
their names provoked the hatred of the entire German bourgeoisie, [while] mine was hardly known by a dozen opponents."[103]

The day after their sentencing, Liebknecht and Bebel
issued a joint statement in which they still denied any intent
to commit high treason "in the sense of the legal code." If
they were guilty, they said, so was "every party that is not
at that moment in power." To them, the trial only proved
that the legal system of Germany was "nothing but a means
of class rule and class oppression." "To us personally the

result is a matter of indifference," they continued. "These proceedings have done so infinitely much for the dissemination of our ideas that we gladly will take a few years in prison. . . ." Before they went to jail, they exhorted their followers, "Social democracy stands above the court. Our party will live, grow and triumph."[104]

Chapter 7
Uniting the Workers' Movement

THE ABORTIVE APPROACH TO UNITY IN 1872-73

During its first decade, the German workers' movement led a
confused political life, being antagonistic toward the established order but also being bitterly divided against itself.
No impersonal, irresistible force dictated that this internal
schism would be healed. On the contrary, the European experience suggests the normality of a fragmented workers' movement.
Consolidation has more often followed than preceded revolution. Yet the party in Germany overcame its internal differences early in its development to become an envied model of
class discipline and solidarity. This achievement towers
as Wilhelm Liebknecht's greatest service to his cause. It
was a success stolen from the makings of disaster, for in
the months before the unity agreement was fashioned, a mass
desertion to the ADAV threatened to rip through the ranks
of Liebknecht's party.

The reasons that induced many of Liebknecht's comrades
to consider an accommodation with the ADAV were as numerous
as they were persuasive. First, many Eisenachers were maverick
Lassalleans. Little would be needed to prod them back toward
the Lassallean fold. Already, in 1869, the apparent differences between their former and present political homes had
begun to dwindle. In that year the Basel resolutions had

severed the tie between the SDAP and the bourgeois *Volks-partei*. Thenceforth both the ADAV and the SDAP preened themselves as purely proletarian parties. Shortly thereafter, Prussia's victory over France and the consequent creation of a *kleindeutsch* German empire had mooted the previously divisive argument about national unification. Almost simultaneously, a third barrier to unification fell away. On 26 March 1871, *Der Sozialdemokrat* announced Schweitzer's "irrevocable" resignation as president of the ADAV. Now he returned to the life of a playwright, until his death from tuberculosis in July 1875.

Liebknecht was delighted at Schweitzer's withdrawal, but others were more jubilant still. Prominent Eisenacher leaders like August Geib and Theodor Yorck had abandoned the ADAV primarily as a protest against Schweitzer's intraparty coup d'etat in 1869. In 1871 they saw their nemesis resign. A year later, the ADAV party congress censured its former president for serving the forces of reaction.[1] These events had to encourage the maverick Lassalleans in the SDAP to consider a reconciliation with their erstwhile comrades in the ADAV.

At this critical moment, the two Eisenachers who should have offered the staunchest resistance to an Eisenacher capitulation to the Lassalleans were incapacitated by their conviction for conspiracy to commit high treason. On 15 June 1872, Liebknecht began serving his two-year sentence. Bebel joined him in the fortress at Hubertusburg shortly thereafter. Two months after the prison doors slammed shut behind Liebknecht, the annual SDAP Congress convened at Mainz. With no recorded opposition, the assembled delegates resolved that the ADAV was, "according to its socialist principles," the "only natural

ally" of the SDAP. To foster cooperation with its former
rival, this convention authorized the Eisenacher Executive
Committee to seek a *prinzipielles Zusammengehen immer von
Neuem* with the Lassalleans.[2]

Until this time, *Der Volksstaat* had been Liebknecht's
most effective tool for preserving his party's adversary attitude toward the Lassalleans. Under his guidance, for example,
Der Volksstaat had relegated Schweitzer's resignation to a
small item on page two, where it was called a mere "comedy,"[3]
and in the following months the newspaper had continued its
occasional sniping at the ADAV.[4] By the autumn of 1872, many
Eisenachers thought such attacks among fellow socialists were
purely self-destructive. For them, the old, bitter charges
and countercharges of treachery and corruption that fouled
the rival party presses evoked only frustration. Reflecting
a widespread exasperation with the pugnacity of *Der Volksstaat*,
Yorck remarked at the 1872 congress, "The relationship between
the Executive Committee and the editorial staff needs regulation. The editors must never act without authorization; they
are servants of the party like every other official." With
Liebknecht in jail, the party directors, many of whom were
ex-ADAVers, hoped to muzzle their newspaper and consummate
a rapprochement with the Lassallean league. To that end,
they secured a resolution from the Mainz Congress directing
Der Volksstaat "immediately to suspend every polemic against
the ADAV and its leaders, and to answer any new hostility
from them with silence."[5]

At the editorial office of *Der Volksstaat*, Liebknecht's
friend and former codefendant Adolf Hepner continued the fight
against the Lassalleans. Liebknecht and Bebel shored up Hepner's morale and defenses in a variety of ways. Liebknecht's

wife, Natalie, smuggled a regular correspondence with Hepner
in and out of the prison, because government officials read
the regular mails. Hepner occasionally visited Hubertusburg
himself to converse with the two socialist inmates. Liebknecht
encouraged Marx and Engels to support Hepner in his fight
against Lassalleanism. Liebknecht wrote argumentative letters
to the pro-Lassallean members of the Eisenacher Executive
Committee. Therein he maintained the continuing need for
an "antithetical" relationship toward the Lassallean teachings.
Calling the "Schweitzer-Wagener" current "one-sided social
sectarian social democracy," he insisted that the SDAP needed
to stress political democracy and combat Lassalle's statism.
Otherwise the entire workers' movement might become a tool
of the reactionaries.[6] Finally, and covertly, Liebknecht
and Bebel helped Hepner to devise a scheme to subvert the
1872 SDAP Congress's bid for a merger with the Lassalleans.

On 28 September, *Der Volksstaat* published its own version
of a unification offer to the Lassalleans. It was signed
simply "The Editors," but Bebel later acknowledged that he
and Liebknecht were the authors.[7] Their proposals set surprisingly modest preconditions for a merger. First, the ADAV
"expressly and unequivocally" would have to acknowledge that
the SDAP was a social democratic party. Henceforth the
Lassalleans would have to call the SDAP by its proper name,
instead of the irritating "Liebknecht-Bebel People's Party."
Second, the ADAV would have to cease its attacks upon Marx's
International. If these two conditions were met, Liebknecht
and Bebel proposed a joint congress of both factions. "If
a unification, i.e., merger is not possible," they continued,
"then at least a common program must be laid down and the
forms arranged within which a common action (in elections,

agitation, etc.) can occur." To oversee the execution of
the agreement, they proposed that a joint committee immediately be elected from both factions.

Even while they extended this olive branch, the Hubertusburg inmates insured that the Lassalleans would reject it. At
their instigation, the same issue of *Der Volksstaat* that contained the unity proposal also printed a flagrant insult to the
Lassallean creed. In this way Liebknecht doubtless hoped to
illustrate the differences in principle between the SDAP and
the ADAV, without having to define these differences in a
lecture to his own comrades.

In a recent editorial, the refurbished and reorganized
central organ of the ADAV, *Der Neue Sozialdemokrat*, had admitted
that Lassalle had underestimated the cost of state help for
productive associations. Accordingly, the editor had tripled
Lassalle's estimate from 100 million to 300 million marks.
Der Volksstaat now sarcastically commented that 1,000 million
would be insufficient to achieve anything of importance on
the cooperative route; the SDAP, the editors opined, had never
believed that a "solution to the social question" could be
found "on the path proposed by Lassalle." Outraged, *Der Neue
Sozialdemokrat* screamed that the Bebel-Liebknecht People's
Party had defamed Lassalle. In response, *Der Volksstaat* simply
reaffirmed its conviction that productive associations were
"not realizable." As a result of this editorial exchange, the
Berlin chapter of the ADAV combatively resolved that every
nonmember, including the Eisenachers, was a class enemy.

Confronted by this eruption of hostility, the SDAP Executive Committee had to furl its white flag and scurry back
behind its own trenches. In a public announcement, it warned
that the preparations for unity would be terminated unless the

Berlin ADAV withdrew its provocative resolution.[8] That action
was not forthcoming, and the unity movement languished. In
his prison cell, Liebknecht heaved a sigh of relief.

Yet the vigor of the Lassallean sympathy among the SDAP
leadership dictated that the drive for a merger would not
dissipate after this single unsuccessful attempt. Already
by the end of November, Liebknecht again saw his faction verging
on disintegration. "We must exert every effort to hold the
party together . . . ," he wrote to Engels.[9]

Despite Liebknecht's strident protests, the executive
committee and the control committee compelled *Der Volksstaat*
to publish a new unity proposal in mid-December. Headlined
"On Unity of the German Workers' Party," (a title already
implying the existence of a single party), this front-page,
two-part editorial reported an ever-increasing popular clamor
for a merger. After reviewing the platforms of the ADAV and
the SDAP, it concluded, "no differences in principle exist
between the two programs. . . ." *Der Volksstaat* then explicitly called for an immediate unity congress to be arranged
jointly by the leadership of both factions.[10]

Unable to corral this second stampede toward a merger
by direct argumentation, Liebknecht again employed subtle
means to achieve his aim. By coincidence, a few weeks earlier
he had received a letter from Schweitzer. This unexpected
missive conceded that the Eisenachers were socialists after
all, and it concluded with a plea to set aside personal
animosity and to work resolutely for unification.[11]

For several weeks Liebknecht pondered how he might best
employ this serendipitous document. He suspected that the
letter constituted an attempt by Schweitzer to regain some
political influence.[12] But he also knew it could be used to

confound the maverick Lassalleans in his own executive committee. Surely Yorck, Geib and the others would greatly
resent Schweitzer's reappearance, and just as certainly they
would be wary of any course the erstwhile dictator plotted.
Liebknecht knew too that the ADAV itself would hardly heed
the advice of the man it had recently voted to censure and
expel. Because Schweitzer's letter seemed likely to diminish
enthusiasm for unification in all camps, Liebknecht instructed
Hepner to print it. On 4 January 1873, it appeared in *Der
Volksstaat*.

Like its predecessor in September, this bit of sabotage
by Liebknecht produced some short-lived consternation, but
it had no permanent effect. Within weeks after its appearance,
the party directors again were browbeating poor Hepner, order-
ing him to be conciliatory to the ADAV and to adopt an editorial
style more like that of *Der Neue Sozialdemokrat*.[13] When Hepner
proved intractable, the executive committee imported its own
protégé, Wilhelm Blos, to supplant him as editor-in-chief.[14]

In the spring of 1873, observing from London, Engels
believed that the SDAP was slipping from the grasp of the
Marxists.[15] Even as the Lassalleans joined the Bakuninists
in battering the IWA into oblivion, most Eisenachers also
threatened to defect to Marx's enemies. There was little
Liebknecht could do to prevent that calamity. Trying to calm
Engels' fears, he asserted that "the Executive Committee has
no *right* to violate [the independence of] the editorial staff,
and, more importantly, it does not have the *power*,"[16] but
Liebknecht's own continued influence on *Der Volksstaat* was
highly doubtful at that moment. Hepner had just been expelled
from Leipzig by the police, and Blos had assumed the editorship of the SDAP's central organ. A colleague of Bracke from

Brunswick, Blos was expected to encourage the rush toward
Lassalleanism.

Two factors, neither of which Liebknecht controlled,
saved him from disaster in 1873. First, Blos contradicted
expectations. In a private communication to Liebknecht, he
announced that he had actually approved of Hepner's tactics.
As an editor, he continued, he had to reject the executive
committee's heavy-handed attempts to dictate to the party
press.[17] Immensely relieved, Liebknecht quickly established
a close working relationship with Blos. That tie saved
Liebknecht's ability to influence *Der Volksstaat*.

Second, the ADAV also helped Liebknecht to checkmate
the Eisenacher directorate in 1873. At its party congress
late in May, the Lassallean league haughtily rejected any
suggestion of a political marriage to the SDAP. Instead it
passed a resolution dismissing the Eisenachers as die-hard
disciples of Schulze-Delitzsch who treacherously sought to
split the workers' movement. This same resolution declared
that the tactics, program and organization of the ADAV and
the SDAP were absolutely irreconcilable. Only three Lassallean
delegates voted against this insulting resolution.[18]

Thus the ADAV turned its back on the entreaties of the
Eisenacher Executive Committee. The 1874 Lassallean convention repeated the rebuff. In their awkward attempt to court
the ADAV, Liebknecht's comrades resembled nothing more than
unrequited suitors. A sidelong glance, a nod of the head
from the Lassalleans, and Liebknecht might have left Hubertusburg to find most of his party gone.[19]

The abortive approach to unity in 1872-73 has been
neglected in previous accounts of the eventual fusion of the
SDAP and the ADAV. That oversight has left a crucial part

of Liebknecht's motivation obscured. Throughout 1874 and
into 1875, he continued to worry that much of his political
following might desert him for the enemy. Consequently, he
war far more eager to organize a merger with the Lassalleans
than he would have been if he could have relied upon the solidarity of his own faction.

LIEBKNECHT'S PROMOTION OF THE MERGER

Meanwhile, the pressures for a merger from members of the
Eisenacher movement continued to mount, and for the first
time tentative signs of reciprocity glimmered within the Lassallean ranks. The growing trade union movement had taken
steps to transcend the schism in the workers' movement as
early as 1873. In the umbrella union organization in Hamburg,
the Lassallean Kapell brothers worked alongside SDAP chieftains
August Geib and Ignaz Auer.[20] In the spring of 1874, in various spots throughout Germany, Lassalleans and Eisenachers
spontaneously surged toward cooperation. Contemporary observers remarked that the clamor for amalgamation of the two
factions was becoming irresistible.[21] Even in Berlin, where
the two groups recently had bloodied each other in street
brawls, the SDAP decided to back the Lassallean candidate
in the runoff ballot for the Reichstag.[22] Der Volksstaat
reported the election results nationwide, lumping ADAV and
SDAP votes into a single total for "our" party. It gloated
over the election of ten reichsfeindlich deputies, a figure
that included both SDAP and ADAV mandates.[23]

In addition to encouraging cooperation to elect the largest
possible number of socialist deputies, the 1874 Reichstag

elections promoted accommodation between the SDAP and the
ADAV in other ways. The total vote for each party was almost
equal. From 1871 to 1874, the ADAV backers had tripled from
60,466 to 180, 319. The SDAP vote increased even more dramatically, from 41,461 to 171,351.[24] (Liebknecht regained his
Reichstag seat in this election.) Viewing these results,
neither party could expect its rival to disappear on its own
accord. Instead, the leaders of both parties were tossed
together into the Reichstag, where they had an opportunity
to recognize that they agreed on almost every issue.

The German police also studied the 1874 election figures.
Alarmed by the socialist recovery (the two factions together
polled almost 7 percent of the total vote), the authorities
escalated their harassment of both parties with orders of
dissolution, decrees of deportation, and hundreds of court
cases. During the first seven months of 1874, in Prussia
alone, for the ADAV alone, eighty-seven members faced 104
trials. They received sentences totalling over 217 months.
In June, the entire ADAV in Prussia was ordered to disband
for violating the law of associations. The authorities
escorted the Lassallean president, Wilhelm Hasenclever, off
to jail for a six-month term.[25]

This aggressive onslaught diluted the lingering pro-
Prussian and statist sympathies among the Lassalleans. It
also demonstrated the vulnerability of the centralized and
dictatorial ADAV organization. As Liebknecht later recalled,
"What healthy human understanding and the feelings of [pro-
letarian] solidarity left wanting [to achieve unification
of the workers' movement], the organs of state power supplied.
. . . Through their persecution they drove both bodies of
[worker] troops together against the common enemy."[26]

As these legions of socialists were herded off to jail,
Liebknecht's imprisonment ended. In May 1874, he left
Hubertusburg. He was thus free to attend his first party
congress since 1871. When his comrades convened at Coburg
in mid-July, Liebknecht seized the opportunity for a public
statement of his reasons for still opposing Lassalleanism.

First he spoke of party organization. Trying to rekindle
memories of Schweitzer's presidency, he pointed out that the
ADAV still subscribed to a dictatorial party structure. That
authoritarian edifice, hallowed by the last testament of their
first and fallen leader, stood as an infallible ideal for
Lasalleans. The democratic Eisenachers, Liebknecht argued,
ridiculed all pretense to infallibility. They considered
socialism to be an evolving science rather than a catechism
of faith. The ADAV, he continued, was "nationalistic,"
"sectarian," and wallowed in a disgusting cult of personality
worship around Lassalle. By contrast, the SDAP was an international proletarian movement that placed principles above
personalities.

Considering these contrasts, Liebknecht advised against
an immediate amalgamation with the Lassalleans. He knew,
however, that some concession to the Lassallean forces in
his own party had to be made. He therefore endorsed a pro-
crastinating resolution offered by Chairman Geib. This statement, adopted with no recorded opposition, reiterated the
SDAP inclination toward a merger, but instead of immediate
and decisive steps toward that end, it simply directed the
Eisenacher party officials to suggest at the next congress a
method for obtaining the desired unity.[27] Summarizing this
outcome in a letter to Engels, Liebknecht asserted that his
party had abandoned the ideal of "unification (*Vereinigung*):
Only a *tactical* unity (*Einigung*) can be considered."[28]

Within three months, events inside the ADAV made Liebknecht revise this estimation. In the autumn of 1874, the
first genuine opportunity for negotiations with the Lassalleans
as an equal rather than as a supplicant presented itself to
Liebknecht. Because of the shaky status of his own party, he
believed that he had to plunge into these deliberations.

The opportunity originated in fratricidal squabbles that
shook the ADAV at its annual congress from 26 May to 5 June
1874. The epigones who succeeded Schweitzer in the leadership of this party had engaged in ceaseless bickering for
years. Especially obstreperous among these intriguers was
Carl Tölcke, who briefly had presided over the ADAV in 1866
and who currently was that party's vice-president. At the
1874 convocation, the numerous enemies of the chronically
factious Tölcke rallied together in an unsuccessful attempt
to strip him of office and power. After this insult, the
sulking Tölcke sought a strategy to avenge himself upon his
detractors.

In consultation with President Hasenclever, who languished
in jail from July onward, Tölcke planned to approach the Eisenachers with a proposal for unification.[29] Hasenclever's motives
in this matter are unclear, but Tölcke sought only to advance
himself, for at the ADAV congress only weeks earlier he had
denounced "unification or even a peaceful co-existence" with
the SDAP.[30] Yet in October he scurried throughout Germany,
drumming up support for a congress to unite the workers'
movement.

A fortuitous rivalry inside the ADAV leadership thus
presented the first chink in the Lassallean armor, that thick
defense that previously had repulsed all the importunings
of the Eisenachers. Liebknecht skillfully pried that chink
open and extracted the whole ADAV.

On 10 October, Tölcke visited Liebknecht in Leipzig.
With great urgency, he recommended that a unity congress be
held on 15 November. However, Liebknecht held back. Aside
from his reservation about the Lassallean program and organization, he recognized that Tölcke was a schismatic who had
little influence with the ADAV membership. He especially
worried that the ADAV newspaper, which was read faithfully
by almost every party member, remained in the hands of Tölcke's
archrival, Wilhelm Hasselmann. Liebknecht remembered all too
well how Schweitzer's control of *Der Sozialdemokrat* had allowed
him to survive the intraparty fracas in 1865, and was now convinced that if "only the *head* of the ADAV (in the form of
Der Neue Sozialdemokrat) remained, the amputated members would
soon grow back. . . ."[31]

Fortunately for Liebknecht, Tölcke's ploy panicked his
rivals in the ADAV leadership. The day after Tölcke's visit,
Liebknecht received a similar initiative from Friedrich
Fritzsche, the Lassallean union leader, who also claimed to
speak on behalf of Hasselmann. Thus courted by all of his
enemies, a joyous Liebknecht wrote to Bebel that the ADAV
was "completely *en deroute*."[32] Two weeks later he informed
Marx of the happy changes in the German movement. Lest his
mentor worry about the direction of future developments,
Liebknecht wrote, "We take things very coolly and shall not
allow ourselves to be corrupted."[33]

Early in November, the six Eisenacher deputies to the
Reichstag met with their three Lassallean counterparts in
Berlin.[34] Public evidence of an impending accommodation was
soon forthcoming. On 21 November, in a speech to the Reichstag, Liebknecht referred to all nine socialist deputies as
members of a single *Fraktion*.[35] More remarkably, a few days

later the ADAV newspaper published the stenographic report
of Liebknecht's speech on page one. Shortly thereafter, the
SDAP central organ reciprocated by giving front-page coverage
to a speech by Hasselmann.[36] Never before had these party
papers given such favorable attention to the speeches of their
rivals.

On 11 December, the two party organs published simultaneous
and practially identical statements announcing the initiation
of negotiations for unity. Hasenclever signed the announcement
in *Der Neue Sozialdemokrat*. August Geib and Ignaz Auer, the
SDAP chairman and secretary, respectively, signed in *Der Volksstaat*. Both announcements described initiatives from the
other side that had called for agreement as quickly as possible.
"Energetic steps" had been taken "to prepare the agreement
on a completely healthy foundation and in a manner legal for
both participants." The simultaneous publication indicated
that each side had already accepted the equality of its rival
for the impending negotiations.

Another meeting of Reichstag deputies, this time joined
by comrades in both factions from Berlin, occurred on 15 December. At that session, a brief and potentially explosive discussion concerning the program of the future party occurred.
But instead of a thorough debate, Hasselmann hailed the class
struggle, everyone cheered, and the subject evaporated.[37]
Those present then elected delegates to a conference that
was later to write a program proposal. Each faction elected
nine representatives, thus again acknowledging the equality
of the participants.

The Eisenacher delegation included no one whose influence
could rival that of Liebknecht. August Bebel was not included
because he remained in jail. Wilhelm Bracke was excluded,

possibly because of his recently publicized hostility to the
Lassallean productive associations. The Eisenachers who did
join Liebknecht, younger men like Ignaz Auer, Eduard Bernstein, and Julius Motteler, deferred to his leadership.

By the end of December, Liebknecht and the Lassalleans
had committed their parties to a complete fusion. Indeed,
the form of the future organization had already been decided.
Although it was not ratified publicly for another five months,
Der Volksstaat accurately outlined this structure on 30 December 1874. Despite his earlier statements, public and private,
Liebknecht had gone far beyond tactical unity (*Einigung*) to
support complete unification (*Vereinigung*). On 1 January
1875, he urged an assembly in Berlin, "If you find people who
still want to thwart the unification (*Vereinigung*), throw
them overboard, whoever they may be!"[38]

Liebknecht's tactical about-face in the autumn of 1874
was harshly criticized by Karl Marx. From his vantage point
in London, Marx believed that the Lassallean band was disintegrating. That once virile organization, he thought, was suffering the inevitable decay that he predicted for all "sectarian"
factions. Because they were constructed in ignorance of the
principles of scientific socialism and bogged down in a cult
of personality around their founder, Marx taught that sectarian
organizations had no chance to lead the proletariat past its
infancy. Because of his theoretical viewpoint, and because
Liebknecht had reported the feuding within the ADAV, Marx
thought that concessions to the Lassallean leaders were unnecessary by 1874. With more patience, Marx assumed that Liebknecht
could have dictated terms to a defunct rival.[39]

Yet only negotiation with the ADAV promised to produce
a united socialist party. Liebknecht rejected the patient

path of negotiating with Tölcke for several reasons. First,
as noted above, the ADAV newspaper would have continued to
beckon any and all deserters to return to the Lassallean band.
Second, Liebknecht had once before plotted with Lassallean
defectors against the established ADAV leadership. At Eisenach
in 1869, dozens of illustrious Lassalleans had joined Liebknecht, and yet the ADAV survived. Tölcke, an isolated renegade
with little popular support, could not have dealt a more
serious blow to the ADAV than did desertion by the far more
numerous defectors five years earlier.

From Liebknecht's perspective, perpetuation of that rift
was dangerous enough by itself. Only months earlier, a large
part of the Eisenacher leadership had threatened to secede
to the Lassalleans. Resolutions from the SDAP Congresses
of 1872, 1873, and 1874 indicated the continuing willingness
of most party members to support such a move. The ADAV leadership was no more unstable than its Eisenacher counterpart, and
if Liebknecht had delayed too much longer in 1874, his own
party might have bolted.

Although battles in the Lassallean governing councils
did provide an opportunity for Liebknecht to negotiate for
unity, that infighting occurred within a sound party. Com-
parative statistics for the strengths of the ADAV and the
SDAP show how futile it would have been for Liebknecht to
wait for the ADAV to collapse.

Membership figures for the SDAP and the ADAV between
1870 and 1875 indicate a phenomenal surge in ADAV membership
in 1872-73 and a somewhat smaller percentage gain for the SDAP
in the same time period. There followed a fairly stable
membership total for both parties from 1873 to 1875. In this
constant ratio, the ADAV enjoyed an approximate 5:3 advantage.

The 1875 figures, verified by a joint commission from both factions, do indicate a slight decline in ADAV membership.[40] But considering the intensity of government repression in the Lassallean stronghold of Prussia, a regression of only 12.4 percent indicates vitality, not weakness. The 1875 membership figures for the ADAV and SDAP were only four percent and one percent less than the 1873 figures, respectively.

It might be recalled at this point that the Reichstag elections of 1874 demonstrated substantial growth and approximately parity for both parties. Though the ADAV enjoyed a slight superiority in popular appeal, the SDAP won more mandates because its strength was geographically concentrated in central Germany. Circulation figures for the respective party presses reconfirm the approximate equality between the two factions.[41] However, the Lassalleans always boasted a better financial record than the Eisenachers. For example, *Der Neue Sozialdemokrat* always earned a profit.[42] *Der Volksstaat* ran a perennial deficit.[43] In the most important source of income for both factions, member contributions, the ADAV apparently enjoyed approximately the same 5:3 advantage over its rival that it held in membership.[44] On the eve of unification, observers in the Eisenacher party still envied the efficiency and wealth of their competitor.[45]

These statistics certainly contradict Marx's estimation made from his London exile. Later, when Marx's objections were well known, Liebknecht reflected on his decision to merge with the Lassalleans: "At that time in 1874-75 every thread ran through my hands," he asserted, "and I know of no one who had an opportunity to consider the opposing power factors . . . more exactly than I."[46]

THE ORGANIZATION AND THE PROGRAM FOR A UNITED PARTY

Inseparable from Liebknecht's pondering of the various paths
to unity was a consideration of the terms under which such
a merger would be arranged. First and most important in
Liebknecht's own mind was the establishment of a democratic
organizational structure. He believed that free debate in
such an organization would eventually eradicate the Lassallean
misconceptions. As corollaries to his organizational objective, he aimed to eliminate the aura of infallibility and
cult of personality around Lassalle, and to subject the ADAV
newspaper to the guidance of the united party. Both of these
points would facilitate the articulation of a scientifically
socialist creed. For Liebknecht, at this moment, the construction of a suitable arena for ideological debate was more
important than the imposition of specific ideological formulations.

Liebknecht and his Lassallean counterparts had hammered
out their organizational differences by the end of 1874. The
organization statute that they wrote thoroughly repudiated
the Lassallean dictatorial principle. In conformity with
the Eisenacher structure, the annual congress, elected directly
by the membership, would be the sovereign authority in the
newly united part. At each congress, the delegates would
choose a location for the executive (*Vorstand*) and a separate
site for a control commission. Comrades in each of these
cities then would choose the membership of the two committees.
The actual administration of the party comprised a labyrinth
of checks and balances, the traditional democratic defense
against dictatorship. The control commission would audit
the work of the *Vorstand* and hear complaints from party members.

In the event that these two bodies disagreed, a third committee from still another city would head the arbitration. An absolute majority of any two of these bodies would suffice to dictate a settlement and even to depose members of the third.

Two further provisions of the statute consummated the victory of Eisenacher-style intraparty democracy over Lassallean authoritarianism. To insure popular control of the annual congresses, the executive, the control commission and the editors of the central organ would be allowed to send only two delegates each. Moreover, echoing the Eisenach Program, the editor and staff of the party newspapers were barred from the party administration, and their newspapers were obligated to mirror opinion inside the party.[47]

The democratic organization must be counted as a tremendous triumph for Liebknecht and his faction. The centralized Lassallean dictatorship, inspired by the testament of the founder of the party, had been thoroughly vanquished. To preserve this victory, Liebknecht was ready to be flexible on programmatic matters.

Liebknecht's willingness to compromise was based on his need for the approval of his peers. The pressure for agreement inherent in any small group's discussion probably accentuated Liebknecht's own inclination to avoid disagreement.[48] Once deliberations with the Lassalleans were under way, Liebknecht almost instinctively assumed his role as an affective leader, smoothing ruffled feathers on all sides. His dedication to unification helped to congeal the previously warring parties during the tense months to come.

On 14 February, nine delegates from each faction met at Gotha, just a few miles from Eisenach in central Germany, where a relatively liberal local regime offered protection

against government harassment. The agenda of this pre-congress
called for the composition of a theoretical platform for the
united socialist party. According to Eduard Bernstein, who
attended the meeting for the Eisenachers, Liebknecht brought
the only written program proposal to the congress.[49] But
before deliberations began, the Lassallean representatives
held a separate meeting in which they agreed to insist upon
the insertion of several Lassallean slogans as their price
for a merger.[50]

The resulting draft was thus a compromise. Although
Liebknecht was its principal author, it included several points
with which he personally disagreed. To Engels he conceded,
"without the unity we could have prepared a more radical program, but *this* faulty program *with* unity is a thousand times
dearer to me than the most perfect program *without* unity."[51]
As with all true compromises, both parties suffered some dissatisfaction. At the unity congress in May, the Lassallean
leader, Hasenclever, too expressed his personal distaste for
parts of the program. But, he continued, "in the interest
of unity one was compelled to consider the views and principles of both directions. . . ."[52]

All differences were either reconciled or balanced out
at the Gotha pre-congress in only two days. On 19 February,
Der Volksstaat reported that the negotiations had "proceeded
to the complete satisfaction of all participants." The program
proposal appeared in both *Der Volksstaat* and *Der Neue Sozialdemokrat* on 7 March 1875.

The draft opens with five paragraphs articulating general
theoretical principles. The first sentence of the draft
asserted that because labor is the source of "all wealth and
all civilization," the worker should be entitled to the

undiminished fruits of his efforts. Contemporary society
is characterized by monopolistic ownership of the instruments of labor by the capitalist class. The dependence bred
by this monopoly is "the cause of misery and servitude in
all forms." To emancipate labor, the program demanded collective ownership of these instruments of labor. Turning from
production to distribution, the program advised that social
regulation of consumption be instituted to insure "a just
distribution of the product of labor." In the realm of tactics, the program draft decreed that all other classes comprise "a reactionary mass" against which the workers must
struggle; the working class would have to liberate itself.
The program then acknowledged the national state as the framework for current political struggle, but it also affirmed
the party's ultimate aspiration toward an international brotherhood of peoples.

In Part II of the program, the socialists announced that
they would fight for the "free state and the socialist society
with all legal means." They also called for "abolition of
the wage system with the iron law of wages" (a phrase that
was both grammatically and theoretically perplexing). More
generally, they demanded the "elimination of all social and
political inequality."

To achieve a solution of the social issue, the "German
Workers' Party" advocated "productive associations with state
help under democratic control of the working people." These
associations were to spread throughout society, providing
a presumably peaceful transition to socialism. A list of
additional specific demands concluded the program. The usual
democratic calls for freedom of the press and assembly, a

democratic franchise and a citizen militia were included.
The program also called for a maximum normal working day (of
undefined length) and a progressive income tax to replace
all other taxes.[53]

Liebknecht had been remiss in keeping his closest friends
informed about the evolution of the content of this program
draft. Because he had entered Hubertusburg later than Liebknecht, and because an additional nine-month sentence had
been added to his term for a separate offense, when the draft
was written Bebel still sat in prison. On 23 February, he
complained to Engels that all he knew about the unity proceedings was what he read in the newspapers. Bebel asked Engels
what he had heard. "Unfortunately we are exactly in your
situation," Engels responded a month later. "Neither Liebknecht nor anyone else has given us any report. . . ." However, by that time he had read the program proposal printed
in *Der Volksstaat*. "It has astonished us more than a little,"
he added.[54] In this letter to Bebel, Engels presented a
lengthy criticism of the platform draft, concluding that "unity
on *this* basis will not last a year." He sent a similar critique
to Liebknecht, to which the latter first found the time and
inclination to respond on 21 April.

In defending his recent actions, Liebknecht acknowledged
several flaws that marred the present composition of the program. He promised to try to improve some of them at the congress.
Specifically he named the "bad composition of the 'national'
paragraph, the iron law of wages, the freedom of conscience,
etc."; the productive associations he thought would be more
difficult to purge, but he promised that a "less Lassallean
form" would be found for that demand too.[55]

At the congress, Liebknecht anonymously submitted a list

of almost twenty amendments, nine of which were adopted. In
the most important substantive change that resulted from his
suggestions, the statement of the international commitment
of the party was strengthened, but attempts to alter or delete
Lassallean slogans, including the productive associations
and the designation of all nonsocialists as a reactionary
mass, failed.[56]

Liebknecht did not fight hard for his amendments. In
broad outline he already had accepted the draft. If it could
not be modified without jeopardizing the merger, he had decided
to accept the program as it stood. Already on 23 April, he
had told Engels that the draft meant "the *complete* victory
of 'Marxian' communism over Lassallean sectarianism. And
to achieve this victory, I would have been prepared for still
further concessions. . . ."[57] Liebknecht properly pointed
out that the new draft was no worse than the Eisenacher program,
which also had been a compromise with Lassalleanism. He could
not understand why acceptable tactics in 1869 had become
unacceptable in 1875.

Marx and Engels had changed their tactics regarding doctrinal compromise during the last decade. In formulating
a platform for the International in 1864, Marx had made numerous
ideological concessions to the variety of opinion in that
body. He intended to reform its opinions from within, but
his plan had miscarried. Instead of experiencing a growing
dedication to Marxist principles, the IWA had been devastated
by the war between Bakunin and Marx. The Londoners learned
from that experience that one does not fraternize with doctrinal
enemies in a single organization. As Engels told Bebel in
1873, the International had gone *kaputt durch die Einigung.*[58]

The doctrinal fight with Bakunin explains the intensity

of the attack by Marx and Engels on Liebknecht's program draft.
Marx provided the connection in a letter he sent to Bracke
on 5 May. His denunciation of the program was "essential,"
Marx said, "since party enemies abroad cherish the carefully
nurtured view . . . that we [Marx and Engels] secretly direct
the movement of the so-called Eisenacher party from here.
For example in a recently published Russian sheet, Bakunin
makes me responsible not only for every program etc. of that
party, but even for every step that Liebknecht has taken since
the days of his cooperation with the People's Party." Marx
refused to be blamed for Liebknecht's most recent escapade,
especially because he rejected precisely those points that
the anarchists would be most likely to attack. He told Bracke
that he and Engels regrettably would be forced to publish
a "short declaration" renouncing responsibility or even agreement with Liebknecht's work.[59]

Marx objected to the Gotha compromise partly because
the ADAV had joined Bakunin in his crusade against Marx. The
painful slanders against Marx published in *Der Neue Sozialdemokrat* must have still rankled. Having at last tossed the ADAV
into the dustbin labelled "sectarians," Marx must have been
horrified to see the Eisenachers join them. The experiences
and needs of Marx and Liebknecht inescapably led them to different conclusions regarding the advisability of doctrinal
compromise with the Lassalleans.

Along with his letter of 5 May to Bracke, Marx sent his
famous *Critique of the Gotha Program*. Apparently he still
hoped to be able to influence the finished program, because
he asked Bracke to circulate the *Critique* to Geib, Auer, Bebel,
and Liebknecht.[60] Marx's *Critique* left few words of the official draft unscathed. He found numerous misleading or

imprecise statements in the proposal. For example, he noted
that labor alone is hardly the only source of "wealth and
civilization." Natural resources comprise an obvious contradiction to this assertion. He next criticized several
phrases that he attributed to the Lassallean influence; the
"reactionary mass," the "undiminished products of labor,"
the "iron law of wages," and the state-sponsored productive
associations. He missed an affirmation that present capitalist
production created the material preconditions that would enable
the workers to achieve a socialist society. Marx then attacked
the acknowledgment of the nation-state, which he also attributed to the deleterious influence of Lassalle. Many of these
points Liebknecht had already anticipated in his letter of
23 April to Engels, but the *Critique* explicitly stated two
other ideas that went beyond Marx's earlier writings.

    First, Marx challenged the phrase, "just distribution
of the products of labor." He pointed out that bourgeois
economists tout the justice of distribution under capitalism.
Marx said that although distributive justice dominated the
thought of many contemporary European socialists, it played
no role in scientific socialism.[61] Marx next denied that
the communist revolution would introduce an equal distribution
of goods. That notion must have shocked Marx's readers in
1875. Marx explained that "the right of producers is *proportional* to what their labor produces; the equality is that
the labor wil be measured by the same standard." Communism
would recognize no class differences, but it would recognize
and reward differences in individual achievement. Only after
human alienation from labor had eventually been eliminated
could the slogan become, "From each according to his abilities, to each according to his needs." For the moment, Marx

advised the German socialists that "in order to avoid all
misunderstandings, the rights must be unequal instead of equal."

Marx made a second startling point when he discussed
the attitude toward the state in Liebknecht's draft.   The
draft promised to strive for the "free state and the socialist society with all legal means." Marx pounced upon those
last two words, for it was impossible to demand democratic
government from an autocracy and still expect to use only
"legal means." For the first time, he moaned, the German
workers' movement had expressly disavowed violent revolution.
Continuing in this political vein, Marx collared the term,
"free state." Noting the ambiguity of that expression, he
sneered that an autocracy like Russia could well be called
a "free state," because the government suffered no popular
limitations. Ignoring the legal limitations within which
Liebknecht labored, Marx advised the German socialists unequivocally to call for a "democratic republic." Marx next described
the transition from capitalism to communism. That social
transformation would call forth a transitional state, and he
boldly labelled it the "revolutionary dictatorship of the
proletariat."

Marx's *Critique* illustrated a vital problem that Liebknecht
faced throughout his career: the reconciliation of theory
with practice. In his study in London, Marx faced no such difficulty in 1875. He was free to compose a commentary that
reflected only his own ideas, but Liebknecht had to write his
party platform in collaboration with the Lassalleans and within
the constraints of German law. In that effort, he had to compromise his principles somewhat.

Because the Gotha Program originated in compromise, Marx's
Critique cannot be taken simply as an exposé of Liebknecht's

shortcomings as a theoretician. On the contrary, Liebknecht agreed with almost all of the points that Marx made, saying only that such theoretical clarity was impossible to achieve in the present circumstances. On one issue, however, Liebknecht rejected his mentor's teaching altogether. He never accepted the necessity of a dictatorship of the proletariat.

Marx's opposition to the Gotha Program provokes a nagging historiographical question that bears directly upon Liebknecht's skill as a spokesman for scientific socialism: Was it conceivable that a program more to Marx's liking *could* have been composed and adopted in Germany in 1875? For Marx's *Critique* to have had any chance for implementation, some element in the German movement needed a fairly sophisticated understanding of scientific socialism.[62] Either Liebknecht suppressed that element and accepted a program that was a step backward; or Marx was naive to expect better results.

Given this choice, the most recent Marxist investigator of these events has tried hard to depict a substantial Marxist understanding in the Eisenacher group. Prominent in his evidence are the many writings by Marx and Engels in *Der Volksstaat*. During the five years from 1870 to 1874, approximately one out of every four issues of Liebknecht's newspaper published a piece by Marx or Engels.[63] Liebknecht believed that these articles rippled outward and influenced party politics and theory.[64]

To balance this impression, however, one must remember the remaining content of *Der Volksstaat*. Engels complained that Liebknecht uncritically accepted any and all material in order to fill his pages; "only here and there something readable," he muttered. For his part, Marx complained of the "half-educated phantasies of philistines" that dotted

Der Volksstaat.[65] Significantly, the material composed in Germany upset Marx and Engels.

Likewise speeches by SDAP leaders include evidence for and against a Marxist understanding in that party. For example, some parts of Liebknecht's speeches often sounded Marxist (as has been noted from time to time in preceding chapters). But he also lapsed into heterodoxy rather frequently, even advocating state-sponsored productive associations as a peaceful means of transition to socialism.[66] Similar contradictory conclusions can be drawn about most apparently Marxist statements by other SDAP leaders.

Addressing the need for a clearer statement of party principles, the 1873 SDAP Congress elected a five-member panel to propose a revision of the Eisenacher platform. (Although he still sat in prison, Liebknecht was among the members elected for this task.) The meanderings of this program committee bolster the case against a budding Marxist awareness in the SDAP. When the 1874 congress convened, Liebknecht told the delegates that "no special movement for recasting the program has manifested itself, and a final formulation is still not possible today because no clarity exists in the matter."[67] A lively discussion of the program issue ensued, but no consensus for any set of changes emerged. So the sly chairman Geib asked the delegates to table the matter for yet another year. Liebknecht seconded Geib's suggestions, and the delegates agreed.[68]

Left to itself, unmolested by compromises with the ADAV, the SDAP repeatedly failed to devise a more scientific program. There simply was no constituency advocating a thoroughly Marxist perspective. Liebknecht was as sophisticated a student of Marx as the SDAP had in 1874, and his theoretical imprecision

is manifest. Regarding the rest of his party, all contemporary observers agreed that the ideas of Lassalle, not those
of Marx, comprised the core of whatever theoretical understanding there was in German socialism.

Because of Lassalle's persistent popularity, Liebknecht
previously had warned Engels of the need for a "certain fore-
bearance toward the Lassallean prejudices."[69] Bebel was more
blunt. He told Engels that Lassalle's writings were "twenty
times more widespread in Germany than any other socialist
writing."[70] Underscoring this point, on 16 January 1874,
Der Volksstaat advertised the list of pamphlets available
from its press. The list offered one essay by Bebel, two
each by J. P. Becker and Marx, three by Engels, four by Liebknecht and twenty by Lassalle. This in the Eisenacher paper!
Against this ideological backdrop, it would be ridiculous
to attribute the murkiness of the Gotha Program solely to
corruption from the ADAV.

In the SDAP, there were no indigenously produced Marxist
alternatives to Liebknecht's draft. In the two and one-half
months that elapsed between the publication of the program
proposal and the convocation of the congress called to ratify
it, only two challenges to the draft surfaced. Neither came
to much.

First, Carl Tölcke made one more feeble try to resurrect
his influence. On 11 April, he convened a separatist meeting
of social democrats in his long-time bailiwick around Dortmund.
There he menacingly declared that acceptance of the official
draft was "impossible." A few of his objections corresponded
to those made by Marx, but his flabby counterproposal also
included a complete disavowal of economic determinism.[71]

Der Neue Sozialdemokrat branded Tölcke's sparsely attended congress as schismatic. The unity of the workers' movement, the ADAV sheet insisted, was "already completed."[72] The absence of popular support for Tölcke in the wake of this Dortmund congress indicates how weak his position had been all along. He capitulated well before the upcoming congress, saying he would accept any program that promised unity, "even if it was only a piece of white paper with a balled fist on it."[73]

Within Liebknecht's faction, two prominent persons also objected to the official draft. Wilhelm Bracke, who recently had authored a pamphlet criticizing the Lassallean productive associations,[74] now complained about the concessions to Lassallean "errors" in the Gotha Program. In correspondence with Engels and with Bebel, he tried to arrange the composition of a competing draft.[75] Bebel was the second dissident. When he first read the official platform, he promptly penned his own countersuggestion. He completed his manifesto by the end of March and mailed it off to the SDAP Executive Committee.[76]

Although this document has been lost, the surviving evidence indicates that it was not a viable alternative to the draft Liebknecht endorsed. Auer recalled that Bebel's long-winded proposal ran to eighteen pages.[77] Bracke frankly told Bebel that such a detailed blueprint of the socialist future had no place in the party program.[78] Even Bebel subsequently conceded that his draft would have made a better brochure than party platform.[79] Because Bracke came up with no better proposal, he stayed away from the unity congress. Bebel, who attended, voted for Liebknecht's version.

The conclusion of this excursus into the intellectual environment that yielded the Gotha Program is unambiguous: short of having Marx write the program himself, there was

no possibility that an advanced statement of Marxist principles
could have originated in Germany. Contemporary observers
agreed that the 1875 platform reflected quite accurately the
theoretical understanding of both participants to the compromise.[80] A comment from Adolf Hepner, who certainly belonged
in the camp of Marx's supporters inside the SDAP, may serve
as a final underlining for this lengthy discussion. On 14
June 1875, Hepner wrote to Liebknecht: "Engels is certainly
put out over a few program concessions that you made to the
Lassalleans, though they are hardly too noteworthy. . . .
Without Engels I would not have even noticed them."[81]

THE GOTHA CONGRESS

When 56 Eisenachers and 73 Lassalleans crowded together into
a single beer hall at Gotha in order to ratify the merger,
tensions were bound to be high, and the whole project hung
precariously in the balance. The leadership of both parties
had worked out careful compromises on most contentious issues
in advance, hoping thereby to preserve a spirit of harmony.
Fearing the solidification of antagonistic viewpoints, they
quenched an initial idea to hold separate congresses of each
party before the joint assembly met.[82] Instead a preliminary
session elected a committee from both factions to prepare
an order of business. Three Lassalleans sat with Bebel and
Liebknecht on this body.[83] This ratio recognized the majority
of Lassallean mandates at Gotha: 15,322 ADAV to 9,121 SDAP.
     Placing the program first on the agenda, this committee
chose Liebknecht and Hasselmann to be co-referees.[84] The
proceedings started on 24 May. The morning session passed

with mainly procedural business being discussed. Liebknecht
then opened the afternoon meeting with a speech that lasted
hours. In his remarks, he explained and defended every sentence of the program draft and openly admitted the compromise
nature of the proposal. No one, he said, could expect complete satisfaction. Calling for understanding and future cooper
ation, he concluded: "The program is no stone dogma, no paper
Pope, but rather it will be altered whenever one finds it necessary."[85] Liebknecht's speech sealed the agreement.[86] Hasselmann, his co-referee, even declined to speak, saying he completely endorsed Liebknecht's review.

Still, in the ensuing discussion, the fragility of the
compromise became apparent. When Bebel questioned the wisdom
of calling all nonsocialist parties a single "reactionary
mass," Hasselmann leaped to the defense of that slogan. By
a vote of 58 to 50 the delegates defeated Bebel's proposal
to modify the phrase. In this roll call, few if any delegates
crossed their old party lines. The Lassalleans proved equally
able to keep the phrase, the "iron law of wages," in the adopted
program. In a third contest, Hasselmann successfully defended
the state-sponsored productive associations against attacks
based on Bracke's pamphlet.[87]

Despite his promise to Engels that the congress would
correct certain errors in the draft, including these three
matters, Liebknecht did not publicly support the efforts to
modify any of these points. Without his backing, given the
strength of the two factions at Gotha, the outcome of these
three votes was never in doubt.

Thus, the delegates at Gotha made few changes in the
program draft. The only major alteration adopted at the Gotha
Congress strengthened the commitment of the newly united party

to the international proletariat. In accordance with this
change, the proposed party name was changed from *Deutsche
Arbeiterpartei* to *Sozialistiche Arbeiterpartei Deutschlands*
(SAP). In another move remarkably progressive for the 1870s,
the plank endorsing a democratic suffrage was altered to include
all adult citizens, instead of adult "men."[88] All other modifications were either merely editorial or unimportant.

Faced with this *fait accompli*, the various critics of
Liebknecht's handiwork fell silent. Neither Bracke nor Bebel
wanted to cripple the new party. Besides, the optimism and
prosperous times generated by the marriage between the Lassalleans and the Eisenachers soon converted these men into
supporters of the compromise. Already in June 1875, Bracke
wrote to Engels with an encouraging report on the state of
the SAP. "Our theoretical insight," he asserted, has "already
penetrated the greater part of the Lassalleans."[89]

Bebel also quickly assumed a positive attitude toward
the organization established at Gotha. He left the long criticism that Engels had sent him in March unanswered for six
months. When he did at last respond, he admitted that the
Gotha Program had its faults, but he insisted that no further
concessions could have been won from the Lassalleans. Regarding
the new party, he expressed satisfaction, especially with
party finances. He told Engels that the whole relationship
to the Lassalleans was a "question of education."[90]

By the time Bebel wrote his memoirs, he glossed his own
brief opposition to the Gotha program. Thirty-five years
after the event, he recalled that "it was no easy task to
agree with the two old men in London. What we saw as clever
calculation, adept tactics, they saw as weakness and irresponsible complaisance; ultimately, the fact of the unification was the main point."[91]

Marx and Engels, on the other hand, never reconciled themselves to the Gotha compromise, but they did keep their criticisms private. Engels explained that the absence of other attacks on the program—presumably from the anarchists—enabled him and Marx to withhold their censure.[92] Nevertheless, he retained the opinion that the program was "in the highest degree unordered, confused, incoherent, illogical and disgraceful."[93] He was convinced that unity would not endure, and he blamed Liebknecht for ruining the workers' movement. Both Marx and Engels attributed every subsequent crisis in the SAP to the faulty foundation laid at Gotha.[94] They never again fully trusted Liebknecht.

Tiring of criticism from these friends, Liebknecht wrote to Bracke as the Gotha Congress concluded, "Yes, write to the Londoners. We have broken the principle of infallibility. By withdrawal from the party and denunciation of the same, Marx and Engels will put themselves *outside the workers' movement.*"[95] That fact may also have helped persuade the London exiles to keep their reservations to themselves.

LIEBKNECHT'S INTRAPARTY SUCCESSES AFTER THE GOTHA CONGRESS

The unity achieved at Gotha invigorated the German workers' movement. Between the 1875 and 1876 congresses, membership soared by 54 percent, from 24,443 to 37,747.[96] The total socialist vote in the next Reichstag election, held in 1877, increased 40 percent over the combined total for the two factions in 1874, with the SAP polling almost half a million votes. Party finances also improved substantially, allowing Liebknecht and the other party leaders each to have a monthly

income that usually exceeded 300 marks.[97] The circulation
of the party press also more than doubled over the SDAP and
ADAV total in the year after the merger at Gotha. By 1876,
it approached 100,000. Two years later that figure had swollen
to 150,000. By that time, the party underwrote 42 periodicals.[98]

Liebknecht's strategy of compromise obviously fostered
the growth of the German workers' movement. But did his tactics
promote his own leadership or a Lassallean victory? The answer
to that question lies in the elected party leadership and in
the party press.

The original executive committee (*Vorstand*) of the SAP
reflected the 3:2 advantage for the Lassalleans that had characterized the committee that directed the Gotha Congress. At
Gotha, Bebel himself had suggested this ratio. On the *Vorstand*,
the ADAV President, Hasenclever, was chosen as chairman. Two
other Lassalleans became vice-chairman and secretary. For the
Eisenachers, Geib claimed the treasury and Auer became the
second secretary. Neither Liebknecht nor Bebel served on this
body for the same reason that they had not been included on
the Eisenacher Executive: the party statute barred party
editors from the directorate.

To counterbalance the numerical advantages of the Lassalleans in the *Vorstand*, the first two positions on the control
commission were given to Eisenachers from Leipzig. Bebel chaired
the body and a renegade from the ADAV named Petzold was his
alternate.[99] This group had the important power to audit the
executive committee and to hear complaints about its actions.

Nevertheless, had power in the SAP remained distributed
in this fashion, one might wonder how much Liebknecht had
really won at Gotha. Fortunately, within five months after
the merger a chain of events greatly reduced Lassallean influence and correspondingly magnified that of Liebknecht's friends.

The first important shift in power came on 5 October
1875. On that day, Hasenclever announced his resignation
as party chairman. He presently edited the *Hamburg-Altonaer
Volksblatt*. Because the organization statute forbade him
to do that and to serve on the executive, he had to choose.
Because the *Volksblatt* enjoyed prestige and one of the largest
circulations in the party, Hasenclever decided to become a
full-time editor.

Under Bebel's guidance, the control commission selected
Hasenclever's successor. It appointed a lesser-known Lassallean in Hamburg, Heinrich Brasch.[100] Because Brasch was a
relative unknown, he exerted far less influence than Hasenclever.
Consequently, the Lassallean presence in the executive committee was diminished. In letters to Engels, Liebknecht crowed,
"Hasenclever has resigned and the whole *Vorstand* is honorable
[Eisenacher]." Any further Lassallean moves, Liebknecht said,
would be merely a "spasmodic quiver after the head has been
cut off."[101]

During 1877, police harassment crippled the operation
of the executive committee. As a body relatively immune from
prosecution, the Reichstag *Fraktion* of the SAP sidled into
the leadership role. From the 1874 election it inherited
a composition of six Eisenachers and only three Lassalleans.
The SAP won twelve mandates in 1877, of which former Eisenachers held eight.[102] Inside the SAP *Fraktion*, the leadership of Liebknecht and Bebel was unchallenged. Here then
was another front on which Liebknecht and his faction enjoyed
a victory.

Paralleling this significant shift in the structure of
the elected leadership came a reorganization of the party's
press that completed the Eisenacher triumph. Even before the

merger, Liebknecht had held *Der Neue Sozialdemokrat* to be
the most potent proselytizer for Lassalleanism.[103] Now that
he had brought that sheet into his house, he began a surrep-
titious campaign to smother it.

Both the Eisenachers and the Lassalleans had long recognized the great importance of the party press. It was expected
to educate party members, to be a clearinghouse of information,
and to cement the various geographical regions together. Furthermore, it earned money for the party and gave paying jobs to its
agitators. But to pursue these various tasks, the Lassalleans
and the Eisenachers had devised press structures that were
diametrically opposite. In the ADAV from 1867 to 1871, the
party president had controlled the only party journal as his
private property. After Schweitzer's resignation, Hasenclever
retained this prerogative of owning *Der Neue Sozialdemokrat*.
The Lassalleans, as part of their devotion to centralization,
established only this single party mouthpiece. Liebknecht
and the Eisenachers, by contrast, always had strictly separated
editorial and administrative positions in their party. They
also encouraged the establishment of numerous autonomous local
socialist sheets. Although Liebknecht edited the SDAP central
organ, he consistently favored the creation of provincial
newspapers, for these papers could do the work of a "dozen
flesh and blood agitators."[104]

At Gotha, the Eisenacher press arrangements prevailed.
Editors were barred from the executive committee, and all
thirteen Eisenacher sheets were retained. Liebknecht believed
this outcome constituted a monumental victory. He thought
that *Der Neue Sozialdemokrat* soon would cease to be a danger,
because it was no longer the sole source of information for
former members of the ADAV.

Before the Gotha Congress, Liebknecht hoped that both
Der Neue Sozialdemokrat and his own paper, *Der Volksstaat*,
would be reduced to local newspapers for Berlin and Leipzig.
He preferred a new and unsullied central organ to be founded
in Hamburg. Unfortunately, Hasenclever and Hasselmann insisted
upon Berlin. Because no agreement could be reached, Liebknecht
endorsed a plan to retain both the ADAV and the SDAP papers
as dual central organs.[105] Liebknecht's compromise probably
saved *Der Volksstaat*, for the Gotha debate indicates that
most delegates favored Berlin, home of *Der Neue Sozialdemokrat*,
as the site for the central organ.

After this shaky start, Liebknecht assumed the offensive
against *Der Neue Sozialdemokrat*. In November 1875, he arranged
the founding of a second party newspaper in Berlin. Only
Eisenachers staffed the enterprise. Liebknecht confided the
purpose of this venture to Engels: "gradually to make *Der
Neue Sozialdemokrat* superfluous, so that *Der Volksstaat* will
become the only central organ."[106] The Prussian police helped
Liebknecht's campaign along in March 1876. At that time they
applied the 1874 prohibition of the ADAV to the SAP throughout
all Prussian territory. In a desperate attempt to save itself,
on 2 April, *Der Neue Sozialdemokrat* dropped its subtitle that
defined it as an official organ of the SAP. In the ongoing
discussion about creating a single central organ, the opponents
of Berlin now had a compelling argument. They used it successfully at the second SAP congress, again held at Gotha in August
1876.

At that meeting, Wilhelm Hasselmann, editor of *Der Neue
Sozialdemokrat*, rallied the partisans of Berlin as the site
for the leading party paper. Bebel led the proponents of
Leipzig. For both sides, government repression became the
central issue. Hasselmann argued that it would be cowardice

to withdraw from Berlin under pressure from the Prussian police.
Arguing that police pressure prevented the publication of
an adequate newspaper in Berlin, Bebel said a single central
organ should appear in Leipzig. Thirty-eight delegates agreed
with Hasselmann, but forty-nine supported Bebel.[107] So Leipzig
and Liebknecht emerged triumphant. *Der Neue Sozialdemokrat*
simply ceased publication on 27 September 1876. On 1 October,
the new central organ, co-edited by Liebknecht and Wilhelm
Hasenclever, made its debut in Leipzig. It was christened
Vorwärts.

Wilhelm Bracke, who formerly had been a harsh critic
of Liebknecht's compromise at Gotha, recognized what a victory this restructuring of the party press was. After the
1876 party congress voted to destroy *Der Neue Sozialdemokrat*
and to create *Vorwärts*, he predicted that this new central
organ of the SAP would become "the organ of Misters Bebel
and Liebknecht. . . ." Combined with the realignment in the
party leadership described above, this change meant that Eisenachers henceforth would control the future of the socialist
movement in Germany. Bracke, reflecting his satisfaction
with that development, wrote to Engels, "Thereby the unity
is sealed. . . ."[108]

LIEBKNECHT AS THE ARCHITECT OF UNITY

In 1874, when the prospect of a merger with the Lassalleans
on acceptable terms first emerged, Liebknecht's initial reaction had been to rely once again on the tattered but tested
program of the International Workingman's Association. Later
he wrote to Engels, "if the International had not made such

a shameful fiasco, we would have been spared all difficulties,
for we [the SDAP and the ADAV] could have mutually accepted
the program of the International as the basis of the German
program."[109] Since that easy option was unavailable, Liebknecht had had to hammer out a new platform in the heat of
action. To him, the construction of a suitable arena for
future theoretical discussion assumed first priority. Always
a democrat, he assumed that free discussions and party elections
would insure the eventual triumph of socialist truth. So when
he won Lassallean agreement to a decentralized organizational
structure resting upon intraparty popular sovereignty, he
believed that any ideological errors in the party platform
could be corrected later. Ten years earlier, under similar
circumstances Marx himself had dived into deep ideological
compromises in founding the International. Liebknecht had
copied this tactic at Eisenach in 1869, and did so again in
1875. Later he wrote, "It was necessary to choose between
a scientific council and a socialist unity congress."[110]
Everything in his experience and personality urged him to
opt for the latter.

Liebknecht always called the Gotha compromise his "greatest service" to his party.[111] Marx's celebrated criticism
notwithstanding, the Gotha Program did incorporate much of
the most advanced socialist thought of its day. In translation, it was adopted by workers' parties in Belgium, Bohemia,
Denmark, the Netherlands, Portugal, Switzerland, and Spain.[112]
Moreover, its adoption saved German socialism from the fragmentation that paralyzed other European workers' movements. At
last the workers could forget their fratricidal war and concentrate on external enemies. As those enemies prepared a ruthless repression of German socialism, Liebknecht's work at
Gotha gave the SAP a chance for survival.

Chapter 8

Surviving Outlawry and
Repelling the Anarchists

In some ways the formative years of the Socialist Workers'
Party parallels Liebknecht's experiences during his revolutionary apprenticeship three decades earlier. Early in their
careers, both Liebknecht and the SAP clashed with the government. Thirty years after Liebknecht's adventures in the 1848
revolution, the German Empire assaulted the SAP with legislation that outlawed almost all of its activities. As
Liebknecht had done in 1849, the SAP fled underground, with
many of its important functions falling to comrades in exile.
A dozen years had passed in this way for Liebknecht in London
in the 1850s, and the same period transpired for the outlawed
SAP in the 1880s. In both cases, the ideas of scientific
socialism established a beachhead during the difficult years
of repression. When illegality ended for the SAP, the party,
like Liebknecht in the 1860s, returned to legal politics
wiser, stronger, and more determined than ever.

INCIPIENT TENDENCIES TOWARD MODERATION

Bismarck's regime did not tolerate successful political dissent. In constructing the *Kaiserreich* the chancellor had
intended to extend the privileges of Prussia's ruling elite

over all of Germany. From the hour of its birth, in arresting the entire Eisenacher leadership and in crushing the Paris Commune, his government had been at war with socialism.

Sometimes government repression backfired. Liebknecht's trial for high treason, for example, had helped the party recover its vigor after the devastation wrought by the Franco-Prussian War. Nevertheless, Bismarck did not relent. Liebknecht found himself in court repeatedly during the latter 1870s. In the summer of 1877, he served a two-month sentence for the nebulous offense of "insulting a government official." A year later he suffered a twelve-week term in jail on the same charge.[1]

Meanwhile the government broadened its vendetta against the socialist leaders to include an attack on the whole party organization. The weapon wielded was the 1854 Prussian Law of Associations, which empowered the authorities to disband any political union they chose. In 1874, the police in Prussia proscribed both the Lassallean and the Eisenacher parties. Simultaneously, Bismarck's lieutenants sought to persuade the Reichstag to take action against the red menace. By 1876, the Reichstag had rejected three separate proposals to sharpen the laws against subversion.[2] Frustrated on the legislative route, the government continued to rely on available police measures. On 30 March 1876, less than a year after the birth of the SAP, the Prussian police ordered the party to dissolve in all areas under its jurisdiction.

This repression intensified the tactical confusion in Liebknecht's party. On the one hand, it confirmed the revolutionary diagnosis of the class nature of the present government; it thereby stifled any urges toward constructive but piecemeal reform efforts. On the other hand, it encouraged

the moderate socialists who wanted the SAP to preserve the
limited freedom and influence it presently enjoyed.

For Liebknecht, as for his party, it is difficult to
sort out these two responses, for they sometimes coexisted
even in the same person. The stultifying atmosphere of German
politics certainly substantiated Liebknecht's long-standing
diagnosis that the bourgeoisie had capitulated to caesarism.
All nonsocialist parties, Liebknecht alleged, had coalesced
into a common crusade against the socialists.[3] Usually,
he saw no hope for a voluntary abdication of power by the
oppressive, privileged ruling class.[4] The unspoken but definitely implied alternative he conjured was violent revolution.

These observations notwithstanding, there is evidence
that the commitment to violent revolution in Liebknecht and
in his party was wavering somewhat in the wake of the Gotha
compromise. For the first time, the official party platform
of 1875 bound the socialists to work for their aims only
with "legal means." Conforming to this prescription, the
social democratic leaders increasingly emphasized elections
and parliamentary activity. When the government ordered
the SAP to disband in 1876, the leadership responded by converting itself into a "Central Electoral Committee," ostensibly
organized only for electioneering. A manifesto from that
committee proclaimed that only one reply could appropriately
answer the provocations from the Prussian police: double
the number of socialist votes received in 1874 at the 1877
election.[5]

Vote and talk; given its minority status, there was
little else the SAP could do. With so much of its activity
revolving around the Reichstag, Liebknecht's party inevitably
gave the impression of one that was inching toward peaceful

politics. When addressing only party members, or at party
congresses, or in his party newspaper, Liebknecht usually
reiterated his old antiparliamentary position. To these
audiences of committed comrades, he confided that participation in elections and in the Reichstag was worthwhile only
for agitational purposes.[6] But on the campaign trail or in
the Reichstag itself, he sounded a different note. Always
he distinguished between the *Scheinparlamentarismus* of the
German Empire and a theoretical "genuine parliamentarism"
in which the elected representatives of the people really
ruled. In the latter institution, he asserted, "We were
and always are prepared to cooperate if one earnestly offers
a hand for reform. . . ."[7]

Even in the imperfect German parliament, a tentative
trend toward moderation can be seen in Liebknecht's career.
In his first term in the Reichstag from 1867 to 1871, Liebknecht always had spoken briefly. After his reelection in
1874, a marked change occurred. He and his comrades in the
socialist *Fraktion* became incapable of making a short statement. They also addressed a much broader range of issues.
Sheer weight of verbiage indicates a growing involvement
for the SAP in parliamentary activity.

The purpose of this participation remained agitational,
but not always in a negative sense. Liebknecht continued
to denounce government proposals with arguments based on
the very nature of the Reich. For example, in 1875 in a
speech to the Reichstag he coined the uncompromising slogan,
"Not one cent for the present system. . . !"[8] About the
same time, he and the other party leaders saw the need to
make positive counterproposals to the existing order. Accordingly, in 1876, the socialist *Fraktion* introduced a bill to

establish independent relief funds for workers who were sick
or unemployed. The following year the SAP submitted a proposal
for a comprehensive labor regulation law, which called for
changes such as a ten-hour workday, a mandatory Sunday holiday, improved factory inspection, and the like.[9] Originating
in the practical demands of the Gotha Program, these ideas
were hardly revolutionary, even in 1877. Yet the party was
very proud of them. Liebknecht's newspaper, *Vorwärts*, displayed them as main agitational attractions in 1876 and 1877.[10]

In sitting in a parliament at all, the SAP was trekking
through a virgin tactical territory. With the exception of a
few short-lived assemblies in 1848-49, revolutionary socialists
had entered elected legislative assemblies only within the
last decade. Liebknecht's party made the first attempt ever
by friends of Marx to cope with the electoral and legislative
process in a bourgeois society. No precedents could be consulted. So the SAP carved out its theory in public practice.
Self-contradiction was inevitable, and the government's campaign
of repression only exacerbated the party's uncertainty.

In addition to government repression and the novel opportunity to work in the Reichstag, other reasons contributed
to a creeping moderation in the stance of Liebknecht's party
after the Gotha compromise. The Lassallean contingent brought
with it a more positive attitude toward the existing state and
its capacity for reform than had characterized the Eisenacher
party. Besides, with less than 10 percent of the voters
choosing socialist candidates in 1877, the party leaders knew
that any resort to violence would have been premature. In its
current situation, the SAP enjoyed full coffers, a complement
of forty-two periodicals and an electoral backing of a half-
million votes; no socialist leader wanted to squander these
carefully accumulated assets.

Liebknecht worked diligently and patiently to beef up
the percentage of Germans who endorsed socialism. After
the inspirational triumph of his 1872 trial for high treason,
he tried on several occasions to rekindle a national sympathy
for socialism with noneconomic issues. In 1876, he published
his pamphlet circumstantially proving that Bismarck had falsified the Ems Dispatch.[11] About the same time, he conducted
a campaign of editorials and speeches denouncing government
tampering with the mail.[12] In a third attempt to incite a
public beyond socialist circles, he composed some shaky lectures on German foreign policy concerning the festering eastern
question.[13]

These efforts, none too successful in themselves, are
nevertheless significant indicators of a tentative, new direction in Liebknecht's politics. He, like his party, strived
to attract a broader segment of German public opinion. In
tugging his convictions in that direction, he inevitably
loosened their roots in the soil of militant socialism.

Liebknecht's rising personal status may also have eroded
any lingering readiness he had for violent revolution. In
international socialism, Liebknecht was by far the best-
known representative of his party. Until the early 1880s,
he retained a virtual monopoly on personal contact with Marx
and Engels, and his comrades agreed that he was the intellectual leader of the SAP.[14] As his principal power base, he
continued, along with Hasenclever, to edit the party's central
organ. Almost 12,000 individuals subscribed to *Vorwärts*,
and many more read the paper. He was also the best and most
prolific pamphleteer in the party. His services as a public
speaker were in constant demand, causing him to spend far
more time away from Leipzig than at home. Independent of

elected party office, Liebknecht was a *Volkstribun*.

In the SAP *Reichstagsfraktion*, he and Bebel dominated the private party meetings. The *Fraktion* had no firm organization because a group of ten delegates could cooperate informally, and theoretically all deputies were equal. In practice, however, the younger party representatives deferred to their more experienced elders.[15] Thus, Bebel and Liebknecht made the most frequent and the longest speeches on behalf of their party, and their speeches received correspondingly extensive coverage in *Vorwärts*.

As his party life prospered, so his private life also assumed a new stability. By the mid-1870s he had lived in Leipzig for a decade, and enjoyed the companionship of numerous friends. In 1877, he was elected to the Saxon State legislature. A legal technicality about residency requirements disbarred him at that time, but two years later he was reelected and assumed his seat.

Financially, Liebknecht at last became prosperous. Having survived on starvation budgets since his return to Germany, in the mid-1870s he began to reap some rewards from the success of his party. From his editorship of *Vorwärts* and of a weekly supplement called *Die Neue Welt*, he earned between 250 and 400 marks per month. The party paid him an additional 80 to 100 marks per month as a stipend for his services in the Reichstag. (The German government did not compensate deputies until after Liebknecht's death.) Thus Liebknecht's income had soared to about six times that of the average worker he represented. In future years it would become larger still. Moreover, as a Reichstag deputy, he enjoyed free railroad travel throughout the country, and the party underwrote his other travel expenses, including trips to London in 1878 and 1880.[16]

Liebknecht's home life necessarily suffered under the demands of public agitation and occasional imprisonments. His prolonged absences and preoccupation with politics sometimes exasperated his wife. In August of 1877, she complained to Engels that her husband had just left jail two weeks earlier, had gone to Darmstadt the day before for another trial and faced still another court appearance two weeks hence. "It is obvious that with this restless, agitated life of my husband, our family life cannot prosper."[17] Still, despite these personal disappointments, she loved and respected her husband, and shared his commitment to social democracy. For his part, Liebknecht's affection for his wife radiates from the numerous letters that he wrote to her and the children. On this firm foundation, their marriage endured the heavy strains that came with Liebknecht's career. Despite the celebration of Liebknecht's forty-third and Natalie's thirty-third birthday in the year of their marriage, they subsequently added five sons to the two daughters Liebknecht had from his first marriage. The second, and eventually most famous of these sons, was born almost simultaneously with the German Empire. Liebknecht ecstatically christened him in the lengthy German fashion Karl Paul Friedrich August. Thus, Marx and Engels lent their names to this future revolutionary hero, and they were his godfathers.[18] Meanwhile, Liebknecht's oldest daughter, Alice, married the rising socialist leader Bruno Geiser. In 1878, Liebknecht became a grandfather.

Liebknecht cherished all of his children. There was nothing of the stern and distant disciplinarian in him. On the contrary, whenever he could steal time to be alone with his family, he was a warm and supportive parent, showing the same patient attitude he had exhibited as a teacher in

Zurich thirty years earlier.[19] A devoted, if somewhat harried, paterfamilias, Liebknecht was determined to provide security for his progeny.

Age, family, money, and prestige bred moderation. Between 1875 and 1878, Liebknecht had many reasons, both tactical and tangible, to postpone his revolutionary plans.

THE IMPOSITION OF THE ANTISOCIALIST LAW

Whatever delicate tendencies toward moderation had sprouted inside the SAP were soon frozen by the antisocialist law that the Reichstag passed in 1878. In that year, two attempts to assassinate the kaiser gave Bismarck the opportunity he awaited. On 11 May, a tinker from Leipzig named Max Hödel fired his pistol at Wilhelm I as the kaiser strolled along Unter den Linden. Hödel missed completely, but Bismarck took more careful aim. On that very day he telegraphed one of his state ministers, "Shouldn't we use the assassination attempt as the occasion for an immediate bill against the socialists and their press?"[20]

Hödel's act had put the SAP in a vulnerable position, for he had been a member of the party in Leipzig. *Vorwärts* insisted that the unstable Hödel had been expelled from the SAP four weeks before his crime in Berlin; it also stressed that the party condemned all "Putsch attempts, conspiracies, assassination attempts and similar mad pranks."[21] These defenses notwithstanding, the government's indictment of Hödel gleefully noted that he had "taken instruction at the Leipzig Workers' Educational Society, directed by the Reichstag Deputy Liebknecht."[22]

With such tactics, Bismarck hoped to persuade the Reichstag to ban the German socialist movement. Yet in the legislature, the National Liberals and the Progressives together comprised almost half of the membership. Neither of these parties wanted exceptional legislation against the socialists. Two National Liberal leaders, Rudolf von Bennigsen and Eduard Lasker, approached Liebknecht and his comrades in the SAP *Fraktion* with a plan to defeat Bismarck's proposal. To avoid irritating an already indignant public, the socialists were to restrain their rhetoric against the antisocialist bill. The liberal parties then would vote against it.[23]

The worried socialists agreed. Accordingly, when the Reichstag debated the law, only Liebknecht spoke for the SAP, and he made one of the shortest speeches of his career. His remarks, prepared collectively by his *Fraktion*, condemned the government's attempt to use the deed of a madman as an excuse to strike at a party that condemned murder in every form. Further participation in this debate, Liebknecht concluded, was beneath the dignity of a social democrat, and no provocation would force him to reenter the discussion.[24]

The low profile assumed by the socialists permitted the bourgeois liberal parties to vote against the law. Only fifty-seven deputies, almost all from the two conservative factions, voted for this first antisocialist law. Two hundred fifty-one voted against it.[25]

Nine days after the Reichstag rebuffed Bismarck, another assassination attempt was made on the kaiser. On Sunday, 2 June, as Wilhelm I paraded in an open carriage, a Dr. Karl Nobiling shot at him from the window of a house on Unter den Linden. Nobiling hit his mark. The badly bleeding kaiser was hustled back to his palace, where he eventually recovered.

Nobiling, after firing at the kaiser, shot himself.
Although he survived in a coma for three months, he never
was properly interrogated. *Vorwärts* speculated that Hödel's
well-publicized and spectacular attempt might have inspired
emulation by Nobiling. The SAP journal asserted defensively
that Nobiling had no connection with social democracy.
Although a resident of Leipzig, he was a National Liberal,
not a socialist.[26] Yet Bismarck and his loyal newspapers
unleashed a slanderous campaign against the socialists, blaming
them for this second assassination attempt. In this hateful
atmosphere, the chancellor ordered a dissolution of the Reichstag and new elections.

The SAP was desperate. Forsaking usual practice, the
party ran candidates only where it had some hope for a victory.[27] Consequently, the total socialist vote declined
by over 50,000. Worse, the party lost three of its twelve
mandates. At least Liebknecht and Bebel both retained their
seats.

When the new Reichstag convened, Bismarck had an assembly
ready to vote for an antisocialist law. Punished for its
rejection of the first exceptional law and for its vague
connections with Nobiling, the National Liberals had lost
29 of their 128 mandates. The Progressives had likewise
dwindled from 50 to 39. The two conservative parties, by
contrast, garnered 38 additional deputies. Henceforth, liberalism lost its already limited influence in the ruling circles
of the empire.

The antisocialist law that Bismarck now submitted for
legislative approval banned all associations that preached
socialist or communist ideals. All assemblies where such
ideas were discussed were likewise proscribed. No socialist

thoughts could be printed in Germany. The law provided for
the proclamation of a "minor state of siege" wherever local
officials deemed the public order to be threatened. In "siege"
areas, police could deport individuals, prohibit all assemblies,
and confiscate any printed matter. A special National Grievance
Commission was established to hear complaints about the enforcement of the law, but in its twelve years of operation, it over-
turned administrative actions in only 7 percent of the hundreds
of cases it heard.[28]

The law contained one important loophole. Election
campaigns and Reichstag mandates were left open to socialists.
Protection of Reichstag immunities apparently was required to
induce the deputies to pass the law. This unblocked avenue
of legal action ultimately allowed the SAP to survive without
reducing itself to a tiny, underground revolutionary conspiracy.

Recognizing the inevitability of passage for this antisocialist law, the SAP deputies in the Reichstag became defiant.
The mortally ill Wilhelm Bracke exclaimed, *Wir pfeifen auf das
Gesetz!* Somewhat more somberly, Liebknecht warned of a day of
reckoning, when the German people would demand retribution for
this "assault on its welfare, on its freedom, on its honor."[29]

The vote on the law followed party lines. On 19 October,
the beaten National Liberals joined the conservative parties
to cast 221 votes for the antisocialist law. The Catholic
Center Party, itself a victim of recent legal harassment, the
Progressives, Germany's feeble liberal conscience, and the
social democrats cast a combined 149 votes against. The law
became effective on 21 October 1878.

Although the SAP leaders had known that the antisocialist
law would pass the Reichstag, strangely they made no plans
to circumvent it. On 17 September, a full month before approval

of the law, the *Fraktion* traveled to Hamburg to confer with
the Central Electoral Committee. Chairman August Geib, now
ailing too, advocated surrender. In any event, he promised
to resign. Geib's pessimism was contagious, and the leaders
voted to dissolve the party.[30] On 21 October, *Vorwärts* printed
a statement signed by four members of the party's Central
Electoral Committee. Therein they announced their decision
to disband even before the antisocialist law went into effect,
saying that they would no longer accept official correspondence
or financial contributions. "Systematic agitation is over,"
they said. Of the once elaborate socialist organization in
Germany, only the *Fraktion*, spared by Bismarck's legislative
proposal, remained.

In late summer, Liebknecht was tried and convicted for
insulting a government official. On 29 October, one week
after the antisocialist law became effective, he entered
prison to serve his three-month sentence. Nevertheless, he
should share in any criticism of the remarkable spinelessness
of the socialist leadership in its time of crisis. Collectively, the leaders defaulted, leaving the party rudderless,
breathlessly awaiting enforcement of the law.

The first blow was almost lethal. All socialist organizations, including the growing trade unions, were disbanded.
Government officials immediately proclaimed a minor state
of siege in Berlin and expelled sixty-seven men from the
capital. Hoping to avoid proscription, the forty-two SAP
journals meekly dropped all political commentary. Their
circumspection was useless. Within days every socialist
publication was banned. When editors appealed, saying they
had given no offense to the law after 21 October, the authorities applied its provisions ex post facto. *Vorwärts*, for

example, was innocent of any offense after implementation of
the exceptional legislation, but it was still shut down. The
National Grievance Commission, in reviewing *Vorwärts'* appeal,
rejected it, saying the newspaper was "notoriously the mouthpiece of Liebknecht, who as the friend and student of Marx
first represented the communist, anti-national and atheistic
direction within the party. . . ."[31]

Considering the circumstances of 1878, the party could
not have launched a counterstrike against the state. In
addition to tangible weaknesses, it had no theory justifying
minority revolution. Indeed it had no notion of organizing
a revolution at all. In October 1879, a statement of the
SAP *Fraktion* written by Liebknecht proclaimed, "We do not
need to destroy Bismarck's system. We will let it destroy
itself. . . . State and society . . . of natural necessity
grow into socialism."[32] Such deterministic rhetoric left
the party without a militant purpose.

Perhaps the nature of the legal action also contributed
to the timidity of the socialist leadership. Although the
party had withstood police harassment for years, in 1878
the elected delegates of the people outlawed socialism. The
passivity of Liebknecht's party was probably partly rooted
in a fear of public hostility. The peaceful tactics the
SAP adopted were designed to placate the populace. Accordingly, avoidance of confrontation became a source of pride
for the social democrats. When the authorities expelled
those sixty-seven socialists from Berlin, they issued a manifesto warning "Do not allow yourselves to be provoked!"[33]
That watchword became the motto of the persecuted party.
In December, Liebknecht reported to Engels that this compliant
attitude was achieving its aim. Public opinion, which had

been so hostile to the SAP after Nobiling's attempt on Wilhelm
I, increasingly sympathized with the victims of the antisocialist law.[34]

Two other considerations explain, if not justify, the
nonresistance of the SAP leadership in 1878. On a personal
level, the dissolution of the party destroyed the livelihood
of every party chief. Decisiveness and fortitude are much
to expect from men who do not know how they will feed their
families.[35] On a theoretical level, the Gotha Program obligated the party to work for socialism only with "legal means."
The leadership needed time to decide what to do when the
Reichstag deprived the SAP of almost every legal means.

TACTICAL CONFUSION AND THE CREATION OF DER SOZIALDEMOKRAT

For a time, the SAP leaders apparently hoped to persuade
the Reichstag to repeal the antisocialist law by promising
that the social democrats posed no threat to the existing
order. In a speech that Liebknecht delivered in the Reichstag
on 17 March 1879, he denied "most emphatically" that the
SAP aspired to the "overthrow of the existing state and social
order." He asserted that the antisocialist law had driven
the social democrats "from the path of organic reform." He
called the SAP a "reform party in the strictest sense of
the word, and not a party that wants to make forceful revolution, which after all is an absurdity."[36]

Liebknecht's unqualified moderation provoked a tempest
of private and public protest from socialists. An incredulous
Bebel disavowed any foreknowledge of Liebknecht's speech.[37]
Engels could hardly believe Liebknecht's attitude.[38] A secret

party congress held in 1880 criticized Liebknecht for his
abandonment of revolution in that speech. Liebknecht tried
to explain away the impact of his words, saying he had intended
only to counsel against violence.[39] Six years later, in the
Reichstag, he tried to depict his 1879 speech as a powerful
rallying cry for fundamental social change.[40] Liebknecht
may have meant to issue such a cry, but his speech sounded
more like a call to retreat. Much as in his 1869 denunciation
of parliamentary activity, Liebknecht again had frightfully
overstated his intention.

    But Liebknecht was not alone in his panicked flight
to the right. In May 1879, when the Reichstag debated Bismarck's proposal for a protective tariff, two SAP deputies
actually spoke approvingly of the idea. Although the party
had never resolved its confusion about protectionism, the
Gotha Program explicitly condemned indirect taxes, and as
a gesture of protest against how the German government spent
its money, social democratic deputies had never voted for
a revenue bill in the Reichstag. Max Kayser and Friedrich
Fritzsche, the two socialist representatives with protec-
tionist sympathies, stalked the outer limits of permissible
socialist practice. On a more purely theoretical level,
Liebknecht's party was tugging at its revolutionary moorings.
In *Das Jahrbuch für Sozialwissenschaft und Sozialpolitik*,
an abstract journal loosely aligned with the SAP, an unsigned
article advocated minimizing talk of the final aim of socialism.
The article, widely thought to reflect official party opinion,
frankly called for blurring the distinction between social
democracy and the parties of bourgeois reform.[41]

    In November 1879, Liebknecht's action for many party
comrades symbolized the deterioration of his revolutionary

commitment. Having been reelected to the Saxon *Landtag*,
he found it necessary to swear allegiance to the king of
Saxony in order to assume his seat in the legislature. Rather
than refuse and thus bar himself from a useful public forum,
Liebknecht performed the distasteful ritual.[42]

Inevitably, the mounting evidence of reticence about
revolutionary ideals provoked charges of opportunism and
even of cowardice from some comrades. While the established
leadership tiptoed to avoid forfeiting the few prerogatives
remaining for socialist deputies, the oppressed lower echelons
had nothing left to lose. Criticism soon seeped upward from
those ranks.

The first voice to chastise the moderation of the *Fraktion*
was an exile newspaper called *Die Laterne*. It was founded in
Brussels on 15 December 1878 by Liebknecht's old friend, Carl
Hirsch,[43] a party veteran who had worked with Liebknecht on
Der Volksstaat. By early 1879, Liebknecht was contributing
lead articles, editing manuscripts submitted by others, and
funneling correspondence from comrades in Germany to *Die
Laterne*.[44]

In a signed letter printed in that journal, Liebknecht
asked party members to believe that it was a "thousand times
easier to scream revolutionary tirades far from the shooting
than to manage the battle here on the spot."[45] Now Hirsch
was Liebknecht's friend, but he was not his orderly. Although
he allowed Liebknecht to publish self-justifications such as
this one in his sheet, from the perspective of an exile he
gradually came to question the quiescent attitude of the SAP
Fraktion. In April 1879, he printed a challenge to the official leadership's incantation of the reformist liturgy, branding
it as a retreat. Specifically he blasted the SAP deputies who

endorsed Bismarck's tariff, asserting that the party chieftains required a critical and independent press to protect
them from the pitfall of opportunism.[46]

In London another exile organ, *Die Freiheit*, joined in
this criticism. The paper was edited by Johann Most, a one-
time Reichstag deputy for the SAP who had considerable
experience in the party press. Prior to the imposition of
the antisocialist law, he had helped to guide the *Berliner
Freie Presse* to a position of prominence. A stormy personality,
he had quarreled with other party leaders over editorial
policy and tactical issues before, and he had detested Liebknecht since their first meeting in 1871.[47]

Most had been in prison when the antisocialist law was
voted. Released on 16 December, he was immediately expelled
from Berlin. Traveling to Hamburg, he was advised by the
demoralized socialists there to go into exile. Settling
on London, he somehow gathered the resources for a newspaper,
which first appeared on 3 January 1879.

Until May, *Die Freiheit* restrained its criticism of the
SAP *Fraktion*, but after *Die Laterne* had broken the implicit
taboo in intraparty dissent, Most vigorously reasserted the
party's revolutionary heritage. He used quotations from
Marx, from Lassalle, and from Liebknecht's 1869 denunciation
of parliamentarism to lend authority to his arguments. By
September, *Die Freiheit* openly asserted that a "policy of
opportunism" threatened the party. "Only a revolutionary
act" could salvage Germany, *Die Freiheit* thundered.[48] Most's
deviation from the policies of the *Fraktion* escalated into
hostile confrontation. In December he ridiculed Liebknecht's
oath of allegiance to the Saxon king.[49] Early in 1880, Most
summarized his disagreement with his erstwhile comrades:

"We are convinced more than before that revolutionary ideas
must be preached sharper and sharper to the proletariat--the
group of Liebknecht and consorts holds the time proper to
declare social democracy as a reform party. . . ."[50]

Without a newspaper they could rely upon to counter
these attacks, the SAP deputies were in danger of becoming
leaders without a following. Police reports composed in
1880 asserted that, in Berlin at least, Most's influence
matched that of the established party leadership.[51] His
position was reinforced by a tacit alliance with Wilhelm
Hasselmann, the renegade Lassallean and Reichstag deputy
who had been at war with the party directors since 1877.
This powerful challenge at last shook the *Fraktion* from its
lethargy and generated the organizational resurrection of
the German workers' movement.

The harsh enforcement of the antisocialist law both
hindered and helped the SAP reorganization. On the one hand,
it ultimately drove over eighty leading socialist agitators,
editors, and even Reichstag deputies from Germany. On the
other hand, the hardships it wrought engendered efforts at
mutual support. These efforts became the skeleton of a new
party structure.

The first clandestine organization congealed as a fund-
raising enterprise to support the men deported from Berlin
and their families. Leaders in Leipzig quickly constructed
a national coordination for the project. Political functions
soon accompanied the humanitarian efforts. By early 1879,
Liebknecht, Bebel, Hasenclever, and Bruno Geiser, Liebknecht's
son-in-law, led a relief committee that served as a crystalli-
zation point for socialists throughout Germany.[52]

Elections provided a second legal opportunity to demonstrate

the vitality of the SAP. In a few by-elections early in
1879, the social democrats were unable to win new mandates,
but they did poll thousands of votes. In the summer, two
more important electoral contests occurred. A pair of SAP
mandates were thrown open to by-election by Bracke's terminal
illness and Reimer's unexpected death. The socialists were
elated when they successfully defended both seats.[53]

Yet the established party leaders still lacked a reliable
way to communicate with the party faithful. Liebknecht had
urged the establishment of a party newspaper in exile as
early as October 1878.[54] Initially, working with Hirsch, he
had hoped to tailor *Die Laterne* to that role, but the caustic
criticism carried in its spring issues changed his mind.
Along with the other members of the SAP *Fraktion*, Liebknecht
came to believe in the need for a paper directly supervised
by the deputies.

To Engels he explained the "most pressing reason" for
founding an official party organ in exile: "Most's attacks
in his *Freiheit* and those of Comrade Carl Hirsch in his *Laterne*
have shown us that persons who stand outside a certain circle
of endeavor cannot in all cases have a proper judgment of
what is necessary inside the same, yes . . . even if they
want to be completely objective." He explained that the
deputies had "absolutely no influence" on those two newspapers
and consequently could not induce their editors to follow the
tactics devised in Germany. He concluded that the party
required a paper upon which the *Fraktion* could exercise
"decisive influence."[55]

Some of the SAP leaders feared that establishing an
official organ in exile would intensify police repression.
In mid-July 1879, in Hamburg, Liebknecht met with the men who

had sponsored the dissolution of the party, and persuaded
them to endorse the foundation of a newspaper in exile.[56]
The initial money came from Karl Hochberg, a wealthy Berlin
philanthropist who had coauthored the "Three-Star Article"
in the *Jahrbuch für Sozialwissenschaft*. Despite his financial
help, he had no influence over the paper.

There was some debate about where to locate the new
sheet. Liebknecht favored London because its laws promised
freedom from harassment.[57] Zurich, which Bebel favored,[58]
had shown its vulnerability to German pressure in 1850, when
the Bundesrat expelled Liebknecht and the other German refugees.
Nevertheless, its proximity promised easier logistics. That
argument apparently vanquished Liebknecht's reservations,
for the deputies chose Zurich as the site for the party's
new prolocutor.

The *Fraktion* vested ultimate authority over the newspaper in a three-man committee comprised of Liebknecht, Bebel,
and Fritzsche. Liebknecht was the obvious choice for actual
editor, but his services were more necessary in Berlin and
Leipzig. As Bebel remarked, the party did not intend to
"transfer the center of gravity entirely abroad."[59] Thus,
Liebknecht was given paramount responsibility for the "direction" of the publication, acting as personal liaison between
the *Fraktion* and the editorial staff, the embodiment of the
deputies' determination to dominate the newspaper. Implicit in
his office were the duty to write frequent lead articles and
the power to dictate general editorial policy. Every edition
was supposed to pass his scrutiny before publication.[60]

To handle the mechanics of organizing the paper, the
Fraktion dispatched Eduard Bernstein, C. A. Schramm, and
Louis Viereck to Zurich. But the deputies sought a person

with more journalistic credentials for the job of editor.
The position was filled in a slippery selection between two
candidates.

Liebknecht favored Carl Hirsch. Marx and Engels shared
his preference. Despite some friction with *Die Laterne*,
Liebknecht believed his old friend had served the party well.
For lack of money, Hirsch's paper had folded on 26 June 1879.
He was thus available for the new venture. In mid-August,
Liebknecht was certain that his friend had been offered and
had accepted the editorship of the Zurich paper.[61]

Meanwhile, supporters of Georg von Vollmar plotted to
secure his appointment to this important post. A Bavarian
soldier who had fought in the Franco-Prussian War, Vollmar
had converted to socialism in the wake of Liebknecht's trial
for high treason. He had first approached Liebknecht about
working for the party in 1874, but he did not receive a party
job until 1877. Early that year, he assumed the editorship
of an SAP newspaper in Dresden. However, his editorial
experience was quite limited because he quickly earned a
ten-month jail term for violating the press code.[62] Despite
his near-novice status as a journalist, Bebel, Bernstein,
Schramm, and Viereck decided to back him for the editorship
of the exile newspaper.

Ideology cannot explain why Bebel and the three sub-
alterns at Zurich preferred Vollmar over Hirsch. In 1879,
both candidates were members of the radical wing of the party.
Nor could organizational experience have promoted one candidate
over the other; neither had ever been a member of the SAP
Fraktion or any other SAP leadership body. The only plausible
explanation for this preference is the one that Bernstein
gave to Hirsch: residual resentment concerning Hirsch's

criticisms in *Die Laterne*.[63] Bebel and his allies managed
to persuade Hirsch that, if he accepted the editorship, he
would have to labor under constant censorship by others.[64]
Refusing to accept this arrangement, Hirsch withdrew and
Vollmar won the appointment.

The selection of Vollmar meant little in terms of ideology,
but it did affect who controlled the party newspaper. Although
Liebknecht was official director of the journal, Bebel now
had won the influence of an individual who owed him a debt of
gratitude. The voluminous correspondence between Bebel and
Vollmar during the next two years shows that the former fully
exploited that connection.[65]

The appointment of Vollmar also contributed to the growing
estrangement between Marx and Engels, on the one hand, and the
SAP directors, on the other. With some reason, the Londoners
thought that Hirsch had been abused by the *Fraktion* because of
his hard line against reformism. Distressed by this and other
evidence of the party's drift away from revolutionary principles,
Marx and Engels refused to contribute to the new party paper.[66]
Thus, they broke a ten-year tradition of lending their writings
to Liebknecht's editorial enterprises. A year later, Liebknecht
traveled to London to try to change their minds,[67] but he did
not succeed. Not until 1882, after a nonsocialist journalist
charged that Marx and Engels had abandoned the SAP, did Engels
at last acknowledge his affiliation with that party's official
journal.[68] In the intervening three years, neither he nor Marx
wrote anything for the Zurich newspaper.

The aging and unhealthy Marx offered little guidance to
the German movement in its tactical confusion. Engels gave
advice in private correspondence, primarily with Liebknecht and
Bebel, later with Bernstein too. But in general, Liebknecht

and the SAP had to hack their way through the unmapped political
territory of outlaw status in Imperial Germany on their own.

THE WYDEN CONGRESS

Defining doctrine was inextricably connected with reasserting
organizational hierarchy. Both tasks required the expulsion
of Johann Most as a first step. There is some evidence that
Most made an offer of cooperation to Liebknecht in August 1879,
but Liebknecht rebuffed him. Thereafter Most made no pretence
to work on behalf of the party.[69] Instead he struck directly
at the roots of the *Fraktion*'s position, arguing that electoral
politics and genuine proletarian parties had nothing in common.
Especially embarrassing for Liebknecht was Most's use of his
1869 denunciation of the Reichstag to disparage participation
in elections to the national legislature.[70] Most's agitation
contributed to a 50 percent decline in the socialist vote in
the 1880 Berlin communal elections and to a 29 percent reduction in the SAP's Reichstag vote a year later.[71] Small wonder
that Bebel said Most's defeat was a "question of existence" for
the party.[72]

Under Liebknecht's guidance, the *Fraktion*'s new journal
wasted no time in counterattacking *Die Freiheit*. Christened
with the familiar name, *Der Sozialdemokrat*, its initial number
appeared almost a year after the imposition of the antisocialist
law on 28 September 1879. The editors explained that *Der
Sozialdemokrat* was not the "usual private undertaking but
rather so to speak an official central organ of the party"
and declared that one purpose for the creation of this newspaper was to "correct uncertainties and lies about German

social democracy that were circulating in the press." The
first two pages of each of the next three numbers carried
a long, comprehensive exculpation of the recent actions by
the *Fraktion*.[73] Liebknecht wrote this critically important
piece. From the outset, much of the content of *Der Sozialdemokrat* came from Liebknecht's pen, and all of it received
his editorial approval before publication.

As Most escalated his insults against the SAP deputies,
Liebknecht directed *Der Sozialdemokrat* to respond. On 6
December, *Die Freiheit* sarcastically hailed the SAP leaders
for at last establishing a newspaper. Unfortunately, Most
lamented, it was just as spineless as its creators. A week
later he exclaimed, "Whoever recognizes the necessity of
revolutionary propaganda will acknowledge *Die Freiheit* as
his organ. . . ."[74] *Der Sozialdemokrat* responded by cursing
Most's "separatist aspirations," threatening to "amputate"
him "like a gangrenous limb from the body of social democracy."[75]

The rhetorical battle raged through the spring of 1880.
Each issue of *Die Freiheit* reached approximately 500 subscribers,[76] but surely many more read that paper. *Der Sozialdemokrat*,
by contrast, smuggled 1,054 copies of its first issues into
Germany and sent another 300 abroad. By the summer of 1880
its circulation totalled 2,236, of which 1,600 went to the
fatherland.[77] Clearly the newspaper that Liebknecht supervised was winning the crucial contest for subscribers.

Buoyed by this success, the *Fraktion* moved to organize
its forces, to regularize its ad hoc arrangement and to purge
Most, Hasselmann, and their ideas from the SAP. Now expulsions were exceedingly rare in the history of Liebknecht's
party. Only seven individuals suffered such punishment in

Liebknecht's lifetime, and extraordinary indiscipline provoked each ejection.[78] Nevertheless, by 1880, the whole *Fraktion*, including the usually conciliatory Liebknecht, had decided that Most and Hasselmann had forfeited their claim to party membership, but the party had no precedents and no defined mechanism to legitimize an expulsion. With the *Fraktion* itself under attack, its members needed a broader mandate for action than their own collective consent could provide. Consequently, Liebknecht and his colleagues concluded that a congress was imperative.

To organize that gathering, Liebknecht journeyed to Zurich in May 1880.[79] However, contrary to his plans Most learned that the proposed meeting would be held in Rohrsbach, Switzerland, and he hurried to the scene. Liebknecht had not anticipated Most's presence; he wanted a congress to produce solidarity, not arguments and a possible schism. On 16 May, claiming that police informants had infiltrated the proposed assembly, *Der Sozialdemokrat* announced that the gathering would be postponed. Most then turned his trip into an agitational triumph. At a meeting in Zurich that was attended by dozens of local comrades and by the staff of *Der Sozialdemokrat*, he forced through a resolution demanding a cease-fire between the official SAP journal and his own newspaper. He then returned to London, from where he assured his readers that the Swiss socialists shared the ideas expressed in *Die Freiheit*.[8]

The shaken SAP leaders regrouped to set up another secret assembly. Liebknecht remained in Switzerland to make the local arrangements. This time he chose a castle at Wyden near Zurich as the site, but he kept the date and location confidential. Anyone wishing to attend had to write to *Der Sozialdemokrat* to receive information about the congress. These precautions may

have been designed, as *Der Sozialdemokrat* explained, to avoid
discovery by the police,[81] but as a beneficial side effect,
the secrecy excluded disciples of Hasselmann and Most. Certainly no one expected those two mavericks to accept when
Der Sozialdemokrat belatedly but ostentatiously extended
them an invitation to attend the congress.[82]

The survival of the established socialist leadership
was at stake as Liebknecht supervised the preparations for
the Wyden Congress. His mustering of forces against Hasselmann and Most did not pass uncontested. Late in May a group
of Berlin comrades sent him a protest in which they denied
the right of the *Fraktion* or *Der Sozialdemokrat* to expel any
party member. They also demanded that their declaration
be published in the party paper. Simultaneously they sent
a similar statement to Most, who gladly printed it in *Die
Freiheit*.[83]

Liebknecht temporarily suppressed the statement of the
Berlin radicals. Before publication, he extorted two pledges
from its authors: they must acknowledge *Der Sozialdemokrat*
as the only official party organ, and they must promise to
obey decisions of the party congress. Only after securing
these assurances, did Liebknecht pass the protest along to
Vollmar for publication.[84] On 8 August, *Der Sozialdemokrat*
at last printed the declaration from Berlin, along with the
important promises of loyalty and obedience.

Twelve days later, fifty-six German socialists arrived
by various circuitous routes at Wyden Castle. The elaborate
precautions to evade the police were futile; the Prussian
authorities received a detailed report on the congress shortly
after it adjourned.[85] The secrecy was more successful in
screening out supporters of Hasselmann and Most. Even so,

the official protocol printed by the party after the congress
had adjourned admitted that the debate on the fate of these
two radicals as well as the discussion of other issues "occasionally assumed a very agitated tone."[86]

Already on 27 June, *Der Sozialdemokrat* had declared
Hasselmann separated from the party. In the Reichstag, that
renegade had announced his solidarity with the tempestuous
Russian anarchists. "These words," *Der Sozialdemokrat* said,
"mean a statement of separation from the party and especially
from us." This repudiation was signed by the whole *Fraktion*
(except Hartmann, who thought the time inopportune for expulsions).[87] The Wyden Congress ratified the ejection of Hasselmann with only three opposing votes, one of which came from
a police spy.[88] Most fared just as poorly. After denunciations
by Liebknecht, Bebel, and Vollmar, only two delegates, both
from Berlin, dared to vote against this excommunication.[89]

The influence of these two radicals did not evaporate
immediately, but it did wither within a year. The acts of
a party congress, legitimized by a decade of precedence,
apparently persuaded German socialists to desert Most and
Hasselmann. *Die Freiheit* derided the Wyden Congress as an
illegitimate assembly of "literary, student and administrative
elements," but several earlier congresses had been attended
by fewer delegates. Furthermore, almost every important
national leader attended the gathering. As always, it is
difficult to guarantee that the congress mirrored membership
opinion, but this assembly did have sufficient influence to
insure that its actions would be accepted. Thus, no significant number of Germans answered Most's call for support from
those who did not want "to figure as cadavers under the
Liebknechtschaft."[90]

The ejections at Wyden are an important landmark in
Liebknecht's career. He and the other SAP leaders had successfully defended their own positions against a very serious
challenge. While protecting themselves, they had also managed
to maintain the recently won party unity. Finally, they had
routed the first serious attempt by putative anarchists to
convert the German workers' movement. As part of the aftershock, a nervous defense against anarchism continued to charac-
terize Liebknecht's agitation for the rest of his career.

Beyond the self-definition in negative terms achieved
by excommunications, the delegates at Wyden did little to
delineate new theory and tactics for their outlaw situation.
Consuming almost an entire day of the deliberations, several
speakers disparaged the conduct of the party's Reichstag
deputies when the antisocialist law was implemented. Bernstein said frankly that the leaders had "lost their heads"
and left the party "without any direction."[91] Comrades from
radical Berlin even introduced a resolution of no confidence
in the *Fraktion*, singling out Liebknecht, Kayser, Bebel,
and Hasenclever for special criticism.

The deputies designated Liebknecht to defend them at
the congress. In this role, he claimed that some comrades
misunderstood the word "revolutionary." It did not mean
only "expressions of force." (What else it might mean, Liebknecht did not say.) Objectively, he asserted the party had
no chance to overthrow the government; a *Putsch* would mean
suicide for the SAP. Under these circumstances, all the
party could do was to maintain its class character and uphold
its principles. That, he said, had been achieved.[92] When a
Berlin delegate pursued his criticism of the *Fraktion*, Liebknecht bluntly charged that the delegate did not represent

the opinion of the Berlin membership.[93] After Liebknecht's
remarks, a vote of confidence in the *Fraktion* was substituted
for the Berliners' motion of censure. It passed unanimously.[94]

After having glossed the matter of tactics, the delegates
turned to theory and discussed modifications to the Gotha
Program. The sketchy record of the debate does not indicate
that theoretical considerations motivated the proposed changes.
On the contrary, the delegates merely wanted to adapt the
Gotha Program to the illegal status of the party. They decided,
therefore, to forego a thorough program revision. Instead,
they voted unanimously simply to delete the restriction,
"legal means," from the program's description of party tactics.[95]

The Wyden Congress then discussed the organization of
the outlaw party. Rejecting a proposal to resurrect their
1875 structure in secret, the delegates instead left local
problems to the discretion of the local comrades. On a
national level, they ratified the assumption of official
leadership by the *Fraktion*. If a deputy should lose his
mandate, he would nonetheless continue to be considered a
member of this leadership. (Apparently the deputies did not
face the 1881 Reichstag elections with confidence.) The
Fraktion would elect a five-member committee or *Vorstand* to
oversee the affairs of the party. *Der Sozialdemokrat* was
confirmed in its role as official party organ.[96] The paper
and its growing distribution network constituted the only
institutional link between the national and local organizations. The relationship between *Der Sozialdemokrat* and the
Vorstand received no clarification.

The delegates at Wyden thus ratified the emergency arrangements that Liebknecht, Bebel, and their closest comrades had

made. The executive committee continued almost identical
in personnel with the Leipzig relief committee that they
had organized early in 1879. Through his direction of *Der
Sozialdemokrat* and his membership in the *Vorstand*, Liebknecht
remained the most influential man in the party.

THE 1881 ELECTIONS

In 1881, having weathered the squalls of intraparty controversy, the SAP awaited a verdict on its viability in the
upcoming Reichstag elections. Determined to handicap the
socialists in the voting as much as possible, the authorities
escalated their harassment. In the autumn of 1880, they
hauled Liebknecht to court again. For the third time in
three years they charged him with insulting a government
official. Convicted again, his sentence was doubled from
the previous instance to six months, which he served from
November 1880 to May 1881.[97]

Hardly had Liebknecht returned to family and friends in
Leipzig when the police struck again. For some time the
authorities had eyed the burgeoning activities of the SAP
leadership in Leipzig. To scatter this group, they issued
an edict on 29 June. Liebknecht, Bebel, Hasenclever, and
twenty-eight other social democrats were ordered to leave
Leipzig immediately.[98] Liebknecht and Bebel found asylum
in the small town of Borsdorf just outside the Leipzig jurisdiction. For the next three years, the two friends shared
a house there. They left their families behind.

Along with the other exiles, they issued a manifesto
denouncing the injustice of their deportation. To preserve

the organization, they directed party members in the future
to send their money and correspondence to Julie Bebel, Natalie
Liebknecht, or Clara Hasenclever.[99] On the frequent occasions
when the women went to Borsdorf to visit, they carried the
party's business with them.

The timing of this expulsion was well calculated. The
Reichstag elections were scheduled for October. During two
of the four previous Reichstag campaigns, Liebknecht and
Bebel had been in jail. The 1878 election, conducted in
the midst of the assassination attempt turmoil, again crippled
the socialists. Only once, in 1877, had the socialist leaders
conducted a relatively unmolested campaign. Their success in
that election taught Bismarck to avoid similar laxity in the
future.

More difficult conditions for electioneering than those
that faced the SAP in 1881 are hard to imagine. Government
repression had driven dozens of the party's agitators into
exile. Not only radicals, like Most and Hasselmann, but
also veteran moderates and founders of the party, like Vahlteich and Fritzsche, had fled to the freer atmosphere of
America. Potential voters had joined the flight of leaders.
Almost half a million disgruntled Germans abandoned the fatherland between 1879 and 1881.[100] Among those who remained,
Most advocated abstention from the "comedy" of the "election
swindle" and thereby further reduced the socialist tally.[101]

Against such obstacles, the SAP mustered less than three-
fourths as many votes as it had collected three years earlier.
Fortunately, success in garnering mandates dispelled some
of the gloom in the party. Social democrats won thirteen
seats in 1881, all in runoff contests. Two of these, from
Offenbach and Mainz, were both won by Liebknecht. Because

Liebknecht had lost in his old Stollberg-Schneeburg district, he had to choose between these two new conquests. Recalling that Natalie's father had represented Offenbach at the Frankfurt Parliament, Liebknecht chose that district.[102] Bebel, who had been defeated in Berlin, tried to claim the Mainz mandate in the by-election. He was unsuccessful, thus suffering the first interruption in his parliamentary career since it began in 1867.

Bebel's defeat symbolizes the nadir of the fortunes of the SAP. Membership, finances, voting strength, organizational structure, all had wasted to fragile skeletons. After 1881, the party began a remarkably speedy and irreversible recovery. Bismarck had delivered his most vicious blow, and the kernel for future growth had survived.

By contrast, Liebknecht stood at the peak of his career in December 1881. He directed the party newspaper, sat on the executive committee, and with Bebel absent, dominated the *Fraktion*. During the next five years he would have to use all his skill in all these offices helping to hold his party together.

Chapter 9
Avoiding Schism

IDEOLOGY AND ORGANIZATION

Ideology and organization are indivisible. Beliefs not only
affect such organizational matters as how a party reaches
decisions, but the way a party reaches decisions also influences
the meaning of its programmatic statements. For Liebknecht's
SAP, the term social democracy encapsuled its goals and its
structural procedures; and most nineteenth-century radicals
acknowledged the interdependence between socialism, representative government, and civil liberties. Like Marx, Liebknecht
and his comrades believed socialism to be the fulfillment of
bourgeois democracy.

Accordingly, German social democrats preached democracy
for society, and they practiced it in their own party business.
At Gotha in 1875, the Eisenacher prescription for intraparty
popular sovereignty vanquished the authoritarian tradition
of Lassalle. The annual SAP congress, with its unlimited
freedom of discussion and decision and with its right to
elect the party directors, implemented the sovereignty of the
membership.

Even before the onset of the antisocialist law, the
formal organization statute of the SAP depicted something
less than the real decision-making process of that party.

Congresses met only once a year. A multitude of matters
had to be handled in the interim. Consequently, the leadership sometimes committed the party and consulted the members
only afterward. To complicate the story of SAP decision-making
further, divisions within the leadership were common, and they
were seldom resolved by appeals to a formal organization chart.
The party leaders wanted to stand united before their external
enemies. Among themselves, therefore, they discussed, negotiated, cajoled, and threatened. Seldom was consensus achieved
by dictating along prescribed lines of authority.

The imposition of the antisocialist law heightened this
amorphous character of the SAP's decision-making process.
During the twelve years of outlawry, only three full party
congresses convened. The one legal socialist body in Germany,
the *Reichstagsfraktion*, picked up the dangling reins of party
leadership. Although this body was elected democratically
at least every three years, it was the choice of unaffiliated
German voters, not just party comrades. Conflicts between
these deputies, who had to please a broad spectrum of voters,
and their party constituents, who were convinced socialists,
were inescapable.

The ensuing arguments were all the more dangerous because,
during the 1880s, the party lacked a formal organization
statute that specified how to settle disputes. Communication
was a problem too. To insure that their decisions reached
their comrades, the deputies founded *Der Sozialdemokrat*. Significantly, they devised no open mechanism to learn the attitudes of the SAP members. Instead, they relied upon individual
and informal discussions with locally influential *Vertrauens-
männer*. Dissatisfied with this arrangement, some comrades
wanted to convert the party newspaper into an open forum for

discussion, to invert its original function, and to make
it an instrument for membership guidance to the party chiefs.
Duels between the deputies and *Der Sozialdemokrat* about this
intention produced a patchwork of ad hoc arrangements, congress
resolutions and tediously negotiated declarations.

Interwoven with the organizational debate surrounding
the newspaper was an escalating argument about the revolutionary purpose of the SAP. The cleavage on this issue corresponded
to the organizational fracture, with the *Fraktion* gravitating
toward moderation and *Der Sozialdemokrat* mouthing an increasingly strident radicalism. From 1880 to 1885, these two themes
of organizational and ideological dissonance joined in a fugue
of increasing intensity. Most fundamentally, both contentious
issues concerned the persistent question of how to accommodate
revolutionary socialist ideals to daily, nonviolent political
action.

As a member of the *Fraktionsvorstand* and as overseer
of *Der Sozialdemokrat*, Liebknecht stood at the center of
the organizational strife. His convictions and his predilection for intraparty compromise led him toward the middle
ground in the doctrinal debate too. As passions waxed and
tempers flared all around him, Liebknecht balanced precariously
between the two diverging camps. Always he sought to placate
personal hostilities, to deflate the importance of ideological
disagreements, and to compromise organizational controversies.
His peacemaking posture left him looking uncertain, vacillating,
and sometimes even mealymouthed, but his labor prevented a
schism in his party.

PEACEFUL REFORM OR VIOLENT REVOLUTION, REVISITED

The organizational and ideological brawls that rocked the
SAP in the first half of the 1880s were repetitive. Issues
simply refused to be resolved. Exploding disagreement would
drive the party apart until some half-measure contained the
quarrel. Tensions temporarily would relax, but then some
new provocation would divide the party members further apart
than before. In each of these cycles, which concerned the
most basic principles of the party, *Der Sozialdemokrat* supported radicalism. In that corner, it at least gave the
appearance of having most party members behind it. In the
other corner, the majority in the *Fraktion* fought for moderation.

In this chronic quarrel *Der Sozialdemokrat* stood for:
(1) free speech, which also meant freedom from *Fraktion* control for the editors in Zurich; (2) defiant resistance to
the antisocialist law, including risking nonviolent provocations that might intensify repression; (3) maintenance of
an absolutely uncompromising attitude toward all the legislative proposals of Bismarck's government; and (4) belief
in the imminence of a successful communist revolution, probably
within a decade.

The moderate majority in the *Fraktion* advocated: (1)
discipline and democratic centralism, which would allow the
deputies to censor *Der Sozialdemokrat*; (2) compliance with
the antisocialist law in the hope that the exceptional legislation against the socialists might be repealed or at least
relaxed; (3) limited cooperation with the government on laws
that promised to benefit the working class; and (4) recognition that a successful socialist revolution was far off.

The moderate position congealed as a response to novel and challenging developments in the Reichstag. On 17 November 1881, Kaiser Wilhelm I opened the legislative session with a call for a program to care for German workers during illness, accident, and old age. With this fanfare, Bismarck's ministry launched a system of social welfare that was unrivaled anywhere during the nineteenth century. Liebknecht, incidentally, had foreseen this development. Three years earlier he had predicted to Engels, "In all probability Bismarck will undertake *Lassallean experiments* and try to create a 'national' socialist party."[1]

The government accompanied its legislative proposals with an announcement that the antisocialist law would be less rigorously enforced. This so-called mild practice of repression was meant to encourage moderate socialists to renounce revolution. For example, the authorities now tolerated "colorless" newspapers edited by known socialists, so long as the content was not subversive.[2] When several SAP deputies took this opportunity to establish and edit basically nonsocialist sheets, the government already had scored a victory.

Liebknecht's party was ill-equipped to resist these conciliatory gestures from the state. Liebknecht personally had always insisted that democratization was a precondition for genuine social reform, but not all of his comrades shared his viewpoint. In the mid-1880s, many socialists thought that socialism meant merely the opposite of Manchester liberalism. They only wanted paternalism to replace the night watchman.[3]

As Bismarck enticed the SAP from the right, the social democratic deputies experienced an equally strong stimulus

repelling them from the left. Anarchism was stalking through
Europe, and the German socialists anxiously dissociated themselves from the indiscriminate violence of the bomb throwers.
While disavowing the anarchists, the SAP announced that it
wanted the "organization of labor by the state, the concentration of all economic might in the hands of the state, the
most extreme development of the power of the state, against
which the anarchists want the *abolition* of the *state*."[4]

Liebknecht's own public comments on social reform and
the state vacillated between the moderate and radical positions. The resulting impression is self-contradictory. The
events of 1878 had taught Liebknecht that socialists could
be punished for the violent acts of nonsocialists, so in
the wake of the assassination of Czar Alexander II, Liebknecht
nervously emphasized that revolution did not necessarily
imply violence. To distinguish himself further from the
anarchists, he stressed that socialism required organization.
Although he charged that the "police-bureaucratic element"
removed Bismarck's social welfare program "*himmelweit* from
genuine democratic socialism," Liebknecht never attacked
the state per se. On the contrary, he even proclaimed "We
are state socialists. Whether one calls [the future social
organization] a state or not is in any case a matter of indifference to me--I do not fight over words."[5]

On the other hand, and in the same speeches in which
these pronouncements appeared, Liebknecht sounded a more
strident note. In a warning against Bismarck's half measures,
he reminded his listeners that the "solution of the social
question is only possible through *the action of the working
class itself*."[6] Commenting briefly on what caused social
misery, he traced its origins to an "incongruity between

production and consumption and in our present system of wage
labor. From these causes, springs the unequal distribution
of wealth, mass poverty on one hand, and great wealth in a
few hands on the other. Whoever takes social reform earnestly
in hand must apply the lever here, must eliminate this incongruity between production and consumption, and the exploitation of the worker by capital. *That is social reform*," he
exclaimed, "and, if completely applied, also *social revolution*. What the Herr Reichschancellor presents as social
reform has absolutely nothing to do with genuine social
reform."[7]

AUTONOMY FOR LIEBKNECHT'S NEWSPAPER

In trying to orient itself on Bismarck's latest challenge,
the social welfare state, the SAP *Fraktion* inevitably experienced strains on its internal unity. The structures of
human interaction, political or otherwise, have a powerful
sort of inertia. To alter routines, to pose new tasks, is
to risk tearing off part of the old group and leaving the
rest behind. Bebel, the SAP's instrumental or task-oriented
leader, tried to define a radical response to Bismarck's
ploy. Most members of the *Fraktion* resisted. Thus a heavy
burden fell upon Liebknecht, the affective leader who traditionally had worked hardest to hold the party together. Persistently, he tried to assuage those who were outmaneuvered
or outvoted, hoping thereby to maintain the facade of unity,
but in 1885, Bebel was outvoted. When he threatened to go
his own way, Liebknecht could only desperately try to conceal
the conflict and to counsel socialist solidarity. The emerging

inability of the two *alte Kämpfer* to work together left the SAP extremely vulnerable to schism.

That dangerous condition developed slowly but inexorably. The first collision between the *Fraktion* and *Der Sozialdemokrat* occurred in 1880, at a time when Bebel and Liebknecht were not yet estranged. Georg von Vollmar, the editor in 1880, published a call for a clandestine, conspiratorial organization in Germany. Generally he disparaged the prospects for peaceful reform. The *Fraktion* leaders, all still timid toward the German government, were indignant at Vollmar's irresponsible provocation. One of their number, Ignaz Auer, a wan and sickly man who already had endured a dozen hard years' experience in Liebknecht's political faction, wrote an explicit denial of Vollmar's position and directed *Der Sozialdemokrat* to publish it immediately. Vollmar dared to criticize Auer by name in subsequent issues, and he soon was removed from his position as editor.[8]

In 1880, all members of the *Fraktion* agreed that *Der Sozialdemokrat* had no right to challenge the SAP deputies. The newspaper had been founded specifically to protect the deputies from abuse in other exile journals. Even Bebel, who had jockeyed Vollmar into office, adamantly defended the *Fraktion*'s power to censor the newspaper. In a letter to the Zurich staff, he said that "every official document must be submitted to us [the *Fraktion*] and be published only if and as we determine. Without such a procedure, conflicts are inevitable. . . ."[9] Because Vollmar refused to accept the *Fraktion*'s overlordship, and because no one in the *Fraktion* endorsed his independence, he had no choice but to resign. He did so at the end of 1880, after only one year in office.

Choosing his replacement was not easy. Liebknecht, along with Marx and Engels, still favored Carl Hirsch. But as it turned out, the obstreperous Hirsch refused to accept the job unless *Der Sozialdemokrat* moved to London. Bebel and Liebknecht decided to treat that demand as a refusal of the editorship.

Lacking another man with sufficient journalistic competence to become editor-in-chief, the *Fraktion* decided that Liebknecht would have to assume the "chief direction of the paper" and "write lead articles and the political overview." Karl Kautsky, an Austrian socialist then residing in Zurich, would handle the correspondence and the "technicalities" of printing.[10] Kautsky was a balding, bearded, and bespectacled twenty-seven-year-old who had had only minimal contact with the German socialist movement. Acutely aware of his novice status, he declined even this modest position.[11]

Liebknecht, imprisoned from November 1880 to May 1881, could not go to Zurich to become editor-in-chief, so Eduard Bernstein, previously an assistant to Vollmar, became managing editor of *Der Sozialdemokrat* by default. Five years older than Kautsky, Bernstein had a decade of experience in the socialist movement in Berlin. In 1879, he had come to Zurich as a personal secretary for the philanthropic Karl Hochberg. His management of *Der Sozialdemokrat* began with the second issue in January 1881, but as late as July of that year, members of the *Fraktion* still treated his appointment as temporary.[1]

Liebknecht's relationship with Bernstein and the newspaper began as a close and cooperative one. Later, Bernstein recalled that Liebknecht had been his *gleichberechtigt* coeditor.[1] In 1881 and 1882, *Der Sozialdemokrat* printed twenty-two major articles signed with one of Liebknecht's pseudonyms. (He

called himself selim, backward for *miles*, which is Latin
for soldier, or he signed his pieces "ml.")[14] He wrote many
other prominent essays that were unsigned. Furthermore,
in August 1881, after his expulsion from Leipzig, Liebknecht
went to Zurich and took over actual editorship of the newspaper for a month and a half.[15] Presumably he was imparting
some of his experience to the younger staff. Subsequently,
Liebknecht traveled often to Zurich to regulate editorial
matters, maintaining a regular correspondence with Bernstein
and with others on the staff. He retained the right, which
he occasionally exercised, to censor material proposed for
publication.

Gradually, however, Liebknecht's position became awkward.
He had one foot firmly planted in Zurich and the other in
Berlin in the *Fraktion*. When these two cities declared war,
Liebknecht had to be a skillful diplomat to avoid becoming
a casualty. The battle began when Bernstein emulated Vollmar,
challenging the moderates in the *Fraktion*, but Bernstein's
challenge was far more serious, for Bebel and Engels lent
him their support.

Sometime between the autumn of 1880 and that of 1881,
Bebel revised his opinion about the right of the *Fraktion*
to dictate to *Der Sozialdemokrat*. Having been defeated in
his bid for reelection to the Reichstag not once but twice
in 1881, he may have questioned the legitimacy of voting
by the whole public as a path to power in a revolutionary
party. Probably his relationship with Engels, which prospered
after their personal meeting in December 1880, also contributed
to his about-face. Engels certainly used his letters to
encourage Bebel to break with the "bourgeois elements" in the
party, and he encouraged him to use *Der Sozialdemokrat* as his

weapon in the struggle. In the event of a rupture, Engels
promised that he and Marx would back the "left wing of the
party."[16] Under Engels' tutelage, Bebel came to believe
that many members of the SAP *Fraktion* suffered from "battle
fatigue" and had forgotten the class nature of society.[17]

Meanwhile Bernstein devised a strategy whereby the radical
posse could use *Der Sozialdemokrat* to arrest the drift toward
moderation of most of the SAP deputies. Alone, the newspaper
had neither a mandate nor power. To succeed, Bernstein needed
to demonstrate that what *Der Sozialdemokrat* said in criticism
of the *Fraktion* sprang not from the editorial staff but rather
from the party membership. It was necessary to convert a
lopsided bout between *Fraktion* and newspaper (the outcome
of which Vollmar's fate foretold) into a more promising clash
between the membership and the leaders. To achieve that
transformation, Bernstein and Engels planned to attack the
Fraktion with a campaign of letters from German comrades,
printed in *Der Sozialdemokrat*.[18]

This scheme had a good chance of success because some
deputies in the twelve-member *Fraktion* would side with Bernstein. Vollmar, who had been elected to the Reichstag in
1881 after resigning from *Der Sozialdemokrat*, surely would;
so would Bebel, who retained his voice in the leadership
despite his electoral defeat. Bernstein also calculated
that Liebknecht would back him on the issue of free expression
for party members.[19]

The excuse for a showdown was offered by two SAP deputies
on 10 December 1881. During a parliamentary debate on the
enforcement of the antisocialist law, government officials
quoted the most revolutionary statements from *Der Sozialdemokrat* to establish the need for ruthless repression of subver-

sives. Embarrassed by the militant tone of their newspaper, Hasenclever and Blos denied responsibility for the remarks in it.[20] *Der Sozialdemokrat* responded with an energetic defense of its position as official party newspaper. In an article menacingly entitled "Either-Or," Bernstein blasted Blos and Hasenclever by name. Correctly, he charged that a disavowal of the newspaper violated the decisions of the Wyden Congress. The next issue of the central organ printed a contrite "letter from Berlin," assuring the readers that the official nature of *Der Sozialdemokrat* would be reasserted publicly in the Reichstag at the first opportunity.[21]

A month elapsed while Bernstein considered his next move. On 19 January 1882, his plan began to unfold. Cleverly giving his critics the first word, he printed a bitter complaint from Blos and a separate statement from one of his sympathizers in Hamburg. These comments provided the pretext for publication of letters condemning Blos and Hasenclever. Several of the ensuing correspondents broadened the issue into an assault on parliamentary activity in general. *Der Sozialdemokrat* shrewdly entitled the column carrying these letters, "How the Party Members Judge."[22]

As overseer of *Der Sozialdemokrat*, Liebknecht played a pivotal role in the resolution of this assault on the authority of the *Fraktion*. Bernstein remarked that Liebknecht, Bebel, Vollmar, and two other deputies advocated a decisive public repudiation of Blos and Hasenclever.[23] Such a stand conforms to Liebknecht's long advocacy of an independent editorial voice while he worked on *Der Volksstaat* and *Vorwärts*. In any case, Liebknecht helped to author a *Fraktion* declaration on this matter that constituted a great victory for *Der Sozialdemokrat*, and it appeared in the newspaper on 16 February 1882.

The declaration began with a direct rebuff to the recent disavowals of the Zurich sheet. "*Der Sozialdemokrat* is the official organ of German social democracy," it said straightforwardly, and the newspaper had the "purpose and task of keeping the party comrades on course . . . and of defending the principles of the party." Hereby the newspaper gained a published mandate to define doctrine. Its power apparently at least equaled the *Fraktion*'s in this regard. This resolution of 16 February further directed *Der Sozialdemokrat* "to be a true mirror of the views and currents" inside the party. To that end, the editors were asked to print all membership contributions that did not violate the party's "principles and interests." Thus did the *Fraktion* legitimize Bernstein's recent tactic against itself.

A more complete victory for the newspaper would be hard to imagine. Bernstein had achieved the position that Carl Hirsch had set out for the exile press in 1879: to act as an "indicator of what the party expects [from the leaders]."[24]

THE *FRAKTION* REASSERTS ITS EDITORIAL CONTROL

The new mandate had hardly been implemented when Bernstein lashed out at another *Fraktion* moderate. The target this time was Bruno Geiser, who happened to be Liebknecht's son-in-law. Encouraged by Engels, on 13 April 1882, in an article entitled "Show Your Colors," *Der Sozialdemokrat* blasted Geiser for deserting party principles.[25]

Liebknecht's response set the pattern for his subsequent mediating efforts between the *Fraktion* and the newspaper. He simply tried to bury the polemic. When interment proved impossible, he insisted that the altercation be kept brief, factual, and limited. In Zurich, Bernstein resented what he described as Liebknecht's "mania for hushing up."[26] As a result, the spirit of cooperation between Liebknecht and the editorial staff eroded.

Back in Berlin, the moderates in the *Fraktion*, who were after all a majority, were determined to stop the incessant sniping from their own newspaper. On 19 August 1882, all twelve SAP deputies marched off to Zurich to impose a new regulation upon the editorial staff. Bebel and Auer accompanied them, even though they had both lost their mandates in the 1881 election.

At the meeting, more a trial than a peace conference, veteran chieftain Hasenclever put the matter plainly: "It is rebellion if the editorial staff says it cannot work under the direction of the *Fraktion*." Blos, another victim of the recent tirades in *Der Sozialdemokrat*, insisted that the "newspaper must subordinate itself to the *Fraktion*. . . ." One by one, the other moderates attacked the editors. Weaving the ideological and organizational issues together, they lambasted the paper for its prediction of imminent revolution, a forecast that most of the deputies found ludicrous.

Bebel, Bernstein, Vollmar, and one other unidentified deputy were the only vocal defenders of the newspaper at the Zurich meeting. Bebel extolled the press as the only channel for the party members to articulate their viewpoints. He rebuked the *Fraktion* for wanting to play dictator in the party. He even alluded to the possibility of a schism if the undemocratic manner of the moderate deputies continued. For his part, Bernstein freely accepted personal responsibility for the attacks on Blos, Hasenclever, and Geiser.

Specifically, he defended his right to print letters from
German comrades that criticized the leadership. Reasserting
the need for an autonomous party press, he self-righteously
refused to submit to "the censorship of the *Fraktion*."

Although the issue was thus clearly drawn, it is difficult to discern Liebknecht's stance from the choppy minutes
of the Zurich meeting. He conceded that *Der Sozialdemokrat*
had to serve the whole party, not just the deputies, but
his conclusion conveys only ambiguity: "The editorial staff
has the right to criticize but should not bring itself into
opposition to the party leadership."

Auer and Blos submitted a resolution that was much more
explicit. It stated: "1) The party organ is to subordinate
itself . . . to the decisions of party congresses and the
consequent instructions of party officials. In contested
cases, a court of arbitration or, where possible, a congress
will decide. 2) Before publication, articles . . . that
contain insulting attacks on party comrades must be circulated to the inner party leadership, without whose consent
they cannot be published." Bebel and Bernstein voted against
this reaffirmation of *Fraktion* prerogatives. Liebknecht
joined the majority in passing it.[27]

In spirit if not in letter, the Zurich resolution contradicted the statement published in *Der Sozialdemokrat* the
preceding 16 February. The Zurich resolution muzzled the
paper; the 16 February declaration had empowered it to criticize the leaders. At the time of their compositions, Liebknecht favored both. The only consistency in his position
is that he swam with the tide of the moment. At the Zurich
meeting in August, in the midst of a *Fraktion* incensed about
insubordination, he forsook editorial independence, thinking
that he fostered unity by siding with the majority.

LIEBKNECHT AND BEBEL TAKE DIFFERENT TACKS

Eight months later, Liebknecht had an opportunity to clarify
his position. In March 1883, the SAP convened its second
complete congress since the onset of the antisocialist law.
At that time, sixty delegates, many of whom had never played
a role in the national leadership before,[28] sneaked off to
Denmark to discuss party tactics, theory, and organization.

The Copenhagen Congress, although it debated the proper
ideological reply to state socialism at some length, was
strangely silent concerning the festering organizational
dispute between the *Fraktion* and *Der Sozialdemokrat*. The
"entire position" of both the deputies and the newspaper
was approved.[29]

Bebel confided to Engels that at Copenhagen "it came
to a rather lively discussion between both directions. . . .
But what shocked me most, is that Liebknecht, who should
have come forth sharply here, instead did everything possible
to conceal and to soften the antagonism."[30] Bernstein confirmed this account: "And as we began to discuss the antagonisms
openly Liebknecht stepped in at the most inopportune moment
and gave a lecture about unity: 'There are no antagonisms
among us, and whoever speaks of such is a traitor!'"[31] Thus,
it was Liebknecht's fault--or achievement--that the Copenhagen
Congress produced no more decisive stand on the various intraparty disagreements.

Bernstein was quite dissatisfied with the irresolution
of the Copenhagen Congress. Just a few weeks after it adjourned,
he tried once again to entice Liebknecht into his camp on the
organizational issue. He began with the proposition that the
greatest possible freedom of the press was "in the interest

of the party," especially because several of the *Fraktion*
members suffered from "Prussianization." Noting the confrontation at Copenhagen between himself and the moderate
deputies, he voiced his resentment over the lack of support
from Liebknecht. "Do you then constantly want to limit yourself to the [Zurich] agreement and not even once to attack?"
Hoping to goad Liebknecht into action, Bernstein expressed
his hope that soon he and Liebknecht would "again swim together
against the tide."[32]

Behind Bernstein's and Bebel's insistence upon editorial
independence lay the desire for doctrinal correctness. Behind
their urgent desire for doctrinal correctness lay the expectation of imminent revolution. "By [18]89 we will probably
be at the goal," Bebel predicted in 1883, "i.e., then the
great international crash will occur. . . . Ultimately, with
a skillful jerk, the whole rubbish heap will tumble down like
a house of cards."[33] In preparation for the decisive moment,
Bebel, Engels, and Bernstein conspired to purge the party
of its doubtful deputies.

At the same time, many of the SAP deputies were becoming
even more moderate. In the "colorless" newspapers left to
them by Bismarck, they inched perceptibly closer to the government's social welfare package.[34] Success in the 1884 Reichstag
election reinforced this tendency. The SAP vote total climbed
from 311,961 to 549,990. Mandates doubled to twenty-four.
These quantitative gains restored the party's confidence in
future electoral victories. With that confidence came a
greater acceptance of patient, peaceful tactics, at least
among the leaders who benefited from the elections.

However, the enlarged size of the *Fraktion* also undermined its cohesiveness. As one deputy remarked to Liebknecht,

"When we had 12 Deputies, sure there were lively debates in the *Fraktion*. With 24 the situation changes. This large number is not so easy to bring under one roof."[35] When the deputies gathered for their first meeting, Liebknecht called their operation *Fraktions-Anarchie*.[36]

By tradition, a simple vote was supposed to settle all disputes inside the *Fraktion*. Then all members supported the majority decision. Never had the *Fraktion* publicly split on a vote in the Reichstag. After all, according to the common belief of the party, there could be only one correct socialist tactic on any given issue. Great skills at negotiation and propitiation had always been needed to persuade outvoted deputies to support the majority position in silence. Deference to Liebknecht and Bebel, the cooperation and unity of those two men, and the relatively small number of people involved had allowed the *Fraktion* to avoid public disagreement in the past. In 1884, the situation changed.

Instead, an air of acrimony permeated the party's leadership. The veil of unity became embarrassingly threadbare; even the nonsocialist press speculated about the imminent fragmentation of the SAP. These reports had more foundation than their authors possibly could have known. Animosity was so great inside the *Fraktion* that some SAP leaders celebrated the electoral defeat of some of their comrades in the 1884 voting.[37] Rivalries inside the party's few legal newspapers festered, and changes of personnel required the most delicate negotiations.[38]

In December 1884, Bebel privately condemned the "policy of opportunism" pursued by most of his colleagues in the leadership. "If the majority does not come to recognize its totally false path," he vowed, "*dann fuhrt dies schliess-*

lich zum krach."[39] Bernstein and Engels had already agreed
somehow to purge the party of its opportunists. In 1884,
Karl Kautsky joined the other three radicals in a correspondence of contempt for the *Fraktion* majority. The Zurich-
based coalition, although clearly a minority among the leaders,
firmly believed that the party membership backed the radical
side. Party unity at the leadership level accordingly had
little value for these men. By the autumn of 1884, they were
spoiling for a showdown.[40]

After the 1884 election, with only the flimsiest evidence,
Bebel privately charged Hasenclever with making an electoral
deal with the conservatives. If true, Bebel's charge meant
that Hasenclever had violated an explicit resolution of the
Copenhagen Congress. Only six months earlier, the *Fraktion*
had expelled one of its members, Moritz Rittinghausen, for
refusing to submit to party discipline. In mid-November,
Hasenclever confided his fears to Auer that Bebel planned
another "expulsion à la Rittinghausen."[41]

Bebel had launched a jihad against Hasenclever. To
Liebknecht, he compared Hasenclever to Schweitzer in his
betrayal of class solidarity. ". . . I am through with H.,
and I will protest against every position of trust that he
is given. . . . I repeat, I know no restraint . . . !"[42]

Both Bebel and Hasenclever recognized that Liebknecht's
support was indispensable, so like Bebel, Hasenclever tried
to win Liebknecht's help. In private letters to Liebknecht,
he accused Bebel of "again playing party dictator," adding
his hope that a *Fraktion* caucus soon would "take him from
his high horse." To that end, he urged that the *Fraktion*
initiate some stringent disciplinary procedures, both to
manage its larger numbers and to punish those who irrespon-
sibly slandered party comrades.[43]

Hasenclever persuaded Liebknecht. On 15 November, Bebel fumed to Liebknecht that he was amazed at the rapidity with which Liebknecht changed sides, even in the "most important and fixed things." Liebknecht had criticized Bebel's "schoolmasterly" attitude. Upset by his friend's chiding, Bebel vented his frustration at years of Liebknecht's tutelage and patronage. He complained that in the past two years Liebknecht often had adopted a tone against him, "even in the presence of third persons," that "wounded him deeply." He charged that Liebknecht insultingly and hostilely rejected nine out of every ten independent proposals that he made. The resulting "enmity and irascibility," he warned, had hurt the party "because it makes calm conversation and regular operation impossible!"[44]

Two months earlier, Bebel had left Borsdorf and his shared home with Liebknecht to settle in Plauen, a suburb of Dresden. Liebknecht remained in Borsdorf for the duration of the antisocialist law. Bebel explained his move as an effort to resume a more normal life with his family.[45] Although he did not mention any conflict with Liebknecht, the strained relationship probably contributed to his decision to move.

The separation of the two most prominent SAP leaders multiplied the chances for serious division in the party. At a time when extensive discussion, close cooperation, and quick decisions were imperative, Bebel and Liebknecht had to rely upon postal communication. After living apart for a year, Bebel told Engels that he and Liebknecht disagreed "in almost every question as soon as we discussed it in letters." He found Liebknecht's "mania for hushing up" disputes intolerable.[46]

Estranged even from his oldest comrade-in-arms, Bebel
became increasingly bitter toward the moderates in the *Fraktion*. After the 1884 elections had returned those astounding
twenty-four mandates to the SAP, Bebel confided to Liebknecht
that, the more he thought about it, the more parliament appeared
to be "a good school of bemirement [*Versumpfung*]."[47] He emphasized his own isolation by saying, "With the exception of
[Paul] Singer, I trust no one in Berlin, and Singer is weak,
he believes in the honesty of people and allows himself to be
misused."[48]

THE STEAMSHIP SUBSIDY CONTROVERSY AND ITS AFTERSHOCKS

As Liebknecht piloted the *Fraktion* through these shoals of
personal conflict, Bismarck launched another of his economic
projects. In 1884-85, the Iron Chancellor indulged in colonialism. To fatten the profits from his adventures, he asked
the Reichstag to approve a subsidy for steamship lines to
various overseas locations, including Germany's colonies.
The prospect of increased employment in ship construction
enticed the SAP *Fraktion* to consider the proposal. Some
socialists even approved of colonial ventures,[49] and most
members of the *Fraktion* pretended not to see any issue of
principle at stake in the steamship subsidy. They wanted
to vote for the subsidy on two conditions: if the two colonial
lines were deleted, leaving only routes to Australia and East
Asia, and if the subsidy would finance construction of new
steamships rather than the maintenance of existing crafts.[50]
A radical minority led by Bebel denounced this viewpoint.
These intransigents interpreted the pliability of the

Fraktion majority as one more sign of the yawing engendered
by parliamentary activity.

The *Fraktion* now encountered a wrenching test of its
cohesion. Preliminary discussions proved that unanimity
on the steamship subsidy would be hard to secure. So, on
11 December 1884, the *Fraktion* issued an interim statement,
saying that the subsidy involved no issue of principle and
that the deputies would continue to weigh their stance based
on practical criteria.[51] After four more days of wrangling,
on 15 December, in a private vote, the deputies divided about
eighteen to six in favor of the subsidy (with the conditions
noted above). Another two weeks of intra-*Fraktion* debate
changed no one's mind.[52] On the contrary, opinions hardened.
The majority even began to hold separate conferences to which
the radicals were not invited.[53]

Viewing the steamship subsidy as a gift to the ruling
class, Liebknecht voted against it on both ballots in the
Fraktion. Nevertheless, as usual, he worked to reconcile
the differences between his moderate and radical comrades.[54]
Trying desperately to please everyone, early in January he
used his position on *Der Sozialdemokrat* to publish a striking
suggestion, whereby he hoped to scuttle the whole debate.
Oddly, Engels was his ally in this project.

Initially *Der Sozialdemokrat* had ignored the intra-
Fraktion quarrel over the subsidy. As late as 1 January
1885, it offered dispassionate reports that the subsidy had
a fair chance for passage in the whole Reichstag. In the
next issue, Liebknecht floated his proposal. In prefatory
remarks, he insisted that the steamship subsidy involved
no question of principle. The overriding consideration had
to be the preservation of party unity and the avoidance of

even the appearance of support for Bismarck's programs. To achieve these goals, he presented an idea from "one of our most trustworthy and competent comrades." Its author was Engels.

Unlike Bebel and Bernstein, Engels saw the steamship subsidy as a relatively unimportant issue. To help the party retain its frayed facade of unity, Engels suggested the following tack: that the SAP offer to exchange its twenty-four votes on the steamship subsidy for a five million mark appropriation to install workers' cooperatives on the royal domains in Prussia.[55] Engels surely realized that the Reichstag would never approve this deal, so there is some doubt about whether he intended his proposal to be taken seriously. He probably meant to tear away the government's mask of pretended concern for the worker and to preserve the unanimity of the SAP *Fraktion*.[56] Surely those were Liebknecht's goals in relaying the suggestion to the membership.

Bebel and Bernstein both were surprised by Engels' suggestion, and both rejected it. Bernstein told his London mentor that the subsidy constituted a "'test' case for the general political position of our party. . . . Our people must finally show their colors."[57] Far from opening an exit from the steamship subsidy controversy, Liebknecht's essay ignited a war of words that made compromise even less likely.

In challenging the moderates in the *Fraktion*, Bernstein again employed the tested tactic of letters from the membership. Suspiciously enough, the first public protest by party members against any compromise on the steamship subsidy surfaced at an assembly in Zurich. Realizing the doubts this location might provoke, Bernstein admitted to Liebknecht that he had attended that meeting, but he swore that he had not

instigated the protest. Shifting to a more offensive stance,
Bernstein told Liebknecht that he hoped the voice of the
masses would persuade the *Fraktion* to abandon its tentative
support for Bismarck's program.[58]

To encourage emulation, the editorial staff of *Der Sozialdemokrat* shipped about twenty offprints of the Zurich resolution to local leaders in Germany.[59] Inside Germany, Bebel
incited similar resolutions at various secret local meetings
of socialists.[60] Because the resulting declarations contained no personally insulting remarks and because they did
not violate party principles, Liebknecht agreed to publish
some of them in *Der Sozialdemokrat*.

The resolution of the Zurich comrades appeared on 22
January. It asked the *Fraktion* to reject the steamship bill
"for principle as well as for tactical reasons." The resolution offered four reasons for its position: (1) the subsidy fostered colonialism; (2) it contradicted the program
of the SAP by strengthening the state; (3) it served the
industrialists, not the workers; and (4) SAP approval would
indicate an endorsement of state socialism. Additional mis-
sives critical of the subsidy and the *Fraktion*, several of
which were from Germany, trickled through *Der Sozialdemokrat*
in February. Yet these few printed statements cannot establish any clear mandate from the membership.[61]

One exceptionally important contretemps occurred in
the newspaper during these weeks. On 29 January, when Auer
published a renewed defense of the subsidy, Bernstein inserted
an editorial footnote declaring that "under no circumstances
can our party endorse the steamship subsidy."[62] With Bernstein's personal intrusion into the controversy, the character
of the debate promised to revert from a dispute between leaders

and followers to a power struggle between the SAP deputies
and the party newspaper.

On 20 March, despite eleven embarrassing absences, those
SAP representatives present in the Reichstag unanimously
rejected the steamship subsidy. Because Bismarck had refused
to consider the two conditions the socialists had set for
approval of the subsidy, the whole intraparty debate had
turned out to be moot, but now the leadership had something
else to argue about: control of the party press.

In a familiar transformation, the controversy now mutated
from ideology back to organization. Early in March, the
Fraktion had elected a five-member commission, all moderates,
to propose a new regulation of *Der Sozialdemokrat*. After a
two-week investigation, on the day of voting against the subsidy, the commission reported to the remaining deputies.[63]

At this gathering, Liebknecht endorsed the moderates'
contention that the party newspaper should, at least in theory,
be subordinate to the elected party leaders. Every organization statute of his party since 1869 had incorporated this
hierarchy. Liebknecht had labored for ten years as an editor
under this restriction. Now he was amazed that anyone would
question the right of the *Fraktion* to dictate to *Der Sozialdemokrat*, especially because the latter had been created
to serve the former.[64] Liebknecht therefore even offered
a few suggestions to toughen the directive that the deputies
dispatched to Zurich. He pressed for a ban on "plebiscites
and the *appel au peuple* (à la Schweitzer)" that had been
the basis for the protests printed in the party organ. Wanting
to stifle public disagreement, he also favored the prohibition
of an editorial response to the *Fraktion* declaration.[65]

Liebknecht abstained on the actual vote on this matter.
He always did so when the *Fraktion* discussed the newspaper.
Bebel and Vollmar, the two most relentless defenders of Bernstein, did not even attend this meeting of 20 March. They
knew the conclusion was foregone. Only one unidentified
vote was cast against the new *Fraktion* directive.[66]

This ukase ordered *Der Sozialdemokrat* to submit to the
direction of the deputies. Specifically, it prohibited publication of further comments from the membership on the steamship subsidy affair. Ignaz Auer sent Bernstein an abusive
letter along with this declaration in which he ordered publication of the directive in the next issue.[67] Liebknecht
urged Bernstein to comply with these provisions, implying
that worse consequences might follow if he resisted.[68]

Bernstein ignored Liebknecht's advice and Auer's demands.
Instead, he fired off a haughty rebuke to the deputies. *Der
Sozialdemokrat* was "in no way the organ of the *Fraktion*,"
he insisted, "but rather of the party. . . ." Free expression
was an inaliable right of the latter, and he told the deputies
to reconsider their ultimatum; otherwise, he would resign.[69]

The pedantic tone of Bernstein's letter further incensed
the moderate deputies.[70] Auer complained to Liebknecht of
the "rebellion" in Zurich, and he suggested that Liebknecht
and Karl Grillenberger, a *Fraktion* moderate and member of
the *Vorstand*, go to Zurich and straighten the matter out.[71]
To insure the success of Liebknecht's mission, the deputies
gave him full power to take all steps necessary to protect
the hegemony of the *Fraktion*.

Liebknecht's attitude against the editorial staff had
hardened by the time he came to Zurich. He had begun to
suspect the goodwill of Bernstein and his colleagues, and

he began to discern a challenge to his own authority in Bernstein's insubordination. In his only concession to Bernstein in their meeting on 30 March, he agreed to insert into the *Fraktion*'s declaration a disclaimer of any intent to censor the party press,[72] but the remainder of the statement robbed that amendment of any meaning.

On 2 April, *Der Sozialdemokrat* published the *Fraktion* directive. It still bore the date 20 March 1885. Although it conceded the right of the newspaper to "independent criticism," it forbade publication of commentary that would belittle the efforts of the SAP deputies "in the eyes of far-removed party comrades." The deputies specifically ordered the newspaper "under no circumstances to oppose the *Fraktion*." In a direct assault on Bernstein's intentions, the declaration concluded, "it is not the newspaper that should determine the attitude of the *Fraktion*; on the contrary, the *Fraktion* must control the attitude of the newspaper."

In private, Bebel vehemently denounced this *Fraktion* order. To Bernstein and his staff, he conveyed his unreserved support.[73] To Liebknecht, he complained that the *Fraktion* was trying to establish a "dictatorship." Neither the editorial staff nor the deputies determined the stance of the party organ. "The party principles and the party program determine that."[74] Bebel had completed a remarkable reversal since 1880. Five years earlier, he and the whole *Fraktion* had demanded obedience from *Der Sozialdemokrat*. Now, in 1885, in a formal letter to the *Fraktion*, he denied the power of the deputies to interfere with freedom of the press. Succinctly he noted that the *Fraktion* was proscribing freedom of expression for comrades while the party platform promised it for everyone. For this reason, Bebel frankly said he did

not consider himself bound by the deputies' declaration.
If the *Fraktion* enforced its censorship, Bebel threatened
to "appeal to the party."[75] He had no doubt that the membership would back him on this issue.[76]

As he had in the steamship subsidy controversy, Liebknecht
squirmed toward some middle ground on the organizational conflict between *Der Sozialdemokrat* and the *Fraktion* majority.
He told Bernstein he believed that the declaration of 2 April
maintained both Bernstein's personal honor and party principles.
On 5 April, he wrote to his coeditor, "If we stand together we
can avoid further collisions." On 9 April, he counseled "only
cool blood. Everything will be all right." Two days later,
he promised that an upcoming session of the *Fraktion* would
produce "satisfaction on all sides." Repeatedly he directed
Bernstein to delay publication of any response to the *Fraktion*
declaration. Simultaneously, he sought the consent of the
moderate deputies to printing objective and temperate letters
from party members.[77] Meanwhile, to all concerned he professed to see no issue of principle separating the warring
factions.

For his part, Bebel had despaired of working for his
viewpoint inside the *Fraktion*. He left Berlin and, in search
of the voice of the membership, arrived at Frankfurt am Main
on April 12. With Bebel present, a secret assembly of socialists met that day and passed an incredibly vituperative resolution blasting the *Fraktion*.[78] The Frankfurt radicals sent
their resolution to Zurich for publication.

As usual, Liebknecht received the proof of the 16 April
issue of *Der Sozialdemokrat* before it was circulated. This
edition demolished his plans for peace in the party. On 15
April, he had reminded Bernstein, "We want peace, and an

honorable peace." One day later, he wrote to the editor,
"I no longer understand you. How could you, after you promised to publish nothing before the *Fraktion* made a decision,
publish a declaration [presumably the Frankfurt Resolution]
that simply continues the conflict and brings the *Fraktion*
into hateful opposition to the entire party."[79]

To deal with the present crisis, Liebknecht communicated
an emergency decision of the *Fraktionsvorstand* to Bernstein.
(Presumably, Bebel was not consulted, but the remaining four
members, including Liebknecht, agreed to these demands.)
First, Bernstein would have to submit all resolutions from
the members to prior censorship by Liebknecht. Second, the
current issue of the paper would go to press without the
Frankfurt Resolution. Third, the *Fraktionsvorstand* would
send an emissary to Zurich to dictate further conditions
of a settlement.[80] Liebknecht himself again trudged off
on this latter task, which he referred to as an *Executions-
reise.*[81]

Once again accompanied by Grillenberger, Liebknecht
arrived in Zurich determined to end the polemic once and
for all. To that end, he agreed to publish all protests
against the 2 April *Fraktion* statement, including the abusive
and controversial Frankfurt Resolution, in the 23 April issue
of the paper.[82] The editorial staff agreed to append a footnote admonishing the Frankfurters for the "animosity" of
their resolution. The delegates of the *Fraktion*, Liebknecht
and Grillenberger, wrote that publication of the Frankfurt
protest proved the tolerance of the *Fraktion*.

A joint statement prepared by Liebknecht, Grillenberger,
and the editors followed the Frankfurt Resolution. This
declaration in the 23 April issue disavowed any intention by

anyone to inhibit free expression. Nevertheless, the new
statement explained, critics had to observe reasonable limits
to avoid crippling the party. If the authority of the elected
leaders were undermined, the party would disintegrate. Once
the leaders made a decision, therefore, the members were
bound to support it, just as the minority of the *Fraktion* subordinated itself to the majority. Thus the steamship subsidy
debate, combined with the issue of free speech, precipitated
a concise statement of the doctrine of democratic centralism.

Liebknecht vigorously enforced his authority to censor
the resolutions from members during the next few weeks. Bernstein obeyed orders and sent all material to his *Fraktion*
overseer.[83] Fairly innocuous comments from the local comrades
were permitted to appear until the 7 May issue. Then *Der
Sozialdemokrat* announced that no further resolutions would
be published; the occasion for the debate had been resolved,
and it would be "foolish" to continue the argument.

Bernstein chafed painfully under this censorship regulation. All the editorial independence he had won during
the preceding four years seemed to be slipping away. In
urgent letters to Liebknecht, he drew his colleague's attention to another smoldering intraparty battle where he hoped
to be able to reconquer his freedom of action. Recognizing
where his strength lay, Bernstein picked a spot where *Der
Sozialdemokrat* could again side with the membership against
the leadership.

This particular squabble originated with the obnoxious
Frankfurt Resolution that had been published on 23 April.
It so happened that Frankfurt was represented in the Reichstag
by one of the moderate socialists, Karl Frohme. Understandably, Frohme took the resolution by some of his constituents

as a personal affront. So, in a public statement printed in a nonsocialist newspaper, he characterized their declaration as the work of a "few dozen harmless, inexperienced young men."[84]

To this allegation, Bebel felt compelled to reply. He believed that Frohme had broken the unwritten agreement to a cease-fire that followed the 23 April declaration in *Der Sozialdemokrat*. Furthermore, he had attended the controversial meeting in Frankfurt that authored the resolution, and he was determined to defend its integrity. He therefore demanded an opportunity for rebuttal in *Der Sozialdemokrat*.[85] Simultaneously, Bernstein seconded his demand. "If the party organ is bound to silence in all such compromises to our cause," he cried to Liebknecht in exasperation, "it would actually be better if we had no organ."[86] On 14 May, unable to restrain himself any longer, Bernstein published Frohme's original allegation and a reply from Bebel.

Liebknecht did not want the polemic in the newspaper. At that moment he had completed delicate negotiations that promised to balance the interests of radicals and moderates. By threatening his own resignation, he had persuaded the *Fraktion* to approve publication of a resolution from some London socialists that was critical of recent *Fraktion* policy, but he meant that one last publication to end the matter. He told Bernstein, "A continuation of the publications would require denials, which in the interest of the party I want to prevent at any price."[87] Concerning the Bebel-Frohme polemic, he saw no reason for the local affairs of Frankfurt to pollute the national newspaper. Besides, he suspected that the resolution was, as Frohme had alleged, the work of "only a few men."[88]

Bernstein's publication on this matter without Liebknecht's approval directly challenged Liebknecht's authority over *Der Sozialdemokrat*. In justifying his independent action, Bernstein asserted that he, not Liebknecht, bore responsibility for the paper. He demanded editorial freedom, saying he would not lend his name to a newspaper that did not reflect his ideas. He protested that Liebknecht's domination threatened to reduce him to a "strawman," an editor in name only.[89]

Bebel sent Liebknecht a similar indictment of his "dictatorial" pretensions toward the editorial staff. He noted that Bernstein, not Liebknecht, had borne the brunt of *Fraktion* criticism at the Zurich and Copenhagen assemblies in 1882 and 1883. It hardly seemed fair, therefore, that Liebknecht should set editorial policy.[90]

Broadening the issue in his correspondence with Liebknecht, Bebel used every argument he could muster to shake his old friend off the fence and into the radical camp. Beginning in May, he pointed to the potential for an irrevocable split in the party.[91] In July, he repeated his observation that two currents in the SAP had been diverging "gradually and for a long time." To him, the fight over the criticism in *Der Sozialdemokrat* was only the most recent stage in the embourgeoisement of the deputies. He filled his letters to Liebknecht with abuse of the "ambition," the "conceit," and the "place-hunting" among the deputies. He argued that the "opportunist" attempt to alter the entire orientation of the party demanded "'orthodoxy' and dedication to principle" on the part of the true socialists. Bebel especially chastised Liebknecht for reversing his earlier antiparliamentary stand. He attacked Liebknecht's moderation in the Reichstag and the Saxon *Landtag*, remarking that

Liebknecht had "completed a considerable shift to the right.
As your earlier position overshot the mark to the left, so
your current position errs to the right." Bebel invited
Liebknecht to rejoin him in the fight against the majority
as they had done "in 1870 and 1871."[92]

Bebel meshed his logical arguments with a clever psychological campaign. Playing upon Liebknecht's need for approval
and support from his friends, Bebel sent him a painfully
plaintive letter he had received from a close friend of
Liebknecht on the Zurich staff. Therein that comrade complained bitterly about the way he had been treated by Liebknecht. Bebel said he showed Liebknecht the letter to reveal
"what one of your best friends, *who would have gone through
fire for you, thinks about you now. . . .*" Bebel also reported
a letter from Bernstein, in which the latter complained "most
bitterly" about the way Liebknecht had treated him. To clinch
his appeal to personal loyalty, he declared, "If it comes to
a rupture, I will stand in the most decisive manner on the
side of the Zurichers, and so will Engels; and concerning
the party members, I have no worries."[93]

Bebel's tactics at this time stand in clear contrast
to those of Liebknecht. He told Liebknecht that it was a
grave mistake when the "existing antagonism is continually
covered up. . . . This may foster harmony, but it destroys
the unity and the strength of the party."[94] Strategically,
he confided to other friends that he always tried to put
his opponents in the wrong before attacking. Then he was
relentless. "In party matters, I never let myself be directed
by personal sympathies and antipathies," he boasted.[95] Such
ruthlessness led Auer to complain that "not a single drop of
diplomatic blood" flowed in Bebel's veins.[96]

Liebknecht's more pliable attitude did not result from ignorance of the issues involved in the 1885 melee. "The conflict revolves only around the correct measure of parliamentarism," he told a group of comrades in London. He admitted that theory dictated abstention from all parliamentary activity other than agitation, but in practice, even "the best comrades" could disagree. Liebknecht was fond of saying that the dispute involved tactics, not principles. Because principles were not at stake, he urged flexibility and cautioned against expulsions and schism, citing the "dismal example of the French [socialists], where everyone believes everyone else to be a traitor and consequently no strong party can develop."[97]

Behind Bebel's back, Liebknecht tried to minimize his friend's stubbornness. He told the *Fraktion*, for example, that Bebel's protest against the 2 April declaration resulted from nervousness and overwork. In Zurich, he distorted Bebel's views into an endorsement of *Fraktion* control over *Der Sozialdemokrat*.[98]

Liebknecht pursued the same aim of appeasement in direct correspondence with Bebel. Wanting nothing more than an amicable end to the discord, he shared none of Bebel's zeal about the terms of settlement. On 28 May, he asked, "But should we *force a break over this silly polemic about the Fraktion declaration? That is the question!*"[99] The next day, in a lengthy epistle on unity to Bebel, he pleaded, "Despite my best efforts, I cannot understand what actually separates us." He knew that his jurisdictional squabble with Bernstein could not have seriously alienated Bebel. "That I strive for dictatorship," Liebknecht wrote, "you yourself do not believe." Liebknecht insisted that he had worked for a settlement honorable to all disputants. In

self-justification, he asserted that he opposed the degen-
eration of the party and the repression of free expression
at least as vigorously as Bebel. Almost desperately, Liebknecht queried, "What do you want? Do you want the break
or not? . . . If not, then you must help finally to stop
the insults in the newspaper."[100]

Contemporaries recognized that the opposite directions
in which Bebel and Liebknecht pulled permitted the schism
in the *Fraktion* to approach finality. Had the two *alte
Kämpfer* stood together, no combination of deputies could
have challenged their authority.[101] Liebknecht too recognized the pivotal importance of his relationship to Bebel.
"Only if we two oppose each other can there be a break in
the party," he admonished his old friend.[102]

Despite the ideological chasm separating moderates and
radicals in the *Fraktion*, the habit of democratic centralism
continued. Neither group wanted the stigma attached to break-
ing party discipline. Bebel's enormous prestige allowed him
to convert this reservation from a consensus-seeking mechanism
into an obstacle to the will of the majority. A lesser-
known or weaker deputy could have been browbeaten into submission. Otherwise he would have been expelled. Bernstein
believed that only Liebknecht's stubborn neutrality prevented
Bebel from achieving the opposite feat: browbeating the
majority into submission and stealing the party for himself.[103]

Largely because of Liebknecht's efforts to blur the lines
of battle, this conflict in 1885 dragged on for months, and
the outcome was inconclusive. Regarding the Bebel-Frohme
polemic, Liebknecht suggested that the *Fraktion* function as
a court of arbitration. Bebel refused to put his case before
that unfriendly tribunal, suggesting instead that a party

congress be convened to settle the altercation.[104] As it
turned out, neither forum convened, and the polemic found
no final resolution. Instead, as Liebknecht had wanted,
both sides disengaged and a cease-fire slipped unobtrusively
into place. On 2 July, *Fraktion* moderates printed a final,
temperate self-defense in *Der Sozialdemokrat*. Neither editorial comment nor counterresolution ensued. In private
correspondence, even Bebel and Bernstein acknowledged the
wisdom of allowing the argument to fade away.[105]

A consummate politician, Bebel knew when enough had
been achieved. The *Fraktion* had received a beating from
the members. *Der Sozialdemokrat* had established its ability
to act vigorously and, if necessary, unilaterally. To drive
for total victory at that moment would have made Bebel and
the radicals the obvious aggressor. A schism under those
conditions might have produced unfavorable results. Specu-
latively, Bebel may also have known that he was vulnerable
in his fight with Frohme; perhaps a small clique *had* authored
the Frankfurt Resolution. In mid-June, Bebel counseled the
Zurich staff to drop the matter.[106]

Uncharacteristic resistance from Liebknecht may also
have influenced Bebel's tactical retreat in June. The organizational challenge from Bernstein at last provoked a firm
response from Liebknecht. "You are in error concerning our
mutual position," Liebknecht told his Zurich colleague. "*I
have full responsibility* for the paper to the German party,
especially to the *party leadership*, and it is therefore necessary that you work in harmony with me--otherwise we cannot
work together." He complained that during April and May,
Bernstein had broken every agreement he had constructed.
He would not let himself be played the fool, "not even *by my*

best friends. If this continues *I will resign or demand your removal.* My patience is exhausted."[107]

Bebel would not have risked a schism unless he could have counted on Liebknecht. When prospects for that alliance receded, the radicals temporarily relented. Though Bernstein did not abandon the position that he had been held responsible for the content of *Der Sozialdemokrat* in the past, he no longer challenged Liebknecht's interpretation of their current relationship. On 6 June, he wrote to Liebknecht expressing his satisfaction that their friendship was restored. "Hopefully the era of misunderstanding is now past."[108] By the end of the month, the reconciliation between Bebel, Bernstein, and Liebknecht was common knowledge in the party.[109]

LIEBKNECHT LANDS IN THE RADICAL CAMP

If being a leader means defining goals and commanding a following to march toward them, then Liebknecht looked very little like a leader in this intraparty melee in the first half of 1885, but the whole notion of leadership, when scrutinized closely, appears to have soft edges. Through peer pressure, group norms, and the like, participation in the socialist leadership exerted a powerful influence on all of its members. Especially for a personality like Liebknecht, it sometimes could even persuade one to advocate a viewpoint that differed from his own convictions. Moreover, for a democratic leader like Liebknecht, the voice of the membership could be a forceful spur in new directions. Through such influences, the leader can sometimes become the led.

In the second half of 1885, the cumulative force of these

pressures nudged Liebknecht leftward. In the first place, despite public proclamations that the *Fraktion* controlled the party newspaper, *Der Sozialdemokrat* continued its campaign against what it called opportunism. Sometimes it published letters from comrades; sometimes it lashed out on its own.[110] Steadfastly, it challenged any deputy who drifted rightward.

At the same time, Liebknecht's friends in the leadership circle maintained their appeal that he join them in the radical camp. Bebel warned Liebknecht that he would receive no thanks for his mediating posture, and he was right. Everyone resented Liebknecht's vacillation.[111] Feeling discomfort from prolonged fence-straddling, after the intense controversy receded, Liebknecht rolled toward Bebel's camp. Bebel claimed that he had taught his old comrade the error of eternal compromise. To Engels, he confided that he had shaken Liebknecht's tendency to trace all antagonism back to "personal intrigues and mis-understandings."[112]

Two additional causes may help to explain Liebknecht's conversion to the radical cause. In the autumn of 1885, he was convicted for insulting fellow members of the Reichs-tag and sentenced to four weeks' imprisonment. Partly as a result, he lost his bid for reelection to the Saxon *Landtag* in October.[113] Soured on the state and on elections, Liebknecht stalked toward a more decisively leftist position.

As was his custom, he used the enforced inactivity of prison as an opportunity to write and research. The result of his labor offered proof of his leftward migration, for it was an assault on the latest heresy of the *Fraktion* moderates. Louis Viereck, a moderate SAP deputy, edited a colorless sheet in Germany called *Recht auf Arbeit*, a slogan borrowed from Bismarck. In the fall of 1885, he, Hasenclever, Blos,

Frohme, and other moderates latched onto the restriction
of working hours as the panacea for the ills of capitalism.
Their agitation for the so-called *Normalarbeitstag* had a
distinguished lineage linking it directly to Karl Marx. But
the *Fraktion* moderates inflated Marx's argument and asserted
that an eight-hour day would eliminate virtually all the
evils of capitalism.[114] The radical wing contested this
position, and the nonsocialist press again predicted a rupture
in the SAP.[115]

In prison, Liebknecht researched and wrote a distinguished
series of articles concerning the *Normalarbeitstag* for *Der
Sozialdemokrat*. These essays, published in late October
and early November, carefully followed Marx's argumentation
in *Capital*. Liebknecht conceded to the moderates that limitation of the working day offered a valuable agitational
tool because it clearly demonstrated the antagonism between
capitalists and proletariat, but he warned against overesti-
mating the results to be obtained from the institution of
an eight- or ten-hour day. He asserted that the industrialists
would circumvent the reduction of the working day by exploit-
ing the available labor more intensely. According to Liebknecht, an eight-hour day could not eliminate unemployment,
much less cure the anarchy of production inherent in private
ownership of the means of production; only collective ownership could achieve that result.[116]

In London, Engels was delighted with this evidence of
Liebknecht's conversion. He thought that Liebknecht's recent
arrest and his fear of falling between two stools in the
Fraktion had made him renounce his servile efforts at intraparty diplomacy. Engels was especially pleased that Liebknecht had publicized the "half-forgotten *Capital*."[117]

Viereck and the *Fraktion* moderates were as angry as
Engels was elated. In *Recht auf Arbeit* Viereck erroneously
charged that Liebknecht had abandoned the *Normalarbeitstag*
as an agitational weapon. His newspaper began a series of
articles in praise of Johann Karl Rodbertus, a nonsocialist
economist who posited a central role for the state in the
elimination of social ills. Viereck also tried to revive
the intraparty organizational dispute by protesting against
the pretensions to infallibility in *Der Sozialdemokrat*.[118]

Liebknecht had cast his lot with the radicals on this
issue, and he now pursued the moderates with a vengeance.
He at last believed that something more important than party
unity was at stake. In an unusual signed statement in the
central organ, he complained that *Recht auf Arbeit* had distorted his meaning. He had simply pointed out the possi-
bilities and limitations of the *Normalarbeitstag*; he had
not denied its educational usefulness. He lambasted Viereck
for trying "to shove Rodbertus into the place of Marx." He
even wrote a fifth article in his series for *Der Sozialdemokrat*,
expanding his evidence on the restricted impact of a maximum
working day and challenging Viereck to prove him wrong. In an
extraordinary second signed statement in the official party
organ in mid-November, Liebknecht warned, "If our party marches
to a Saarbücken by denial of its scientific and principled
standpoint, it will certainly be in danger of ultimately finding its Sedan."[119]

At last clear lines were drawn on a matter of theory:
would the SAP be a revolutionary Marxist party or would it
follow Rodbertus and Bismarck along the path of state-sponsored
social reform? Viereck tried to improve the prospects for the
latter course by elevating Rodbertus to the level of a respect-

able rival to Marx,[120] and he complemented his ideological offensive with a renewed effort to split the SAP *Fraktion*. In January 1886, Bebel informed Liebknecht that several deputies, including Hasenclever, had decided to side with Viereck.[121]

Bernstein, under Engels' guidance, printed numerous articles against Rodbertus in *Der Sozialdemokrat* during the spring of 1886. In the *Fraktion*, Viereck and his friends were unable to withstand the reunited authority of Bebel and Liebknecht.[122] A police report for July 1886, a usually reliable source of information, reported that Bebel had triumphed over Frohme, Viereck, and the moderates. It correctly predicted that Viereck would be expelled from the party. The spy concluded, "The entire attitude of the party proves that the radical direction is the dominant."[123] Surely Liebknecht's shift of position contributed greatly to that result.

MOTIVATIONS AND ACHIEVEMENTS OF A CONCILIATOR

This protracted furor inside the SAP did not produce a conclusive victory for any person or principle. In any organization, conflict only rarely yields perfect resolution. When it does, the result often is schism.[124] Usually conflicts are managed rather than resolved. Successful management can produce constructive by-products, like the restructuring of internal power relationships to conform to changing personnel or the reexamination and revitalization of a group's goals.[125] Liebknecht's labors in 1885 kept conflict within tolerable bounds and allowed it to perform these important tasks.

The work of a conciliator required him to understate the

importance of the issues at stake. To cool passions and
to preserve some room for maneuver, Liebknecht insisted that
the 1885 controversy "absolutely does not involve matters
of principle."[126] If not ideology, then what did motivate
Liebknecht?

Liebknecht's personality predisposed him toward accommodation. He valued the good opinion of all of his colleagues
and worked to keep it. The Gotha compromise offered an additional incentive for Liebknecht to work as a peacemaker.
As the chief architect of that arrangement, Liebknecht had
a vested interest in maintaining it. If the SAP disintegrated,
he would have to reexamine critically his own actions of a
decade earlier, and might have to concede that his detractors--
Marx, Engels, Bebel, and Bracke--had been right. Liebknecht's
dedication to compromise was motivated also by money. Bebel
estimated that Liebknecht's various literary, editorial, and
agitational enterprises earned him an incredible 7,000 marks
a year in 1885.[127] That income, which put Liebknecht among
the highest-paid people in the nation, was derived from the
socialist party. If the party exploded, Liebknecht might
have plummeted into poverty.

Still more important than any of these reasons was
the fact that Liebknecht had transcended sectarian politics.
He saw the important enemy of his beliefs outside the socialist party. Among comrades, he encouraged free discussion,
and he celebrated the invigorating effect of boisterous argument. His perception may well have been right. Surface
signs of health for a political party, such as ideological
consensus or a stable leadership, may actually conceal organizational and intellectual sterility. Vigorous political
infighting may reflect vitality, confidence, and creativity,

thereby exemplifying a dialectical procedure in the pursuit of a proper ideological orientation. Keeping these necessary arguments within the bounds of constructive disagreement was Liebknecht's service to his party in the 1880s.

In these battles, a decisive Bebel rode a wave of protests from party members to a standoff against the majority of his colleagues in the *Fraktion*. Despite the apparent checkmate, his crusade produced perceptible changes in party structure and creed. Although *Der Sozialdemokrat* had been created to serve the *Fraktion*, it successfully asserted its right to criticize its creator. This practice arose despite the final 23 April proclamation that asserted the continued right of the *Fraktion* to control the party organ. Ideologically, Bebel commented that the conflict "cleared the heads of the majority and showed them what the mood of the party is."[128] The radical position emerged with the strong moral authority that membership approval gives in a democratic party. Liebknecht delayed the radical surge with his peacemaking politics. When he finally supported the left wing of the party with his articles on the *Normalarbeitstag*, the moderates could only scurry to some temporary cover.

But it would be a mistake to think that arguments about these matters had ended. *Fraktion* members continued to clash with each other and with *Der Sozialdemokrat* about the content of the official party press.[129] More acrimonious battles about the relationship of the elected party leaders and the central organ occurred in the 1890s,[130] and Liebknecht's party never settled its debate about revolutionary theory and tactics--at least until those issues finally exploded into schism in 1917.

Looking back on the legendary "heroic years" of the 1880s, Bebel mused to Liebknecht, "Who invented the image of the iron bars, as if the anti-socialist law held us together? Not I!"[131] With justifiable pride, near the end of his life Liebknecht recalled how his skillful negotiating between radicals and moderates had helped to keep the SAP from coming unglued in 1885.[132] Without his efforts at pacification, the rupture that eventually shattered socialist solidarity in Germany might well have happened three decades earlier.

Chapter 10
Losing Influence and
Gaining Prestige

When Liebknecht celebrated his sixtieth birthday in 1886,
he must have noticed how time had thinned the ranks of his
generation in the socialist movement. Marx, Lassalle, and
Schweitzer were dead. At Liebknecht's heels, a new cohort,
comprised of men at least fifteen years his junior, clamored
for their turn to lead the SAP. Slowly, they nudged Liebknecht
from the inner sanctum of party decision making.

Yet Liebknecht did not retire, nor did he become a useless vestige. His intraparty role changed, but it did not
wither. In the international arena, where he increasingly
concentrated his efforts, he was influential and enjoyed
a prestige unsurpassed by anyone, and the German comrades
beyond the leadership circle continued to revere him as much
as any of their leaders. What Liebknecht lost in his sixties
was his role as affective leader, his function as conciliator
and go-between among the party chiefs. Compensating for
that forfeiture, Liebknecht became both the symbol and international spokesman for socialist unity, tradition and strength.
He became the elder statesman of the workers' movement.

AN AGITATIONAL TRIP TO THE USA

Liebknecht had always been cosmopolitan, a true internationalist; but earlier in his career, he had thought it best
to establish his socialist party within the emerging national
framework of Germany. Consequently, he had done little to
organize for Marx's International Workingman's Association
in the 1860s. Two decades later, having established a viable
movement in his fatherland, he redirected his attention toward
resuscitating the socialist international. In the autumn of
1886, symbolic of his shifting priorities, he undertook an
extended agitational trip to the United States.

Forty years had elapsed since young Liebknecht had con-
templated immigration to Wisconsin. Now he came to the New
World not as a derelict or a refugee but rather as a respected
political figure. While millions of his countrymen endured
this passage to America one-way in the disgusting conditions
of steerage, Liebknecht shared a comfortable round trip cabin
with friends, paid for with part of the money people in the
United States paid to hear him speak.

Liebknecht had two reasons for travelling to the United
States: to spread the socialist gospel and to raise money
for the next Reichstag campaign. To achieve these ends, he
stayed over three months, from late August to mid-December.
He was accompanied by Marx's daughter, Eleanor, and her husband, the English socialist, Edward Aveling. Because a mass
trial and conviction of nine other SAP leaders had decimated
the party's home front, no one else could be spared from
Germany to accompany them.[1]

After a brief stopover in London to visit with Engels,
Liebknecht and the Avelings arrived in New York on 13 September.

At the dock, they were greeted by impressive delegations from numerous German labor organizations. That evening a reception was held at Liebknecht's hotel, the Metropolitan House, on East Fourth Street. The festivities included fireworks and the singing of revolutionary songs. The organizers then herded the guests into a procession at whose head was carried a red banner. On that standard, with some irony, large silver letters proclaimed: "Ferdinand Lassalle, 1863." The whole company of several hundred socialists followed it off to a nearby beerhall, where they passed the evening in drinking and speech making.[2]

Liebknecht remained in and around New York until the end of September, addressing several rallies in the large German émigré community. Each time he drew several thousand listeners.[3] Then, on 30 September, he set out on a two-month whirlwind tour of fifteen states, during which he gave speeches in over thirty cities.

During the first three weeks, Liebknecht's tour was reasonably paced. Travelling by train, he spoke to gatherings every day or two at a different New England town, but on 24 October, when he swung west from Albany toward Buffalo, the distances between engagements became longer and longer. After practically whistle-stopping through the metropolitan centers on the Great Lakes, he arrived in Milwaukee on 6 November. In the following seven days, he sped through Davenport, Quincy, St. Louis and Indianapolis. He then headed toward New York via a more southerly route, stopping to speak in Cincinnati, Pittsburgh, Baltimore, Washington, D.C., and other smaller cities.[4] At each stop, Liebknecht's listeners were enthusiastic and generous. On this tour, Liebknecht raised 16,000 marks for the SAP, an amount that compares favorably with the average annual party revenue of 31,000 marks between 1884 and 1887.[5]

Yet not all German expatriates welcomed Liebknecht.
Some, like Liebknecht's old antagonist Johann Most, seethed
with militant anarchism. These extremists detested the discipline and restraint that Liebknecht represented. In *Die
Freiheit*, which Most had transplanted to Chicago, he now
blasted Liebknecht as a "scoundrel" and ridiculed the whole
SAP leadership as the "upper eunuchs." His correspondents
in various American cities reported untrue accounts of Liebknecht's speeches, saying that they were poorly attended,
unenthusiastically received, and preached capitulation to
the ruling classes.[6] These stories were picked up and circulated by the press back in Europe.[7]

From a social democratic viewpoint, Liebknecht's arrival
in America came at a most inopportune time. On 4 May 1886,
terrorists had exploded a bomb at the Haymarket in Chicago.
Eleven random deaths resulted. The police responded by arresting an almost equally random seven anarchists, all of whom
were condemned to be hanged. In leftist circles everywhere,
this travesty of justice provoked sympathy for the imprisoned
Chicago seven.

Now Liebknecht had been invited to the United States by
the Labor Party, a social democratic emulator of the SAP,
partly to help in exterminating anarchism. In 1886, unfortunately for Liebknecht and his sponsors, Most and the other
anarchists wore the protective cloak of martyrdom. Liebknecht
therefore had to criticize anarchism with care.

His actions in Chicago show how he met this challenge.
Directly after his arrival, he went to the jail where the
seven anarchists were held, introduced himself to the surprised prisoners, and expressed his personal sympathy for
their plight. The next day he explained his actions to an

assembly of 3,000 at the *Vorwärts* gymnasium. He said he
had visited the condemned men "not because they are anarchists but rather because they are representatives of the
proletariat. . . ." He pitied them as victims of class justice and then launched his exposition upon the correct politics
for proletarians.

Anarchism, he lectured, erred by advocating the disintegration of society. Its individualistic violence reflected
its ignorance of the social, of the collective nature of
the workers' struggle. Vigorously repudiating terrorist
tactics, he stressed that "nothing could be accomplished . . .
without the support of popular sentiment." Turning to the
ultimate socialist vision, he explained that the workers must
collect, combine and coordinate the productive forces of
society. Only in this organized way could the material preconditions for a better life for the working class be created.[8]

So strongly did Liebknecht repudiate violence in America
that the German consul in Washington characterized him as a
Friedensprediger,[9] but his remarks only echoed the disavowals
of anarchist "propoganda of the deed" that he already had
trumpeted in the Reichstag and elsewhere.[10] Taken together,
these rebuffs to the anarchists illustrate once again how
strongly specific agitational needs colored Liebknecht's
public pronouncements.

But Liebknecht also criticized the institutions of piecemeal reform. Attacking trade unionism, he said the workers
had to aim at more than "merely getting a little higher price
for labor,"[11] and he denounced the American political system.
In Cincinnati, he proclaimed, "Instead of crowned heads you
have here in America capitalists and monopolies—railroad
rings and the money power—which rule everywhere and control

your officials in every department."[12] To reform this evil
situation, Liebknecht proposed the formation of a massive
socialist party, not individualistic terrorism.

While sailing back to Germany, Liebknecht wrote down
his impressions of the United States. A few months later,
these reflections were published as a substantial volume
entitled *Ein Blick in Die Neue Welt*. This book illustrated
how Liebknecht used foreign examples to serve domestic agitational purposes.

In this travelogue, unlike his speeches in America,
Liebknecht's admiration of the United States was unlimited.
Alluding to the recently erected Statue of Liberty that beckoned
the oppressed from all countries, he praised the absence of
nationalism in melting-pot America. He lauded America's
passive foreign policy, observing "live and let live is their
principle." He extolled America's freedom from the chains
of tradition that fettered progress in Europe. On more specific matters he said, "On the average I am convinced that the
American children read, write and calculate better than the
German children who have completed the *Volksschule*." "The
poorly paid workers here," he alleged, "as a rule are always
still better paid than ours." He reported that, in America,
there was less drunkenness and that the hotels were cleaner
than in Germany. He even called the open coaches in the
American trains a "triumph of the principle of equality"
over the class-segregated European railroads.

Other aspects of Liebknecht's panegyric were less innocuous. He naively congratulated Buffalo Bill for rendering
"great service to his government in the Indian Wars." He
asserted that the American woman was "socially completely
equal to man" and was "on the way to achieving political

equality also. . . ." And he only gave evidence against the persistence of racial prejudice. In his entire book, he made only two criticisms of the United States: the neglect of factory legislation and the failure of Democrats and Republicans clearly to define their programs. Condemnations of capitalism and reports of class struggle were not part of Liebknecht's image of the New World. Instead, he depicted the ceaseless evolution of freedom in the United States and closed his book with the confident prediction, "The Fatherland of Lincoln and 'old' John Brown will break the sceptre of the 'Almighty Dollar!'"[13]

Liebknecht's enthusiastic account reflected little penetration of American life and still less of socialist theory. In a manner reminiscent of utopians from Thomas More to Etienne Cabet, he depicted aspects of his own vision of an ideal society as if they currently were practiced in the far-off land he described.

Some critics accused Liebknecht of encouraging emigration with his book. There can be no doubt that he sincerely found much in America that he preferred to German practices. Yet there was another, tactical reason for his laudatory tone. His old friend, Robert Schweichel, noted that Liebknecht intended his book to help introduce "the best characteristics of America into Germany."[14] Liebknecht recognized that viewing one's own country as the best in the world breeds complacency, if not contentment. In his agitation, therefore, he invariably reported that the countries he visited surpassed Germany in freedom, culture, industry, education, cleanliness, and happiness of the citizenry. On the other hand, in England in the 1850s and in the United States in 1886, he bluntly told his audiences they were no better off than the Germans.

When Liebknecht returned to Germany on 11 December 1886, he had reason to be pleased with his trip. He had raised a good deal of money, he had successfully confronted the anarchists, he had boosted socialist prospects in the New World, and he had broadened his background. The insights derived from the voyage may also have encouraged him to help resurrect the organization of the socialist international.

RESURRECTING THE SOCIALIST INTERNATIONAL

The next congress of the SAP, which met at St. Gall in Switzerland in October 1887, endorsed the convocation of an international assembly of working class representatives. British and French initiatives with the same purpose surfaced almost simultaneously. Outlawed in their own country, the German social democrats allowed the British Trade Union Congress to exert leadership. In 1888 a brief meeting in London sponsored by that organization authorized a French socialist faction to arrange a larger congress for Paris the next year.

On the German side, preparations devolved almost exclusively upon Liebknecht. Some of his party comrades, having observed the potpourri of anarchist, reformist, and trade-unionist opinion at the London gathering, would have preferred to see the whole idea of an international congress disappear.[15] Reinforcing this predisposition was the fact that the London conference had designated the Possibilists to prepare the Paris meeting. The decentralized and heterodox Possibilists were moderate socialist rivals to the struggling Marxist group, the *Parti Ouvrier*, in France.[16] Divisions between these feuding factions threatened to abort the Second International.

Liebknecht worked hard to circumvent the disagreements
among the French socialists. Hoping that a preconference
might be able to reconcile them, he invited representatives
of both groups to meet with him and Bebel on neutral ground,
at the Hague, in February 1889.[17] Recalling Liebknecht's
concessions to the Lassalleans at Gotha, Engels and the French
Marxists feared that this confabulation at the Hague might
permanently contaminate the new international,[18] but despite
Liebknecht's willingness to bargain, the Possibilists feared
a Marxist trap and refused to attend. Alone at the Hague,
Bebel, Liebknecht and delegates from the *Parti Ouvrier* simply
authorized themselves to organize a competing congress that
would undermine the Possibilists' assembly.

On the centennial of Bastille Day, two ostensibly international working-class congresses convened in Paris. The
gathering sponsored by Liebknecht, the SAP and the *Parti
Ouvrier* drew approximately 400 delegates from twenty countries
as far away as Argentina. Despite some anti-French prejudice
in his own party, Liebknecht had prodded eighty-one Germans
into attending.[19] By acclamation, the predominantly French
and German assembly chose Liebknecht and the French socialist,
Eduard Vaillant, as cochairmen.

Shaking hands with Vaillant to symbolize international
working-class unity, Liebknecht disregarded the various shades
of socialism present at the meeting as well as the existence
of a separate Possibilist congress a few blocks away. "It is
the proudest moment of my life," he told the delegates, "to
stand here and to see the fulfillment of the ideal . . . ,
proletarians of all countries, unite."[20] During this first
session, when some indiscreet delegates broached the issue
of unity with the Possibilists, Liebknecht rose to defend

the convocation of a separate assembly. The Possibilists had
been invited into a common congress at the Hague, he explained,
and indeed the doors to the present meeting still stood open
to them, but it was "entirely impossible to demand amalgamation at any price." Later, he proposed a resolution approving
the work of the Hague precongress and the organization of the
present meeting. Balloting by nation, the delegates accepted
it by a vote of twelve to six.[21]

In other business, the delegates to the Paris Congress
called for the abolition of the standing army by the substitution of a citizen militia. Mirroring Liebknecht's lifelong
conviction, they called "peace the first and indispensable
precondition for worker-emancipation." They also called
for international labor legislation, including the prohibition of child labor and the eight-hour work day. To promote
these goals, the congress endorsed an international demonstration of proletarian solidarity on 1 May 1890.

Although it made no formal declaration in this regard,
the Paris Congress, which Liebknecht helped to arrange, became
the founding assembly for the Second International. That
organization, for years lacking its own bureaucracy, survived
as a web of personal connections among the socialist leaders
of the various countries. In the 1890s, Liebknecht stood
at the center of that web. At each of the next three congresses of the International that convened during his lifetime, Liebknecht appeared as a prominent speaker. On other
occasions he travelled frequently to France, England, Austria
and the Netherlands, dispensing advice, preaching unity, and
promoting the cause of social democracy.[22] In its eulogy
to Liebknecht, the German party paper stressed how irreplace-
able his loss was for the International. "Wherever a difficult

question emerged, wherever misunderstandings impeded agree-
ment--a trip by Liebknecht brought everything back into balance
again. At the international congresses, where the differences
often dashed together fiercely, . . . his experience and his
gift for accommodation and conciliation brought the matters
quickly back into balance again."[23] Liebknecht also conducted
a constant and voluminous correspondence with European socialists.[24] In 1896, even Mustafa Kemal wrote to him respectfully
asking for his advice about the proper course for the Ottoman
Empire in Egypt.[25] In the last few years of the nineteenth
century, no one commanded more admiration among Europe's lower
classes and their leaders than did Liebknecht.

Liebknecht jealously guarded his position as the sole link
between the International and the German party. In 1894, Bebel
complained to Engels, "To meddle with Liebknecht in his foreign
connections is simply impossible. No one knows to whom he write
or what he writes; he talks to no one about that. . . ."[26]

Liebknecht paid a price for his monopoly on the German
part of the business of the International. The time spent
on affairs abroad decreased the attention he could give to
leading the SAP. Thus, success in the international arena
became one of several causes that diluted Liebknecht's authority in the upper echelons of his own party.

LIEBKNECHT SUFFERS ELECTORAL DEFEAT

By the time Liebknecht helped to found the Second International,
his dominance inside his own national organization already had
eroded somewhat. The Reichstag elections of February 1887 had
dealt him one serious blow. In that balloting, which was

heavily influenced by Bismarck's jingoistic manipulations, the
party lost thirteen of its twenty-four mandates. Liebknecht
was among the losers. In his Offenbach district, his share
of the vote collapsed from 44 percent on the first ballot
in 1884 to 35 percent in 1887. Other veteran leaders, including Auer, Blos, Geiser, Viereck and Vollmar, also lost their
seats; but defeat cost Liebknecht more. The 1865 order expelling him from Prussia still was in force. Since his election
to the Reichstag in 1874, the immunities conferred on deputies
had allowed him to travel freely to Berlin. Now, after his
defeat in 1887, he could not participate in the deliberations
of the SAP *Fraktion* because he could not come to Berlin.
Consequently, his seat on the five-member *Fraktionvorstand*
fell to Bebel, who had not served on that body since 1885.[27]

Fortunately, Liebknecht managed to return to the Reichstag
before the next general election in 1890. The opportunity
arose when a fatal illness struck Wilhelm Hasenclever. Hasenclever, who was eight years younger than Liebknecht (but
older than any of the other SAP deputies), suffered a stroke
late in 1887. Exacerbated by alcoholism, his health failed
entirely in 1888.[28] That summer, he resigned his Reichstag
mandate; the former ADAV president died in July 1889.

Hasenclever had represented Berlin's Sixth Reichstag
electoral district, a seat the party had held on and off
for a decade. To replace him, the local party nominated
Liebknecht. Even though he could not visit Berlin to campaign,
the party had such strength in this district that Liebknecht
triumphed on the first ballot in the August 30 by-election.[29]
Shortly thereafter he replaced Hasenclever on the *Vorstand*.[30]

Altogether, Liebknecht had been absent from the official
party directorate for eighteen months. Combined with his

simultaneous diversion by the affairs of the Second International, this hiatus helped reduce his authority inside the SAP leadership.

EFFECTS OF THE RETURN TO LEGALITY ON LIEBKNECHT

Meanwhile, a third transformation that would alter Liebknecht's intraparty role occurred in the government offices on the Wilhelmsstrasse. In 1888, an active and ambitious Wilhelm II ascended Germany's throne. The young emperor was eager to become a popular, paternalistic monarch by somehow attracting the working class to himself. To that end, he personally negotiated with striking coal miners in 1889, and he even sponsored an international congress of government officials to discuss labor legislation in Berlin on 15–29 March 1890.[31] These conciliatory gestures understandably led the members of the Reichstag to suspect that their monarch no longer supported the antisocialist law. After intricate parliamentary maneuvers and bitter behind-the-scenes battles, on 25 January 1890, the Reichstag voted 169 to 98 against extension of the exceptional legislation, which expired on 30 September.

The antisocialist law had driven the SAP organization underground and caused much suffering among party members. During the twelve years of outlawry, over 1,500 socialists were jailed for sentences totaling over 1,000 years. Nearly 900 men were expelled from their homes under the provisions of the minor state of siege. Many of the exiles, usually capable party leaders, left Germany forever as a result of the persecution.[32]

Yet, these hardships notwithstanding, the German workers'

movement was far stronger in 1890 than it had been twelve
years earlier. In the Reichstag elections of March 1890,
the SAP polled nearly one and a half million votes, which
was 20 percent of the total vote cast. In the Sixth District
in Berlin, Liebknecht won a first ballot victory with 62
percent of the vote. Including his mandate, the social democrats won thirty-five seats. Both ballots and deputies for
the SAP had tripled since 1878.

Like his party, Liebknecht had both suffered and grown
during the 1880s. While the exceptional legislation had
been in force, he had endured fourteen months in jail on
various charges. For nine years, he had endured expulsion
from his home and separation from his family, but from a
political perspective, the 1880s constitute the apex of his
career. Never had the party needed the services of an affective leader more. Harassed from outside, confused and divided,
without an accepted formal organization, the SAP had needed
someone with Liebknecht's interpersonal skills simply to
hold it together.

These conditions that made Liebknecht indispensable
began to disappear around 1890. With the return of legality,
the party promptly provided itself with a thoroughly articulated organization statute, replete with precise mechanisms
for settling disputes. Liebknecht's informal services as
a negotiator henceforth would be less necessary. They also
were less feasible in a *Fraktion* that swelled to fifty members
by mid-decade. In addition, the resumption of annual party
congresses allowed a free interchange of ideas and a resolution of conflicts by open, democratic ballots. In this environment, Liebknecht's talent for papering over disagreements
became less of a desideratum. Finally, when a legion of loyal

bureaucrats began to swarm around the prospering party structure, Liebknecht's unceremonious operations outside of official
channels became obsolete.[33]

APPOINTMENT AS EDITOR-IN-CHIEF OF *VORWÄRTS*

The adoption of a more bureaucratic style of leadership for
German social democracy and the concomitant displacement
of Liebknecht occurred gradually. In 1890, Liebknecht maintained an appearance of great intraparty power. The other
party chiefs agreed that he should man one of the most influential posts at their disposal, the editorship of the revived
central newspaper. That office had provided the foundation
for Liebknecht's power before 1878, and it had the potential
to do so again.

Yet Liebknecht was less than eager to relocate in Berlin
in order to edit the publication. Showing signs of waning
ambition, he raised numerous personal objections to the move.
During the preceding twenty-five years, he and his family had
settled comfortably in Leipzig. Natalie had no desire to
brave the bustle of Berlin, which was five times larger than
her present hometown. If the Liebknechts were transplanted,
his wife worried that he would be overworked, that the schools
would not be good enough for her children (the youngest of
whom still was only twelve), that the cost of living would be
too high, and so on. Liebknecht almost let these considerations undermine his career as a national political leader.

Because the party desperately needed Liebknecht's journalistic experience, Bebel pleaded with both Liebknecht and his
wife to come to the capital. He promised an annual salary of

7,000 marks and minimal work--a couple of hours a day,--for
the chief editorship of the central organ and then warned
that if Liebknecht remained in Leipzig, he would "set himself
aside and in the second rank [of the leadership]."[34] Over-
coming their initial hesitation, the Liebknechts decided in
mid-June that they would resettle in Berlin.[35]

Initially, the ensuing events confirmed the wisdom of
Liebknecht's choice and promised well for his future work.
At the SAP Congress in October 1890, as an aftershock of
the unresolved organizational controversy of 1885, the delegates tried to inject additional authority and independence
into Liebknecht's position as editor-in-chief. That attempt
came during the debate about the organization statute proposed
by the veteran party leaders.

Concerning national leadership and the position of the
party press, the 1890 organization proposal mainly reaffirmed
pre-1878 tradition. According to its provisions, annual
party congresses would elect five directors who in turn would
manage party business and "control the principled position of
the party organs. . . ." In the one contentious innovation
suggested in this proposal, the *Fraktion* would be empowered
to elect the control commission, which in turn would audit
the *Vorstand* and arbitrate intraparty disputes.[36]

This proposal incensed party comrades who for years
had defended *Der Sozialdemokrat* against censorship by the
Fraktion.[37] At the 1890 congress, Party Secretary Auer tried
to overcome the objections of these critics. Wearing his
long, scraggly beard and still looking pale from a recent
incapacitating illness, Auer softly protested that the leadership intended no suppression of free expression among comrades.
He pointed out that close supervision of each party journal

would be impossible because over sixty socialist sheets already
had sprouted into existence. Nevertheless, he explained, the
party needed the authority to withdraw official endorsement
from a newspaper that consistently violated socialist principles.[38]

Auer's arguments alone probably could not have convinced
the delegates to approve the right of the *Vorstand* to set
editorial policy. The congress at Halle took two further
actions to defend the press against censorship; only then
did it ratify the organization proposal, including the *Vorstand*'s editorial powers. First, the delegates amputated
the control commission from the *Fraktion*. They decreed that
the control commission would be elected by the party congress
and not by the deputies. Thus, the *Fraktion* as a body lost
all formal authority inside the party after 1890.[39] Second,
the delegates insisted upon their right to ratify the selection of Liebknecht as editor-in-chief. "He [Liebknecht]
must not be viewed as an employee of the party directorate,"
Grillenberger argued and therefore moved that Liebknecht be
confirmed by the congress as editor, that he be invited to
all sessions of the *Vorstand* and be given an advisory voice
in its deliberations, and that he be *gleichberechtigt mit
dem Parteivorstande*. The delegates unanimously endorsed
this resolution.[40] They intended that any future arguments
between the five elected directors and the editor-in-chief
would produce a standoff, as had happened in 1885. The control commission, now elected by the congress, would decide
such disagreements.

With these changes, the wary delegates ratified the
organization proposal. Among its provisions was a change
of name for the party, to *Sozialdemokratische Partei Deutsch-*

lands (SPD). The statute directed that, beginning on 1
January 1891, the existing colorless newspaper of the Berlin
comrades, the *Berliner Volksblatt*, would be promoted to a
dual role, serving as both local and national organ. Recalling the name of the SAP's pre-1878 standard bearer, it was
christened *Vorwärts*. Even before the change of name, Liebknecht slipped into the editorship.

In Liebknecht, the delegates at Halle had found a dedicated defender of free expression within their party. Liebknecht plainly stated his own conception of the correct function for the central organ in a reprimand he directed to
the staff of *Der Sozialdemokrat* in 1885: "As *comrades* you
have the same right as every other comrade to judge, to condemn, and to attack, but as *editors* of the party organ you
do not have the right to take sides within the party."[41]
When squabbles erupted among fellow socialists, Liebknecht's
Vorwärts hailed the invigorating effect of debate, adding
that socialists were "too good democrats" to tolerate the
"intellectual autocracy" implicit in a newspaper that dictated orthodoxy in all disputes.[42] "The central organ belongs
to the entire party," Liebknecht pointed out in 1896," and
if various currents prevail in the party, . . . I do not
consider myself entitled to condemn or to excommunicate
deviating opinions from my editorial desk." He likened his
open editorial policy to democratic government, contrasting
it to "monarchical-caesarian" rule that "prescribes ideas
from above."[43]

Liebknecht followed his guidelines when *Vorwärts* faced
its first intraparty fracas. Building upon the well-
established tradition of radicalism in Berlin, a small but
vocal coterie known as *Die Jungen* began to criticize what

they saw as the corruption and opportunism of the veteran
party leadership. Their concerns, voiced with increasing
stridency beginning in 1890, illustrated the continuity of
the issues that occupied the party in the 1890s with those
of a decade earlier.[44]

Antiparliamentarism held *Die Jungen* together.[45] In
the *Berliner Volkstribune*, in the *Sächsische Arbeiterzeitung*,
and in the *Magdeburger Volksstimme*, spokesmen for this radical faction cried that the appropriate sphere of activity
for socialists lay outside the Reichstag, in strikes and
other direct action. Most embarrassing for Liebknecht,
Die Jungen resurrected his 1869 denunciation of the Reichstag
as support for their own antiparliamentary position.[46]

As the leaders most specifically attacked by these radicals, Bebel and Liebknecht led the counterattack. Carrying
the fight to the enemy, Bebel addressed rallies in the radical
strongholds of Dresden, Magdeburg, and Berlin. In each public
meeting, he secured the passage of a resolution endorsing
the *Fraktion* against the insurgents.[47]

Liebknecht's labors were less productive. After initially
and typically dismissing *Die Jungen* as unimportant,[48] he wrote
a letter to a Danish socialist in which he denounced the
radicals as a "borderline flock of sheep" of "downright comic
insignificance." The Danes indiscreetly published this letter.
Their gaffe enabled the *Berliner Volkstribune* and the *Sächsische
Arbeiterzeitung* to howl about the impropriety of airing intraparty spats in the foreign press—and in a "Possibilist" sheet
at that.[49] Fairly detached observers like Engels and Auer
agreed that Liebknecht was handling the intraparty insurgency
with "uncommon clumsiness."[50]

So routing *Die Jungen* at the Halle Congress became a matter of much importance. Including the organization debate, which reflected the radicals' contempt for the *Fraktion*, arguments about the competency of the current leaders raged for three days at this gathering. When *Die Jungen* denounced parliament, Liebknecht equated them with the anarchists. "Any ass can throw a bomb," he lashed out. Explicitly disavowing his 1869 antiparliamentary tirade, he asserted that agitation among the masses had proven to be the proper path to power.[51] A year later, when the SPD again had to argue with *Die Jungen*, Liebknecht repeated his repudiation of his 1869 position. "Bismarck lies crushed on the ground, and social democracy is the strongest party in Germany. Is that not a potent proof for the worth of the present tactics?"[52] Its patience exhausted by the intemperance of the radical attacks, this 1891 SPD congress voted to expel the leaders of *Die Jungen*.[53]

Already the *Vorstand* had exercised its right to control the party newspapers by removing the radical editors from the *Sächsische Arbeiterzeitung*.[54] The *Berliner Volkstribune*, which the radicals owned, simply drifted away from the party. To combat this embarrassing oracle for extremism in Berlin, the *Vorstand* was more determined than ever to wield *Vorwärts* in its own interests.[55] But under Liebknecht's guidance, the central organ hardly mentioned the commotion surrounding *Die Jungen*.

Liebknecht had consciously decided not to use his newspaper against the rebels. When criticized for the indecisiveness of *Vorwärts* at the 1891 party congress, he explained, "My principle is, within the party there is no party for me. And even Herr Werner [a champion of *Die Jungen*], as long as he is in the party, has for me as editor of *Vorwärts* exactly the same right to have his opinions taken into consideration as my friend Bebel."[56]

Liebknecht's commitment to unfettered expression within the socialist fraternity frustrated some of his friends who wanted to guide the SPD toward a more Marxist outlook. Karl Kautsky is one example. In 1883, Liebknecht had helped him become editor of the SAP's theoretical journal, *Die Neue Zeit*. However, around 1890, Kautsky revised his earlier respect for Liebknecht and became quite critical of him in his private correspondence. He called Liebknecht's editing of *Vorwärts* "downright laughable."[57] To Engels he commented, "It is actually incredible how incapable of judgment the man [Liebknecht] has become. . . . His alleged tolerance follows only as a consequence that he reads nothing at all, not even the newspapers for which he writes."[58]

Engels shared Kautsky's disgust with *Vorwärts*, adding "never had a large party such a miserable organ,"[59] but Engels professed not to be surprised by Liebknecht's shortcomings. From his perspective in London, he thought that Liebknecht had vegetated in Borsdorf; meanwhile, the party had become ever more sophisticated in its appreciation of scientific socialism. "He has remained the same," Engels alleged; "they [the party comrades] have developed further. . . . With *Der Volksstaat* etc. he did no better, but there others helped him to hold the paper up. . . ."[60] In April 1891, Engels observed that "the decisive role in the party is transferring more and more to Bebel, and that is very good. Bebel is a cool, clear head, who has educated himself in theory entirely differently from Liebknecht."[61]

Bebel also growled some harsh complaints about his old friend. He resented the failure of *Vorwärts* to repudiate *Die Jungen*, and he predicted that continued indecisiveness in the central organ would lead to the "intellectual castration"

of the SPD.[62] So intemperate did some of Bebel's private
remarks become that he asked Engels to destroy his recent
letters lest they eventually be published and embarrass
Liebknecht.[63]

Reflecting Liebknecht's senescence, *Der Alte* replaced
Soldat as the familiar appellation for Liebknecht in the
correspondence among Bebel, Kautsky and Engels. That "the
old man" meant something less than total respect is indicated by the avoidance of that nickname in direct correspondence with Liebknecht.[64]

Even Party Secretary Ignaz Auer, who was hardly orthodox
himself, agreed that Liebknecht had botched his job on *Vorwärts*. Auer bemoaned the central organ's vacillation concerning the tactical conundrums that confronted the social
democrats. To Vollmar he remarked, "*Der Alte* has, aside
from his well-known peculiarities--innumerable good qualities,
but he is not a newspaper editor. Of an editor-in-chief
he has nothing about him but the name."[65]

Convinced that Liebknecht had become a hindrance to
the maturation of the SPD, Bebel, Engels, Kautsky and Auer
combined to sabotage his ideological and organizational influence. An opportunity to depose *Der Alte* as the party's reigning
theoretician came when the SPD adopted a new program in 1891.

DEFEAT ON THE ERFURT PROGRAM

The first thorough attempt to revise the Gotha Program had
been launched in 1887, when the St. Gall Congress empowered
Liebknecht, Bebel and Auer to propose a draft for a new platform at the next party conclave.[66] A severe illness that

struck Auer, and Liebknecht's distractions in preparing for
the Second International, scuttled this effort. At the 1890
congress, Liebknecht could only confess that nothing had
been accomplished as yet. He did, however, probe the shortcomings of the current program, borrowing freely from Marx's
unpublished *Critique* as he guided the delegates through this
discussion. At his suggestion, the Halle Congress then directed
the *Vorstand* to submit a revised declaration of principles at
the 1891 congress.[67]

Engels sat in the wings, watching Liebknecht's plagiarism.
He resented the covert application of Marx's ideas, and he
wanted to be sure that Marx's advice from 1875 found full
incorporation in the new party platform, so he decided to
publish the *Critique*.[68] Searching for a forum, he settled
upon *Die Neue Zeit*.

Karl Kautsky had edited this monthly theoretical journal
since its founding in 1883. Originally Liebknecht had overseen his work, just as he did *Der Sozialdemokrat*, but after
the first two years he ceased to take an interest in the
magazine. He did not even write an article for Kautsky's
venture between 1886 and 1890.[69] Thus, Kautsky enjoyed full
autonomy on *Die Neue Zeit*.

To overcome any residual hesitations Kautsky might have
had about publishing Marx's *Critique*, Engels threatened to
publish the essay elsewhere if the German press offered no
opportunity.[70] As it turned out, Kautsky needed little persuasion. After reading the *Critique*, he was enthralled at
the prospect of exposing Liebknecht's deficiencies as a
theoretician.[71]

Publication of the *Critique* alone would have sufficed
to embarrass Liebknecht. Engels also included the abusive

personal letter that Marx had sent to Bracke along with his
more objective evaluation of the Gotha Program. In a brief
introduction dated 6 January 1891, Engels claimed that he
had deleted some of the sharper personal expressions in Marx's
letter. Actually, he added the adjectives "criminal" and
"unscrupulous" to reinforce the anger of Marx's condemnation
of Liebknecht's 1875 actions.[72]

Kautsky informed no one of the planned publication until
the *Critique* had gone to press late in January. Privately he
chortled that publication would be a direct slap at the "old
Lassalleans and Liebknecht."[73] At the last moment, he noticed
from the date on the *Critique* that Bebel was still in prison
at Hubertusburg when it was circulated. Intending to enlist
the support of an irate Bebel in his crusade against heterodoxy, Kautsky sent him excerpts from the forthcoming publication.

Instead of endorsing Kautsky's exposé, Bebel sided with
Liebknecht and dispatched a telegraphic order to halt publication. Along with the other members of the *Vorstand*, he
feared that Marx's *Critique* would rekindle the rebellion
of *Die Jungen*,[74] but Bebel's telegram arrived too late, and
the party at last learned Marx's opinion of Liebknecht's
handiwork at Gotha.

Without comment, shortly after its appearance in *Die
Neue Zeit*, Liebknecht printed Marx's *Critique* in *Vorwärts*.
Another two weeks passed before he mustered an editorial
discussion of the matter. In response, Liebknecht first
asserted that publication of the *Critique* proved the SPD
had "nothing to hide and feared no criticism." Second, he
chastised *Die Neue Zeit* for revealing private comments for
exploitation by the enemies of social democracy. Third, he

noted how the *Critique* destroyed the image of the German workers' movement as a puppet in Marx's hand, observing that the SPD accorded infallibility to no one. Fourth, he insisted that the unity achieved at Gotha had been the basis for the subsequent success of the socialist party. The achievement of the merger thus could "only redound to the honor of the participants." Finally, *Vorwärts* added a declaration from the *Vorstand* disavowing foreknowledge and expressing disapproval of Kautsky's publication of a private document.[75]

With proper party etiquette, *Die Neue Zeit* reprinted Liebknecht's remarks and the *Vorstand*'s disavowal. Kautsky publicly assumed full responsibility for the publication.[76] For a short time, he and Engels considered rebutting Liebknecht's self-justification, but they ultimately decided that their purposes already had been served.[77] Liebknecht's doctrinal impurity had been exposed, and the authors of the next party program could not ignore Marx's *Critique*. As a nasty by-product of this incident, relations between Liebknecht and Kautsky and Engels deteriorated.[78]

This assault on Liebknecht's reputation as a theoretician was only a premonition of a more serious setback yet to come. Within a few months, Kautsky and Engels combined with Bebel to destroy Liebknecht's proposal for the new party program.

Leading up to this rebuff, the *Vorstand* first asked Bebel and Liebknecht each to write a separate program draft. They completed their tasks by the end of May 1891. The executive committee reviewed the two proposals and then asked Liebknecht to compose a revision incorporating elements of both drafts. He did so by mid-June. The directors next circulated Liebknecht's version to members of the *Fraktion* and to Engels, Kautsky and Bernstein. The recipients were

asked to keep the proposal "strictly confidential" and to
return their suggestions for alteration no later than 27
June.[79]

Although the initial drafts by Bebel and Liebknecht
have been lost, this interim proposal from June 1891 has
survived. Since Liebknecht rather than Bebel wrote the document, it seems reasonable to assume that the outcome was
largely his rather than Bebel's work.

The interim proposal began with the proposition that
the separation of workers from their means of production
had split society into two classes: "the working and the
possessing." In the hands of the owners, the means of production had become a means of exploitation. "Political disenfranchisement, social misery, physical atrophy and spiritual
degradation" originated in the dependence of the workers
upon the capitalists. There was an acceleration of the concentration of wealth in the hands of a few capitalists and
a concomitant spread of poverty among the proletariat. The
directionless capitalist mode of production insured the continuation of cyclical depressions and consequent "unrest
and confusion" in society. Collective ownership of the means
of production would remedy this situation. "Capitalist society
itself has created the material and intellectual preconditions"
for that transformation. The document called for an independent proletarian party and reiterated the international character of the socialist struggle. Influenced by Bismarck's
social legislation, this draft declared that "the social
democratic party has nothing in common with the so-called
state socialism. . . ." The long theoretical section was
followed by the traditional list of practical demands. The
only marked changes in the immediate demands since 1875 were

a more specific program of factory legislation, a call for
limiting the working day to eight hours, and an explicit
endorsement of female suffrage.[80]

Liebknecht's interim draft removed many of the fallacies
that Marx had found in the Gotha Program. Most noticeably,
all positive references to the state or to state aid for
productive associations had vanished. "Just distribution
of goods" and references to equality in the future communist
state also had disappeared.[81] These important modifications
notwithstanding, this draft still bore Liebknecht's distinc-
tive imprint. As in the Gotha Program, the interim draft
set forth a list of evils and urged the party to remedy them.
Concomitantly, it understated the inevitable dialectical
evolution of a social order carrying within it the seeds
of its own *Aufhebung*.

Several recipients of this draft made suggestions for
changes, but the most comprehensive critique came from Engels.
He began with a tribute to the vast improvement the interim
draft showed over the Gotha Program. He observed that "specifically Lassallean and vulgar-socialist" phrases had been
eliminated; he commented that the theoretical portion stood
"completely on the foundation of today's science." Engels
then questioned a few minor imprecisions in the first part
of the program. Most of these challenges were easily met
with alterations in a revised *Vorstand* draft. In his one
vigorous and substantive criticism, Engels complained that
the draft lacked coherent political demands. The "free state"
recommended in the Gotha Program had been abandoned, but
nothing had replaced it. Engels feared that, without a specific
demand for a democratic republic, the party would be indeci-
sive in time of crisis. If a republic could not be openly

called for, Engels advised the use of a phrase such as "concentration of all political power in the hands of popular representatives."[82]

When *Vorwärts* first published the evolving program proposal on 4 July 1891, several of the modifications suggested by Engels had already been made. In the only major disparity, the draft still lacked a demand for a republic, but that omission was not just Liebknecht's responsibility. Bebel told Engels that so flagrant a challenge to the German monarchy would be unwise for a party so recently returned to legality.[83]

In mid-July, Liebknecht's role as resident theoretician for the SPD still seemed secure, but then, unexpectedly, in *Die Neue Zeit* Kautsky critically commented upon the *Vorstand* draft. The first three of his essays reviewed the evolution of socialist theory, especially praising Marx's discovery of the "laws of development." Then, Kautsky unveiled his own counterproposal to the *Vorstand* draft. Succinctly, he summarized the difference between his own draft and the official one. His draft, he explained, introduced communism "as a necessity resulting directly from the historical trend of capitalist production methods." The *Vorstand* proposal, on the other hand, derived communism "not from the character of current production, but rather from the character of our party. . . . The train of thought in the proposal of the Party Executive is as follows: the current method of production creates unbearable conditions; therefore we must eliminate them. . . . In our opinion, the correct train of thought is this: the current method of production creates unbearable conditions; it also creates, however, the possibility and necessity of communism. . . ."[84] Symbolizing this difference in accent, the initial sentence in Kautsky's draft heralded the dubious and deleterious conception that some "natural necessity" decreed the transformation of private property into collective ownership.

In large measure, the differences between the two drafts revolved around the role of the party, or in more abstract terms, around voluntarism and determinism. In Liebknecht's version, the "goal and task" of the party was defined as "the ending of [the evils of capitalism], which become more unbearable daily, by the elimination of their cause, and the achievement of the liberation of the working class."[85] For Kautsky, the "task" of the SPD was more passive: "to mold this struggle of the working class into a conscious and united [one] and to show [the working class] its naturally necessary goal."[86]

Perhaps these divergent emphases can be ascribed partly to the different roles of the authors. As an agitator, Liebknecht needed to convince his audience to be active, to undertake the struggle, or at least to vote for the SPD. To justify his own career as an organizer and agitator, he had to believe in an activist role for the party. By contrast, Kautsky devoted his life to the study of theories and laws of development. He had never addressed a workers' assembly, never edited a publication aimed at a mass audience, and never held any elected office in the party or the state. He was a scholar, and his program draft stressed the lesson he had learned--the theoretical certainty of a socialist victory.[87]

Yet Liebknecht's and Kautsky's drafts had their similarities. Both were Marxist, even though neither satisfied Engels' important request to include the demand for a republic. Kautsky incorporated the practical demands from Liebknecht's draft with virtually no changes. As for the different interpretations of the role of the party, that was a riddle that was not resolved in Liebknecht's lifetime.

At the outset, Kautsky's draft had little prospect for adoption. As a lone theoretician, he found little support against the combined opinion of the directors and Liebknecht. Bebel rejected this draft on 12 July.[88] But in the intervening three months before the party congress at Erfurt, Bebel reversed his position, probably as a result of Engels' support for Kautsky's version.

Shortly before the 1891 congress at Erfurt, Chairman Bebel called a conference of twenty-one party leaders from all parts of Germany to discuss the program question. If possible, he wanted to win a united endorsement of Kautsky's draft before the full party congress met.[89] In the conference, the delegates followed Bebel's lead and voted seventeen to four to accept Kautsky's version as the officially sponsored draft.

This defeat upset Liebknecht greatly, and he threatened to withdraw as referee for the program at Erfurt. Because the order of business had already been published with Liebknecht designated as reviewer for the program discussion, his withdrawal would have caused considerable embarrassment. In the end, he accepted the job to maintain party unity. The conference then entrusted him, Vollmar, and Kautsky with the final editing of the program. They made no significant alterations.[90]

At the Erfurt Congress, Liebknecht delivered a three-hour endorsement of Kautsky's program. His speech amounted to a point-by-point illustration of the superiority of Kautsky's version over his own.[91] Engels remarked to Bebel, "It was a

bitter pill for Liebknecht that *he* had to make the report on
the new program in which the last remains not only of Lassalleanism but also of his beloved *Volkspartei* phrases were
expunged. I hope a gently inclined plane will be found upon
which Liebknecht gradually can be slid into retirement--he
has aged notably in the party."[92]

Liebknecht's long speech came on the last day of a seven-
day congress.[93] Exhausted by six tiring days of tactical
controversy, the delegates spent little time on theory.
Instead, after Liebknecht's remarks, the congress voted unanimously to accept Kautsky's draft without amendment. Thus
did the world's largest socialist party ratify a program
that was, in its theoretical section at least, sophisticatedly
Marxist. The Erfurt Program, which remained the official
foundation of party ideology until 1918, has rightly been
called the most significant party document of Wilhelmine
Germany.[94]

The manner of adoption and the content of the Erfurt
Program indicated a significant shift in the character of
German social democracy. Kautsky, a theorist without practical political experience, had composed the SPD platform.
That event demonstrated the growing importance of theory
in German socialism. It also signaled the penetration of
a theory more determinist than that likely to be sponsored
by working politicians. Kautsky's victory and Liebknecht's
defeat were symbolic of an incipient disjunction between
theory and practice in the SPD.

The adoption of the Erfurt Program also reflected Liebknecht's changing role in the SPD. Although his program
draft was acknowledged as scientifically correct by no less
an authority than Engels, it suffered an overwhelming rejection

in the program committee. That defeat resulted from the
theoretical opposition of Kautsky and Engels; Bebel's political muscle implemented that opposition. Characteristically,
Liebknecht sacrificed his own position in 1891 for the sake
of party solidarity.

Unfortunately, this incident was only the first of several
painful episodes that plagued Liebknecht's last decade of
political activity. Even as he was stripped of his mantle of
chief theoretician, his detractors also conspired to make him
a figurehead of *Vorwärts*.

LOSS OF CONTROL OVER *VORWÄRTS*

The party had a dual expectation of *Vorwärts*. At the Halle
Congress, Auer explained that party newspapers not only would
have to spread socialism but also would have to "form the
essential backbone of the party in pecuniary respects."[95]   In
this financial category, the central organ flourished. Under
Liebknecht's guidance subscriptions doubled, reaching over
50,000 by the mid-1890s. Proceeds from the subscriptions
and from advertising generated an average annual profit exceeding 51,000 marks, a sum sufficient to cover the deficit incurred
by the entire remainder of the socialist press.[96]

Preaching doctrine to the faithful posed a harder task
for Liebknecht, particularly since party members disagreed
so persistently about the content of the socialist creed.
Nevertheless, Auer and Bebel, who dominated the *Vorstand*,
thought that a better job in this regard could be done if
Liebknecht were somehow circumvented. Beginning in 1891, they
led the executive committee in a series of assaults upon

Liebknecht's authority. By 1896, they had demolished the editor-in-chief's control over his own newspaper.

Bebel announced the first steps in this campaign in a letter to Liebknecht in September 1891. Lest Liebknecht overlook the reason for the new directive, Bebel remarked that the executive committee unanimously agreed that *Vorwärts* "must become what it hitherto has not been: the leading paper of the party, charting a course. The vacillation and hesitation, which disgrace us before all men capable of thinking, must cease." Bebel blamed some of the irresolution of the central organ on the editorial staff. Among his assistants, Liebknecht had hired his son-in-law, Bruno Geiser, and his former co-worker and current moderate champion, Wilhelm Blos. Bebel ordered the banishment of both men from the staff. For the remainder of the decade, the *Vorstand*, not Liebknecht, decided who would become assistant editors at *Vorwärts*. In the same directive in 1891, Bebel provided a means to insure close executive committee supervision of *Vorwärts*. "Every evening in the future between 6 and 8," he told Liebknecht, "Auer will come to the editorial office and see to it that notices and replies in the party interest appear in the paper, and [that], on the other hand, no false reports appear."[97]

For the following decade, Auer supervised *Vorwärts* in much the same way that Liebknecht had overseen *Der Sozial-demokrat* during the preceding ten years. Although he denied acting as a censor for the central organ, Auer wrote his own lead articles and altered those written by staff members, even those by Liebknecht.[98] The party paid Auer a monthly supplement of 125 marks--half the pay of an assistant editor-- to insure a "close connection between *Parteivorstand* and central organ."[99]

In evaluating Liebknecht's journalism in the 1890s,
one must remember (1) that his newspaper could print nothing
that evoked *Vorstand* disapproval, and (2) that the *Vorstand*
sometimes inserted copy without Liebknecht's approval. In
1894, for example, *Vorwärts* published a highly edited version
of a new work by Engels. Engels was indignant because the
way his work was compressed made him sound like an apostle
of peaceful evolution, and he blamed the calamity on Liebknecht. Actually, the *Vorstand* had moderated Engels' tone
out of fear of renewed repression.[100]

The respective roles of Auer and Liebknecht inevitably
created tension. Auer, it should be remembered, was twenty
years younger than Liebknecht. In December 1892, he thoroughly
rewrote one of Liebknecht's lead articles. *Der Alte* vented
his frustration to Party Cochairman Paul Singer, complaining,
"Every line I write, is submitted to a censorship more reactionary than the police in 1848." He warned that he would
no longer tolerate Auer's interference. "To be sure, he
believes that I've grown 'too old,' but he will discover
that I am still in the position to survive the struggle with
him and others." He cried that *Vorwärts* had become "a hell"
for him, adding that he would have resigned long ago if it
were not for the needs of his family. Finally, he asked
Singer to return the letter; he wanted his sons to "read it
after my death so that they will not become party slaves
too."[101] The relationship between Auer and Liebknecht never
really improved, and confrontations occurred throughout the
decade.[102]

The leadership hesitated to ask Liebknecht to retire
both out of consideration of his decades of service to the
party and because of his continued popularity with the

membership. Engels observed that, if retired, Liebknecht
"would be in Leipzig--historical irony--the social democratic
Bismarck of Friedrichsruh, and ultimately there would be a
row."[103] Still, the executive committee thought that it
might be possible to implant someone in Liebknecht's staff
who would take over the actual editing of *Vorwärts*.

Liebknecht's conception of his own duties as editor-
in-chief gave hope to this maneuver. He disagreed with the
usual "German" notion of a chief editor as one "who cares
for the entire combination, who personally handles all the
material and all the specifics." Because he was determined
to continue his career as a Reichstag deputy and as a busy
public speaker, he preferred to think of editorship in the
grand style. To him, an editor-in-chief should write occasional lead articles and leave it to others to prepare a
paper "in his spirit."[104]

The party directors encouraged Liebknecht in this predilection. Bebel had promised that Liebknecht would have to
work only two hours daily at *Vorwärts*. Citing the demands
of Liebknecht's many other party jobs, Auer urged him to
let more of the work devolve upon his assistants.[105] Then,
in the autumn of 1891, Bebel and Auer tried to smuggle Carl
Hirsch into the staff. Privately they admitted their plan
to make Hirsch actual editor-in-chief.[106] The executive
committee's ploy was poorly camouflaged. Even the bourgeois
press observed that Liebknecht was being surreptitiously
retired. Perhaps out of consideration for his friend's feelings, Hirsch withdrew.[107]

Undeterred, the *Vorstand* tried again to find a suitable
"assistant" for Liebknecht. In February 1892, they hired the
promising young journalist, Bruno Schoenlank. But after a year

away from Berlin convalescing from an illness, Schoenlank resigned from *Vorwärts* to run for the Reichstag.[108] Liebknecht privately gloated that he had thwarted Schoenlank's bid to become "actual chief editor, with me as *roi fainéant*."[109]

With Liebknecht fully aware of the machinations against him, Bebel made him a blunt offer. "We urged him in the most direct way to continue to keep title and salary but to abdicate the actual work to another," Bebel told Engels. Liebknecht refused.[110]

Having failed to supplant Liebknecht, at the 1893 *Parteitag* the executive committee promoted the creation of a weekly central organ.[111] Kautsky hoped Liebknecht would be kicked upstairs into the editorship of this journal,[112] but the directors decided instead to make an end run around *Vorwärts* by emphasizing the new magazine. At their instigation the congress in 1893 voted 134 to 66 to launch the weekly publication. Every member of the elected leadership endorsed the project. Liebknecht voted against it.[113]

The weekly, christened *Der Sozialdemokrat*, first appeared on 25 January 1894. Under the editorship of Adolf Braun, a subsequent assistant on *Vorwärts*, it floundered. Its circulation never exceeded 6,000, only one-tenth of *Vorwärts'* subscriptions. Furthermore, and more damning from the *Vorstand* viewpoint, it emulated Liebknecht's manner of impartial reporting of all sides in party debates. Recognizing an ideological and a fiscal failure, the *Vorstand* persuaded the 1895 party congress to jettison *Der Sozialdemokrat*.[114]

Exasperated by these repeated miscarriages, Bebel and Auer now opted for a fifth-column attack upon the editor-in-chief of *Vorwärts*. Since 1891 the *Vorstand* had reserved the right to appoint Liebknecht's staff. Utilization of

that prerogative insured that the assistant editors owed
their allegiance to Bebel and Auer rather than to Liebknecht.
In 1896, the former two men joined forces with the *Vorwärts*
staff to launch a palace revolution against *Der Alte*. This
time they obliterated his authority on the central organ.

The excuse for the staff revolt came during the continuing
debate over the proper role for trade unions in socialist
agitation. At the General Congress of Trade Unions in 1896,
Dr. Max Quarck, a close friend of Liebknecht who was a member
of the moderate wing of the party, secured passage of a resolution requesting a larger role for unions in political agitation.[115] Liebknecht was absent from his desk at *Vorwärts* at
this time, attending a congress of the Second International
in London. The remaining editors, led by Auer, directed
Vorwärts into its most decisive stand of the decade. Taking
issue with Quarck's request, Auer authored articles arguing
that political agitation was the function of the party alone;
the unions should be limited to improving the economic condition of the workers. Subsequently, the polemic in *Vorwärts*
degenerated into a personal attack on Quarck, charging that
he was but a recent convert to socialism, typical of the
academic sort that preferred bourgeois reform to proletarian
revolution.[116]

From London, Liebknecht sent a signed statement to his
staff disavowing the "nature and style" of the polemic against
his friend Quarck. In response, Adolf Braun and the other
assistants threatened collective resignation if they were
not allowed to express their own opinions in *Vorwärts*.[117]
For the public, they published Liebknecht's statement along
with one of their own. In their declaration they said a
newspaper with a dictatorial chief was "unworthy of social

democracy." They then called upon the *Vorstand* to adjudicate
the dispute between their boss and themselves.[118]

Liebknecht had no defenders on the *Vorstand*. Bebel
and Auer eagerly sided with the staff. Even Liebknecht's
confidant and financial advisor, Co-chairman Singer, agreed
with the other four directors and backed the assistants against
Liebknecht. Considerately, Singer wrote gentle letters to
Natalie, pleading with her to convince her husband that the
current happenings were not part of some plot to harass or
to castrate him politically.[119] But the outcome of this
Quarck affair was precisely that: the emasculation of Liebknecht in his role as editor of *Vorwärts*. On 19 September,
in a front-page declaration, the party directors announced
that after "long negotiation . . . , the great majority
[apparently of the *Vorstand* and the editorial staff] stands
by the position represented by the editorial staff of *Vorwärts* in the [Quarck] matter."

Liebknecht tried to salvage his authority at the 1896
party congress. At that meeting, he and Quarck both demanded
a *Parteitag* censure of the personal insults in *Vorwärts*, but
their cause was doomed. Auer took the floor to justify the
central organ's attacks, revealing that he had authored the
first of them. Bebel followed and announced his diametrical
opposition to Liebknecht with regard not only to the Quarck
controversy but also to the issue of staff independence.
Next, three delegates from Berlin spoke, and each endorsed
the assistant editors against Liebknecht. They also praised
the paper for taking a stand at last instead of continuing
to play the impartial referee.[120] The congress then rejected
Liebknecht's call for a censure of his coworkers. Thus Quarck
was left without satisfaction and Liebknecht without control
over his own staff.

Ironically, *Vorstand* interference at *Vorwärts*, which had been intended to stiffen the backbone of the central organ, was partly responsible for its subsequent reticence on important issues. In 1899, Bebel grumbled privately to Liebknecht about Auer's manifest drift toward reformism and the deleterious effect his attitudes had upon *Vorwärts*.[121] A few months later, *Der Alte* reciprocated with a complaint that the "opportunist and reactionary" majority among his assistant editors had vetoed publication of an article he had written against revisionism. "I find it obvious," he said, "that viewpoints other than my own find expression [in *Vorwärts*]. Only I cannot permit that all other than opportunist viewpoints are excluded."[122] Protesting that he had been reduced to a "strawman," he threatened to resign unless his authority was restored. Liebknecht never found satisfaction for this complaint.

Unfortunately for Liebknecht, the *Vorstand* and his staff were only two of four agencies that circumscribed his power on *Vorwärts*. The Berlin comrades, whose subscriptions amounted to some 90 percent of the central organ's total, successfully insisted upon ever-increasing authority for a locally elected press commission. By 1899, it had been given a voice absolutely equal to the *Vorstand* in all affairs of the paper. If the Berlin Press Commission and the *Vorstand* failed to agree, the control commission was to cast a deciding vote between them.[123] These regulations did not even mention a role for the editor-in-chief.

The annual congresses constituted the fourth agency that limited Liebknecht's authority on *Vorwärts*. Every one of these gatherings during the 1890s spent hours debating the content, format, finances, and personnel decisions of

Liebknecht's newspaper. At the 1893 *Parteitag*, the delegates
spent an incredible two days castigating *Vorwärts*. Sometimes
comrades proposed simple resolutions to reduce the price of
the central organ or to delete foreign expressions from the
newspaper. More seriously, others demanded more decisive
theoretical guidance from *Vorwärts*.[124] Always Liebknecht's
competence was at issue.

Liebknecht was accustomed to such strictures; they had
accompanied his journalistic labors of the 1870s, too. He
had developed numerous explanations with which to defend
himself: the overlapping jurisdictions among the *Vorstand*,
the Berlin Press Commission and the editorial staff inevitably
caused confusion; the small number of experienced journalists
available to the party limited the quality of the newspaper;
the disagreements within the party concerning socialist theory
precluded a single editorial line for *Vorwärts*; and so on.[125]

Sometimes Liebknecht shrugged off the faultfinding,
saying, "To edit democratically is in any case more difficult
then to edit in a bourgeois manner--precisely as a democratic
government is more difficult than an absolute or bureaucratic
one,"[126] but at the 1898 congress his equanimity momentarily
deserted him. Battered by Bebel and the *Vorstand*, betrayed
by his own staff, harassed by his Berlin readers, and now
beleaguered by Bernstein's famous attempt to revise Marx, he
exclaimed before the delegates, "I can say that in recent
years since I have been editor of *Vorwärts*, I have had more
friction and vexation than in my entire previous political
life."[127]

THE REASONS FOR LIEBKNECHT'S LOSS OF AUTHORITY

Specific characteristics and specific mistakes of Liebknecht
account for the sudden decline in his influence. Liebknecht
did not play the intraparty political game very skillfully.
For example, he wasted the mandate "equal to" the *Vorstand*
that the 1890 party congress bestowed upon him. Conceivably
he could have brought his battles with Bebel and Auer before
any party congress early in the decade. Had he couched the
issue as one of free speech, the congress might well have
forced Bebel and Auer to retreat (much as Bebel had forced
the *Fraktion* to back off from *Der Sozialdemokrat* during the
preceding decade). Instead, through insufficient vigilance,
Liebknecht permitted a steady erosion of his position. Especially important was the loss of the right to appoint his
own staff on *Vorwärts*. Instead of hiring loyal seconds,
he soon became isolated from the staff of the newspaper.

Liebknecht was equally careless toward sessions of the
Vorstand. The 1890 congress explicitly authorized him to
attend every meeting. Secretary Auer invited him to each
one,[128] but whenever Liebknecht attended, discussion focused
on the faults of *Vorwärts*. Refusing to confront criticism,
Liebknecht avoided sessions of the *Vorstand* altogether, thus
abandoning the most important mechanism for intraparty action
into the hands of his detractors.

Had he been a ruthless editor, Liebknecht might have
compensated for this bureaucratic loss with journalistic
agressiveness. Early in the decade, he could have used *Vorwärts* to expose and scatter the advancing skirmishers of
the executive committee, but Liebknecht was constitutionally
unable to fight this kind of battle. Despite his blustering

private threats, he simply could not wage war inside the
socialist camp. The nature of his personality and his intense
devotion to party unity dictated that Liebknecht's invective
flowed only against the external enemies of social democracy.

Irresolution already had cost Liebknecht part of his power
in 1885. Although his facile footwork may have helped to hold
his party together during the steamship subsidy controversy, it
also cost him much of his political credit. By siding first
with the moderates and then with the radicals, he had alienated
both camps. Similar vacillation characterized his career in the
1890s, with similar debilitating consequences for his authority.

Other mistakes from the 1880s loom large in retrospect.
For a variety of reasons, some of which lay beyond his control,
Liebknecht allowed his supervisory rights on *Der Sozialdemokrat*
to atrophy during the latter half of the 1880s. In 1888, the
Swiss authorities reacted to German pressure by expelling *Der
Sozialdemokrat*. The paper then migrated to London, a relocation
that stretched Liebknecht's supervision beyond its effective
range. His visits to the staff, his lead articles, and his right
to preview each edition all evaporated as the decade drew to a
close.[129] A similar pattern of events occurred with *Die Neue
Zeit*. When that theoretical journal was founded in 1883, the
Fraktion gave Liebknecht the same supervisory rights over it
that he enjoyed over *Der Sozialdemokrat*. Karl Kautsky served
as Liebknecht's lieutenant, doing the actual editing.
Initially Liebknecht wrote frequently for *Die Neue Zeit* and
he edited much of the copy,[130] but Kautsky gradually followed
Bernstein, asserting ever more editorial independence for himself. In 1885, while Liebknecht was preoccupied with the
steamship subsidy, Kautsky began overriding his supervisor's
decisions about what should and should not be published.[131]
With only a lukewarm protest, Liebknecht allowed this rebellion

to succeed. In the latter 1880s, he did not even write for
Die Neue Zeit, much less oversee it.

Age contributed to Liebknecht's decline in influence.
Physical limitations began to handicap him. In the mid-
1880s, he still relished a schedule that sometimes included
nine speeches and incorporated twenty-five hours of train
travel in only six days.[132] By the time he neared his seven-
ties, he could no longer sustain that pace. Friends solici-
tous for his health began to limit the length of his public
addresses to less than an hour.[133] In the Reichstag, he
spoke with decreasing length and frequency. In general,
even though he worked with awe-inspiring dedication up until
the hour of his death, he no longer could accomplish as much
as a younger man.

The party had aged too, and in so doing it had changed.
From a tiny faction desperately courting each recruit, German
social democracy had grown into a prosperous organization
able to attract talent with tangible rewards. It dispensed
hundreds of editorial positions, each of which carred handsome salaries. For its elite, it could promise election
to the Reichstag, almost regardless of personal attractive-
ness. Rewards like these enabled the party to generate an
almost self-sustaining appeal. And the threat of withholding
these rewards provided a potent disciplinary procedure for
the SPD.

In a successful party like German social democracy,
Liebknecht's style of leadership inexorably sinks into obso-
lescence. His writings and speeches were suited to converting
outsiders to socialism, not to honing doctrine for the faithful. His conciliatory, flexible nature meshed best with
an embryonic party structure, where personal ties were more

important than material rewards or bureaucratic channels.
Liebknecht needed a small and amorphous leadership circle
to excel as an affective leader. About 1890, the conditions conducive to his success faded.

The passing years brought personal changes in Liebknecht's comrades that also contributed to his decline. A
sample of twenty-four party directors, deputies and theore-
ticians who led the SPD in the mid-1890s averaged an age
of forty-four. Of these twenty-four, Bebel was the oldest,
turning fifty-five at mid-decade. In 1896, Liebknecht turned
seventy. His age, which initially had earned him the deference of this younger generation, eventually excluded him
from it.[134] When individuals discard their deference to
their teachers, sometimes conflict between mentor and protégé occurs. Liebknecht's collision with Marx over the Gotha
Compromise illustrates this pattern, as does Bebel's battle
with Liebknecht over the steamship subsidy.

Because Liebknecht had always relied upon Bebel's organizational talents, Bebel's emancipation from Liebknecht's
tutelage is a major reason for the latter's decline. In
his memoirs Bebel recalled how he had only slowly and with
difficulty been able to free himself from Liebknecht's
"apodictal nature." And then, he said, "we sometimes collided
hard. . . ."[135] On his side, Liebknecht resented Bebel's
newly found independence and personal influence. By the
mid-1890s, their long-standing friendship just barely survived.[136]

Similar transformations affected Liebknecht's relationship with both Karl Kautsky and Eduard Bernstein. Both men
had enlisted in the party under Liebknecht's patronage; both
initially admired Liebknecht's talents, including his intellect;

but both eventually disparaged his abilities as a theoretician and even as a tactical leader.[137] By the later 1890s, *Der Alte* had fought bitterly and publicly with both men.

Looking backward slightly, the meteoric rise of Paul Singer to national leadership confirms this pattern of an emerging younger generation of leaders. In 1878, Liebknecht had guided Singer, a wealthy and portly merchant eighteen years his junior, into the socialist fold.[138] From the outset, Singer's financial resources fueled his ascension. He generously used money from his clothing establishment in Berlin to support the families of exiles during the 1880s, and he helped party leaders with their expenses. He even helped Liebknecht establish an investment portfolio.[139] In the surprisingly successful election campaign of 1884, Singer won his first Reichstag mandate. Soon his colleagues elected him to the *Fraktionsvorstand*. In mid-1886, the police expelled Singer from his home in Berlin, and in a fateful move, he joined Bebel at Plauen and they became close friends. To some extent, Singer supplanted Liebknecht as Bebel's most trusted associate.

In the autumn of 1886, with Bebel in prison and Liebknecht abroad, Singer took over the administration of the party. He proved quite capable. In 1887, when electoral defeat handicapped several other socialist leaders, including Liebknecht, and when death or illness eliminated Hasenclever, Kayser, Auer, and still others, Singer strode into the highest echelon of party leadership.[140] In the short span of three years, this *grossbourgeois* was catapulted from local to national prominence. Throughout the 1890s, he chaired the annual party congresses. Furthermore, for that whole decade he shared the cochairmanship of the *Vorstand* with Bebel.

Politics abhors a vacuum. Liebknecht would not have lost influence if someone else had not been prepared and able to exercise it. In the last decade of Liebknecht's life, others already were dividing his inheritance. To a large extent, Singer and Auer were wedged into his position of intraparty leadership alongside Bebel. Kautsky and Bernstein fought over the role of theoretician.

In addition to their own ambitions, these men were bold enough to challenge Liebknecht because they were encouraged by Friedrich Engels. Liebknecht and Marx were closer than Liebknecht and Engels. To judge from the correspondence between the exiles, Marx seems to have been more tolerant of Liebknecht's shortcomings than was Engels. Until his death in 1883, Marx relied upon Liebknecht as his official informant on German affairs. The situation changed when Marx died. The relationship between Engels and Liebknecht certainly was one of comradeship, but it was suffused with an undercurrent of rivalry. Both men viewed themselves as Marx's most important heir. In his memoir of Marx, Liebknecht jealously noted that no one, not even Engels, had visited as often with Marx in the 1850s as he had. In the same source, written just after Engels' death, Liebknecht called Marx the "most affable of men"; Engels was flawed by a "somewhat military curtness which defied contradiction. . . ."[141] In a eulogy to Engels, Liebknecht admitted to only two disagreements with Marx, but he said that he quarreled with Engels "rather often."[142]

Engels had his complaints about Liebknecht too. To Bebel he lampooned Liebknecht's ridiculous optimism and his annoying failure to report any unpleasant news. "You will understand, that a really businesslike and factual correspondence as I have conducted for years with you and with Bernstein was simply impossible [with Liebknecht]."[143] In 1889, Engels told a friend in France that Bebel was "ten times more important than Liebknecht."[144] A year later he informed a comrade in America that he never formed a firm view on German affairs until he read Bebel's opinion on the matter.[145] The respect was mutual. In his memoirs, Bebel, who had hardly known Marx, described Engels most affectionately. Unique among his numerous character sketches, he found not a single fault in Engels.[146]

Engels used his correspondence to encourage Bebel and Bernstein to defy the *Fraktion*. In personal contact he likewise promoted the independence of Kautsky and Singer. In a sense, these second-generation German leaders appealed to a man with even greater experience and even more handsome theoretical credentials than Liebknecht.

Thus, in the latter 1880s, a new configuration of political authority emerged inside German social democracy. A diagram of that leadership would show that Liebknecht shifted from the center to a station of secondary importance. During the 1890s, *Der Alte* sometimes could pit one of the new chieftains against the others and thereby win a victory for the viewpoint he represented, but whenever the new generation stood united against him, as on the Erfurt Program or in the Quarck controversy, he was defeated.

Chapter II
Liebknecht's Legacy

CONTINUING GOVERNMENT REPRESSION

On 22 March 1890, an embittered but unbowed Bismarck left
Berlin for exile at Friedrichsruh. His failure to tame Lieb-
knecht's party had played an important part in his downfall.
Six months later, after an absence of thirty-five years,
Liebknecht returned to the Prussian capital.

Having outlasted the Iron Chancellor, Liebknecht and
his party had high hopes for further victories, and success
did materialize; SPD votes soared 48 percent from 1890 to
1898, when the party amassed over 2 million votes; socialist
mandates multiplied from 35 to 56 in the same period; and
during the 1890s, party investments in presses, offices,
and other things swelled from 164,645 to almost half a million
marks.[1] Yet, for two reasons, the social democratic upsurge
symbolized by Bismarck's banishment and Liebknecht's return
to Berlin produced no further fundamental changes in Germany's
political structure during the lifetimes of either of these
archenemies.

In the first place, despite changes in personnel in
some ministries, the Imperial Government continued staunchly
to defend its undemocratic nature. On the twenty-fifth anni-
versary of the Prussian victory at Sedan, Wilhelm II himself

denounced social democracy as "a rabble . . . not worthy
of being called German." One month after this insulting
comment from the kaiser, Liebknecht exclaimed to the SPD
Congress, "Under the protection of the highest authorities
in the state, . . . the social democrats have been challenged
to a life and death battle. . . ."[2] Enthusiastic applause
interrupted his speech at this point, so he never got to
say what he thought should be done about this "challenge."
Nevertheless, for these vaguely audacious remarks, government
agents hauled Liebknecht into court, where they charged him
with insulting the kaiser. The judge sentenced him to a
four-month prison term.[3]

This personal misfortune comprised only a tiny part
of Wilhelm II's continuing campaign against the socialists.
Although the Reichstag rejected a renewed antisocialist law
in 1894, the courts and the police pursued the subversives
relentlessly. In one twelve-month period in the mid-1890s,
SPD party members were sentenced to more than 118 years of
imprisonment and were fined more than 28,000 marks.[4]

Simultaneously, the kaiser slammed the door on the possibility of a peaceful evolution toward social democracy. Far
from allowing a gradual accretion of power in the Reichstag
after Bismarck's dismissal, Wilhelm II continued to undermine
the independence and authority of his legislature, even con-
templating a coup d'etat to undo the constitution entirely.
Skillfully, he and his new ministers exported domestic concerns
with a dangerously effective exploitation of nationalism.[5]

Trying to unmask Germany's reactionary, militaristic
government, Liebknecht rose in the Reichstag to denounce
the kaiser's proposal for a costly navy for Germany. On
12 June 1900, he blasted that bill as a "campaign of robbery

against the German people." The shocked President of the
Reichstag hastily rapped his gavel. Sternly he called Liebknecht to order for applying insulting terminology to a government legislative proposal. "In the German Reichstag," Liebknecht snapped, "one cannot speak the truth without being
called to order!" The indignant president rapped his gavel
again, calling Liebknecht to order a second time. According
to the rules of the Reichstag, Liebknecht now lost the floor.[6]
This complaint against militarism and the ensuing critique
of censorship were the last comments Liebknecht ever uttered
in Germany's legislature.

Government repression in Germany, which wore so many
guises and pervaded politics so thoroughly, is still only
half an explanation of the failure of the SPD to translate
its increasing popular appeal into real political power.
A second reason lies in the character of Liebknecht's party.
To summarize Liebknecht's legacy, the rest of this chapter
will probe the limitations of vision and decision that crippled
Der Alte and his comrades in their quest to implement social
democracy.

LIEBKNECHT'S PROSPERITY AND ITS POSSIBLE CONSEQUENCES

Three interrelated conditions contributed to the unwillingness
of the SPD to seek power more aggressively in the 1890s.
First, some party leaders lost sight of the party's ultimate
revolutionary goal. For them, consciously or unconsciously,
the organization became an end in itself. Second, the party
lacked the decisiveness to strike out on any bold new tactical
trail. That indecision resulted partly from fear of wasting

the hard-won organization through schism or a failed insurrection, and partly it resulted from the incapacitating practice of intraparty democracy. Finally, the foregoing conditions hindered the SPD in developing a precise plan of *how*
it should come to power. Illustrations of these three points
should clarify them.

In the German workers' movement, as in any organization,
there was a stubborn tendency to substitute perpetuation
of the structure for the original purpose of the association.[7]
Material prosperity may have reinforced that tendency. Consider for example the transformation in Liebknecht since
he had been expelled, penniless and without prospects, from
Berlin in 1865. Twenty-five years later, he returned a well-
to-do political leader. In July 1890, he and his wife leased
an expensive apartment in a new building at 160 Kantstrasse.
Even the wealthy Paul Singer was appalled at the rent they
paid for this domicile, 1,750 marks a year.[8] That figure
for rent was more than twice the average annual wage of
Germany's workers. While the working class huddled in tene-
ments in northern Berlin, the Liebknechts settled into
fashionable Charlottenburg on the western side of the city.
Kanstrasse ran diagonally to the Kurfürstendamm, just southwest of the pleasant Tiergarten. This home of the nouveau
riche was culturally and geographically miles removed from
Deputy Liebknecht's constituents in Berlin's sixth electoral
district.[9] Liebknecht had traveled much more than the four
kilometers that separated his 1890 address from the humble
apartment he had left on the Neuenbergerstrasse in 1865.
He now earned about 10,000 marks a year, and he thought he
needed and deserved every pfennig of his salary.

Contemporaries outside the SPD noticed the enrichment

of the socialist leadership. Eager for revenge, in 1892,
a newspaper edited by *Die Jungen* charged that the party paid
Liebknecht 12,000 marks per year for his editing of *Vorwärts*.
That accusation provoked an uproar at the next congress of
the SPD.

The controversy erupted when delegates from Hamburg
proposed that no party functionary receive more than 2,500
marks for his or her services. That resolution jeopardized
the standard of living of many party leaders. Bebel, for
example, earned 3,600 marks every year from *Die Neue Zeit*,
though he wrote very little for that journal; the Dietz Publishing House also paid him several thousand marks annual
interest on an original investment of 15,000 marks he made
in 1889. Like Liebknecht, Bebel also received 3,000 marks
a year from the party as a Reichstag deputy. He received
an additional 3,000 for serving as cochairman. Thus Bebel's
income easily exceeded 10,000 marks a year.[10] To the sources
of income shared by several party leaders, Liebknecht added
royalties from his numerous pamphlets and payments to his
wife for translations of foreign works. (In 1890, the party
paid her 1,000 marks for a single translation!)[11]

Party wealth made socialist agitation a bustling business. The editors of all major party newspapers earned at
least 5,000 marks a year. Indeed, one of Liebknecht's friends
turned down a position as an assistant on *Vorwärts* because
it paid only 6,000.[12] Even minor party posts carried a salary
of 1,800. To keep these figures in perspective, one should
recall that the average German worker earned only about 700
marks a year during the early 1890s.[13] During this 1892
wage debate, the membership protested against a bureaucracy
prospering at its expense. The complaints consumed a full
day of the congress's deliberations.

During the course of this discussion Liebknecht defended himself. "My salary will appear high to some, but I cannot possibly make do with less if I am to give my children the training they need in order to be prepared for the struggle for existence. . . ." [During the 1890s, two of Liebknecht's sons earned law degrees and one, a doctorate in philosophy.] Continuing, Liebknecht either lied or deluded himself when he told the assembly, "I live as a proletarian and have proletarian needs. . . ." As he wandered deeper into self-justification, Liebknecht commented that he could earn three times as much if he worked outside the party. Becoming aggressive, Liebknecht charged that the assembled delegates were "so to speak aristocrats among the workers, I mean according to income. . . . What would you say if the weavers demanded that no one should have a higher income than themselves?"[14]

Liebknecht's counterattack deflated the enthusiasm of some delegates for this discussion. Bebel shamed the rest into silence by pointing out that Liebknecht at last was being compensated for a lifetime of deprivation in service to socialism.[15] With that, the wage debate faded, having produced no result. It flared occasionally at future congresses, but with no more effect,[16] and party functionaries, many of whom had never spent a day in poverty, continued to prosper.

In discussing matters of salary, delegates to the various congresses surveyed only the surface of what may have been an ugly scandal. Bebel was not alone in living handsomely off investments. On 9 March 1891, Paul Singer wrote to Natalie Liebknecht that her husband had "recently given me 1000 mk with the instruction to add it to the other money that I administer for him."[17] Apparently Singer, an experienced

merchant himself, managed a substantial investment portfolio
for his comrade.

Unfortunately, the nature of Liebknecht's investments
cannot be reconstructed; the money may even have been pumped
into party enterprises, although it seems unlikely that Singer's
services would have been required for such ventures inside the
SPD. Wherever Liebknecht had stored his surplus cash, it constituted an anchor inhibiting any possible drift toward
violent revolution. If he held shares in capitalist enterprises, materially he would have stood to lose much if capitalism were overthrown. If his money lay in socialist businesses, a failed revolutionary gamble could cost him not only
his considerable annual salary but also his investment portfolio. In either case, Liebknecht and the other leaders
of the SPD had sound financial reasons for shying away from
the insurrectionary stroke. If, as Marx averred, one's economic position predetermines one's politics, then Liebknecht
and these other prospering socialists might have done better
to hold their own standard and style of living closer to
that of the class they claimed to represent.

DEVOTION TO THE OLD ORGANIZATION AND THE TESTED TACTICS

Because the party provided for them so well, the SPD leaders
were perhaps less eager than they should have been to reconsider their tactics for the acquisition of national political
power. Liebknecht had practiced obfuscation on divisive tactical issues before, but in the 1890s his predilection spread to
the party as a whole. Although individuals sometimes urged
resolution, the collective unwillingness or inability of the

socialists to grapple decisively with fundamental matters of strategy and principle manifested itself repeatedly during this decade. On the few occasions when the party did reach a conclusion about a controversial problem, it always upheld the old tactics against proposed changes. The fate of *Die Jungen*, which was discussed in the previous chapter, illustrates this pattern. The simultaneous onslaught of reformism provides a second and longer lasting example.

Reformism, the substitution of piecemeal change for revolutionary upheaval and thorough transformation, burrowed into the SPD from several directions. To some extent it could feed on remarks made by Liebknecht. In his long career he had often suggested a gradual evolution into socialism; and typically he asserted that "reform and revolution are not opposites in principle. . . ."[18] When the antisocialist law expired, some other socialists thought the prospects for peaceful change had vastly improved. Georg von Vollmar succinctly summarized his reaction to the so-called New Course for Germany's government: "To good will, an open hand; to bad [will], the fist!"[19] In a remarkable anticipation of Eduard Bernstein's more famous revision of Marx, Vollmar admitted at the 1891 congress, "The achievement of the immediate demands [of the party program] is the main point for me, . . . because this gradual evolution is the naturally indicated path of progressive transition."[20]

At the Erfurt Congress, all the national party chiefs attacked Vollmar. Joining in the rampage against reformism, Liebknecht said Vollmar's mistake lay in believing that the nature of the government had changed in 1890. "What Vollmar has forgotten is that a compromise between capitalism and socialism is not possible and that all other parties stand

on the foundation of capitalism." Tacking far to the left,
Liebknecht even threatened to join *Die Jungen*, who at that
moment still menaced the party, if a strong rebuke to Vollmar
was not adopted. Vollmar defended himself and his gradualist
strategy by urging the delegates "not to gamble with our
exemplary organization," but the delegates ignored his caveat.
Unanimously they adopted a resolution repudiating the Bavarian's
innovative tactical prescriptions. "There is no reason to
change the previous tactics of the party," it said straightforwardly.[21]

This 1891 rebuff did not silence Vollmar. A year later
he indicated his continued movement to the right. In an
interview that he gave to a French journal, *Revue bleu*, Vollmar
asserted that many provisions of the Erfurt Program might be
seen as an "approximation to state socialism."[22]

With unusual alacrity and zeal, Liebknecht used *Vorwärts*
to denounce Vollmar's latest heterodoxy. In attacking Vollmar,
Liebknecht reasserted his traditional view of party doctrine
with a vengeance. Blasting Vollmar by name in *Vorwärts*,
Liebknecht denied any connection between state socialism
and the SPD. When Vollmar protested that his interview had
been mistranslated, Liebknecht's newspaper dismissed that
excuse, noting that "every year in the political dog days
a new pronunciamiento and controversy from Vollmar; every
year, a step further to the right."[23]

Meanwhile, behind the scenes, Liebknecht persuaded Vollmar to retreat, at least temporarily. The two protagonists
unveiled their formula for reconciliation at the 1892 party
congress, jointly introducing a resolution that branded state
socialism and social democracy as "irreconcilable opposites."
When Vollmar explained that he accepted this declaration

"for the benefit and in the interest of our party,"[24] its
passage was assured. Thus, for the second straight year,
Liebknecht had helped to persuade the SPD Congress to reject
an attempt to restructure its tactics and ideology.

Before this episode, Liebknecht and Vollmar had not
been particularly close friends. *Der Alte* disliked Vollmar's
personal ambition and privately criticized him for failing
to study socialist theory at all,[25] but early in 1893, he
wrote to the Bavarian chief: "Your readiness to endorse
my resolution proposal immediately made the best impression
on me." Liebknecht asserted that his "main effectiveness
in the leadership of the party from the beginning" had been
"to create the maximum elbow-room for everybody and to let
no one put his person in the foreground--I had the terrible
example of France in mind."[26] The next time the issue of
reformism arose, Liebknecht believed that Bebel was putting
his person in the foreground and raising the spectre of a
French-style schism. Fearing for the all-important unity
of his party, this time Liebknecht sided with Vollmar.

The third round in this chronic battle about reformism
began on 2 June 1894, when the socialist delegation in the
Bavarian *Landtag* actually voted for the state budget.[27] At
the party congress at Frankfurt in October, Liebknecht joined
Auer, Bebel and Singer in sponsoring a resolution censuring
the Bavarian action, but after long debate and intricate
parliamentary maneuvering, the delegates voted it down. The
Münchener Post rejoiced that no iron strictures had been
forged concerning tactics. After all, it continued, "according to *Liebknecht's* expression, tactics can be changed every
day."[28] The Frankfurt Congress then catered to the southern
German representatives by endorsing Vollmar's call for a party

platform aimed at rural voters. A fifteen-member commission
including Bebel, Liebknecht and Vollmar was elected to draft
a proposal for the 1895 convention. The mandating resolution
instructed them to offer a "fundamental reform activity to
alleviate the distress of peasants and agricultural workers."[29]

After consulting with Engels, Bebel concluded that the
outcome of the Frankfurt Congress imperiled the revolutionary
stance of the SPD.[30] At a public meeting in the second Reichstag electoral district in Berlin on 15 November, he bemoaned
the "dilution" of party principle by "petty bourgeois" elements that had flocked to the SPD since the expiration of the
antisocialist law. Specifically, he criticized Vollmar's
rightward drift from his Eldorado speeches, through his *Revue
bleu* interview in 1892, culminating in the Bavarian socialists'
approval of the state budget. In scathing terms he challenged
Vollmar's assertion that Bavarian conditions required a special
strategy, dismissing this argument as "*spiessbürgerliche Par-
tikularismus.*"[31]

Since Bebel's speech received a full reprint in the
central organ, the southern Germans quickly charged that
Vorwärts had conspired with the party chairman to discredit
Vollmar. The editors indignantly denied that accusation,
claiming that *Vorwärts* had always felt obligated to maintain
the "strictest neutrality" in discussions "inside the party."
On 17 November 1894, it promised to offer an impartial forum
for all viewpoints. Accordingly, for the next few weeks,
Vorwärts prominently featured articles from Bebel and from
his critics.[32]

Meanwhile, in private correspondence, Liebknecht tried
desperately to muffle this controversy. To Vollmar's Bavarian
colleague Grillenberger, Liebknecht whispered that he had

already chastised Bebel for his "folly." "That I disagree
with him, anyone can read in *Vorwärts*--in and between the
lines. But that is secondary, the main matter now is to
prevent evil consequences. And for that we need before all
else cool blood. . . . I appeal on your old friendship to
do all you can to hold the conflict within the bounds of
comradeship. . . ." In particular, Liebknecht asked the
Bavarians to issue only a brief declaration now and to await
convocation of the *Reichstagsfraktion* in three weeks to arbitrate the dispute.[33] Meanwhile, to muzzle Bebel, Liebknecht
tried to enlist Engels' support. On 16 November, he asked
the London exile to persuade Bebel to soften his attacks on
Vollmar and the Bavarian socialists. Otherwise, Liebknecht
asserted, "Bebel will endanger his position with the party."[34]

Publicly, in *Vorwärts*, Liebknecht balanced gingerly
between schism and abandonment of principle. On 23 November,
his newspaper answered Bavarian demands for a statement of
position by referring its readers to two earlier lead articles
on the Frankfurt *Parteitag*. "What was said in those," the
editors said, "stands in diametrical opposition" to Bebel's
recent speech. This front-page essay continued, "Everyone
will understand that it cannot be pleasant for the chief
editor of *Vorwärts*, who has fought for a quarter century
shoulder to shoulder with Bebel, . . . immediately to throw
the whole weight of the central organ of the party into the
scales against an old friend." The next day, *Vorwärts* revised
this rebuke to Bebel considerably. The editors now claimed
that they differed with Bebel only in his generally pessimis-
tic view of recent party history and not on the specific
matter of south German tactics.[35] At last, on 29 November,
Liebknecht employed the unusual device of a signed statement

in *Vorwärts* to define his own position. Again he asserted
that party interest dictated editorial neutrality for the
central party organ. As a personal opinion, however, he
bemoaned the "tone" of Bebel's speech, and he disagreed with
his depiction of a deteriorating party. But on the two issues
of budget approval and agrarian tactics, he claimed to stand
"exactly on the same position as Bebel."

For another week the central organ reprinted comments
from Vollmar's *Münchener Post*, "*Gegenerklärungen*" by Bebel,
and assorted letters from party members and comments from
the socialist press. Then quite abruptly, on 7 December,
this smorgasbord of opinion vanished from *Vorwärts* as coverage
of a renewed government legislative attack on the SPD filled
the first four pages. Two days earlier the Reichstag had
convened, and the threat of outlawry now forced the SPD to
close ranks. On 8 December, *Vorwärts* printed a declaration
signed by the four members of the *Vorstand* other than Bebel
in which they explained that Bebel had not discussed his
speech in advance with his colleagues. Consequently, the
declaration concluded that Bebel had not spoken "in his office
as a *Vorstand* member." An unrepentant *Schlüsserklärung* from
Bebel followed, and with that the furor disappeared from
the pages of the socialist press.[36] Henceforth, when party
members requested space in the central organ to address the
agrarian issue, Liebknecht pointed to the declaration of a
cease-fire by the *Fraktion* and denied the request.[37]

Although the public debate ended, a large store of ill
will remained. Bebel's friends, Kautsky, Singer and Engels,
were irritated at Liebknecht for opposing Bebel.[38] Bebel
himself believed that selfish resentment toward his rise
in the party had provoked Liebknecht's opposition.[39]

Liebknecht also felt aggrieved, and the friendship between the two *alte Kämpfer* disintegrated further.[40]

All the conflict about agrarian tactics produced no result. At the 1895 congress, the agrarian commission introduced its program draft, but the delegates voted it down.[41] Thus, after four years of debate spawned by Vollmar's provocative politics, the SPD had done nothing to modify or to clarify tactics.

Liebknecht contributed much to that indecision. Initially, by his staunch opposition, he helped to quench Vollmar's invitation to reformism. Then, by negotiating, by temporizing and by compromising, he crippled Bebel's campaign against Vollmar. By refusing to take sides in *Vorwärts*, he muddied all attempts at doctrinal clarification, and by his own vacillation he caused confusion in others.

The floundering through the agrarian question in 1894-95 illustrates how the division between Bebel and Liebknecht intensified the tactical paralysis of the SPD. Repeatedly during the 1890s, these two comrades pulled the SPD in opposite directions. In 1894, Bebel took the more determinedly radical stance, with Liebknecht being the more appeasing and moderate. Three years later, on the issue of participation in elections for the Prussian *Landtag*, they switched sides, but they still disagreed.

Throughout Liebknecht's lifetime, the Prussian legislature remained an uncontaminated bastion of antisocialist thought and actions. Unlike several of the other German states, Prussia's *Landtag* had admitted no social democrats. A three-class electoral system that weighed votes according to taxes paid constituted the barrier to socialist success. Traditionally, the SPD abstained from the undemocratic

Prussian elections as a gesture of contempt. However, in
1897, several party leaders initiated a campaign to reverse
this policy. Because of the recent crippling assaults by
the Prussian police, and because of a narrowly defeated
attempt to adopt an antisocialist law for the Prussian state,
some social democratic chiefs thought their party needed
at least a few voices in the Prussian legislature.[42] Thus,
at the 1897 party congress, Bebel proposed a resolution autho-
rizing that participation.

Liebknecht opposed this change in party policy. Arguing
that the basic political situation in Germany had not been
altered, he reasoned that party tactics should not change
either.[43] To implement his viewpoint, Liebknecht backed
an amendment that was designed to gut Bebel's resolution
by flatly prohibiting any election deals between the SPD
and other parties. When the congress endorsed this amendment
by a vote of 146 to 64, Chairman Singer interpreted this
outcome to mean that socialists could vote only for socialist
candidates in the Prussian *Landtag* elections.[44] He thereby
implied that participation would be a mere numerical demonstration without hope of electing representatives.

Bebel believed that his resolution had been sabotaged
by a cheap parliamentary trick. As in 1894, he now tried
to undo an outcome of the party congress that displeased
him. Choosing Kautsky's *Die Neue Zeit* as his forum, in November 1897, he renewed his plea for unrestricted participation
in the elections. In a rather heated article, he reasoned
that the ban on compromises made effective participation
impossible; hence the *Parteitag* resolution became self-
contradictory. The *Fraktion*, therefore, should issue a clarifying directive before the next election in Prussia, coming
up in 1898.[45]

Finding Bebel's logic incredible, Liebknecht responded
in *Die Neue Zeit*. In his article entitled "*Fraktion über
Parteitag?*," he accused Bebel of trying to establish a dictatorship within the party. Liebknecht claimed that, "as
if by autosuggestion," Bebel had confused the will of the
party congress with his own desires. Liebknecht reasoned
that the congress had done with the prohibition of compromises
exactly what it intended to do: invalidate the main resolution endorsing participation in the elections. In a direct
challenge to Bebel, Liebknecht defended the principal of
democratic centralism: "as a member of a democratic party,
unless the party violates its principles, one must adhere
to the majority."[46]

After this exchange, which was reprinted in *Vorwärts*
for a wider readership,[47] Bebel's suggestion withered for
lack of support. Indeed, no further public discussion of
the *Landtag* matter occurred until the summer of 1898. It
seems likely that the SPD discouraged internecine disputes
in the interim in order to present a united front for the
1898 Reichstag election.

After another elating victory in that balloting, the
SPD returned to the Prussian *Landtag* issue. Liebknecht's
newspaper began the renewed discussion with its lead article
on 13 August. In that essay, *Vorwärts* encouraged party comrades in each electoral district to decide for themselves
whether or not to participate in the Prussian elections,
for the balloting was nigh. On 23 August, abandoning its
customary neutrality, the central organ actually stated its
editorial opposition to preelection agreements with nonsocialists. On the next day, *Vorwärts* gave several pages
to a report of a meeting of Berlin comrades that overwhelmingly

rejected electoral participation under any circumstances.[48]
Trying to counter this negative stance, Bebel published a
signed article urging the remaining Prussian party members
to ignore the example of their Berlin comrades and to decide
for participation,[49] but the Prussian party members chose
to follow Liebknecht rather than Bebel on this issue. By
a ratio of two to one, the local assemblies throughout Prussia
rejected participation.[50]

Cooperating with the powerful Berlin Press Commission,
Liebknecht engineered this outcome. Violating his own publicly stated policy, he used his newspaper to instigate not
just discussion but even decision on a matter that stood
on the agenda of the next party congress. Thus, when the
1898 congress convened, it faced a *fait accompli* in Prussian
abstention from the *Landtag* elections. Trying to put the
best face on an embarrassing situation, the delegates appointed
a fifteen-member commission to hammer out a resolution on this
matter for consideration by the congress. The Prussian majority, including Liebknecht, on this committee proposed that
"directives from above" be avoided and that each electoral
district be left with freedom of choice.[51] As sole referee,
Liebknecht spoke briefly on behalf of this resolution. The
delegates adopted it by a large majority.[52] Of course, this
decision was not the last word on the Prussian *Landtag* elections. As usual, conflict proved chronic; future party congresses would repeat these debates, but for the moment, the
viewpoint Liebknecht represented had triumphed.

The outcome of this controversy proved that Liebknecht
still could win intraparty battles even this late in his
career.[53] His success stemmed in part from his alliance with
inertia. The SPD in the 1890s preferred to avoid decisions;

when it did decide, it tended to avoid innovation. This
same pattern was manifest in Bernstein's challenge to Marx.
On this controversy, Bebel and Liebknecht were reunited in
opposition to change.

In an essay that appeared in *Die Neue Zeit* in 1898,
the formerly radical Bernstein wrote, "I confess it plainly,
I have extraordinarily little feeling or interest for that
which one usually understands by the final goal of socialism!
This goal, whatever it may be, is nothing to me; the movement, everything. . . ."[54] This position disgusted Liebknecht.
By early 1897, he already complained privately about how
English liberalism had eroded Bernstein's socialist ideals.[55]
In June of that year he confided to a friend, "I no longer
read what he [Bernstein] writes; I have always already read
it in the *Daily Chronicle* [a liberal English newspaper]."[56]

Despite Liebknecht's personal opinion, his newspaper
was slow to respond to Bernstein. Contributing to this delay
were Liebknecht's notorious irresolution as editor-in-chief
and his incarceration for *lèse majesté*. At last, in March
1898, Liebknecht persuaded Kautsky--who had been reluctant
to challenge his old friend Bernstein[57]--to compose a series
of antirevisionist articles for *Vorwärts*. Typically, Liebknecht then allowed Bernstein to use the central organ for
rebuttal.[58]

With the exception of a single local socialist sheet,
these *Vorwärts* articles were the only attacks on revisionism
in the SPD press in the spring of 1898.[59] The issue languished
until the following October, when Rosa Luxemburg began sniping
at the central organ for its toleration of Bernstein. First
in the *Sächsische Arbeiterzeitung* and subsequently in the
Leipziger Volkzeitung, she charged that Liebknecht's attempts

to maintain unity at all costs had rendered the central organ
of the party useless.[60] The party congress, meeting on 3
October at Stuttgart, also chastised both *Vorwärts* and *Die
Neue Zeit* for failing to repudiate revisionism.[61]

At that assembly, Liebknecht lambasted Bernstein, just
as he had attacked Vollmar six years earlier. Echoing Bebel's
1894 complaints, he worried that petty bourgeois elements
had sneaked into the SPD and diluted its socialist commitment. These elements, he predicted, "could not be relied
upon at the decisive moment."[62] Still in his conclusion
at the congress, Liebknecht crept back toward a middle ground
between Bernstein and Luxemburg. "Out of Bernstein's mouth
. . . the words have fallen: 'The movement is everything to
me; the final goal, nothing!' That is an enormous stupidity.
For that would be movement without a goal. A planless wander-
ing. Comrade Luxemburg has said the opposite: 'The final
goal is everything to me; the movement, nothing!' How is
the final goal to be reached without movement? No: movement
and final goal--movement *toward* final goal, that is the correct solution, and the final goal is the *overthrow of the
capitalist society*. (Stormy applause followed)."[63]

In the following months, Liebknecht continued his personal crusade against Bernstein. In speeches and pamphlets,
he reasserted that "class struggle is the starting point
of the whole modern labor movement."[64] When the French socialist Alexander-Etienne Millerand joined a predominantly bourgeois government in France a year later, Liebknecht threw
up his hands at the international spread of *Bernsteinerei*.
To a group of French Marxists he wrote, "a socialist who
enters a bourgeois ministry either deserts to the enemy,
or he surrenders to the enemy. In either case, . . . [he]
separates himself from us, the fighting socialists."[65]

Inside his own party, Liebknecht was exasperated that
no firmer action was taken against Bernstein. He fretted
that Bebel had lost credibility in this conflict when he
continued to endorse participation in the Prussian *Landtag*
elections. "Whoever exercises *Bernsteinerei* in practice
cannot conquer Bernstein in theory," he quipped.[66] Liebknecht
would have liked to use *Vorwärts* as decisively in battling
Bernstein as he had used it in the *Landtag* issue a year
earlier. Unfortunately, the steps the *Vorstand* had taken
earlier to invigorate the central organ now handcuffed Liebknecht. The majority on the *Vorstand* and the majority on
Liebknecht's editorial staff vetoed a campaign against revisionism.[67] Thus, Liebknecht could only use his position
as a *Volkstribun* to fence with his former coeditor. He did
that vigorously. At the 1899 congress, he spoke in behalf
of a resolution reaffirming the tried and tested tactics
of the party. "Under the old banner, with the old goals
we have won thousands of victories! . . . Should we abandon
this basis of struggle? A deviation from our program, from
our tactics . . . means in fact to defer the final goal,
to retard the struggle, to prolong the battle, to postpone
the victory. Therefore rally to the old program and the
old tactics!"[68] Responding with enthusiastic applause, the
delegates endorsed a declaration that again repudiated any
change in party tactics or principles.

THE PATH TO POWER

During the last decade of his life, while debate about principles and strategy rocked the SPD, Liebknecht insistently

inhibited innovation. After exhibiting remarkable flexibility in the 1860s and 1870s, his ideas seem to have hardened. In the 1880s, when the challenge from anarchism arose, he hurried to extinguish that deviation. A decade later, when the threat flared on the right, he proved equally determined to defend party precedents. But what were those precedents concerning the path to power? Between direct individualistic action and reformism, how did Liebknecht plan for the SPD to transform society into socialism?

First, he rejected any form of conspiratorial action by a minority. Since the futility of 1848, he had been determined to build majority support before the next try at revolution. "The time of conspiracies, of putsches, of street battles is over," he wrote in 1894.[69] Recruitment was the work he pursued, and education remained the major tool. Accordingly, in the early 1890s, Liebknecht instigated the establishment of a school for party agitators in Berlin. Explaining his action in *Die Neue Zeit*, he wrote, "The will of the working people will be implemented--if it is a clear and goal-conscious will."[70]

Voluntary and enlightened mass participation in the revolutionary process was Liebknecht's aim. For him, the manipulative dictatorship of the proletariat always remained an embarrassing and incongruous part of Marxism. He flatly and publicly denied that his party subscribed to it.[71] In 1898 he wrote, "The democratic state is the only feasible form for a society organized on a socialist basis."[72] On another occasion in 1899 he elaborated, saying "To be a social democrat means more than being a republican. One can be a republican without wanting to eliminate class rule. But whoever wants to eliminate class rule is obviously a republican."[73] Liebknecht insisted that economic inequality be eliminated too. Otherwise "economic dependence would make all political freedom purely illusory and rob it of its practical worth."[74]

Freedom and socialism meshed comfortably in Liebknecht's thought. Because he believed that the proletariat ultimately would encompass the vast majority of society, and because he believed with Marx that class predetermined one's politics, he believed that majority support for democratic socialism was inevitable. For the same reasons he saw no need to attract nonproletarian voters.

There are obvious problems and lacunae in Liebknecht's sketchy scheme of how the socialists would come to power. For example, he refused to say whether violence would be needed to achieve communism. Instead, averring that the final goal could be reached either by fundamental reforms or by precipitate revolution, he left the option for or against force to the enemies of social democracy.[75] Likewise, Liebknecht did not clarify the commitment expected of members of his party. Were they to be gun-toting rebels and convinced communists, or were they to be merely passive spectators and lukewarm advocates of change? Liebknecht seems to have paid insufficient attention to the possibility that internal indecision could disable his party at the revolutionary moment, especially if it had grown large enough to enlist a majority in society. Instead he studied the growing socialist tally in each Reichstag election and proclaimed somewhat naively, "More followers, more power!"[76]

Still it would be wrong to say that Liebknecht lacked a theory of *Machtergreifung*.[77] He suggested that an unsuccessful war or some similar crisis might provoke a successful

socialist insurrection.[78] In the meantime, he watched the
increase of socialist sympathies in Germany and awaited
majority support. He never doubted that a final showdown
and an ultimate victory for socialism lay in the future.

There was no apparent imperative demanding revision
of Liebknecht's "receivership" strategy in the nineteenth
century.[79] Socialist ballots increased from election to
election, almost reaching a majority. Far from being sterile,
the tactics were successful, and it would have been imprudent
to tamper with them.

The main tasks for the SPD appeared to be education,
recruitment and the maintenance of party solidarity and
working-class orientation. Liebknecht excelled at them.
While most nineteenth-century socialist movements indulged
in sectarian debates and adolescent rivalries, the German
movement crystallized rapidly and resisted subsequent schism
until 1917. The history of this *Arbeiterbewegung* might well
have been more faction-ridden if Liebknecht--or someone quite
like him--had not played the role of affective leader so
skillfully.

THE ULTIMATE SCHISM

On the morning of 7 August 1900, Wilhelm Liebknecht died.
Working until after midnight in his office at *Vorwärts* the
previous evening, he had showed no awareness of illness. A
few hours later he suffered a violent stroke. That morning
his newspaper morbidly reported how his struggle with death
had tossed him from his bed. For the next week, the first
few pages of each issue of *Vorwärts* were filled with the

catalog of Liebknecht's achievements and with mourning for
the loss of a warm, patient, tolerant and yet resolute
champion of the oppressed. On 12 August, Liebknecht's massive
funeral procession, fifty thousand strong and headed by dozens
of domestic and international socialist leaders, left his
home on Kantstrasse and wound through the streets of Berlin.
Speeches at his graveside in Friedrichsfelde echoed through
the afternoon. The SPD buried *Der Alte* with all the pomp
and dignity it could muster.[80]

"What was Liebknecht to the party?" the assistant editors
at *Vorwärts* asked rhetorically. "He was the party itself.
In him, the history of the modern workers' movement is
embodied," they answered.[81] Liebknecht embodied the establishment and growing pains, the suffering and the success
of the German workers' movement in its first stage of development. He had helped to elevate a struggling sect into the
world's largest socialist party, and he had done so as a
tolerant, democratic leader. His democracy was of a sort
recognizable to everyone: he respected the rights of the
individual, including the right to hold divergent viewpoints;
he almost completely refused to exercise intraparty censorship or ostracism; he tried to lead by building a consensus
rather than by the force of his own will; and all his efforts
aimed at winning the voluntary endorsement of social democracy
by a majority in the whole society.

The passage of time has shown that Liebknecht's success
carried a profound internal contradiction. Many of the recruits
and still more of the voters that the SPD attracted in his
lifetime only vaguely shared party principles. After his
death, strategic arguments about how the social democrats
should come to power and what they should do once there tore

the SPD apart. Indeed, in a variety of ways, the unresolved fraticidal arguments among Liebknecht's political descendants tore his whole nation apart.

In 1918, when the Second Empire collapsed under the strain of defeat in World War I, Liebknecht's party fractured into two warring camps. That division flawed democracy in Germany from its inception, and it helped facilitate the rise of fascism. The ensuing dictatorship provoked the Second World War, and as a result of that catastrophe, the territory Bismarck had welded together is today partitioned between two rival regimes.

In East Germany, the government is decisively Marxist-Leninist, brandishing the dictatorship of the proletariat and thoroughly socializing its economy under state management. In West Germany, the regime is reformist, practicing bourgeois democracy and tolerating a continuation of capitalism.[82] Both of these directions originated in the intraparty schism during World War I, and both of these current German governments boast of descent from Wilhelm Liebknecht. With his stubborn devotion to conciliation, one can almost imagine Liebknecht trying to soothe the historial grievances between these two parts of his fatherland and summoning them both toward international socialist solidarity.

Appendices

APPENDIX 1. LIEBKNECHT'S PRISON RECORD[1]

Offense	Sentence or Procedure	Dates Served
Insurrection against the Baden government	Investigative detention	Sept. 1848– May 1849
Conspiracy to assassinate a government official	Investigative detention	2-5 June 1849
Violation of Swiss neutrality	Expulsion	20 Feb.– 1 April 1850 (served before expulsion)
Violation of ban from Prussian territory	3 months	19 Oct. 1866– 17 Jan. 1867
Circulation of ideas dangerous to the state	3 weeks	16 Nov.– 7 Dec. 1869
Conspiracy to commit high treason	Investigative detention	17 Dec. 1870– 28 Mar. 1871
Circulation of ideas dangerous to the state	4 weeks	Aug.–Sept. 1871
Conspiracy to commit high treason	2 years	15 June 1872– 15 Apr. 1874 (2 months imprisonment during investigation credited)
Publicly insulting a government official	3 weeks	Sentenced in 1872; served May 1874

Offense	Sentence or Procedure	Dates Served
Same	2 months	June-Aug. 1877
Same	12 weeks	Oct. 1878- Jan. 1879
Same	6 months	10 Nov. 1880- 15 May 1881
Authoring a socialist election flier	2 months	17 Oct.- 17 Dec. 1882
Insulting the Bundesrat	2 months (reduced to 1 month)	3 Sept.- 3 Oct. 1883
Insulting members of the Reichstag	4 weeks	Sept.-Oct. 1885
Lèse majesté	4 months	Nov. 1897- Mar. 1898

---

[1]Most information here presented is derived from a record of the Polizeiamt der Stadt Leipzig, dated 11 July 1893, in Liebknecht Archive, 448, IISH.

APPENDIX 2. PARTY PROGRAMS

Excerpt from the Provisional Statute
of the International Workingman's Association
28 Sept. 1864

In consideration

that the emancipation of the working classes must be
won by the working class itself; that the struggle for the
emancipation of the working class is not a struggle for class
privileges and monopolies, but rather for equal rights and
duties and for the abrogation of all class dominion;

that the economic dependence of the workers on the appro-
priators of the tools of labor, i.e. the sources of life,
lies at the root of servitude in all its forms--of all social
misery, of all intellectual atrophy and of political dependence;

that the economic emancipation of the working class is
therefore the great final purpose to which the political
movement is to be subordinated as a means;

that all previous attempts directed toward this goal
have shattered on the lack of unity among the various branches
of labor in each country and on the absence of a brotherly
alliance among the working classes of various lands;

that the emancipation of the working class is neither
a local, nor a national, but rather a social task, which
encompasses all lands in which the modern social order exists,
and whose solution depends upon the practical and theoretical
cooperation of the most advanced lands; . . .

From IML, ed., *Die I. Internationale*, p. 13.

Nuremberg Program (1868)

The fifth German Workers' Society Congress assembled at Nuremberg declares its agreement with the program of the International Workingman's Association in the following points.
    1. The emancipation of the working classes must be won by the working classes themselves. The struggle for the emancipation of the working classes is not a struggle for class privileges and monopolies, but rather for equal rights and equal duties and for the abolition of all class dominion.
    2. The economic dependence of the man of labor on the monopolists (the exclusive owners) of the implements of labor builds the foundation of servitude in every form, of social misery, of intellectual degradation and of political dependence.
    3. Political freedom is the most indispensable precondition of the economic liberation of the working classes. Hence the social question is inseparable from the political, its resolution is dependent on the latter and is only possible in the democratic state.
    Further in consideration:
    that all previous efforts directed toward economic emancipation have shattered on the lack of solidarity among the various branches of labor in each land and the absence of a brotherly bond of unity among the working classes of various lands; that the emancipation of labor is neither a local nor a national but rather a social problem which encompasses all lands in which there is a modern social order, and whose solution depends on the practical and theoretical participation of the most advanced countries, the fifth German Workers' Society Congress resolves its union with the International Workingman's Association.

Original German text in Mommsen, ed., *Parteiprogramme*, pp. 310-11.

Eisenach Program Draft (1869)

   I. The Social Democratic Party of Germany strives for the
establishment of the free people's state.

  II. Every member of the social democratic party pledges himself to defend the following principles with his entire
strength:

    1. The present political and social conditions are un-
just in the highest degree and therefore are to be
combatted with the greatest energy.

    2. The struggle for the liberation of the working classes
is not a struggle for class privileges and prerogatives, but rather for equal rights and equal duties
and for the abolition of all class dominion.

    3. The economic dependence of the worker on the capitalist
builds the foundation of servitude in every form, and
therefore the Social Democratic Party strives for the
full product of his labor for every worker by the abolition of the present manner of production (wage system).

    4. Political freedom is the most indispensable precon-
dition for the liberation of the working classes.
Hence the social question is inseparable from the
political, its resolution is dependent on the latter
and is only possible in the democratic state.

    5. In consideration that the political and economic
liberation of the working class is only possible
if it conducts the struggle together and in a centralized way, the Social Democratic Party of Germany provides itself with a centralized organization, which,
however, also enables every individual to make his
influence effective for the welfare of the whole.

    6. In consideration that the liberation of labor is
neither a local nor a national but rather a social
task that encompasses all countries in which there is
a modern social order, the Social Democratic Party of
Germany considers itself, insofar as the laws of
association allow, as a branch of the International
Workingman's Association, adhering to its aspirations.

  III. To be considered as the immediate demands in the agitation of the Social Democratic Party are:

    1. Bestowal of universal, equal, direct and secret suf-
frage on all adult men at least 20 years of age in
elections for the parliament, the legislatures of the
individual states, the provincial and communal representatives as for all remaining representative bodies.

2. Introduction of direct legislation (referendum) by the people.
3. Abrogation of all prerogatives of rank, of property, of birth and confession.
4. Establishment of a militia in place of the standing army.
5. Separation of the church from the state, and separation of the school from the church.
6. Obligatory and free education in people's schools.
7. Independence of the courts, introduction of jury trials and introduction of public and oral juridical proceedings.
8. Complete freedom of the press, the freest rights of assembly, association and organization, introduction of the maximum working day, prohibition of child labor.
9. Elimination of indirect taxes and introduction of a single, direct, progressive income tax.

The organization statute followed immediately. This proposal is translated from the original German text in the *Demokratische Wochenblatt*, 31 July 1869, *Beilage*. A German text of the version adopted at the Eisenach Congress can be found in Mommsen, ed., *Parteiprogramme*, pp. 311-12.

Gotha Program Draft (1875)

I. Labor is the source of all wealth and of all culture,
   and since useful labor is possible only in the society
   and through the society, the undiminished product of
   labor belongs, according to equal rights, to all members
   of society.

   In the present society the means of labor are the monopoly
   of the capitalist class; the consequent dependence of
   the working class is the cause of misery and servitude in
   all forms.

   The liberation of labor demands the elevation of the
   means of labor into the common property of society and
   the cooperative regulation of collective labor with
   just distribution of the product of labor.

   The liberation of labor must be the work of the working
   class, in contrast to which all other classes are only
   a reactionary mass.

   The working class works for its liberation first of
   all in the framework of the present national state,
   recognizing that the necessary result of its endeavor,
   which is common to the workers of all civilized countries, must be the international fraternity of nations.

II. Proceeding from these principles, the German Workers'
   Party strives with all legal means for the free state
   and the socialist society, the abolition of the wage
   system with the iron law of wages, and of exploitation
   in every form, and the elimination of all social and
   political inequality.

   The German Workers' Party, in order to pave the way
   for the solution of the social question, demands the
   establishment of productive associations with state
   help under the democratic control of the working people.
   The productive associations for industry and agricul-
   ture are to be called into life to such an extent that
   the socialist organization of collective labor will
   grow out of them.

   The German Workers' Party demands as the free foundation
   of the state:
   1. Universal, equal, direct and secret suffrage for
      all men 21 years of age for all elections in the
      state and community.

2. Direct legislation by the people with the right of proposal and repudiation.
3. Universal military service. Militia in place of the standing army. Decision on war and peace by the people.
4. Elimination of all exceptional laws, especially the press, association and assembly laws.
5. Administration of justice by the people. Free administration of justice.

The German Workers' Party demands as the intellectual and ethical foundation of the state:

1. Universal and equal popular education by the state. Compulsory attendance. Free instruction.
2. Scientific freedom. Freedom of knowledge.

The German Workers' Party demands as the economic foundation of the state:

A single progressive income tax for state and community in the place of all existing taxes, especially the indirect taxes.

The German Workers' Party demands for the defense of the working class against the power of capital within the present society:

1. Free organization.
2. A maximum working day and prohibition of work on Sunday.
3. Restriction of female and prohibition of child labor.
4. State supervision of factory workshop and domestic industry.
5. Regulation of prison labor.
6. An effective employers' liability act.

The original German text of this draft is taken from the *Protokoll* of the Gotha Congress, pp. 3–4. The final version may be found in German in Mommsen, ed., *Parteiprogramme*, pp. 313–14. An English translation is available in Lidtke, *Outlawed Party*, pp. 333–34.

Vorstand Draft for the Erfurt Program (1891)

The separation of workers from the means of labor--agricultural land, mines, quarries, pits, machines and tools, means of commerce--and their transformation into the sole ownership of a part of the members of society has led to the cleavage of society into two classes: the working and the possessing.

In the hands of the owners (monopolists), the means of labor necessary for the existence of society have become means of exploitation. The consequent dependence of the workers on the owners of the means of labor is the foundation of servitude in every form: political disenfranchisement, social misery, physical atrophy and mental degradation.

Under the dominion of the owners--capitalists, large landowners, bourgeoisie--the accumulation of means of labor and riches gained through exploitation in the hands of the capitalists accelerates with growing rapidity--ever more unequal becomes the distribution of the products of labor, ever greater the number and misery of the proletariat, ever more enormous the army of superfluous workers, ever sharper the class antagonisms, ever more bitter the class struggle that divides modern society into two opposing camps, the common feature of all industrial countries.

The planlessness rooted in the essence of capitalist private production breeds those ever longer-lasting crises and work stoppages that worsen the situation of the workers, cause the ruin of broad strata of the population, result in general economic and political uncertainty and plunge the entire society into unrest and confusion.

To terminate this condition, which daily becomes more unbearable, by eliminating the cause, and to achieve the liberation of the working class, is the goal and the task of Social Democracy.

The Social Democratic Party of Germany accordingly strives for the transformation of the means of labor--agricultural land, mines, quarries, pits, machines and tools, means of commerce--into the common property of society and the transformation of capitalist private production into socialist common production, for which the capitalist society itself has created the material and intellectual preconditions.

The liberation of the working class can only be the work of the working class itself because all other classes and parties stand on the foundation of capitalism and, in spite of the conflicts of interest among them, nevertheless have as a common goal the maintenance and strengthening of capitalism.

In the awareness that the liberation of the working class is not a national but rather a social task in which the workers of all civilized countries share an equal interest and whose solution can only be obtained through international cooperation, the Social Democratic Party of Germany feels and declares itself to be one with the class-conscious workers of all other countries.

The Social Democratic Party has nothing in common with the so-called state socialism: the system of fiscal nationalization which puts the state in the place of the private entrepreneur but allows the dual yoke of economic exploitation and political repression to oppress the worker.

The Social Democratic Party fights not for new class prerogatives but rather for the elimination of class dominion and for equal rights for all without regard to sex or parentage. In its struggle for the liberation of the working class, the struggle for the liberation of mankind, Social Democracy underwrites all demands, measures and institutions that are suited to improve the situation of the people in general and the working class in particular.

The Social Democratic Party of Germany therefore makes the following demands:

1. Universal, equal direct suffrage with secret balloting for all citizens over 21 years old without regard to sex for all elections and votes. Introduction of the proportional electoral system; appointment of elections and votes on a Sunday or holiday.
2. Direct legislation by the people, that is, popular right of proposal and rejection.
3. Decision on war and peace by the elected representatives of the people. Establishment of an international court of arbitration.
4. Abolition of all laws that limit or repress free expression of opinion and the right of association and assembly.
5. Abolition of all contributions from public means to ecclesiastical and religious purposes. The ecclesiastical and religious communities are to be considered as private associations.
6. Secularization of the schools. Obligatory attendance at public schools. Free instruction and educational materials in all public educational institutions.
7. Education for universal military service. Militia in place of the standing army.
8. Free administration of justice and legal counsel. Administration of justice by popularly elected judges.

9. Free medical treatment and medicines.
10. Progressive income, capital and inheritance tax for the defrayal of all public expenses, insofar as these are covered by taxes. Abolition of all indirect taxes, tariffs and other economic measures that sacrifice the interests of the whole to the interests of a privileged minority.

For the protection of the working class, the Social Democratic Party of Germany demands:

1. An effective national and international worker protection legislation on the following foundation:
   a. Establishment of a normal working day of at most eight hours;
   b. Prohibition of factory work for children under 14 years;
   c. Prohibition of night work, except for such industries that by their nature, for technical reasons or reasons of the public welfare, require night work;
   d. Prohibition of female labor in branches of industry whose manner of operation harms the organism of the woman;
   e. Prohibition of night work for women and young workers under 18 years;
   f. An uninterrupted rest period of at least 36 hours in every week for every worker;
   g. Prohibition of the truck system;
   h. Supervision of all workshops and industrial concerns, including domestic industry by inspectors paid by the state.
2. Guarantee of the right of organization against encroachment by the entrepreneur.
3. Assumption of the entire workers' insurance by the state, with controlling voice in the administration given to the participants.

For regulation and supervision of labor conditions, the Social Democratic Party of Germany demands a State Labor Office, Regional Labor offices and the creation of labor secretariats, whose members are to be chosen half from the workers, the rest from the entrepreneurs.

This draft is taken from the Kampffmeyer Archive, ASD. It has been reprinted in Horst Bartel, "Der interne Juni-Entwurf zum Erfurter Programm," *Beiträge zur Geschichte der deutschen Arbeiterbewegung, 10* (Sonderheft, 1968), 173-75. The original German text of the adopted version as well as the *Vorstand* draft modified to include Engels's suggestions may be compared in the *1891 SPD Protokoll*. An English translation of the adopted version is available in Lidtke, *Outlawed Party*, pp. 335-38.

Notes

PREFACE

1. See his disagreement with Bebel over the interpretation of the intraparty feud in 1885, revealed in Bebel to Liebknecht, 1 Dec. 1898, Bebel Archive 34a, IISH. See also his protest that Auer had falsified the story of the Gotha compromise in Liebknecht to Bebel, 30 May 1900, ibid. For a public example of these early historiographical disagreements, see the article by Franz Mehring in *Die Neue Zeit*, 15/1 (1896–97), 705–706 and Liebknecht's heated rebuttal in *Vorwärts*, 7 Mar. 1897.

2. See *HVP*, pp. 28-29, 53-54; also Wilhelm Liebknecht, *Karl Marx zum Gedächtnis* (Nuremberg, 1896), p. 40; letter from Liebknecht to the staff of *Die Neue Zeit*, 15/1 (1896-97), 543; signed statement by Liebknecht in *Vorwärts*, 13 Feb. 1891.

CHAPTER 1

1. Karl E. Demandt, *Geschichte des Landes Hessen* (2d. ed.; Cassell & Basel, 1972), pp. 561-66.

2. A good account of the operation of the secret societies at Giessen is in Ludwig Weickhardt, *Dr. Friedrich Ludwig Weidig* (Butzbach, 1969), pp. 10 ff.

3. Demandt, *Geschichte des Landes Hessen*, 567-68; Weickhardt, *Weidig*, 16-17.

4. Concerning Buchner, see John L. Snell and Hans A. Schmidt, *The Democratic Movement in Germany, 1789-1914* (Chapel Hill, 1976), pp. 32-35.

5. "Giessen: Vergangenheit und Gegenwart," brochure published without bibliographical information by the Giessen Stadtmuseum.

6. The original research into the family background was done by Friedrich Wilhelm Weitershaus, who shared his data with me in 1973. He subsequently published his findings as "Die Liebknechts: Eine thuringischehessische Beamtenfamilie," *Mitteilungen des Oberhessischen Geschichtsvereins*, 40 (1975), 93-144. See also Weitershaus's *Wilhelm Liebknecht: Eine Biographie* (Gutersloh & Giessen, 1976), pp. 23-24.

7. This story is told in Paul Kampffmeyer, *Wilhelm Liebknecht: der Soldat der Revolution* (Berlin, n.d.), p. 4.

8. Weitershaus, *Liebknecht*, 24-25. Wilhelm may also have lost his younger sister about this same time.

9. Wilhelm Liebknecht, "Aus der Jugendzeit," *Neuer Welt Kalendar für 1900*, 36.

10. Quote in Erwin Knauss, "Wilhelm Liebknecht und seine Jugendzeit in der Stadt und an der Universität in Giessen," *Heimat im Bild*, Mar. 1976, no pagination. See also Robert Schweichel, "Zum Gedächtnis Wilhelm Liebknechts," *Die Neue Zeit*, 19/2 (1900-1901), 530-41, and Robert Schweichel, "Wilhelm Liebknecht--Ein Charakterbild," *Neue Welt Kalendar für 1902*, 35. Since Schweichel was among Liebknecht's closest adult friends, his observation that Wilhelm was a "quiet youth" raised "without love" deserves consideration.

11. Wilhelm Liebknecht, "In der Lehre," *Neue Deutsche Rundschau*, 9 (no. 4, April 1898), 397. See also *Robert Blum und seine Zeit* (3d. ed.; Nuremberg, 1896), p. 132, and

Liebknecht to Hirsch undated [early 1873], in Georg Eckert,
ed., *Wilhelm Liebknechts Briefwechsel mit deutschen Sozialdemokraten*, vol. 1: *1862-1878* (Assen, 1973), p. 539 (hereinafter cited as LBDS).

12. Weickhardt, *Weidig*, *passim*, also anonymous, *Der
Tod des Pfarrers Dr. Friedrich Ludwig Weidig: Ein achten-
mässiger und urkundlich belegter Beitrag zur Beurtheilung
des geheimen Strafprozess und der politischen Zustände Deutschlands* (Zurich & Winterhur, 1843), especially pp. 68, 74-75,
81-96. See also Harold Braun, "Friedrich Ludwig Weidig--Der
Turnvater Hessens," *Stadion*, 3 (no.1), 90-116.

13. For a discussion of my reservations about psycho-
biography, see Raymond Dominick, "Freudian Fallacies and
Their Implications for Psychohistory," paper read at the
June 1979 meeting of the Canadian Society for Cultural and
Intellectual History. For a recently published and quite
thorough critique of psychohistory in general, see David
E. Stannard, *Shrinking History: On Freud and the Failure of
Psychohistory* (New York, 1980).

14. Liebknecht, "Aus der Jugendzeit," p. 40, tells
the story of his loss on the passage to America. Liebknecht,
"Anno 1849. Aus der Schweizer Flüchtlingszeit," *Die Neue
Welt Kalendar. 1899*, 36, says he worked as a "volunteer"
at Fröbel's School. Liebknecht, "Aus meiner Schulmeisterzeit," *Neue Welt Kalendar für 1901*, 45, describes his loans.

15. Liebknecht Archiv, 441/1-2, IISH.

16. Enrollment documents from Giessen University are
cited in "Wilhelm Liebknecht," *Oberhessische Volkszeitung*,
1 May 1926.

17. It subsequently became characteristic for Liebknecht,
whenever confronted by difficulty, to consider immigration.
If psychological theories about regression have any validity,
such behavior may have stemmed from his childhood and adolescent
experiences of relocating when he lost parental figures.

18. Price statistics are from B. R. Mitchell, *European
Historical Statistics, 1750-1970* (New York, 1975), p. 742.
For a description of the potato rebellion and its background,
see Theodore Hamerow, *Restoration, Revolution, Reaction:
Economics and Politics in Germany, 1815-1871* (Princeton,
N.J., 1966), pp. 80-86. See also Gerhard Masur, *Imperial
Berlin* (New York, 1970), p. 42.

19. Liebknecht Archive, 442, 443, 444, IISH.

20. Liebknecht, "In der Lehre," 399; "Aus der Jugendzeit," 36.

21. F. M. Markham, ed. & trs., *Comte de Saint-Simon
(1760-1825): Selected Writings* (Oxford, 1952), in its introduction offers a good summary of Saint-Simon's writings and
influence.

22. Wilhelm Liebknecht, *Erinnerungen eines Soldaten der Revolution*, ed. IML (Berlin, 1976), p. 199. Also Kurt Adamy, "Ein Soldat der Revolution," *BGA*, 13 (no. 5, 1971), 813.

23. Liebknecht, "Aus der Jugendzeit," 35.

24. Ibid., 36.

25. In an article on the literary movement, "jungste Deutschland," Liebknecht recalled his poetic efforts; *Die Neue Zeit*, 9/2, (1890-1891), 44. With relief, he commented that all of his poems had been lost.

26. Liebknecht, "In der Lehre," 399.

27. Liebknecht to Vollmar, 26 Dec. 1892, Vollmar Archive, 1283, IISH. Also Liebknecht, *Erinnerungen*, p. 40.

28. Gerhard Beinbeck, "Ein 'Soldat der Revolution'; Zur Wilhelm Liebknechts 150. Geburtstag," *Hessische Heimat*, 27 Mar. 1976, 25.

29. Ibid., 26; also Knauss, "Liebknecht und seine Jugendzeit."

30. Knauss, "Liebknecht und seine Jugendzeit," describes previous strikes of this sort.

31. Liebknecht, *Erinnerungen*, p. 53.

32. The petition of the students, including Liebknecht's signature as #12 out of 57, is reproduced in Beinbeck, "'Soldat der Revolution,'" 26.

33. Liebknecht, "In der Lehre," 403, stresses the insult implied by the use of the diminutive. Fifty years later, he recalled it vividly. Furthermore, he attributed it to his unusually small stature. Although overcompensation for short-ness is probably an oversimplified and overworked notion, it may have played a role in Liebknecht's drive to become a leader.

34. Unfortunately the protocols for the Giessen Senate for 1845 and 1846 have been misplaced or destroyed. The records for 1844 and 1847 are preserved in the Giessen Stadt-archiv. But the accounts by Liebknecht and subsequent reporters all agree that the townspeople pressured the university offi-cials to yield.

35. Demandt, *Geschichte des Landes Hessen*, 572-73.

36. Hans Brumme, ed., *Wilhelm Liebknecht: Wissen ist Macht und Macht ist Wissen und andere bildungs-politisch-pädogogisch Aeusserungen* (Berlin, 1968), pp. 182, 400-403.

37. Liebknecht Archive, 445/1-2, IISH.

38. Liebknecht, "Aus der Jugendzeit," 35-36. A search of the *Deputationsprotokolle* for the university of Marburg indicates that a student named Liebknecht had quite a succession of disciplinary actions in the autumn and winter of 1847.

Because Wilhelm Liebknecht was in Zurich at that time, unless the record is misdated, this cannot refer to him. The record is in the Hessiches Staatsarchiv at Marburg.

39. Liebknecht, "Aus der Jugendzeit," 37-38.
40. Ibid., 38.

CHAPTER 2

1. Liebknecht, "Aus der Jugendzeit," 39-40.
2. Ernst Nobs, *Aus Wilhelm Liebknechts Jugendjahren* (Zurich, n.d.), p. 12.
3. Liebknecht, "Aus meiner Schulmeisterzeit," 44-45.
4. Liebknecht, *Erinnerungen*, 41. See also Brumme, ed., *Liebknecht Wissen ist Macht*, pp. 183-86.
5. Liebknecht, "Aus der Jugendzeit," 41.
6. Nobs, *Aus Liebknechts Jugendjahren*, p. 34, claims to have found ninety-six articles. Since the file I used was incomplete, his count may be more accurate than mine. Nevertheless, I can testify to the existence of only sixty-five.
7. *Mannheimer Abendzeitung*, 30 Oct. 1847.
8. Ibid., 21 Nov. 1847.
9. Ibid., 13 Jan. 1848.
10. Ibid., 7 Feb. 1848.
11. Ibid., 13 Jan. 1848. See also 19 and 24 Jan. 1848 for similar emphasis on educational reform.
12. Snell and Schmitt incorrectly state that Liebknecht was not concerned with class conflict and the economic reorganization of society. *The Democratic Movement in Germany*, p. 191.
13. *Mannheimer Abendzeitung*, 31 Dec. 1847; see also 23 Jan. 1848. Nobs, *Aus Liebknechts Jugendjahren*, argues throughout that Liebknecht was a thoroughgoing socialist before the 1848 revolution. To buttress his case, he quotes extensive excerpts from Liebknecht's articles. Unfortunately, these very articles are the ones that were missing from the only file of this newspaper available to me. Because I distrust Nobs's bias, I have not quoted from his text in my narrative. The interested reader can examine a strongly worded testimony to socialism in Nobs, p. 49, that the author cites to the *Mannheimer Abendzeitung*, 12 Jan. and 11 Feb. 1848.
14. *Mannheimer Abendzeitung*, 15 Jan. 1848.
15. Ibid., 17 Feb. 1848.
16. Liebknecht, *Robert Blum*, p. 479; also, Liebknecht, *Erinnerungen*, p. 247.
17. *Mannheimer Abendzeitung*, 4 Mar. 1848.
18. Ibid., 14 Mar. 1848.

19. Otto von Corvin, *Erinnerungen aus meinem Leben*, 4 vols., 3d ed. (Leipzig, 1880), vol. 2, pp. 303-28, gives an excellent account of the legion.

20. Wilhelm Blos, *Badische Revolutionsgeschichte aus den Jahren 1848 und 1849* (Mannheim, 1910) was especially informative for the perspective of this narrative.

21. Ibid., pp. 12-20. See also the following useful accounts: Charles W. Dahlinger, *The German Revolution of 1849* (New York, 1903), p. 16; Snell and Schmidt, *The Democratic Movement in Germany*, pp. 89-91; Dorothy C. Vogel, "Historiographical Analysis of the Baden Revolutions of 1848-1849" (New York University, Unpublished Ph.D. Dissertation, 1970), pp. 54-58.

22. Corvin, *Erinnerungen*, vol. 2, p. 332.

23. Detlev Roberty, "Ein Soldat der Revolution," *Neue Welt Kalendar für 1897*, 66. Liebknecht's last report in the *Mannheimer Abendzeitung*, without dateline, appeared 28 Mar. 1848.

24. Photocopies of documents of the Democratic Union were supplied by the Bundesarchiv at Bern; see documents E 21/180, Bd. 2, and E 21/180A, Bd. 2. See also the report issued by the Swiss Bundesrat, *Bericht und Beschlusse des schweizerischen Bundesrathes in Sachen der deutschen Arbeiterverein in der Schweiz* (Zurich, 1850), pp. 16-21. It should be stressed that this society was a democratic and not a workers' organization, and apparently it had no ties to the worker organizations described in Peter Noyes, *Organization and Revolution: Working-Class Associations in the German Revolution of 1848-49* (Princeton, 1966).

25. Koppel S. Pinson, *Modern Germany*, 2d. ed. (New York, 1966), pp. 81-84. On Struve, see also Viet Valentin, *1848: Chapters of German History* (Archon, 1965), p. 99; and Dahlinger, *The German Revolution*, pp. 103 ff.

26. Liebknecht to Struve, 20 June 1864, says "Although our paths separated fourteen years ago, we have still pursued essentially the same goal since then. In any case I have never ceased respecting you and loving you as a good friend." In Bundesarchiv, Aussenstelle Frankfurt, Nachlass Gustav von Struve, Packet 27, Briefe 28. Liebknecht also spoke highly of Struve in "Anno 1849," 34-35.

27. Gustav von Struve, *Geschichte der drei Volkserhebungen in Baden* (Bern, 1849), pp. 96-133. See also Vogel, "Historiographical Analysis," 59-64; and Blos, *Badische Revolutionsgeschichte*, pp. 40-44.

28. Quoted in Friedrich Engels, "Die Deutsche Reichsverfassungskampagne," MEW, vol. 7, p. 162.

29. Wilhelm Liebknecht, "Drei Tage in den Kasematten von Rastatt," *Neue Welt Kalendar*. *1895*, 43; also Wilhelm Liebknecht, "Ein Weib und ein Mann," in Emma Adler, ed., *Neues Buch der Jugend* (Vienna, 1912), pp. 183-85.

30. Corvin, *Erinnerungen*, 2, pp. 437-40, alleges that Struve was both "insane" and an unwitting tool of the reactionaries. Blos, *Badische Revolutionsgeschichte*, p. 46, calls the venture "comic." Vogel, "Historiographical Analysis," 248, says most commentators agree that the September *Putsch* was the "least wise and praiseworthy" of the three revolts in Baden.

31. Snell and Schmidt, *Democratic Movement*, p. 105.

32. In the *Grossherzoglich Badisches Regierungsblatt*, 64 Jahrgang, No. 1-83, the order proclaiming martial law is dated 23 Sept. 1848, even before the battle of Staufen. Blos, *Badische Revolutionsgeschichte*, pp. 44-45, reports the guerillas' arrest and fortuitous escape from courts martial. Struve recalls his arrest in a handwritten draft for his memoir, p. 121, in Bundesarchiv, Aussenstelle Frankfurt, Nachlass Struve. When Wilhelm Liebknecht's son, Karl, was apprehended during a misfiring revolution in Berlin eighty years later, his captors killed him outright and threw his body into a canal.

33. GLA, Abteilung 240 has records of cases for over 500 persons investigated and tried in 1849 and 1850. Struve's records survive, perhaps because his trial actually occurred. Unfortunately I found no record of Liebknecht, but his papers probably were lost or destroyed when revolution inundated his trial at Freiburg. The total of 3,500 is calculated by the number of prisoners taken in the various battles.

34. GLA, Abt. 241/22.

35. Schweichel, "Zum Gedächtnis Liebknechts," 542.

36. Valentin, *1848*, pp. 392-93; and Dahlinger, *German Revolution*, pp. 28-32.

37. Blos, *Badische Revolutionsgeschichte*, pp. 74-77.

38. Ibid., p. 78. Also see Vogel, "Historiographical Analysis," 64-72; and Dahlinger, *German Revolution*, pp. 34-39.

39. Liebknecht, "Drei Tage," 43; Struve, *Geschichte der Volkserhebungen*, p. 154.

40. Blos, *Badische Revolutionsgeschichte*, pp. 79-81; Dahlinger, *German Revolution*, pp. 44-73.

41. Responsibility for the defeat of the revolution in Baden is a subject of controversy. Friedrich Engels stressed the potential for a revolution that controlled an entire state. At the same time, he noted that the ultimate fate of the Baden insurrection depended upon the viability of the revolutions in Paris and in Hungary. In any case, a

decisive offensive was absolutely indispensable, and according to Engels, Brentano bears a heavy burden of blame for
failing to launch it: see his *Germany: Revolution and Counter-
Revolution* (Chicago, 1967), pp. 233-34, and his "Die deutsche
Reichsverfassungskampagne," especially pp. 131, 133-44.
Dahlinger, *The German Revolution*, pp. 100-103, is far more
sympathetic toward Brentano's fear of a terror in Baden.
Without elaboration, Dahlinger says that the demoralized
troops blamed their early defeats on Struve. He implies
that this animosity explained Struve's removal from the State
Council. Vogel, "Historiographical Analysis," 72-79, reasserts
the counterrevolutionary orientation of Brentano's actions,
including the dismissal of Struve. Liebknecht of course was
hostile to Brentano in his recollections. He had no doubt
that a decisive offensive offered the only hope for the revolution. See his "Drei Tage," 44.

    42. Liebknecht, "Drei Tage," 44.

    43. Ibid. See also Struve's recollection in his hand-
written memoir, p. 123, in Bundesarchiv, Aussenstelle Frankfurt, Nachlass Struve.

    44. Vogel, "Historiographical Analysis," 160-86.

    45. Liebknecht, "Drei Tage," 45.

    46. Struve, *Geschichte der Volkserhebungen*, pp. 203-
207; Blos, *Badische Revolutionsgeschichte*, p. 90. For Liebknecht's recollection, see "Drei Tage," 45-46.

    47. Liebknecht, "Drei Tage," 45-46.

    48. Vogel, "Historiographical Analysis," 258.

    49. Engels, "Die deutsche Reichsverfassungskampagne,"
pp. 185-90; Blos, *Badische Revolutionsgeschichte*, pp. 92-111.

    50. Engels, "Die deutsche Reichsverfassungskampagne,"
pp. 192-93, reflects Engels's bitterness at Struve's flip-
flop, for he was still among the soldiers in the field who
were abandoned by this decision. Indeed, Engels's commentary
in this article often challenges Struve's account; see also
pp. 179-82. For Struve's recollection, see his handwritten
memoir in the Bundesarchiv, Aussenstelle Frankfurt, Nachlass
Struve, pp. 87-89, or his *Geschichte der Volkserhebungen*.

    51. Liebknecht, "Anno 1849," 31-32.

    52. Blos, *Badische Revolutionsgeschichte*, pp. 114-26.

    53. See Bibliography, p. xxx.

    54. For examples of Liebknecht's use of history to
highlight current abuses, see Liebknecht, *Robert Blum*, p.
132, and *Robert Owen: Sein Leben und sozialpolitisches Wirken*
(Nuremberg, 1892), p. 132.

    Sometimes his writings have to be understood as thinly
veiled metaphors. In "Drei Tage," pp. 46-47, he recalls his

vain attempts as a youth to warn the faction's veterans,
Struve and Becker, about an impending counterrevolutionary
coup. Clues abound that he spoke in a parable. The symbolic
meaning concerned the intraparty leftist movement of the
1890s, called *Die Jungen*, who tried to warn the veteran leaders
against a drift into opportunism.

Liebknecht's writings, despite their tendentious nature,
are less dogmatic than current Marxist historiography. In
Robert Blum, pp. 73-74, for example, he was very charitable
to his subject, asserting that Blum had to be judged by the
standards of his day. Eugene Neuman, *Restoration Radical:
Robert Blum and the Challenge of German Democracy, 1807-48*
(Boston, 1974), pp. 9-10, argues that Liebknecht greatly
exaggerated Blum's dedication to socialism. Neuman underestimates that dedication, and his own evidence on pp. 149-
50 supports this contention.

55. For specific attacks on Sybel and Treitschke, see
Wilhelm Liebknecht, *Zum Jübeljahr der Märzrevolution* (Berlin,
1898), p. 64. For his disagreement with Hans Blum, the son
of Robert, see "Anno 1849," 34.

56. Liebknecht, *Zum Jübeljahr*, p. 67.

57. Ibid., p. 84.

58. Ibid., pp. 84, 90; see also Liebknecht, *Robert
Blum*, p. 324.

59. Liebknecht, *Erinnerungen*, pp. 194-97.

60. Wilhelm Liebknecht, "Zu Trutz and Schutz" (5th
ed.; Hottingen-Zurich, 1883 [1871]), pp. 18-19, said that
all popular revolutions from the Peasants' War to 1848 had
been defensive in nature. In a speech to the Reichstag in
1882, he asserted that government repression (like the antisocialist law then in force) provoked revolution: VdR, 24
Jan. 1882, 66, p. 923.

61. Liebknecht's introduction to *Der Hochverrathsprozess
wider Liebknecht, Bebel, Hepner vor dem Schwurgericht zu
Leipzig von 11. bis 26. März 1872* (Berlin, 1894), p. 42.
(Hereinafter this source will be abbreviated *HVP*.)

62. Wilhelm Liebknecht, "Hochverrath und Revolution,"
Sozialdemokratische Bibliothek, vol. 2, Hefte 14-24 (Hottingen-
Zurich, 1887-1888), p. 11.

63. Liebknecht, *Robert Blum*, p. 392; see also pp. 479-80.

CHAPTER 3

1. Andrew Lees, *Revolution and Reflection: Intellectual
Change in Germany during the 1850's* (The Hague, 1974), passim.

2. Liebknecht, "Anno 1849," 33.

3. Ibid., 35-36.

4. Struve's handwritten memoir, p. 90, in Bundesarchiv, Aussenstelle Frankfurt, Nachlass Struve, describes the various people present at Geneva.

5. Wilhelm Liebknecht, *Karl Marx: Biographical Memoirs*, trans. by Ernest Untermann (Chicago, 1904), p. 70.

6. Liebknecht, "Anno 1849," 36-37. Signs of emerging class consciousness already existed in a circular of the Zurich Democratic Union dated a year earlier, 20 Aug. 1848; but the animosity toward middle-class liberals is much more explicit in one dated 2 Oct. 1849. Both circulars may be read in Swiss Bundesrat, *Bericht und Beschlussen in Sachen der Arbeiterverein*, pp. 24-27, 47. For similar developments about the same time in Germany itself, see Noyes, *Organization and Revolution*, p. 277.

7. Franklin S. Haiman, *Group Leadership and Democratic Action* (Boston, 1950), p. 10; Alvin Gouldner, ed., *Studies in Leadership* (New York, 1965), pp. 21-27, 41-42; and Bernard Bass, *Leadership Psychology and Organizational Behavior* (New York, 1960), pp. 18, 21. A less sophisticated account of the connection between personality and leadership is presented in Bruce Mazlish, *The Revolutionary Ascetic* (New York, 1976), pp. 5-6 and passim. Mazlish suggests that typical successful revolutionary leaders have few "libidinal ties" to their comrades because they displace their libido onto the revolution. This conception surely misses Liebknecht's type of leadership.

8. Bass, *Leadership Psychology*, p. 156; Sidney Verba, *Small Groups and Political Behavior* (Princeton, N.J., 1961), pp. 143-44 and passim.

9. Comments by Franz Mehring in *Archiv für die Geschichte des Sozialismus und der Arbeiterbewegung* (Leipzig, 1911-30), vol. 1, p. 118; and vol. 4, p. 304; Eduard Bernstein, *Aus den Jahren meines Exils* (Berlin, 1918), pp. 136-39.

10. Engels to Lafargue, 13 Dec. 1886, in Friedrich Engels, Paul and Laura Lafargue, *Correspondence*, trans. by Yvonne Kapp (Moscow, 1959-60), vol. 1, p. 401; also see Engels to Bebel, 10/11 May 1883, in Werner Blumenberg, ed., *August Bebels Briefwechsel mit Friedrich Engels* (The Hague, 1965), pp. 158-59.

11. Robert Schweichel, "Wilhelm Liebknecht als Schriftsteller," *Die Neue Welt* (no. 42, 1900), 333; also Engels to Sorge, 3 Mar. 1887, in MEW, vol. 36, p. 623.

12. See Liebknecht, "Anno 1849," 31; and sample the collection, Liebknecht, *Erinnerungen*.

13. For an American newspaper reporter's description of Liebknecht's rational oratorical style, see the *Cincinnati Commercial Gazette*, 15 Nov. 1886.

14. Liebknecht, *Marx*, pp. 86–87.

15. Bern Bundesarchiv, E21/184B, Bd. 2. See also Swiss Bundesrat, *Bericht und Beschlusse in Sachen der Arbeiterverein*, pp. 35–37; and Balser, *Sozial-Demokratie*, vol. 1, pp. 261–64.

16. Bern Bundesarchiv, E21/184B, Bd. 2.

17. Ibid.

18. Ibid. See also Swiss Bundesrat, *Bericht und Beschlusse*, pp. 55–56.

19. Bern Bundesarchiv, E21/180A, Bd. 2; also Swiss Bundesrat, *Bericht und Beschlusse*, pp. 41–43.

20. Liebknecht, "Anno 1849," 36–37.

21. Nobs, *Liebknechts Jugendjahren*, pp. 98–123; Liebknecht, "Aus der Jugendzeit," 35; Balser, *Sozial-Demokratie*, vol. 1, p. 260.

22. "Briefe von Wilhelm Liebknecht aus dem Jahren 1850," *Die Neue Zeit*, 31/2 (1912–13), 1028. See also Swiss Bundesrat, *Bericht und Beschlusse*, p. 5; and Liebknecht, "Anno 1849," 38.

23. Nobs, *Liebknechts Jugendjahren*, pp. 112, 122–23; Swiss Bundesrat, *Bericht und Beschlusse*, pp. 56–57; Balser, *Sozial-Demokratie*, vol. 1, 266–67.

24. Liebknecht, "Anno 1849," 38.

25. Mitchell, *European Historical Statistics*.

26. Geoffrey Trease, *London* (New York, 1975), pp. 190 ff.; and Francis Sheppard, *London 1808–1870* (Berkeley & Los Angeles, 1971), pp. 276–77. I would also like to thank Professor Vladimir Steffel for sharing with me some of his insights about mid-nineteenth-century London.

27. Liebknecht to Engels, 19 Jan. 1853, in Georg Eckert, ed., *Wilhelm Liebknechts Briefwechsel mit Karl Marx und Friedrich Engels* (The Hague, 1963), p. 26. (Hereinafter this source will be abbreviated LBME.) See also the letters from Liebknecht to the Cotta'sche Buchhlandlung, 5 Jan. 1857, 31 Mar., 31 Aug., 2 Dec. 1858, in Cotta Archiv (Stiftung der Stuttgarten Zeitung), Schiller-Nationalmuseum, Marbach a.N. (Hereinafter cited as Cotta Archiv.)

28. Lutz, "Liebknecht als Sozialist," 71, mistakenly construes Liebknecht's praise for England in the 1870s, after he had returned to Germany, as evidence that he admired England in the 1850s. Actually, Liebknecht consistently exaggerated his admiration for foreign examples in order to heighten discontent in Germany.

29. Liebknecht, *Marx*, p. 149.

30. Articles by Liebknecht, signed //, in the Augsburg
Allgemeine Zeitung, 3 May 1856 and 3 July 1858. See similar
sentiments in one article by Liebknecht in the *Osnabrücker
Zeitung*, 19 May 1864.

31. Wilhelm Liebknecht, "Ein Bild aus dem Londoner
Fluchtlingsleben," *Die Neue Welt Kalendar. 1896*, 38–39.

32. Liebknecht, *Marx*, pp. 52–58. Also Balser, *Sozial-
Demokratie*, vol. 1, pp. 221–22.

33. Liebknecht, *Marx*, pp. 11–12.

34. See the letters from Marx's daughter to Liebknecht
in LBME, pp. 413–27.

35. Liebknecht, *Marx*, pp. 53–118.

36. In his letter to the Cotta'sche Buchhandlung of
1861, he lists his address as 3 Ronburgh Terrace in Kentish
Town; in Cotta Archiv.

37. The English translation of Liebknecht, *Marx*, p. 6,
has deleted the emphasis that Engels saw Marx "only nearly"
as much as Liebknecht. Grammatical simplification may explain
the deletion. In any case, my citation for this passage is
taken from the German, *Karl Marx zum Gedächtnis* (Nuremberg,
1896), pp. iii–iv. All other citations to this source will
again refer to the English translation.

38. Liebknecht, *Marx*, p. 72. Liebknecht names these
fights: (1) the argument in the early 1850s concerning the
Workers' Educational Society in London; and (2) the debate
over the Gotha Program in 1875. Three other major disputes
included: (1) differences over the proper tactics concerning
national unification and the left-liberals in Germany, 1866–71.
This dispute was compounded by what Marx saw as Liebknecht's
neglect of the International Workingman's Association; (2)
disagreement about tactics concerning Bakunin's threat to
the International in 1872–73; and (3) misunderstandings surrounding the founding of *Der Sozialdemokrat* in 1879–80. This
list does not include less important squabbles such as the
personal spat in the spring of 1870, even though that tiff
interrupted the correspondence between Marx and Liebknecht
for several months.

39. Marx to Engels, 6 Jan. 1851 and 10 March 1853,
in MEW, vol. 27, p. 156, and vol. 28, p. 224. See vol. 29
for the omission of Liebknecht from Apr. 1857 to Aug. 1858.

40. Quoted in Gerhard Beinbeck, "Ein 'Soldat der Revolution': Zu Wilhelm Liebknechts 150. Geburtstag." *Hessische
Heimat*, 27 Mar. 1976, p. 27. Liebknecht himself also quoted
this remark in *Marx*, p. 81.

41. Liebknecht's introductory comments in HVP, pp.
28–29.

42. Present-day Marxists emphasize the debt that Lieb-
knecht owed to Marx and stress his role as a transmitter of
Marxism to the German workers' movement. For examples of
this viewpoint, see Karl-Heinz Leidigkeit, *Wilhelm Liebknecht
und August Bebel in der deutschen Arbeiterbewegung, 1862-1869*
(Berlin, 1957), p. 35; Adamy, "Soldat der Revolution," 814;
Vadim Chubinskii, *Wilhelm Liebknecht* (Moscow, 1968), p. 20;
Joseph Schleifstein et al., *150 Jahre: Wilhelm Liebknecht
29 März 1826 - Giessen* (Frankfurt a.Main, 1976), p. 7. Non-
Marxists (and some nonorthodox Marxists) prefer to minimize
Liebknecht's allegiance to Marx. Eduard Bernstein, the pro-
genitor of all subsequent revisionism, began this tendency by
saying he thought Liebknecht had "not read very much or very
intensively" and labeling him a "socialist of the French
school": *Aus dem Jahren meines Exils*, pp. 136-37. Karl
Kautsky seconded the depiction of Liebknecht as a second-
rate theoretician who knew "nothing of Marxism, neither
economic nor historical": in Benedikt Kautsky, *Karl Kautskys
Briefwechsel mit Friedrich Engels* (Vienna, 1955), p. 165.
See also Karl Kautsky, *Erinnerungen und Erörterungen* (The
Hague, 1960), p. 375. This viewpoint constitutes the thrust
of current West German writing about Liebknecht. See Hans-
Joseph Steinberg, *Sozialismus und deutsche Sozialdemokratie*
(Hannover, 1967), pp. 14-15.
    43. Minutes of the meeting are in Gerhard Becker, "Der
'Neue Arbeiter-Verein in London' 1852," *Zeitschrift für
Geschichtswissenschaft*, 14 (no. 1, 1966), 85-97.
    44. Liebknecht to Marx, 13 May 1870, in LBME, pp. 100-
101.
    45. Liebknecht to Marx, 2 Oct. 1868, Marx/Engels Archive,
D3146, IISH.
    For almost identical pleas for a division of labor,
see Liebknecht to Marx, 13 Nov. 1869, in Erich Kundel, "Aus
dem Briefwechsel der 'Volksstaat'--Redaktion mit Karl Marx
und Friedrich Engels," BGA 9 (no. 4, 1969), 652; Liebknecht,
Marx, pp. 8-9; Vetter Niemand (pseudonym for Liebknecht),
"Trutz-Eisenstirn. Erzieherisches aus Puttkamerum," in
Sozialdemokratische Bibliothek (London, 1889-90), vol. 3,
p. 23.
    46. Liebknecht to Vollmar, 15 Jan. 1893, Vollmar Archive,
1283, IISH.
    47. See, for example, Engels to Bernstein, 27 Feb./1
Mar. 1883, in Helmut Hirsch, ed., *Eduard Bernstein's Briefwechsel mit Friedrich Engels* (Assen, 1970), p. 194.
    48. Marx to Kugelmann, 5 Dec. 1868, in *Marx's Letters
to Dr. Kugelmann*, trs. anon. (London, n.d.), pp. 81-82. A

similar opinion is expressed in Engels to Marx, 10 April 1868, in MEW, vol. 32, p. 56.

49. Liebknecht, "Trutz-Eisenstern," 12-13.

50. In Robert Tucker, ed., *The Marx-Engels Reader* (New York, 1972), p. 109.

51. See the introduction to *Der Bund der Kommunisten. Dokumente und Materialen* (Berlin, 1970), vol. 1, pp. 46-49. In Karl Marx and Friedrich Engels, *The Cologne Communist Trial*, tr. Rodney Livingston (New York, 1971), pp. 22-25, the introduction is also useful. Also see David McLellan, *Karl Marx* (New York, et al., 1973), pp. 246-52. When Marx's comrades in Cologne were convicted in 1852, primary among the forged evidence was a diary of minutes supposedly written by H. [sic] Liebknecht. Discrediting that document is a major part of Marx's denunciation of the trial; see Marx and Engels, *The Cologne Communist Trial*, pp. 88-90, 99.

52. Marx to Lassalle, 6 Nov. 1859, in MEW, vol. 19, p. 619, only slightly overstates the truth in saying Marx had no connections to any of the exile factions since 1851.

53. See the German translation of Wadim Tschubinskii, *Wilhelm Liebknecht* (Berlin, 1973), pp. 32-33.

54. Brumme, ed., *Wilhelm Liebknecht*, pp. 186-87.

55. *Das Volk*, 21 May 1859, used the enrollment of three new members to demonstrate that membership was "growing rapidly."

56. Liebknecht, *Marx*, p. 72. Contemporary evidence of an argument in 1858/59 is in Marx to Engels, 17 Dec. 1858, 18 May 1859, in MEW, vol. 19, pp. 377, 433-34, 440, and in Liebknecht to Frau Marx, undated (summer 1859), in LBME, p. 27.

57. Marx to Lassalle, 6 Nov. 1859, in MEW, vol. 19, p. 619.

58. Marx to Engels, 18 and 24 May 1859, in MEW, vol. 19, pp. 433-34, 440. The formal announcement that Marx and Engels had become contributors appeared in *Das Volk*, 11 June 1859.

59. Liebknecht, *Marx*, pp. 100-104, describes Urquhart's extraordinary influence upon Marx and himself. A signed article by Liebknecht in *Vorwärts*, 10 March 1897, concerning the eastern situation demonstrates the extent of Urquhart's influence.

60. *Das Volk*, 4 June, 6 and 20 Aug. 1859.

61. Ibid., 14 May 1859.

62. Ibid., 13 Aug. 1859.

63. Marx to Engels, 25 May and 26 Aug. 1859; Engels to Marx, 25 July 1859, in MEW, vol. 19, pp. 443, 476, 465, respectively.

64. Theodore Zeldin, *The Political System of Napoleon III* (London, 1958). Allan Mitchell, "Bonapartism as a Model for Bismarckian Politics," *Journal of Modern History*, 41 (No. 2, June 1977), 181-99, strangely does not point out that Marx, Liebknecht and other contemporary leftists were the first to use Bonapartism as a model for analyzing Bismarck's policies.

65. The best account I have found for the Vogt affair is in the introductory comments by Manfred Häckel, *Ferdinand Freiligraths Briefwechsel mit Marx und Engels*, 2 vols. (Berlin, 1968), vol. 1, pp. lxxxvii-lxxxviii.

66. *Das Volk*, 14 May 1859.

67. The charge from the *Schweizer Handelscourier*, datelined Bern, 23 May 1859, was reproduced in *Das Volk*, 11 June 1859. On 18 June, *Das Volk* reasserted its original charge that Napoleon had bribed Vogt.

68. Häckel, ed., *Freiligrath's Briefwechsel mit Marx*, vol. 1, p. ixc.

69. Marx to Freiligrath, 23 Feb. 1860, in ibid., p. 129. See also Marx to Engels, 5 Oct. 1859, in MEW, vol. 19, p. 493.

70. Marx to Liebknecht, 17 Sept. 1859, in LBME, pp. 27-30. See also Marx to Lassalle, 6 Nov. 1859, in Gustav Mayer, ed., *Ferdinand Lasalle: Nachgelassene Briefe und Schriften*, 4 vols. (Stuttgart, 1922), vol. 3, pp. 228-32.

71. Häckel, ed., *Freiligrath's Briefwechsel mit Marx*, vol. 2, pp. 157, 160-61.

72. McLellan, *Marx*, pp. 311-15.

73. Quoted in Maximilien Rubel and Margaret Manale, *Marx Without Myth* (New York, 1976), p. 161.

74. Häckel, ed., *Freiligrath's Breifwechsel mit Marx*, vol. 1, p. xcii. Liebknecht gloated over the evidence in *Marx*, p. 35.

75. Marx to Engels, 9 Apr. 1860, in MEW, vol. 30, p. 44. See also LBDS, vol. 1, p. 53, note 2.

76. Liebknecht to Cotta'sche Buchhandlung, 8 June 1861, Cotta Archive.

77. Marx to Engels, 10 Oct. 1854, in MEW, vol. 18, p. 396.

78. Weitershaus, *Liebknecht*, pp. 67-68.

79. Marx to Engels, 10 Apr. 1856, in MEW, vol. 19, p. 49, remarked, "Liebknecht has finally come to something, namely to a little Liebknecht."

80. Weitershaus, *Liebknecht*, pp. 76-81. In a letter to Motteler, 24 June 1897, in Liebknecht Archive, 37/142, IISH, Liebknecht answered an inquiry about Alice's birthdate as being on 26 November 1856. He must have been in error

about the year, for every other surviving document indicates
1857. See the Leipzig police dossier of Aug. 1871 in the
Arno Kapp Nachlass, Mappe IV, AsD.

81. Walter Schmidt, "Die Kommunisten und der preussische
Amnestieerlass vom 12. Januar 1861," *Zeitschrift für Geschichtswissenschaft*, 25 (no. 9, 1977), 1066-79. Schmidt points out
that Marx's petition for the reinstatement of citizenship
was denied. He does not discuss Liebknecht.

CHAPTER 4

1. Brass to Liebknecht, 11 Nov. 1861, in Georg Eckert,
ed., *Liebknecht's Briefwechsel mit deutschen Sozialdemokraten*
(Assen, 1973) (hereinafter this source will be abbreviated
LBDS), vol. 1, p. 789, establishes that Liebknecht already
was writing for the *Norddeutsche Allgemeine*.
2. Brass to Liebknecht, 7 May 1862, in ibid., p. 790.
3. Brass to Liebknecht, 6 June 1862, in ibid., p. 791.
4. Brass to Liebknecht, 7 July 1862, in ibid., p. 792.
5. Brass to Liebknecht, 14, 26 July 1862, in ibid.,
pp. 793-94. The exact date of Liebknecht's arrival in Berlin
cannot be established. On 12 Sept. 1862, he wrote to his
daughter, Alice, from Berlin, so he had arrived before that
date; Liebknecht Archive, 348/2, IISH.
6. For Bismarck's relationship to Brass's newspaper,
see Irene Fischer-Frauendienst, *Bismarcks Pressepolitik*
(Munster, 1973), pp. 49, 52, 59. See also Eleanor L. Turk,
"The Press of Imperial Germany," *Central European History*,
10 (no. 4, Dec. 1977), 334, note 8. For Bismarck's later
bribery of Fröbel, see Prussian Foreign Office, Acta betreffend
die Einwirkung auf die Presse im Interesse Preussens, A959,
vol. 3, A2594, A2900, and A3757, vol. 4.
7. Liebknecht to Cotta'sche Buchhandlung, 6 Nov. 1862,
in Schiller-Nationalmuseum.
8. Liebknecht, *Erinnerungen*, pp. 303-304; Schweichel,
"Liebknecht als Schriftsteller," 332. See also Liebknecht's
public explanation of these events in the *Allgemeine deutsche
Arbeiter-Zeitung*, 20 May 1866.
9. Brass to Liebknecht, 20 Nov. 1862, in LBDS, vol.
1, p. 795.
10. Quoted in Leidigkeit, *Liebknecht und Bebel*, p. 38.
11. Hamerow, *Restoration, Revolution, Reaction*, pp. 241-
42; Eugene N. Anderson, *The Social and Political Conflict in
Prussia, 1858-1864* (Lincoln, Neb., 1954), p. 12.

12. Anderson, *Social and Political Conflict*, p. 316, notes how the idea of producers' cooperatives meshed with the guild mentality. Bernard H. Moss, *The Origins of the French Labor Movement, 1830-1914* (Berkeley, 1976), pp. 3-4, properly castigates historians for the scant attention usually given to the cooperative movement.

13. On Schulze-Delitzsch, see Bernhard Schulze, "Zur linksliberalen Ideologie und Politik: Ein Beitrag zur politischen Biographie Schulze-Delitzsch," in Horst Bartel and Ernst Engelberg, eds., *Der grosspreussischmilitaristische Reichsgründung 1871* (Berlin, 1971), pp. 271-307. From a Marxist perspective, Schulze explains the current political implications of the various historical interpretations of the work of Schulze-Delitzsch. See also Gerd Fesser, *Linksliberalismus und Arbeiterbewegung* (Berlin, 1976), pp. 34-35; and Anderson, *Political and Social Conflict*, pp. 231-32, 295-97.

14. Lees, *Revolution and Reflection*, pp. 155-61; Theodore S. Hamerow, *The Social Foundations of German Unification*, vol. 2: *Struggles and Accomplishments* (Princeton, N.J., 1969), pp. 206-207.

15. See Hamerow, *Social Foundations*, vol. 2, p. 86.

16. Ibid., pp. 216-18.

17. Fesser, *Linksliberalismus und Arbeiterbewegung*, vii-xi, provides a Marxist survey of the literature on the issue of integration of the working class.

18. Liebknecht to Engels, 11 Dec. 1867, in LBME, pp. 82-83, explains that, although he did not make actual alliances with the particularists, he did everything he could to keep their wounds festering, including allowing them occasional use of his newspaper.

19. Leidigkeit, *Liebknecht und Bebel*, pp. 91-93, discusses Engels's tactical advice and notes how it corresponded to Liebknecht's statements and actions. This work is generally excellent concerning Liebknecht's career in the 1860s.

20. See Georg Eckert, ed., *Wilhelm Liebknecht: Leitartikel und Beiträge in der Osnabrücker Zeitung 1864-1866* (Hildesheim, 1975) (hereinafter this source will be abbreviated LLBOZ), pp. 2-3. Günther Ebersold, "Die Stellung Wilhelm Liebknecht and August Bebel zur deutschen Frage 1863 bis 1870" (Heidelberg, Unpublished Ph.D. Dissertation, 1963), uses bourgeois newspapers, including some that were unavailable to me, to reconstruct Liebknecht's agitation in the 1860s.

21. Quoted in LLBOZ, p. 3.

22. *Osnabrücker Zeitung*, 2 June 1865, in ibid., p. 402. In this article and others Liebknecht used the concept of caesarism and Bonapartism interchangeably to describe Bismarck's actions.

23. *Osnabrücker Zeitung*, 9 Aug. 1864, in LLBOZ, pp. 121-22.

24. Ibid., 29 Oct. 1864, p. 209.

25. To illustrate the consistency of his opinion, see ibid., 13 June 1864, 13, 20 October 1865, pp. 65, 525, 531.

26. Ibid., 13 Apr. 1866, p. 684.

27. Ibid., 16 Mar. 1866, pp. 662-63.

28. Ibid., 18 May 1864, pp. 27-28.

29. Liebknecht to Engels, 11 Dec. 1867 and 27 Apr. 1870, in LBME, pp. 81, 98. For a discussion of how the national issue permeated Liebknecht's politics in the 1860s, see Werner Conze and Dieter Groh, *Die Arbeiterbewegung in der nationalen Bewegung* (Stuttgart, 1966), especially pp. 57, 61-62, 67. Ebersold, "Die Stellung Liebknechts," pp. 105, 192, properly stresses that Liebknecht's anti-Prussianism stemmed from his revolutionary commitment.

30. LBME is sadly incomplete, especially for the 1860s. This condition may have fostered the false impression that Liebknecht and Marx did not maintain a close tie once Liebknecht left London. Recent publications of additional letters correct this distortion. Seventeen Liebknecht to Marx letters are in IML, ed. *Die I. Internationale in Deutschland (1864-1872): Dokumente und Materialen* (Berlin, 1964). Also, many letters that were formerly unavailable to western scholars have recently been photocopied from the holdings of the IML in Berlin and deposited at the IISH. Excellent use of these letters is made in Lothar Petry, *Die Erste Internationale in der Berliner Arbeiterbewegung* (Erlangen, 1975).

31. For an incisive commentary on the historiography of the revived workers' movement, see the essay by Shlomo Na'aman in Otto Büsch and Hans Herzfeldt, eds., *Die frühsozialstische Bünde in der Geschichte der deutschen Arbeiterbewegung* (Berlin, 1975), pp. 60-63. Although I agree with Na'aman that continuity with 1848 is undeniable, a younger generation, including August Bebel, Julius Vahlteich, and Eduard Bernstein, did not recognize the 1848 roots of their movement. See the essays by the former two in *Die Gründung und Entwicklung der deutschen Sozialdemokratie* (Leipzig, 1913), pp. 3, 15, and Eduard Bernstein, *Die Geschichte der Berliner Arbeiterbewegung* (Berlin, 1907), vol. 1, p. 92. Liebknecht's contribution constitutes evidence of the

continuing influence of 1848. Na'aman stands in contradiction to the implications of Frolinde Balser, *Sozial-
Demokratie 1848/49-1863*, 2 vols. (Stuttgart, 1962), where it
is argued that the roots of the revived workers' movement
were purely reformist and completely dissociated from Marx.

32. Shlomo Na'aman, *Die Konstituierung der deutschen
Arbeiterbewegung 1862/63* (Assen, 1975), pp. 26-28. See Klaus
Gerteis, *Leopold Sonnemann* (Frankfurt am Main, 1970), pp.
35-37, for an account of this tendency in Frankfurt.

33. Fesser, *Linksliberalismus und Arbeiterbewegung*,
pp. 28-29; August Bebel, *Aus meinem Leben* (Berlin, 1953),
vol. 1, p. 72 (hereinafter this source will be abbreviated
AML); Na'aman, *Die Konstituierung*, p. 59. Interestingly
enough Na'aman's older work, *Lassalle* (Hannover, 1970), p.
542, implies that Eichler only later entered Bismarck's
employ.

34. The decree is in Balser, *Sozial-Demokratie*, vol.
2, 597-98.

35. The distorting impact of these various legal limi-
tations comprises a major thesis of Richard W. Reichard,
Crippled from Birth: German Social Democracy, 1844-1870
(Ames, Iowa, 1969).

36. Marx to Lassalle, 30 Jan. 1860, in MEW, vol. 30,
439, defended Liebknecht against this charge. For a discussion of Lassalle's position on the 1859 diplomatic situation, see Na'aman, *Lassalle*, pp. 305-306. Liebknecht recalled
this spat in his *Marx*, p. 111.

37. Na'aman, *Lassalle*, p. 672.

38. Ibid., pp. 528-33; also Na'aman, *Die Konstituierung*,
pp. 61-67. Lassalle's role in reviving the workers' movement
has generated much debate. Na'aman's well-informed books
stress the ferment in the working class before Lassalle began
his agitation. Nevertheless, the popular cliché still sur-
vives that Lassalle founded the movement singlehandedly.
For one example, see Robert Wesson, *Why Marxism?* (New York,
1976), p. 41. Reformist socialists who hope to deprecate
Marx's influence have long exaggerated Lassalle's contribution;
for an example see Carlton J. H. Hayes, "German Socialism
Reconsidered," *American Historical Review*, 23 (no. 1., Oct.
1917), 65-66. See Fred Oelssner, *Das Kompromiss von Gotha
und seine Lehren* (Berlin, 1950), pp. 11-12; and Fesser,
Linksliberalismus und Arbeiterbewegung, passim, for a critique
of that viewpoint. The exaggeration of Lassalle's influence
can be traced back to Franz Mehring and his influential
Geschichte der deutschen Sozialdemokratie. Mehring was no
friend of Liebknecht or Bebel, and his panegyrics to Lassalle

were partially designed to undercut the reputation of those two rivals. Furthermore, being a Prussian himself, Mehring was less than objective about Lassalle's service to Bismarck. Finally, Mehring saw organizational laxity and flirtation with the bourgeoisie as two contemporary weaknesses of his party. Praise for Lassalle's policies could be used to combat those weaknesses. For a brief but typical example of his bias, see his article in *Archiv für die Geschichte des Sozialismus und der Arbeiterbewegung*, vol. 1 (1911), pp. 101-33. Some of the reasons for Mehring's bias are discussed in Glen R. McDougall, "Franz Mehring: Politics and History in the Making of Radical German Social Democracy, 1869-1903" (Unpublished Ph.D. Dissertation, Columbia, 1976), especially chapter 2. McDougall does not, however, provide a thorough critique of the inaccuracies in Mehring's work.

39. With obvious distaste Liebknecht recalled Lassalle's "expensively furnished home," in Liebknecht, "Zwei Pioniere," 132.

40. Eduard Bernstein, ed., *Ferdinand Lassalle's Gesammelte Reden und Schriften* (Berlin, 1919), vol. 3, pp. 41-92.

41. Lassalle to Hatzfeld, 6 Mar. 1863, in ibid., vol. 4, 340-41.

42. Bismarck to Lassalle, 11 May 1863, in Gustav Mayer, *Bismarck und Lassalle* (Berlin, 1928), p. 59.

43. Lassalle to Bismarck, 8 June 1863, in ibid., pp. 59-62.

44. Lassalle to Bismarck, 19 Nov. 1863, in Mayer, *Bismarck und Lassalle*, pp. 79-80; Na'aman, *Lassalle*, p. 722.

45. Quoted in Na'aman, *Lassalle*, p. 728.

46. Ibid., p. 560; Na'aman, *Die Konstituierung*, pp. 147-48; Fesser, *Linksliberalismus und Arbeiterbewegung*, pp. 53-54; Gerteis, *Sonnemann*, pp. 38-40; Bebel, AML, vol. 1, p. 92. The list of delegates in attendance and the number of members they claimed to represent is reprinted in Balser, *Sozial-demokratie*, vol. 2, 602-604.

47. Fesser, *Linksliberalismus und Arbeiterbewegung*, pp. 38-39.

48. Lassalle to Hatzfeldt, 19 Oct. 1863, in Gustav Mayer, *Ferdinand Lassalle: Nachgelassene Briefe und Schriften* (Stuttgart and Berlin, 1922), vol. 4, pp. 348-49. See also Petry, *Die Erste Internationale*, p. 47.

49. Petry, *Die Erste Internationale*, pp. 48-49.

50. Liebknecht to Marx, 1 May 1863, in ibid., p. 39.

51. Liebknecht to Marx, 16 Oct. 1863, in ibid., p. 41.

52. Liebknecht to Marx, 16 Oct. and 13 Nov. 1863, in

ibid., pp. 48-49; see also Liebknecht, "Zwei Pioniere," 132.

53. The worst offender, and a work with which I consistently disagree, is Gustav Mayer, *Johann Baptiste von Schweitzer und die Sozialdemokratie* (Jena, 1909), pp. 103, 112, 153, 237. The same position is asserted in Kurt Brandis, *Die deutsche Sozialdemokratie bis zum Fall des Sozialistengesetz* (Leipzig, 1931), p. 26. The most solidly proven counterargument, based on Liebknecht's unpublished letters to Marx, is Petry, *Die Erste Internationale*.

54. Liebknecht to Marx, 12 June 1864, in LBME, pp. 37-38; Liebknecht, *Erinnerungen*, p. 313.

55. Liebknecht to Marx, 3 June 1864, in LBME, pp. 33-34.

56. Petry, *Die Erste Internationale*, pp. 54 ff.; August Vogt and Liebknecht to Julius Vahlteich, 15 Aug. 1864, in LBDS, vol. 1, 6-9; also ibid., p. 9, note 8.

57. Na'aman, *Lassalle*, p. 747, erroneously asserts that Liebknecht and Lassalle had no disagreement about organizational principles. In the letter of 15 Aug. 1864 to Vahlteich, in LBDS, vol. 1, pp. 6-9, Liebknecht and Vogt make it clear that they intended to use the party congress against the president. Vogt to Vahlteich, 19 July 1864, specifically promised to try to abolish the "burdensome dictatorship"; in LBDS, vol. 1, pp. 3-4, note 3. Because Liebknecht and Vogt worked closely together at building the anti-Lassallean opposition, and because they penned several joint letters to Vahlteich, it can be assumed that Liebknecht was aware of the contents of this letter and approved it. Besides, in every organization in which Liebknecht had a say about structure, he advocated a collective and diffuse leadership and frequent, powerful party congresses. For Liebknecht's advice to avoid a schism at present, see the letter that he and Vogt wrote to Vahlteich, 10 Aug. 1864, in LBDS, vol. 1, pp. 4-5.

58. Na'aman, *Lassalle*, pp. 786-88.

59. Ibid., p. 787; Petry, *Die Erste Internationale*, pp. 60-61.

60. Marx to Karl Klings, 4 Oct. 1864; Marx to Carl Siebel, 22 Dec. 1864, in IML, ed., *Die I. Internationale*, pp. 17-18, 22-23.

61. Liebknecht to Marx, 16 Feb. 1865, in LBDS, vol. 1, 51, note 4.

62. Liebknecht to Marx, 1 Apr. 1865, in ibid., 63-65, note 2.

63. Leidigkeit, *Liebknecht und Bebel*, p. 59. No evidence has been found to substantiate that Hatzfeldt urged the Prussian government to deport Liebknecht.

64. These events are summarized by Bernstein in
Lassalle's Gesammelte Reden, vol. 3, pp. 314-21. See also
Bebel, AML, vol. 2, 229-30.
65. Petry, *Die Erste Internationale*, p. 63.
66. Gustav Mayer, "Der Allgemeine Deutsche Arbeiterverein und die Krisis 1866," *Archiv für Sozialwissenschaft und
Sozialpolitik*, 57 (1927), pp. 167-75. This evidence was
given to Mayer by an employee at the Prussian Archive. Mayer
does not claim to have made an exhaustive search himself for
additional proof of Schweitzer's connection to Bismarck.
This evidence directly contradicts Mayer's older work,
Schweitzer, pp. 128-29, where he said Schweitzer's whole
character argued against his acceptance of money from Bismarck.
That error does not speak well for Mayer's general interpretation of Schweitzer's character. Oddly enough, even in the
older biography, Mayer was aware that Schweitzer had asked
Bismarck for an interview; see pp. 180-85. For Mayer, such
advances were perfectly compatible with socialist agitation.
Even in "Der Allgemeine Deutsche Arbeiterverein," Mayer
refuses to change his basic evaluation of Schweitzer as an
honorable political leader.
67. For example, see Liebknecht to Moses Hess, 28 Nov.
1869, in Edmund Silberner, ed., *Moses Hess Briefwechsel*, p. 590.
68. *Protokoll der Generalversammlung des Allgemeinen
deutschen Arbeitervereins zu Berlin vom 22. bis 25. Mai
1872* (no publication information given), pp. 8-11, 36, 40.
For Bebel's allegations against Schweitzer, see AML, vol.
2, pp. 10-11, 30.
69. Richard Lipinski, *Die Sozialdemokratie von ihren
Anfängen bis zur Gegenwart* (Berlin, 1927), vol. 1, p. 203;
Bebel, AML, vol. 2, p. 45.
70. Bismarck to Minister of Commerce Itzenplitz, 17
Nov. 1871, quoted in Erich Kundel, "Der Kampf der Sozialdemokratischen Arbeiterpartei gegen den Bakuninismus von der
Londoner Konferenz 1871 bis zum Haager Kongress 1872," BGA,
6 (1964), 124.
71. Quoted in Petry, *Die Erste Internationale*, p. 65.
72. Ibid., p. 67.
73. *Der Sozialdemokrat*, 15 Dec. 1864.
74. Marx to Kugelmann, 23 Feb. 1865, in *Letters to
Dr. Kugelmann*, pp. 27-30.
75. *Der Sozialdemokrat*, 15 Dec. 1864.
76. Liebknecht to Marx, 20 Dec. 1864, in IML, ed., *Die
I. Internationale*, pp. 19-21.
77. Liebknecht to Marx, undated [beginning of Feb.
1865], in LBME, p. 40. A good account of the controversy

arising from Paris is in Edmund Silberner, *Moses Hess* (Leiden, 1966), pp. 514-15.

78. *Der Sozialdemokrat*, 21 Dec. 1864.

79. Ibid., 27 Jan. 1865.

80. Ibid., 5 Feb. 1865.

81. Ibid., 17 Feb. 1865.

82. In this connection, one may study a clear example of Franz Mehring's biased history in his *Karl Marx* (London, 1936), pp. 330-33, where he tries to argue that Schweitzer, in these articles on Bismarck's ministry, did not mean to support the government. Mehring dismisses Liebknecht as an "old '48er" who had little sense for political reality.

83. Liebknecht to Marx, undated [beginning of Feb. 1865], in LBME, pp. 40-42.

84. The making of Liebknecht's decision to resign is revealed in his letter to Marx, written in several installments, 14-17 Feb. 1865, in Petry, *Die Erste Internationale*, pp. 72-75. Schweichel to Liebknecht, 28 Feb. 1865, in LBDS, vol. 1, p. 49, congratulates Liebknecht on the break.

85. MEW, vol. 16, p. 79. The declaration was printed in *Der Sozialdemokrat*, 3 Mar. 1865, and in the *Allgemeine deutsche Arbeiter-Zeitung*, 12 Mar. 1865. A fuller explanation of the reasons for his resignation was published by Marx in the *Berliner Reform*, 15 March 1865, reprinted in IML, *Die I. Internationale*, pp. 46-49. In his memoirs, Bebel erroneously asserted that Marx and Engels resigned from *Der Sozialdemokrat* before Liebknecht did; see AML, vol. 2, pp. 24-25. In Mayer, *Schweitzer*, pp. 120-21, this error was magnified: "To save himself Liebknecht joined his London friends [in resigning]," Mayer wrote. Mayer later corrected himself in his biography of Engels.

86. The additional resignations, like those of Marx and Engels, were announced in *Der Sozialdemokrat*; for example, 8 Mar. 1865. Moses Hess, who had written the denunciation of the IWA's Paris agent, was the one contributor who did not resign. Indeed, Hess published a rather bitter attack on Marx at this time. A year later, however, he too broke with Schweitzer over his endorsement of Bismarck. See Silberner, *Hess*, pp. 547-53.

87. Kurt Koszyk, *Die Presse der deutschen Sozialdemokratie* (Hannover, 1966), p. 63.

88. Liebknecht to Engels, 4 and 8 Apr. 1865, in LBME, pp. 54, 56.

89. The speech is reprinted in Engelberg, ed., *Im Widerstreit um die Reichsgründung* (Berlin, 1970), pp. 218-21.

90. Liebknecht to Engels, 25 Mar. 1865, in LBME, pp. 48-49, reports how he faced down Schweitzer at a meeting of the Berlin organization. See also Petry, *Die Erste Internationale*, p. 90.

91. The announcement was printed in *Der Sozialdemokrat*, 31 Mar. 1865.

92. Bernstein, *Geschichte der Berliner Arbeiterbewegung*, vol. 1, p. 134. See Liebknecht's account in his letters to Engels, 29 Mar. and 4 Apr., 1865, in LBME, pp. 51, 53.

93. *Allgemeine deutsche Arbeiter-Zeitung*, 9 Apr. 1865. Even *Der Sozialdemokrat*, 14 Apr. 1865, admitted the loss of a substantial number of members, though of course it claimed that the majority continued to be loyal to Becker and Schweitzer. Reichard, *Crippled from Birth*, p. 192, underestimates the depth and breadth of this challenge to Schweitzer. Silberner, *Hess*, pp. 519-20, makes the same mistake. With a remarkable lapse in critical interpretation, Silberner quotes *Der Sozialdemokrat* and Bernard Becker to prove that the intraparty rebellion had few followers.

94. Liebknecht to Engels, 8 Apr. 1865, in LBME, p. 56.

95. For examples, see Liebknecht to Marx, 20 Dec. 1864, 3 May 1865, in IML, ed., *Die I. Internationale*, pp. 20, 54. Also the letters quoted in Petry, *Die Erste Internationale*, p. 44.

96. Liebknecht, "Zwei Pioniere," 132.

97. Marx to Liebknecht, 24 June 1865, in LBME, p. 58. See also Liebknecht to Engels, 30 Aug. 1865, in ibid., p. 62.

98. For evidence of Liebknecht's role in preparing this occurrence, see Sigfrid Meyer to Liebknecht, 25 Oct., 13 Nov. 1865, in LBDS, vol. 1, pp. 116, 118-19.

99. Liebknecht tried to enlist Vahlteich, who was one of his few Lassallean acquaintances outside Berlin, for the current struggle. Vahlteich declined for personal reasons; Vahlteich to Liebknecht, 19 Mar. 1865, in LBDS, vol. 1, pp. 55-59.

100. Liebknecht to Engels, 29 Mar. 1865, in LBME, pp. 51-52.

101. Liebknecht to Cotta'sche Buchhandlung, undated, Schiller-Nationalmuseum.

102. Liebknecht, *Erinnerungen*, pp. 27-28; Werner Muehlbradt, "Wilhelm Liebknecht und die Gründung der deutschen Sozialdemokratie (1862-1875)" (Unpublished Ph.D. Dissertation, Göttingen, 1950), pp. 65-68. *Der Sozialdemokrat* announced his expulsion on 7 July 1865. In its commentary on 23 July 1865, the *Allgemeine deutsche Arbeiter-Zeitung* attributed his expulsion to his opposition to the Junkers and to Lassalleanism.

103. Bernstein, *Geschichte der Berliner Arbeiterbewegung*, vol. 1, p. 134.

CHAPTER 5

1. Liebknecht to Marx, 6 Feb. 1866, and Liebknecht to J. P. Becker, 8 Feb. 1866, in IML, ed., *Die I. Internationale*, pp. 106-108.
2. Jürgen Kuczynski, *A Short History of Labor Conditions under Industrial Capitalism in Germany* (London, 1945), p. 66. See also Petry, *Die Erste Internationale*, pp. 22-25. For information on urbanization, see Alan S. Milward and S. B. Saul, *The Development of the Economies of Continental Europe* (London, 1977), p. 45.
3. Seymour Lipset, "Leadership in New Social Movements," in Gouldner, ed., *Studies in Leadership*, p. 362, points out the indispensability of recruitment of such a large and formerly integrated segment of society if a radical party is to succeed in building a mass base.
4. Liebknecht describes these events in a letter to Engels, 30 Aug. 1865, in LBME, p. 60.
5. For observations on the Saxon economy, see Germany, Kaiserliche Statistischen Amt, *Statistische Jahrbuch für das Deutsche Reich* (Berlin, 1880), I. Jahrgang, pp. 15, 177. For figures on the artisans, see Helga Grebing, *Geschichte der deutschen Arbeiterbewegung* (Munich, 1966), p. 16.
6. Liebknecht, "Ein Sohn des Volkes," *Der Neue Welt Kalendar, 1898*, 68.
7. Liebknecht to Engels, 30 Aug. 1865, in LBME, p. 62.
8. For comments on Sonnemann, see Gerteis, *Sonnemann*, esp. pp. 43-44; and Nicholas Martin Hope, *The Alternative to German Unification: The Anti-Prussian Party, Frankfurt, Nassau, and the Two Hessen, 1859-1867* (Wiesbaden, 1973), pp. 245-56. On 12 and 26 Feb. 1865, announcements from the executive committee in the *Allgemeine deutsche Arbeiter-Zeitung* were signed by Sonnemann as Vorsitzender. For general observation on the role of liberals in creating the VDAV, see Gustav Mayer, *Die Trennung der proletarischen von der bürgerlichen Demokratie in Deutschland (1863-1870)* (Leipzig, 1911), pp. 14-20; and Heinz Hümmler, *Opposition gegen Lassalle: Die revolutionäre proletarische Opposition im Allgemeinen Deutschen Arbeiterverein 1862/63-1866* (Berlin, 1963), pp. 209-11.
9. IML, *Geschichte der deutschen Arbeiterbewegung Chronik* (Berlin, 1965), vol. 1, p. 67; Leidigkeit, *Liebknecht*

und Bebel, pp. 67–70; Hümmler, *Opposition gegen Lassalle*, pp. 188–92; Fesser, *Linksliberalismus und Arbeiterbewegung*, p. 55; Gunter Benser, *Zur Herausbildung der Eisenacher Partei* (Berlin, 1956), p. 47.

10. Bebel, AML, vol. 1, pp. 17–78.

11. Ibid., pp. 124–27. See also William H. Maehl, *August Bebel: Shadow Emperor of the German Workers* (Philadelphia, 1980), pp. 38–40.

12. Liebknecht mentions his first meeting with Bebel only briefly in "Sohn des Volkes," 68. The letter from Bebel to Liebknecht on 11 Jan. 1866, in LBDS, vol. 1, pp. 145–46, still exhibits a formal tone.

13. Bebel, AML, vol. 1, pp. 128, 131.

14. Ibid., p. 129.

15. Michael J. Olmsted, *The Small Group* (New York, 1959), pp. 127–28, 131; and Verba, *Small Groups and Political Behavior*, passim.

16. On the founding of the DVP, see Hope, *Alternative to German Unification*, pp. 48–53, 256–89; and Gerhard Eisfeld, *Die Entstehung der liberalen Parteien in Deutschland 1858–1870* (Hannover, 1969), pp. 139–41; for Liebknecht's role, see Muehlbradt, "Liebknecht," 79–81.

17. Quoted in Ebersold, "Die Stellung Liebknechts und Bebels," 105. See also IML, ed., *Geschichte der deutschen Arbeiterbewegung Chronik*, vol. 1, p. 69. Maehl, *Bebel*, p. 47, calls Liebknecht's position "anti-national," and derides the "patent Austrophilism" of the VDAV. I think Maehl misreads the circumstances of the 1860s, confusing *grossdeutsch* and Austrophile and forgetting that German-speaking Austrians had as much claim to inclusion in a German Reich as did the Bavarians, Hannoverians or Prussians.

18. Bebel, AML, vol. 1, p. 150; Leidigkeit, *Liebknecht und Bebel*, pp. 102–103.

19. Bebel, AML, vol. 1, pp. 66–68, 117; Karl Kautsky, *Sozialisten und Krieg* (Prague, 1937), pp. 165–67; Horst Bartel, ed., *Arbeiterbewegung und Reichsgründung* (Berlin, 1971), p. 56.

20. William I to Bismarck, 11 Apr. 1866, in *The Correspondence of William I and Bismarck*, tr. J. A. Ford, 2 vols. (New York, 1903), vol. 1, p. 63.

21. See the colorful account in Paul Goldschmidt, *Berlin in Geschichte und Gegenwart* (Berlin, 1910), pp. 274–75.

22. *Der Sozialdemokrat*, 3 June 1866. The article was part of a series that also appeared on 18, 20, 25 May. See also the report of a speech by Schweitzer given at Leipzig on 16 June, in ibid., 19 June 1866.

23. Liebknecht to Marx, undated in LBME, pp. 75-76; cf. Liebknecht to Marx, 5 June 1866, in IML, ed., *Die I. Internationale*, p. 124; and *Allgemeine deutsche Arbeiter-Zeitung*, final issue on 8 Aug. 1866. See also Bebel, "Erinnerungen an Liebknecht," 3323; and Leidigkeit, *Liebknecht und Bebel*, p. 106.

24. Bebel, AML, vol. 1, pp. 160-61.

25. The Chemnitz Program is in Wilhelm Mommsen, ed., *Deutsche Parteiprogramme* (Munich, 1960), pp. 307-308.

26. Liebknecht to Becker, 3 Aug. 1867, in LBDS, vol. 1, p. 215. Liebknecht said, "Point 4 of our Chemnitz Program shows that the People's Party is socialist. . . ." He must have meant Point 5, which is quoted in the text above.

27. *Der Sozialdemokrat*, 8 Oct. 1869; also 17, 19, 26 Feb. 1869.

28. Engels to Marx, 25 July 1866, in MEW, vol. 31, p. 241.

29. Engels to Marx, 29 Jan., 18 Mar. 1869, in ibid., vol. 32, pp. 252, 281. See also Josef Schleifstein, "Der Kampf von Marx und Engels für die Herausbildung und Festigung der selbständingen revolutionären Massenpartei der deutschen Arbeiterklasse in den Jahren 1859 bis 1871," *Wissenschaftliche Zeitschrift der Karl-Marx Universität Leipzig*, 4 (1954-55, no. 5), 422. Contrast to the policy that Marx pursued in 1848-49, as described in *Der Bund der Kommunisten*, pp. 35-36. At the earlier time, he virtually abandoned class politics and concentrated his efforts in democratic societies. His neglect of the proletarian viewpoint even led to a schism with Andreas Gottschalk in Cologne. In the latter 1860s, Liebknecht followed a course of action that Marx had approved a decade or so earlier but had since renounced. It would therefore be a misleading oversimplification to call Liebknecht's tactics a violation of Marxist doctrine. Marx thought new tactics were needed to meet a new situation. Because the old objectives had yet to be reached, Liebknecht thought the old tactics should be retained. Still, following the lead of Marx and Engels, modern Marxists continue to chastise Liebknecht for formulating a common program with the left-liberals. See Leidigkeit, *Liebknecht und Bebel*, p. 108; Brumme, *Liebknecht*, p. 20; Benser, *Zur Herausbildung der Eisenacher Partei*, p. 14.

30. Liebknecht to Engels, 20 June 1868, LBME, p. 87.

31. Liebknecht's attitude can be reconstructed from these sources: Liebknecht to Marx, 22 July 1865, Marx/Engels Archive, D3155, IISH: Statement of the Ausschuss of the People's Party in Saxony, signed by Bebel, Liebknecht and

Freytag, undated in Liebknecht Addenda, 73/1, IISH; Liebknecht to Quarck, 23 Dec. 1898, in Quarck Nachlass, 210,
ASD; report of a speech by Liebknecht in *Demokratische Wochenblatt*, 7 Aug. 1869.
   32. Speech by Liebknecht reported in *Demokratische
Wochenblatt*, 7 Aug. 1869.
   33. Ibid. Also 4 Jan., 8, 22 Feb. and 28 Mar. 1868
in ibid.
   34. Bebel, AML, vol. 2, p. 61.
   35. Marx to Kuglemann, 6 Apr. 1868, in MEW, vol. 32,
pp. 542-43. A similar sentiment is expressed in Engels to
Marx, 22 May 1868, in ibid., 90. Cf. Liebknecht to Engels,
5, 27 Apr. 1870, in LBME, pp. 95, 98.
   36. Liebknecht to Gottschald, 22 Feb. 1867, in LBDS,
vol. 1, p. 210.
   37. *Demokratische Wochenblatt*, 6 June 1868 and 22 May
1869. A good secondary account of Liebknecht's agitation
is in Ebersold, "Die Stellung Liebknechts und Bebel," 138-46.
   38. Marx to Engels, 4 Nov. 1864, in MEW, vol. 31, p.
16. Excerpts from the program of the IWA may be examined
in Appendix 2.
   39. Roger Morgan, *The German Social Democrats and the
First International* (Cambridge, 1965), p. 99. The same erroneous interpretation appears in Reichard, *Crippled from Birth*,
p. 192. The best evidence for Liebknecht's activities on
behalf of Marx's organization appear in his letters to his
friend in London. Aside from the incomplete LBME, see the
letters from Liebknecht to Marx, especially those of 29 Apr.,
3 May, 1865, 21 Jan., 8 Feb., and 5 June 1866, in IML, ed.,
Die I. Internationale, pp. 52, 54, 101, 107, 124. This volume
carries a 1964 publication date. Before that time, the letters
were held by the IML in East Berlin and were unavailable to
western scholars. Morgan's work appeared in 1965, so perhaps
he did not have an opportunity to see these letters before
publishing his own work. That circumstance could help to
explain why he underestimated Liebknecht's labors for the IWA.
Letters in LBDS also corroborate Liebknecht's efforts on
behalf of the International. This work first appeared in
1973. Nevertheless, unlike the Liebknecht/Marx letters mentioned above, the letters in LBDS have long been accessible
to western scholars at the IISH.
   40. Julius Braunthal, *History of the International*,
trs. Henry Collins and Kenneth Mitchell, 2 vols. (New York
and Washington, 1967), vol. 1, p. 110. Wolfgang Schmierer,
*Von der Arbeiterbildung zur Arbeiterpolitik: Die Anfänge
der Arbeiterbewegung in Wurttemberg 1862/63-1878* (Hannover,

1970), p. 131, flatly contradicts Morgan, *Social Democrats*, where it is asserted that the IWA was gaining grass roots support, culminating in the adoption of the International's program at Nuremberg. Morgan cites Stuttgart as a specific example of growing support and Schmierer denies the accuracy of that example.

41. Engels to Theodor Cuno 7-[8] May 1872, in MEW, vol. 30, p. 461.

42. For complaints by Marx that Liebknecht did not work hard enough on behalf of the IWA, see Marx to Engels, 8 Jan. 1868, 29 Mar., 18 Nov. 1869, in MEW, vol. 32, pp. 12, 290, 394. These remarks may have encouraged Morgan, *German Social Democrats*, pp. 98-99, to underestimate Liebknecht's contribution to the IWA. Still, it is a treacherous inductive leap to move from complaints originating in England to the assertion that "the International played a very minor role in his [Liebknecht's] activities."

43. LBME, pp. 90-91. See also Marx to Liebknecht, 15 Jan. 1866, in ibid., pp. 71-72, for the earlier authorization to deal directly with the General Council. I agree with Morgan, *German Social Democrats*, pp. 85-86, where it is pointed out how the Londoners regularly failed to back Becker.

44. Liebknecht to Marx, 8 Feb. 1866, in LBDS, vol. 1, p. 159, note 3. For evidence of his work for the IWA in Berlin, see his letters to Sigfrid Meyer, 25 Sept., 13 Nov. 1865, in ibid., pp. 116, 119-20.

45. Wilhelm Liebknecht, "Zwei Pioniere," *Die Neue Welt*, no. 17 (1900), 132.

46. Regarding *Capital*, see Liebknecht to Engels, 11 Dec. 1867, in LBME, p. 86.

47. Liebknecht to Engels, 20 Jan. 1868, in ibid., p. 88; Liebknecht to Becker, undated, in LBDS, vol. 1, pp. 216-17.

48. Liebknecht to Marx, 22 Jan. 1869, in Marx/Engels Archive, D3149, IISH.

49. Liebknecht to Becker, 3 Aug. 1867, in IML, ed., *Die I. Internationale*, pp. 167-68, justifies his concentration on political rather than social agitation by citing the need to offer a counterexample to the ADAV.

50. Bebel to Becker, 9 Oct. 1868, in AML, vol. 1, p. 170.

51. Liebknecht to Becker, 8 Feb. 1866, in IML, ed., *Die I. Internationale*, p. 106.

52. Liebknecht to Engels, 20 Jan. 1868, in LBME, p. 87. An undated circular for the Ausschuss of the People's party in Saxony, signed by Bebel, Freitag and Liebknecht, points to the "extremely fortunate success" of the *Demokratische*

Wochenblatt, saying its circulation had reached 1,100 subscribers after only nine months of publication; Liebknecht
Addenda, 73/1, IISH. Liebknecht exaggerated the count to
1,300 in a letter to Engels of 29 Mar. 1868, in LBME, p. 90.
For a yardstick of comparison, circulation of Becker's *Vorbote* was about 500; see Kurt Koszyk, *Deutsche Presse in 19
Jahrhundert*, 2 vols. (Berlin, 1966), vol. 2, p. 191.
    53. Engels to Marx, 1 Mar., 22 Oct. 1868; Marx to Engels,
21 Apr. 1868, in MEW, vol. 32, pp. 36, 188, 64, respectively.
    54. *Demokratische Wochenblatt*, 4 Jan. 1868.
    55. Ibid., 21, 28 Mar. 1868.
    56. Ibid., 1, 15, 29 Aug., 5 Sept. 1868.
    57. Ibid., 14 Aug. 1869.
    58. Bebel to Becker, 9 Oct. 1867, in IML, ed., *Die
I. Internationale*, p. 181.
    59. In Mommsen, *Parteiprogramme*, pp. 308-10. See also
Der Sozialdemokrat, 30 Sept. 1866; 6 Sept. 1868, 10 Feb.
1869, all of which stress the indivisibility of political
and social struggle and the importance of political freedom.
The first two explicitly call for a "People's State."
    60. Ibid., 22 Jan.-6 May 1868; Marx to Engels, 23 Mar.
1868, in MEW, vol. 32, p. 50.
    61. Liebknecht to Marx, 17 July 1868, in IML, ed.,
Die I. Internationale, pp. 224-26.
    62. Bebel, AML, vol. 1, p. 180; see also Bebel, "Erin-
nerungen an Liebknecht," 3324.
    63. Bebel, "Natalie Liebknecht," *Die Neue Zeit*, 27/
1 (1908-09), 693-94.
    64. Liebknecht to Marx, 17 July 1868, in IML, ed.,
Die I. Internationale, p. 224. See also Friedericke Seipp
to Liebknecht, 16 Dec. 1867, and Magdalene Landolt to Liebknecht, 19 Feb. 1868, both in Liebknecht Archive, 301/1-2,
217, respectively, IISH.
    65. Bebel, "Natalie Liebknecht," 693-94.
    66. This remark was made by a delegate named Thorade;
see the Nuremberg Protocol in HVP, p. 775.
    67. See the protocol in HVP, p. 759. See also Bebel,
AML, vol. 1, pp. 181, 191.
    68. The Nuremberg Program is in Appendix 2. For an
1867 modification of the IWA statute, see IML, ed., *Die I.
Internationale*, p. 170. I disagree with Maehl, *Bebel*, pp.
59-61, who denies the working class orientation and socialist
nature of the Nuremberg program.
    69. Nuremberg Protocol in HVP, pp. 760-82.
    70. HVP, pp. 789-90.
    71. Schmierer, *Von der Arbeiterbildung*, pp. 20, 127-59;

Jorg Schadt, *Die Sozialdemokratische Partei in Baden* (Hannover, 1971), p. 30.

72. *Demokratische Wochenblatt*, 26 Sept. 1868. See also Bebel, AML, vol. 1, pp. 189-90.

73. *Demokratische Wochenblatt*, 19 Sept. 1868.

74. Statistics in *European Historical Statistics*, pp. 185, 742.

75. Werner Ettelt and Hans-Dieter Krause, *Der Kampf um eine marxistische Gewerkschaftspolitik in der deutschen Arbeiterbewegung 1868 bis 1878* (Berlin, 1975), pp. 44-47.

76. *Der Sozialdemokrat*, 4, 6, 9, 11, 13, 16, 18, 26 Sept. 1868. As usual, I disagree with the account of these events in Mayer, *Schweitzer*, pp. 216-34. Mayer ignores Schweitzer's double-dealing completely. For a detailed account of the machinations of Schweitzer to co-opt Fritzsche and his cigar workers union, see Ettelt and Krause, *Kampf um eine marxistische Gewerkschaftspolitik*, pp. 65-72, and the speech by Tölcke in the *1872 ADAV Protokoll*, p. 5.

77. Ettelt and Krause, *Kampf um eine marxistische Gewerkschaftspolitik*, pp. 74-75.

78. Ibid., pp. 84-85; also Petry, *Die Erste Internationale*, pp. 166-73.

79. Ettelt and Krause, *Kampf um eine marxistische Gewerkschaftspolitik*, pp. 104-10, 124-26.

80. *Demokratische Wochenblatt*, 26 Sept. 1868. See Liebknecht's summary of the events of September 1868 in his report to the congress of the IWA at Basel in September 1869, printed in IML, ed., *Die I. Internationale*, pp. 420-21.

81. Liebknecht to Marx, 16 Sept. 1868, in Marx/Engels Archive, D3144, IISH.

82. Liebknecht to Marx, 2 Oct. 1868, in Marx/Engels Archive, D3146, IISH.

83. Marx to Engels, 29 July, 29 Sept. 1868, in MEW, vol. 32, pp. 128, 169,

84. Marx to Schweitzer, 13 Oct. 1868, in ibid., pp. 568-71.

85. Marx to Engels, 19, 21, 23, 25 Sept., 10 Oct. 1868, Engels to Marx, 24 Sept. 1868, in ibid., pp. 155-64, 179-80.

86. Liebknecht to Marx, 17 Dec. 1868, in Petry, *Die Erste Internationale*, p. 190.

87. For example, see *Demokratische Wochenblatt*, 3 Oct. 1868, 13 Feb. 1869.

88. Ibid., 6 March 1869. See also ibid., 6 Feb. 1869; and Bebel, AML, vol. 2, p. 61.

89. *Demokratische Wochenblatt*, 20 Feb. 1869; also 27 Feb. 1869.

90. Bebel, AML, vol. 1, pp. 213 ff.

91. Schweitzer suppressed publication of a protocol for the Barmen-Elberfeld meeting. The only record was printed in *Der Sozialdemokrat*, 2, 4 Apr. 1869. These reports have been reprinted in Arno Herzig, ed., *Carl Wilhelm Tölcke: Presseberichte zur Entwicklung der deutschen Sozialdemokratie 1848-1893* (Munich, 1976), pp. 58-61.

92. *Der Sozialdemokrat*, 4 Apr. 1869.

93. Ibid., 30 Apr. 1869; Bebel, AML, vol. 2, p. 66; Herzig, ed., *Tölcke's Presseberichte*, pp. 78-80.

94. *Demokratische Wochenblatt*, 3 Apr. 1869. The account in Bebel, AML, vol. 2, pp. 64-67, says he negotiated a cease-fire with Schweitzer on 8 April and that the newspapers of both factions published the declarations simultaneously on 16 April. Schweitzer's *Sozialdemokrat* did delay until 16 April in printing its acknowledgment of the cease-fire.

95. Liebknecht to Marx, 3 Apr. 1869, in IML, ed., *Die I. Internationale*, p. 323.

96. Liebknecht to Becker, 7 Apr. 1869, in LBDS, vol. 1, p. 243.

97. Bebel to Liebknecht, undated Apr. 1869, in ibid., pp. 245-46. See also IML, ed., *Geschichte der Arbeiterbewegung Chronik*, vol. 1, p. 82. Bebel's memoir skips over the details. However, he does say that he rejected a proposal by Schweitzer to ban all contact between leaders of the two factions; AML, vol. 2, p. 285.

98. *Der Sozialdemokrat*, 18 June 1869. Even Mehring, who usually was a fan of Schweitzer, called this reunion an "unworthy comedy"; in *Archiv für die Geschichte des Sozialismus und der Arbeiterbewegung*, 1 (1911), 132.

99. See Bracke to Liebknecht, 24 June 1869, Bracke to Bebel, 26 June 1869, in Heinrich Gemkow, "Im Kampf um die Gründung der Partei. Unveröffentlichte Briefe an Bebel und Liebknecht (Juni bis August 1869)," BGA, 11 (no. 4, 1969), 628-31. See also Bracke's account in *Der Lassalle'sche Vorschlag. Ein Wort an den 4. Congress der social-demokratischen Arbeiterpartei. (Einberufen auf den 23. August 1873 nach Eisenach)* (Brunswick, 1873), pp. 54-55; and Bebel's accounts in AML, vol. 2, pp. 70-71, and "Erinnerungen an Liebknecht," 3324.

100. Liebknecht to Marx, 17 Aug. 1869, in IML, ed., *Die I. Internationale*, p. 414. See also Liebknecht to Hess, 28 Nov. 1869, in Edmund Silberner, ed., *Moses Hess Briefwechsel* ('S-Gravenhage, 1959), p. 590. For discussion of the resulting self-censorship in the *Demokratische Wochenblatt*, see Erich Kundel, "Die Mitarbeit von Karl Marx und Friedrich

Engels am Zentralorgan der Eisenacher Partei 'Der Volkstaat,'"
BGA, 10 (1968, Sonderheft), 98-136.

101. *Demokratische Wochenblatt*, 10 July 1869.

102. Liebknecht to Marx, 29 June 1869, in IML, ed.,
Die I. Internationale, p. 361.

103. Liebknecht to Marx, 22 Jan. 1869, in Marx/Engels
Archive, D3149, IISH.

104. Liebknecht to Marx, 29 June 1869, in IML, ed.,
Die I. Internationale, p. 362. See also Liebknecht to Marx,
17 Aug. 1869, in ibid., p. 413.

105. Becker's proposal is reprinted in *Protokoll über
die Verhandlungen des Allgemeine deutschen Sozial-demo-
kratischen Arbeiterpartei zu Eisenach am 7., 8. und 9. August
1869* (Leipzig, 1869), pp. 19-21. (Hereinafter the protocols
of the various SDAP congresses will be cited only with appropriate year and page references.)

106. Liebknecht to Marx, 29 June 1869, in IML, ed.,
Die I. Internationale, p. 362; Bebel, AML, vol. 2, p. 82;
Bebel to Marx, 30 July 1869, thanks Marx for his support,
in Blumenberg, ed., *Bebels Briefwechsel mit Engels*, pp. 12-13.

107. Institut of Marxism-Leninism of the C.C., C.P.S.U.,
ed., *The General Council of the First International 1864-
1872: Minutes*, 5 vols. (Moscow, n.d.), vol. 3, p. 137.

108. Engels to Theodor Cuno, 7-8 May 1872, in MEW,
vol. 33, p. 461.

109. Liebknecht to Marx, 17 Aug. 1869, in IML, ed.,
Die I. Internationale, p. 413.

110. *Der Vorbote*, Aug. 1869, pp. 114-17.

111. *SDAP Protokoll, 1869*, p. 72.

112. Geib to Bebel, 21 July 1869, in Heinrich Gemkow,
"Im Kampf um die Gründung der Partei," 633. See also Hess
to Becker, 10 Aug. 1869, in Silberner, ed., *Hess Briefwechsel*, p. 584.

113. *Demokratische Wochenblatt*, 26 June, 3, 10, 17
July 1869.

114. Oberwinder to Liebknecht, 1 July 1869, in LBDS,
vol. 1, p. 251.

115. Reported in *Demokratische Wochenblatt*, 28 July
and 7 Aug. 1869, and in *Frankfurter Zeitung*, 28 July 1869.

116. Liebknecht to Bebel, 25 July 1869, in LBDS, vol.
1, p. 254.

117. *SDAP Protokoll, 1869*, pp. 76-82.

118. Ibid., pp. 1-13.

119. *Der Sozialdemokrat*, 10, 13, 15, 20, 25, 27 Aug.
1869.

120. The organization statute is in Wilhelm Schröder, *Geschichte der sozialdemokratischen Parteiorganization in Deutschland* (Dresden, 1912), p. 68. For Liebknecht's remarks, see *SDAP Protokoll, 1869*, p. 53.

121. Letters from Bracke and Geib in July 1869 to Bebel indicate that the statute and program originated with Bebel; see Gemkow, "Im Kampf um die Gründung," especially p. 622. At the congress itself, Bebel dominated the debate on the statute; see *SDAP Protokoll, 1869*, passim. See also Bebel, AML, vol. 2, p. 81.

122. *SDAP Protokoll, 1869*, p. 31.

123. The Eisenach Program draft is in Appendix 2. For the addition of point ten, see *SDAP Protokoll, 1869*, pp. 32, 37.

124. *SDAP Protokoll, 1869*, pp. 54-55.

125. Sonnemann's *Frankfurter Zeitung* gave a compressed but thorough and impartial account of the Eisenach Congress in its issues of 10 and 11 Aug. 1869. *Geschichte der Frankfurter Zeitung* (Frankfurt am Main, 1906), pp. 170-71, asserts that Sonnemann was fairly content with the outcome of the Eisenach Congre

126. The resolutions were printed in *Demokratische Wochenblatt*, 29 Sept. 1869.

127. In the stenographic report carried by the *Frankfurter Zeitung*, 13 Sept. 1869. *Verhandlungen des IV. Congresses des internationalen Arbeiterbundes in Basel 7-11 September 1869* (Basel, 1869), pp. 45-57, contains a greatly compressed and sometimes confusing report of the debate on this issue. Liebknecht's position is not well defined in this source, but he voted for the two controversial resolutions. Gary P. Steenson, *Karl Kautsky 1854-1938: Marxism in the Classical Years* (Pittsburgh, 1978), p. 102, erroneously asserts that Liebknecht voted against these resolutions.

128. The reaction of the SDAP makes it clear that criticism from the DVP and its press was intense. Unfortunately, of the various DVP-affiliated sheets only the *Frankfurter Zeitung* was available. It was surprisingly silent on this explosive issue. After a stenographic report of the congress, it carried no further comment on the Basel resolutions during September. Apparently Sonnemann still was trying to maintain the tie between the SDAP and the DVP.

129. *Der Volksstaat*, 3 Nov. 1869.

130. *Demokratische Wochenblatt*, 29 Sept. 1869.

131. *Der Volksstaat*, 13, 23 Oct. 1869.

132. Maehl, *Bebel*, p. 66, erroneously asserts that Bebel was elected to the five-member executive committee at Eisenach. The members in Brunswick elected five local men to the executive; see *Demokratische Wochenblatt*, 28 Aug. 1869.

133. Liebknecht to Bracke, 17 Nov. 1869, in HVP, pp. 196-97. Also Liebknecht to Bonhorst, Oct. 1869, in ibid., pp. 195-96

134. Mayer, *Trennung der proletarischen von der burgerlichen Demokratie*, pp. 51-52; and Jutta Seidel, *Wilhelm Bracke:
Vom Lassalleaner zum Marxisten* (Berlin, 1966), pp. 63-64.
Both note the opinion of the majority in the executive committee. The evidence for the position of Spier and Bonhorst
is in *Der Volksstaat*, 30 Oct., 3 Nov. 1869.

135. See Appendix 1 for Liebknecht's prison record.

136. *Der Sozialdemokrat*, 3 Oct. 1869. For similar
attacks, see the issues of 26 Sept., 15, 17, 20, 23 and 27
Oct. 1869.

137. Hugo Eckert, *Liberal oder Sozialdemokratie: Frühgeschichte der Nurnberger-Arbeiterbewegung* (Stuttgart, 1968),
pp. 162-66; Bebel, AML, vol. 2, pp. 101-104.

138. *Der Volksstaat*, 15 Jan. 1870.

139. Bebel's essays were subsequently published as a
pamphlet, "Unsere Ziele: Ein Streitschrift gegen die 'Demokratische Korrespondenz'" (Leipzig, 1874); for this quotation,
see pp. 16-17.

140. Reported in *Der Volksstaat*, 22 Jan. 1870.

141. Wilhelm Liebknecht, "Zur Grund- und Bodenfrage"
(Leipzig, 1876), p. 20.

142. Ibid., p. 26.

143. Ibid., p. 130. To document the wretched rural
conditions in England, Liebknecht quoted extensively from
Marx's *Capital*; see pp. 43-54 in Liebknecht's pamphlet.

144. Ibid., pp. 68-70.

145. Ibid., p. 170.

146. Ibid., p. 177.

147. Ibid., p. 190.

148. *SDAP Protokoll*, pp. 10, 12, 15-18. (The pagination in the first twenty pages of this source is unusual;
only every other page is numbered.) Maehl, *Bebel*, pp. 69-72,
tries to play down this break with the left-liberals, mys-
teriously calling the appearance of the schism a "propagandistic ruse."

149. Fritz Brupbacher, *Marx und Bakunin* (Berlin-
Wilmersdorf, 1922), pp. 42, 52-60. See also the correspondence between Marx and Bakunin reprinted in MEW, vol. 18,
pp. 12-15; also K. J. Kenafik, *Michael Bakunin and Karl
Marx* (Melbourne, 1948), pp. 72-79.

150. The best summary I have seen of the differences
between Marx and Bakunin is in Brupbacher, *Marx und Bakunin*,
pp. 55, 72-73, 86-88. Marx himself juxtaposed his reliance
upon legal agitation to Bakunin's conspiratorial predilections;
see MEW, vol. 18, p. 346. The differing views on the state
held by Marx and Bakunin are elucidated in Shlomo Avineri,

The Social and Political Thought of Karl Marx (Cambridge, 1968), pp. 208, 237-39, and passim. For Marx's assertion during this battle with Bakunin of the necessity of a dictatorship of the proletariat, see Richard N. Hunt, *The Political Ideas of Marx and Engels* (Pittsburg, 1974), vol. 1, pp. 307-28.

151. Liebknecht to Marx, 7 Sept. 1869, in IML, ed., *Die I. Internationale*, p. 423.

152. Protocol summary in *Frankfurter Zeitung*, 8 Sept. 1869.

153. Bakunin to Becker, 4 Aug. 1869, ed. by Rjasanoff, in *Archiv für die Geschichte des Sozialismus und der Arbeiterbewegung*, 5 (1915), 191-92; Brupbacher, *Marx und Bakunin*, pp. 79-80; Silberner, *Hess*, pp. 598-600.

154. Brupbacher, *Marx und Bakunin*, pp. 72-78, 103-105, 109-11.

155. Marx's views on sectarianism are scattered throughout his works, but they remained consistent. Compare Karl Marx and Friedrich Engels, *Communist Manifesto*, ed. by D. A. Drennan (Woodbury, N. Y., 1972), pp. 186-88, with Marx, "Alleged Splits in the International," in MEW, vol. 18, pp. 33-34.

156. Karl Marx, "Konfidentielle Mittheilung," in MEW, vol. 16, p. 418. See also the comments by Marx in a session of the General Council in December 1869, in IML of the C.C., C.P.S.U., ed., *The General Council of the First International*, vol. 3, p. 195.

157. Liebknecht to Marx, 20 Apr. 1870, Marx/Engels Archive, D3160, IISH.

158. Liebknecht to the Eisenacher executive committee, 6 May 1870, in LBDS, vol. 1, p. 310. See also Marx to the executive committee, 14 June 1870, in IML, ed., *Die I. Internationale*, pp. 485-86; also the report of the SDAP executive committee to the General Council in ibid., pp. 501-502.

159. Liebknecht to Engels, 8 Dec. 1871, in Marx/Engels Archive, L3450, IISH.

160. Brupbacher, *Marx und Bakunin*, pp. 117-23.

161. Ibid., pp. 127-28. For the Marxist viewpoint on these events, see Kundel, "Der Kampf der Sozialdemokratischen Arbeiterpartei gegen den Bakuninismus," 116.

162. Henry Collins and Chimen Abramsky, *Karl Marx and the British Labor Movement* (London, 1965), pp. 236-39; Samuel Bernstein, *The Beginnings of Marxian Socialism in France* (New York, 1965), pp. 92-103.

163. *Der Neue Sozialdemokrat*, 3 Dec. 1871 and 7 Jan.
1872. See also Liebknecht to Engels, 10 Jan. 1872, and Engels
to Liebknecht, 18 Jan. 1872, in IML, ed., *Die I. Internationale*,
pp. 625, 629.
164. The use of the IWA to attack the Eisenachers is
especially apparent in *Der Neue Sozialdemokrat*, 8 Dec. 1871;
see also 15 Nov., 6, 8, 11 Dec. 1872. These articles criticizing Marx in the ADAV journal have been collected and published in Ernst Schraepler, "Der Zerfall der Ersten Internationale im Spiegel des 'Neuen Social-Demokrat,'" *Archiv
für Sozialgeschichte*, 3 (1963), 508-59.
165. Marx to Gustav Kwasnewsky, 25 Sept. 1871, in Boris
Nikolayewsky, "Karl Marx und die Berliner Sektion der I.
Internationale," Sonderdruck of *Die Gesellschaft* (1933),
260-61; Marx to Liebknecht, 17 Nov. 1871, in LBME, pp. 141-43.
166. Liebknecht to Engels, 8 Dec. 1871, in Marx/Engels
Archive, L3450, IISH.
167. Liebknecht to Engels, 18 Dec. 1871, in ibid., L3451.

CHAPTER 6

1. See Appendix 1 for Liebknecht's prison record and
dates of incarceration.
2. Liebknecht to Ernestine, 17 Nov. 1866, in LBDS, vol.
1, p. 199.
3. Documents in Liebknecht Archive, 351 and 377, IISH.
See also the numerous letters to Ernestine in LBDS, vol. 1,
pp. 190-203.
4. Adolf Landolt to Ernestine, 24 Oct. 1866, Friedericke
Seipp [Wilhelm's sister] to Ernestine, 24 Oct. 1866, and
Magdalene Landolt to Ernestine, 2 Feb. 1867, all in Liebknecht
Archive, 353/1, 369/1-2, 356/5-6, respectively, IISH.
5. Liebknecht to Reinhold Schlingmann, 19 March 1867,
in LBDS, vol. 1, pp. 211-12.
6. Liebknecht to Metzner, 8 June 1867, in ibid., p. 212.
7. Reported in *Demokratische Wochenblatt*, 20 June 1868.
8. Without evidence, Ernst Huber, *Deutsche Verfassungsgeschichte seit 1789*, 4 vols. (Stuttgart, 1957-1969), vol.
3, pp. 655 ff., argues that the constitution was a "compromise"
between the demands of the member governments and the changes
made by the Constituent Assembly. In my opinion, such a
viewpoint greatly understates the determining role that Bismarck played. For corroboration, see Otto Becker, *Bismarcks
Ringen um Deutschlands Gestaltung* (Heidelberg, 1958), passim;
and Gordon Craig, *Germany 1866-1945* (New York, 1978), p. 12.

9. *Demokratische Wochenblatt*, 4 Apr. 1868. See also
Liebknecht's speech, "On the Political Position of Social
Democracy Particularly with Respect to the Reichstag" (Moscow,
n.d.), especially p. 32. For a statement of his private
sentiments, see Liebknecht to Engels, 27 Apr. 1870, in LBME,
p. 98.

10. Liebknecht, "On the Political Position." See also
Demokratische Wochenblatt, 15 May, 3 July, 7 Aug. 1869.

11. VdR, 17 Oct. 1867, vol. 3, p. 451. See also his
speech in *Protokoll über den ersten Congress der Sozialdemokratischen Arbeiterpartei zu Stuttgart on 4, 5, 6, und 7
June 1870* (Leipzig, 1870), pp. 11-12.

12. An 1869 speech by Liebknecht, quoted in Kurt Eisner,
Wilhelm Liebknecht (Berlin, 1906), p. 68.

13. Speech by Liebknecht reprinted in *Demokratische
Wochenblatt*, 4 Apr. 1868. See also ibid., 4 Jan. 1868.
For further information on the Tariff Parliament, see Bebel,
AML, vol. 1, p. 178; and Leidigkeit, *Liebknecht und Bebel*,
pp. 123-24.

14. Liebknecht to Marx, 8 Oct. 1867, in IML, ed.,
Die I. Internationale, p. 179. Schweitzer's legislative
proposal is reprinted in *Aus der Waffenkammer des Sozialismus: Eine Sammlung alter und neuer Propaganda-Schriften*,
ed. by the staff of the *Volksstimme*, 12 vols. (Frankfurt
am Main, 1903-10), vol. 10, pp. 20-28.

15. VdR, 18 Oct. 1867, vol. 3, p. 470. See also
Liebknecht to Marx, 19 Oct. 1867, in IML, ed., *Die I. Internationale*, p. 193.

16. VdR, 17, 21 Oct. 1867, vol. 3, pp. 451, 562-63.

17. Resolution reproduced in Bebel, AML, vol. 2, pp.
105-106. Writing in *Die Neue Zeit*, 30/2 (1911-12), 89, Bebel
said "to my knowledge there was not a single prominent man
in the entire party who shared Liebknecht's earlier views
about parliamentarism." The 1870 resolution squarely contradicts this assertion by Bebel.

18. HVP, pp. 26-27, 445-46, 465.

19. In the secondary literature, see Weitershaus,
Liebknecht, p. 145, where it is argued that "in the last
decade of his life Liebknecht came to the insight that a
continuous, positive parliamentary participation could be
useful for his party and for success with the voters." Marga
Beyer, "Wilhelm Liebknechts Kampf gegen den Opportunismus
in letzten Jahrzehnt seines Lebens," BGA, 18 (1976, no. 1),
92-101, sees Liebknecht developing a hard line against reformism at exactly the same time Weitershaus sees moderation.

20. VdR, 2 Apr. 1886, vol. 83, p. 1840.

21. A remarkable shift in the Marxist-Leninist answer
to this question has occurred in recent years. Representing
the older viewpoint, Heinz Beike, *Die deutsche Arbeiterbewegung und der Krieg von 1870-1871* (Berlin, 1957), p. 29
and passim, stresses the progressive nature of the war up
until the battle of Sedan and chastizes Bebel and Liebknecht
for failing to support it. By contrast, Marga Beyer and
Gerhard Winkler, *Revolutionäre Arbeitereinheit: Eisenach-
Gotha-Erfurt* (Berlin, 1975), pp. 44-48, celebrates the heroic
proletarian opposition from the outset of the war. The change
in East German interpretation may have been provoked by Conze
and Groh, *Die Arbeiterbewegung in der nationalen Bewegung*,
especially pp. 102-103. This non-Marxist treatment, published
in 1966, used the evidence of SDAP support for the early part
of the war to prove that the working class in Germany was
not alienated from "the nation" early in 1870. These authors
imply that only the events of 1870-71 drove the workers away
from a gradual integration into the united Germany. Such an
interpretation, refuting the irreconcilability of class conflicts and the inevitability of proletarian independence,
is anathema to Marxist-Leninists. Thus ideological scholars
in the East may have reinterpreted the events surrounding
the outbreak of the war to clarify their disagreement with
Conze and Groh.
22. For example, see the *Augsburger Allgemeine Zeitung*,
11, 31 July; 1, 5 Aug. 1859. Almost every issue of *Das Volk*
contained an anti-Napoleonic piece. See above, chapter 3,
p. 51.
23. *Demokratische Wochenblatt*, 28 Nov. 1868. For similar
comments, see also ibid., 25 Apr., 2 May, 31 Oct. and 19 Dec.
1868.
24. Ibid., 2 Jan. 1869.
25. The Nuremberg Protocol is in HVP, p. 788.
26. Published in *Der Volksstaat*, 20 July 1870. A slightly
different version, also dated 17 July and signed by Bebel,
Liebknecht, Louis Eckstein, and Carl Demmler was sent to Moses
Hess in Paris; see *Hess Briefwechsel*, pp. 603-604.
27. *Der Volksstaat*, 20, 23 July 1870.
28. Bebel, "Erinnerungen an Liebknecht," 3325.
29. Bebel, AML, vol. 2, p. 158.
30. Bebel's statement in the Reichstag about his written
statement was made 21 July 1870, VdR, vol. 14, p. 14. The
statement itself was printed in *Der Volksstaat*, 23 July 1870,
on p. 4. Karl Kautsky, *Sozialismus von den Hussiten bis zum
Völkerbund* (Prague, 1973), pp. 190-91, claims that in 1870,
no socialist questioned the duty of citizens to support a
defensive war. Kautsky was wrong. Liebknecht and Bebel

opposed the war regardless of who was responsible. William
H. Maehl, "Bebel and the Origins of German Parliamentary
Socialism During the Franco-Prussian War," *Studies in History
and Society*, 1 (no. 2, Autumn 1976), 35, asserts that this
declaration rejecting the war credits "contained nothing
of a revolutionary assault," and even more curiously, that
it "subordinated principle to tactical considerations." I
obviously disagree.

31. *Der Sozialdemokrat*, 17, 22 July 1870.

32. Beike, *Arbeiterbewegung und Krieg*, pp. 24-26.

33. *Der Volksstaat*, 13 July 1870.

34. LBDS, vol. 1, pp. 324-25. There are additional
letters here of 17 and 20 July that underscore this directive.

35. Manifesto in Beike, *Arbeiterbewegung und Krieg*,
p. 93.

36. Bracke to Geib, 29 July 1870, in Wilhelm Bracke,
*Der Braunschweiger Ausschuss der social-demokratischen
Arbeiter-Partei im Lötzen und vor dem Gericht* (Brunswick,
1872), p. 5.

37. Telegram from Bracke to Spier, 22 July 1870, in
Eckert, "Korrespondenz des Braunschweiger Ausschusses," 132.

38. Bracke to Geib, 1 Sept. 1870, in Bracke, *Braunschweiger Ausschuss vor dem Gericht*, pp. 142-43.

39. Marx to Engels, 20 July 1870, in MEW, vol. 33,
p. 5.

40. Liebknecht to Marx, 13 Aug. 1870, in Kundel, "Briefwechsel der 'Volksstaat'-Redaktion mit Marx und Engels," 653.

41. Marx to Ausschuss of SDAP, 2 Aug. 1870, in HVP,
p. 337.

42. Marx to Liebknecht, 29 July 1870, in LBME, p. 115;
Engels to Marx, 15 Aug. 1870; Marx to Engels, 17 Aug. 1870,
in MEW, vol. 33, pp. 39-43.

43. See Liebknecht's account of this frightening incident in HVP, pp. 9-11.

44. Quoted in Beike, *Arbeiterbewegung und Krieg*, p. 34.

45. *Der Volksstaat*, 20, 23 July, 10 Aug. 1870.

46. Ibid., 23 July 1870. See also Carl Ludecke to
Liebknecht, ca. August 1870; and Bracke to Liebknecht, 4
Sept. 1870, in LBDS, vol. 1, pp. 334-40.

47. *Der Volksstaat*, 7 Aug. 1870.

48. *Der Vorbote*, Aug. 1870.

49. Conze and Groh, *Arbeiterbewegung in der nationalen
Bewegung*, pp. 86-95. They disparage proletarian internationalism altogether and claim that even Bebel and Liebknecht
were motivated by narrow hatred of Prussia, not by genuine
internationalism. Petry, *Die Erste Internationale*, p. 314,

reports prowar proletarian sentiment in Berlin. Other public opposition to the war, on the other hand, remains relatively unexplored. It did exist and deserves more scholarly attention. For a beginning, see Ernst Engelberg, *Im Widerstreit um die Reichsgründung* (Berlin, 1970).

50. *Der Volksstaat*, 17, 20 Aug. 1872. See also Wilhelm Liebknecht, "Die Emser Depesche, oder wie Kriege gemacht werden" (Nuremberg, 1895). Bebel, AML, vol. 2, p. 149, claims that he, not Liebknecht, authored these articles. Bebel gives no explanation of why he allowed Liebknecht to publish the brochure under his name. For this reason and because Bebel's memoir was published after Liebknecht's death, I am dubious of Bebel's assertion. The initial articles actually were coauthored by Bebel and Liebknecht. Both men sat together in prison at Hubertusburg in 1873, and they talked daily. Surely they collaborated on this important project. However, the 1876 additions were Liebknecht's alone; Bebel does not even claim to have authored those parts.

51. Liebknecht, "Emser Depesche," p. iii.

52. Bebel to Engels, 24 Nov. 1892, in Blumenberg, ed., *Bebels Briefwechsel mit Engels*, p. 624.

53. Liebknecht to Bracke, 5 Sept. 1870, quoted in Muehlbradt, "Liebknecht," 196-97. This letter is not included in LBDS.

54. Shortly before the composition of this document, Bracke had received Marx's letter outlining his views on the war. Parts of Marx's letter were incorporated into this manifesto. See Bracke, *Braunschweiger Ausschuss vor dem Gericht*, p. 7; Marx to Engels, 2 Sept. 1870, in MEW, vol. 33, p. 50; Bonhorst to Liebknecht, 3 Sept. 1870, in HVP, p. 334.

55. The complete manifesto is reprinted in Beike, *Arbeiterbewegung und Krieg*, pp. 101-107.

56. Liebknecht to the executive committee, Sept. 1870, in LBDS, vol. 1, p. 340.

57. Beike, *Arbeiterbewegung und Krieg*, p. 59.

58. *Der Volksstaat*, 11 Sept. 1870.

59. VdR, 26 Nov. 1870, vol. 15, pp. 18-20.

60. *SDAP Protokoll, 1871*, p. 1, identifies a man from Leipzig named Gabriel as delivering this report in the name of a provisional executive committee. The financial records may be examined in *Sozialdemokratische Arbeiter-Partei. Kassenbericht. Von Beginn der Agitation für den Eisenacher Congress bis zum Schluss des Jahres 1869*, pp. 2-9; *vom 1. Januar bis 31. Mai 1870*, pp. 3-10; *vom 23. September 1870 bis 31. Januar 1872*, p. 3; *vom 1. Februar bis 31. August 1872*, p. 5.

61. Membership figures are in each *SDAP Protokoll,*
1870, pp. 51-52; *1871*, pp. 233-34; *1872*, p. 35; *1873*, p.
80; *1874*, p. 104.
62. *Der Volksstaat*, 26 Oct. 1870.
63. *SDAP Protokoll, 1871*, pp. 1, 80. *Der Volksstaat*
published a claim of 2,790 subscribers on 29 March 1871. By
way of comparison, circulation for the ADAV central organ
stood at about 5,000 in 1869. It fell to 2,800 early in 1871
but had rebounded to 5,200 by the end of the year; see Koszyk,
Deutsche Presse, vol. 2, p. 63.
64. Letters between Otto Freytag and Liebknecht, 17
Jan., 24 Feb. 1871 and undated, in LBDS, vol. 1, pp. 374-78.
65. For information on Minkwitz, see LBDS, vol. 1,
pp. 271, note 2, 377-78.
66. *Der Volksstaat*, 17 Sept. 1870.
67. Ibid., 5, 15 Apr. 1871.
68. Ibid., 12 Apr. 1871. Liebknecht similarly disparaged the constitutional charade in Berlin in VdR, 9 Dec.
1870, vol. 15, p. 153.
69. Quoted in Horst Bartel, et al., *August Bebel: Eine*
Biographie (Berlin, 1863), pp. 59-60.
70. *Der Volksstaat*, 1 Jan. 1873.
71. Quoted in Eisner, *Liebknecht*, p. 90. Maehl, *Bebel*,
pp. 84-87, argues that Bebel's devotion to parliamentary
tactics as the proper path to socialism began in 1871 as
a result of similar insights. I think Maehl puts the date
for Bebel's transformation far too early. As late as the
mid-1880s, Bebel had still not come to terms with parliamentarism.
72. The indictment is in Bracke, *Braunschweiger Ausschuss*
vor dem Gericht, pp. 61-65.
73. Ibid., p. 151.
74. Ibid., p. 99.
75. Ibid., p. 99, 102 and passim.
76. Heinrich Leonard, *Wilhelm Bracke: Leben und Wirken*
(Brunswick, 1930), p. 49.
77. Wilhelm Liebknecht, "Zu Trutz und Schutz: Festrede
gehalten zum Stiftungsfest des Crimmitschauer Volksvereins
am 22. Oktober 1871" (Hottingen-Zurich, 1883), 17.
78. Ibid., pp. 21-30.
79. Liebknecht, "Trutz-Eisenstirn," vol. 2, pp. 21-22.
80. Speech of 2 Apr. 1886, VdR, vol. 83, p. 1840.
81. Wilhelm Liebknecht, *Robert Owen: Sein Leben und*
Wirken (Nuremberg, 1892), pp. 68-80. This brief book is based
on essays that Liebknecht wrote in 1874 and 1876.

82. Liebknecht, "Zu Trutz und Schutz," 17; see also pp. 3, 18-19.

83. The various government plans for a coup are discussed in Gerhard A. Ritter, *Die Arbeiterbewegung im Wilhelminischen Reich* (Berlin-Dahlem, 1959), pp. 27-30; see also p. 43 for Liebknecht's argument that the growth of socialism would force a counterrevolutionary coup.

84. Liebknecht, "Zur Grund- und Bodenfrage," 170.

85. Wilhelm Liebknecht, "Wissen ist Macht--Macht ist Wissen: Festrede gehalten zum Stiftungsfest des Dresdener Bildungs-Vereins am 5. Februar 1872" (Berlin, 1894), 24.

86. Ibid., pp. 43-44.

87. HVP, p. 89.

88. Ibid., p. 69.

89. Ibid., pp. 76-77.

90. Ibid., pp. 139-40.

91. For another account of the trial by Liebknecht, see "Hochverrath und Revolution," *Sozialdemokratische Bibliothek* (Hottingen-Zurich, 1887/88), vol. 2, Heft 14-24, p. 15.

92. HVP, pp. 452-53.

93. Ibid., p. 107.

94. Ibid., pp. 372-73.

95. Liebknecht, "Hochverrath und Revolution," 30.

96. See for example the *Volks-Zeitung* of Berlin, 19 Mar. 1872, p. 1.

97. *National-Zeitung* of Berlin, 22 Mar. 1872.

98. For examples of left-liberal defenses of Liebknecht, Bebel, and Hepner, see *Volks-Zeitung*, 19 Mar. 1872, and *Frankfurter Zeitung*, 28 Mar. 1872.

99. HVP, p. 62.

100. *Kladderadatsch*, 24 Mar. 1872. The poem apparently was modeled on Ferdinand Freiligrath's "Trotz Alledem."

101. Engels to Liebknecht, 23 Apr. 1872, in LBME, p. 158; Carl Hirsch to Liebknecht, 31 Mar. 1872, Wilhelm Eichoff to Liebknecht, 31 Mar. 1872, Carl Demmler to Liebknecht, 24 Apr. 1872, in LBDS, vol. 1, pp. 410, 412, 419.

102. Jacoby sent a letter to *Der Volksstaat*, dated 2 Apr. 1872, announcing his enrollment in the SDAP as a result of the trial; in *Johann Jacoby Briefwechsel/1850-1877*, edited by Edmund Silberner (Bonn, 1978), p. 574. See Liebknecht's ecstatic comment on this recruit in his letter to Engels, 4 Apr. 1872, in Marx/Engels Archive, L3465, IISH. On Vollmar's conversion, see Paul Kampffmeyer, *Georg von Vollmar* (Munich, 1930), p. 10.

103. HVP, pp. 640-41.

104. *Der Volksstaat*, 30 Mar. 1872.

CHAPTER 7

1. *ADAV Protokoll, 1872*, p. 41.
2. *SDAP Protokoll, 1871*, pp. 42-43.
3. *Der Volksstaat*, 1 Apr. 1871.
4. For example, see ibid., 28 June; 1, 12, July 1871.
5. *SDAP Protokoll, 1872*, pp. 24, 42-43.
6. Liebknecht to Geib, 5 Dec. 1872, LBDS, vol. 1, pp. 445-46.
7. *Der Volksstaat*, 28 Sept. 1872. Bebel acknowledges that he and Liebknecht wrote this statement in AML, vol. 2, pp. 254-55. Maehl, *Bebel*, p. 102, believes that the offer was sincere. See the following comments in the text for my interpretation.
8. *Der Neue Sozialdemokrat*, 11 Oct. 1872; *Der Volksstaat*, 28 Sept., 16 Oct. 1872.
9. Liebknecht to Engels, 30 Nov. 1872, in LBDS, vol. 1, p. 445, note 1.
10. *Der Volksstaat*, 14 Dec. 1872. See also 18 Dec. 1872.
11. Mayer, *Schweitzer*, p. 417, explains that Schweitzer wrote the letter at the insistence of two unidentified ADAV leaders. Mayer incorrectly asserts that Liebknecht favored immediate publication but was restrained by the SDAP Executive Committee.
12. Liebknecht to Engels, 30 Nov. and 15 Dec. 1872, Marx/Engels Archive, L3479 and L3480, IISH.
13. Reported in Engels to Bebel, 20 June 1873, in MEW, vol. 33, pp. 588-89.
14. Blos to Liebknecht, 2 May 1873, LBDS, vol. 1, p. 485.
15. Engels to Sorge, 3 May 1872, in MEW, vol. 33, p. 583.
16. Liebknecht to Engels, 6 May 1873, in Kundel, "Aus dem Briefwechsel der 'Volksstaat'--Redaktion," 656-57.
17. Blos to Liebknecht, 2 May 1873, LBDS, vol. 1, p. 485.
18. Discussion of this matter is sprinkled through the *ADAV Protokoll, 1873*, pp. 5, 7, 10, 15-19, 25, 40-41, 51-58.
19. For the impact of the ADAV rebuff, see Geib's comment in *SDAP Protokoll, 1874*, p. 24. See also Liebknecht to Engels, 6 May 1873, in Kundel, "Aus dem Briefwechsel der 'Volksstaat'--Redaktion," 656, where Liebknecht asserts that the danger of a Lassallean secession has passed.

20. Ettelt and Krause, *Kampf um eine marxistische Gewerkschaftspolitik*, pp. 450, 454-56.

21. Bebel, AML, vol. 2, p. 284; Wilhelm Blos, *Denkwürdigkeiten eines Sozialdemokraten*, 2 vols. (Munich, 1914), vol. 1, pp. 186-87.

22. Bernstein, *Geschichte der Berliner Arbeiterbewegung*, vol. 1, pp. 286-87; also Bernstein, *Sozialdemokratische Lehrjahre* (Berlin, 1928), pp. 33-34. For an account of similar local cooperation in Stuttgart, see Schmierer, *Von Arbeiterbildung zur Arbeiterpolitik*, pp. 188-89.

23. *Der Volksstaat*, 13 Mar. 1874; see also 25 Jan. 1874.

24. IML, ed., *Geschichte der deutschen Arbeiterbewegung*, 3 vols. (Berlin, 1965), vol. 1, pp. 92, 103.

25. Schröder, *Geschichte der Parteiorganization*, pp. 19-20; Bernstein, *Geschichte der Berliner Arbeiterbewegung*, vol. 1, pp. 295-96; Kundel, *Marx und Engels im Kampf um Arbeitereinheit*, p. 89.

26. Introduction to HVP, p. 53.

27. *SDAP Protokoll, 1874*, pp. 90-92.

28. Liebknecht to Engels, 28 July 1874, in Kundel, "Zum Vereinigungsprozess von Eisenachern and Lassalleanern. Unveröffentlichte Briefe von Wilhelm Liebknecht und Hermann Ramm an Karl Marx und Friedrich Engels," BGA, 18 (no. 6, 1976), 1038; *SDAP Protokoll, 1874*, 91-92. See also Kundel, *Marx und Engels im Kampf um Arbeitereinheit*, pp. 56-58.

29. Kundel, *Marx und Engels im Kampf um Arbeitereinheit*, p. 103; see also Tölcke, *Presseberichte*, p. 266. The abortive attack on Tölcke at the congress can be discerned in *ADAV Protokoll, 1874*, pp. 71-79, 87, 121-22. It is quite difficult, however, to reconstruct the fight at the party congress because the protocol is cryptic and censored. For admissions of censorship at an earlier congress, see *ADAV Protokoll, 1871*, pp. 12-14.

30. *ADAV Protokoll, 1874*, p. 34.

31. Liebknecht to Engels, 21 Apr. 1875, in Kundel, "Zum Vereinigungsprozess," 1041. See also Liebknecht to Bebel, 11 Oct. 1874, in LBDS, vol. 1, p. 583. Mehring, *Marx*, pp. 508-509, mistakenly says Liebknecht "jumped at" Tölcke's unity bid. For a reassertion of the "cool reception" that Tölcke received, see Hermann Ramm to Engels, 22 Oct. 1874, in Kundel, "Zum Vereinigungsprozess," 1040.

32. Liebknecht to Bebel, 11 Oct. 1874, LBDS, vol. 1, p. 583. See also Kundel, *Marx und Engels im Kampf um Arbeitereinheit*, pp. 105-106.

33. Liebknecht to Marx, 26 Oct. 1874, in Kundel, "Zum Vereinigungsprozess," 1040.

34. Geib to Marx, 8 Nov. 1874, in Tölcke, *Presse-berichte*, pp. 223-24.

35. VdR, vol. 34, p. 244. Despite the election of ten socialists in 1874, only nine sat in the Reichstag because Johann Jacoby had resigned his mandate.

36. *Der Neue Sozialdemokrat*, 27 Nov. 1874; and *Der Volksstaat*, 6 Dec. 1874.

37. Eduard Bernstein, "Zur Vorgeschichte des Gothaer Programms," *Die Neue Zeit*, 15/1 (1896-97), 469.

38. Quoted in Weitershaus, *Liebknecht*, p. 157.

39. Marx to Bracke, 5 May 1875, in Marx and Engels, *Briefwechsel mit Wilhelm Bracke (1869-1880)*, ed. by Heinrich Gemkow (Berlin, 1963), p. 46. Current Marxist interpretations vigorously defend Marx's viewpoint; see Kundel, *Marx und Engels im Kampf um Arbeitereinheit*, pp. 58-72; and Beyer and Winkler, *Revolutionäre Arbeitereinheit*, p. 59.

40. Membership figures for both parties can be found in the annual party congress protocols. Kundel, *Marx und Engels im Kampf um Arbeitereinheit*, p. 269, includes several thousand *unrepresented* members for the 1874 ADAV Congress in his comparison with the 1875 ADAV figure. Consequently, he calculates a 30 percent decline in ADAV membership from 1874 to 1875. This manipulation is totally misleading. Of course the SDAP did not let the ADAV claim any unrepresented delegates at the 1875 congress.

41. Wilhelm Blos, who edited *Der Volksstaat*, credited the ADAV journal with 20,000 subscribers; *Denkwürdigkeiten*, vol. 1, p. 145. Schröder, *Geschichte der Parteiorganization*, pp. 6, 13, offers the more specific figure of 21,154 in 1872. Kundel, *Marx und Engels im Kampf um Arbeitereinheit*, pp. 58-59, reports 16,524 subscribers early in 1874. *Der Volksstaat*, 18 Jan. 1874, claimed a circulation of 6,396, but the SDAP also had 13 additional local sheets; their circulation usually remained under 1,000; Rolf Engelsing, *Massenpublikum und Journalistentum im 19. Jahrhundert in Nordwestdeutschland* (Berlin, 1966), pp. 92-93.

42. *ADAV Protokoll, 1873*, pp. 95-102, indicates a surplus of 1,599 thalers from Apr. 1872 to Apr. 1873. *Sozialistische Arbeiterpartei Deutschlands. Abrechnung vom 1 Juni bis 30 September 1875*, p. 15, shows a profit of 4,091 marks from June to September 1875.

43. *SDAP Kassenbericht, 20 April-10 July 1874*, p. 7; *16 Nov. 1874-28 Feb. 1875*, p. 4.

44. I have been unable to locate complete financial

reports for the ADAV, but some comparison is possible on
the basis of reports in *ADAV Protokoll, 1873*, p. 95. This
source reports a total income of 5,420 thalers for the period
Apr. 1872 to Apr. 1873. *SDAP Kassenberichten* report an income
of 2,822 thalers for the longer period Feb. 1872 to March
1873. If these figures remained generally true, then the
ADAV had a tremendous financial advantage over its rival.
    45. Bernstein to Liebknecht, undated in 1874, LBDS,
vol. 1, pp. 546–47.
    46. Liebknecht letter to the editor in *Die Neue Zeit*,
15/1 (1896–97), 543.
    47. The organization statute may be read in Schröder,
Geschichte der Parteiorganization, pp. 70–72. Schröder makes
the absolutely insupportable assertion that this statute
represented a victory for Lassallean principles, pp. 22–23.
Kundel, *Marx und Engels im Kampf um Arbeitereinheit*, pp.
214–15, minimizes Liebknecht's success on the organization
issue, saying that even delegates at the 1874 ADAV Congress
wanted a more democratic organization. The point, however,
is that these dissidents were a very small minority in the
ADAV.
    48. Verba, *Small Groups and Political Behavior*, pp.
22–26, points out the potent pressures for accommodation
and conformity in small group decision making.
    49. Bernstein, *Sozialdemokratische Lehrjahre*, p. 45.
    50. Liebknecht to Engels, 21 Apr. 1875, in Kundel,
"Zum Vereinigungsprozess," 1041. Eduard Bernstein overlooked
this fact in his recollections, thereby implying that the
theoretical opaqueness of the Gotha Program stemmed mainly
from Liebknecht; Bernstein, *Sozialdemokratische Lehrjahre*,
p. 45; and Bernstein, "Zur Vorgeschichte," 470. Bernstein's
accounts may have been deliberately misleading. In retrospect, he knew that Marx detested the Gotha Program. If
the errors Marx criticized were Liebknecht's own mistakes
and not the result of Lassallean pressure, Liebknecht's heterodoxy would be established. Then Bernstein's own subsequent
revision of Marx would mesh well with party tradition. Bernstein's contemporary analysis was more accurate than his
recollection. In a letter to Bebel on 19 Jan. 1875, he
wrote, "Unfortunately the people are such stubborn Lassalleans, that we must make concessions in this regard"; see
Bebel, AML, vol. 2, p. 276. To underline this point and
hopefully to erase any doubts about Lassallean insistence
upon their slogans, see Ramm to Engels, 24 May 1875, in
Kundel, "Zum Vereinigungsprozess," 1044.

51. Liebknecht to Engels, 23 Apr. 1875, in Kundel, "Zum Vereinigungsprozess," 1043.

52. *Protokoll des Vereinigungs-Congresses der Sozial-demokraten Deutschlands. Abeghalten zu Gotha, vom 22. bis 27. Mai 1875* (Leipzig, 1875), p. 30.

53. The program draft is in Appendix 2.

54. Bebel to Engels, 23 Feb. 1875, and Engels to Bebel 18/28 Mar. 1875, in Blumenberg, ed., *Bebels Briefwechsel mit Engels*, pp. 26-35.

55. Liebknecht to Engels, 21 Apr. 1875, in Kundel, "Zum Vereinigungsprozess," 1041-52.

56. The resolutions, identified only as submissions of "Leipzig party comrades," appear in *Protokoll des Verein-igungs-Congresses*, pp. 11-12.

57. Liebknecht to Engels, 23 Apr. 1875, in Kundel, "Zum Vereinigungsprozess," 1043.

58. Engels to Bebel, 20 June 1873, in *Bebels Brief-wechsel mit Engels*, pp. 19-22.

59. Marx to Bracke, 5 May 1875, in MEW, vol. 34, p. 137. See also Engels to Bebel, 18/28 Mar. 1875, in ibid., p. 129. In bold contradiction of all evidence, Kundel, *Marx und Engels im Kampf um Arbeitereinheit*, p. 194, asserts that "the argument with anarchism played hardly any role in . . . Marx and Engels' criticism." Marx's fight with Bakunin inspired much of his critique of the Gotha Program; see Raymond Dominick, "A Compromise Between Theory and Practice? Karl Marx, German Social Democrats and the Gotha Program of 1875" (Rocky Mountain Social Science Association, 1974). Hunt, *Political Ideas of Marx and Engels*, vol. 1, especially pp. 317-28, thoroughly documented this same point.

60. There has been some disagreement about whether or not Bebel saw the *Critique*. *Vorwärts*, 1 Feb. 1891, says he did not. In light of new evidence, Erich Kundel, "Neue Bracke-Briefe. Briefe zum Vereinigungskongress 1875," BGA (no. 4, 1977), 616, suspects that he did. In any case he read Engels's extensive criticism of the Gotha Program in the letter of 18/28 March 1875. All the other designated recipients of the *Critique* definitely saw it before the Gotha Congress.

61. The *Critique* is reproduced in Mommsen, *Parteipro-gramme*, pp. 315-32. For an insightful discussion of dis-tributive justice in the thought of Marx, see Robert C. Tucker, *The Marxian Revolutionary Idea* (New York, 1969), pp. 37-53. A recent collection of essays discussing other points of theoretical interest in the *Critique* is in Wolfgang Heinrichs, et al., *Aktuelle Bedeutung der Marxschen Randglossen zum Gothaer Programm* (Berlin, 1976).

62. Kundel, *Marx und Engels im Kampf um Arbeitereinheit*,
p. 144, acknowledges that Marx's *Critique* was "absolutely
senseless," unless the SDAP was theoretically more Marxist
than the ADAV. Were the Eisenachers more scientific than
their rivals? The historiographical dividing line on this
issue originally did not reflect the ideology of the historian. For non-Marxist-Leninist studies that see both Eisenachers and the ADAV as Lassallean, see Brandis, *Deutsche
Sozialdemokratie*, p. 46, and Steinberg, *Sozialismus und Sozialdemokratie*, pp. 13, 19–20. The latter even asserts that the
ADAV understood Marx better than Liebknecht's faction. That
assertion is also made by Mayer, *Schweitzer*, passim. Marxists
also formerly accepted the theoretical equality of the two
factions; Mehring, *Geschichte der Sozialdemokratie*, vol.
2, pp. 447–53, and Benser, *Herausbildung der Eisenacher Partei*,
p. 79. Kundel, *Marx und Engels im Kampf um die revolutionäre
Arbeitereinheit*, reasons much more closely than any of these
other historians, and his study is by far the best account
of the Gotha Congress that is available. It is seriously
marred, however, by the unfailing effort to prove that Marx
was right and Liebknecht was wrong. Not all Marxist-Leninists
share Kundel's harsh verdict of Liebknecht. Chubinskii,
Liebknecht, pp. 114–15, takes a much more tolerant view of
the need for action that confronted Liebknecht. He cites
Lenin to buttress his argument. Perhaps Kundel and Chubinskii
differ in their relative deference to Marx and to Lenin.
63. Kundel, "Mitarbeit von Marx und Engels am Zentralorgan der Eisenacher Partei," 133–35.
64. Liebknecht to Engels, 25 Mar. 1873, Marx/Engels
Archive, L3484, IISH.
65. Engels to Marx, 21 Sept. 1874; Marx to Sorge, 4
Aug. 1874, in MEW, vol. 33, pp. 119, 636.
66. Liebknecht, "Zu Trutz und Schutz," p. 30.
67. *SDAP Protokoll, 1874*, p. 79.
68. Ibid., pp. 75–79.
69. Liebknecht to Engels, May 1873, in Kundel, "Briefwechsel der 'Volksstaat'--Redaktion mit Marx und Engels," 658.
70. Bebel to Engels, 19 May 1873, *Bebels Briefwechsel
mit Engels*, pp. 14–15. See also these testimonies to Lassalle's
influence: remarks by Grillenberger quoted in Georg Gärtner,
Karl Grillenberger (Nuremberg, 1930), p. 72; Blos, *Denkwürdigkeiten*, vol. 1, p. 114; Kautsky, *Erinnerungen*, p. 306.
71. *Der Volksstaat*, 30 Apr. 1875. Kundel, *Marx und
Engels im Kampf um Arbeitereinheit*, pp. 259–62, attempts
to depict Tölcke's schism as another lost opportunity to avoid
compromise with Lassalleanism. This is a distortion on two

counts. First, Tölcke's program draft, though free of
Lasalleanism, barely qualifies as a socialist program. Second,
there is no evidence that Tölcke had any significant following.
Indeed, his easy capitulation indicates the opposite.

72. *Der Neue Sozialdemokrat*, 30 Apr. 1875.

73. Quoted in Bernstein, "Vorgeschichte des Gothaer
Programms," 470.

74. Wilhelm Bracke, *Der Lassalle'sche Vorschlag* (Brunswick, 1873).

75. Bracke to Bebel, 23 Mar. 1875, in Kundel, "Neue
Bracke-Briefe," 613; Bracke to Engels, 25 Mar. 1875, in *Marx
und Engels Briefwechsel mit Bracke*, pp. 31 ff.

76. Bebel to Liebknecht, 27 Mar. 1875, LBDS, vol. 1,
pp. 630-31.

77. *Protokoll über die Verhandlungen des Parteitages
der Sozialdemokratischen Partei Deutschlands. Abgehalten
zu Dresden von 13. bis 20. September 1903* (Berlin, 1903),
p. 371.

78. Bracke to Bebel, 10 May 1875, in Kundel, "Neue
Bracke-Briefe," 616.

79. Bebel, AML, vol. 2, p. 278.

80. Bernstein, *Sozialdemokratische Lehrjahre*, p. 46;
and Kautsky, *Erinnerungen*, p. 306.

81. Hepner to Liebknecht, 14 June 1875, quoted in Kundel,
Marx und Engels im Kampf um Arbeitereinheit, p. 249.

82. *Der Volksstaat*, 9 Apr. 1875, and *Der Neue Sozialdemokrat*, 21 Apr. 1875, both referred to separate conferences for each party. On 25 Apr. *Der Neue Sozialdemokrat*
announced that the separate ADAV congress would be postponed
until after the unity congress. In fact it was never held.
See the discussion of this matter in *Protokoll des Vereinigungs-Congresses*, pp. 23-27.

83. *Protokoll des Vereinigungs-Congresses*, pp. 13, 18.

84. Ibid., p. 30.

85. Ibid., p. 38.

86. See Bracke to Engels, 28 June 1875, in *Marx und
Engels Briefwechsel mit Bracke*, p. 77.

87. *Protokoll des Vereinigungs-Congresses*, pp. 38-42.

88. Ibid., pp. 49-50.

89. Bracke to Engels, 28 June 1875, in *Marx und Engels
Briefwechsel mit Bracke*, p. 78.

90. Bebel to Engels, 21 Sept. 1875, in *Bebels Briefwechsel mit Engels*, pp. 35-36. This was Bebel's first response
to Engels's critique six months earlier in March 1875; see ibid.,
pp. 27-35. The inordinate delay led Gustav Mayer erroneously
to conclude that Bebel never answered Engels's critique and

consequently must not have received it; Mayer, *Friedrich Engels* (The Hague, 1934), vol. 2, p. 277.

91. Bebel, AML, vol. 2, p. 295.

92. Engels to Bracke, 11 Oct. 1875, in *Marx und Engels Briefwechsel mit Bracke*, p. 82; Engels to Bebel, 12 Oct. 1875, in *Bebels Briefwechsel mit Engels*, p. 38. Eike Kopf, "Die reaktionäre Marxkritik nach dem Gothaer Programm der deutschen Sozialdemokratie," *Deutsche Zeitschrift für Philosophie*, 23 (no. 5, 1975), 712, asserts that most bourgeois commentators stressed the revolutionary nature of the Gotha Program.

93. Engels to Bebel, 12 Oct. 1875, in *Bebels Briefwechsel mit Engels*, pp. 37-38.

94. Engels to Bracke, 11 Oct. 1875, *Marx und Engels Briefwechsel mit Bracke*, p. 81; Engels to Liebknecht, 31 July 1877, in LBME, p. 235; Marx to F. A. Sorge, 19 Oct. 1877, in *Breife und Auszüge aus Briefen von Joh. Phil. Becker, Jos. Dietzgen, Friedrich Engels, Karl Marx u. A. an F.A. Sorge und Andere* (Stuttgart, 1906), p. 159.

95. Liebknecht to Bracke, 26 May 1875, LBDS, vol. 1, p. 638.

96. *Protokoll des Vereinigungs-Congresses*, pp. 14, 17; *Protokoll des Socialisten-Congresses zu Gotha vom 19. bis 23. August 1876* (Berlin, 1876), p. 23. (Hereinafter protocols of the SAP will be cited only as *SAP Protokoll* with appropriate year and page references.)

97. This financial estimate is based on the annual SDAP *Kassenberichten* and the SAP *Abrechnungen*, both of which are available at the IISH.

98. *SAP Protokoll 1877*, p. 18; Koszyk, *Presse der Sozialdemokratie*, pp. 8-9, 114.

99. Reported in *Der Neue Sozialdemokrat*, 18 June 1875.

100. *Der Volksstaat*, 17 Oct. 1875.

101. Liebknecht to Engels, 25 Oct. 1875, in Marx/Engels Archive, L3500, IISH.

102. *Fraktion* lists may be examined for each legislature period in Adolf Neumann-Hofer, *Die Entwicklung der Sozialdemokratie bei den Wählen zum Deutschen Reichstage* (Berlin, 1903), p. 46, for the 1877 list.

103. Liebknecht to Engels, 21, 24 Apr. 1875, in Kundel, "Zum Vereinigungsprozess," 1041-43.

104. *SDAP Protokoll, 1874*, p. 84.

105. *Protokoll des Vereinigungs-Congresses*, pp. 56-68. For the final arrangements concerning the two party organs, see Schröder, *Geschichte der Parteiorganization*, pp. 72-73.

106. Liebknecht to Engels, 16 Nov. 1875, Marx/Engels Archive, L3502, IISH.

107. *SAP Protokoll, 1875*, pp. 71-77.

108. Bracke to Engels, 31 Aug. 1876, in Bebel, AML, vol. 2, pp. 329-30.

109. Liebknecht to Engels, 21 Apr. 1875, in Kundel, "Zum Vereinigungsprozess," 1042.

110. *Vorwärts*, 13 Feb. 1891.

111. For Liebknecht's evaluation of Gotha, see his introduction to HVP, pp. 28-29, 53-54; *Marx zum Gedächtnis*, p. 40; letter from Liebknecht to staff of *Die Neue Zeit*, 15/1 (1896-97), 543; signed statement by Liebknecht in *Vorwärts*, 13 Feb. 1891.

112. Beyer and Winkler, *Revolutionäre Arbeitereinheit*, p. 82.

CHAPTER 8

1. See Appendix 1. Between 1874 and 1878, Liebknecht's newspapers had 43 press offenses in various categories; Hans-Wolfgang Wetzel, *Presseinnenpolitik im Bismarckreich (1874-1890)* (Bern, 1975), p. 304.

2. Wolfgang Pack, *Das parlamentarische Ringen um das Sozialistengesetz Bismarcks 1878-1890* (Dusseldorf, 1961), p. 16. For an example of socialist reaction, see *Der Volksstaat*, 6-18 Feb. 1876.

3. Liebknecht, *Das Briefgeheimnis vor dem Deutschen Reichstag* (Berlin, 1878), p. 61.

4. Liebknecht, *Robert Owen*, pp. 68-71.

5. Quoted in Schröder, *Geschichte der Parteiorganization*, p. 25.

6. For example, see his speech in *SDAP Protokoll, 1874*, p. 34.

7. VdR, 10 Apr. 1878, vol. 48, p. 883.

8. Ibid., 22 Nov. 1875, vol. 38, pp. 263-67.

9. The proposal is reproduced in Blos, *Denkwürdigkeiten*, vol. 1, pp. 231, 273-81.

10. *Der Volksstaat*, 23, 25 Feb., 3, 5, 8, 10 Mar. 1876; *Vorwärts*, 11, 13, 25, 27 Apr., 13 May 1877. The delegates to the 1876 congress had demanded a labor protection bill; see *Protokoll des Socialisten-Congresses zu Gotha vom 19. bis. 23. August 1876* (Berlin, 1876), pp. 32-33. (Hereinafter this source will be cited as *SAP Protokoll* with appropriate year and page reference.)

11. See the discussion above in Chapter 6, p. 180 ff.

12. Liebknecht, *Das Briefgehemnis*, collects the speeches he made on this subject in the Reichstag.

13. Wilhelm Liebknecht, *Zur orientalische Frage; oder, soll Europa kosakisch werden?* (Leipzig, 1878). See also his speech in VdR, 19 Feb. 1878, vol. 47, pp. 111-14. Liebknecht's ideas originated in Marx's analysis; see Liebknecht to Marx, 8 Feb. 1878, in Marx/Engels Archive, D3180, IISH.

14. For example, see Auer to Liebknecht, 5 Aug. 1876, in LBDS, vol. 1, p. 691; and Kautsky, *Erinnerungen*, pp. 374-75.

15. Blos, *Denkwürdigkeiten*, vol. 1, p. 224.

16. Concerning Liebknecht's travel expenses, see Geib to Liebknecht, 19 Feb. and 10 Apr. 1878, in LBDS, vol. 1, pp. 775, 778-79. For records of Liebknecht's salary as a journalist, see the various *Kassenberichten* of the SDAP and the *Abrechnungen* of the SAP, printed copies of which are preserved at the IISH. For comparison with average wages, see Ashok V. Desai, *Real Wages in Germany, 1871-1913* (Oxford, 1968), and R. Kuczynski, *Arbeitslohn und Arbeitszeit in Europa und Amerika 1870-1909* (Berlin, 1913).

17. Natalie Liebknecht to Engels, 28 Aug. 1877 in LBME, p. 238. For other similar complaints see LBME, pp. 279, 299.

18. Baptismal certificate in Liebknecht Archive, Packet 451, IISH. See also Liebknecht to Engels, 28 Aug. 1871, Marx/Engels Archive, L3445, IISH; the same packet includes a separate letter to Marx asking him to be a godfather too.

19. Heinz Wohlgemuth, *Karl Liebknecht: Eine Biographie* (Berlin, 1973), provides a sensitive portrait of the Liebknecht family circle.

20. Germany, Foreign office, *Acta betreffend den Erlass eines Gesetzes gegen die gemeingefahrlichen Bestrebungen der Sozialdemokratie*, reel 104, A2928.

21. *Vorwärts*, 15, 17 May 1878.

22. Quoted in ibid., 14 July 1878.

23. Eduard Bernstein, *Ignaz Auer: Eine Gedenkschrift* (Berlin, 1907), pp. 33-34; Blos, *Denkwürdigkeiten*, vol. 1, p. 241.

24. VdR, 23 May 1878, vol. 48, p. 1497.

25. Pack, *Parlamentarische Ringen um das Sozialistengesetz*, pp. 29-50.

26. *Vorwärts*, 7 June 1878.

27. Ibid., 16, 23 June 1878.

28. The text of the law is reproduced in Vernon L. Lidtke, *The Outlawed Party: Social Democracy in Germany, 1878-1890* (Princeton, 1966), pp. 339-45. The information on the National Grievance Commission is from Wetzel, *Presseinnenpolitik*, pp. 189-91, 197.

29. VdR, 18 Oct. 1878, vol. 51, pp. 350-51.

30. Bebel, AML, vol. 3, pp. 23-24; Ignaz Auer, *Von Gotha bis Wyden* (Berlin, 1901), p. 15; Auer, *Nach Zehn Jahren*, pp. 83-84, 95.

31. Quoted in Leo Stern, ed., *Der Kampf der deutschen Sozialdemokratie in der Zeit des Sozialistengesetzes 1878-1890--Die Tätigkeit der Reichs-Commission* (Berlin, 1956), vol. 3/1, pp. 42-44.

32. "Rechenschaftsbericht der sozialdemokratischen Mitglieder des deutschen Reichstages" (Zurich, 1879), p.

33. Proof of Liebknecht's authorship is in Liebknecht to Vollmar, ca. 12 Oct. 1879, Vollmar Archive, 1283, IISH. For a secondary source that argues persuasively that neither the leadership nor the membership of the SAP believed in violent revolution, see Manfried Scharrer, *Arbeiterbewegung im Obrigkeitsstaat* (Berlin, 1976), especially p. 44.

33. Quoted in Bernstein, *Geschichte der Berliner Arbeiterbewegung*, vol. 2, pp. 14-15, 27. Also *Vorwärts*, 23 June 1878.

34. Liebknecht to Engels, 2 Dec. 1878, Marx/Engels Archive, L3564, IISH.

35. Bebel notes this fact in AML, vol. 3, pp. 28-29.

36. VdR, 17 Mar. 1879, vol. 81, pp. 441-43.

37. Bebel to Bracke, 24 May 1879, in Gemkow, ed., *Marx und Engels Briefwechsel mit Bracke*, p. 185. See also Bebel's advice in the letter to Liebknecht, 9 Feb. 1879, in Liebknecht Archive, 65/14, IISH.

38. Engels to J. P. Becker, 1 July 1879, MEW, vol. 34, p. 382.

39. Wyden Congress Protokoll, Motteler Archive, 1478/28-29, IISH.

40. VdR, 4 Mar. 1885, vol. 81, p. 1542.

41. The article was entitled "Rückblicke auf die sozialistische Bewegung in Deutschland. Kritische Aphorismen von ***," *Jahrbuch für Sozialwissenschaft und Sozialpolitik*, 1. Jahrgang, 1. Hefte, 1879, 75-96. The authorship is discussed in Karl Kautsky, Jr., ed., *August Bebels Briefwechsel mit Karl Kautsky* (Vienna, 1955), p. 5; Bernstein, *Sozialdemokratische Lehrjahre*, pp. 78-79, disavows authorship of the article. Nevertheless, Pierre Angel, *Eduard Bernstein et l'évolution du socialisme allemand* (Paris, 1961), pp. 63-64, insists that Bernstein wrote the article. Angel is unconvincing to me. Karl Hochberg, Karl Schramm, and Karl Flesch appear to have been the authors.

42. See his justifications in *Der Sozialdemokrat*, 16 Nov. and 21 Dec. 1879. See also Hirsch to Liebknecht, 21 Nov. 1879, in Liebknecht Archive, 177/47-48, where Hirsch warns of criticism from radical comrades for this act.

43. Ursula Hermann, "Die Sozialistische Arbeiterpartei Deutschlands und das Ausnagmegesetz und zum Anteil der Zeitung 'Die Laterne,'" BGA, 15 (no. 3, 1973), 613.

44. Ibid., pp. 612-35. See also Liebknecht to Engels, 30 Oct., 23 Dec. 1878, in LBME, pp. 258, 263; also Dietzgen to Liebknecht, undated, in Ursula Hermann, "Briefe von Joseph Dietzgen an Wilhelm Liebknecht und der Redaktion 'Volksstaats,'" BGA, 13 (no. 2, 1971), 253.

45. Die Laterne, 1 June 1879. Liebknecht's letter is datelined 10 May.

46. Ibid., 27 Apr. 1879, pp. 535-47.

47. On Most, see John Most, Memoiren, 4 vols. (New York, 1903-1907); unfortunately vol. 3 ends in 1878 before Most left Germany, and vol. 4 is a recapitulation of his trial and imprisonment 1874-76. He does recount his bitter recollection of his first meeting with Liebknecht in vol. 3, p. 7. For further information on Most, see the sympathetic account by Rudolph Rocker, Johann Most (Berlin, 1924). For accounts of conflicts with party leaders before 1878, see Bernstein, Auer, pp. 29-31, and Bernstein, Sozialdemokratische Lehrjahre, pp. 84-85.

48. Die Freiheit, 3 May, 13 Sept. 1879.

49. Ibid., 27 Dec. 1879.

50. Ibid., 28 Feb. 1880.

51. Police reports of 10 June and 31 Dec. 1880 quoted in Reinhard Höhn, Die vaterlandlosen Gesellen: Der Sozialismus im Licht der Geheimberichte der preussische Polizei 1878-1914 (Cologne, 1964), pp. 37-62.

52. Police report of 29 Dec. 1879 in ibid., p. 24. Also Auer, Nach zehn Jahren, p. 100; and Bebel, AML, vol. 3, p. 31. Heinrich Gemkow and Ursula Hermann, "Bebel, die Partei und das Sozialistengesetz," BGA, 20 (no. 5, 1978), 645, uses this mutual support effort to argue that the party, and especially Bebel, reacted decisively to the onset of the antisocialist law. In my opinion, these authors misrepresent the true situation by overlooking the substantial evidence of confusion and indecision.

53. Engels to Liebknecht, 1 Mar. 1879, LBME, p. 263, expresses his delight at an earlier by-election success in Breslau, remarking that it should help the party to rally against the antisocialist law. See also Bebel, AML, vol. 3, p. 37, and Auer, Nach Zehn Jahren, p. 105, for the impact of the later Reichstag elections. A police report of 12 Jan. 1882 stresses the importance of elections in resurrecting the workers' movement; in Hohn, Die vaterlandlosen Gesellen, p. 97.

54. Liebknecht to Engels, 30 Oct. 1878, in LBME, p. 258.

55. Liebknecht and Fritzsche to Engels, 21 Oct. 1879, in LBME, pp. 272-73.

56. Bebel, AML, vol. 3, pp. 49-50.

57. Liebknecht to Engels, 30 Oct. 1878, in LBME, p. 268.

58. Bebel, AML, vol. 3, p. 49.

59. Bebel to Vollmar, 27 July 1879, in Vollmar Archive, 194, IISH.

60. For information on Liebknecht's role on *Der Sozial-demokrat*, see Bebel, AML, vol. 3, p. 52; Bernstein, *Sozial-demokratische Lehrjahre*, p. 119; Bernstein, *Aus den Jahren meines Exils*, pp. 114-15.

61. Liebknecht to Vollmar, 13 Aug. 1879, Vollmar Archive, 1283, IISH.

62. Reinhard Jansen, *Georg von Vollmar* (Dusseldorf, 1958), pp. 13-16.

63. Bernstein, *Sozialdemokratische Lehrjahre*, p. 89.

64. Bebel to Vollmar, 17 July 1879, in Bebel, AML, vol. 3, p. 50. Horst Bartel, et al., "'Der Sozialdemokrat'--Entwicklung und historische Stellung" (Berlin, 1970), p. 5; this editorial comment on the recent reproduction of *Der Sozialdemokrat* blames only the Zurich "opportunists" for discouraging Hirsch. The authors ignore Bebel's role in instigating this action.

65. Vollmar Archive, 194, IISH. Although Bebel did have considerable influence on *Der Sozialdemokrat*, Maehl, *Bebel*, p. 163, errs in asserting that Bebel chaired the editorial board.

66. Marx and Engels's circular letter to the leaders of the SAP, 17/18 Sept. 1879, in MEW, vol. 34, p. 408; Engels to J. P. Becker, 19 Dec. 1879, in ibid., p. 432; Bebel to Vollmar, 16 Aug. 1879, in Vollmar Archive, 194, IISH.

67. Engels to J. P. Becker, 12 Oct. 1880, and Marx to Sorge, 5 Nov. 1880, in MEW, vol. 34, pp. 470, 474.

68. MEW, vol. 35, p. 479 note.

69. Liebknecht to Vollmar, 20 Oct. 1879, Vollmar Archive, 1283, IISH. Most apparently tried for cooperation in August. *Die Freiheit*, 16 Aug. 1879, gave a quite favorable review to Bebel's *Frau und Sozialismus*. Liebknecht was not alone in rebuffing Most; see Auer to Vollmar, 3 Dec. 1879, in Vollmar Archive, 131, IISH.

70. *Die Freiheit*, 29 May 1880, 30 July 1881.

71. Bernstein, *Geschichte der Berliner Arbeiterbewegung*, vol. 2, pp. 46-48, reports an almost 50 percent drop in

voter participation in the communal elections. *Die Freiheit*,
5 Nov. 1881, gloats over the Reichstag election outcome.
Lidtke, *Outlawed Party*, p. 162, concentrates on Adolf
Stoecker's anti-Semitic agitation to explain the reduction
in the SAP vote, ignoring Most altogether. In fact, the
lost votes went not to Stoecker but to abstention, which
was what Most advocated. After a steadily rising level of
voter participation from 1871 to 1878, the number of votes
cast in 1881 fell by over half a million, even though the
number of eligible voters stayed about the same. Compared
to this precipitate decline, the small total won by Stoecker's
party seems almost inconsequential.

72. Bebel to Vollmar, 24 Aug. 1879, quoted in Ernst
Engelberg, *Revolutionäre Politik und rote Feldpost 1878-
1890* (Berlin, 1959), p. 39. Despite this evidence, Maehl,
Bebel, pp. 146-48, insists that Most was a "minor annoyance"
with very few followers.

73. *Der Sozialdemokrat*, 5, 12, 19 and 26 Oct. 1879.

74. *Die Freiheit*, 6 and 13 Dec. 1879.

75. *Der Sozialdemokrat*, 14 Dec. 1879.

76. This estimate is based on a financial statement
published by *Die Freiheit*, 18 Oct. 1879. Quarterly income
from subscriptions slightly exceeded 47 pounds. Quarterly
subscriptions cost 2 shillings. This indicates 470 subscribers.

77. Circulation statistics for *Der Sozialdemokrat* are
in the Motteler Archive, IISH. On the method of smuggling
the paper into Germany, see Ernst Engelberg, *Revolutionäre
Politik und rote Feldpost 1878-1890*, passim.

78. The four instances are Most, Hasselmann (both 1880),
Moritz Rittinghausen (1884), Bruno Geiser and Louis Viereck
(1887), and the leaders of *Die Jungen*, Werner and Wildberger
(1891). There were, of course, many more cases of withdrawal.

79. Liebknecht to Vollmar, 19 Apr. 1880, Vollmar Archive,
1283, IISH.

80. *Die Freiheit*, 29 May 1880. Bebel, AML, vol. 3,
pp. 129-30, claims that discovery by the police forced post-
ponement of the congress. Bernstein, *Sozialdemokratische
Lehrjahre*, pp. 103-105, ignores the planned congress and
reports only that Most came to Switzerland to create a radical
rival to the SAP. Rocker, *Most*, p. 76, argues convincingly
that the congress was abandoned only because Most proved
to be strong enough to defeat the SAP leaders. *Der Sozialdemokrat*, 30 May 1880, printed the agreement to a cease-
fire that Most pushed through in an assembly under the very
noses of the SAP editorial staff.

81. *Der Sozialdemokrat*, 20 June 1880.

82. Ibid., 11 July 1880.

83. *Die Freiheit*, 5 June 1880.

84. Liebknecht to Vollmar, 26 July 1880, Vollmar Archive, 1283, IISH.

85. Report in Stern, ed., *Kampf der Sozialdemokratie*, 3/1, 398.

86. *Protokoll des Kongresses der deutschen Sozial-demokratie: Abgehalten auf Schloss Wyden in der Schweiz von 20. bis 23. August 1880* (Zurich, 1880), p. 4.

87. *Der Sozialdemokrat*, 27 June 1880. Important back-ground to this expulsion is in a declaration signed by Bebel and Liebknecht, dated 12 Nov. 1879, in the Stadt und Landes-bibliothek at Dortmund, Atg. 15074. This document stresses Hasselmann's insubordination in founding a newspaper without *Fraktion* authorization. See also Bebel to Auer, 13 Nov. 1879 and 25 May 1880, also in the Stadt und Landesbibliothek at Dortmund, Atg. 15074.

88. "Wyden Congress Protokoll," Motteler Archive, 1478/31-38, IISH. This document is fuller than the published protocol, and it also identifies speakers by name. See also Günther Bers, *Wilhelm Hasselmann, 1844-1916* (Cologne, 1973), p. 53; and Stern, ed., *Kampf der Sozialdemokratie*, 3/1, 398.

89. "Wyden Congress Protokoll," Motteler Archive, 1478/26-38.

90. *Die Freiheit*, 4 Sept. 1880.

91. "Wyden Congress Protokoll," Motteler Archive, 1478/4.

92. Ibid., 1478/34. The printed protocol, *Protokoll des Kongresses der deutschen Sozialdemokratie*, pp. 43-44, has been changed from the original by Bebel in an apparent effort to make Liebknecht sound more revolutionary.

93. "Wyden Congress Protokoll," Motteler Achive, 1478/37.

94. Ibid., 1478/34, 37.

95. "Wyden Congress Protokoll," Motteler Archive, 1478/12, IISH. Modern Marxist historians usually exaggerate the sig-nificance of the program change, asserting that it indicated a reassertion of true revolutionary spirit or the penetration of Marxism into the SAP. For example, see Wolfgang Schröder and Gustav Seeber, "Zur Vorbereitung des Erfurter Programms," *Zeitschrift für Geschichtswissenschaft*, 14 (no. 7, 1966), 1118-19; Heinrich Gemkow, *Friedrich Engels Hilfe beim Sieg der deutschen Sozialdemokratie über das Sozialistengesetz* (Berlin, 1957), p. 57. A more reasonable argument is offered in Steinberg, *Sozialismus und Sozialdemokratie*, p. 66. The deletion of "legal means" merely recognized the new situation

of the party. At most, it removed a very feeble barrier
to the notion of violent revolution.

96. "Wyden Congress Protokoll," Motteler Archive,
1478/38-40. A police report in Höhn, *Die vaterlandlosen
Gesellen*, observes that the delegates agreed to allow members
of the *Vorstand* to continue in office even if they were not
reelected.

97. See Appendix 1.

98. Höhn, *Die vaterlandlosen Gesellen*, p. 78; and Dieter
Fricke, *Bismarcks Prätorianer: Die Berliner politische Polizei
im Kampf gegen die deutsche Arbeiterbewegung (1871-1898)* (Berlin,
1962), p. 102.

99. *Der Sozialdemokrat*, 7 July 1881.

100. Bebel, AML, vol. 3, pp. 43, 158.

101. *Die Freiheit*, 21 Aug., 8 Oct. 1881.

102. Bebel, "Natalie Liebknecht," 693.

CHAPTER 9

1. Liebknecht to Engels, 30 Oct. 1878, in LBME, p.
258. For brief summaries of the content of Bismarck's program, see William O. Henderson, *The Rise of German Industrial
Power, 1834-1914* (London, 1975), pp. 231-32, or Jurgen Kuczynski,
*A Short History of Labor Conditions under Industrial Capitalism
in Germany* (London, 1945), pp. 172-73. For more thorough
treatments, W. H. Dawson, *Bismarck and State Socialism* (London,
1890), or Annie Ashley, *The Social Policy of Bismarck* (London,
n.d.).

2. Good evidence on the reduction of harassment of
newspapers is in Wetzel, *Presseinnenpolitik*, pp. 213-14.

3. Mayer, *Engels*, vol. 2, pp. 361-62.

4. Bebel, ed., *Die Sozialdemokratie im deutschen Reichstag: Wahlaufrufe, III, Die Sozialdemokratische Wahlaufrufe
für die Reichstagswählen 1881, 1884, 1887* (Berlin, 1908), p.
211.

5. VdR, 2 Apr. 1886, vol. 88, p. 1845.

6. Ibid., 4 Mar. 1885, vol. 81, p. 1541.

7. Ibid., 21 Mar. 1884, vol. 75, p. 191. Lidtke, *Outlawed Party*, p. 214, asserts that "rather suddenly, in the
middle of the eighties, Liebknecht concluded that parliamentary institutions were useful not only for propaganda but
also as essential instruments for the achievement of a socialist society." Yet no permanent shift in Liebknecht's attitude
occurred. In the 1880s and 1890s, his attitude toward parliamentarism continued to change as circumstances dictated.

8. Paul Kampffmeyer, *Georg von Vollmar* (Munich, 1930), p. 25; also *Der Sozialdemokrat*, 17, 31 Oct., 7 Nov., 5, 19, 26 Dec. 1880.

9. Bebel to Motteler, 18 Sept. 1880, in Bebel Archive, 40/9-11, IISH. See also Bebel to Vollmar, 21 Sept., 25 Oct., 1880, in Vollmar Archive, 194, IISH.

10. Bebel to Engels, 26 Dec. 1880, in *Bebels Briefwechsel mit Engels*, p. 100. See also Bebel to Vollmar, 26 Dec. 1880, in Vollmar Archive, 194, IISH.

11. Karl Kautsky's remarks, reprinted in *Engels Briefwechsel mit Kautsky*, p. 8.

12. Auer to Hasenclever, 27 July 1881, Liebknecht Archive, 170/12, IISH. See also Bernstein, *Sozialdemokratische Lehrjahre*, p. 118.

13. Bernstein, *Aus den Jahren meines Exils*, pp. 114-15.

14. Bernstein, *Sozialdemokratische Lahrjahre*, p. 114.

15. Bernstein to Engels, 9 Sept. 1881, in *Bernsteins Briefwechsel mit Engels*, p. 33.

16. Engels to Bebel, 21 June 1882, in *Bebels Briefwechsel mit Engels*, p. 126.

17. Bebel to Auer, 4 Jan. 1882, in AML, vol. 3, p. 199.

18. Bernstein to Engels, 12 Jan. 1882, and Engels to Bernstein, 25/31 Jan. 1882, in *Bernsteins Briefwechsel mit Engels*, pp. 65, 69.

19. Bernstein to Engels, 17 Feb. 1882, in ibid., p. 75.

20. VdR, 10 Dec. 1881, vol. 55, pp. 246-308, 316-17.

21. *Der Sozialdemokrat*, 15, 22 Dec. 1881.

22. Ibid., 2, 23 Feb., 2 Mar., 6 Apr. 1882.

23. Bernstein to Engels, 17 Feb. 1882, in *Bernsteins Briefwechsel mit Engels*, p. 75.

24. *Die Laterne*, 27 Apr. 1879.

25. See also Engels to Bernstein, 17 Apr. 1882, in *Bernsteins Briefwechsel mit Engels*, p. 89.

26. Bernstein to Engels, 12 Jan. 1882; see also 27 Apr. 1882, in ibid., pp. 66-67, 92-93.

27. The original copy of the Zurich Protocol was in the Motteler Archive, 1479, IISH. Although the handwritten copy has been unaccountably misplaced, a typewritten copy prepared by Professor Vernon Lidtke is available. Professor Lidtke has assured me that his copy accurately reflects the original. Both are choppy and cryptic.

28. Police report of 30 July 1883 in Höhn, *Die vaterlandlosen Gesellen*, pp. 170-71.

29. *Protokoll über den Kongress der deutschen Sozialdemokratie in Kopenhagen. Abgehalten von 29. März bis 2. April 1883* (Hottingen-Zurich, 1883), pp. 27-30.

30. Bebel to Engels, 2 May 1883, in *Bebels Briefwechsel mit Engels*, pp. 154-55.

31. Bernstein to Engels, 31 May 1883, in *Bernsteins Briefwechsel mit Engels*, p. 209.

32. Bernstein to Liebknecht, 4 June 1883, in Liebknecht Archive, 69/6-7, IISH.

33. Bebel to Hermann Schlüter, 24 Nov. 1884, in Bebel Archive, 40/27-28, IISH.

34. For example, see *Berliner Volksblatt*, 1, 7 Jan. 1885.

35. Dietz to Liebknecht, 23 Feb. 1885, in Liebknecht Addenda, 16/18-20, IISH.

36. Liebknecht to Kautsky, 18 Nov. 1885, in Kautsky Archive, 515, 532, IISH.

37. Bebel to Liebknecht, 15 Nov. 1884, in Liebknecht Archive, 65/26-38, IISH.

38. For example, see Kautsky to Engels, 7, 11 Apr., 29 May, 23 June 1884, in *Engels Briefwechsel mit Kautsky*, pp. 107, 109, 118, 125.

39. Bebel to Schlüter, 15 Dec. 1884, in Bebel Archive, 43/30-31, IISH.

40. Bebel to Engels, 8 June 1884, in *Bebels Briefwechsel mit Engels*, p. 184; Engels to Bernstein, 5 June 1884, Bernstein to Engels, 16 July 1884, in *Bernsteins Briefwechsel mit Engels*, pp. 271-72, 285; Kautsky to Engels, 5 Aug., 14 Sept. 1883, 15 Apr. 1884, Engels to Kautsky, 18 Sept. 1883, in *Engels Briefwechsel mit Kautsky*, pp. 80-82, 110, 111; Kautsky to Bebel, 8 Nov. 1884, in *Bebels Briefwechsel mit Kautsky*, p. 24. I disagree completely with Maehl, *Bebel*, pp. 151, 173, and 179, where it is asserted that Bebel played the role of a "bridge" between the SAP left and right and that he tried to avoid a schism.

41. Hasenclever to Auer, 13 Nov. 1884, Liebknecht Archive, 61/26-27, IISH.

42. Bebel to Liebknecht, 10 Nov. 1884, Liebknecht Archive, 65/24-25, IISH. See also Bebel to Motteler, 17 Nov. 1884, in Bebel Archive, 40/54-55, IISH.

43. Hasenclever to Liebknecht, 11, 14 Nov. 1884, Liebknecht Addenda, 38/15-17, 20-22, IISH.

44. Bebel to Liebknecht, 15 Nov. 1884, in Liebknecht Archive, 65/26-28, IISH.

45. Bebel to Engels, 3 Oct. 1884, in *Bebels Briefwechsel mit Engels*, p. 185.

46. Bebel to Engels, 19 Sept. 1885, ibid., p. 236.

47. Bebel to Liebknecht, 28 Dec. 1884, Liebknecht Archive, 65/32-33, IISH.

48. Bebel to Liebknecht, 17 Nov. 1884, ibid., 65/29-30.

49. Hans-Christoph Schröder, *Sozialismus und Imperial-ismus* (Hannover, 1968), p. 125.
50. Blos, *Denkwürdigkeiten*, vol. 2, pp. 126-27.
51. *Der Sozialdemokrat*, 11 Dec. 1884.
52. Bebel to Schlüter, 15 Dec. 1884, in Bebel Archive, 43/30-31, IISH; Bebel to Engels, 28 Dec. 1884, in *Bebels Briefwechsel mit Engels*, pp. 206-207. This debate is well summarized in Schröder, *Sozialismus und Imperialismus*, pp. 127-36.
53. Bebel's reflections quoted in Helmut Hirsch, ed., *August Bebel: Sein Leben in Dokumenten, Reden und Schriften* (Cologne, 1968), pp. 396-97.
54. Bebel to Engels, 28 Dec. 1884, in *Bebels Brief-wechsel mit Engels*, pp. 206-207.
55. *Der Sozialdemokrat*, 8 Jan. 1885. Bebel and Lieb-knecht later argued about whether Engels had intended his proposal for publication. Liebknecht, of course, insisted that Engels had approved publication. The relevant material is collected in the Bebel Archive, 34a, IISH.
56. Engels to Bebel, 30 Dec. 1884, in *Bebels Brief-wechsel mit Engels*, pp. 211-12. See also the article by Franz Mehring in *Die Neue Zeit*, 20/1 (1901-1902), p. 227, and Bebel to Motteler, 12 Jan. 1885, in Bebel Archive, 40/50, IISH.
57. Bernstein to Engels, 15 Jan. 1885, *Bernsteins Brief-wechsel mit Engels*, p. 317. See also the editorial comment in *Bebels Briefwechsel mit Engels*, p. xx.
58. Bernstein to Liebknecht, 13, 21 Jan. 1885, Lieb-knecht Archive, 69/8-9, 69/10-11, IISH.
59. Motteler discusses circulating the Zurich resolu-tion in marginal comments on a letter from Bebel to Bern-stein, 31 Mar. 1885, Kampffmeyer Archive, 2, AsD. In the text of the letter, even Bebel found Motteler's action provoca-tive. *Der Sozialdemokrat*, 2 Apr. 1885, contains a complaint from the *Fraktion* about this circulation.
60. Bebel to Motteler, 19 Jan., 7 Feb. 1885, in Bebel Archive, 40/60, 63-64, IISH.
61. The declarations can be examined in *Der Sozialdemo-krat* during the entire month of February. The exile origin of the initial protests is emphasized in Blos, *Denkwürdig-keiten*, vol. 2, p. 129.
62. *Der Sozialdemokrat*, 29 Jan. 1885.
63. Bernstein to Kautsky, 6 Mar., 1 Apr. 1885, Kautsky Archive, 505/32, 505/36, IISH; see also Bebel to Kautsky, 16 Mar. 1885, in *Bebels Briefwechsel mit Kautsky*, p. 37. See also Horst Bartel, et al., "*Der Sozialdemokrat*--Entwicklung

und historische Stellung," (Berlin, 1970), pp. 19-20.

64. Undated letter fragment by Liebknecht, Kampffmeyer Archive, 58, AsD.

65. Liebknecht to Bernstein, 20 Mar. 1885, in ibid., 9, AsD.

66. Ibid.

67. Bernstein to Kautsky, 1 Apr. 1885, Kautsky Archive, 505/36, IISH.

68. Liebknecht to Bernstein, 20 Mar. 1885, Kampffmeyer Archive, 9, AsD.

69. Bernstein, *Sozialdemokratische Lehrjahre*, p. 159.

70. Even Bebel found the tone offensive. See Bebel to Bernstein, 31 Mar. 1885, Kampffmeyer Archive, 2, AsD.

71. Auer to Liebknecht, 27 Mar. 1885, Liebknecht Archive, 61/29-30, IISH. Paul Singer shared Auer's indignation; see Singer to Bernstein, 26 Mar. 1885, Kampffmeyer Archive, 1, AsD.

72. Bernstein, *Sozialdemokratische Lehrjahre*, p. 160. Bernstein to Kautsky, 1 Apr. 1885, Kautsky Archive, 505/36, IISH, says that what stood in the 2 Apr. declaration was "only a weak idea of what stood in the original." If that is true, the original must have been outrageous.

73. Bebel to Bernstein, 31 Mar. 1885, Kampffmeyer Archive, 2, AsD; also Bebel to Motteler, 3 Apr. 1885, Bebel Archive, 40/69, IISH.

74. Bebel to Liebknecht, 1 Apr. 1885, Liebknecht Archive, 65/36-37, IISH.

75. Bebel to SAP *Fraktion*, 5 Apr. 1885, Bebel Archive, 42, IISH.

76. Bebel to Kautsky, 16 Mar. 1885, in *Bebels Briefwechsel mit Kautsky*, p. 37; Bebel to Engels, 19 June 1885, in *Bebels Briefwechsel mit Engels*, p. 225.

77. Liebknecht to Bernstein, 5, 9, 11, 15, Apr. 1885, Kampffmeyer Archive, 10, 11, 12, 13, AsD.

78. Bebel to Bernstein, 12 Apr. 1885, in ibid., 3, AsD.

79. Liebknecht to Bernstein, 15, 16 Apr. 1885, ibid., 13, 14, AsD.

80. Liebknecht to Bernstein, 16 Apr. 1885, ibid., 14, AsD. See also Kampffmeyer, *Vollmar*, p. 59.

81. Liebknecht to Motteler, 31 May 1885, Liebknecht Archive, 37/9-11, IISH.

82. Liebknecht's permission for publication was explicitly noted in a later statement by Bebel in *Der Sozialdemokrat*, 21 May 1885.

83. Liebknecht to Bernstein, 28 Apr. 1885, Kampffmeyer

Archive, 15, AsD; Bernstein to Liebknecht, 25 Apr. 2, 9, 15
May 1885, Liebknecht Archive, 69/14, 15-16, 19-21, 25-28,
IISH.
    84. Quoted in *Der Sozialdemokrat*, 14 May 1885; see
also Blos, *Denkwürdigkeiten*, vol. 2, pp. 132-34. See also
Singer to Liebknecht, 26 May 1885, in Liebknecht Addenda,
62/28-31, IISH.
    85. Bebel to Liebknecht, 9 May 1885, Liebknecht Archive,
65/41-42, IISH.
    86. Bernstein to Liebknecht, 9 May 1885, ibid., 69/19-21.
    87. Liebknecht to Bernstein, 14 May 1885, Kampffmeyer
Archive, 16, AsD.
    88. Liebknecht to Motteler, 8 May 1885, Liebknecht
Archive, 37/6, IISH.
    89. Bernstein to Liebknecht, 17 May 1885, ibid.,
69/29-32.
    90. Bebel to Liebknecht, 30 May 1885, ibid., 65/48-49.
    91. Bebel to Liebknecht, 24 May 1885, ibid., 65/45-46.
    92. Bebel to Liebknecht, 26 July, 5 Aug. 1885, ibid.,
65/58-59, 85-86. This latter letter is misdated on its packet
in the archive. Similar sentiments are in Bebel to Liebknecht,
7, 9 Aug. 1885, ibid., 65/60, 61-62.
    93. Bebel to Liebknecht, 27 May 1885, Liebknecht
Archive, 65/47, IISH. The letter from Motteler to Bebel that
was included in this correspondence is in the Liebknecht
Archive, 65/156, IISH.
    94. Bebel to Liebknecht, 26 July 1885, ibid., 65/58-59.
    95. Bebel to Motteler, 17 Aug. 1884, Bebel Archive,
40/43-44, IISH; also Bebel to Bernstein, 31 Mar. 1885,
Kampffmeyer Archive, 2, AsD.
    96. Auer to Liebknecht, 25 Nov. 1884, Liebknecht
Archive, 61/23-25, IISH.
    97. Liebknecht to London Comrades, 10 July 1885, ibid.,
37/16-17, IISH.
    98. See Bebel's complaint about these actions in his
letter to Liebknecht, 28 Apr. 1885, ibid., 65/39-40.
    99. Liebknecht to Bebel and the Zurich staff, 28 May
1885, Bebel Archive, 127/2-3, IISH.
    100. Liebknecht to Bebel, 29 May 1885, Liebknecht Archive,
22, IISH.
    101. Bernstein makes his diagnosis to Engels, 15 Jan.
1885, in *Bernsteins Briefwechsel mit Engels*, p. 318.
    102. Liebknecht to Bebel and the Zurich staff, 28 May
1885, Bebel Archive, 127/2-3, IISH.
    103. Bernstein to Engels, 15 Jan. 1885, in *Bernsteins
Briefwechsel mit Engels*, p. 318.

104. Bebel to Liebknecht, 28 June, 5, 12 July 1885, Liebknecht Archive, 65/53, 55, 56; also Bebel to Vollmar, 11 July 1885, Vollmar Archive, 194, IISH.

105. Bernstein to Liebknecht, 13 June, 5 July 1885, Liebknecht Archive, 69/38-41, 48-49, IISH; Bebel to Vollmar, 8, 14 June 1885, Vollmar Archive, 194, IISH; Bebel to Motteler, 13 June 1885, Bebel Archive, 40/75-76, IISH.

106. Bebel to Motteler, 13 June 1885, in Bebel Archive, 40/75-76, IISH; Bernstein to Liebknecht, 13 June 1885, in Liebknecht Archive, 69/38-41, IISH.

107. Liebknecht to Bernstein, undated [ca. 1 June 1885], Kampffmeyer Archive, 23, AsD; Liebknecht to Bebel and the Zurich staff, 28 May 1885, Bebel Archive, 127/2-3, IISH.

108. Bernstein to Liebknecht, 6 June 1885, Liebknecht Archive, 69/35-37, IISH.

109. Kautsky to Bernstein, 30 June 1885, in Eduard Bernstein, ed., *Die Briefe von Friedrich Engels an Eduard Bernstein, mit Briefen von Karl Kautsky an Ebendenselben* (Berlin, 1925), p. 170.

110. *Der Sozialdemokrat*, 20 Aug., 3, 18 Sept., 22 Oct. 1885. See also Engels to Bernstein, 15 May 1885, in *Bernsteins Briefwechsel mit Engels*, p. 321.

111. Bebel to Liebknecht, 6 Apr. 1885, Liebknecht Archive, 65/38, IISH; also Bebel to Engels, 7 Dec. 1885, in *Bebels Briefwechsel mit Engels*, p. 247; Bebel to Kautsky, 22 Feb. 1885, in *Bebels Briefwechsel mit Kautsky*, p. 31; Kautsky to Engels, 21 Aug. 1885, in *Engels Briefwechsel mit Kautsky*, p. 182.

112. Bebel to Engels, 19 June 1885, in *Bebels Briefwechsel mit Engels*, p. 224.

113. Liebknecht to Kautsky, 31 Oct. 1885, in Kautsky Archive, 515, 531, IISH. See also Appendix 1.

114. Ulrich Hess, "Louis Viereck und seine Münchner Blätter für Arbeiter 1882-1889," *Dortmünder Beiträge zur Zeitungsforschung*, 6 (1961), 27-28.

115. Clippings in Kampffmeyer Nachlass, 63, AsD.

116. *Der Sozialdemokrat*, 22, 29 Oct., 5, 12 Nov. 1885.

117. Engels to Bebel, 17 Nov. 1885, in *Bebels Briefwechsel mit Engels*, pp. 243-44.

118. *Recht auf Arbeit*, 11 Nov. 1885.

119. *Der Sozialdemokrat*, 11, 19, 26 Nov. 1885.

120. The ideological implications of this dispute are treated in some detail in Steinberg, *Sozialismus und Sozialdemokratie*, pp. 36-37, and in Vernon Lidtke, "German Social Democracy and German State Socialism," *International Review of Social History*, 9 (1964), 220-24. See also Steenson, *Kautsky*, pp. 68-70.

121. Bebel to Liebknecht, 8 Jan. 1886, in Liebknecht Archive, 65/64-65, IISH. The political background of Viereck's maneuvers is discussed in the introduction to Paul Mayer, *Bruno Schoenlank 1859-1901: Reformer der Sozialdemokratischen Tagespresse* (Hannover, 1971), pp. 28-29.

122. Bebel to Engels, 7 Dec. 1885, in *Bebels Briefwechsel mit Engels*, p. 247.

123. Report dated 24 July 1886, in Höhn, *Die vaterlandlosen Gesellen*, pp. 265-67.

124. Richard H. Hall, *Organizations: Structure and Process* (Englewood Cliffs, N.J., 1972), p. 238; Louis R. Pondy, "Organizational Conflict: Concepts and Models," *Administrative Science Quarterly*, 12 (no. 2, Sept. 1967), 305.

125. Lewis A. Coser, *The Functions of Social Conflict* (Glencoe, Ill., 1964), pp. 151-57.

126. For example, see Liebknecht to Kautsky, 2 May 1885, in Kautsky Archive, 515, 530, IISH.

127. Bebel to Motteler, 13 June 1885, in Bebel Archive, 40/75-76, IISH.

128. Bebel to Engels, 5 July 1885, in *Bebels Briefwechsel mit Engels*, p. 230.

129. Auer to Liebknecht, 27 Apr. 1886, in Liebknecht Archive, 61/37-38, IISH, is already quarreling about editorial policies for *Der Sozialdemokrat*. At the next party congress, Chairman Singer deliberately squelched any discussion of the relationship between the *Fraktion* and the newspaper; see *Verhandlungen des Parteitages der deutschen Sozialdemokratie in St. Gallen* (Hottingen-Zurich, 1888), p. 16 and passim.

130. See Raymond H. Dominick, "Democracy or Socialism: A Case Study of *Vorwärts* in the 1890s," *Central European History*, 10 (Dec. 1977), pp. 286-311.

131. Bebel to Liebknecht, 1 Dec. 1898, in Bebel Archive, 34a, IISH.

132. See his statements in Bebel Archive, 34a, IISH.

CHAPTER 10

1. On the trial, see Bernstein, *Auer*, pp. 50-51.

2. Report in the *New York Sun*, 14 Sept. 1886.

3. Ibid., 20, 21, 23 Sept. 1886.

4. Itinerary is compiled from Wilhelm Liebknecht, *Ein Blick in die Neue Welt* (Stuttgart, 1887).

5. Note in Blumenberg, ed., *Bebels Briefwechsel mit*

Engels, p. 263 note. Average revenue figures for the SAP are taken from *Verhandlungen des Parteitages der deutschen Sozialdemokratie in St. Gallen* (Hottingen-Zurich, 1888), p. 9

6. *Die Freiheit*, 11, 27 Sept.; 9, 23 Oct. 1886. Similar sentiments appeared in the anarchist *Chicagoer Arbeiter-Zeitung*, 5 and 6 Nov. 1886. Rocker, *Most*, p. 334, accepts these biased accounts as accurate, calling Liebknecht's trip a "total failure." German police reports said Liebknecht's agitation was quite successful; see Gerhard Becker, "Die Agitationsreise Wilhelm Liebknecht durch die USA 1886," *Zeitschrift für Geschichtswissenschaft*, 15 (no. 5, 1967), 842-62, and Karl Obermann, "Die Amerikareise Wilhelm Liebknechts im Jahre 1886," *Zeitschrift für Geschichtswissenschaft*, 14 (no. 4, 1966), 614-15.

7. Singer to Liebknecht, 4 Oct. 1886, in Liebknecht Addenda, 62/52-55, IISH. In *Der Sozialdemokrat*, 5 Nov. 1886, Liebknecht published a signed statement repudiating all the "lies" circulating about his trip.

8. Synthesized from reports in *Illinois Staats-Zeitung*, 6 Nov. 1886, and *Cincinnati Commercial Gazette*, 15 Nov. 1886. See also *Chicago Weekly News*, 11 Nov. 1886.

9. Becker, "Die Agitationsreise Liebknecht," 851-62. See also excerpts from the colorless socialist newspapers in Stern, ed., *Kampf der deutschen Sozialdemokratie*, pp. 230-32, 234-35.

10. VdR, 31 Jan. 1885, vol. 80, p. 1032. For similar denunciations of anarchism, see Vetter Niemand [pseud. for Liebknecht], *Trutz-Eisenstirn*, vol. 1, pp. 4-7, 25, 57, 59. Liebknecht also was the referee against anarchism at the St. Gall Congress in 1887; see *SAP Protokoll, 1887*, pp. 39-43.

11. *New York Sun*, 23 Sept. 1886.

12. *Cincinnati Commercial Gazette*, 14 Nov. 1886.

13. Liebknecht, *Ein Blick*, pp. 46-52, 79, 99-102, 124, 150, 163, 281-82.

14. Schweichel, "Liebknecht als Schriftsteller," 334. Liebknecht's tactics fit very well the thesis of John L. Snell, "The World of German Democracy, 1789-1914," *The Historian*, 31 (Aug. 1969), 521-38, where it is argued that foreign example played a significant role in influencing German attitudes toward democracy and republican state forms.

15. Kautsky to Liebknecht, 19 Apr. 1888, in Liebknecht Archive, 189/25-26, IISH.

16. For background, see Bernard Moss, *The Origins of the French Labor Movement, 1830-1914* (Berkeley, 1976), pp. 100-119.

17. A source for Liebknecht's efforts is LBME, pp. 316-17, 322-38. See also *Bebels Briefwechsel mit Engels*, pp. 344-53. For secondary accounts, see James Joll, *The Second International, 1889-1914* (New York, 1956), pp. 30-35; and Braunthal, *History of the International*, vol. 1, p. 198.

18. See the whole Engels-Lafargue exchange in *Correspondence*, vol. 1, pp. 146-295.

19. Grillenberger to Liebknecht, 15 June 1889, and Singer to Liebknecht, 16 Nov. 1888 and 31 July 1889, in Liebknecht Addenda, 32/32-33 and 62/147-49 and 190-91, IISH, all exhibit anti-French sentiments.

20. *Protokoll des Internationalen Arbeiter-Congresses zu Paris. Abgehalten vom 14. bis 30. Juli 1889* (Nuremberg, 1890), pp. 2-5. See also Joll, *Second International*, pp. 36-37.

21. *Protokoll des Internationalen Arbeiter-Congresses 1889*, pp. 5, 15-16.

22. For examples of and comments on his travel, see Lafargue to Engels, 5 Oct. 1892 and 23 Mar. 1893, in Engels and Lafargue, *Correspondence*, vol. 3, pp. 197, 253; Liebknecht, "Acht Tage in Holland," *Die Neue Zeit*, 15/22 (1898-99), 110-12.

23. *Vorwärts*, 10 Aug. 1900.

24. In the Liebknecht Archive, IISH, see no. 259 for correspondence with Lafargue, no. 257 for Millerand, no. 165 for Guesde, no. 75 for Bonnier, and no. 325 for Vaillant.

25. Kemal to Liebknecht, 24 Sept. 1896, in Liebknecht Archive, 188/1-2, IISH.

26. Bebel to Engels, 15 Oct. 1894, in *Bebels Briefwechsel mit Engels*, p. 777.

27. *Der Sozialdemokrat*, 29 Jan. and 29 Apr. 1887, reflects the altered composition of the *Vorstand*.

28. Singer to Liebknecht, 28 Nov. 1887, in Liebknecht Archive, 62/86-89, IISH, refers to Hasenclever's alcoholism as contributing to a stroke.

29. Bernstein, *Geschichte der Berliner Arbeiterbewegung*, vol. 2, pp. 246-47.

30. *Der Sozialdemokrat*, 23 Nov. 1889.

31. For Wilhelm II's labor conference, see *Die Protokoll der Internationalen Arbeiterschutzkonferenz. Im amtlichen Auftrag* (Leipzig, 1890). There is a good account of the expiration of the antisocialist law in Gordon Craig, *Germany, 1866-1945* (New York, 1978), pp. 171-78.

32. Record of expulsions in Lipinski, *Sozialdemokratie von ihren Anfängen*, vol. 2, p. 51. For other impact, see Mehring, *Geschichte der Sozialdemokratie*, pp. 673-75.

33. For sociological generalizations asserting the inevitability that bureaucratic types replace successful agitators, see Gouldner, ed., *Studies in Leadership*, pp. 64–65, 77–78.

34. Bebel to Natalie Liebknecht, 2 June 1890, in Liebknecht Archive, 396/13–15, IISH. See also Bebel to Engels, 2 June 1890, in *Bebels Briefwechsel mit Engels*, pp. 394–95; Bebel to Liebknecht, 27 May 1890, in Liebknecht Archive, 65/98, IISH; and Engels to Natalie Liebknecht, 19 June 1890, in LBME, pp. 369–70.

35. Bebel to Natalie Liebknecht, 16 June 1890, Liebknecht Archive, 396/17–18 and Bebel to Hirsch, 5 July 1890, in the Stadt und Landesbibliothek at Dortmund, document no. 15282.

36. The proposal appeared in the *Berliner Volkstribune*, 9 Aug. 1890. For Bebel's role in formulating this proposal, see Marga Beyer, "August Bebels Statutentwurf aus dem Jahre 1890," BGA, 19 (no. 3, 1977), 421–29. I have found no information on Liebknecht's role in preparing the proposal.

37. *Protokoll über die Verhandlungen des Parteitages der Sozialdemokratischen Partei Deutschlands. Abgehalten zu Halle a.s. vom 12. bis 18. Oktober 1890* (Berlin, 1890), pp. 134–37, 143–45. (Hereinafter this source will be cited as *SPD Protokoll* with appropriate year and page references.) See also Dirk H. Müller, *Idealismus und Revolution: Zur Opposition der Jungen gegen dem Sozialdemokratischen Parteivorstand 1890 bis 1894* (Berlin, 1975), p. 54.

38. *SPD Protokoll, 1890*, pp. 124–25, 156–57, 238–39.

39. Müller, *Idealismus und Revolution*, p. 75.

40. *SPD Protokoll, 1890*, p. 264. For a comment on the gradual growth of *Vorstand* control over the press, see Dieter Groh, *Negative Integration und revolutionärer Attentismus* (Frankfurt am Main, 1973), pp. 138–39. For a thorough discussion of this issue during the 1890s, see Dominick, "Democracy or Socialism," 286–311.

41. Liebknecht to Julius Motteler, 16 July 1885, in Liebknecht Archive, 37/18–19, IISH.

42. *Vorwärts*, 23 Nov. 1894.

43. *SPD Protokoll, 1896*, pp. 100–101, 114–16.

44. The importance of the expiration of the antisocialist law as a landmark in the history of Liebknecht's party can easily be exaggerated. To concentrate on that date obscures the numerous factors other than state policy that influenced the evolution of the SPD: for example, electoral success, the growing industrial work force and consequent growth in labor unions, arguments with the anarchists, and

continued schooling in Marxism. The imposition of the law
created a stir in the party, but its expiration really raised
no new issues. For a comment illustrating the continuity
of issues from 1885 to 1890, see Auer to Liebknecht, 4 April
1890, in Liebknecht Archive, 61/50-51, IISH. This continuity
is stressed in Peter Wienand, "Revoluzzer und Revisionisten:
Die 'Jungen' in der Sozialdemokratie vor der Jahrhundertwende," *Politische Vierteljahresschrift*, 17 (no. 2, 1976),
208-10.

45. For the long-standing background to antiparliamen-
tarism, see *Der Sozialdemokrat*, 12 Nov. 1886, and Bernstein,
Geschichte der Berliner Arbeiterbewegung, vol. 2, pp. 267-
68. On *Die Jungen* generally, see Müller, *Idealismus und
Revolution*, especially pp. 2-3, 45-46, Hans-Manfred Bock,
"Die 'Literaten- und Studenten-Revolte' der Jungen in der
SPD um 1890," *Das Argument*, 13 (Mar., 1971), 22-41, and
Wienand, "Revoluzzer und Revisionisten."

46. *Berliner Volkstribune*, 16, 23 Aug., 27 Sept. 1890;
Sächsische Arbeiter-Zeitung, 13 Aug. 1890.

47. Bebel to Vollmar, 27 July 1890, in Vollmar Archive,
194, IISH; Bernstein, *Geschichte der Berliner Arbeiterbewegung*, vol. 2, pp. 305-27; Bock, "'Literaten- und Studenten-
Revolte,'" 26-27.

48. Liebknecht to Motteler, 28 Apr. 1890, Liebknecht
Archive, 37/36, IISH.

49. *Berliner Volkstribune*, 23 Aug. 1890; *Sächsische
Arbeiter-Zeitung*, 31 Aug. 1890; Adler to Liebknecht, 14 Sept.
1890 and Liebknecht to Adler, 16 Sept. 1890, in Friedrich
Adler, ed., *Victor Adlers Briefwechsel mit August Bebel und
Karl Kautsky, sowie Briefe von und an Ignaz Auer, Eduard
Bernstein, Adolf Braun, Heinrich Dietz, Friedrich Ebert,
Wilhelm Liebknecht, Hermann Müller und Paul Singer* (Vienna,
1954), pp. 60-62.

50. Engels to Lafargue, 27 Aug. 1890, in Engels and
Lafargue, *Correspondence*, vol. 2, p. 387; Auer to Liebknecht,
12 Aug. 1890, in Liebknecht Archive, 61/63-64.

51. *SPD Protokoll, 1890*, pp. 95-97.

52. *SPD Protokoll, 1891*, pp. 204-205.

53. Ibid., pp. 61-67; Müller, *Idealismus und Revolution*, pp. 108-109; Bock, "'Literaten- und Studenten-Revolte,'"
28; Ritter, *Arbeiterbewegung im wilhelminischen Reich*, pp.
86-87; Wienand, "Revoluzzer und Revisionisten," 216.

54. *Sächsische Arbeiter-Zeitung*, 31 Aug. 1891.

55. Singer to Liebknecht, 15 Sept. 1890, in Liebknecht
Addenda, 62/276-78, IISH.

56. *SPD Protokoll, 1891*, pp. 128-29.

57. Kautsky to Adler, 5 Aug. 1891, in *Adlers Brief-wechsel mit Bebel und Kautsky*, pp. 75–76; see also Kautsky to Engels, 7 Mar., 5 Apr., and 26 Sept. 1891, in *Engels Brief-wechsel mit Kautsky*, pp. 285, 292, 306.

58. Kautsky to Engels, 26 Sept. 1891, in *Engels Brief-wechsel mit Kautsky*, p. 306; see also Kautsky to Engels, 18 Feb. 1891, in ibid., p. 279. For Kautsky's argument against tolerance of heterodoxy in the official party press, see *Die Neue Zeit*, 14/1 (1895–96), 113.

59. Engels to Lafargue, 30 Mar. 1891, in Engels and Lafargue, *Correspondence*, vol. 3, p. 41; see also Engels to Sorge, 2 Sept. 1891, in MEW, vol. 37, pp. 149–50.

60. Engels to Kautsky, 13 June 1891, in *Engels Brief-wechsel mit Kautsky*, p. 301.

61. Engels to Sorge, 8 Apr. 1891, in MEW, vol. 38, p. 80.

62. Bebel to Engels, 24 Oct. 1891, in *Bebels Briefwechsel mit Engels*, pp. 459–60.

63. Bebel to Engels, 12 Sept. 1891, in ibid., p. 430.

64. See the editorial comments in Karl Kautsky, Jr., ed., *August Bebels Briefwechsel mit Karl Kautsky* (Assen, 1971), p. xxiv. In his letters *to* Liebknecht, Kautsky always called him "Lieber Freund"; moreover, he never used the informal "Du" but rather the formal "Sie." In the whole correspondence between Bebel and Liebknecht, only two instances occur where Bebel called his friend "lieber Alte." "Lieber Freund" was the usual form of address.

65. Auer to Vollmar, 6(?) Aug. 1891, in Vollmar Archive, 131, IISH.

66. *SAP Protokoll, 1887*, p. 47.

67. *SPD Protokoll, 1890*, p. 181.

68. Mayer, *Engels*, vol. 2, pp. 480–81; see also Engels to Lafargue, 10 Feb. 1891, in Engels and Lafargue, *Corre-spondence*, vol. 3, p. 30.

69. Kautsky, *Erinnerungen*, pp. 524–25, 534–35.

70. Engels to Kautsky, 7 Jan. 1891, in *Engels Brief-wechsel mit Kautsky*, p. 268.

71. Kautsky to Engels, 8 Jan. 1891, in ibid., p. 269. See also Steenson, *Kautsky,* pp. 94–95.

72. *Die Neue Zeit*, 9/1 (1890–91), 561–62; the changes made by Engels are noted in the copy of the *Critique* in Mommsen, ed., *Parteiprogramme*, p. 325.

73. Kautsky to Adler, 26 Jan. 1891, in *Adlers Brief-wechsel*, p. 69.

74. Bebel to Kautsky, 26 Mar. 1891, in *Bebels Brief-wechsel mit Kautsky*, p. 76; see also Singer to Liebknecht,

8 July 1891, in Liebknecht Addenda, 62/305-307, IISH.

75. *Vorwärts*, 13 Feb. 1891.

76. *Die Neue Zeit*, 9/1 (1890-91), 683-86; see also Kautsky to Liebknecht, 25 Feb. 1891, in Liebknecht Archive, 189/28, IISH.

77. Kautsky to Engels, 9 Feb., 21 Mar. 1891, Engels to Kautsky, 17 Mar. 1891, in *Engels Briefwechsel mit Kautsky*, pp. 276, 288-89.

78. LBME (if it is complete for this period) shows a dramatic drop in the frequency of Liebknecht-Engels correspondence in 1891 and 1892. It rebounded somewhat in 1893 and 1894. The average length of Kautsky to Liebknecht letters fell by half after this affair; see Liebknecht Archive, 189, IISH. There is an enormous gap in the surviving Liebknecht to Kautsky correspondence from 1888 to 1894; see Kautsky Archive, DXV 503-65, IISH.

79. There are several erroneous accounts of the genesis of the various program drafts. Horst Bartel, *Friedrich Engels Kampf für die Schaffung einer marxistischen Arbeiterpartei in Deutschland* (Berlin, 1956), pp. 54-56, displays two common misconceptions: (1) that Bebel authored the *Vorstand* draft, and (2) that Engels assisted Kautsky in preparing his draft. Ritter, *Arbeiterbewegung*, p. 95, erroneously claims that Bernstein authored the practical demands for the adopted Erfurt Program. He probably incorporated this error from Kautsky's account in Benedikt Kautsky, ed., *Ein Leben fur den Sozialismus: Erinnerungen an Karl Kautsky* (Hannover, 1954), p. 21. The incorrectness of this assertion can be demonstrated by comparing the adopted Erfurt Program with Liebknecht's draft in Appendix 2. Nevertheless, the mistake is repeated in the recently published Steenson, *Kautsky*, p. 99. The actual sequence of events as described in the text has been reconstructed from Bebel to Adler, 7 July 1891, in *Adlers Briefwechsel*, p. 74, Bebel to Engels, 18 June 1891, in *Bebels Briefwechsel mit Engels*, pp. 420-21, and a speech by Bebel reported in *Vorwärts*, 18 July 1891, 1. *Beilage*.

80. See Appendix 2.

81. See the discussion of Marx's *Critique of the Gotha Program* in Chapter 7 of this work.

82. Friedrich Engels, "Zur Kritik des sozialdemokratischen Programmentwurfs 1891," *Die Neue Zeit*, 20/1 (1901-1902), 5-13.

83. Bebel to Engels, 12 July 1891, in *Bebels Briefwechsel mit Engels*, p. 424.

84. *Die Neue Zeit*, 9/2 (1890-91), 786-87; see also

ibid., pp. 506-10, 723-30, 749-58, 814-27. The revised Vorstand draft may be compared with Kautsky's version in *SPD
Protokoll, 1891*, pp. 13-19.
    85. See Appendix 2.
    86. *Die Neue Zeit*, 9/2 (1890-91), 826.
    87. The rigid determinism of the Erfurt Program is
noted in Ritter, *Arbeiterbewegung*, p. 97, Brandis, *Deutsche
Sozialdemokratie*, pp. 102-103, and Erich Matthias, *Kautsky
und der Kautskyanismus* (Tubingen, n.d.), p. 163. Steenson,
Kautsky, pp. 7, 252 and passim, asserts that Kautsky tried
to balance voluntarism and determinism in his work. That
assertion may be accurate for Kautsky's career as a whole,
but determinism clearly vanquished voluntarism in his version
of the Erfurt Program.
    88. Bebel to Engels, 12 July 1891, in *Bebels Brief-
wechsel mit Engels*, p. 423.
    89. Bebel to Engels, 9 Oct. 1891, in ibid., p. 449.
The 21 members of the program commission are identified
in *SPD Protokoll, 1891*, p. 16. The way they were selected
is not explained.
    90. Kautsky to Engels, 30 Oct. 1891, in *Engels Brief-
wechsel mit Kautsky*, p. 314.
    91. *SPD Protokoll, 1891*, pp. 330-57. The speech is
reprinted without change in Wilhelm Liebknecht, *Socialism:
What It Is and What It Seeks to Accomplish*, trs. by May
Wood Simons (Chicago, 1901), pp. 35-64.
    92. Engels to Bebel, 24/26 Oct. 1891, in *Bebels Brief-
wechsel mit Engels*, p. 462.
    93. *SPD Protokoll, 1891*, pp. 357-58.
    94. Huber, *Deutsche Verfassungsgeschichte*, vol. 4,
pp. 109-110.
    95. *SPD Protokoll, 1890*, p. 127.
    96. Financial reports for *Vorwärts* and the other party
newspaper were published in each annual party congress
protocol.
    97. Bebel to Liebknecht, 22 Sept. 1891, Liebknecht
Archive, 65/115-16, IISH.
    98. Auer denied acting as a censor in a letter to
Max Quarck, 11 Jan. 1899, Quarck Archive, 7, AsD. For
evidence of Auer's actual censorship, see his letters to
Liebknecht, 19 Mar. 1891, and 14 June 1897, in Liebknecht
Archive, 65/132, IISH.
    99. *SPD Protokoll, 1894*, p. 68.
    100. Engels to Lafargue, 3 Apr. 1895, in Engels and
Lafargue, *Correspondence*, vol. 3, p. 373; Engels to Kautsky,

1 Apr. 1895, in *Engels Briefwechsel mit Kautsky*, p. 429.
For evidence of *Vorstand* editing, see Engels to Fischer,
8 Mar. 1895, in MEW, vol. 39, pp. 424-26, 605 note. See
also Steinberg, *Sozialismus und Sozialdemokratie*, p. 70.

101. Liebknecht to Singer, 9 Dec. 1892, Liebknecht
Archive, 41, IISH.

102. Liebknecht to Quarck, 3 May 1893; 16, 18 Dec.
1898; 1, 4 Jan. 1899; Quarck Archive, 139, 208, 209, 213,
214, AsD.

103. Engels to Kautsky, 30 Apr. 1891, in Benedikt
Kautsky, ed., *Engels Briefwechsel mit Kautsky*, pp. 295-96.

104. *SPD Protokoll, 1896*, p. 99.

105. Auer to Liebknecht, 5 Jan. 1891, in Liebknecht
Archive, 61/73-74, IISH.

106. Bebel to Engels, 12, 29 Sept. 1891, in *Bebels
Briefwechsel mit Engels*, pp. 430, 434, 435.

107. See the announcement in *Vorwärts*, 11 Nov. 1891.

108. Paul Mayer, ed., *Bruno Schoenlank 1859-1901* (Hannover, 1971), p. 48. See also Liebknecht to Motteler, 10
Feb. 1893, in Liebknecht Archive, 37/40-41, IISH.

109. Liebknecht to Quarck, 1 Nov. 1893, in Quarck
Archive, 158a, AsD.

110. Bebel to Engels, 13 Nov. 1893, in *Bebels Briefwechsel mit Engels*, p. 730.

111. The idea had already been twice proposed and
defeated: see *SPD Protokoll, 1891*, pp. 291-97; *SPD Protokoll,
1892*, pp. 16, 18, 253-57.

112. Kautsky to Adler, 13 Oct. 1893, in *Adlers Briefwechsel*, p. 122; Kautsky to Engels, 26 Nov. 1892, 11 Oct.
1893, in *Engels Briefwechsel mit Kautsky*, pp. 372, 388.

113. *SPD Protokoll, 1893*, pp. 17-18, 150.

114. Dieter Fricke, *Zur Organization und Tätigkeit
der deutschen Arbeiterbewegung (1890-1914)* (Leipzig, 1962),
pp. 139-40. For examples of *Der Sozialdemokrat*'s imitation
of *Vorwärts*' open editorial style, see its *Beiläge* for 29
Nov. and 6 Dec. 1894.

115. Ritter, *Arbeiterbewegung im wilhelminischen Reich*,
p. 154.

116. *Vorwärts*, 24 July, 16, 22, 25 Aug. 1896.

117. Adolf Braun to Liebknecht, 24, 26 Aug. 1896,
in Liebknecht Archive, 83a/34-35, 36, IISH; Robert Schmidt,
August Enders, Wilhelm Schröder, August Jacobey (?), and
Hugo Pötzsch to Liebknecht, 24 Aug. 1896, in ibid., 294a/1-2,
IISH.

118. *Vorwärts*, 30 Aug. 1896.

119. Singer to Natalie Liebknecht, 7 Sept. 1896, in

Liebknecht Archive, 419/13-14, IISH; also Singer to Liebknecht, 28 Aug. 1896, in Liebknecht Archive, 62/361-64,
IISH.

120. *SPD Protokoll, 1896*, pp. 76-78, 86-90, 102, 104,
107, 111.

121. Bebel to Liebknecht, 28 Mar. 1899, in Liebknecht
Archive, 65/142-43, IISH.

122. Liebknecht to Bebel, 30 May 1900, Bebel Archive,
127/12-13, IISH. See also a second letter on the same day,
ibid., 127/14-15.

123. *SPD Protokoll, 1891*, pp. 34-35, 92-93, 230-31;
ibid., *1897*, pp. 61, 69, 174; ibid., *1899*, p. 8.

124. *SPD Protokoll, 1892*, pp. 15-19, 96-98, 107-108,
272-75; ibid., *1893*, pp. 15, 16, 21, 112-13, 115-16, 121-
47, 272-75; ibid., *1896*, pp. 93-98; ibid., *1897*, pp. 94-
107, 114; ibid., *1898*, pp. 60-61, 212-14.

125. Ibid., *1896*, p. 115; ibid., *1898*, p. 133; ibid.,
1899, p. 286.

126. Liebknecht to Quarck, 1 Jan. 1893, Quarck Archive,
160, AsD.

127. *SPD Protokoll, 1898*, p. 133.

128. Auer to Liebknecht, 22, 23 Nov. (misdated on
packet as 23 Feb.) 1890, 22 Jan., 19, 21, 25 Mar., 4 Apr.,
28 May 1891, in Liebknecht Archive, 61/72, 45, 77-78, 81,
82, 83, 84-85, 87-88, 89-90, IISH.

129. As late as 1888 Liebknecht still occasionally
counseled the paper; see Bebel to Engels, 8 Mar. 1888, in
Bebels Briefwechsel mit Engels, p. 322. But evidence of
his intervention is generally conspicuous by its absence.

130. For evidence see Liebknecht to Kautsky, 2 Feb.,
7 Apr. 1884, in Kautsky Archive, DXV 513, 515, IISH; and
Kautsky to Liebknecht, 5 June 1883, 6, 18 Nov. 1884, in
Liebknecht Archive, 189/4, 5-7, 8-9, IISH. Steenson, *Kautsky*,
p. 50, overstates Kautsky's independence at the outset of
this editorial venture, and Steenson's own subsequent comments make it clear that in the mid-1880s Kautsky could
not appoint his own staff at *Die Neue Zeit*.

131. Liebknecht to Kautsky, 21 Feb. 1885, in Kautsky
Archive, DXV 527, IISH; Kautsky to Liebknecht, 18, 24 Feb.
1885, in Liebknecht Archive, 189/15-16, 17-18, IISH.

132. Liebknecht to Kautsky, 10 Oct. 1884, in Kautsky
Archive, DXV 253, IISH.

133. Eleanor Marx-Aveling to Natalie Liebknecht, 14
May 1896, in LBME, p. 449.

134. The age problem was compounded by the influx
of still younger men at lower party ranks. See Wilfred

Henze, "Die Deligierten der Parteikongresse der Sozialistischen Arbeiterpartei Deutschlands unter dem Sozialistengesetz," ZFG, 28 (no. 8, 1980), 760-74.
    135. Bebel, AML, vol. 1, p. 126.
    136. Bebel to Engels, 24 Apr. 1894, in *Bebels Brief-
wechsel mit Engels*, p. 760; Bebel to Adler, 18 Nov. 1896,
in *Adlers Briefwechsel*, p. 223; Bebel to Kautsky, 3 Dec.
1894, in *Bebels Briefwechsel mit Kautsky*, p. 82; Liebknecht
to Quarck, 8 Dec. 1893, in Quarck Archive, 164, AsD.
    137. Kautsky to Bebel, 14 Feb. 1885, in *Bebels Brief-
wechsel mit Kautsky*, p. 28, shows great respect for Liebknecht. Contrast to the opinions in Kautsky, *Erinnerungen*,
pp. 374, 470-72.
    138. Liebknecht to Engels, 17 Nov. 1898, in LBME,
p. 262.
    139. Heinrich Gemkow, *Paul Singer* (Berlin, 1957),
pp. 18-19. See also Singer to Liebknecht, 21 June 1888,
in Liebknecht Addenda, 62/120-21, IISH.
    140. Police report of 22 Dec. 1887, quoted in Hirsch,
Bebel, p. 393.
    141. Quoted in LBME, p. 8.
    142. Reprinted in Liebknecht, *Marx*, p. 110. For other
evidence of tension between Engels and Liebknecht, see Liebknecht, "Anno 1849," and Liebknecht, *Erinnerungen*, pp. 194-
98. See also the editorial comments in LBME, p. 315.
    143. Engels to Bebel, 10 Nov. 1883, in *Bebels Briefwech-
sel mit Engels*, pp. 158-59.
    144. Engels to Lafargue, 16 Nov. 1889, in Engels and
Lafargue, *Correspondence*, vol. 2, p. 341.
    145. Engels to Sorge, 27 Sept. 1890, in MEW, vol.
37, p. 478.
    146. Bebel, AML, vol. 3, p. 153.

CHAPTER 11

    1. Paul Hirsch and Bruno Borchardt, *Die Sozialdemo-
kratie und die Wählen zum deutschen Reichstag* (Berlin, 1912),
p. 23; Ritter, *Arbeiterbewegung*, p. 230.
    2. Wilhelm Liebknecht, *Speeches of Wilhelm Liebknecht*,
trs. anon. (New York, 1928), p. 77. See also Alex Hall,
Scandal, Sensation and Social Democracy (Cambridge, 1977),
p. 57.
    3. *Der Prozess Liebknecht. Verhandlungen wegen
Majestäts-Beleidigung vor dem Landgericht zu Breslau am
Donnerstag, den 14. November 1895* (Berlin, 1895).

4. Alex Hall, "The War of Words: Anti-socialist Offensives and Counter-propaganda in Wilhelmine Germany, 1890-1914," *Journal of Contemporary History*, 11 (no. 2 & 3, 1976), 36, note 15. See also Hall's *Scandal, Sensation and Social Democracy*, p. 55.

5. Still illuminating for this study is Eckart Kehr, *Schlachtflottenbau und Parteipolitik* (Berlin, 1930). On the plotting of a coup by government officials, see Ritter, *Arbeiterbewegung*, passim.

6. VdR, 12 June 1900, vol. 171, p. 6028.

7. Concerning this tendency, see Peter M. Blau, *Bureaucracy in Modern Society* (New York, 1956).

8. Singer to Liebknecht, 15 July 1890, in Liebknecht Addenda, 62/242-43, IISH. See also Engels to Lafargue, 18 Sept. 1893, in Engels and Lafargue, *Correspondence*, vol. 3, pp. 292-94.

9. *Berlin, Potsdam und Umgebungen* (Berlin, 1894), p. 229, has a map of the city. It also contains descriptions of various neighborhoods, including Charlottenburg. See also Masur, *Imperial Berlin*, p. 74.

10. Mayer, *Schoenlank*, p. 117; Bronder, "Organization und Fuhrung," pp. 177, 181; and Maehl, *Bebel*, pp. 361, 367.

11. See Dietz to Liebknecht, 22 May 1888 and 23 Dec. 1890, in Liebknecht Addenda, 16/25-26, 57-58, IISH.

12. Liebknecht to Quarck, 29 July, 22 Aug., 8 Nov. 1893, Quarck Archive, 150, 152, 159, AsD. For other salary information, see Mayer, *Schoenlank*, pp. 65-66; Koszyk, *Deutsche Presse*, p. 201; Ritter, *Arbeiterbewegung*, pp. 63-64.

13. Ashok V. Desai, *Real Wages in Germany, 1871-1913* (Oxford, 1968), p. 125.

14. *SPD Protokoll, 1892*, pp. 121-23.

15. Ibid., pp. 114-15. For other relevant remarks see pp. 91-94.

16. *SPD Protokoll, 1894*, pp. 69-84; *SPD Protokoll, 1895*, p. 13.

17. Singer to Natalie Liebknecht, 9 Mar. 1891, Liebknecht Archive, 419/5, IISH.

18. Liebknecht, *Trutz-Eisenstern*, vol. 2, p. 27, see also pp. 9-10, 17-18, 21, 28. Also VdR, 7 Feb. 1893, vol. 128, p. 897.

19. Georg von Vollmar, "Über die nächsten Aufgaben der deutschen Sozialdemokratie" (Munich, 1891), pp. 5-7, 18. For general observations on the origins of reformism, see Georg Fülberth, "Zur Genese des Revisionismus in der deutschen Sozialdemokratie vor 1914," *Das Argument*, 13 (no. 1/2, 1971), 1-21, and David S. Rosen, "German Social

Democracy Between Bismarck and Bernstein: Georg von Vollmar
and the Reformist Controversy, 1890-1895" (Unpublished Ph.D.
Dissertation: University of Wisconsin, 1975), especially
pp. 139-44.

20. *SPD Protokoll, 1891*, p. 182. See also *Münchener
Post*, 4 Aug. 1891.

21. *SPD Protokoll, 1891*, especially pp. 190, 208-209,
223-24, 244. Ritter, *Arbeiterbewegung*, p. 92, describes
this resolution as a "*nichtsagende Kompromissresolution.*"
The evidence contradicts Ritter. The debate shows plainly
how directly this resolution repudiated Vollmar. The *Münchener Post*, 28 Oct. 1891, observed correctly that with
this resolution the party congress had rejected Vollmar's
viewpoint.

22. *Vorwärts*, 2 July 1891; Georg von Vollmar, "Über
Staatssocialismus" (Nuremberg, 1892), p. 7.

23. *Vorwärts*, 6, 12, 21, 28 July 1892.

24. *SPD Protokoll, 1892*, pp. 173-90.

25. Liebknecht to Kautsky, 6 May 1885, in Kautsky Archive,
DXV 529, IISH.

26. Liebknecht to Vollmar, 15 Jan. 1893, in Vollmar
Archive, 1283, IISH.

27. Hans Georg Lehmann, *Die Agrarfrage in der Theorie
und Praxis der deutschen und internationalen Sozialdemokratie*
(Tübingen, 1970), is an excellent source for this whole
controversy in 1894-95.

28. *Münchener Post*, 27 Oct. 1894.

29. *Protokoll, 1894*, pp. 109-35, 157.

30. The hypothesis that Engels encouraged Bebel's attack
is well argued in Lehmann, *Agrarfrage*, pp. 117-18.

31. *Vorwärts*, 16 Nov. 1894, *1. Beilage*.

32. Ibid., 15 Nov., 1 Dec. 1894.

33. Liebknecht to Grillenberger, 17 Nov. 1894, in
Liebknecht Archive, 27, IISH; see also Liebknecht to Vollmar,
22 Nov. 1894, in Vollmar Archive, 1283, IISH.

34. Liebknecht to Engels, 16 Nov. 1894, in LBME, pp.
394-95.

35. *Vorwärts*, 24 Nov. 1894.

36. Lehmann, *Agrarfrage*, pp. 125-40, interprets the
cease-fire as an unqualified victory for Bebel, but the
outcome seems more like a draw.

37. Liebknecht to Kautsky, 8 Dec. 1894, in Kautsky
Archive, DXV 544, IISH.

38. Kautsky to Engels, 24 Nov. 1894, in *Engels Briefwechsel mit Kautsky*, p. 417; Kautsky to Adler, 21 Nov. 1894,

in *Adlers Briefwechsel*, p. 161; Singer to Adler, 26 Nov. 1894, in ibid., pp. 163-64.

39. Bebel to Kautsky, 3 Dec. 1894, in *Bebels Briefwechsel mit Kautsky*, p. 82; Bebel to Engels, 15 Nov. 1894, in *Bebels Briefwechsel mit Engels*, pp. 780-82.

40. Bebel to Engels, 24 Apr. 1894, in *Bebels Briefwechsel mit Engels*, p. 760, indicates that the relationship between Bebel and Liebknecht was very strained even before the Vollmar crisis. Bebel to Adler, 18 Nov. 1896, in *Adlers Briefwechsel*, p. 223, says that all personal contact between the Bebel and Liebknecht families had ceased.

41. *SPD Protokoll, 1895*, pp. 176-77. On interpreting this vote, I disagree with Lehmann, *Agrarfrage*, p. 196, where it is asserted that the votes of the "small" delegates led to defeat for the program. Actually, with the exception of Bebel and Liebknecht, all members of the national leadership voted against the agrarian program. For Kautsky's role, see Steenson, *Kautsky*, pp. 106-10.

42. *Die Neue Zeit*, 13/2 (1896-97), 275-82. For evidence of increasing repression, see *Vorwärts*, 17, 19, 20 May 1896, and *SPD Protokoll, 1896*, pp. 20-21.

43. *SPD Protokoll, 1897*, pp. 177-81.

44. Ibid., *1897*, pp. 68-70.

45. *Die Neue Zeit*, 16/1 (1897-98), 196-99.

46. Ibid., 264-69. See also Liebknecht to Kautsky, 10 Nov. 1897, in Kautsky Archive, DXV 555, IISH.

47. *Vorwärts*, 10, 16, 24 Nov. 1897.

48. Ibid., 24 Aug. 1898.

49. Ibid., 1 Sept. 1898.

50. Ibid., 24 Sept. 1898.

51. Members of the committee are listed in *SPD Protokoll, 1898*, p. 10, but there is no explanation of how they were selected.

52. Ibid., pp. 161-62.

53. Ritter, *Arbeiterbewegung*, pp. 92-93, asserts that Liebknecht's role as party leader was already "practically played out" in the early 1890s. I think Ritter's assertion is an exaggeration. It follows that Ritter handles this instance of Liebknecht's success, the Prussian *Landtag* matter, in a confused and distorted way, saying that the 1897 outcome reflected only some vague "unclarity" and the "anachronism" of Liebknecht, ibid., p. 182. Ritter completely neglects the overwhelming Prussian opposition to participation.

54. Quoted in Thomas Meyer, *Bernsteins Konstruktiver Sozialismus* (Berlin, 1977), p. 296. Meyer presents a thoughtful and thorough exposition of Bernstein's ideas.

55. Liebknecht to Kautsky, 22 Feb. 1897, in Kautsky Archive, DXV 548, IISH.

56. Liebknecht to Motteler, 24 June 1897, in Liebknecht Archive, 37/142, IISH; see also Liebknecht to Kautsky, 2 Apr. 1897, in Kautsky Archive, DXV 551, IISH.

57. Kautsky, *Ein Leben für dem Sozialismus*, p. 24, and Steenson, *Kautsky*, pp. 121-22.

58. *Vorwärts*, 16, 17, 18 Mar., 8, 11, 12, 18, 21, 26 Apr. 1898.

59. Winifred B. Scharlau and Zbynek A. Zeman, *Freibeuter der Revolution: Parvus Helphand* (Cologne, 1964), pp. 49-51.

60. J. P. Nettl, *Rosa Luxemburg*, 2 vols. (London, 1966), vol. 1, pp. 156-61. See especially Luxemburg's article from 22 Sept. 1898 in the *Leipziger Volkszeitung*.

61. *SPD Protokoll, 1898*, pp. 113-16, 126-27, 132.

62. Liebknecht, *On the Political Position of Social Democracy . . . No Compromises*, p. 64.

63. *SPD Protokoll, 1898*, pp. 134-35.

64. Liebknecht, *On the Political Position of Social Democracy . . . No Compromises*, p. 83.

65. Liebknecht to the *Parti Ouvrier Français* at Epernay, 10 Aug. 1899, in IML, ed., *Dokumente und Materialen zur Geschichte der deutschen Arbeiterbewegung*, vol. 4: *März 1898-Juli 1914* (Berlin, 1967), pp. 31-32.

66. Liebknecht to unidentified comrades abroad, 12 Aug. 1899, document no. 12387 in the Stadt und Landesbibliothek at Dortmund. At the 1899 party congress Bebel had persuaded the deputies to authorize (but not to mandate) cooperation with other parties in *Landtag* elections. This resolution passed 205 to 34, with Liebknecht being among the small group of dissidents; see *SPD Protokoll, 1899*, pp. 67, 242. See also Liebknecht to Motteler, 12 Aug. 1899, in Liebknecht Archive, 37/219-20, IISH.

67. Liebknecht to Motteler, 29 June 1900, in ibid., 37/273-74; Liebknecht to Bebel, 2 letters both dated 30 May 1900, in Bebel Archive, 127/12-13, 14-15, IISH.

68. *SPD Protokoll, 1899*, p. 156.

69. Liebknecht, HVP, p. 41. This comment was not made at the trial but rather in the introduction written in March 1894. See also ibid., p. 43.

70. *Die Neue Zeit*, 9/1 (1890-91), 583-85. See also ibid., p. 711; *Vorwärts*, 15 Jan. 1891; and Bernstein, *Geschichte der Berliner Arbeiterbewegung*, vol. 3, pp. 390-92.

71. VdR, 21 Apr. 1891, vol. 107, p. 2475.

72. Liebknecht, *On the Political Position of Social Democracy . . . No Compromises*, p. 77.

73. *SDAP Protokoll, 1870*, p. 13.

74. Wilhelm Liebknecht, *Socialism: What It Is and What It Seeks to Accomplish*, trs. May Wood Simons (Chicago, 1901), p. 14. See also a speech by Liebknecht, 7 Feb. 1893, in VdR, vol. 128, p. 897.

75. *SPD Protokoll, 1899*, pp. 152-53.

76. Liebknecht, *Trutz-Eisenstirn*, vol. 2, p. 58.

77. Muehlbradt, "Liebknecht," p. 319, explicitly asserts that Liebknecht did lack a theory of how the SPD should come to power.

78. Speech quoted in Eisner, *Liebknecht*, pp. 86-87.

79. For investigations of this relatively passive attitude of the SPD, see Peter Nettl, "The German Social Democratic Party, 1890-1914, as a Political Model," *Past and Present*, 30 (Apr. 1965), 65-69, and Dieter Groh, *Negative Integration und revolutionäre Attentismus* (Frankfurt am Main, 1973).

80. *Vorwärts*, 7, 9, 10, 11 Aug. 1900. There is a photograph of Liebknecht's funeral procession in Bernstein, *Geschichte der Berliner Arbeiterbewegung*, vol. 3, facing p. 416.

81. *Vorwärts*, 7 Aug. 1900.

82. Andreas Dorpalen, "Marxism and National Unity: The Case of Germany," *The Review of Politics*, 39 (no. 4, Oct. 1977), 505-20, discusses the present, increasingly rigid division of the German nation as the outgrowth of internal class divisions dating back to Bismarck's *Reichsgründung*.

Bibliography

No comprehensive survey of the literature concerning nine-teenth-century German Social Democracy can be undertaken here. As in the text, the purpose is to illuminate the career of Wilhelm Liebknecht, and the sources for even this more modest enterprise constitute an embarrassment of riches.

UNPUBLISHED MATERIALS

Access to part of the unpublished Liebknecht correspondence has been, until recent times, a problem. A substantial bloc of letters lies in the Institut für Marxismus-Leninismus (IML) in Berlin, and the directors of that institution twice denied me permission to examine their holdings. Fortunately, the International Institute for Social History (IISH), in Amsterdam, which always has opened its resources to me most cordially, recently arranged an exchange of photocopied documents with the IML, and in this way its holdings concerning Liebknecht have grown considerably. For example, in the Marx-Engels Archive at the IISH, the *Briefwechsel* with Lieb-knecht has been augmented by approximately 50 percent since Eckert published his edition of that correspondence in 1963. This East-West exchange has been arranged to permit publi-cation of Eckert's last project, *Wilhelm Liebknechts Brief-wechsel mit deutschen Sozialdemokraten*. Only the first volume, which includes the IISH holdings through 1878, had been com-pleted when Eckert died in 1974. Götz Langkau, co-director of the Mitteleuropäischer Abteilung of the IISH, has indicated that both the exchange and the publication of Liebknecht's letters will continue for several years. An additional pub-lication of Liebknecht's correspondence with foreign social-ists is planned. This biography of Liebknecht is based on an examination of the post-1878 letters and photocopies at the IISH in *Handschrift*.

The Liebknecht Archive offers the largest relevant collection among the many *Nachlässe* in the IISH. In addition to
personal documents concerning his education and legal resi-
dences, it includes a smattering of family correspondence
among Liebknecht and his spouses, siblings, and children.
There are also substantial *Briefwechsels* with the following
colleagues in the SPD leadership: Auer, Bebel, Adolf and
Heinrich Braun, Hirsch, Kautsky, Mehring, Motteler, and
Schlüter. For documentation of Liebknecht's influence in
the Second International, there are exchanges with Aveling,
Bonnier, Guesde, Vaillant, and others. A recently added group
of photocopies, the "Liebknecht Addenda," includes letters
by and to Dietz, Grillenberger, Hasenclever, Schoenlank,
Singer, and other, lesser-known comrades. All Liebknecht-
Vollmar correspondence is in the IISH's Vollmar Archive. At
the Institute, I also surveyed the various correspondence
in the Bebel and Kautsky *Nachlässe* for comment concerning
Liebknecht's career. The Motteler Archive contains unpublished party protocols from the 1880s that comprise an indispensable source.

The Archive der sozialen Demokratie (AsD) at Bonn-Bad
Godesberg also proved to be an invaluable resource, especially
concerning the *Dampfersubventionsstreit* of 1885. In the
Kampffmeyer Nachlass are letters from various party leaders
during the spring of that year, including fifteen from Liebknecht to Bernstein. In addition, this collection holds
numerous protests from the membership, only a few of which
were published contemporaneously, and some of which still
have not been printed in scholarly journals. The Quarck
Nachlass at the AsD preserves 110 Liebknecht to Quarck letters
from the 1890s. Also useful were the collections for Arno
Kapp, Hermann Molkenbuhr, Carl Oertel, and Bruno Schoenlank,
as well as a small selection entitled "Photocopies from the
Hauptstaatsarchiv, Dusseldorf, concerning Rittinghausen."

In Karlsruhe, I visited the Generallandesarchiv (GLA)
in search of information concerning the 1848 revolution.
Abteilung 241 yielded much evidence about Struve and the
Baden revolution in general, even mentioning Ernestine Landolt,
but unfortunately no record of Liebknecht's incarceration
was preserved. The Adolf Geck Nachlass, 69NI/1032 & 1033, at
the GLA included a small Liebknecht correspondence.

The Stadtarchiv at Frankfurt owns a Quarck Nachlass
containing exchanges with several party leaders, including
Liebknecht. In the Bundesarchiv, Aussenstelle Frankfurt,
in the Struve Nachlass, two letters from Liebknecht (Paket
27, Briefe 28) documenting the association between him and
Struve have been preserved.

I surveyed Abteilung 407, no. 182 at the nearby Hessisches
Hauptstaatsarchiv in Wiesbaden, looking for police reports of
clandestine socialist meetings in and around Frankfurt in the
1880s, and found several useful documents.

The Stadtarchiv at Giessen provided a folio of information, primarily newspaper clippings and capsule biographies
of Liebknecht from the local SPD press on the occasion of
his hundredth and hundred and fiftieth birthdays. Unfortunately, the city and university records relating to the
student strike of 1846 have been destroyed or misplaced.
A visit to the Hessisches Staatsarchiv at Marburg had the
purpose of uncovering documentation of Liebknecht's trouble
with the university authorities there. The *Deputations-
protocol*, volumes 18 and 19, record disciplinary action against
a student named Liebknecht, but since this occurred in the
autumn of 1847, when Wilhelm was in Zurich, it must have been
a different Liebknecht.

The Stadt und Landesbibliothek in Dortmund holds a small
collection of Liebknecht letters, and it conveniently shares
a building with the Institut für Zeitungsforschung, where
numerous newspapers used in this study were found.

The Schiller-Nationalmuseum, Marbach a. N., kindly provided photocopies of letters from Liebknecht to the Cotta'sche
Buchhandlung from its Cotta-Archiv (Stiftung der Stuttgarter
Zeitung). The Bundesarchiv in Bern supplied copies of the
circular letters that Liebknecht sent to the various *Vereine*
in Switzerland between 1848 and 1850 (E21/180, Bd. 2; 180A,
Bd. 2; 181, Bd. 1; 184B, Bd. 2).

PUBLISHED CORRESPONDENCE

Collections Including Letters By and To Liebknecht

"Briefe von Wilhelm Liebknecht aus dem Jahre 1850." *Die
    Neue Zeit*, 31/2 (1912-13), 1028-29.
Eckert, Georg, ed. "Aus der Korrespondenz des Braunschweiger
    Ausschusses der Sozialdemokratischen Arbeiter-Partei."
    Sonderdruck of *Braunschweige Jahrbuch*, 45 (1964), 107-49.
_____. *Wilhelm Liebknechts Briefwechsel mit deutschen Sozial-
    demokraten*. vol. 1; *1862-1878*. Assen: Van Gorcum & Co.,
    1973.
_____. *Wilhelm Liebknechts Briefwechsel mit Karl Marx und
    Friedrich Engels*. The Hague: Mouton & Co., 1963.
Gemkow, Heinrich. "Im Kampf um die Gründung der Partei.
    Unveröffentlichte Briefe an Bebel und Liebknecht (Juni
    bis August 1869)." BGA, 11 (no. 4, 1969), 620-39.

Gemkow, Heinrich, and Hofmann, Gudrun eds. "Aus den Anfängen
    der Eisenacher Partei. Unveröffentlichte Briefe an
    Bebel und Liebknecht." BGA, 18 (no. 5, 1976), 843-71.
Hermann, Ursula. "Briefe von Joseph Dietzgen an Wilhelm
    Liebknecht und die Redaktion 'Volksstaats.'" BGA, 13
    (no. 2, 1971), 241-53.
IML, ed. *Die I. Internationale in Deutschland (1864-1872).*
    Dokument und Materialen. Berlin: Dietz Verlag, 1964.
Kundel, Erich. "Aus dem Briefwechsel der 'Volksstaats'-
    Redaktion mit Karl Marx und Friedrich Engels." BGA
    11 (no. 4, 1969), 639-63.
_____. "Die 'Volksstaat'-Redaktion in den Wochen vor dem
    Haager Kongress: Unveröffentlichte Briefe von Adolf
    Hepner und Wilhelm Liebknecht an Friedrich Engels."
    BGA, 15 (no. 2, 1973), 283-304.
_____. "Zum Vereinigungsprozess von Eisenachern und
    Lassalleanern. Unveröffentlichte Briefe von Wilhelm
    Liebknecht und Hermann Ramm an Karl Marx und Friedrich
    Engels." BGA, 18 (no. 6, 1976), 1029-44.

Published Correspondence of Liebknecht's Comrades

Adler, Victor. *Aufsätze, Reden und Briefe.* Vol. 1. Vienna:
    Wiener Volksbuchhandlung, 1922.
_____. *Briefwechsel mit August Bebel und Karl Kautsky,*
    sowie Briefe von und an Ignaz Auer, Eduard Bernstein,
    Adolph Braun, Heinrich Dietz, Friedrich Ebert, Wilhelm
    Liebknecht, Hermann Muller und Paul Singer. Ed. Friedrich
    Adler. Vienna: Wiener Volksbuchhandlung, 1954.
Bebel, August. *Briefwechsel mit Friedrich Engels.* Ed. Werner
    Blumenberg. The Hague: Mouton & Co., 1965.
_____. *Briefwechsel mit Karl Kautsky.* Ed. Karl Kautsky,
    Jr. Assen: Van Gorcum & Co., 1971.
Bernstein, Eduard. *Briefwechsel mit Friedrich Engels.* Ed.
    Helmut Hirsch. Assen: Van Gorcum & Co., 1970.
Briefe und Auszüge aus Briefen von Joh. Phil. Becker, Jos.
    Dietzgen, Friedrich Engels, Karl Marx u. A. an F.A.
    Sorge und Andere. Stuttgart: J.H.W. Dietz Nachfolger,
    1906.
Eckert, George, ed. *Aus den Anfängen der Braunschweiger*
    Arbeiterbewegung. Unveröffentlichte Bracke-Briefe.
    Brunswick: Albert Limback Verlag, 1965.
Engels, Friedrich. *Briefwechsel mit Karl Kautsky.* Ed.
    Benedikt Kautsky. Vienna: Danubia Verlag, 1955.

_____. *Vergessene Briefe*. *(Briefe an Johann Philipp Becker.) Ein Beitrag zum hundertjährigen Geburtstag.* Ed. Emil Eichhorn. Berlin: A. Seekof & Co., n.d.

_____, Lafargue, Paul, and Lafargue, Laura. *Correspondence.* Trs. Yvonne Kapp. 3 vols. Moscow: Foreign Languages Publishing House, 1959-60.

Freiligrath, Ferdinand. *Briefwechsel mit Marx und Engels.* Ed. and int. Manfred Häckel. 2 vols. Berlin: Akademie-Verlag, 1968.

Gemkow, Heinrich. "Drei unbekannte Bebel-Briefe aus dem Gefängnis." BGA, 7 (no. 1, 1965), 44-53.

Hess, Moses. *Briefwechsel.* Ed. Edmund Silberner. The Hague: Mouton & Co., 1959.

Kundel, Erich. "Neue Bracke-Briefe zum Vereinigungskongress 1875," BGA, 19 (no. 4, 1977), 605-16.

Luxemburg, Rosa. *Briefe an Karl und Luise Kautsky. (1896-1918).* Ed. Luise Kautsky. Berlin: E. Laub'sche Verlagsbuchhandlung, 1923.

Marx, Karl. *Letters to Dr. Kugelmann.* London: Martin Lawrence, n.d.

_____. *Werke*. Ed. Institut für Marxismus-Leninismus, Berlin. Berlin: Dietz Verlag, 1956-71.

_____, and Engels, Friedrich. *Briefwechsel mit Wilhelm Bracke (1869-1880)*. Ed. Heinrich Gemkow. Berlin: Dietz Verlag, 1963.

PUBLISHED DOCUMENTS

This category of sources includes a variety of records authored by workers' organizations and by the Swiss and German governments. The material available steadily grows for each successive stage of Liebknecht's career. Concerning Liebknecht's expulsion from Switzerland, see Switzerland, Bundesrat, *Bericht und Beschlusse des Schweizerischen Bundesrathes in Sachen der deutschen Arbeiterverein in der Schweiz* (Zurich: Fr. Schultess, 1850). For his activity during his London exile, see Gerhard Becker, "Der 'Neue Arbeiter-Verein in London' 1852," *Zeitschrift für Geschichtswissenschaft*, 14 (no. 1, 1966), 74-97, which publishes the minutes of meetings at which Liebknecht sometimes spoke. *Der Bund der Kommunisten: Dokumente und Materialen*, ed. Institut für Marxismus-Leninismus (Berlin: Dietz Verlag, 1970), was available only in its first volume, covering up to 1849, and consequently was useful only for background information. Karl Marx and Friedrich

Engels, *The Cologne Communist Trial*, trs. Rodney Livingston
(New York: International Publishers, 1971), helps to unravel
Liebknecht's role in that tangled affair.

Protocols of party congresses become an important tool
for reconstructing Liebknecht's endeavors after he returned
to Germany. I surveyed the *Allgemeine deutsche Arbeiter-
Verein Protokolle* for 1866 and 1870-74, all of which are
available at the IISH. Wilhelm Schröder, ed., *Handbuch der
sozialdemokratischen Parteitage von 1863 bis 1909* (Munich:
G. Birk & Co., 1910), includes important excerpts from numerous gatherings, all arranged and indexed topically. The SDAP
Protokolle, 1869-74, and the *Kassenberichten* for the same
period were all published contemporaneously and are now preserved at the IISH and elsewhere, as are the SAP Parteitag
records and *Abrechnungen* for 1875-78. Stenographic reports
of three of the congresses held during the era of the antisocialist law were published in the 1880s at Zurich: Wyden
in 1880, Copenhagen in 1883, and St. Gaul in 1887. The first
two appeared without the names of participants or speakers
and should therefore be supplemented with the fuller records
in the Motteler Archive, IISH. The same archive contains
a protocol of the 1882 gathering at Zurich that was attended
by the SAP *Reichstagsfraktion* and the editorial staff of
Der Sozialdemokrat. This document exists now only in a typewritten transcript prepared by Vernon Lidtke; the original
has been lost. It has never been published. All party protocols for the SPD, 1890-1900, were printed in Berlin by the
Buchhandlung Vorwärts and are available at numerous libraries.

Beginning in 1898, the SPD *Fraktion* kept minutes of
its meetings, and these now have been edited by Erich Matthias
and Eberhard Pikart, *Die Reichstagsfraktion der deutschen
Sozialdemokratie 1898 bis 1918* (Dusseldorf: Droste Verlag,
1966).

Records of the operation and proceedings of the first
two socialist internationals are indispensable for a biography
of Liebknecht. Most important for the early period is Institut
für Marxismus-Leninismus, ed., *Die I. Internationale in Deutschland (1864-1872)* (Berlin: Dietz Verlag, 1964). This
documentary collection contains many previously unpublished
letters exchanged among Liebknecht, Marx, and Engels. Additional useful material is printed in Institute of Marxism-
Leninism of the C.C., C.P.S.U., ed., *The General Council of
the First International, 1864-1872: Minutes*, 5 vols. (Moscow:
Progress Publishers, n.d.). Hans Gerth, ed. and trs., *The
First International: Minutes of the Hague Congress of 1872*

(Madison: Univ. of Wisconsin Press, 1958), contributes information to the same subject. Of special interest for Liebknecht's actions is *Die Verhandlungen des IV. Congresses
des internationalen Arbeiterbundes in Basel 7-11 September
1869* (Basel: G.A. Bonfantine, 1869). This document, like
most of the protocols for the first international, is so
terse that it almost seems cryptic. Fortunately, newspaper
reports are usually available to supplement these scanty
accounts.

The summaries of the speeches became fuller in the
stenographic reports of the Second International. *Protokoll
des Internationalen Arbeiter-Congresses zu Paris. Abgehalten
vom 14 bis 20 Juli 1889* (Nuremberg: Wörlein & Co., 1890)
contains a preface by Liebknecht testifying to the importance
he attached to the International. Along with *Verhandlungen
und Beschlüsse des Internationalen Sozialistischen Arbeiter-
und Gewerkschafts-Kongresses zu London . . . 1896* (Berlin:
Vorwärts, 1896), this source provides convincing evidence
of Liebknecht's importance in the international socialist
movement.

Authorities of the Second German Empire also kept records
that aid in reconstructing Liebknecht's career. In this
regard, records of three trials were available and useful
to me:

*Der Braunschweiger Ausschuss der sozialdemokratischen Arbeiter-
Partei im Lötzen und vor dem Gericht.* Brunswick:
Braunschweiger Volksfreund, 1872, with a preface by
Wilhelm Bracke, Jr.
*Der Hochverraths-prozess wider Liebknecht, Bebel, Hepner
vor dem Schwurgericht zu Leipzig vom 11. bis 26. März
1872.* Berlin: Vorwärts, 1894.
*Der Prozess Liebknecht. Verhandlung wegen Majestäts-Beleidi-
gung vor dem Landgericht zu Breslau am Donnerstag dem
14. November 1895.* Berlin: Vorwärts, 1895.

More general documentation of the repression of socialists
is presented in the following sources:

Höhn, Reinhard. *Die vaterlandlosen Gesellen. Der Sozialismus
im Licht der Geheimberichte der preussischen Polizei
1878-1914.* Cologne and Opladen: Westdeutscher Verlag,
1964.
Krieter, W. *Die geheime Organization der sozialdemokratischen
Partei.* Magdeburg: Albert Rathke, 1887.

Lipinski, Richard. *Dokumente zum Sozialistengesetz. Mater-
    ialen nach amtlichen Akten.* Berlin: Vorwärts, 1928.
Stern, Leo, ed. *Der Kampf der deutschen Sozialdemokratie
    in der Zeit des Sozialistengesetz 1878-1890--Die Tätig-
    keit der Reichscommission.* Berlin: Rütten & Loening,
    1956.

This evidence demonstrates that police infiltration of the
socialist party, especially during the 1880s, was remarkably
successful and provided quite accurate information to the
government.
    For sheer quantity of Liebknecht's words, the richest
single source is the stenographic record of the proceedings
of the Reichstag, both of the North German Confederation
and the Second German Empire, where Liebknecht held a seat
for all but four of the years between 1867 and 1900.

CONTEMPORARY WRITINGS BY LIEBKNECHT

Although there are no collected works for the elder Liebknecht (as there are for his son, Karl), all major compositions are available. Since he wrote for so many publications,
both German and foreign, I cannot claim to have read everything he published (indeed, it is my firm conviction that
such a claim will never honestly be made), but the following list, combined with the newspapers cited below, comprises
a broad foundation upon which to rebuild a summary of Liebknecht's ideas and actions.

Liebknecht, Wilhelm. *Ein Blick in Die Neue Welt.* Stuttgart:
    J.H.W. Dietz, 1887.
_____. "Das Brief-Geheimnis vor dem Deutsche Reichstag.
    Nach dem amtlichen Stenographischen Berichten. Mit
    einem Nachwort von W. Liebknecht." Berlin: Allgemeine
    Deutsche Associations-Buchdruckerei, 1878.
_____. *Die Emser Depesche oder wie Kriege gemacht werden.*
    Nuremberg: Wörlein & Co., 1895.
_____. "Hochverrath und Revolution." *Sozialdemokratische
    Bibliothek: Sammlung von Abhandlung über Theorie und
    Geschichte des Sozialismus.* Vol. 2, Heft 14-24. Hot-
    tingen-Zurich: Verlag der Volksbuchhandlung, 1887-88.
_____. "On the Political Position of Social Democracy
    Particularly with Respect to the Reichstag. No Com-
    promises, No Election Deals." Moscow: Foreign Languages

Publishing House, n.d. These speeches were made in 1869 and 1899 respectively.

_____. "Die Orientdebatte im deutschen Reichstag (vollständig nach dem amtlichen stenographischen Bericht)." Leipzig: Commissions-Verlag von R.E. Höhme, [1878].

_____. "Rede über die Kölner Parteitag mit besonderer Berücksichtigung der Gewerkschaftsbewegung, gehalten zu Bielefeld am 29. Oktober 1893." Bielefeld: Volkswacht, 1893.

_____. *Reden.* Ed. Kurt Kersten. Berlin: Neuer Deutscher Verlag, 1925.

_____. *Robert Blum und seine Zeit.* 3d ed. Nuremberg: Wörlein & Co., 1896.

_____. *Robert Owen. Sein Leben und sozialpolitisches Wirken. Zwei ausgegrabene Skizzen.* Nuremberg: Wörlein & Co., 1892.

_____. "Ein Sohn des Volks." *Der Neue Welt Kalendar 1896,* 68-70.

_____. *Socialism: What It Is and What It Seeks to Accomplish.* Trs. May Wood Simons. Chicago: Charles H. Kerr & Co., 1901.

_____. *Speeches of Wilhelm Liebknecht.* Trs. and ed. anon. New York: International Publishers, 1928.

Niemand, Vetter [pseudonym for Liebknecht]. "Trutz-Eisenstirn. Erzieherisches aus Puttkamerum. Ein vierblättriges Broschüren-Kleeblatt nebst mit einem Anhang." *Socialdemokratische Bibliothek.* Vol. 3, Heft 25-34. London: German Cooperative Printing & Publishing Co., 1888-90.

Liebknecht, Wilhelm. *Volksfremdwörterbuch.* 10th ed. Stuttgart: Dietz Nochfolger, 1908.

_____. "Weltpolitik, Chinawirren, Transvaalkrieg. Ein Rede gehalten zu Dresden in 'Trianon' am 28 Juli 1900." Dresden: Kaden & Co., 1900.

_____. "Wissen ist Macht--Macht ist Wissen. Festrede gehalten zum Stiftungsfest des Dresdener Bildungs-Vereins am 5. Februar 1882." Berlin: Vorwärts, 1894.

_____. "Zu Trutz und Schutz: Festrede gehalten zum Stiftungsfest des Crimmitschauer Volksvereins am 22. Oktober 1871." 5th ed. Hottingen-Zurich: Verlag der Schweizerischen Volksbuchhandlung, 1883.

_____. "Zum 18. März und Verwandtes." Nuremberg: Wörlein & Co., 1893.

_____. *Zum Jubeljahr der Märzrevolution.* Berlin: Vorwärts, 1898.

_____. *Zur Grund- und Bodenfrage.* 2d ed. Leipzig: Genossenschaftsbuchdruckerei, 1876.

_____. *Zur orientalischen Frage; oder, Soll Europa kosakisch werden? Ein Mahnwort an das deutsche Volk.* Leipzig: Commissions-Verlag von R. E. Höhme, [1878].

_____. "Zwei Pioniere." *Die Neue Welt. Illustrierte Unterhaltungsbeilage.* Nr. 17. 1900, 131-34.

Several of these essays, which are sometimes quite difficult to find, have been collected and published by Wolfgang Schröder under the title *Wilhelm Liebknecht. Kleine politische Schriften* (Leipzig: Philipp Reclam jun., 1976).

MEMOIR MATERIAL BY LIEBKNECHT

Unlike his closest comrade, August Bebel, Liebknecht never found time to write about any of his life's work that occurred after his return to Germany in 1862. Late in life, however, he did publish a few short articles about his experiences in the *tolle Jahren,* 1848-49, and subsequent years of exile. These articles were virtually inaccessible until the recent publication, Institut für Marxismus-Leninismus, ed., *Wilhelm Liebknecht: Erinnerungen eines Soldaten der Revolution* (Berlin: Dietz Verlag, 1976). The only significant supplement to this collection is Liebknecht's *Karl Marx: Biographical Memoirs,* trs. Ernest Untermann (Chicago: Charles H. Kerr & Co., 1906).

MEMOIRS BY LIEBKNECHT'S COLLEAGUES AND RIVALS

Ignaz Auer has lately become the centerpiece of several studies that view the history of the German workers' movement as a record of emancipation from theory, and his two party histories do tell the story with very little reference to Marxism; see *Nach zehn Jahren: Material und glossen zur Geschichte des Sozialistengesetz* (Nuremberg: Fränkische Verlagsanstalt, 1913), and *Von Gotha bis Wyden* (Berlin: Sozialistische Monatshefte, 1901). August Bebel's three-volume memoir, covering only up to 1882, has been a mainstay for all subsequent investigators: *Aus meinem Leben* (Berlin: Dietz Verlag, 1953). In my text, I have indicated several disagreements that I have with Bebel's narrative, in matters both factual and interpretive. Eduard Bernstein produced the following memoirs: *Aus den Jahren meines Exils.*

Erinnerungen eines Sozialisten, 4th ed. (Berlin: Erich
Reiss Verlag, 1918); *Sozialdemokratische Lehrjahre* (Berlin:
Der Buchkreis, 1928); *Von der Sekte zur Partei; Die deutsche
Sozialdemokratie einst und jetzt* (Jena: Eugen Diederichs,
1911); and "Zur Vorgeschichte des Gothaer Programms," *Die
Neue Zeit*, 15/1 (1896-97), 466-72. As with Auer's works,
Bernstein's recollections buttress the interpretation of
German socialists as radical reformers rather than Marxist
revolutionaries. The same ideological cant colors Wilhelm
Blos, *Denkwürdigkeiten eines Sozialdemokraten*, 2 vols. (Munich:
G. Birk & Co., 1914). More attention is paid to theory in
Karl Kautsky's *Erinnerungen und Erörterungen*, ed. Benedikt
Kautsky (The Hague: Mouton & Co., 1960), but this source
unfortunately terminates in 1883. Furthermore, I find Kautsky's
disparagement of the theoretical capabilities of all his
Marxist forerunners in Germany, including Liebknecht, to be
self-serving and overstated. There is also a short essay by
Kautsky, summarizing his whole career, in Benedikt Kautsky,
ed., *Ein Leben für den Sozialismus: Erinnerungen an Karl
Kautsky* (Hannover: J. H. W. Dietz Nachfolger, 1954). Paul
Mayer recently edited and provided an introduction to Bruno
Schoenlank's diary, a work published under the title of
*Bruno Schoenlank 1859-1901. Reformer der sozialdemokratischen
Tagespresse*. (Hannover: Verlag für Literatur und Zeit-
geschehen, 1971). Some readers will be surprised to find
Franz Mehring's *Geschichte der deutschen Sozialdemokratie*
(Berlin: Dietz Verlag, 1960) listed in this section of
memoir literature, but I suggest that here it rightfully
belongs. Mehring experienced the events he discussed and
emerged with powerful prejudices; the published reactions of
Liebknecht and Bebel in the party press when they read Mehring's
early articles praising Schweitzer prove that his opinions
about party history were strongly contested from the outset.
John Most, *Memoiren*, 4 vols. (New York: John Most Verlag,
1903-07), like so many of these sources, terminates just when
matters are about to become interesting--in this case in 1878.
Philipp Scheidemann, *The Making of New Germany*, trs. J. E.
Mitchell, 2 vols. (New York: D. Appleton & Co., 1929),
includes a brief character sketch of Liebknecht but
otherwise offers little for this biography.
  Concerning the 1848 revolution, I found five accounts
by veterans of the Baden *Reichsverfassungskampagne* to be helpful for background information, although none mention Liebknecht.

Corvin, Otto von. *Erinnerungen aus meinem Leben*. 4 vols.
    Leipzig: Fr. Thiel, 1880.
Engels, Friedrich. *Germany: Revolution and Counter-Revolution*.
    Ed. and int. Leonard Krieger. Chicago: University of
    Chicago Press, 1967.
Froebel, Julius. *Ein Lebenslauf: Aufzeichnungen, Erinnerungen
    und Bekenntnisse*. Stuttgart: I. G. Cotta'schen Buch-
    handlung, 1890.
Schurz, Carl. *Lebenserinnerungen*. Zurich: Manesse Verlag,
    n.d.
Struve, Gustav von. *Geschichte der drei Volkserhebungen in
    Baden*. Bern: Verlag von Jenni, Sohn, 1849.

NEWSPAPERS AND PERIODICALS

The essays of Liebknecht, a prolific journalist, enlivened
the pages of many publications. He either edited or wrote for
all of the following (the dates listed indicate the issues I
perused and are not necessarily the inclusive dates of publication):

Allgemeine deutsche Arbeiter-Zeitung. Coburg, 1865-66.
Allgemeine Zeitung. Augsburg. 1855-60.
Berliner Volksblatt. 1884-90.
Demokratisches Wochenblatt. Leipzig. 1868-69.
Mannheimer Abendzeitung. Sept. 1847-Mar. 1848.
Die Laterne. Brussels. Dec. 1878-June 1879.
*Wilhelm Liebknechts Leitartikel und Beiträge in der Osna-
    brücker Zeitung 1864-1866*. Ed. Georg Eckert (Hildesheim:
    August Lax Verlagsbuchhandlung, 1975).
Sozialistische Monatshefte. Berlin. 1897-1900.
Die Neue Welt. Leipzig and Berlin. 1876-1902.
Die Neue Zeit. Stuttgart. 1883-1900.
Der Sozialdemokrat. Zurich and London. 1879-90.
Der Volksstaat. Leipzig. 1869-76.
Vorwärts. Central-Organ der Sozialdemokratie Deutschland.
    Leipzig. 1876-78.
Vorwärts. Berliner Volksblatt. 1891-1900.
Das Volk. London. May-Aug. 1859.

These additional party sheets were read for the dates
indicated:

Der arme Conrad. 1876.
Berliner Freie Presse. July-Dec. 1876.
Leipziger Volkszeitung. Isolated issues, 1894-1901.

Das Recht auf Arbeit. Oct.-Dec. 1885.
Sächsische Arbeiterzeitung. Isolated numbers, 1890-92.
*Der Sozialdemokrat. Wochenblatt der sozialdemokratischen
    Partei Deutschlands.* 1894-95.
Der Vorbote. 1869.
Die Zukunft. 1877-78.

Newspapers edited by Liebknecht's socialist rivals and
surveyed for this study include:

Berliner Volks-Tribune. Jan. 1890-Dec. 1891.
Freiheit. London. Jan. 1879-Dec. 1881.
Der Sozialdemokrat. Berlin. 1864-71.
Neuer Sozial-Demokrat. Berlin. 1871-76.

The following bourgeois sheets were examined in individual numbers to sample the nonsocialist perspective on
important events in Liebknecht's life:

Frankfurter Zeitung.
Kölnische Zeitung.
National-Zeitung. Berlin.
Volks-Zeitung. Berlin.

SECONDARY WORKS SPECIFICALLY CONCERNING LIEBKNECHT

Until quite recently, there existed only one biography of
Wilhelm Liebknecht. Authored by Kurt Eisner in 1900 as a
eulogy to the fallen leader, *Wilhelm Liebknecht: Sein Leben
und Wirken*, 2d ed. (Berlin: Vorwärts, 1906), makes no claim
to objectivity. Nevertheless, the work, with its heroic
depiction of Liebknecht and its merciless abuse of his enemies,
has a romantic appeal.
    The first biography with claims to serious scholarship
is Vadim Chubinskii, *Wilhelm Liebknecht--Soldat Revolutsii*
(Moscow: Mysl, 1968). These claims are somewhat vitiated by
absence of footnotes and bibliography (a few very thin footnotes were added for the German translation of this book,
which appeared in 1973), and by the subordination of Liebknecht's career to the needs of Marxist-Leninist ideology.
Chubinskii illustrates the disturbing practice, common among
East European Marxists, of contrasting Liebknecht's "errors"
to the "correct" stance of Marx and Engels themselves, without
apparently considering the possibility that Liebknecht occasionally was better informed and more perceptive than his
London critics. To the uninitiated, it may be surprising to

learn that Liebknecht is a controversial subject; alas, he is
one strand of the rope used in a tug-of-war between Soviet
Marxists like Chubinskii, on the one hand, and social reformers
in the West German Social Democratic Party, on the other.
Both tendencies seek Liebknecht's posthumous imprimatur for
their policies, hoping thereby to prove themselves legitimate
heirs to the traditions of nineteenth-century social democracy.
The Soviet group, therefore, stresses Liebknecht's close
ties to Marx, his dedication to class struggle and his unwaver-
ing belief in the necessity of revolution to obtain the final
goal of socialism. The collection of essays in Joseph Schleifstein, et al., *150 Jahre: Wilhelm Liebknecht 29 März 1826-
Giessen* (Frankfurt am Main: Marxistische Blätter, 1976),
swims in this historiographical current, hoping that the in-
tonation of Liebknecht's revolutionary dedication will rouse
the slumbering masses at least to indignation, if not to action.

Friedrich Wilhelm Weitershaus, *Wilhelm Liebknecht: Das
unruhige Leben eines Sozialdemokraten* (Giessen: Brühlsche
Universitätsdruckerei, 1976), stands at the opposite historiographical pole. In his interpretation, the revolutionary
aspects of Liebknecht's career are treated as aberrations or
not at all. For example, Weitershaus devotes ten pages to
Wilhelm's youth in Geissen but treats the events of 1848-
49 in only three. A treatment of Liebknecht as a social
reformer would be defensible if the author took cognizance
of the opposite viewpoint in the historical literature and
refuted it, but after his prefatory remarks, Weitershaus
demonstrates no awareness, in footnotes or bibliography, of
the controversies through which he wades. But to stress the
author's bias is to give a false impression of this book, for
it is mainly a rich collection of photographs, photocopies
of documents, and excerpts from speeches and letters. It
lacks a coherent thesis.

A specialized study with a decidedly socialist viewpoint
is Ernst Nobs, *Aus Wilhelm Liebknechts Jugendjahren* (Zurich:
Genossenschafts-Buchhandlung, [1926]). This source employs
Swiss police archives and Liebknecht's newspaper articles
to trace the young socialist's political development between
1847 and 1850.

Hans Brumme, *Wilhelm Liebknecht. Wissen ist Macht--
Macht ist Wissen und andere bildungspolitisch--pädagogische
Aeusserungen* (Berlin: Volk und Wissen Volkseigener Verlag,
1968), introduces a collection of Liebknecht's speeches with
an examination of his contribution to pedagogical knowledge
through Marxism.

Gunter Ebersold, "Die Stellung Wilhelm Liebknechts

und August Bebels zur deutschen Frage 1863 bis 1870"
(Unpublished Ph.D. Dissertation, Heidelberg, 1963), actually
focuses almost exclusively on Liebknecht, using his writings
for various bourgeois newspapers to establish his attitude.
Ebersold is useful in documenting Liebknecht's uncompromising
anti-Prussianism, but like most Western scholars he underestimates the revolutionary premises that led Liebknecht to
his stance on the national issue. His argument that Liebknecht aimed only at the creation of a *Volkspartei* and was
forced into pursuit of independent worker politics by rivalry
with the ADAV is simply unsupportable. A valuable corrective
is Karl-Heinz Leidigkeit's *Wilhelm Liebknecht und August
Bebel in der deutschen Arbeiterbewegung 1862-1869* (Berlin:
Rütten & Loening, 1957), where the author stresses--and
perhaps exaggerates a bit--Liebknecht's work on behalf of
socialism.

   Two West German dissertations, which remain unpublished,
deserve mention only because they have influenced subsequent
interpretations. Margarete Lutz, "Wilhelm Liebknecht als
Sozialist im Deutschen Reichstag" (Tubingen, 1951), is polluted by the worst kind of cold war assumptions. In part
2 of her work, the author loses all semblance of detachment,
asserting that dictatorship is inherent in socialism, that
Liebknecht's ideas prove the "danger of social democracy,"
and that an antisocialist law constitutes reasonable self-
defense against such a threat. Equally distressing from
a scholarly viewpoint is Lutz's treatment of Liebknecht's
ideas between 1869 and 1900 as an immutable edifice which
rested on a foundation mixed from 1848 republicanism and
a small dose of Saint-Simon. To read Lutz, one would think
that Liebknecht hardly knew of Karl Marx; one would never
learn how Liebknecht's ideas evolved--and sometimes contradicted themselves--during his long career. Werner Muehlbradt's
"Wilhelm Liebknecht und die Gründung der deutschen Sozialdemokratie (1862-1875)" (Göttingen, 1950), is more solid, but
it tries to tell Liebknecht's story without having read his
correspondence, and consequently is quite thin in describing
motivation and is blind to major points of disagreement within
Liebknecht's faction.

   The following shorter studies were helpful in various
parts of my work:

Adamy, Kurt. "Sie hat sich um die grosse Sache des Prole-
     tariats verdient gemacht. Natalie Liebknecht." BGA,
     16 (no. 4, 1974), 672-77.

_____. "Ein Soldat der Revolution." BGA, 13 (no. 5, 1971), 812-22.

Aveling, Edward. *Wilhelm Liebknecht and the social-democratic movement in Germany. On behalf of the Zurich Committee for the International Workers and Trade Union Congress, London, July 26 to August 1. 1896.* London: Twentieth Century Press, n.d.

Bartel, Horst. "Wilhelm Liebknecht und das Erfurter Programm." BGA, 8 (no. 6, 1966), 974-95.

Bebel, August. "Erinnerungen an Liebknecht." *Beilage zum Wahre Jacob.* Nr. 368. 1900.

_____. "Natalie Liebknecht." *Die Neue Zeit*, 37/1 (1908-1909), 693-94.

Becker, Gerhard. "Die Agitationsreise Wilhelm Liebknecht durch die USA 1886." *Zeitschrift fur Geschichtswissenschaft*, 15 (no. 5, 1967), 842-62.

Beinbeck, Gerhard. "Ein 'Soldat der Revolution': Zu Wilhelm Liebknechts 150. Geburtstag," *Hessische Heimat*, 27 Mar. 1976.

Beyer, Marga. "Wilhelm Liebknechts Kampf gegen den Opportunismus im letzten Jahrzehnt seines Lebens." BGA, 18 (no. 1, 1976), 92-101.

_____. "Wilhelm Liebknechts Schreiben an die italienischen Sozialisten vom November 1898." BGA, 18 (no. 1, 1976), 70-72.

Chubinskii, Vadim. "Russische Ausgaben von Reden und Schriften Wilhelm Liebknecht und ihre Einsatz in revolutionäre Kampf," BGA, 17 (no. 1, 1975), 103-109.

_____. "W. I. Lenin über Wilhelm Liebknecht," BGA, 19 (no. 2, 1977), 243-52.

Kampffmeyer, Paul. *Wilhelm Liebknecht, der Soldat der Revolution.* Berlin: Bezirksverband Berlin, n.d.

_____. "Wilhelm Liebknechts Leben und Werk." *Arbeiter-Bildung: Schriftenreihe des Reichsausschusses für sozialistische Bildungsarbeit.* Nr. 10. 1926.

Knauss, Ervin. "Wilhelm Liebknecht und seine Jugendzeit in der Stadt und an der Universität in Giessen." *Heimat im Bild.* Mar. 1976.

Koch, Wilhelm. "Einiges über alte Giessen Geschlechter." *Giessen 1248-1948. Siebenhundert Jahre Giessen im Wort und Bild.* Giessen: Brühlsche Universitätsdruckerei, 1948.

Marcu, Valeriu. *Wilhelm Liebknecht: Ein Bild der deutschen Arbeiterbewegung.* Berlin: E. Laub'sche Verlagsbuchhandlung, 1926.

Mayer, Gustav. *Aus der Welt des Sozialismus: Kleine Historische Aufsätze*. Berlin: Weltgeist-Bücher, [1926].

Obermann, Karl. "Die Amerikareise Wilhelm Liebknechts im Jahre 1886." *Zeitschrift für Geschichtswissenschaft*, 14 (no. 4, 1966), 611-17.

Roberty, Detlev. "Ein Soldat der Revolution." *Neue Welt Kalendar, 1897*.

Schweichel, Robert. "Zum Gedächtnis Wilhelm Liebknechts." *Die Neue Zeit*, 19/2 (1900-1901), 539-44, 571-76, 602-608.

_____. "Wilhelm Liebknecht als Schriftssteller." *Die Neue Welt. Illustriertes Unterhaltungsblatt für das Volk*. Nr. 42, 1900, 332-34.

_____. "Wilhelm Liebknecht--Ein Charakterbild." *Neue Welt Kalendar, 1902*.

Tak, P. L. *Liebknecht en Bebel*. Haarlem: n.p., 1889.

"Wilhelm Liebknecht," *Oberhessische Volkszeitung*. 1 May 1926.

Weitershaus, Friedrich Wilhelm. "Die Liebknechts. Eine Thuringischhessische Beamtenfamilie." *Mitteilungen des Oberhessischen Geschichtsvereins*, 60 (1975), 93-144.

OTHER SECONDARY WORKS

Adamiak, Richard. "Marx, Engels, and Dühring." *Journal of the History of Ideas*, 35 (no. 1, Jan.-Mar. 1974), 98-112.

Anderson, Eugene N. *The Social and Political Conflict in Prussia, 1858-1864*. Lincoln, Nebraska: University of Nebraska Press, 1954.

Angel, Pierre. *Eduard Bernstein et l'évolution du socialisme allemand*. Paris: Librarie Marcel Didier, 1961.

Armstrong, Sinclair W. "The Social Democrats and the Unification of Germany." *Journal of Modern History*, 12 (1940), 485-509.

Aus der Waffenkammer des Sozialismus. Eine Sammlung alter und neuer Propaganda-Schriften. Ed. the staff of *Die Volksstimme*. 12 vols. Frankfurt am Main: Union-Druckerei, 1903-10.

Avineri, Shlomo. *The Social and Political Thought of Karl Marx*. Cambridge: Cambridge University Press, 1968.

Balser, Frolinde. *Sozial-Demokratie 1848/49-1863. Die erste deutsche Arbeiterorganization "Allgemeine Arbeiterverbrüderung" nach der Revolution*. Stuttgart: Ernst Klett Verlag, 1962.

Bartel, Horst, ed. *Arbeiterbewegung und Reichsgrundung*. Berlin: Akademie-Verlag, 1971.

_____, et al. *August Bebel. Eine Biographie*. Berlin: Dietz Verlag, 1963.

_____, and Kundel, Erich. "Die Bedeutung der Aufsätze von Friedrich Engels im 'Volksstaat' für den Kampf der deutschen Arbeiterklasse gegen den preussische-deutschen Militarismus in den Jahren 1874/75." *Beiträge zur Geschichte der deutschen Arbeiterbewegung*, 4 (1962) Sonderheft, 219-41.

_____. "Die Durschsetzung des Marxismus in der deutschen Arbeiterbewegung im letzten Drittel des 19. Jahrhundert." *Zeitschrift für Geschichtswissenschaft*, 14 (no. 8, 1966), 1334-71.

_____. *Friedrich Engels Kampf für die Schaffung einer marxistischen Arbeiterpartei in Deutschland*. Berlin: Dietz Verlag, 1956.

_____, and Engelberg, Ernst. *Die grosspreussisch-militaristische Reichsgründung 1871*. Berlin: Akademie Verlag, 1971.

_____. "Die Haltung der revolutionären deutschen Arbeiterbewegung zur Reichsgrundung von 1871." *Zeitschrift für Geschichtswissenschaft*, 16 (no. 4, 1968), 430-42.

_____. "Der interne Juni-Entwurf zum Erfurter Programm." *Beiträge zur Geschichte der deutschen Arbeiterbewegung*, 10 (1968), Sonderheft, 171-75.

_____. *Marx und Engels im Kampf um ein revolutionäres deutsche Parteiorgan, 1879-1890. Zu einigen Problemen der Hilfe von Karl Marx und Friedrich Engels für den Kampf des 'Sozialdemokrat' gegen das Sozialistengesetz*. Berlin: Dietz Verlag, 1961.

_____, et al. *Marxismus und deutsche Arbeiterbewegung. Studien zur sozialistischen Bewegung im letzten Drittel des 19. Jahrhundert*. Berlin: Dietz Verlag, 1970.

_____, et al. "'Der Sozialdemokrat'--Entwicklung und historische Stellung." Berlin: Dietz Verlag, 1970.

Bass, Bernard M. *Leadership, Psychology and Organizational Behavior*. New York: Harper and Brothers, 1960.

Becker, Gerhard. "Der 'neue Arbeiter-Verein in London' 1852." *Zeitschrift für Geschichtswissenschaft*, 14 (no. 1, 1966), 74-97.

Beike, Heinz. *Die deutsche Arbeiterbewegung und der Krieg von 1870-1871*. Berlin: Dietz Verlag, 1957.

Benser, Gunter. *Zur Herausbildung der Eisenacher Partei: Eine Untersuchung über die Entwicklung der Arbeiterbewegung im sächsichen Textilindustriegebiet Glauchau-Meerane*. Berlin: Dietz Verlag, 1956.

Bergmann, Günther. *Das Sozialistengesetz im rechts-Rheinischen Industriegebiet: Ein Beitrag zur Auseinandersetzung zwischen Staat und Sozialdemokratie im Wuppertal und im Bergischen Land 1878-1890.* Hannover: Verlag für Literatur und Zeitgeschehen, 1970.

Berlin, Potsdam und Umgebungen. Berlin: Verlag von Albert Goldschmidt, 1894.

Bernstein, Eduard, ed. *Ferdinand Lassalle, Gesammelte Reden und Schriften.* 12 vols. Berlin: Paul Cassirer, 1919.

_____. *Die Geschichte der Berliner Arbeiterbewegung. Ein Kapital zur Geschichte der deutschen Sozialdemokratie.* Berlin: Vorwärts, 1907-10.

Bers, Günter. *Wilhelm Hasselmann, 1844-1916. Sozialrevolutionärer Agitator und Abgeordneter des Deutschen Reichstages.* Cologne: Einhorn Presse, 1973.

Berthold, Lothar and Neef, Helmut. *Der Kampf von Karl Marx und Friedrich Engels um die revolutionäre Partei der deutschen Arbeiterklasse: mit einem Dokutmentenanhang.* Berlin: Dietz Verlag, 1966.

Beyer, Marga. "August Bebels Statutentwurf aus dem Jahre 1890." *Beiträge zur Geschichte der Arbeiterbewegung,* 19 (no. 3, 1977), 421-29.

_____, and Winkler, Gerhard. *Revolutionäre Arbeitereinheit: Eisenach--Gotha--Erfurt.* Berlin: Dietz Verlag, 1975.

Bock, Hans Manfred. "Die 'Literaten- und Studenten-Revolte' der Jungen in der SPD um 1890." *Das Argument,* 13 (Mar. 1971), 22-41.

Bracke, Wilhelm, Jr. *Der Lassalle'sche Vorschlag.* Brunswick: Druck und Verlag von W. Bracke, Jr., 1873.

Brandis, Kurt. *Die deutsche Sozialdemokratie bis zum Fall des Sozialistengesetz.* Leipzig: Verlag von C.L. Hirschfeld, 1931.

Braun, Herald. "Friedrick Ludwig Weidig--Der Turnvater Hessens." *Stadion,* 3 (no. 1, 1977), 90-116.

Braunthal, Julius. *History of the International.* Trs. Henry Collins and Kenneth Mitchell. 2 vols. New York & Washington: Frederick A. Praeger, 1976.

Bronder, Dietrich. "Organization und Führung der sozialistischen Arbeiterbewegung im Deutschen Reich, 1890-1914." Unpublished Ph.D. Dissertation, Georg-August-Universität zu Göttingen, 1952.

Brown, E.H., with Brown, Margaret H. *A Century of Pay. The Course of Pay and Production in France, Germany, Sweden, the United Kingdom, and the United States of America, 1860-1960.* New York: St. Martin's Press, 1968.

Brupbacher, Fritz. *Marx und Bakunin: Ein Beitrag zur Geschichte der Internationalen Arbeiterassoziation.* Berlin-Wilmersdorf: Verlag der Wochenschrift Die Aktion, 1922.

Bry, Gerhard. *Wages in Germany, 1871-1945.* Princeton, N.J.: Princeton University Press, 1960.

Büsch, Otto, and Herzfeld, Hans, eds. *Die frühsozialistische Bünde in der Geschichte der deutschen Arbeiterbewegung.* Berlin: Colloquium Verlag, 1975.

Carlson, Andrew R. *Anarchism in Germany.* Metuchen, N.J.: Scarecrow Press, 1972.

Collins, Henry, and Abramsky, Chimen. *Karl Marx and the British Labor Movement: Years of the First International.* London: Macmillan and Co., 1965.

Conze, Werner, and Groh, Dieter. *Die Arbeiterbewegung in der nationalen Bewegung. Die deutsche Sozialdemokratie vor, während und nach der Reichsgründung.* Stuttgart: Ernst Klett Verlag, 1966.

Curtis, Michael, ed. *Marxism.* New York: Atherton Press, 1970.

Dawson, William Harbutt. *Bismarck and State Socialism: An Exposition of the Social and Economic Legislation of Germany since 1870.* London: Swan Sonnenschein & Co., 1890.

_____. *German Socialism and Ferdinand Lassalle: A Biographical History of the German Socialistic Movements During This Century.* London: Swan Sonnenschein & Co., 1888.

Demandt, Karl E. *Geschichte des Landes Hessen.* 2d ed. Kassel and Basel: Börenreiter Verlag, 1972.

Desai, Ashok V. *Real Wages in Germany, 1871-1913.* Oxford: Clarendon Press, 1968.

Domann, Peter. *Sozialdemokratie und Kaisertum unter Wilhelm II.* Wiesbaden: Steiner Verlag, 1974.

Dominick, Raymond. "Democracy vs Socialism? A Case Study of *Vorwärts* in the 1890's." *Central European History,* 10 (no. 4, Dec. 1977), 286-311.

_____. "Freudian Fallacies and Their Implications for Psychohistory." Paper read at the June 1979 meeting of the Canadian Society for Cultural and Intellectual History.

Dorpalen, Andreas. "Marxism and National Unity: The Case of Germany." *The Review of Politics,* 39 (no. 4, Oct. 1977), 505-20.

Ebersold, Günther. "Die Stellung Wilhelm Liebknechts und August Bebels zur deutschen Frage 1863 bis 1870." Unpublished Ph.D. Dissertation, Ruprecht-Karl-Universität in Heidelberg, 1963.

Eckert, Georg. *Die Braunschweiger Arbeiterbewegung unter dem Sozialistengesetz.* Brunswick: Waisenhaus Buchdruckerei und Verlag, 1961.

_____. "Der Rechenschaftsbericht der Sozialdemokratischen Arbeiter-Partei für den Stuttgarter Parteitag Juni 1870." *Archiv für Sozialgeschichte*, 3 (1963), 497-508.

_____. *Wilhelm Bracke und die Anfänge der Braunschweiger Arbeiterbewegung.* Brunswick: n.p., 1957.

Eckert, Hugo. *Liberal oder Sozialdemokratie? Frühgeschichte der Nürnberger Arbeiterbewegung.* Stuttgart: Ernst Klett Verlag, 1968.

Eisfeld, Gerhard. *Die Entstehung der liberalen Parteien in Deutschland 1858-1870.* Hannover: Verlag für Literatur und Zeitgeschehen, 1969.

Engelberg, Ernst, ed. *Im Widerstreit um die Reichsgründung.* Berlin: VEB Deutscher Verlag der Wissenschaft, 1970.

_____. *Revolutionäre Politik und rote Feldpost, 1878-1890.* Berlin: Akademie-Verlag, 1959.

Engels, Friedrich. *Anti-Dühring. Herr Eugen Dühring's Revolution in Science.* 3d ed. Moscow: Foreign Languages Publishing House, 1962.

_____. "Zur Kritik des sozialdemokratischen Programmentwurfs 1891." *Die Neue Zeit*, 20 (1901-1902), 5-13.

Engelsing, Rolf. *Massenpublikum und Journalistentum im 19. Jahrhundert in Nordwestdeutschland.* Berlin: Duncker & Humboldt, 1966.

Ettelt, Werner, and Krause, Hans-Dieter. *Der Kampf um eine marxistische Gewerkschaftspolitik in der deutschen Arbeiterbewegung 1868 bis 1878.* Berlin: Verlag Tribüne, 1975.

Eyck, Erich. *Das persönliche Regiment Wilhelms II.* Zurich: Eugen Rentsch Verlag, 1948.

Fesser, Gerd. *Linksliberalismus und Arbeiterbewegung: Die Stellung der Deutschen Fortschrittspartei zur Arbeiterbewegung 1861-1866.* Berlin: Akademie Verlag, 1976.

Fischer-Frauendienst, Irene. *Bismarcks Pressepolitik.* Münster: Verlag C. J. Fahle, 1963.

Förster, Alfred. *Zur Geschichte der deutschen Gewerkschaftsbewegung 1871 bis 1890.* Berlin: Verlag Tribüne, 1962.

Fricke, Dieter. *Bismarcks Prätorianer. Die Berliner politische Polizei im Kampf gegen die deutsche Arbeiterbewegung (1871-1898).* Berlin: Rütten & Loening, 1962.

_____. *Zur Organization und Tätigkeit der deutschen Arbeiterbewegung (1890-1914).* Leipzig: VEB Verlag Enzyklopädii, 1962.

Fulberth, Georg. "Zur Genese des Revisionismus in der deut-
    schen Sozialdemokratie vor 1914." *Das Argument*, 13
    (Mar. 1971), 1-21.
Gärtner, Georg. *Karl Grillenberger: Lebensbild eines
    Kämpfer für Volksrecht und Volksfreiheit.* Nuremberg:
    Fränkische Verlagsanstalt und Buchdruckerei, 1930.
Gay, Peter. *The Dilemma of Democratic Socialism: Eduard
    Bernstein's Challenge to Marx.* New York: Collier
    Books, 1962.
Gemkow, Heinrich, and Hermann, Ursula. "Bebel, die Partei
    und das Sozialistengesetz." *Beiträge zur Geschichte
    der Arbeiterbewegung*, 20 (no. 5, 1978), 643-54.
_____, et al. *Friedrich Engels: Eine Biographie.* Berlin:
    Dietz Verlag, 1970.
_____. *Friedrich Engels' Hilfe beim Sieg der deutschen
    Sozialdemokratie über das Sozialistengesetz.* Berlin:
    Dietz Verlag, 1957.
_____, et al. *Karl Marx: Eine Biographie.* Berlin:
    Dietz Verlag, 1967.
_____. *Paul Singer, ein bedeutender Führer der deutschen
    Arbeiterbewegung: Mit einer Auswahl aus seinen Reden
    und Schriften.* Berlin: Dietz Verlag, 1957.
Gerteis, Klaus. *Leopold Sonnemann. Ein Beitrag zur Geschichte
    des demokratischen Nationalstaatsgedankens in Deutsch-
    land.* Frankfurt am Main: Verlag Waldemar Kramer, 1970.
Geschichte der Frankfurter Zeitung 1856 bis 1906. Ed. Verlag
    der Frankfurter Zeitung. Frankfurt am Main: Druckerei
    von August Osterrieth, 1906.
"Giessen: Vergangenheit und Gegenwart." Pub. Giessen Stadt-
    museum without bibliographical information.
Goldschmidt, Paul. *Berlin in Geschichte und Gegenwart.*
    Berlin: Verlag von Julius Springer, 1910.
Gouldner, Alvin W., ed. *Studies in Leadership: Leadership
    and Democratic Action.* New York: Russell and Russell,
    1965.
Grebing, Helga. *The History of the German Labor Movement:
    A Survey, With a Chapter on Foreign Policy by Mary Saran.*
    Tr. Edith Körner. London: Oswald Wolff, Ltd., 1969.
Greer, Scott A. *Social Organization.* New York: Random
    House, 1955.
Groh, Dieter. *Negative Integration und revolutionärer Atten-
    tismus. Die deutsche Sozialdemokratie am Vorabend des
    Ersten Weltkrieges.* Frankfurt am Main: Propylaen,
    1973.
Grohall, Ulrich, ed. *Dokumente der deutschen Arbeiterbewegung*

zur Journalistik. Vol. 1. *Vormärz bis 1905.* Berlin:
VEB Deutscher Verlag der Wissenschaft, 1961.

Die Gründung una Entwicklung der deutschen Sozialdemokratie:
Festschrift der Leipziger Arbeiter zum 23. Mai 1913.
Ed. Bezirksvorstand der sozialdemokratischen Partei
Leipzigs. Leipzig: Kommissionsverlag der Leipziger
Buchdruckerei Aktiengesellschaft, 1913.

Gustafsson, Bo. *Marxismus und Revisionismus: Eduard Bern-*
steins Kritik des Marxismus und ihre ideengeschichtliche
Voraussetzungen. Frankfurt am Main: Europäische Verlags-
ansalt, 1972.

Guttsman, W.L. *The German Social Democratic Party, 1875-1933.*
London: George Allen & Unwin, 1981.

Hackethal, Eberhard. "Der Allgemeine Deutsche Arbeiterverein
unter dem Einfluss der Pariser Commune." *Zeitschrift*
für Geschichtswissenschaft, 16 (no. 4, 1968), 443-61.

Haiman, Franklin S. *Group Leadership and Democratic Action.*
Boston: Houghton Miflin, 1950.

Hall, Alex. *Scandal, Sensation and Social Democracy: The*
SPD Press and Wilhelmine Germany. Cambridge: Cambridge
University Press, 1977.

_____. "The War of Words: Anti-socialist Offensives and
Counter-propaganda in Wilhelmine Germany, 1890-1914."
Journal of Contemporary History, 11 (nos. 2 & 3, Jul.
1976), 11-42.

Hamerow, Theodore S. *The Social Foundations of German*
Unification, 1858-1871. 2 vols. Princeton, N.J.:
Princeton University Press, 1969-72.

Hayes, Carlton J.H. "German Socialism Reconsidered."
American Historical Review, 23 (no. 1, Oct. 1917),
62-101.

Heidegger, Herman. *Die deutsche Sozialdemokratie und der*
nationale Staat, 1870-1920: Unter besonderer Berück-
sichtigung des Kriegs- und Revolutionsjahre. Göttingen:
Musterschmidt Verlag, 1956.

Hellfaier, Karl-Alexander. *Die deutsche Sozialdemokratie*
während des Sozialistengesetzes 1878-1890. Ein Beitrag
zur Geschichte ihrer illegalen Organisations- und
Agitationsformen. Berlin: VEB Deutscher Verlag der
Wissenschaft, 1958.

Henderson, William O. *The Life of Friedrich Engels.* 2 vols.
London: Frank Cass, 1971.

_____. *The Rise of German Industrial Power, 1834-1914.*
London: Temple Smith, 1975.

Henze, Wilfried. "Die Delegierten der Parteikongresse der
Sozialistichen Arbeiterpartei Deutschlands unter dem

Sozialistengesetz." *Zeitschrift für Geschichtswissen-schaft*, 28 (no. 8, 1980), 760-74.

Herrmann, Ursula, and Malik, Dieter. *Das revolutionäre Erbe der Eisenacher*. Berlin: Dietz Verlag, 1969.

_____. "Die Sozialistische Arbeiterpartei Deutschlands und das Ausnahmegesetz und zum Anteil der Zeitung 'Die Laterne.'" *Beiträge zur Geschichte der Arbeiterbewegung*, 15 (no. 3, 1973), 606-29.

Hess, Ulrich. "Louis Vierick und seine Münchner Blätter für Arbeiter, 1882-1889." *Dortmünder Beiträge zur Zeitungsforschung*, 6 (1961), 1-50.

Hirsch, Helmut, ed. *August Bebel: Sein Leben in Dokumente, Reden und Schriften*. Cologne and Berlin: Kiepenheuer & Witsch, 1968.

Hirsch, Paul. *Die Sozialdemokratie im Wahlkreis Teltow-Beeskow-Storkow-Charlottenburg. Auf Grund der amtlichen Statistik der Reichstags-Wahlen von 1890, 1893 und 1903 bearbeitet*. 3d ed. Charlottenburg: Wilhelm Eberhardt Verlag, 1904.

_____, and Borchardt, Bruno. *Die Sozialdemokratie und die Wahlen zum deutschen Reichstage*. Berlin: Buchhandlung Vorwärts, 1912.

Hochdorf, Max. *August Bebel. Geschichte einer politischen Vernunft*. Berlin: Verlag für Kulturpolitik, 1956.

Höhle, Thomas. *Franz Mehring: Sein Weg zum Marxismus 1869-1891*. Berlin: Rütten & Loening, 1956.

Hope, Nicholas Martin. *The Alternative to German Unification. The Anti-Prussian Party, Frankfurt, Nassau, and the Two Hessen, 1859-1867*. Wiesbaden: Franz Steiner Verlag, 1973.

Huber, Ernst Rudolph. *Deutsche Verfassungsgeschichte seit 1789*. 4 vols. Stuttgart: W. Kohlhammer Verlag, 1957-69.

Hummler, Heinz. *Opposition gegen Lassalle. Die revolutionäre proletarische Opposition im Allgemeinen Deutschen Arbeiterverein 1862/63-1866*. Berlin: Rütten & Loening, 1963.

Hunt, Richard N. *The Political Ideas of Marx and Engels*. Vol. 1: *Marxism and Totalitarian Democracy, 1818-1850*. Pittsburgh, Pa.: University of Pittsburgh Press, 1974.

Institut für Marxismus-Leninismus, ed. *Beiträge zur Marx/Engels Forschung*. Berlin: Dietz Verlag, 1968.

_____. `Dokumente und Materialen zur Geschichte der deutschen Arbeiterbewegung*. Vol. 4: *März 1898-Juli 1914*. Berlin: Dietz Verlag, 1967.

_____. *Geschichte der Deutschen Arbeiterbewegung*. Berlin: Dietz Verlag, 1966.

_____. *Mohr und General: Erinerungen an Marx und Engels*.

Berlin: Dietz Verlag, 1964.

Jansen, Reinhard. *Georg von Vollmar. Eine politische Biographie.* Dusseldorf: Droste Verlag, 1958.

Joll, James. *The Second International, 1889-1914.* New York: Praeger, 1956.

Kampffmeyer, Paul. *Georg von Vollmar.* Munich: G. Birk & Co., 1930.

Kantorowicz, Ludwig. *Die sozialdemokratische Presse Deutschlands: Eine soziologische Untersuchung.* Tubingen: J.C.B. Mohr, 1922.

Kautsky, Benedikt, ed. *Ein Leben für den Sozialismus. Erinnerungen an Karl Kautsky.* Hannover: J.H.W. Dietz Nachfolger, 1954.

Kautsky, Karl. *Friedrich Engels. Sein Leben, sein Wirken, Seine Schriften.* 2d ed. Berlin: Vorwärts, 1908.

_____. *Sozialisten und Krieg: Ein Beitrag zur Ideengeschichte des Sozialismus von den Hussiten bis zum Volkerbund.* Prague: Orbis-Verlag, 1937.

Kenafick, K.J. *Michael Bakunin and Karl Marx.* Melbourne: Excelsior Printing Works, 1948.

Klühs, Franz. *Der Aufstieg. Führer durch die Geschichte der deutschen Arbeiterbewegung.* 3d ed. Berlin: J.H.W. Dietz Nachfolger, 1930.

_____. *August Bebel. Der Mann und sein Werk.* Berlin: J.H.W. Dietz, 1923.

Koch, Wilhelm. "Einiges über alte Giessen Geschlechter." *Giessen 1848-1948. Seibenhundert Jahre Giessen in Wort und Bild.* Ed. Karl Glöckner. Giessen: Brühlsche Universitätsdruckerei, 1948.

Koepscke, Cordula. *Sozialismus in Deutschland.* Munich: Günter Olzog Verlag, 1970.

Kopf, Eike. "Die reaktionäre Marxkritik nach dem Gothaer Programm der deutschen Sozialdemokratie," *Deutsche Zeitschrift für Philosophie*, 23 (no. 5, 1975), 706-13.

Koszyk, Kurt. *Deutsche Presse im 19. Jahrhundert. Geschichte der deutschen Presse.* 2 vols. Berlin: Colloquium Verlag, 1966.

_____. *Die Presse der deutschen Sozialdemokratie. Eine Bibliographie.* Hannover: Verlag für Literatur und Zeitgeschehen, 1966.

Kuczynski, Jürgen. *A Short History of Labor Conditions Under Industrial Capitalism in Germany: 1800 to the Present Day.* London: Frederick Muller Ltd., 1945.

Kuczynski, R. *Arbeitslohn und Arbeitszeit in Europa und Amerika 1870-1909.* Berlin: Verlag von Julius Springer, 1913.

Kundel, Erich. "Der Kampf der Sozialdemokratischen Arbeiterpartei gegen den Bakuninismum von der Londoner Konferenz
1871 bis zum Haager Kongress 1872." *Beiträge zur
Geschichte der deutschen Arbeiterbewegung*, 6 (1960),
111-41.

————. *Marx und Engels im Kampf um die revolutionäre Arbeitereinheit. Zur Geschichte des Gothaer Vereinigungskongresses
von 1875*. Berlin: Dietz Verlag, 1962.

————. "Die Mitarbeit von Karl Marx und Friedrich Engels am
Zentralorgan der Eisenacher Partei 'Der Volksstaat.' Mit
einer chronologischen Uebersicht." *Beiträge zur Geschichte
der deutschen Arbeiterbewegung*, 10, Sonderheft, 1968,
98-136.

Lademacher, Horst. "Zu den Anfängen der Deutsche Sozialdemokratie 1863-1878. Probleme ihrer Geschichtsschreibung."
International Review of Social History, 14 (nos. 2 & 3,
1959), 239-60, 367-93.

Landauer, Carl. *European Socialism: A History of Ideas and
Movements from the Industrial Revolution to Hitler's
Seizure of Power*. 2 vols. Berkeley: University of
California Press, 1959.

Laschitza, Annelius. "Karl Kautsky und der Zentrismus."
Beiträge zur Geschichte der deutschen Arbeiterbewegung,
10 (no. 5, 1968).

Lees, Andrew. *Revolution and Reflection: Intellectual Change
in Germany During the 1850's*. The Hague: Martinus
Nijhoff, 1974.

Lehmann, Hans Georg. *Die Agrarfrage in der Theorie und Praxis
der deutschen und internationalen Sozialdemokratie*.
Tubingen: J.C.B. Mohr, 1970.

Lehning, Arthur. "Michael Bakounine: Theorie et Pratique du
Federalisme Anti-Etatique en 1870-71." *International
Review of Social History*, 17 (nos. 1 & 2, 1972), 455-73.

Leidigkeit, Karl-Heinz. *Wilhelm Liebknecht und August Bebel
in der deutschen Arbeiterbewegung, 1862-1869*. Berlin:
Rütten & Loening, 1957.

Leonard, Heinrich. *Wilhelm Bracke: Leben und Wirken.
Gedenkschrift zum fünfzigsten Todestag am 27. April
1930*. Brunswick: H. Reike, 1930.

Lidtke, Vernon L. "German Social Democracy and German State
Socialism, 1876-1884." *International Review of Social
History*, 9, 1964, 202-25.

————. *The Outlawed Party: Social Democracy in Germany,
1878-1890*. Princeton, N.J.: Princeton University
Press, 1966.

Lipinski, Richard. *Die Sozialdemokratie von ihren Anfängen bis zur Gegenwart. Eine Gedrängte Darstellung für Funktionäre und Lernende.* 2 vols. Berlin: J.H.W. Dietz, 1927-1928.

Maehl, William Harvey. *August Bebel: Shadow Emperor of the German Workers.* Philadelphia: The American Philosophical Society, 1980.

_____. "Bebel and the Origins of German Parliamentary Socialism During the Franco-Prussian War." *Studies in History and Society,* 1 (no. 2, 1976), 22-40.

Markham, F.M.H., ed. and tr. *Henri Comte de Saint-Simon (1760-1825): Selected Writings.* Oxford: Basil Blackwell, 1952.

Marks, Harry J. "The Sources of Reformism in the Social Democratic Party of Germany, 1890-1914." *Journal of Modern History,* 11 (Sept., 1939), 334-52.

Marx, Karl. *The Civil War in France.* London: Martin Lawrence, Ltd., 1933.

_____. *Critique of the Gotha Program.* New York: International Publishers, 1933.

Masur, Gerhard. *Imperial Berlin.* New York: Basic Books, 1970.

Matthias, Erich. "Kautsky und der Kautskyanismus." *Marxismusstudien, Sonderdruck,* Tubingen: J.C.B. Mohr, n.d.

Mayer, Gustav. "Der Allgemeine Deutsche Arbeiterverein und die Krisis 1866." *Archiv für Sozialwissenschaft und Sozialpolitik,* 57 (1927), 167-75.

_____. *Bismarck und Lassalle: Ihr Briefwechsel und Ihre Gespräche.* Berlin: Dietz Nachfolger, 1928.

_____, ed. *Ferdinand Lassalle: Nachgelassene Briefe und Schriften.* Stuttgart and Berlin: Deutsche Verlags-Anstalt, 1922.

_____. *Friedrich Engels: Eine Biographie.* The Hague: Martinus Nijhoff, 1934.

_____. *Johann Baptiste von Schweitzer und die Sozialdemokratie: Ein Beitrag zur Geschichte der deutschen Arbeiterbewegung.* Jena: Verlag von Gustav Fischer, 1909.

_____. *Die Trennung der proletarischen von der burgerlichen Demokratie in Deutschland (1863-1870).* Leipzig: Verlag von C.L. Hirschfeld, 1911.

Mayer, Paul. "Die Geschichte des sozialdemokratischen Parteiarchivs und das Schicksal des Marx-Engels-Nachlass." *Archiv für Sozialgeschichte,* 6/7 (1966-67), 5-112.

McDougall, Glen R. "Franz Mehring: Politics and History in the Making of Radical German Social Democracy, 1869-1903." Unpublished Ph.D. Dissertation, Columbia University, 1976.

McLellan, David. *Karl Marx: His Life and Thought.* New York: Harper and Row, 1973.

Mehring, Franz. *Karl Marx: The Story of His Life.* Tr. Edward Fitzgerald. London: George Allen & Unwin Ltd., 1936.

_____. *Politische Publizistik 1891 bis 1904.* Ed. Josef Schleifstein. Berlin: Dietz Verlag, 1964.

Merker, Paul. *Sozialdemokratie und Gewerkschaften 1890-1920.* Berlin: Dietz Verlag, 1949.

Meyer, Karl W. *Karl Liebknecht: Man Without a Country.* Washington, D.C.: Public Affairs Press, 1967.

Meyer, Thomas. *Bernsteins konstruktiver Sozialismus: Eduard Bernsteins Beitrag zur Theorie des Sozialismus.* Berlin: J.H.W. Dietz Nachfolger, 1977.

Meyer, R. *Der Emancipationskampf des Vierten Standes.* Berlin: Verlag von August Schindler, 1874.

Michels, Robert. "Die deutsche Sozialdemokratie im internationale Verbande: Eine kritische Untersuchung." *Archiv für Sozialwissenschaft.* Vol. 25.

_____. *Zur Soziologie des Parteiwesens in der modernen Demokratie. Untersuchungen über die oligarchischen Tendenzen des Gruppenlebens.* 2d ed. Leipzig: Alfred Kröner Verlag, 1925.

Miller, Susanne. *Das Problem der Freiheit im Sozialismus. Freiheit, Staat und Revolution in der Programmatik der Sozialdemokratie von Lassalle bis zum Revisionismusstreit.* 2d ed. Frankfurt am Main: Europäische Verlagsanstalt, 1964.

Milward, Alan S., and Saul, S. B. *The Development of the Economies of Continental Europe, 1850-1914.* London: George Allen & Unwin Ltd., 1977.

Mishark, John W. *The Road to Revolution: German Marxism and World War I - 1914-1919.* Detroit: Moira Books, 1967.

Mitchell, Allan. "Bonapartism as a Model for Bismarckian Politics." *Journal of Modern History,* 41 (no. 2, June 1977), 181-99.

Mitchell, B.R. *European Historical Statistics, 1750-1970.* New York: Columbia University Press, 1975.

Mommsen, Wilhelm, ed. *Deutsche Parteiprogramme.* Munich: Isar Verlag, 1960.

Moore, Robert L. "European Socialists and the American Promised Land, 1880-1917." Unpublished Ph.D. Dissertation, Yale, 1968.

Morgan, Roger. *The German Social Democrats and the First International.* Cambridge: Cambridge University Press, 1965.

_____. "The Significance of Johann Philipp Becker's Geneva Central Committee for the Development of the I.W.A. in Germany." *La Première International: L'Institution, L'Implantation, Le Rayonnement*. Paris: Editions du Centre National de la Recherche Scientifique, 1968.

Moring, Karl-Ernst. *Die Sozialdemokratische Partei in Bremen 1890-1914. Reformismus und Radikalismus in der Sozialdemokratischen Partei Bremens*. Hannover: Verlag für Literatur und Zeitgeschehen, 1968.

Moss, Bernard H. *The Origins of the French Labor Movement 1830-1914: The Socialism of Skilled Workers*. Berkeley: University of California Press, 1976.

Müller, Dirk H. *Idealismus und Revolution: Zur Opposition der Jungen gegen den Sozialdemokratischen Parteivorstand 1890 bis 1894*. Berlin:, Colloquium Verlag, 1975.

Muser, Gerhard. *Statistische Untersuchung über die Zeitungen Deutschlands 1885-1914*. Leipzig: Verlag von Emmanuel Reinicke, 1918.

Na'aman, Shlomo, with Harstick, H.P. *Die Konstituierung der deutschen Arbeiterbewegung 1862/63: Darstellung und Dokumentation*. Assen: Van Gorcum, 1975.

Na'aman, Shlomo. *Lassalle*. Hannover: Verlag für Literatur und Zeitgeschehen, 1970.

Neef, Helmut. *Zur Geschichte der deutschen Arbeiterbewegung im 19. Jahrhundert*. Berlin: Dietz Verlag, 1962.

Nettl, Peter. "The German Social Democratic Party 1890-1914 as a Political Model." *Past and Present* (April, 1965), 65-95.

_____. *Rosa Luxemburg*. 2 vols. London: Oxford University Press, 1966.

Neumann-Hofer, Adolf. *Die Entwicklung der Sozialdemokratie bei den Wählen zum Deutschen Reichstage, 1871-1903*. 3d ed. Berlin: Verlag von Conrad Skopnik, 1903.

Newman, Eugene. *Restoration Radical: Robert Blum and the Challenge of German Democracy, 1807-1848*. Boston: Branden Press, 1974.

Nichols, J. Alden. *Germany After Bismarck. The Caprivi Era, 1890-1894*. Cambridge, Mass.: Harvard University Press, 1958.

Nikolajewsky, Boris. "Karl Marx und die Berliner Sektion der I. Internationale: Unveröffentlichte Briefe von Karl Marx." *Die Gesellschaft*, 10 (1933), 252-64.

Nipperdey, Thomas. *Die Organisation der deutschen Parteien vor 1918*. Dusseldorf: Droste Verlag, 1961.

Noyes, Paul H. *Organization and Revolution: Working-Class Associations in the German Revolution of 1848-49*. Princeton, N.J.: Princeton University Press, 1966.

Obermann, Karl, et al., eds. *Biographische Lexikon zur Deutschen Geschichte*. Berlin: Deutscher Verlag der Wissenschaft, 1967.

_____, and Hermann, Ursula. *Friedrich Engels und die internationale Arbeiterbewegung*. Berlin: Akademie-Verlag, 1962.

Oelssner, Fred. *Das Kompromiss von Gotha und seine Lehren*. Berlin: Dietz Verlag, 1950.

Olmsted, Michael S. *The Small Group*. New York: Random House, 1959.

Opitz, Waldtraut. "Friedrich Engels und die deutsche Sozialdemokratie in den Jahren 1890/91." *Zeitschrift für Geschichtswissenschaft*, 17 (no. 11, 1969), 1403-15.

Osterroth, Franz. *Biographisches Lexikon des Sozialismus*. 2 vols. Hannover: J.H.W. Dietz Nachfolger, 1960.

Pack, Wolfgang. *Das Parlamentarische Ringen um das Sozialistengesetz Bismarcks 1878-1890*. Dusseldorf: Droste Verlag, 1961.

Petry, Lothar. *Die Erste Internationale in der Berliner Arbeiterbewegung*. Erlangen: Verlag Palm & Enke, 1975.

Pinson, Koppel S. *Modern Germany: Its History and Civilization*. 2d ed. New York: Macmillan Co., 1966.

Ratz, Ursula. *Georg Ledebour 1850-1947: Weg und Wirken eines sozialistischen Politikers*. Berlin: Walter de Gruyter & Co., 1969.

Reichard, Richard W. *Crippled from Birth. German Social Democracy, 1844-1870*. Ames, Iowa: Iowa State University Press, 1969.

Rieger, Isolde. *Die Wilhelminische Presse im Ueberblick 1888-1918*. Munich: Pohl & Co., 1957.

Rikli, Erika. *Der Revisionismus. Ein Revisionsversuch der deutschen marxistischen Theorie (1890-1914)*. Zurich: H. Girsberger Verlag, 1936.

Ritter, Gerhard A. *Die Arbeiterbewegung im Wilhelminischen Reich. Die sozialdemokratische Partei und die freien Gewerkschaften 1890-1900*. Berlin-Dahlem: Colloquium Verlag, 1959.

Rocker, Rudolf. *Johann Most: Das Leben eines Rebellen*. Berlin: Verlag "Der Syndikalist," 1924.

Röhl, J.C.G. *Germany without Bismarck: The Crisis of Government in the Second Reich, 1890-1900*. Berkeley: University of California Press, 1967.

Rosenberg, Arthur. *Democracy and Socialism. A Contribution to the Political History of the Past 150 Years*. Boston: Beacon Press, 1965 [1938].

Roth, Guenther. *The Social Democrats in Imperial Germany:*

    A Study in Working-Class Isolation and National Integration. Totowa, N.J.: Bedminster Press, 1963.

Roth, Rudolf. "Zum Streit um die Dampfersubvention." *Archiv für Sozialgeschichte* (no. 1, 1961), 109-18.

Rosen, David S. "German Social Democracy Between Bismarck and Bernstein: Georg von Vollmar and the Reformist Controversy, 1890-1895." Unpublished Ph.D. Dissertation, University of Wisconsin, 1975.

Rubel, Maximilien, and Manale, Margaret. *Marx Without Myth: A Chronological Study of His Life and Work.* New York: Harper and Row, 1976.

Schade, Franz. *Kurt Eisner und die bayerische Sozialdemokratie.* Hannover: Verlag für Literatur und Zeitgeschehen, 1961.

Schadt, Jörg. *Die Sozialdemokratische Partei in Baden. Von den Anfängen bis zur Jahrhundertwende (1868-1900).* Hannover: Verlag für Literatur und Zeitgeschehen, 1971.

Scharlau, Winfried, and Zeman, Zbynck A. *Freibeuter der Revolution. Parvus-Helphand: Eine politische Biographie.* Cologne: Verlag Wissenschaft und Politik, 1964.

Scharrer, Manfred. *Arbeiterbewegung im Obrigkeitsstaat: SPD und Gewerkschaft nach dem Sozialistengesetz.* Berlin: Rotbuch Verlag, 1976.

Schleifstein, Josef. *Franz Mehring: Sein marxistisches Schaffen 1891-1919.* Berlin: Rütten & Loening, 1959.

_____. "Der Kampf von Marx und Engels für die Herausbildung und Festigung der selbständigen revolutionären Massenpartei der deutschen Arbeiterklasse in den Jahren 1859 bis 1871." *Wissenschaftliche Zeitschrift der Karl-Marx-Universität Leipzig.* 4 (1954-55, 5), 413-38.

Schmidt, Walter. "Die Kommunisten und der preussische Amnestieerlass von 12. Januar 1861." *Zeitschrift für Geschichtswissenschaft*, 15 (no. 9, 1977), 1066-79.

Schmierer, Wolfgang. *Von der Arbeiterbildung zur Arbeiterpolitik. Die Anfänge der Arbeiterbewegung in Wurttemberg 1862/63-1878.* Hannover: Verlag für Literatur und Zeitgeschehen, 1970.

Schorske, Carl E. *German Social Democracy, 1905-1917. The Development of the Great Schism.* Cambridge, Mass.: Harvard University Press, 1955.

Schraepler, Ernst, ed. *August-Bebel-Bibliographie.* Dusseldorf: Droste Verlag, 1962.

_____. *August Bebel: Sozialdemokrat im Kaiserreich.* Göttingen: Musterschmidt-Verlag, 1966.

_____. "Der Zerfall der Ersten Internationale im Spiegel des 'Neuen Sozial-Demokrat.'" *Archiv für Sozialgeschichte*, 3 (1963), 509.

Schröder, Hans-Christoph. *Sozialismus und Imperialismus: Die Auseinandersetzung der deutschen Sozialdemokratie mit dem Imperialismusproblem und der 'Weltpolitik' vor 1914.* Hannover: Verlag für Literatur und Zeitgeschehen, 1968.

Schröder, Wilhelm. *Geschichte der sozialdemokratischen Parteiorganization in Deutschland.* Heft 4 and 5 of *Abhandlungen und Vorträge zur sozialistischen Bildung.* Ed. Max Grunwald. Dresden: Verlag von Kaden & Co., 1912.

Schröder, Wolfgang. *Partei und Gewerkschaften: Die Gewerkschaftsbewegung in der Konzeption der revolutionären Sozialdemokratie 1868/69 bis 1893.* Berlin: Verlag Tribüne, 1975.

_____, and Seeber, Gustav. "Zur Vorbereitung des Erfurter Programms." *Zeitschrift für Geschichtswissenschaft,* 14 (no. 7, 1966), 1117-47.

Schumann, Harry. *Karl Liebknecht: Ein unpolitisches Bild seiner Persönlichkeit.* Dresden: Carl Reissner, 1919.

Seeber, Gustav. *Die deutsche Sozialdemokratie und die Entwicklung ihrer revolutionären Parlamentstaktik von 1867 bis 1893.* Berlin: Dietz Verlag, 1966.

_____, and Wolter, Heinz. "Die Gründung des Deutschen Reiches und die Arbeiterbewegung." *Beiträge zur Geschichte der Arbeiterbewegung,* 13 (no. 1, 1971), 3-22.

Seidel, Jutta. *Wilhelm Bracke: Vom Lassalleaner zum Marxisten.* Berlin: Dietz Verlag, 1966.

Sheppard, Francis. *London 1808-1870.* Berkeley: University of California Press, 1971.

Silberner, Edmund. *Johann Jacoby: Politiker und Mensch.* Bonn-Bad Godesberg: Verlag Neue Gesellschaft, 1976.

_____. *Moses Hess. Geschichte seines Lebens.* Leiden: E.J. Brill, 1966.

Snell, John L., ed. and completed by Hans A. Schmitt. *The Democratic Movement in Germany, 1789-1914.* Chapel Hill, N.C.: University of North Carolina Press, 1976.

_____. "The World of German Democracy, 1789-1914." *The Historian,* 31 (August, 1969), 521-38.

Stannard, David E. *Shrinking History: On Freud and the Failure of Psychohistory.* New York: Oxford University Press, 1980.

Steenson, Gary P. *Karl Kautsky 1854-1938: Marxism in the Classical Years.* Pittsburg, Pa.: University of Pittsburgh Press, 1978.

Steinberg, Hans-Josef. *Sozialismus und deutsche Sozialdemokratie: Zur Ideologie der Partei vor dem I. Welt-*

krieg. Hannover: Verlag für Literatur und Zeitgeschehen, 1967.

Stuchlick, Gerhard. "Die Spende Liebknechts." *Geschichte zur Geschichte*, May, 1966.

Trease, Geoffrey. *London: A Concise History.* New York: Charles Scribner and Sons, 1975.

Trübner, Georg. "Der Deutsche Republikaner Johann Philipp Becker als Mitstreiter für die Erringung demokratischer Ziele in der Schweiz: Ein Beitrag zur Geschichte des Vormärz in Kanton Bern." *International Review of Social History*, 6 (no. 2, 1961).

Tucker, Robert C. *The Marxian Revolutionary Idea.* New York: W.W. Norton and Co., 1969.

Turk, Eleanor L. "The Press of Imperial Germany: A New Role for a Traditional Resource." *Central European History*, 10 (no. 4, Dec. 1977), 329-37.

Valentin, Viet. *1848: Chapters of German History.* Hamden, Conn.: Archon Books, 1965.

Varain, Heinz Josef. *Freie Gewerkschaften, Sozialdemokratie und Staat. Die Politik der Generalkommission unter der Führung Karl Legiens (1890-1920).* Dusseldorf: Droste Verlag, 1956.

Verba, Sidney. *Small Groups and Political Behavior. A Study of Leadership.* Princeton, N.J.: Princeton University Press, 1961.

Vollmar, Georg. "Ueber die nächsten Aufgaben der deutschen Sozialdemokratie." Munich: Druck und Verlag von M. Ernst, 1891.

_____. "Ueber Staatssocialismus." Nuremberg: Verlag von Wörlein & Co., 1892.

Wachenheim, Hedwig. *Die deutsche Arbeiterbewegung 1844 bis 1914.* Cologne: Westdeutscher Verlag, 1967.

Wehler, Hans-Ulrich. *Sozialdemokratie und Nationalstaat. Die deutsche Sozialdemokratie und die Nationalitätenfragen in Deutschland von Karl Marx bis zum Ausbruch des Ersten Weltkriegs.* Wurzburg: Holzner-Verlag, 1962.

Weickhardt, Ludwig. *Dr. Friedrich Ludwig Weidig: Das Lebensbild eines aufrechten deutschen Mannes.* Butzbach: Verlag Ludwig Weickhardt, 1969.

Wendel, Hermann. *August Bebel: Ein Lebensbild für deutsche Arbeiter.* Berlin: Vorwärts, 1913.

Wetzel, Hans-Wolfgang. *Presseinnenpolitik im Bismarckreich (1874-1890): Das Problem der Repression oppositioneller Zeitungen.* Bern: Herbert Lang, 1975.

Wienand, Peter. "Revoluzzer und Revisionisten: Die 'Jungen' in der Sozialdemokratie vor der Jahrhundertwende."

Politische Vierteljahresschrift, 17 (no. 2, 1976), 208-41.

William I. *The Correspondence of William I & Bismarck, with other Letters From and to Prince Bismarck*. Tr. J. A. Ford. 2 vols. New York: Frederick A. Stokes, 1903.

Wohlgemuth, Heinz. *Karl Liebknecht: Eine Biographie*. Berlin: Dietz Verlag, 1973.

Zimmermann, Fritz. "Friedrich Engels' Hilfe für die Deutsche Sozialdemokratie im Kampf gegen den Opportunismus in der Bauernfrage in den neunziger Jahren des 19. Jahrhunderts." *Beiträge zur Geschichte der deutschen Arbeiterbewegung*, 3 (Sonderheft, 1961), 167-87.

Index